ZAGAT
2014

W9-BNS-283

New York City Shopping & Food Lover's Guide

STAFF EDITORS
Randi Gollin & Carol Diuguid

Published and distributed by
Zagat Survey, LLC
76 Ninth Avenue
New York, NY 10011
T: 212.977.6000
E: feedback@zagat.com
www.zagat.com

ACKNOWLEDGMENTS

We sincerely thank the thousands of people who participated in this survey – this guide is really "theirs."

We also thank Anne Bauso (editor), Andrew Murphy (cartographer), Julie Alvin, Katharine Critchlow, Miranda Levenstein, Nancy Bilyeau, Suzanne Blecher, Christa Bourg, Erin Clack, Claire Connors, Leigh Crandall, Renata Espinosa, Lara Ewen, Kimberly Forrest, Katie Hottinger, Kelly McMasters, Craig Nelson, Bernie Onken, Camille Rankin, Lindsay Sammon, Simon Spelling, Victoria Spencer, Kelly Stewart and Mary Zubritsky, as well as the following members of our staff: Anna Hyclak (project manager), Brian Albert, Sean Beachell, Maryanne Bertollo, Reni Chin, Larry Cohn, Nicole Diaz, Jeff Freier, Alison Gainor, Michelle Golden, Marc Henson, Ryutaro Ishikane, Aynsley Karps, Natalie Lebert, Mike Liao, Vivian Ma, Caitlin Miehl, Molly Moker, Polina Paley, Josh Siegel, Albry Smither, Art Yagci, Sharon Yates, Anna Zappia and Kyle Zolner.

ABOUT ZAGAT

In 1979, we asked friends to rate and review restaurants purely for fun. The term "user-generated content" had yet to be coined. That hobby grew into Zagat Survey; 34 years later, we have loyal surveyors around the globe and our content now includes nightlife, shopping, tourist attractions, golf and more. Along the way, we evolved from being a print publisher to a digital content provider. We also produce marketing tools for a wide range of corporate clients, and you can find us on Google+ and just about any other social media network.

Our reviews are based on public opinion surveys. The ratings reflect the average scores given by the survey participants who voted on each establishment. The text is based on quotes from, or paraphrasings of, the surveyors' comments. Phone numbers, addresses and other factual data were correct to the best of our knowledge when published in this guide.

JOIN IN

To improve our guides, we solicit your comments – positive or negative; it's vital that we hear your opinions. Just contact us at nina-tim@zagat.com.

Contents

Ratings & Symbols

	Zagat Top Spot	Name	Symbols		Zagat Ratings			
					QUALITY	DISPLAY	SERVICE	COST

Area, Address & Contact

⨀ Tim & Nina's ◐   ▽ 23 | 20 | 13 | I

Chelsea | 76 Ninth Ave. (bet. 15th & 16th Sts.) | 212-977-6000 | www.zagat.com

Review, surveyor comments in quotes

Tim and Nina lure "throngs of tourists", "do-it-yourself types and discerning design devotees" alike to their "home furnishings mecca", located a "stone's throw from the High Line"; the "swell mix" ranges from "cushy" sleeper sofas (where the owners "sometimes sneak in a nap") to "crazy tchotchkes" like "tasting forks with extendable handles"; if a few nesters squawk that the shelves are "often empty" and the staff "tends to disappear", "dirt-cheap prices" answer most complaints.

Ratings   **Quality, Display** & **Service** are rated on a 30-point scale.

26	–	30	extraordinary to perfection
21	–	25	very good to excellent
16	–	20	good to very good
11	–	15	fair to good
0	–	10	poor to fair
▽			low response	less reliable

Cost   The price range for each store.

| I | Inexpensive | E | Expensive |
| M | Moderate | VE | Very Expensive |

Symbols   ◐   usually open after 8 PM

              ⊄   cash only

Locations   For chains with over 10 locations in NYC, only the flagship address is listed.

What's New

For the first time ever, we've combined NYC Shopping and NYC Food Lover's content into one best-of-the-best volume including 1,789 places. Covering everything from clothing, jewelry, housewares, furniture and electronics stores to bakeries, chocolate shops, butchers, fishmongers and vintners, this guide provides a snapshot of the city's top shopping options.

NEIGHBORHOOD WATCH: Tourist-thronged SoHo became more of a luxury-label magnet, attracting **Balenciaga, Chloé, Saint Laurent Paris** and **Versace.** International expansion raged on with French clothier **IRO** joining Broome Street's hip Gallic fashion pack, Paris import **Le Palais des Thés** setting up on Spring Street (and the UWS), and Switzerland's **Osswald Perfumerie** and a boutique from Peruvian designer **Pamela Gonzales** opening on SoHo's less-trafficked southern fringes. Retail shifts happened elsewhere in town too, with **Tommy Bahama,** cheeky-chic Brit brand **Ted Baker** and **Zara** sibling **Massimo Dutti** hitting Midtown, style-setters **Alice & Olivia** and **Rag & Bone** surfacing in the less-rarefied Meatpacking, and accessible fashion juggernauts – from **Kate Spade** to French chains **Maje** and **Sandro** – joining tony designers like **Armani Junior, Belstaff, Monique Lhuillier** and **Proenza Schouler** on Madison Avenue. The sweets and baked goods scene continued to cook Uptown and Down, with Parisian patisserie **Maison Kayser** debuting on the UES (with more NYC locations on the way), along with multiple branches from Japan's **Royce' Chocolate** and the NJ-born outfits **House of Cupcakes** and **Sugar and Plumm.**

MENSWEAR GRABS SPOTLIGHT: The dapper dude trend showed no sign of abating. New haberdasheries include SoHo's clubby **Carson Street Clothiers** and arty provocateurs **The Askel Project** and **Private Stock,** Madison Avenue's **Lanvin Men** and retro-inspired arrivals such as Midtown's **Fine & Dandy,** the West Village's **J. Press – York Street** and Williamsburg's **H.W. Carter and Sons** and **Pork Pie Hatters.**

OPENING DOORS: Further evidence of NYC's mallification, several shopping-center projects are taking shape around the city. **Brookfield Place,** a remake of the former World Financial Center, is slated to open in 2014, anchored by an upscale grocery store, a dining gallery showcasing the likes of **Sprinkles Cupcakes** and fashion retailers including **Michael Kors.** In the Sandy-ravaged South Street Seaport, **Pier 17** is transforming into a glass-walled mall, while two nearby food markets are in the works. By year's end **Comme des Garçons** is set to unveil **Dover Street Market** in Murray Hill, a seven-story multibrand emporium, modeled after its London and Tokyo counterparts. In Downtown Brooklyn, the open-air, near-moribund **Fulton Street Mall** has been revitalized, signing on tenants like **Brooklyn Industries, H&M** and **Swarovski,** while the four-story **City Point** center nearby, featuring discounter **Century 21** and a high-end supermarket, is scheduled for 2015. And in Crown Heights, **Brooklyn Flea/Smorgasburg** founder Jonathan Butler has partnered with Goldman Sachs to develop a 150,000-sq.-ft. complex to include a food hall with local vendors.

New York, NY
August 1, 2013

Nina and Tim Zagat

Key Newcomers & Neighborhoods

NYC's shopping scene is one of the most vibrant anywhere, with new stores debuting practically every week. Below are our editors' picks among this year's arrivals (see full list on p. 194, 310), which are mapped on the facing page. Following are four handy maps showing standouts, old and new, in the city's retail hotbeds, from the posh East Side to ultrahip Williamsburg. Use our walking tours as a guide or as a springboard for making your own discoveries.

All Good Things | *artisanal foods*
Armani Junior | *status kids*
Belstaff | *British luxe*
Bettie Page | *retro apparel*
Beurre & Sel | *Dorie's cookies*
Breads Bakery | *Euro loaves*
Brian Atwood | *stiletto-central*
Brooklyn Harvest | *W'burg grocer*
Carson St. Clothiers | *guy garb*
Christian Siriano | *fierce fashions*
Creel and Gow | *curiosity shop*
Cutler & Gross | *English specs*
Equipment | *silk blouses*
Everything/Water | *swimsuits galore*
Halston Heritage | *brand revival*
House of Cupcakes | *bakery twins*
H.W. Carter & Sons | *spiffy duds*
Iosselliani | *Italian jewelry*
Ippolita | *colorful bling*
IRO | *Gallic panache*
J. Press – York St. | *new preppy*
Jung Lee | *elegant tableware*
Kurt Geiger | *British kicks*

Lanvin Men | *luxury label*
LeChurro | *Spanish sweets*
Leica | *cool cameras*
Le Palais des Thés | *Parisian tea*
Macaron Parlour | *cute cookies*
Maison Kayser | *chic patisserie*
Massimo Dutti | *Zara's sibling*
Monique Lhuillier | *red-carpet looks*
Osswald Parfumerie | *Swiss scents*
Pain d'Epices | *UWS bakery*
Personnel of NY | *guy/girl style*
Piperlime | *e-tailer-cum-retailer*
Private Stock | *men's gallery*
Proenza Schouler | *boldface designer*
Raleigh | *denim specialist*
Royce' Chocolate | *Japanese bonbons*
Schutz | *Brazilian shoes*
Sugar & Plumm | *sweet emporiums*
Swords-Smith | *Billyburg fashion*
Teavana | *Starbucks does tea*
The Bar at Baublebar | *bold baubles*
Tiberio | *custom local meats*
Tommy Bahama | *tropical style*

WHAT'S NEXT

Baked: Favorite Red Hook sweet spot seeks a Manhattan outpost

Carven: Storied French label slated to join SoHo's Gallic enclave

Lady M Cake: Chichi UES confectioner preps a third branch on Bryant Park

Maison Ladurée: The macaron champ to bake up a SoHo flagship

Maiyet: The luxe side of ethical, artisanal fashion to hit Crosby Street

Orogold Cosmetics: Beauty brand taking a shine to the East 50s

Rebecca Minkoff: Her cult of fashion cool is coming to SoHo

Branches on the way: Anthropologie (Williamsburg), **C. Wonder** (Flatiron), **Fairway** (Chelsea), **J.Crew** (Cobble Hill), **Kate Spade** (UWS's ex Emerald Inn), **Lanvin Men** (SoHo), **Proenza Schouler** (SoHo)

Visit zagat.com

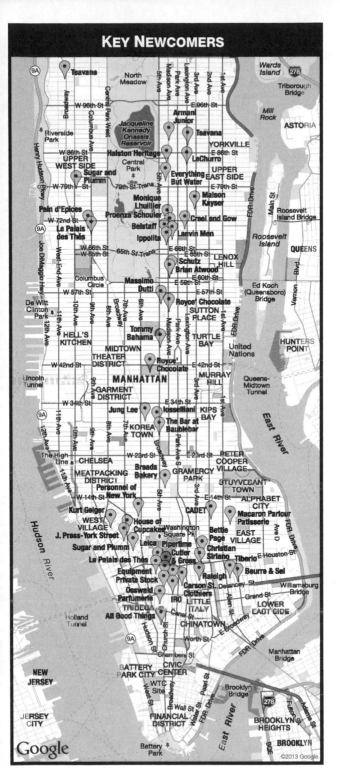

KEY NEWCOMERS

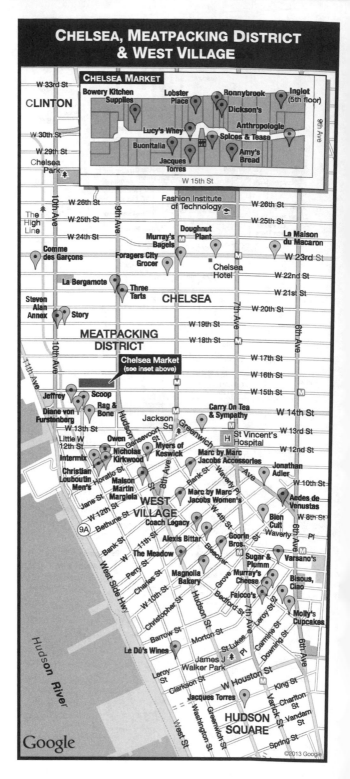

CHELSEA, MEATPACKING DISTRICT & WEST VILLAGE

CHELSEA MARKET

Bowery Kitchen Supplies
Lobster Place
Ronnybrook
Inglot (5th floor)
Dickson's
Anthropologie
Lucy's Whey
Spices & Tease
Buonitalia
Jacques Torres
Amy's Bread

CLINTON

W 33rd St
W 30th St
W 29th St
Chelsea Park
9th Ave
W 15th St

The High Line
W 26th St
W 25th St
W 24th St
Fashion Institute of Technology
W 26th St
W 25th St
La Maison du Macaron
W 23rd St

Comme des Garçons
Murray's Bagels
Doughnut Plant
Chelsea Hotel
W 22nd St

Foragers City Grocer
La Bergamote
Three Tarts
CHELSEA
W 21st St
W 20th St

Steven Alan Annex
Story
W 19th St
W 18th St

MEATPACKING DISTRICT

Chelsea Market (see inset above)

W 17th St
W 16th St
W 15th St

Jeffrey
Scoop
Rag & Bone
Jackson Sq
Carry On Tea & Sympathy
W 14th St

Diane von Furstenberg
W 13th St
W 13th St

Little W 12th St
Owen
Myers of Keswick
St Vincent's Hospital
W 12th St

Intermix
Nicholas Kirkwood
Marc by Marc Jacobs Accessories
Jonathan Adler
W 10th St

Christian Louboutin Men's
Maison Martin Margiela
WEST VILLAGE
Marc by Marc Jacobs Women's
Aedes de Venustas
W 8th St

Coach Legacy
Bien Cuit
Waverly Pl

Alexis Bittar
Goorin Bros.
Varsano's

The Meadow
Sugar & Plumm
Murray's Cheese
Bisous, Ciao

Magnolia Bakery
Faicco's
Molly's Cupcakes

Le Dû's Wines
James J Walker Park
W Houston St

Jacques Torres
HUDSON SQUARE

Hudson River

Google

©2013 Google

SoHo & Surrounds

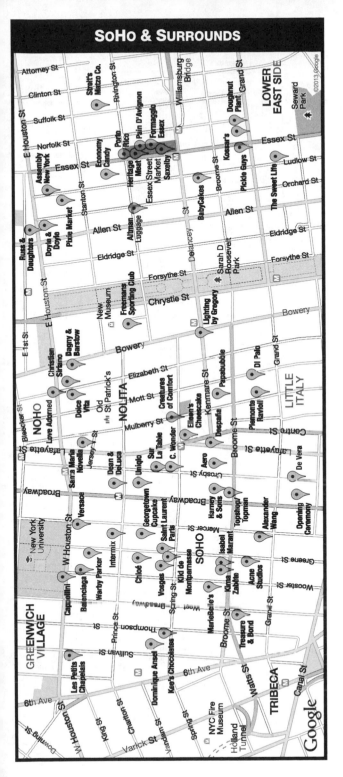

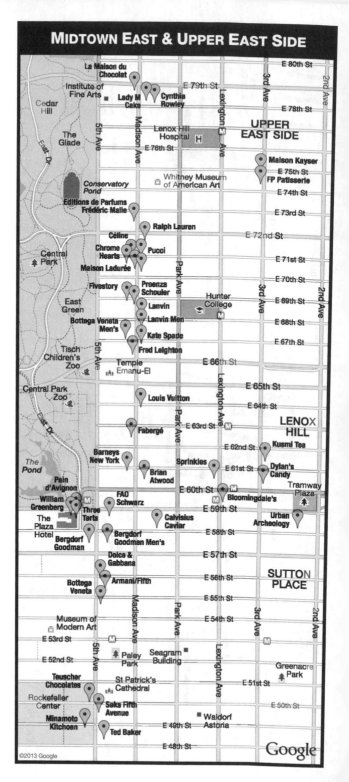

MIDTOWN EAST & UPPER EAST SIDE

La Maison du Chocolat
Institute of Fine Arts
Cedar Hill
Lady M Cakes
Cynthia Rowley
E 79th St
E 80th St
E 78th St
UPPER EAST SIDE
Lenox Hill Hospital H
The Glade
E 76th St
Maison Kayser
E 75th St
FP Patisserie
Conservatory Pond
Whitney Museum of American Art
E 74th St
Editions de Parfums Frédéric Malle
E 73rd St
Ralph Lauren
Céline
E 72nd St
Central Park
Chrome Hearts
Pucci
E 71st St
Maison Ladurée
E 70th St
Fivestory
Proenza Schouler
East Green
Lanvin
Hunter College
E 69th St
Lanvin Men
E 68th St
Bottega Veneta Men's
Kate Spade
E 67th St
Fred Leighton
Tisch Children's Zoo
Temple Emanu-El
E 66th St
E 65th St
Central Park Zoo
Louis Vuitton
E 64th St
LENOX HILL
Fabergé
E 63rd St
Kusmi Tea
Barneys New York
E 62nd St
The Pond
Brian Atwood
Sprinkles
E 61st St
Dylan's Candy
Pain d'Avignon
E 60th St
Bloomingdale's
Tramway Plaza
William Greenberg
FAO Schwarz
E 59th St
Urban Archeology
Three Tarts
Calvisius Caviar
E 58th St
The Plaza Hotel
Bergdorf Goodman
Bergdorf Goodman Men's
E 57th St
Dolce & Gabbana
SUTTON PLACE
E 56th St
Bottega Veneta
Armani/Fifth
E 55th St
Museum of Modern Art
E 54th St
E 53rd St
Paley Park
Seagram Building
E 52nd St
Greenacre Park
Teuscher Chocolates
St Patrick's Cathedral
E 51st St
Rockefeller Center
Saks Fifth Avenue
E 50th St
Minamoto Kitchoan
Waldorf Astoria
Ted Baker
E 49th St
E 48th St

©2013 Google

Google

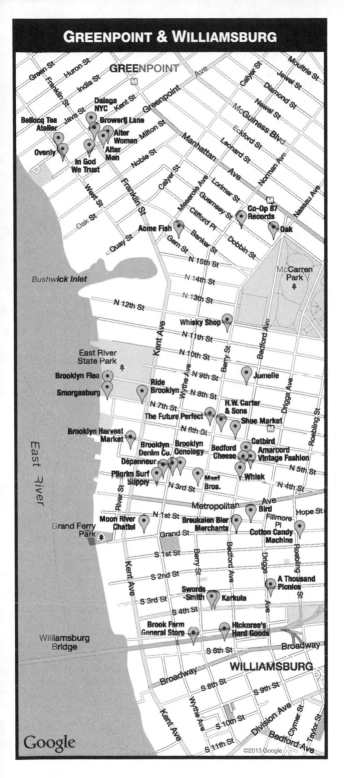

GREENPOINT & WILLIAMSBURG

GREENPOINT

Dalaga NYC
Browerji Lane
Bellocq Tea Atelier
Alter Women
Alter Men
Ovenly
In God We Trust

Co-Op 87 Records
Oak
Acme Fish

Bushwick Inlet

McCarren Park

Whisky Shop

East River State Park
Jumelle
Brooklyn Flea
Ride Brooklyn
Smorgasburg
H.W. Carter & Sons
The Future Perfect
Shoe Market
Brooklyn Harvest Market
Catbird
Brooklyn Denim Co.
Brooklyn Oenology
Bedford Cheese
Amarcord Vintage Fashion
Dépanneur
Pilgrim Surf Supply
Mast Bros.
Whisk

East River

Bird
Moon River Chattel
Breukelen Bier Merchants
Fillmore Pl
Grand Ferry Park
Cotton Candy Machine

A Thousand Picnics

Swords-Smith
Karkula
Brook Farm General Store
Hickoree's Hard Goods
Williamsburg Bridge

WILLIAMSBURG

Broadway

Google

©2013 Google

SHOPPING

Most Popular

FASHION/BEAUTY

1. Anthropologie
2. H&M
3. Sephora
4. Uniqlo
5. Tiffany & Co.
6. Coach
7. Express
8. Victoria's Secret
9. J.Crew
10. Brooks Brothers
11. 7 For All Mankind
12. Zara
13. Ralph Lauren
14. Urban Outfitters
15. Kiehl's
16. Burberry
17. Eileen Fisher
18. Housing Works
19. Michael Kors
20. Harry's Shoes

HOME/GARDEN

1. Bed Bath & Beyond
2. ABC Carpet & Home
3. Williams-Sonoma
4. Crate & Barrel
5. Gracious Home
6. Fishs Eddy
7. Sur La Table
8. Ikea
9. 23rd St. Hardware
10. Muji
11. Broadway Panhandler
12. ABC Carpet/Home (Rugs)
13. ABC Carpet/Outlet
14. CB2
15. A Cook's Companion
16. Marimekko
17. Alessi
18. Beacon Paint
19. Georg Jensen
20. Michael C. Fina

LIFESTYLE

1. Apple Store
2. B&H Photo-Video
3. Amer. Mus. of Natural History
4. Metropolitan Museum Shop
5. American Girl Place
6. J&R Music
7. MoMA Store
8. FAO Schwarz
9. Paragon
10. 42nd St. Photo
11. Adorama Camera
12. Pearl River
13. Jewish Museum Store
14. A.I. Friedman
15. Brooklyn Flea
16. REI
17. String
18. TUMI
19. Lee's Art
20. Bose

DEPARTMENT STORES/MASS MERCHANTS

1. Macy's
2. Bloomingdale's
3. Lord & Taylor
4. Saks Fifth Ave.
5. Costco Warehouse
6. Bergdorf Goodman
7. Target
8. Barneys New York

Top Ratings by Quality

FASHION/BEAUTY

30] Hermès

29] Fred Leighton
Breitling
Fratelli Rossetti*
Hermes Men*
Santa Maria Novella*
Loro Piana
Brunello Cucinelli
Audemars Piguet
David Webb*
IF*
Oscar de la Renta*
Amsale
Cartier
Bottega Veneta
Mikimoto
Brioni
Vera Wang Bridal
Carolina Herrera
Van Cleef & Arpels
Chopard
Harry Winston
Balenciaga
Bergdorf Goodman Men's
Buccellati
Wempe*
Bergdorf Goodman
Journelle
Dior New York
Alexander McQueen

HOME/GARDEN

29] Duxiana
Georg Jensen
Pratesi
Lalique
Korin
Baccarat
Christofle
Bernardaud
D. Porthault
Knoll
Frette

28] Yves Delorme
Pompanoosuc
Greenhouse
Ann Sacks
Moss Bureau*
Zabar's Mezz.
Scully & Scully
Alessi
J.B. Prince

27] Michael C. Fina
Marimekko
John Derian*
Artistic Tile
Canvas
Michael Aram
B&B Italia
Davis & Warshow
Williams-Sonoma
A&G Merch.

LIFESTYLE

29] String
Fountain Pen
Jazz Record Ctr.
Diptyque
Smythson
Apple Store

28] Dinosaur Hill
TUMI
Tender Buttons
Montblanc
B&H Photo-Video
Purl Soho
Bang & Olufsen
Dempsey/Carroll

27] Knitty City
Evolution
Annie's Blue Ribbon
Cotton Candy Machine*
Maclaren*
Tekserve
Crumpler
Adorama Camera
Bose
Sony Style
Frick Collection Shop
Albee Baby
Bicycle Habitat
NY Central Art
International Ctr. Photo*
Arthur Brown

* Indicates a tie with property above; excludes places with low votes

Top Display

29		
Santa Maria Novella	String*
Moss Bureau	Alexander McQueen
Fred Leighton	Chrome Hearts
Issey Miyake	Marni*
David Webb	Amsale
Evolution Store	Hermès
Breitling	Mikimoto
Harry Winston	Salvatore Ferragamo
Buccellati	Tiffany & Co.
Cartier	Comme des Garçons

28		
Baccarat	Jo Malone
Bernardaud	Lalique
Catbird	Bergdorf Goodman
Wempe	D. Porthault
Carolina Herrera	Chanel

Top Service

29		
Buccellati	Harry Winston
Breitling	Etro
Wempe	H. Stern

28		
Mikimoto	Lalique
Audemars Piguet	Goorin Bros.
Greenhouse	Warby Parker
Vera Wang Bridal	JackRabbit Sports

27		
Burberry Brit	Hermès Men
Chopard	Carolina Herrera
Chrome Hearts	Vacheron Constantin
David Webb*	Sabon
Malin + Goetz*	Brooklyn Superhero
Paul Stuart	Oscar de la Renta*
Baccarat	Scully & Scully*
Leonard Opticians	Cartier

TOPS BY CATEGORY

ACCESSORIES

29 Loro Piana
Bottega Veneta
28 Dunhill
Asprey
27 Longchamp

ACTIVEWEAR

27 Patagonia
Lululemon Athletic
26 JackRabbit Sports
25 Athleta
Nike

APPAREL, CHILDREN'S

28 Jacadi
Catimini
Bonpoint
Ralph Lauren Children's
Diesel Kids

APPAREL, MEN'S

29 Hermès Men
Brioni
Paul Stuart
Beretta
28 Turnbull & Asser

APPAREL, MEN/WOMEN

30 Hermès
29 Brunello Cucinelli*
IF
Bogner
Emporio Armani

APPAREL, VINTAGE

25 Ina
24 Amarcord Vintage
23 Mem. Sloan-Kettering
Michael's
22 What Goes Around

APPAREL, WOMEN'S

29 Oscar de la Renta
Bottega Veneta
Carolina Herrera
Balenciaga
Dior New York

ART SUPPLIES

27 New York Central Art
26 Blick Art Materials
Lee's Art
25 A.I. Friedman
24 Pearl Paint

BATH & KITCHEN

28 Ann Sacks
27 Artistic Tile
Davis & Warshow
26 Waterworks
Blackman

BEAUTY/GROOMING

29 Santa Maria Novella
28 Malin + Goetz
Jo Malone
27 New London Pharmacy
Kiehl's

BICYCLES

27 Bicycle Habitat
26 Danny's Cycles
Dixon's Bicycle Shop
Gotham Bikes
24 Adeline Adeline

BRIDAL

29 Amsale
Vera Wang Bridal
Carolina Herrera
25 Kleinfeld
24 Adriennes

CAMERA/VIDEO

28 B&H Photo-Video
27 Adorama Camera
25 Willoughby's
24 Camera Land
23 42nd St. Photo

CHINA/SILVER/CRYSTAL

29 Georg Jensen
Lalique
Baccarat
Christofle
Bernardaud

COOKWARE

29 Korin
28 Zabar's Mezzanine
Alessi
J.B. Prince
27 Williams-Sonoma

DEPARTMENT STORES

29 Bergdorf Goodman Men's
Bergdorf Goodman
28 Barneys New York
27 Saks Fifth Ave.
26 Bloomingdale's

ELECTRONICS

29 Apple Store
28 Bang & Olufsen
27 Tekserve
   Bose
26 Sony Style

EYEWEAR

29 Alain Mikli
28 Oliver Peoples
27 Leonard Opticians
   Morgenthal Frederics
   Warby Parker

FLEA MARKETS

24 Artists & Fleas
21 Brooklyn Flea
20 Malcolm Shabazz
   Hell's Kitchen*
   GreenFlea

FURNITURE/
HOME FURNISHINGS

29 Knoll
28 Pompanoosuc Mills
   Greenhouse
   Moss Bureau
   Scully & Scully

GIFTS/NOVELTIES

29 Diptyque
27 Evolution
   Annie's Blue Ribbon
26 Arcadia Spa & Home
   Met Opera Shop

HANDBAGS

28 Mulberry
27 Anya Hindmarch
   Longchamp
26 Coach
   Coach Legacy

HARDWARE

26 Simon's Hardware
   Beacon Paint
25 Garber Hardware
   Green Depot
   23rd St. Hardware

JEANS

28 Earnest Sewn
   Joe's Jeans
27 Diesel Black Gold
26 AG | Adriano Goldschmied
25 7 For All Mankind

JEWELRY

29 Fred Leighton
   David Webb
   Cartier
   Mikimoto
   Van Cleef & Arpels

KNITTING

29 String
28 Purl Soho
27 Knitty City
23 Yarn Co.

LEGWEAR/LINGERIE

29 Journelle
28 La Perla
   La Petite Coquette
   Wolford
   Cosabella

LIGHTING

27 Arhaus
25 Gracious Home
   Lee's Studio
24 Aero
23 Lighting by Gregory

LINENS

29 Duxiana
   Pratesi
   D. Porthault
   Frette
28 Yves Delorme

LUGGAGE

28 TUMI
27 Crumpler Bags
26 Bric's
   Altman Luggage
22 Flight 001

MUSEUM SHOPS

27 Frick Collection Shop
   International Ctr. Photo
   Amer. Mus. of Natural History
26 Mus. of the City of NY
   Mus. of Arts & Design

SHOES

29 Fratelli Rossetti
   Manolo Blahnik
   Salvatore Ferragamo
28 Christian Louboutin
   John Fluevog

SNEAKERS

27 Bape
    New York Running
26 ASICS
25 Nike
    Adidas

SPORTING GOODS

26 REI
    JackRabbit Sports
    Burton
    Paragon
25 Adidas Sports

STATIONERY

29 Fountain Pen
    Smythson of Bond St.
28 Montblanc
    Dempsey & Carroll
27 Arthur Brown

SWIMWEAR

26 Malia Mills
    Paragon
25 OMO: Norma Kamali
    Vilebrequin
24 Zimmermann

TOYS

28 Dinosaur Hill
26 LEGO
    FAO Schwarz
    American Girl Place
25 Boomerang

WATCHES

29 Breitling
    Audemars Piguet
    Chopard
    Wempe
    Vacheron Constantin

TOPS BY LOCATION

CHELSEA

29 Jazz Record Ctr.
    Knoll
28 Comme des Garçons
    Malin + Goetz
    Steven Alan

EAST 40s

29 Paul Stuart
    Apple Store
28 TUMI
    Allen Edmonds
    Burberry

EAST 50s

29 Duxiana
    Fratelli Rossetti
    Breitling
    Lalique
    Audemars Piguet

EAST 60s

29 Hermès
    Fred Leighton
    Hermès Men
    Georg Jensen
    Pratesi

EAST 70s

29 David Webb
    Christofle

    Bottega Veneta
    Vera Wang Bridal
    Carolina Herrera

EAST 80s

28 TUMI
    Jacadi
    Catimini
    Barbour
    Peter Elliot

EAST 90s

28 Blue Tree
    Bonpoint
26 Intimacy
    Jewish Museum Store
24 Capezio

EAST VILLAGE

28 Dinosaur Hill
27 John Derian
    Kiehl's
    Odin
    New York Central Art

FINANCIAL DISTRICT

30 Hermès
28 TUMI
    Tiffany & Co.
    Canali
24 J&R Music

FLATIRON DISTRICT

29] Journelle
28] TUMI
Ann Sacks
Bang & Olufsen
Dr. Martens

GARMENT DISTRICT

28] Moss Bureau
B&H Photo-Video
26] 30th St. Guitars
Mood
Bare Escentuals

GRAMERCY PARK/ MURRAY HILL

28] J.B. Prince
26] Danny's Cycles
Simon's Hardware
Morgan Library Shop
25] Roche Bobois

GREENWICH VILLAGE

28] La Petite Coquette
27] C.O. Bigelow
26] Aesop
25] Broadway Panhandler
William-Wayne

HARLEM

27] Davis & Warshow
26] Carol's Daughter
25] Studio Museum Shop
24] New York Public Library Shop
20] Malcolm Shabazz

LOWER EAST SIDE

28] Earnest Sewn
27] Doyle & Doyle
26] LES Tenement Mus. Bookshop
Altman Luggage
Hoodie Shop

MEATPACKING DIST.

29] Alexander McQueen
Apple Store
28] La Perla
Christian Louboutin
Marni

NOHO

27] Bond 07 Selima
Bond No. 9
Zacky's
26] Zero/Maria Cornejo
Blick Art Materials

NOLITA

29] Santa Maria Novella
28] John Fluevog
Earnest Sewn Outpost
Steven Alan
27] Crumpler Bags

SOHO

29] IF
Balenciaga
Journelle
Chanel
Bogner

TRIBECA

29] Duxiana
Korin
Fountain Pen
28] Pompanoosuc Mills
Issey Miyake

UNION SQUARE

27] Lululemon Athletic
26] JackRabbit Sports
Paragon
25] Agnès B.
Moscot

WEST 40s

28] TUMI
Allen Edmonds
27] Michael Kors
International Ctr. Photo
Arthur Brown
Longchamp

WEST 50s

29] Bergdorf Goodman
Manolo Blahnik
Knoll
Smythson of Bond St.
27] Ascot Chang

WEST 60s

29] Apple Store
28] TUMI
Burberry Brit
Jacadi
Wolford

WEST 70s

28] TUMI
Bang & Olufsen
Stuart Weitzman
27] Knitty City
Bra Smyth

WEST 80s/90s

28] Malin + Goetz
Zabar's Mezzanine
Steven Alan
27] Albee Baby
Patagonia

WEST VILLAGE

29] Brunello Cucinelli
Diptyque
28] Christian Louboutin
Burberry Brit
Mulberry

OUTER BOROUGHS

BRONX

25] NY Botanical Garden Shop
23] ABC Carpet/Outlet
Macy's
20] BJ's
Loehmann's

BKLYN: BOERUM HILL/ DOWNTOWN

28] Greenhouse
Steven Alan
27] Annie's Blue Ribbon
26] Malia Mills
Carol's Daughter

BKLYN: CARROLL GARDENS/COBBLE HILL

27] Bird
26] Barney's Co-Op
25] Moscot
By Brooklyn
20] Buffalo Exchange

BKLYN: HEIGHTS/DUMBO

26] A Cook's Companion
25] Design Within Reach

23] J. McLaughlin
Zoë

BKLYN: PARK SLOPE

27] Bicycle Habitat
Bird
Lululemon Athletic
26] Clay Pot
Goorin Bros.

BKLYN: WILLIAMSBURG

28] Catbird
27] Cotton Candy Machine
A&G Merch.
Bird*
26] Organic Modernism

QUEENS

27] Michael Kors
Davis & Warshow
26] LEGO
Bare Escentuals
Sam Ash

ARCHITECTURAL INTEREST

Acne Studios
Alexander McQueen
Alexander Wang
Apple Store
Armani Fifth Avenue
Baccarat
Bottega Veneta
Bottega Veneta Men's
Carlos Miele
Carlo Pazolini
Cartier
Comme des Garçons
Derek Lam
Fabergé
Fendi
Fivestory
Henri Bendel
Issey Miyake

IWC Schaffhausen
Lanvin
Lanvin Men
Louis Vuitton
Maison Kitsuné
Mauboussin
Moroso
Neue Galerie Shop
Owen
Prada
Pucci
Ralph Lauren
Rick Owens
Saint Laurent Paris
Story
3.1 Phillilp Lim
Tom Ford
Versace

DESIGNER COLLABORATIONS/ CAPSULE COLLECTIONS

Featuring special, limited-edition joint-label offerings

Adeline Adeline
Adidas
Anthropologie
Assembly NY
Atelier New York
Barneys New York
Brian Atwood
Cappellini
Cole Haan
Crewcuts
Cutler and Gross
Design Within Reach
Earnest Sewn
Equinox Energy Wear
Everything But Water
Galeria Melissa
Ghurka
H&M
Happy Socks
Intermix
Isabel Marant

J.Crew
J.Crew Men's
Knoll
Louis Vuitton
M.A.C. Cosmetics
Madewell
Moncler
Odin
Oliver Peoples
Opening Ceremony
Scoop
Sperry Top-Sider
Stella McCartney
Steven Alan
Stone Fox Bride
Surface to Air
Target
Trina Turk
Uniqlo
Versace
West Elm Market

HOLIDAY DECORATION

ABC Carpet & Home
American Girl Place
Barneys New York
Bergdorf Goodman
Bloomingdale's
Cartier
FAO Schwarz
Harry Winston

Henri Bendel
Lord & Taylor
Macy's
Paul Smith
Ralph Lauren
Saks Fifth Ave.
Sony Style
Tiffany & Co.

MADE IN NYC

Annelore
Assembly New York
A Thousand Picnics
By Brooklyn
By Robert James
Cadet
Courtshop
Erica Weiner

Freemans Sporting Goods
Harlem Haberdashery
In God We Trust
Malin + Goetz
Nanette Lepore
Reformation
Stone Fox Bride
Tucker

Good Values

DEPARTMENT/DISCOUNT MASS MERCHANTS

Bed Bath Beyond
BJ's
Century 21
Costco
Loehmann's
Lord & Taylor
Macy's
Target

FASHION/BEAUTY

Baggu
Beacon's Closet
Bettie Page
Brandy Melville
Buffalo Exchange
Clarks
C.O. Bigelow
Converse
C. Wonder
Dave's Army Navy
Dolce Vita
Express
Goorin Bros.
H&M
Happy Socks
Housing Works
Joe Fresh
Levi's
Lush
M&J
Massimo Dutti
Ray Beauty Supply
Sabon
Sam Edelman
SlapBack
Splendid
Swatch
Trinity Place
Uniqlo
Uno de 50
Warby Parker
Zara

HOME/GARDEN

A Cook's Companion
Aero
Antiques Garage
Beacon Paint
Bowery Kitchen
Brooklyn Kitchen
Broadway Panhandler
CB2
Crate & Barrel
Film Biz Props
Fishs Eddy
Garber Hardware
Green Depot
Greenhouse
Housing Works
Ikea
Janovic
Muji
Pintchik
Tarzian Housewares
23rd St. Hardware
West Elm Market

LIFESTYLE

Academy Records
Alphabets
Altman Luggage
Amer. Mus. of Natural History
Balloon Saloon
B&H Photo-Video
Bleecker St. Records
Brooklyn Museum Shop
Dinosaur Hill
Dixon's Bicycle Shop
Fool's Gold
Jazz Record Ctr.
Knitty City
LES Tenement Mus. Bookshop
M&J Trimming
Mus. City of NY Shop
New York Public Library Shop
Pearl Paint
Pearl River
Studio Museum Shop

SHOPPING
DIRECTORY

| | QUALITY | DISPLAY | SERVICE | COST |

A&G Merch
27 | 24 | 20 | E

Williamsburg | 111 N. Sixth St. (Berry St.) | Brooklyn | 718-388-1779 | www.aandgmerch.com

"Make a room special" courtesy of this "cool" Williamsburg shop, which offers "everything your nest needs" in the way of "modern", mostly eco-friendly furnishings and a "curated selection of household tchotchkes" that showcase "designer flair" "without a hint of irony"; the merch is meant to suit urbanites at a "not-too-expensive" cost – the only problem is, it may "leave you wishing you had a bigger apartment."

Aaron Basha
28 | 26 | 26 | VE

E 60s | 685 Madison Ave. (bet. 61st & 62nd Sts.) | 212-644-1970 | www.aaronbasha.com

"Sometimes ya just gotta have jeweled baby shoes" that "all the new moms wear" declare devotees dazzled by the "darling", whimsical "enameled charms" at this family-owned Madison Avenue jeweler; but there's more than "sweet" collectibles in store – you'll also find "unique", "beautifully designed" pieces that "you won't see coming and going", all purveyed by the "attentive" staff.

Aaron Faber Gallery
27 | 25 | 24 | VE

W 50s | 666 Fifth Ave. (53rd St.) | 212-586-8411 | www.aaronfaber.com

Looky-loos take note: the "superb selection" of modern "designer studio" and estate jewelry, "fabulous" timepieces and other "out-of-the-way delights" at this "unique" glass-and-chrome gallery-esque shop in Midtown is "definitely worth a leisurely browse" and "great for inspiration" even if you "can't afford" the splurge; loyalists "appreciate the education and attention" bestowed by the "wonderful" owners and staff, adding it's "the only place to go for vintage watch repairs and appraisals."

ABC Carpet & Home
26 | 25 | 20 | VE

Flatiron | 888 Broadway (19th St.) | 212-473-3000 | www.abchome.com

Almost a "museum made for shopping", this Flatiron "fantasyland" offers "interior design junkies" seven "sprawling" stories stuffed with a "mélange of furniture styles" including "sustainable" options, "extravagant" chandeliers and "unique trinkets" "from all over the world"; though "sticker shock" is standard and staffers range from "friendly" to "aloof", most consider it a "visual feast" packed with "ideas and inspiration" and "always worth a wander"; P.S. ABC Kitchen and ABC Cocina restaurants are "added bonuses."

ABC Carpet & Home (Carpets/Rugs)
26 | 22 | 21 | E

Flatiron | 881 Broadway (bet. 18th & 19th Sts.) | 212-473-3000 | www.abccarpet.com

Like an "Arabian souk", this Flatiron "magic carpet store" proffers "piles" of "really gorgeous goods", from "tiny throws to mansion-sized" mats in "endless" styles, colors and patterns – "if you can't find a rug you love here, you should just settle for bare floors"; thankfully the staff is "helpful" because the experience can be "overwhelming", and those in the know suggest starting with the "bargains in the basement" because the selection is as "dazzling" as "the bill."

	QUALITY	DISPLAY	SERVICE	COST

ABC Carpet & Home Warehouse Outlet   23 | 17 | 18 | M

Soundview | 1055 Bronx River Ave. (Bruckner Blvd.) | Bronx |
718-842-8772 | www.abchome.com

"Wander" this "huge" discount warehouse offshoot of ABC to find a
"unique" "assortment of rugs", furnishings and more "amazing stuff
you wish your apartment was big enough to hold"; the "showroom is a
bit overwhelming" and many offerings are "still expensive", but "there
are bargains to be found" – "if you have the patience" and are willing
to make the "trek" to the Bronx.

Academy Records   25 | 19 | 22 | M

E Village | 415 E. 12th St. (bet. Ave. A & 1st Ave.) | 212-780-9166
Flatiron | 12 W. 18th St. (bet. 5th & 6th Aves.) | 212-242-3000
Williamsburg | 96 N. Sixth St. (bet. Berry St. & Wythe Ave.) |
Brooklyn | 718-218-8200 ◐

"You'll spend hours if you're not careful" at this "browser-friendly" trio
featuring a "vast selection" of new and secondhand LPs and CDs
across all genres (plus DVDs and Blu-rays), overseen by a "knowledgeable staff" that isn't above "lecturing you if you make a bad
choice"; "opera buffs will be singing like Maria Callas" at the classical-
heavy Flatiron original, while vinyl junkies "keep it spinnin'" at the East
Village and Williamsburg locations.

AC Gears   ▽ 25 | 25 | 21 | M

G Village | 69 E. Eighth St. (B'way) | 212-260-2269 | www.acgears.com
A "unique" nook geared to "gadget-lovers", this sleekly styled Villager
vends "the hottest, trendiest" electronics along with "surprising and
fun knickknacks", mostly imported "straight from Japan" and Europe;
"Mimobot" flash drives, multihued headphones and earbuds, "solar-
charging" backpacks and more offer a profusion of "high-tech presents"
for the cyberphile in your life.

Acne Studios   ▽ 25 | 18 | 20 | E

SoHo | 33 Greene St. (Grand St.) | 212-334-8345 | www.acnestudios.com
Don't let the "terrible name" fool you: this SoHo outpost of the ultrahip
Stockholm-based collective, housed in mirrored, mazelike quarters with
carpeting and fur benches, stocks "gorgeous" guy- and girlwear in minimalist cuts; the standout denim and sportswear are "great for Swedish
bodies and Swedish winters", as are the coveted boots and accessories;
it's "expensive", but these fresh-faced items are "so well worth it!"

A Cook's Companion   26 | 22 | 24 | M

Brooklyn Heights | 197 Atlantic Ave. (bet. Clinton & Court Sts.) |
Brooklyn | 718-852-6901 | www.acookscompanion.com
Home chefs hunting for "basics" and the "unusual" find this Brooklyn
Heights kitchen shop stuffed silly with a "terrific selection" of "fine cookware", bakeware, cutlery, culinary gadgets and more; run by "helpful"
sorts who offer "quality recommendations", it's also "great to browse" –
provided you can "resist temptations"; P.S. closed Tuesdays.

Acorn   ▽ 24 | 21 | 20 | M

Downtown Bklyn | 323 Atlantic Ave. (bet. Hoyt & Smith Sts.) |
Brooklyn | 718-522-3760 | www.acorntoyshop.com
"Hip parents with hip kids" head to this "beautiful" Brooklyn store for
the kind of "adorable", "quirky" toys "you won't find elsewhere"; many

of the offerings are "handcrafted" using environmentally sustainable practices, and the "friendly, welcoming" staff makes you feel as if you're in a "small museum", or at the very least a "very special shop."

Adeline Adeline
24 | 23 | 22 | E

TriBeCa | 147 Reade St. (bet. Greenwich & Hudson Sts.) | 212-227-1150 | www.adelineadeline.com

"Very cute, quirky and 'TriBeCa'-ish", this "uncluttered" boutique bike shop sweeps freewheelers off their feet with its "helpful staff" and European-style city cycles, ranging from family workhorses like Christiania's cargo trike and WorkCycle's iconic Dutch granny styles to Linus' retro roadsters and even collaborations with Kate Spade; the accessories, including checkerboard helmets, rattan baskets and saddles with springs, also veer far away from the pedestrian.

A Détacher
27 | 24 | 22 | E

NoLita | 262 Mott St. (bet. Houston & Prince Sts.) | 212-625-3380 | www.adetacher.com

Owner-cum-curator Monika Kowalska's "beautiful" NoLita shrine, featuring rough-plank floors and a minimalist feel, is a fitting showcase for her deconstructed silhouettes in luxe fabrics; though "expensive", the "elegant, simple hipster wear" is of "excellent quality" and exhibits "great craftsmanship", ensuring it can be worn "year after year"; the handpicked jewelry, accessories and objects are equally rarefied.

Adidas Originals
25 | 24 | 20 | M

SoHo | 136 Wooster St. (bet. Houston & Prince Sts.) | 212-673-0398
Elmhurst | Queens Center Mall | 90-15 Queens Blvd. (bet. 57th & 59th Aves.) | Queens | 718-393-9620 ◐

Adidas Sports Performance ◐

NoHo | 610 Broadway (Houston St.) | 212-529-0081
800-289-2724 | www.adidas.com

No matter their favored game, "fashion-forward sports enthusiasts" sprint to this outfit for "the proper outfits" – from tracksuits to sneaks – bearing the "iconic" "striped" logo; NoHo's Sports Performance branch equips active jocks with practical "athletic gear galore", and its "colorful" SoHo and Queens Center teammates have the Originals "classics covered" along with "the latest hip" "limited editions."

Adidas SLVR
▽ 23 | 22 | 19 | E

SoHo | 108 Wooster St. (bet. Prince & Spring Sts.) | 212-941-6580 | www.slvrstore.adidas.com

Eschewing the familiar trefoil emblem, this recently renovated SoHo destination for team Adidas' tasteful lifestyle brand – think understated threads and hip kicks – falls between the sporty Originals and Performance lines and chichi Y-3; shoppers who "select carefully" and spend liberally emerge from the well-lighted quarters with "cool stuff that not everyone has."

Adorama Camera
27 | 19 | 23 | M

Flatiron | 42 W. 18th St. (bet. 5th & 6th Aves.) | 212-741-0052 | 800-223-2500 | www.adorama.com

Whatever your "esoteric camera-related need", this Flatiron photorama is "one of the best" for equipment "from amateur to pro" ("both new and reconditioned") at "fair prices", not to mention rentals, printing,

	QUALITY	DISPLAY	SERVICE	COST

"photography courses", TVs and entertainment devices; service is "personable" but "no-nonsense", so it's advisable "to know what you're interested in"; P.S. closes at 5 PM Friday and all day Saturday.

Adriennes

24 | 21 | 21 | E

LES | 134 Orchard St. (bet. Delancey & Rivington Sts.) | 212-228-9618 | www.adriennesny.com

"What a pleasurable experience" agree engaged customers who spend a "magic" afternoon trying on dresses at this by-appointment LES bridal mainstay, which recently relocated to new quarters near the original; the special-day wear includes "elegant, beautiful" wedding gowns from NYC-based designers plus "pretty" bridesmaids frocks from Vera Wang and Badgley Mischka, most at "extremely fair prices"; service is "kind" albeit somewhat "disorganized", but they "know the business."

Aedes de Venustas

∇ 29 | 29 | 26 | E

W Village | 9 Christopher St. (bet. 6th Ave. & 7th Ave. S.) | 212-206-8674 | 888-233-3715 | www.aedes.com

"Paradise for fragrance lovers", this "gorgeous" burgundy-and-gold Villager adorned with ornate chandeliers and gilded displays is "stocked to the rafters" with "luxe", "impossible-to-find" European perfumes, room sprays, candles and lotions in pretty packaging; prices tend toward the "high end", but they come with "incredible service" and "awesome" gift-wrapping that add to the simply "divine" experience.

Aero

24 | 22 | 21 | E

SoHo | 419 Broome St. (bet. Crosby & Lafayette Sts.) | 212-966-1500 | www.aerostudios.com

Interior designer Thomas O'Brien's loftlike SoHo furniture boutique and studio is tastefully filled to the brim with an eclectic collection of "gifts, kitchen gadgets and household fixings" for the abode; fans of the clean-lined midcentury and modern offerings – a mix of refurbished antiques, lighting and the home honcho's pieces – swear it's impossible "to leave without one great deal."

Aesop

26 | 23 | 22 | E

E 40s | Grand Central Terminal | 87 E. 42nd St., Graybar Passage (Vanderbilt Ave.) | 212-867-7311
G Village | 60 University Pl. (bet. 10th & 11th Sts.) | 212-505-1511
NoLita | 232 Elizabeth St. (bet. Houston & Prince Sts.) | 212-431-4411
NEW **SoHo** | 438 W. Broadway (bet. Prince & Spring Sts.) | 212-899-3451
877-602-3767 | www.aesop.com

The Australian beauty and grooming brand makes a splash stateside, rolling out its "terrific, natural" products at its Grand Central kiosk and NoLita, SoHo and Village branches; "discerning" enthusiasts delight in the "serene ambiance", "spa"-like smell and "beautifully displayed" signature amber glass bottles of "amazing and effective" hair, skin and body lotions and potions, declaring "what a fantastic import."

AG Adriano Goldschmied

26 | 24 | 22 | E

SoHo | 111 Greene St. (bet. Prince & Spring Sts.) | 212-680-0581
W 70s | 305 Columbus Ave. (bet. 74th & 75th Sts.) | 212-496-5692
www.agjeans.com

"If you find a model that fits you right" from this California-based denim brand it may "last forever" laud loyalists who scoop up "ridiculously comfortable" jeans at this skylit SoHo shop and UWS offshoot; the salespeople recommend "very forgiving" styles that "flatter", and if your sticks need a nip/tuck, there's a free "awesome tailoring" service.

Agent Provocateur   26 | 26 | 22 | VE

E 60s | 675 Madison Ave. (bet. 61st & 62nd Sts.) | 212-840-2436
SoHo | 133 Mercer St. (bet. Prince & Spring Sts.) | 212-965-0229
www.agentprovocateur.com

"Ready to unleash the modern courtesan in you? run don't walk" to this British brand's "sumptuous" East 60s–SoHo pair packed with "stimulating things" like "fancy underpants" and "over-the-top" bras and nighties that are "more form than function"; the "cute" staffers are "easy to chat with about the most unmentionable things", plus when your "guy sees you" in these "sexy" little nothings "it'll blow his . . . mind."

Agnès B.   25 | 22 | 20 | E

E 80s | 1063 Madison Ave. (bet. 80th & 81st Sts.) | 212-570-9333
SoHo | 50 Howard St. (bet. B'way & Mercer St.) | 212-431-1335
Union Sq | 13 E. 16th St. (bet. 5th Ave. & Union Sq. W.) | 212-741-2585
www.agnesb.com

"Unmistakably French" fawn Francophiles who file into this Gallic designer's NYC trio (including the art-filled SoHo branch) for a "taste of Paris"; the "standout" accessories and "classic clothing", including "some of the prettiest blouses ever" and "well-made" staples ("don't underestimate the menswear"), "easily fit into a modern wardrobe" and are "worth collecting"; "whilst not ground breaking", it's "not too conservative either", plus service leans toward "bend over backward."

A.I. Friedman   25 | 22 | 20 | M

Flatiron | 44 W. 18th St. (bet. 5th & 6th Aves.) | 212-243-9000 | 800-736-5676 | www.aifriedman.com

A "playground for creatives", this Flatiron "standby" abounds with "tempting" arts-and-crafts supplies, a "beautiful selection of paper", "fabulous" ready-made picture frames (plus "quality" custom framing via a "courteous staff") and "sleek" studio furniture; the "well-organized" layout is "fun to browse" for "professionals and beginners" alike, and its "winning" character charms even when it's "not cheap."

Akris   29 | 26 | 25 | VE

E 60s | 835 Madison Ave. (bet. 69th & 70th Sts.) | 212-717-1170 | www.akris.ch

"You never go wrong" with this low-key Swiss luxury brand's "classic styles that make you look special" declare devotees who descend on this tri-level Madison Avenue outpost; from fabrics and "little touches" like a lining's hidden polka dots to "great-fitting pants", the wares set the gold standard for minimalist "design that you can't get anywhere else" and are "worth the week's paycheck"; P.S. the "more affordable" collection housed downstairs is "just as chic."

Alain Mikli   29 | 26 | 25 | VE

E 50s | 575 Madison Ave. (bet. 56th & 57th Sts.) | 212-751-6085
E 70s | 1025 Madison Ave. (79th St.) | 212-472-6085
www.mikli.com

Pamper your peepers with "the look you need to be special" at this "chic eyewear" pair on Madison Avenue, where the très "fashionable"

French-made frames are "amazingly styled and engineered" for "sexy" cachet that'll win "compliments from strangers"; designer Philippe Starck's chandeliered boutiques are as "gorgeous" as the goods, but just be sure you're "willing to pay the price" for "the best."

Alan Moss ⊟   ▽ 28 | 27 | 18 | VE

E Village | 436 Lafayette St. (bet. Astor Pl. & 4th St.) | 212-473-1310 | www.alanmossny.com

"Just look and drool" at the "museum"-quality 20th-century furniture, lighting and objets d'art filling the East Village loft space of this namesake dealer extraordinaire; culled from designers of the 1900s–1990s, these antiques and rarities command "expensive prices" that may be more "targeted to deep-pocketed Wall Streeters" than Main Streeters.

A La Vieille Russie   28 | 27 | 26 | VE

E 50s | The Sherry-Netherland | 781 Fifth Ave. (59th St.) | 212-752-1727 | www.alvr.com

With its "old-world atmosphere", this "exquisite" East 50s gallery is an "extraordinary" "window into Czarist Russia", showcasing "rare Fabergé confections", "dazzling displays" of jewelry and other "museum-quality" antiques and art objects; even with the help of an "attentive" staff, some find the level of luxury "forbidding" since "even oligarchs can't afford it" here, but most are content to simply "look" and "dream."

Albee Baby Carriage Co.   27 | 15 | 23 | M

W 90s | 715 Amsterdam Ave. (95th St.) | 212-662-7337 | 877-692-5233 | www.albeebaby.com

"Mamas- and papas"-to-be make pilgrimages to this West 90s "institution", the "go-to source" for "generations" for "everything you need – and don't need" – for baby, including the "best" strollers, cribs, car seats, highchairs, furniture and clothes, all at "very competitive" prices; first-timers can depend on the staff to steer them right, even if the "crowded aisles" may make for a "harried shopping experience."

Alden   ▽ 29 | 22 | 25 | VE

E 40s | 344 Madison Ave. (44th St.) | 212-687-3023 | www.aldenshoe.com

Traditionalists hoof it to this Midtown branch of a circa-1884 New England shoemaker to score "excellent", "long-lasting" men's footwear of "exceptional quality" that's well "worth the price", notably the "all-time" classic "cordovan loafer (with or without tassels)"; the "knowledgeable staff" also handles belts, argyle socks and accessories, while the old-school setting, decorated with black-and-white photos, adds to the "great shopping experience."

Alessi   28 | 27 | 23 | E

E 60s | 30 E. 60th St. (bet. Madison & Park Aves.) | 212-317-9880
SoHo | 130 Greene St. (bet. Houston & Prince Sts.) | 212-941-7300
www.alessi.com

"High art meets classical design" at this SoHo-UES duo vending the Italian innovator's line of "whimsical, modern" housewares and stainless-steel accessories, "standouts worth collecting" by the likes of Michael Graves and Philippe Starck, all sure to "set your kitchen apart"; though "a bit pricey", the "hard-to-resist" pieces are "meant to endure", and the "informative" staff "helps you choose what works best."

	QUALITY	DISPLAY	SERVICE	COST

Alexander McQueen

29 | 28 | 23 | VE

Meatpacking | 417 W. 14th St. (bet. 9th & 10th Aves.) |
212-645-1797 | www.alexandermcqueen.com

"Elegant, tranquil and artfully done", this Meatpacking "fashion won-derland", where "fantasy and unique beauty" are whipped into "exqui-site" gowns, accessories and shoes (orchestrated by the late McQueen's former sidekick, Sarah Burton), underscores the legacy of this "vision-ary" "artist" as the "king of wow"; the "sticker shock" may be a fair trade for "close-ups" of designer creations that "make every woman look like a model", especially for that walk down the "runway carpet"; P.S. plans are underway to move to Madison Avenue.

Alexander Wang

26 | 27 | 24 | VE

SoHo | 103 Grand St. (Mercer St.) | 212-977-9683 |
www.alexanderwang.com

Find some of "the most architectural and edgy shapes" imaginable at this eponymous designer's SoHo bastion of off-duty model chic; the "so-cool" interior is as "unique and minimalist" as the guys' and girls' goods, replete with arty installations and a fox "fur hammock"; "bring your bank account" to afford this "pricey but nicey" collection – or sat-isfy cravings with the lower-priced, comfy T by Alexander Wang line.

Alexis Bittar

26 | 26 | 24 | E

E 80s | 1100 Madison Ave. (bet. 82nd & 83rd Sts.) | 212-249-3581
SoHo | 465 Broome St. (bet. Greene & Mercer Sts.) | 212-625-8340
NEW **W 70s** | 410 Columbus Ave. (bet. 79th & 80th Sts.) | 646-590-4142
W Village | 353 Bleecker St. (W. 10th St.) | 212-727-1093
877-680-9017 | www.alexisbittar.com

The namesake designer's "avant-garde imagination" is on "creative display" at his "treasure-chest-of-marvels" quartet (including a new Columbus Avenue branch) bursting with "beautiful baubles, bangles" and "unique showstoppers"; rock the "chic, lightweight" "conversation pieces" hand-sculpted from Lucite, or the "stunning" semiprecious and vermeil jewels, and you'll "always get compliments"; there's "so much stuff to look at" – thankfully the "enthusiastic" staffers help make "decisions that much smoother."

Alice + Olivia

24 | 24 | 22 | E

E 60s | 755 Madison Ave. (65th St.) | 646-545-2895
NEW **Meatpacking** | 431 W. 14th St. (Washington St.) |
646-747-1232
NEW **SoHo** | 72 Greene St. (bet. Broome & Spring Sts.) |
646-790-8030
W 40s | 80 W. 40th St. (bet. 5th & 6th Aves.) | 212-840-0887
www.aliceandolivia.com

"Need a party dress? look no further" than these "hard-to-resist" chain branches bursting with "adorable frocks in an array of colors"; designer Stacey Bendet "sets the trends before you even know you want it", luring loyalists with "well-constructed" pieces bedecked with "plenty of bling", along with "funky" or "cute yet classic" must-haves that "flatteringly fit most body types."

Allen Edmonds

28 | 24 | 25 | E

E 40s | 24 E. 44th St. (bet. 5th & Madison Aves.) | 212-682-3144
E 50s | 551 Madison Ave. (55th St.) | 212-308-8305

(continued)

Allen Edmonds

W 40s | Rockefeller Ctr. | 1250 Sixth Ave. (bet. 49th & 50th Sts.) | 212-262-4070

NEW **W 40s** | 20 W. 43rd St. (6th Ave.) | 212-687-1635

800-235-2348 | www.allenedmonds.com

"Leading the way in the wingtip movement" with "classic", "American-made" "dress and casual" styles that "last for years", the Midtown branches of this "been-around-forever" men's shoemaker court the corporate crowd; sure, they're "pricey", but the "helpful and knowledgeable" staffers "fit all feet" and they "stand solidly behind their product" with a "refurbishment service" that "makes shoes like new again."

AllSaints Spitalfields

`23` `25` `19` `E`

Meatpacking | 411-417 W. 13th St. (bet. 9th Ave. & Washington St.) | 646-862-3155

SoHo | 512 Broadway (bet. Broome & Spring Sts.) | 646-862-1832 ◐

www.allsaints.com

A "high cool factor" reigns at these mobbed SoHo and Meatpacking branches of a U.K. chain that "excels" in "couture grunge" for guys and gals; the "one-of-a-kind Goth" goods, including "sculpted leather jackets", asymmetrical tops and other "wrinkled, rumpled and faded" pieces, are displayed in an "amazing" warehouse-y setting accented with Singer sewing machines, "echoing the edginess of the clothes."

Aloha Rag

`26` `24` `24` `E`

Hudson Square | 505 Greenwich St. (bet. Canal & Spring Sts.) | 212-925-0882 | www.aloharag.com

Hang loose or dress up at this ultraminimalist, "very unique" Hudson Square boutique, an offshoot of the Hawaii original that surfs the wave of high-end labels with a "myriad of designers" for him and her; no need to wade – the floating racks are "well curated", offering "hip and trendy specialty gear" from "excellent quality" names like Carven, Lanvin and Thomas Wylde, capped with edgy jewelry and accessories.

Alphabets

`25` `25` `21` `M`

E Village | 115 Ave. A (bet. 7th St. & St. Marks Pl.) | 212-475-7250 | 800-419-3989 | www.alphabetsnyc.com

Add some "style and wit" to your lexicon via this "narrow" East Village vendor of "trendy gifts", cards and "cute novelty items" to suit "all types", from "illustrated tees" and retro toys to "snazzy-smelling candles"; when shopping for a "coworker" or "a birthday party", the "creative" curios are bound to "produce a chuckle."

Alter

`26` `25` `26` `M`

Greenpoint | 109 Franklin St. (Greenpoint Ave.) | Brooklyn | 718-784-8818

Greenpoint | 140 Franklin St. (Greenpoint Ave.) | Brooklyn | 718-349-0203

Williamsburg | 407 Graham Ave. (bet. Jackson & Withers Sts.) | Brooklyn | 718-609-0203

www.alterbrooklyn.com

An indie fashion dynasty grows in Brooklyn courtesy of this "hip, cool" trio specializing in wearable yet "edgy apparel" along with "great belts,

| | QUALITY | DISPLAY | SERVICE | COST |

jewelry and shoes"; guys and girls go their own ways on Franklin Street, while Graham Avenue welcomes a coed crew, and all deliver lines with a lotta look – like Cheap Monday, Kill City and Mink Pink – at refreshingly "moderate prices."

Altman Luggage
| 26 | 15 | 21 | M |

LES | 135 Orchard St. (bet. Delancey & Rivington Sts.) | 212-254-7275 | 800-372-3377 | www.altmanluggage.com

When you're getting "ready to pack", seasoned travelers say it's "worth a trip to the Lower East Side" to browse this longtime luggage outlet's "exceptionally large and varied stock" featuring "name brands" at "bargain" prices; an "efficient" crew works the jumbled floor, and those who "need a pen" or desk accessory can bag them in the back; P.S. closed Saturdays.

Amarcord Vintage Fashion
| 24 | 22 | 23 | E |

SoHo | 252 Lafayette St. (bet. Prince & Spring Sts.) | 212-431-4161
Williamsburg | 223 Bedford Ave. (bet. N. 4th & N. 5th Sts.) | Brooklyn | 718-963-4001
www.amarcordvintagefashion.com

A "funky, eclectic" mix of "vintage clothing finds" (mostly '40s to '80s European) is displayed with a "cinematic twist" at these "nicely cu-rated" SoHo-Williamsburg siblings where the Fellini-inspired decor "transports you to Italy in another time"; it's a "real treat" to "play dress-up" with designer pieces in such "great condition", but some connoisseurs feel it can be "too expensive for what it is."

NEW Amelia Toro
| – | – | – | E |

Chelsea | 229 10th Ave. (bet. 23rd & 24th Sts.) | 212-337-8567 | www.ameliatoro.com

The eponymous Bogota-based designer brings her striking, avant-garde attire to this sleek boutique, fittingly set in Chelsea's gallery district; the austere, sprawling space, comprised of concrete floors, aluminum fixtures and bare walls, contrasts with the collection of dramatic black coats, dresses and accessories, all stitched by Latin American artisans from European fabrics.

American Girl Place
| 26 | 27 | 24 | E |

E 40s | 609 Fifth Ave. (49th St.) | 212-371-2220 | 877-247-5223 | www.americangirl.com

A "pilgrimage for the under-10 set", this "doll lover's dreamland" on Fifth Avenue is the stuff of "fantasy"; kids choose a "look-alike" dollie, each equipped with plenty of "backstory", then pick her next "new outfit", treat her to a "hair salon" makeover and a spot of "tea and scones" in the cafe; if grumblers grow "pale looking at the price tags", most "grin and bear it" since this is "a rite of passage."

American Museum of Natural History Shop
| 27 | 26 | 23 | M |

W 70s | American Museum of Natural History | 200 Central Park W. (79th St.) | 212-769-1500 | 800-671-7035 | www.amnh.org

For the "little scientist" or the "young at heart", this triple-tiered store in the "landmark" UWS museum is "a learning experience and a plea-sure" with its "impressive" variety of "fun" "souvenirs" ("all the dino-saurs you could want"), "educational toys", "unique jewelry" and "interesting finds" at "doable prices"; it's a quarry for "offbeat" gifts "whether you're a tourist or a lifelong NYer", but beware "when school's out" and "the masses descend."

American Two Shot

SoHo | 135 Grand St. (Crosby St.) | 212-925-3403 | www.americantwoshot.com

Retail gets a shot in the arm at this whitewashed SoHo gallery/shop/coffee bar that's more than just another chill concept shop for the fashion-forward tribe; the owners, an artist and former Theory employee, curate a host of hip apparel, jewelry, ephemera and artwork, much of it made by their circle of creative friends, balanced by special vintage finds.

Amsale
29 | 28 | 25 | VE

E 50s | 625 Madison Ave., 2nd fl. (bet. 58th & 59th Sts.) | 212-583-1700 | www.amsale.com

"Once you get the appointment, shopping is a breeze" at Amsale Aberra's "bright", loftlike Madison Avenue salon where the "patient" staff makes finding that "one-of-a-kind" wedding gown a "wonderful experience"; fashioned from duchesse satin and silk, the "gorgeous frocks are striking" while the bridesmaids' offerings "don't outshine the bride", and while it's seriously "expensive", the aisle-bound chime it's "very worth it."

Anna Sui
23 | 25 | 21 | E

SoHo | 113 Greene St. (bet. Prince & Spring Sts.) | 212-941-8406 | www.annasui.com

"Happy there's still a tiny piece of the old SoHo left" squeal acolytes who convene at the iconic designer's lushly decorated "black-and purple-lover's paradise" brimming with "edgy, Goth-tinged clothing and a limited but exquisite selection" of footwear sure to satisfy the "hip, young retro-hippie in all of us"; the "fanciful" collection is spot-on "for city girls who want to make a statement", but with so much color and cuteness afoot "a little goes a long way."

NEW Anne et Valentin

NoLita | 2 Prince St. (bet. Bowery & Elizabeth St.) | 212-226-2343 | www.anneetvalentin.com

Iconoclasts find statement-making eyewear, including sunglasses, in quirky styles, color combos and materials at this French company's sharp-looking NoLita nook modeled after its Paris shop; the funky, retro and bohemian frames rest on resin tables and in sleek wall cabinets and can be custom-fitted to flatter your face.

Annelore
24 | 23 | 25 | E

TriBeCa | 18 Jay St. (bet. Greenwich & Hudson Sts.) | 212-775-0077
W Village | 636 Hudson St. (Horatio St.) | 212-255-5574
www.annelorenyc.com

After years of peddling her "beautiful line of women's clothing" at her darling West Village storefront, designer Juliana Cho opened a TriBeCa sibling where she also stitches her artful creations, including day dresses in unusual prints, flowing cocktail frocks and crisp jackets, from top-notch fabrics; prices are reasonable for the quality, and it's "worth a stop in" just to browse the accessories from indie designers.

QUALITY | DISPLAY | SERVICE | COST

Annie's Blue Ribbon General Store   27 | 22 | 24 | M

Downtown Bklyn | 365 State St. (Bond St.) | Brooklyn | 718-522-9848 | www.blueribbongeneralstore.com

Just "browsing" is "a hoot" at this Downtown Brooklyn boutique, where the "fabulous" hodgepodge of "interesting trinkets, toys, candies", "games, kitchen and garden products" and "native Brooklyn" paraphernalia provides "perfect" presents "for anybody or any occasion"; for "really unique items" in the "cutest" setting ever, it's a blue ribbon "winner every time."

Ann Sacks   28 | 27 | 23 | VE

E 50s | 204 E. 58th St. (bet. 2nd & 3rd Aves.) | 212-588-1920
Flatiron | 37 E. 18th St. (bet. B'way & Park Ave.) | 212-529-2800
800-278-8453 | www.annsacks.com

An "excellent source for interior designers as well as homeowners with high taste", this Flatiron–East 50s duo proffers "gorgeous stuff" including "the most beautiful stone" and "creative" tiles, plus plumbing and light fixtures for your kitchen and bathroom; you may "need a second mortgage to pay for it", but it's a "divine" "place to start your dreams of sybaritic" bubble baths, and the staff is "helpful with samples"; P.S. closed Saturdays and Sundays.

Anthropologie ●   23 | 26 | 20 | E

Chelsea | Chelsea Mkt. | 75 Ninth Ave. (bet. 15th & 16th Sts.) | 212-620-3116
E 70s | 1230 Third Ave. (71st St.) | 212-288-1940
Flatiron | 85 Fifth Ave. (16th St.) | 212-627-5885
SoHo | 375 W. Broadway (bet. Broome & Spring Sts.) | 212-343-7070
W 50s | Rockefeller Ctr. | 50 Rockefeller Plaza (50th St.) | 212-246-0386
800-309-2500 | www.anthropologie.com

For the "boho-chic aesthetic" (think *New Girl*'s Zooey Deschanel's "adorkable" wardrobe) head to this "whimsically" "quirky" chain, rated NYC's Most Popular in the Fashion/Beauty category; you'll find everything from "unique" "springtime frocks to fall layers to winter jackets" and "laced among" the togs: "killer accessories" and "eclectic" housewares "made for the rom-com heroine"; a visit "transports you" to a "lifestyle you aspire to live – isn't that what fashion is supposed to do?"; P.S. a Williamsburg branch is in the works.

Antiques Garage ⊘   21 | 16 | 16 | M

Chelsea | 112 W. 25th St. (bet. 6th & 7th Aves.) | 212-243-5343 | www.hellskitchenfleamarket.com

"Surprising finds" await "flea market and antiques junkies" every weekend at this bi-level Chelsea "collector's dream" where some 100 vendors "set up shop" in a former "parking garage", displaying "tons of jewelry, home furnishings, vintage clothing and everything else imaginable"; some offerings may be "more expensive" than expected, but those in the know report "deals – if you really look."

Anya Hindmarch   27 | 25 | 25 | VE

E 60s | 29 E. 60th St. (bet. Madison & Park Aves.) | 212-750-3974 | www.anyahindmarch.com

The "quality statement" handbags created by this London-based accessories designer have a cultlike following on both sides of the pond, luring loyalists to her "tiny" UES storefront; the "cramped setup doesn't hinder" the "accommodating" staffers from "showing you any bag you want", and while the "incredibly well-made and smartly designed" purses, wallets and pouches are "expensive", they're not "out of control"; P.S. a move to Madison is planned for summer 2013.

A.P.C.
25 | 24 | 21 | E

SoHo | 131 Mercer St. (bet. Prince & Spring Sts.) | 212-966-9685
W Village | 267 W. Fourth St. (Perry St.) | 212-755-2523

A.P.C. Surplus

W Village | 92 Perry St. (Bleecker St.) | 646-371-9292
www.apc.fr

"French minimalism at its finest" – "somehow these simple clothes are also quite distinctive" declare guys and gamines who file into designer Jean Touitou's "lovely" wood-planked SoHo shop and smaller West Village sibs; "if you groove on the collection" you want everything from the "long-lasting jeans" to the "unpretentious basics"; *oui*, "it may be a bit expensive", "but so is a trip to Paris" (plus the Surplus store offers discounts on past collections); P.S. a Bond Street branch is in the works.

Apple Store ⦿
29 | 27 | 26 | E

E 40s | 45 Grand Central Terminal | main concourse (Vanderbilt Ave.) | 212-284-1800
E 50s | 767 Fifth Ave. (59th St.) | 212-336-1440
Meatpacking | 401 W. 14th St. (9th Ave.) | 212-444-3400
SoHo | 103 Prince St. (Greene St.) | 212-226-3126
W 60s | 1981 Broadway (67th St.) | 212-209-3400
New Springville | Staten Island Mall | 2655 Richmond Ave.
(bet. Platinum Ave. & Richmond Hill Rd.) | Staten Island | 718-568-2230
800-692-7753 | www.apple.com

You'll "wish you were a nerd all along" at these "jaw-dropping", glass-walled showrooms for Apple's "tantalizing" devices, rated NYC's Most Popular in the Lifestyle category, combining "flashy" "hands-on displays" with "one-stop shopping and support" from a staff of "egghead maestros" who are "unfailingly" helpful for "techies and non-techies alike"; the "cutting-edge" wares "command a hefty price", and the "insane crowds" of "e-nuts" "can be maddening", but "once bitten", it's "futile to resist."

Arcadia Spa & Home
26 | 25 | 25 | E

Chelsea | 249 W. 23rd St. (bet. 7th & 8th Aves.) | 212-243-5358 | www.arcadianyc.com

Find "something to suit everyone" at this "funky" Chelsea gift boutique, a "relaxing" retreat whether or not you enjoy the adjoining spa; the "amazing array" of "wonderfully unique" and "ever-changing" Fair Trade items ranges from birdhouses, Buddhas, candles, crystals and "papier-mâché elephants from Zimbabwe" to natural bath products, fragrances and incense, plus the "incredibly friendly" staffers make shopping "a real treat."

Area Kids
24 | 19 | 19 | E

Williamsburg | 218 Bedford Ave. (N. 5th St.) | Brooklyn | 718-218-8647 | www.areakids.com
Additional locations throughout the NY area

For "unique" children's clothes, shoes, toys and other little goodies you won't find just anywhere, stroller-pushers swear by this "charming", eco-minded local mini-chain that keeps current with "cool" indie and NYC brands, like Appaman, Aden + Anais and Dante Beatrix; although service can be spotty, it's a great "go-to spot" for scooping up last-minute gifts.

Arhaus Furniture ●

27 | 27 | 26 | E

Meatpacking | 410 W. 13th St. (bet. 9th Ave. & Washington St.) | 212-337-9853 | www.arhaus.com

Packed with "high-quality furnishings that make you drool" from all over the world, this massive Meatpacking District design offshoot of the Cleveland-based chain may prompt you to "go home and throw out everything you own just to start all new"; the "gorgeous" antique wood and "loft-style furniture", lighting and accessories sell for "reasonable prices", but changer-uppers admit "it can get expensive when you go for custom fabrics."

Aritzia ●

23 | 23 | 22 | M

NEW **E 50s** | 600 Fifth Ave. (bet. 48th & 49th Sts.) | 212-307-3121 | www.aritzia.com

SoHo | 524 Broadway (Spring St.) | 212-965-2188 | www.aritzia.com

"Even if you don't know what you're looking for, you'll find it" among the racks of "flirty", well-priced womenswear at this Canadian chain's sprawling, two-floor offshoots in SoHo and Rockefeller Center, decorated with crystals, mushrooms and tree stumps to resemble an enchanted forest; if cynics hiss the styles are "hit-or-miss", aficionados assert "you won't see yourself coming and going" in the "trendy" house-label wares.

Armani Fifth Avenue

28 | 27 | 25 | VE

E 50s | 717 Fifth Ave. (56th St.) | 212-339-5950

Giorgio Armani

E 60s | 760 Madison Ave. (65th St.) | 212-988-9191 www.giorgioarmani.com

"There is no rival" to this "king of Italian designers", offering "dynamite dresswear" in "timeless, elegant silhouettes" at these luxury boutiques, with a "gorgeous" Fifth Avenue location housing a "first-class" restaurant and a Madison Avenue shop that's "more like a museum"; the "professional" sales staff is "a pleasure", and while prices may be "heart-stopping", these "divine" creations are "worthwhile lifetime investments."

NEW Armani Junior

- | - | - | E

E 80s | 1223 Madison Ave. (88th St.) | 212-828-6920 | www.armani.com/armanijunior

The Italian fashion house expands its Madison Avenue empire with this lavish, 1,480-sq.-ft. boutique just for junior; the high-end attire and accessories for newborns, toddlers and teens alike manages to be both cute and, of course, stylishly understated, proving that it's never too early to teach tomorrow's fashion plates the fundamentals of Armani.

Armor-Lux

∇ 29 | 28 | 28 | E

NoLita | 232 Mulberry St. (bet. Prince & Spring Sts.) | 917-261-5567 | www.armorlux.com

Hailing from the small French town of Quimper, this NoLita fisherman's fave hocks "high-quality" Breton-style shirts, wool sweaters and pea coats for men, women and even petite sailors; conservative yet current, these maritime-inspired staples unite old-world craftsmanship with a simple striped aesthetic that keeps followers hooked; nautical-inspired scarves, socks and slippers round out the fashionable fare.

Arthur Brown & Brother
27 | 20 | 23 | M

W 40s | 2 W. 45th St. (bet. 5th & 6th Aves.) | 212-575-5555 | 800-772-7367 | www.artbrown.com

"Who said writing is a lost art?" scoff scriveners who deem this "family-owned", 87-year-old Midtown standby "tops" for an ink-redible array of "the finest in pens", whatever the category or price; the "great staff" fosters "real relationships with customers" (and also hosts biannual trade shows), and for those in need of stationery and supplies for a favored quill, "this is the place."

Artistic Tile
27 | 26 | 20 | E

Flatiron | 38 W. 21st St. (bet. 5th & 6th Aves.) | 212-727-9331 | 800-260-8646 | www.artistictile.com

Among "the best showrooms" for "a wide range" of "beautifully crafted tiles for your kitchen and bath", this Flatiron flagship is "wonderful for colorful or classic neutral" selections; the "fabulous displays" make it "a must" for anyone "renovating" or scoping out "great design ideas", while a "knowledgeable" staff that "goes the extra mile" provides the finishing touch.

Artists & Fleas
24 | 23 | 22 | M

Williamsburg | 70 N. Seventh St. (bet. Kent & Wythe Aves.) | Brooklyn | 917-301-5765 | www.artistsandfleas.com

"Not your mother's suburban flea market", this Williamsburg weekend "hodgepodge" boasts an "artistic bent" given its "indie designers" who display their own "one-of-a-kind" "handmade pieces" alongside the usual "vintage clothing, jewelry" and antiques; its "enclosed setting provides for excellent browsing", so curiosity-seekers can "wander in" and scratch up "unique buys" year-round.

Art of Shaving
26 | 24 | 25 | E

E 40s | 373 Madison Ave. (46th St.) | 212-986-2905
E 40s | Grand Central Terminal | 87 E. 42nd St., Lexington Passage (Vanderbilt Ave.) | 212-682-0248
E 50s | 520 Madison Ave. (bet. 53rd & 54th Sts.) | 212-702-9596
E 60s | 141 E. 62nd St. (bet. Lexington & 3rd Aves.) | 212-317-8436
W 60s | Shops at Columbus Circle | 10 Columbus Circle, 2nd fl. (B'way & 60th St.) | 212-823-9410 ◗
W 70s | 2151 Broadway (bet. 75th & 76th Sts.) | 212-362-1493
800-493-2212 | www.theartofshaving.com

A "daily ritual" is "elevated into an art form" at this "luxury" grooming chain, where pampered patrons can indulge in a hot shave by an expert barber or buy "double-edged Merkur blades", "lush aftershave", "quality" skincare products and "unique" gifts and travel sets; while the "handsome" interior is awash in "leather and wood detailing" reminiscent of a vintage barberia, prices are strictly modern.

Ascot Chang
27 | 24 | 25 | VE

W 50s | 110 Central Park S. (bet. 6th & 7th Aves.) | 212-759-3333 | 877-486-9966 | www.ascotchang.com

"Buy fewer shirts, but buy them here" suggest gents who frequent this "top-quality" Hong Kong haberdasher across from Central

Park; sartorialists praise the "fantastic variety of styles", "great fabric assortment and accurate measurements" and just "love the service" offered by the "wonderful" salesfolk; while much of the business is bespoke (it's "first class for handmade formalwear"), off-the-rack items are also "terrific."

Ash Footwear

25 | 25 | 25 | E

SoHo | 44 Mercer St. (bet. Broome & Grand Sts.) | 646-422-7098 | 888-497-6005 | www.ashfootwearusa.com

Hollywood's hipster crowd loves the color-saturated kicks, pumps and boots from this "trendy" shoemaker that blends "incredible" French design with Italian craftsmanship, and everyday guys, gals and even kids can also get in on the action at the brand's "clean, bright" white SoHo shop; the line delivers "awesome" looks "for the price", with cool details like buckles and straps.

AsiaStore at Asia Society Museum

25 | 23 | 23 | E

E 70s | Asia Society Museum | 725 Park Ave. (70th St.) | 212-327-9217 | www.asiastore.org

Like a "little museum inside the museum", this Upper East Side shop's "charming selection" spotlights "gorgeous stuffs of the Orient", including "one-of-a-kind jewelry", handmade "arts and crafts", "silk clothing", books and "Asian-inspired" home decor; it's "a delight to walk through" and a "top-notch resource" for "lovely gifts", assuming you're a mandarin with "money to burn."

ASICS

26 | 24 | 25 | M

W 40s | 51 W. 42nd St. (bet. 5th & 6th Aves.) | 212-354-1908 | www.asicsamerica.com

Athletes in pursuit of "good performance" get down to basics at this Japanese maker of "high-quality running shoes", whose Midtown branch offers countless colorful choices with cushioning, maximum support and other in-demand features, plus a "very helpful" gait assessment "on a treadmill" to pick the kicks that are "right for you"; for footwear that's "comfortable and long-lasting", this is the inside track.

NEW The Askel Project

- | - | - | E

SoHo | 311 W. Broadway (bet. Canal & Grand Sts.) | 888-992-5735 | www.akselparis.com

French men's designer Yazid Aksas brings his flashy brand of European-style shirts and custom-made suits to SoHo with his first-ever brick-and-mortar shop; equally as eye catching as the attire is the sculptural interior, adorned with a store-spanning red installation by architect Gregory Okshteyn and ever-changing murals by emerging artists.

Asprey

28 | 25 | 25 | VE

E 70s | 853 Madison Ave. (bet. 70th & 71st Sts.) | 212-688-1811 | 800-883-2777 | www.asprey.com

"There's nothing more British" than this sleek Madison Avenue import where the "gentle" salesfolk tend to a "high-end" crowd and the tony "top-quality" goods range from porcelain to "outstanding" accessories to jewelry oft "worn by royalty"; if the less-awed wonder "who can afford" the "spectacular" price tags, aspirants quip "have the Bentley pull around", insisting "you get what you pay for."

	QUALITY	DISPLAY	SERVICE	COST

Assembly New York ◐
24 | 23 | 21 | E

LES | 170 Ludlow St. (bet. Houston & Stanton Sts.) | 212-253-5393 | www.assemblynewyork.com

At his über-hip LES haven for futurist utilitarian chic, owner Greg Armas offers style-hunters a tantalizing fusion of obscure European labels, exclusive designer collaborations and handpicked vintage; customers clamor for the house brand collection of understated accessories and unisex pieces hand-sewn in NYC and stay one foot ahead of the fashion pack with unusual finds from lines like Christian Peau, Christophe Lemaire and Illesteva.

Atelier New York
25 | 24 | 25 | E

Hudson Square | 304 Hudson St. (Spring St.) | 212-941-8435 | www.ateliernewyork.com

Minimalist menswear sets the tone at this Hudson Square shrine to the avant-garde, where musicians and other creatives come for cutting-edge, "high-end" clothes and accessories, including store-exclusives, from established labels like Ann Demeulemeester and Yohji Yamamoto, as well as noteworthy new arrivals; dark Masonite floors, black leather couches and white marble tables lend an austere air to the "clever displays" of "fantastic merchandise" for the certified fashionisto.

Athleta ◐
25 | 24 | 24 | E

E 80s | 1517 Third Ave. (86th St.) | 212-249-2072
W 60s | 216 Columbus Ave. (bet. 69th & 70th Sts.) | 212-787-5602
www.athleta.gap.com

You can "look good even before you work out" thanks to these cross-town outlets of the Gap-owned women's activewear retailer, "appealing" sources of "stylish" gym apparel that matches "breathable material" with "feminine designs", as well as "casual" lifestyle clothing for "the Saturday uniform"; although it's "pricey", the merch is "well made" and the staff "helpful", plus there are even "free fitness classes" for on-site motivation.

A Thousand Picnics
24 | 23 | 22 | E

Williamsburg | 171 S. Fourth St. (Driggs Ave.) | Brooklyn | 347-606-8715 | www.coldpicnic.com

Jewelry junkies with a penchant for pieces with bite feast on the cast brass and bronze finds at this brick-walled Williamsburg upstart, a collaboration between the designers of Species by the Thousands and Cold Picnic; African textiles, cave paintings and primitive animals inspire sculptural cuffs and bangles, pendants and stud earrings, with handmade leather totes and clutches rounding out the array of cutting-edge temptations.

Atrium + KITH
23 | 22 | 19 | E

NoHo | 644 Broadway (Bleecker St.) | 212-473-9200 ◐
Prospect Heights | 233 Flatbush Ave. (bet. Dean & Bergen Sts.) | Brooklyn | 347-889-6114
www.atriumnyc.com

NoHo's "go-to place" where style-forward guys and girls "spot the next trend" also boasts a men's offshoot just steps from Brooklyn's Barclays Center; the "frequently changing displays" feature "lots of fantastic denim" from cult makers like Naked & Famous and Prps,

QUALITY DISPLAY SERVICE COST

urban-prepster outerwear from Canada Goose and Penfield and "other unique clothing", plus kicks at shoe cohort KITH, making it well "worth a visit."

Audemars Piguet
29 | 27 | 28 | VE

E 50s | 65 E. 57th St. (bet. Madison & Park Aves.) | 212-688-6644 | 888-214-6858 | www.audemarspiguet.com

"When nothing but the best will do", slip into this East 50s showcase of the legendary manufacturer of prestige Swiss timepieces; the brand's "awesome" world-class watches (from ultrathin crocodile-band models to luxurious high-tech chronographs) "never disappoint" and always make a statement – about how much you're willing to pay to tell time.

Aveda Environmental Lifestyle Store
26 | 23 | 24 | E

E 40s | Grand Central Terminal | 87 E. 42nd St., Lexington Passage (Vanderbilt Ave.) | 212-682-5397
Flatiron | 140 Fifth Ave. (19th St.) | 212-645-4797
SoHo | 20 Vandam St. (bet. 6th Ave. & Varick St.) | 212-473-0280
SoHo | 233 Spring St. (bet. 6th Ave. & Varick St.) | 212-807-1492
SoHo | 456 W. Broadway (bet. Houston & Prince Sts.) | 212-473-0280
W 60s | Shops at Columbus Circle | 10 Columbus Circle, 3rd fl. (B'way & 60th St.) | 212-823-9714
800-644-4831 | www.aveda.com

"Loyal clients" love "shopping, browsing and testing" while sipping on "lovely gratis green tea" at this "soothing", spalike beauty chain, which offers "environmentally conscientious" plant and flower-sourced items for skin and hair; products are "well priced" and "fresh-smelling", and the "gracious" sales staff "really knows what it is talking about both in terms of the extensive product line and company philosophy."

A.W. Kaufman
25 | 15 | 21 | M

LES | 73 Orchard St. (bet. Broome & Grand Sts.) | 212-226-1629 | www.awkaufman.com

At this third-generation Lower East Side purveyor of "beautiful lingerie", the staff "provides excellent service", ensuring fancy panties, PJs and loungewear fit the way their European designers intended (men can do more than ogle – there's sleepwear, robes and tees for them too); fans who concede "the place is a mess" save themselves repeat visits and "call, call, call" to order their unmentionables.

babycottons
▽ 28 | 27 | 25 | E

E 80s | 1236 Madison Ave. (89th St.) | 212-828-8979 | www.babycottons.com

This "elegant" East 80s boutique is awash in "beautiful", "drool-worthy" "classic clothes" for newborns and toddlers spun from "baby-soft" Peruvian pima cotton that "makes everything else feel like hay"; the "staff is so nice", it helps customers recover from the sticker shock that accompanies "prices that match the rest of Madison Avenue."

Baccarat
29 | 28 | 27 | VE

E 60s | 635 Madison Ave. (60th St.) | 212-826-4100 | 800-215-1300 | www.baccarat.com

In anticipation of its 250th anniversary, this luxury brand "favorite" relocated its flagship to the East 60s, showcasing its "dazzling displays" of "gorgeous" French crystal chandeliers, tableware and jewelry in a

| | QUALITY | DISPLAY | SERVICE | COST |

large, lavish space designed by architect Rafael de Cardenas; each piece is "worth the world" (and surely "breaks the bank"), plus acolytes agree that this storied outfit "lives up to its legendary standards" for service and quality, noting it's a "wonderful place" to find a "wedding gift" or that "special" something you will "pass on to your heirs."

NEW Baggu — | — | — | M

Williamsburg | 242 Wythe Ave. (N. 3rd St.) | Brooklyn | 800-605-0759 | www.baggu.com

A bag-lover's paradise, this white-walled Williamsburg newcomer brims with options galore from its house line; choose from signature styles like simply made reusable ripstop nylon carry-alls, plus backpacks and recycled cotton canvas totes and pouches, all rendered in bright colors or playful prints, or punch up your look with soft leather pouch handbags and accessories.

Balenciaga 29 | 27 | 23 | VE

SoHo | 138 Wooster St. (bet. Houston & Prince Sts.) | 212-206-0872 | www.balenciaga.com

Change is afoot for this "high-end" fashion house: Alexander Wang has taken the creative reins from Nicolas Ghesquière, and the NYC flagship is preparing to move from its temporary SoHo digs into a permanent space at 148 Mercer Street, with a men's store at 149 Mercer for good measure; the latest design head's creations draw inspiration from this label's century-old archives, so it will no doubt remain "well worth a visit" for luxury lovers.

Balloon Saloon 22 | 20 | 20 | M

TriBeCa | 133 W. Broadway (Duane St.) | 212-227-3838 | www.balloonsaloon.com

As a "source of goofy gifts", this "overstuffed" TriBeCa party store is among "the most entertaining" around given its "unbelievable selection of helium balloons" floating amid wall-to-wall "goodies", "gags", toys and "cultural kitsch"; its "talented crew" will also arrange and deliver "beautiful" inflated "bouquets" for any occasion "you can think of."

Bally 26 | 23 | 23 | VE

E 50s | 628 Madison Ave. (59th St.) | 212-751-9082 | www.bally.com

Fans of this venerated Swiss brand are anything but neutral when it comes to the understatedly stylish, buttery soft "leather wares" – wingtips, stilettos, handbags, briefcases, belts and more – showcased at its East 50s outpost, where the solicitous staff will "treat you like a princess" or prince; you'll pay royal prices too, since these classics "last and last."

B&B Italia 27 | 25 | 22 | VE

E 50s | A&D Bldg. | 150 E. 58th St. (bet. Lexington & 3rd Aves.) | 212-758-4046

SoHo | 138 Greene St. (bet. Houston & Prince Sts.) | 212-966-3514 800-872-1697 | www.bebitalia.com

"Beautiful furniture" that "would fit right in any apartment in Manhattan" is the allure of these East 50s–SoHo offshoots of the Italian brand purveying "modern" offerings "for the individual who likes contemporary clean lines"; "sleek, comfy pieces" from designers such as Mario Bellini and Patricia Urquiola don't come cheap, but fans of the "high-end", "minimalist" look would "buy it all", if they had the budget; P.S. the East 58th locale is closed weekends.

B&H Photo-Video-Pro Audio

28 | 22 | 23 | M

Garment District | 420 Ninth Ave. (bet. 33rd & 34th Sts.) | 212-444-6615 | 800-606-6969 | www.bhphotovideo.com

With "more cameras than the paparazzi at the Oscars", this "fast-paced" Garment District "destination" is a longtime "gold mine" for "all photo and video needs", where the "exhaustive stock" – carted to check-out via "overhead conveyor belts" – "can't be topped"; the "chaotic" "crowds" can be "dizzying", but the "cordial" staffers "know their stuff" and the "value" makes it "hard to visit and leave empty-handed"; P.S. closes at 1 PM Friday and closed Saturday.

Bang & Olufsen

28 | 26 | 24 | VE

E 70s | 952 Madison Ave. (75th St.) | 212-879-6161
Flatiron | 927 Broadway (bet. 21st & 22nd Sts.) | 212-388-9792
SoHo | 63 Greene St. (bet. Broome & Spring Sts.) | 212-274-1003
W 70s | 330 Columbus Ave. (bet. 75th & 76th Sts.) | 212-501-0926
www.bang-olufsen.com

The "epitome of style" for the "hi-fi buff", this "audio-visual experience" is known for "sleek" Danish "designs matched with top quality" in its "gorgeous" "contemporary" equipment, from "quintessential" sound systems and TVs to speakers that'll "blow your mind"; the "classic showrooms" are overseen by "personally invested" salespeople, and while the "ultraexpensive" price tag may bang up your budget, if you're seeking "the 'wow' factor" you "can't go wrong" here.

Bape Store

27 | 23 | 24 | E

(aka Bathing Ape)

SoHo | 91 Greene St. (bet. Prince & Spring Sts.) | 212-925-0222 | www.bape.com

Still kickin' in bright candy colors despite being sold by its Japanese creator, Nigo, this SoHo shop attracts a cultish crowd that flips for the "amazing", "fun" streetwear and almost "cartoonish" sneakers – many of them "exclusive" and limited-edition; everything's artfully displayed within minimalist two-story digs that look more like a "gallery" than a store, complete with a conveyor belt.

🆕 The Bar at Baublebar

- | - | - | E

Chelsea | 230 Fifth Ave., Ste. 610 (27th St.) | 646-664-4827 | www.baublebar.com

Once an e-commerce–only endeavor, this online jewelry boutique goes brick and mortar with its Fifth Avenue shop, offering all manner of attention-grabbing accessories from both known designers and affordable brands; an extension of the company's headquarters, the sunny space on the sixth floor is currently only open for appointments, but they're easy to schedule online.

Barbour

28 | 22 | 23 | E

E 80s | 1047 Madison Ave. (80th St.) | 212-570-2600
SoHo | 123 Wooster St. (bet. Prince & Spring Sts.) | 212-941-7524
www.barbour.com

It's all "very *Downton Abbey*" at this "charming British" East 80s–SoHo duo proffering "durable outerwear worn by the English" and

QUALITY DISPLAY SERVICE COST

"New England preps", particularly its signature waxed jackets, perfect for "pheasant hunting" or a well-outfitted stroll through "Central Park"; prices are "to the manor born", but the staffers "know everything about everything" and the products are "timeless" and "last forever" (especially if you "re-waterproof"), remaining "staples" in many "Anglophiles'" wardrobes.

Bare Escentuals
26 | 23 | 24 | M

E 60s | 1140 Third Ave. (bet. 66th & 67th Sts.) | 646-537-0070
Garment District | 44 W. 34th St. (bet. 5th & 6th Aves.) | 212-220-1900 ●
W 40s | 1585 Broadway (bet. 47th & 48th Sts.) | 212-220-0414 ●
Elmhurst | Queens Center Mall | 90-15 Queens Blvd. (bet. 57th & 59th Aves.) | Queens | 718-371-3724 ●
800-227-3990 | www.bareescentuals.com

"Best makeup ever!" is the verdict – "once you see the coverage from these light-but-effective natural minerals" made from "natural ingredients" applied to puff-fection with "heavenly" brushes at this chain, "you won't go back to cakey, old-ladyish liquid foundation and/or creme eyeshadows"; the "supremely helpful staff" is "more than happy to give makeovers on-the-spot" and make sure that you don't walk out looking like a "kabuki stage player."

Barneys Co-Op
26 | 22 | 19 | E

SoHo | 116 Wooster St. (bet. Prince & Spring Sts.) | 212-965-9964
W 70s | 2151 Broadway (76th St.) | 646-335-0978
Cobble Hill | 194 Atlantic Ave. (bet. Clinton & Court Sts.) | Brooklyn | 718-637-2234
888-822-7639 | www.barneys.com

A "go-to destination" for "up-to-the-minute" cult-fashion favorites including Acne, A.L.C., Carven and Suno, premium denim and "private-label pieces that shouldn't be overlooked", "Barneys' hip younger sister" is the one the "young and cool" "prefer to pull out their wallet for"; while the merch sports "more modest price tags" than its "posh" parent it's still somewhat "rough" on budgets, and sensitive stylistas hiss that the "super-trendy" staff makes you "feel invisible"; P.S. a rebranding is in the works.

Barneys New York
28 | 26 | 22 | VE

E 60s | 660 Madison Ave. (61st St.) | 212-826-8900 | 888-822-7639 | www.barneys.com

"Folks who shop as a hobby" find this "stylish" Madison Avenue "palace of fashion in NYC" "beautifully curated" with a mix of "high-end" and "cutting-edge designer apparel", from Balenciaga and Haider Ackermann to Lanvin ("all the chicest brands under one roof"), a "fabulous" unisex shoe department and beauty counters that are "a cosmetics junkie's dream" – "even just window shopping is incredibly satisfying"; some diehards praise the "top-notch service", while others caution "dress like a fashionista" or "risk a withering look", and prices, well, "if you win the lottery", "this is the place to go."

The Bathroom
▽ 25 | 28 | 23 | E

W Village | 94 Charles St. (bet. Bleecker & W. 4th Sts.) | 212-929-1449 | 800-856-9223 | www.inthebathroom.com

Shoppers "could spend all day" browsing around this "tiny, cute" West Villager, an English apothecary overflowing with bath, body and home

QUALITY DISPLAY SERVICE COST

items from a wide range of European lines – think Swissco loofahs and Mason Pearson brushes; "the quality of items is well worth the price", and a "knowledgeable" staff guides you through "the mix" with "care and humor."

BCBG Max Azria
24 | 23 | 21 | E

E 40s | 461 Fifth Ave. (40th St.) | 212-991-9777
E 60s | 770 Madison Ave. (66th St.) | 212-717-4225
NEW E 70s | 1290 Third Ave. (74th St.) | 212-991-2056
Flatiron | 168 Fifth Ave. (22nd St.) | 212-989-7307
NEW Garment District | 424 Fifth Ave. (bet. 38th & 39th Sts.) | 212-730-0273 ◐
SoHo | 120 Wooster St. (bet. Prince & Spring Sts.) | 212-625-2723
W 60s | 2003-2005 Broadway (bet. 68th & 69th Sts.) | 212-496-1853
New Springville | Staten Island Mall | 2655 Richmond Ave. (bet. Platinum Ave. & Richmond Hill Rd.) | Staten Island | 718-983-5938 ◐
866-518-2224 | www.bcbg.com

"Forever love" the body-con jersey dresses, "gorgeous prints" and "stunning gowns" confess Max-imistas who also head to this "dream store" chain for "unforgettable" wow looks that "transition from day to night"; what a "lift" Hérve Léger's collection has given the line – it's the "next best thing" to the French designer's original "bandage" frocks – and if prices are "intimidating", well, try "stalking the merchandise" at sale time.

BDDW
25 | 24 | 23 | E

SoHo | 5 Crosby St. (bet. Grand & Howard Sts.) | 212-625-1230 | www.bddw.com

"One of the most transporting" home decor showcases around, this SoHo standout's "handmade American furniture" – beds, tables, seating, mirrors and cabinets – applies heirloom-inspired designs to naturally treated domestic hardwood to yield a "combo of modern and rustic" that's "subtle, pleasing to the eye" and built "to last"; it's "expensive", but the "amazing" display floor alone is "a treasure, even if just for a visit."

Beacon Paint & Hardware
26 | 17 | 24 | M

W 70s | 371 Amsterdam Ave. (bet. 77th & 78th Sts.) | 212-787-1090 | www.beaconpaint.com

"Every neighborhood depends on a hardware store" like this "family-owned" Upper Westsider, a "nostalgic" "survivor" that's "holding its own" after 100-plus years with an "excellent" inventory featuring Benjamin Moore paints and "household repair" supplies (tools, plumbing and electrical) at an "ok price"; with a "friendly" staff to offer "on-target" advice, it's a "resource" the community's "lucky to have."

Beacon's Closet
19 | 17 | 16 | I

G Village | 10 W. 13th St. (bet. 5th & 6th Aves.) | 917-261-4863
Park Slope | 92 Fifth Ave. (Warren St.) | Brooklyn | 718-230-1630 ◐
Williamsburg | 88 N. 11th St. (bet. Berry St. & Wythe Ave.) | Brooklyn | 718-486-0816 ◐
www.beaconscloset.com

"Super-selective buyers" attest that this resale outfit in Brooklyn and the West Village boasting "tons" of "secondhand gems" "organized by color and type of garment" isn't just "a dumping ground for your random castoffs"; "decent prices" and "wicked sales" make it "difficult to leave empty-handed", but a staff that sometimes "dishes out 'tude like it's going out of style" can be challenging for the uninitiated.

Bed Bath & Beyond ❂

| 22 | 20 | 18 | M |

Flatiron | 620 Sixth Ave. (bet. 18th & 19th Sts.) | 212-255-3550 | 800-462-3966 | www.bedbathandbeyond.com
Additional locations throughout the NY area

"Every New Yorker's first place to stop after moving in", this "massive chain" rated NYC's Most Popular in the Home/Garden category, is "a veritable cornucopia of household necessities" that goes "way beyond" bed and bath, ensuring you "always leave with more than you came for", be it "small appliances", "glassware or dinner plates"; shoppers "can find everything but salespeople", but the "huge" selection and good values keep the "crowds" coming.

Behaviour New York

| 26 | 24 | 24 | M |

Chelsea | 160 Ninth Ave. (20th St.) | 646-559-8414
Chelsea | 231 W. 19th St. (8th Ave.) | 212-352-8380
www.behaviournewyork.com

"Unique" and "trendy" menswear boasting slim cuts and dapper details from a wide range of international designers, including Ben Mori and Roberto Collina, is featured at these Chelsea siblings; the gallery-like presentation of goods "grabs your attention with its bright colors and asymmetrical shapes", and the "helpful, cute" employees always make sure that every fashionisto finds exactly what he's looking for.

Belgian Shoes

| 28 | 22 | 25 | VE |

E 50s | 110 E. 55th St. (bet. Lexington & Park Aves.) | 212-755-7372 | www.belgianshoes.com

"Often imitated, never equaled", this East Side vet's "handmade" hard-soled his-and-hers Belgian loafers in suede, patent leather, ostrich, woolens, animal prints and more are "elegant", "super-comfortable" slip-ons sporting a "very particular" design that's "never out of style"; for well-heeled enthusiasts who maintain "it doesn't get any better", the "long wait to get shoes on order" is "the only bummer" – "but patience is a virtue."

NEW Belstaff

| - | - | - | VE |

E 60s | 814 Madison Ave. (bet. 68th & 69th Sts.) | 212-897-1880 | www.belstaff.com

What started nearly a century ago as an English workwear line is now a high-end fashion brand with its first-ever stateside store, a Madison Avenue mecca with a masculine aesthetic courtesy of renowned retail designer William Sofield; stylish sorts can dress for the elements in its famous sturdy waxed cotton jackets or opt for such indulgences as silky women's garments, trim men's blazers and luxe leather accessories.

Benefit Cosmetics

| 27 | 24 | 24 | M |

E 70s | 1301 Third Ave. (bet. 74th & 75th Sts.) | 212-288-4728
SoHo | 454 W. Broadway (bet. Prince & Houston Sts.) | 212-769-1111
www.benefitcosmetics.com

"Hooked" beauty buffs get their cosmetic fix at this San Francisco-based brand's "cute" SoHo–East 70s branches that house "simply wonderful" makeup, skincare and fragrances, plus airbrush tanning and "the best brow bar"; prices aren't the cheapest around, but these products "deliver on what they promise", and staffers are "very generous with the free samples too."

Ben Sherman ●

| 24 | 25 | 23 | E |

SoHo | 96 Spring St. (bet. B'way & Mercer St.) | 212-680-0160 | www.bensherman.com

Anglophiles looking for "the perfect combination of music and fashion rolled into one sexy lifestyle brand" pack this "high-energy" SoHo emporium filled with "hip yet preppy" casual menswear – mod buttondowns, pants and shoes – that makes you "glad your wardrobe was a victim of the British invasion"; "hats off to style" – just remember "you better be really slim to fit into" these clothes "made for stick figures."

Beretta

| 29 | 25 | 26 | VE |

E 60s | 718 Madison Ave. (bet. 63rd & 64th Sts.) | 212-319-3235 | www.berettausa.com

"From fine clothes to firearms", this East 60s outpost of the circa-1526 Italian gun company "is the place" to come for "high-end shooting apparel" thanks to a wide selection of well-made equipment "for the sportsman or woman", and "helpful" staffers who "know their stuff"; the three-story shop modeled after the Beretta family home in Gardone Val Trompia also includes an extensive book selection and a gun gallery that's "fun even for those who don't hunt, shoot or trample the moors."

Bergdorf Goodman

| 29 | 28 | 25 | VE |

W 50s | 754 Fifth Ave. (bet. 57th & 58th Sts.) | 212-753-7300 | 800-558-1855 | www.bergdorfgoodman.com

Truly the "crème de la crème" of department stores, this "one-of-a-kind" Fifth Avenue "institution" is a "mecca" to "chic shoppers" who appreciate the "highly edited" selection of "stunning designer duds" for women, "killer shoe department", a beauty floor "that's the closest thing to nirvana" and "wonderful salespeople" who "know their merchandise"; while you can "find reasonable prices on the fifth floor", in general the "luxurious items" here cost "top dollar", but "if you can't afford the goodies inside" you can at least "admire the stunning, work-of-art" displays, particularly the "spectacular holiday windows."

Bergdorf Goodman Men's

| 29 | 27 | 26 | VE |

E 50s | 745 Fifth Ave. (58th St.) | 212-753-7300 | 800-558-1855 | www.bergdorfgoodman.com

"The piles of cashmere, the rooms of designer wear, the air of pedigree" – yes, it's "a treat to shop" at this "high-end" Fifth Avenue haberdashery across from the women's landmark; "bring your well-stuffed alligator wallet", "spend a fortune" on "luxurious" men's clothing from "exclusive lines" and "custom-measure" suits and furnishings, then "go land that girl, job or whatever you need to look your absolute best for"; P.S. the staff is "incredible", but, some suggest "self-confidence is mandatory" since you may be evaluated "top to bottom."

Bernardaud

| 29 | 28 | 24 | VE |

E 50s | 499 Park Ave. (59th St.) | 212-371-4300 | 800-884-7775 | www.bernardaud.com

"Beautiful things" abound at the Park Avenue home of this venerable French brand known for its "premier" handcrafted porcelain and other "glorious" decorative objets; the "environment of utmost sophistication" enhances the "delightful shopping experience", making visitors "want to walk out with everything on display"; just be prepared to pay a pretty penny – it's "art" for the table, after all.

NEW Bettie Page Clothing ● — | — | — | M

E Village | 303 Bowery (bet. Bleecker & Houston Sts.) | 646-478-7006 | www.bettiepageclothing.com

Nineteen-fifties pinup girl Bettie Page's iconic style is replicated at this Bowery spin-off of a national chain, where retro-inclined, black-banged ladies of the East Village can stock up on jumpers, circle skirts, sheath dresses and high-waisted shorts at reasonable prices; the spacious pink-walled digs are equally transporting, with a video monitor screening the sexpot's burlesque films and an old-school jukebox to boot.

Bicycle Habitat 27 | 21 | 22 | E

Chelsea | 228 Seventh Ave. (bet. 23rd & 24th Sts.) | 212-206-6949
SoHo | 244 Lafayette St. (bet. Prince & Spring Sts.) | 212-431-3315
SoHo | 250 Lafayette St. (bet. Prince & Spring Sts.) | 212-431-3315
Park Slope | 476 Fifth Ave. (11th St.) | Brooklyn | 718-788-2543
www.bicyclehabitat.com

"A bike enthusiast's heaven", these "vital shops" cater to cyclists set on "buying and fitting" new wheels courtesy of "helpful" sorts who'll also provide "everything you need to keep you pedaling", from accessories to "tune-ups"; the "sprawling" SoHo locations divvy up urban/commuter and road/mountain models, while the Park Sloper is especially handy for children's bikes.

Billionaire Boys Club & Ice Cream 24 | 25 | 21 | E

SoHo | 456 W. Broadway (bet. Houston & Prince Sts.) | 212-777-2225 | www.bbcicecream.com

"Get your street cred" at this SoHo shop founded by musician Pharrell Williams and Japanese designer Nigo, boasting one floor with the owners' Ice Cream label and a "sweet confection shop" feel and another showcasing the BBC brand; the "beautiful displays" feature sneaks and "unique/quality casual/sporty-wear" "often worn by hip-hop moguls", but looking dope has its price – expect goods "a little on the high side."

Billy Reid ▽ 25 | 27 | 24 | E

NoHo | 54 Bond St. (bet. Bowery & Lafayette St.) | 212-598-9355 | www.billyreid.com

Tradition with a twist reigns at this languidly elegant bi-level Bond Street townhouse constructed from all salvaged materials, decorated with "fantastic" vintage bric-a-brac and stocked with the Alabama-based designer's "beautiful", "upscale rugged wear" for gents and belles; the natty attire boasts "great workmanship" and gracefully walks the line between "Southern-casual" and "urban" – "this is what real New Yorkers sport" around town.

Bird 27 | 23 | 22 | E

Cobble Hill | 220 Smith St. (Butler St.) | Brooklyn | 718-797-3774
Park Slope | 316 Fifth Ave. (bet. 2nd & 3rd Sts.) | Brooklyn | 718-768-4940
Williamsburg | 203 Grand St. (Bedford Ave.) | Brooklyn | 718-388-1655
www.shopbird.com

"There's nothing that won't cause you to gasp" crow acolytes who "covet" the "beautiful merchandise" at Jen Mankins' "cute" indie trio in Park Slope, Cobble Hill and Williamsburg; you'll find the "right amount of the right pieces" to feather your closet, including "amazing shoes, one-of-a-kind dresses" and jewelry from of-the-moment labels like Isabel Marant, Rachel Comey and Tsumari Chisato, made from "high-quality materials" and of course "on the pricier side."

Bisazza
▽ | 25 | 24 | 21 | VE

SoHo | 43 Greene St. (bet. Broome & Grand Sts.) | 212-334-7130 | www.bisazza.com

"You'll want to do your entire house" in the "gorgeous" glass mosaic tile designs showcased at this sensational SoHo flagship for the fabulous Italian company offering custom creations for posh palazzos, pools and powder rooms; displays are divine and price tags prohibitive, but wandering through this wonderland can really brighten your day.

BJ's ●
20 | 14 | 12 | I

Mott Haven | Bronx Terminal Shopping Ctr. | 610 Exterior St. (150th St.) | Bronx | 718-292-5410
Canarsie | 900 Remsen Ave. (bet. Ave. D & Ditmas Ave.) | Brooklyn | 718-249-1311
East NY | Gateway Shopping Ctr. | 339 Gateway Dr. (Schenck Ave.) | Brooklyn | 718-942-2090
Middle Village | Metro Mall-Middle Vill. | 6626 Metropolitan Ave. (Rentar Plaza) | Queens | 718-326-9080
www.bjs.com

For "no-frills bulk shopping" customers flock to this East Coast whole-sale club chain of "warehouses" to "stock up" on "super-size" "basics" – "from underwear to electronics" to tires and deli meats – all at "bargain" prices; "service could be better", and the combo low prices/endless options can overwhelm: "you must plan well so you don't wind up with thousands of toilet paper rolls!"

Black Fleece ●
▽ | 24 | 21 | 19 | VE

W Village | 351 Bleecker St. (10th St.) | 212-929-2763 | 800-274-1815 | www.brooksbrothers.com

Set in historic West Village digs, this "beautiful" Brooks Brothers lab-oratory showcases the work of menswear magician Thom Browne, whose "high-end" take on the label's archival pieces nets a "nicer cut and cooler patterns" than its "classic" cohort; if some long for "sizes for real men", über-trim sartorialists adore the "excellent" attire, like jackets inspired by '60s sack suits, advising "come here for the quality."

Black Gold Records
▽ | 25 | 19 | 23 | M

Carroll Gardens | 461 Court St. (bet. 4th Pl. & Luquer St.) | Brooklyn | 347-227-8227 | www.blackgoldbrooklyn.com

After chowing down at Carroll Gardens' Frankies Spuntino, duck into this "small, attractive", "very Brooklyn" emporium with an early-1900s "retro" feel purveying java, antiques and scores of record genres; you never know what nugget you'll discover – say, a Stiv Bators 45 or Wu-Tang Clan CD, or even used furniture and oddities – and rounding out the mix: Rook Coffee Roasters' Black Gold Blend coffee.

Blackman
26 | 21 | 21 | E

Flatiron | 85 Fifth Ave., 2nd fl. (16th St.) | 212-337-1000
Flushing | 134-07 Northern Blvd. (bet. College Point Blvd. & Main St.) | Queens | 718-939-7200

(continued)

Blackman

Queens Village | 217-68 Hempstead Ave. (bet. Springfield Blvd. & 217th St.) | Queens | 718-479-5533
800-843-2695 | www.blackman.com

Making a splash with the "wonderful selection and display" at its rambling Flatiron flagship, this stalwart cross-borough plumbing supplier specializes in "high-quality fixtures for kitchen and bath" in "a wide variety of brands"; a few pipe up it's "expensive", but the staff is "knowledgeable" about the "technicalities" – and "if it's not in stock, they can get it"; P.S. appointments suggested.

Bleecker Street Records ❷

24 | 20 | 23 | M

W Village | 239 Bleecker St. (bet. Carmine & Leroy Sts.) | 212-255-7899 | www.bleeckerstreetrecordsnyc.com

Turntable enthusiasts discover one of "the biggest and best selections" of LPs and CDs, "ranging from the mainstream to the obscure" to "out-of-print gems", at this "brilliant" West Village "throwback" staffed with "knowledgeable" people who aren't "like the characters in *High Fidelity*"; "even if you don't own a record player" it's "fun" to "spend a lazy afternoon" "looking at all the vinyl."

Blick Art Materials

26 | 22 | 21 | M

NoHo | 1-5 Bond St. (bet. B'way & Lafayette St.) | 212-533-2444 | www.dickblick.com

"Wow!" – "they have everything" in the way of "quality art supplies" at this "handy" NoHo branch of a national chain where you'll find an "incredible selection" of paints, pencils, canvas, paper and craft materials along with a custom-framing department; "reasonable prices" make it an "excellent resource" that "hobbyists and professionals" alike "love to get lost in."

bliss ❷

25 | 23 | 23 | E

NEW **E 40s** | W Hotel | 541 Lexington Ave. (bet. 49th & 50th Sts.) | 212-401-2001
SoHo | 568 Broadway (bet. Houston & Prince Sts.) | 212-380-4699
NEW **W 50s** | 12 W. 57th St., 3rd fl. (bet. 5th & 6th Aves.) | 212-888-0033
877-862-5477 | www.blissworld.com

"Has your skin ever felt better?" wonder customers who "pamper" themselves with a trip to this "amazing" day spa's retail arm purveying the house line of "wonderful" scrubbing, bubbling, polishing and exfoliating products with "quippy, girlish descriptions"; the potions can be "a little pricey" but it's "worth the splurge" because they're "simply addictive" – this is "bliss indeed."

Bloomingdale's ❷

26 | 24 | 21 | E

E 50s | 1000 Third Ave. (bet. 59th & 60th Sts.) | 212-705-2000

Bloomingdale's SoHo ❷

SoHo | 504 Broadway (bet. Broome & Spring Sts.) | 212-729-5900
800-232-1854 | www.bloomingdales.com

A New York "institution" that "still impresses", the "enormous" East Side "shoppers' paradise" boasts a "broad selection of clothing, accessories, home furnishings" and cosmetics from "every moderate" brand imaginable as well as "trusted long-standing luxury designers", while its "younger, more curated" though "less comprehensive" SoHo sister sure "comes in handy"; staffers are "very helpful once you find one", and the "bright and clean" surroundings also appeal; still, a few find the original a "bit of a madhouse" and "hard to navigate."

Blue & Cream   25 | 23 | 21 | VE

E Village | 1 E. First St. (Bowery) | 212-533-3088 | www.blueandcream.com

What "über-cool clothes" cry trendsetters who pounce on "covetable" cream-of-the-crop designer names like Equipment, IRO and Rag & Bone along with house-brand guy- and girlwear at this "hip", spacious Bowery boutique, an offshoot of the Hamptons favorite; it's "perfect if you need to pick up a last-minute outfit for a night out" on the town, plus the "staff is attentive, not pushy."

Bluemercury Apothecary   26 | 24 | 23 | E

E 70s | 1311 Third Ave. (75th St.) | 212-396-1500
Flatiron | 865 Broadway (bet. 17th & 18th Sts.) | 212-243-8100 ●
W 80s | 2305 Broadway (83rd St.) | 212-799-0500
800-355-6000 | www.bluemercury.com

"More upscale" than other makeup emporiums and "less intimidating" than department stores, this "boutique cosmetics" trio is where beauty buffs head to get "all skincare needs taken care of", stocking up on the luxe likes of NARS, Clinique, Fekkai and Laura Mercier without big markups; staffers "know their stuff", and guests go for "hard-to-come-by" cult items or to "discover something new" – or to take advantage of makeover parties and spa services.

Blue Tree   28 | 27 | 24 | E

E 90s | 1283 Madison Ave. (bet. 91st & 92nd Sts.) | 212-369-2583 | www.bluetreeny.com

"Absolutely charming", this "neighborhood treasure" in Carnegie Hill manages to "perfectly reflect the grace and taste of lovely actress/owner Phoebe Cates Kline" exclaim loyalists; the "unusual and interesting stock" of "attention-getting jewelry", "stylish" clothing and footwear "gems" and "fun, quirky home goods" and toys are expertly "curated", plus "excellent" service (from the proprietress herself) that goes out on a limb heightens the "wonderful" experience.

Bogner   29 | 25 | 24 | VE

SoHo | 380 W. Broadway (bet. Broome & Spring Sts.) | 212-219-2757 | www.bogner.com

For "stylish ski clothes" that "last and last", along with helmets, goggles and shades, après-appropriate clothing and the glam Sônia Bogner women's collection, slalom over to the SoHo home of the German sportswear brand founded by an Olympian; given the "knowledgeable staff" and swanky decor featuring an electric fireplace, a visit here is almost as "wonderful" as a day on the slopes – just expect to pay peak prices for the "best of the best."

Bond No. 9   27 | 26 | 24 | VE

E 70s | 897 Madison Ave. (73rd St.) | 212-794-4480
NEW **Meatpacking** | 863 Washington St. (bet. B'way & Lafayette St.) | 212-206-9907
NoHo | 9 Bond St. (bet. B'way & Lafayette St.) | 212-228-1732

(continued)

Bond No. 9

W Village | 399 Bleecker St. (11th St.) | 212-633-1641
877-273-3369 | www.bondno9.com

"Choose a scent you'll end up making your signature" at this "uniquely New York" perfumery offering custom blends and "playful" products inspired by "famous people and neighborhoods", packaged in "art-quality" bottles; the "Bond girls" are "knowledgeable and eager", and the "must-visit" NoHo flagship boasting iconic flacons is "heaven", making the "splurge" of an experience "worth the investment."

Bond 07 by Selima

27 | 26 | 26 | VE

NoHo | 7 Bond St. (bet. B'way & Lafayette St.) | 212-677-8487 | www.selimaoptique.com

Aficionados of "quality eye frames with French flair" espy chic options galore from optical trendsetter Selima Salaun at her "fantastic" purple-walled NoHo boutique; but there's more to uncover among the "beautiful" displays, including an exclusive house line of hats, out-of-the-ordinary vintage and contemporary apparel, a clutch of Hermès bags and jewelry from local designers, all sold by "helpful" staffers.

Bonobos NYC Guideshop

- | - | - | E

NEW **SoHo** | 35 Crosby St. (bet. Broome & Grand Sts.) | 212-343-4235
Flatiron | 45 W. 25th St. (bet. B'way & 6th Ave.) | 877-294-7737
www.bonobos.com

On a mission to rid the world of saggy seats, proprietor Andy Dunn brings his e-commerce menswear concept to a brick-and-mortar retail shop annexed to his company's fifth-floor Flatiron headquarters and new sherbet-hued SoHo addition; customers can book appointments online, work with in-house stylists, trying on items like signature chinos and lightweight wool suits, then place orders for home delivery.

Bonpoint

28 | 24 | 24 | VE

E 60s | 805 Madison Ave. (bet. 67th & 68th Sts.) | 212-879-0900
E 90s | 1269 Madison Ave. (91st St.) | 212-722-7720
W Village | 392 Bleecker St. (Perry St.) | 212-647-1700
www.bonpoint.com

"The perfect place to spoil" the "little Napoleon or Marie Antoinette in the family", this favorite French brand's boutiques have the market cornered on "statement"-making childrenswear with its "chic" collection of layette essentials, sportswear and party finery in "delicious" fabrics; yes, everything is "outrageously expensive", but *amis* insist it's "worth the splurge" for "gorgeous" ensembles guaranteed to "steal the show."

Bookmarc

∇ 24 | 24 | 20 | M

W Village | 400 Bleecker St. (11th St.) | 212-620-4021 | www.marcjacobs.com

"Marc Jacobs continues his reign of cool" at this "cute" West Villager, which augments an "eclectic" selection of "chic books" – mostly coffee-table affairs on art, music and fashion – with "quirky" geegaws like MJ key chains, totes, necklaces and notebooks; it's an "affordable" go-to for "gifts for your savvy friends", but watch out when the "super-tiny" space gets "overrun by tourists."

Boomerang Toys

25 | 22 | 22 | E

NEW **TriBeCa** | Mercantile Exchange Bldg. | 1 North End Ave. (Vesey St.) | 212-227-7271

TriBeCa | 119 W. Broadway (bet. Duane & Reade Sts.) | 212-226-7650
West Brighton | 646 Forest Ave. (Bement Ave.) | Staten Island | 718-448-0873
www.boomerangtoys.com

"Treat your kids" with a visit to this playful trio, where the "well-curated" selection of "quality toys" – both familiar faves and European imports – is sure to please the toddler-to-tween demo with "nice birthday presents" or impromptu gifts; given such "unique stuff" matched with "primo" service, returning customers say they could use "more places like this."

Bose

27 | 24 | 24 | VE

SoHo | 465 Broadway (Grand St.) | 212-334-3710
NEW **W 50s** | Rockefeller Ctr. | 620 Fifth Ave. (50th St.) | 212-247-8103
W 60s | Shops at Columbus Circle | 10 Columbus Circle, 3rd fl. (B'way & 60th St.) | 212-823-9314 ◑
800-999-2673 | www.bose.com

Choosy audiophiles find "incredible" "aural experiences" at these "boutique" outlets for the "king of high fidelity", a "legend" for the "brilliant sound" of its "unsurpassed" speakers, Wave music systems and "noise-canceling headphones"; of course such "quality" commands a "premium price", but "they stand behind the product", and the "enthusiastic" salesfolk treat you as a "valued customer."

Bottega Veneta

29 | 27 | 25 | VE

E 50s | 699 Fifth Ave. (bet. 54th & 55th Sts.) | 212-371-5511
E 70s | 849 Madison Ave. (bet. 70th & 71st Sts.) | 212-879-4182
www.bottegaveneta.com

Luxury-lovers flock to the Fifth Avenue "favorite" and Madison Avenue addition for "supple, wonderful" leather goods, including "world-class" "signature woven bags" that "feel like butter", from the "top-of-the-line" Italian maker; also on view: a "fabulous selection" of creative director Tomas Maier's "timeless, chic" ready-to-wear delivering "quality with a cool factor" (plus menswear and home furnishings at the East 50 locale) all tended by "gracious" staffers; even dreamers daunted by the "steep prices" enjoy the "aesthetic experience" of seeing "such beautiful objects so tastefully displayed."

Bottega Veneta Men's

- | - | - | VE

E 60s | 23 E. 67th St. (Madison Ave.) | 212-879-5780 |
www.bottegaveneta.com

Joining the brand's flagship and women's boutique, this East 60s men's offshoot, the first location of its kind in the U.S., reflects creative director Tomas Maier's signature store concept of clean lines and creamy carpeting, with an inviting courtyard out back; on offer are ultraupscale suits and formalwear, plus luxurious butter-soft footwear, wallets and, of course, those signature woven-leather duffels.

Bowery Kitchen Supplies

24 | 14 | 17 | M

Chelsea | Chelsea Mkt. | 75 Ninth Ave. (bet. 15th & 16th Sts.) | 212-376-4982 | www.shopbowery.com

"Serious chefs" come to this Chelsea Market spot for a "can't-be-beat" selection of "everything you need for your kitchen, and then some", including "top brand" utensils, glasses and gadgets and a once-a-week knife sharpening station; the staff is "friendly, though hard to get a hold of", and the "tasty sandwich counter" provides respite from the "claustrophobic" clutter that devotees declare an epicurean "treasure hunt."

Brandy Melville
- | - | - | M

SoHo | 518 Broadway (bet. Broome & Spring Sts.) | 646-449-9322 | www.brandymelvilleusa.com

A "must-stop" in SoHo, this Italian brand's city addition is always teeming with young fashionistas rifling through the "sweet feminine designs", T-shirts with provocative sayings, swingy skirts and "great accessories"; the affordable collection boasts a laid-back LA style that's also registered with Hollywood celebs like Miley Cyrus and Karlie Kloss and many items are "one size" eliminating a search for yours; P.S. an UWS branch is in the works.

Bra Smyth
27 | 17 | 23 | E

E 70s | 905 Madison Ave. (bet. 72nd & 73rd Sts.) | 212-772-9400
W 70s | 2177 Broadway (77th St.) | 212-721-5111
800-272-9466 | www.brasmyth.com

Ladies searching for "uplifting solutions" head to these East-West siblings, where an "attentive staff" offers "custom fittings" and "free alterations" so you can "walk out with the perfect bra" that "never lets you down", plus "beautiful" undies, loungewear and swimwear; if quibblers kvetch about "small" quarters and displays that are "not the most alluring", fans find it "comfortable" and appreciate the "personal attention."

Bra*Tenders
25 | 19 | 22 | E

W 40s | 630 Ninth Ave., 6th fl. (bet. 44th & 45th Sts.) | 212-957-7000 | 888-438-2272 | www.bratenders.com

"You may well bump into a Broadway star or two" at this "best of the best" West 40s "industry" foundations shop where the "expert, individual" appointment only service works with many theatrical (and bridal customers) – in fact, "these ladies know how to corral your ladies exactly where you want them"; if you don't render yourself tendered, you could risk "not wearing the correct bra for your size."

Breguet
▽ 29 | 28 | 29 | VE

E 50s | 711 Fifth Ave. (bet. 55th & 56th Sts.) | 646-692-6469
E 60s | 779 Madison Ave. (bet. 66th & 67th Sts.) | 212-288-4014
www.breguet.com

Queen Victoria, "Napoleon and Wellington wore them" – yes, the "magnificent designs and fine craftsmanship" of these "sophisticated watches" "make you feel like royalty" note armchair historians who're as fascinated by the French horologist's collections showcased at its gilded East 50s and East 60s branches as its storied past as the pioneer of the modern, self-winding tourbillion; owned by the Swatch Group and produced in Switzerland, these timepieces remain the pinnacle of elegance – "top-notch is an understatement."

Breitling
29 | 29 | 29 | VE

E 50s | 5 E. 57th St. (bet. 5th & Madison Aves.) | 855-999-1884 | www.breitling.com

This "excellent" Swiss watchmaker's triple-tiered Midtown showroom/ museum/lounge highlights a hard-to-match variety of precision men's timepieces in "beautiful", aviation-derived designs, matched with service that "shows how the other half lives"; yes, "you'll pay dearly", but you'll wind up with "forever" "quality" that's "worth breaking the bank."

NEW Brian Atwood
`- | - | - | VE`

E 60s | 655 Madison Ave. (bet. 60th & 61st Sts.) | 212-415-4739 | www.brianatwood.com

Shoe designer Brian Atwood's Madison Avenue flagship offers the world's largest selection of his swanky stilettos, platforms, wedges and booties, all arranged on illuminated pedestals in a jewel box–like salon setting replete with mirrored walls, gray velvet sofas and a marble entryway; each pair sold here has a gold '655 Madison' plaque embedded on the sole to indicate its illustrious provenance.

Bric's
`26 | 22 | 21 | E`

E 50s | 535 Madison Ave. (bet. 54th & 55th Sts.) | 212-688-4490 | 866-866-3390 | www.brics.it

Chic is the word at this Italian luggage manufacturer's roomy Midtown store, a source for "durable and stylish" suitcases, bags and travel accessories in eye-grabbing designs that "will set you apart" at the baggage carousel; business types can also browse a more conservative line of some of the "best briefcases" around.

Brioni
`29 | 25 | 26 | VE`

E 50s | 55 E. 52nd St. (bet. Madison & Park Aves.) | 212-355-1940
E 50s | 57 E. 57th St. (bet. Madison & Park Aves.) | 212-376-5777
888-778-8775 | www.brioni.it

For "a second skin that spells success", gents flock to this East 50s outfitter that delivers "Italian flair and style at its finest" and "lovely service" to boot; "conservative but beautiful, the suits are exquisite" and cut from only the "best fabrics", and "you just cannot beat" the "impeccable" cotton shirts and "stunning silk ties"; true, you may have to "mortgage your home", especially for the custom-made goods, but once you slip on the "beautiful" attire, "there's no going back."

Broadway Panhandler
`25 | 18 | 18 | M`

G Village | 65 E. Eighth St. (bet. B'way & University Pl.) | 212-966-3434 | 866-266-5927 | www.broadwaypanhandler.com

A "dreamland" for "home cooks", this Village "culinary candy store" packs in an "amazing variety" of brand-name kitchenware, with an "A-to-Z" array encompassing "essentials" to "obscure" gadgetry; the "fair" prices are "even better when they have a sale", and though some pan the "confusing" "clutter", "if they don't have it, you don't need it"; P.S. it's *the* "place to get your knives sharpened."

Brook Farm General Store
`24 | 23 | 23 | M`

Williamsburg | 75 S. Sixth St. (bet. Berry St. & Wythe Ave.) | Brooklyn | 718-388-8642 | www.brookfarmgeneralstore.com

"Off the beaten path" in Brooklyn and tucked under the Williamsburg Bridge lies "the most perfectly curated shop of beauty and utility" that "impresses" with a "very earthy and clean selection" of "interesting products" from kitchenware to shag towels, bedding and vintage finds; browsing is a breeze and some prices painless, prompting devotees to declare "if you're looking to be inspired, this is the store."

| | QUALITY | DISPLAY | SERVICE | COST |

Brooklyn Botanic Garden's Garden Shop $\quad-\mid-\mid-\mid$ M

Prospect Heights | Brooklyn Botanic Gdn. | 990 Washington Ave. (Crown St.) | Brooklyn | 718-622-0963 | www.bbg.org

After marveling at the fragrant flowers in bloom, green thumbs head to the BBG's glass-enclosed gift shop near the Visitor's Center, brimming with pots, planters, pruners, terrariums and garden supplies, along with seasonal plants, bulbs and seeds; rounding out the mix: jewelry, toys and housewares, many from the organization's signature house line.

Brooklyn Circus $\quad$ 25 | 26 | 24 | E

Boerum Hill | 150 Nevins St. (Bergen St.) | Brooklyn | 718-858-0919 | www.thebkcircus.com

"You have to be a special brand of hip" to sport the "fantastic" steam-punk-cum-"upscale-urban" street gear, curated by the borough's own Ouigi Theodore, aka The Bearded Man, at his "small, cozy" Boerum Hill menswear boutique; hard-to-find labels like Creep and the store's "self-branded" BKc varsity-inspired letter jackets and flannel hats make this "unique" shop a tough act to follow – the "window displays alone make you want to know what's inside" the Circus.

Brooklyn Denim Company $\quad$ 24 | 23 | 24 | E

Williamsburg | 85 N. Third St. (Wythe Ave.) | Brooklyn | 718-782-2600 | www.brooklyndenimco.com

"Denim takes on a new life" at Frank Pizzuro's Williamsburg destination with an industrial factory feel that purists consider "one of the best" sources for jeans in NYC; staffers are "experts on their product", helping you pluck the right "style, color and fade" from a curated mix of labels including Adriano Goldschmied, DL1961 and Tellason, plus you can custom-order the perfect pair from the house line BDC and utilize the tailoring services.

Brooklyn Flea $\quad$ 21 | 19 | 21 | M

Fort Greene | 1 Hanson Pl. (Ashland Pl.) | Brooklyn | 718-928-6603
Fort Greene | 176 Lafayette Ave. (bet. Clermont & Vanderbilt Aves.) | Brooklyn | 718-928-6603
Williamsburg | East River State Park | 90 Kent Ave. (N. 7th St.) | Brooklyn | 718-928-6603
www.brooklynflea.com

Weekends are "always entertaining" at these seasonal alfresco markets in Fort Greene and Williamsburg (plus the "magnificent" Skylight One Hanson winter quarters, a soaring "ex-bank"), large-scale venues for browsing "vintage jewelry, clothing", furniture and all manner of "quirky knickknacks" crafted by "local artisans", "gorging" from "top-notch" food vendors adds to the overall "fun" experience, and while the wares are "not the cheapest", you could "spend a day" just "hipster-watching."

Brooklyn Industries ◗ $\quad$ 21 | 21 | 20 | M

Williamsburg | 162 Bedford Ave. (N. 8th St.) | Brooklyn | 718-486-6464 | 800-318-6061 | www.brooklynindustries.com
Additional locations throughout the NY area

"Hipsters" flock to this "local business made good" with locations Brooklyn-wide and even Manhattan, stocking "stylish urban apparel", including "super-soft" tees, dresses, sweaters and denim for men, women and children; while its "indie" threads are "ultracool", followers give biggest props to the trademark "indestructible" totes and "signature messenger bags" boasting the namesake borough's iconic "old water tower" logo.

Brooklyn Kitchen
26 | 24 | 24 | M

Williamsburg | 100 Frost St. (bet. Manhattan & Meeker Aves.) | Brooklyn | 718-389-2982 | www.thebrooklynkitchen.com

"The expert as well as the novice" find it "fun to rummage around" at this "hip" Williamsburg "haven" boasting an "amazing selection" of "top-quality" (if "sort of pricey") kitchen merch, from cookware, knives, tools and appliances to DIY canning supplies and vintage items; other on-site attractions include "wonderful" culinary classes and the "off-the-hook" locally sourced butcher Meat Hook in the back.

Brooklyn Museum Shop
25 | 23 | 22 | M

Prospect Heights | Brooklyn Museum | 200 Eastern Pkwy. (Washington Ave.) | Brooklyn | 718-501-6259 | www.brooklynmuseum.org

"Pick up something to remind you" of your "art tour" at the Brooklyn Museum's "lovely" shop, where the "beautifully displayed" collection of "unusual" jewelry, decorative items, books and reproductions includes both choices inspired by "current exhibitions" and "genuine" handicrafts from across the globe; "fairly reasonable" prices help make it a "go-to" for "original, enchanting gifts."

Brooklyn Superhero Supply Co.
24 | 26 | 27 | I

Park Slope | 372 Fifth Ave. (bet. 5th & 6th Sts.) | Brooklyn | 718-499-9884 | www.superherosupplies.com

"Where else you gonna go to get the ability to run at the speed of light" but this "wonderfully curated" nonprofit Park Slope learning center masking as an "insanely creative" superhero supply store; "bring the kids" (or "your inner kid") and browse for "quirky" goods – "yes, that's anti-gravity powder next to the invisibility capes" – then take the oath that "you'll use your powers for good" upon exiting.

Brooklyn Tailors
- | - | - | E

Williamsburg | 358 Grand St. (bet. Havemeyer St. & Marcy Ave.) | Brooklyn | 347-799-1646 | www.brooklyn-tailors.com

Young creative professionals and arty-types looking to up their style game frequent this Willliamsburg menswear haunt offering handmade garments such as classic striped shirts, linen-cotton button-downs and garment dyed chinos fashioned from fine fabrics and finished with thoughful details, like horn or mother of pearl buttons; for custom wares, including stylish suits in the affordable range, book an appointment at the designers' large studio nearby.

Brooks Brothers
26 | 24 | 24 | E

E 40s | 346 Madison Ave. (44th St.) | 212-682-8800
E 80s | 1180 Madison Ave. (bet. 86th & 87th Sts.) | 212-289-5027
Flatiron | 901 Broadway (20th St.) | 212-228-3580
TriBeCa | 1 Liberty Plaza (Broadway) | 212-267-2400
W 50s | 1270 Sixth Ave. (bet. 50th & 51st Sts.) | 212-247-9374
W 60s | 1934 Broadway (65th St.) | 212-362-2374
W 80s | 2381 Broadway (bet. 87th & 88th Sts.) | 646-505-5280
800-274-1815 | www.brooksbrothers.com

Managing to be "a bastion of old-school style without living in the past", this "classic" chain hasn't lost its touch, with devotees calling it "the gold standard for all-American tailored clothing" thanks to "quality"

QUALITY DISPLAY SERVICE COST

suits and "wrinkle-free" dress button-downs; edgier sorts call the women's fashions "staid" and a handful wish everyone else didn't "have the same shirt", but "excellent service" and "interesting bargains" come sale time keep customers coming back.

Brunello Cucinelli
29 | 25 | 25 | VE

E 60s | 683 Madison Ave. (bet. 61st & 62nd Sts.) | 212-813-0900
W Village | 379 Bleecker St. (bet. Charles & Perry Sts.) | 212-627-9202
www.brunellocucinelli.it

"Drooling is permitted" at this white-walled "luxury" duo Uptown and Down, where "unimaginably" soft, "very European" cashmere sweaters share the racks with "high-end bohemian" slacks and accessories sewn by hand in a provincial Italian town; customer service is "excellent" and staffers makes shoppers "feel at home", but "don't get too attached" to the "gorgeous" merchandise – prices are "stratospheric."

Buccellati
29 | 29 | 29 | VE

E 60s | 810 Madison Ave. (68th St.) | 212-308-2900 | www.buccellati.com

"When only the best Italian silver will do, go" to the venerable Milanese company's "hushed, reserved" tapestry-lined Madison Avenue mecca and indulge suggest *amici* who also praise the "great" staff that's rated No. 1 in NYC for Service; the "sterling stemware and serving pieces are genuine works of art", and the unique jewelry, including "breathtaking" gemstone mosaics, is "fabulous"; *sì*, the wares are also "extravagant" in price, but "worth every dollar" and "perfectly adaptable to modern living."

Buffalo Exchange
20 | 16 | 17 | I

Chelsea | 114 W. 26th St. (bet. 6th & 7th Aves.) | 212-675-3535
E Village | 332 E. 11th St. (bet. 1st & 2nd Aves.) | 212-260-9340
Cobble Hill | 109 Boerum Pl. (bet. Dean & Pacific Sts.) | Brooklyn | 718-403-0490
Williamsburg | 504 Driggs Ave. (9th St.) | Brooklyn | 718-384-6901
www.buffaloexchange.com

"A surprise always awaits you in this treasure chest of a vintage" chain say thrifters who "go with an open eye" to "score deals on designer shoes" and "stylish secondhand clothing", "all clean and in good" shape; "the trendy staff" "buys selectively but is very fair", ensuring that you too will be "trading up to something fab and trendy."

Bulgari
▽ 29 | 28 | 25 | VE

E 50s | 730 Fifth Ave. (57th St.) | 212-315-9000 | 800-285-4274 | www.bulgari.com

Dating back to 1884, this Italian luxury firm known for its meticulous craftsmanship and serpent-inspired and modular designs, spotlights "art that happens to be jewelry" and "competes with the best and often beats them"; the glittering Fifth Avenue flagship also boasts "beautifully displayed" collections of watches, handbags and men's accessories and while the "merchandise is out of this world", so are the prices.

Bump
▽ 26 | 23 | 23 | M

Park Slope | 464 Bergen St. (bet. 5th & Flatbush Aves.) | Brooklyn | 718-638-1960 | www.bumpbrooklyn.com

For some of the "most stylish maternity wear" around, head to Park Slope's "pregnant lady headquarters" on bustling Bergen Steet, run by two moms who believe you don't have to forgo your fashion sense when expecting; the "pleasant", homey space is filled with cute, figure-flattering pieces from a mix of contemporary brands, and since prices are "decent" you won't blow baby's entire college fund.

Burberry
28 | 26 | 25 | VE

E 40s | 444 Madison Ave. (bet. 49th & 50th Sts.) | 212-707-6700
E 50s | 9 E. 57th St. (bet. 5th & Madison Aves.) | 212-407-7100
SoHo | 131 Spring St. (bet. Greene & Wooster Sts.) | 212-925-9300
www.burberry.com

"Much more than the ubiquitous plaid" "that has become just as recognizable as the flag of England itself", these "classy" chain links boast design head Christopher Bailey's "well-tailored", "avant-posh" "riffs on the classics" as well as "very hip" pieces for him and her alike; all this finery is priced for the "swanky" "1%" – but some loyalists say this "British luxury collection" is proof positive that we've "succeeded in life."

Burberry Brit
28 | 27 | 27 | VE

E 50s | 444 Madison Ave. (bet. 49th & 50th Sts.) | 212-707-6700
W 60s | 160 Columbus Ave. (bet. 67th & 68th Sts.) | 212-595-0934
W Village | 367-369 Bleecker St. (Charles St.) | 212-901-3600
Burberry London

E 50s | 444 Madison Ave. (bet. 49th & 50th Sts.) | 212-707-6700
www.burberry.com

Burberry-philes with "fewer years and fewer dollars" who "refuse to be short on style" make a beeline for these "top stops" around town, brand spin-offs that ably deliver "prestige, quality and design", evident in everything from a spot-on trench to a crisp checked shirt; the "extremely helpful" staffers "make you feel so much at ease", you may snap up "multiple things just because of their undivided attention", even if you were "just browsing originally."

Burton Store
26 | 24 | 24 | E

SoHo | 106 Spring St. (Mercer St.) | 212-966-8070 | www.burton.com
Powder-surfers headed "to the mountains" "grab some gear" at this SoHo "snowboarder's paradise", the manufacturer's flagship dealer in decks and "clothes to go with", i.e. a "high-quality" line of outerwear, boots and accessories "that'll certainly last the season"; it's a rustically "hip" setup with "very good customer service" to acclimate newbies.

buybuy BABY ⦿
23 | 20 | 20 | M

Chelsea | 270 Seventh Ave. (bet. 25th & 26th Sts.) | 917-344-1555 | 877-328-9222 | www.buybuybaby.com
"Comprehensive" and "crowded", this Chelsea "megastore" chain offshoot is a "mecca" for expectant parents looking to "stock up" on "everything they need and then some", including "trendy strollers", high chairs and teeny clothing; while some find the layout "easy to navigate", others get "frustrated" when "service is less than expected"; still, everyone agrees that its coupons are "great."

By Brooklyn
23 | 22 | 22 | M

Cobble Hill | 261 Smith St. (Douglass St.) | Brooklyn | 718-643-0606 | www.bybrooklyn.com
During a jaunt through the city's "most creative borough" escape to this "quirky" Cobble Hill shop peddling exclusively made-in-Brooklyn

wares – from skincare, tees, stationery, mugs and jewelry to artisanal foodstuffs including jams, condiments, candy, pickles and even jerky; the local "novelty" items make "one-of-a-kind" gifts for "out-of-towners" (themed baskets are a specialty), but tread lightly during the holidays as the "tiny" space "can get crowded"; P.S. it also offers classes on crafty subjects like perfume-making and block-printing.

By Robert James

- | - | - | M

LES | 74 Orchard St. (bet. Broome & Grand Sts.) | 212-253-2121 ◗
NEW **Williamsburg** | 241 Bedford Ave. (N. 3rd St.) | Brooklyn | 347-529-6392
www.byrobertjames.com

Vintage vinyl records and interesting geegaws lend character to this spacious menswear duo in Williamsburg and the Lower East Side; the handsome classics, including casual and dress shirts boasting unexpected details, screen-printed tees and historically informed jackets and suits with a modern-day feel, are locally made, and the nice young man waiting on you might well be the namesake designer himself.

CADET ◗

- | - | - | E

E Village | 305 E. Ninth St. (bet. 1st & 2nd Aves.) | 646-633-4560
Williamsburg | 46 N. Sixth St. (bet. Kent & Wythe Aves.) | Brooklyn | 718-715-1695
www.cadetusa.com

Co-founded by a former fit specialist for brands like Club Monaco and an e-commerce vet, this line of crisp, tailored menswear is inspired by postwar military design and merchandised in an orderly fashion at its East Village–Williamsburg storefronts; the clothing is crafted at the company's own Brooklyn factory and displayed in a spare space adorned with globes, uniform regalia and a wall-sized image of a Civil War general.

Calvin Klein

26 | 25 | 23 | E

E 60s | 654 Madison Ave. (60th St.) | 212-292-9000 | www.calvinklein.com
The quintessence of "sleek, modern style" confirm followers who file into this "beautiful" Madison Avenue flagship for all things Calvin; with "sophisticated" and, yes, "expensive" understated gowns and slim dresses from creative director Francisco Costa plus some of the "best men's designs" from Italo Zucchelli, including "well-made" suits, "it's easy to put yourself together" here; add in "helpful clerks" and a "relaxing atmosphere", and you've got a "shopping experience" that's "simply perfection."

Calvin Klein Underwear

26 | 22 | 21 | M

SoHo | 104 Prince St. (bet. Greene & Mercer Sts.) | 212-274-1639 | 877-258-7646 | www.cku.com
Stock up on "high-quality" "unmentionables" at the namesake designer's minimalist SoHo standby that "meets and exceeds the need" for more than standard-issue tighty-whities; guys and gals "love" the "large collection" – the well-fitting bras are "sooo comfy" and the briefs and boxers come in scores of "colors and designs"; if a few feel stripped by the prices, most Calvinists claim it's an "affordable alternative."

Calypso

23 | 24 | 22 | E

E 70s | 900 Madison Ave. (bet. 72nd & 73rd Sts.) | 212-535-4100
(continued)

(continued)

Calypso

NoLita | 280 Mott St. (bet. Houston & Prince Sts.) | 212-965-0990
SoHo | 191 Lafayette St. (Broome St.) | 212-941-6512
SoHo | 426 Broome St. (bet. Crosby & Lafayette Sts.) | 212-941-9700
TriBeCa | 137 W. Broadway (bet. Duane & Thomas Sts.) | 212-608-2222
W Village | 654 Hudson St. (Gansevoort St.) | 646-638-3000
866-422-5977 | www.calypsostbarth.com
Selling "beautiful, breezy" washed-silk dresses and cotton tunics in
"wonderful color schemes" and "bohemian" vacation wear that might
"make you jump on the next plane to St. Barts", this "tropical"-inspired
outfitter "is like sunshine" for beach-starved New Yorkers; "considerate"
salespeople won't "breathe down your neck", and though a few find the
"flirty" items "overpriced", costs "drop considerably" during sales.

Calypso Home
26 | 26 | 22 | VE

Little Italy | 407 Broome St. (bet. Centre & Lafayette Sts.) |
212-925-6200 | 866-422-5977 | www.calypsostbarth.com
This "beachy cool" haven for the home in Little Italy shares the same
"lovely" aesthetic as its sibling fashion chain, sporting "earthy-looking"
globally sourced decor in natural fabrics, "very high-end" modern and
vintage-y furniture and "gorgeous" "island-inspired items"; the "unique
pieces add an unusual bit of style to any home", and while pricey, it's
worth it for "something of quality and delight."

Camera Land
24 | 15 | 22 | M

E 50s | 575 Lexington Ave. (bet. 51st & 52nd Sts.) | 212-753-5128 |
866-967-8427 | www.cameralandny.com
They "really know their stuff" at this long-standing "local camera
store" on the East Side, an "un-big box" operation offering "a range
of products" from major names, spanning "point-and-shoots to
professional-grade" gear; prices are "very fair", and whether you're at
the digital-printing kiosks or getting "helpful" advice from the family
owners, "time's never an issue."

Camper
24 | 21 | 20 | E

NEW **E 40s** | 522 Fifth Ave. (bet. 43rd & 44th Sts.) | 212-221-3529
E 50s | 635 Madison Ave. (59th St.) | 212-339-0078
SoHo | 110 Prince St. (Greene St.) | 212-343-4220
SoHo | 125 Prince St. (Wooster St.) | 212-358-1842
www.camper.com
Hipsters and "art"-y types are "hooked on" the "funky", "incredibly
comfortable" footwear for grown-ups and kids from this Spanish
brand beloved for its "whimsical" designs that "last year after year";
the stores' high-concept interiors put the spotlight on the shoes, especially the "awesome" 110 Prince Street locale conceived by Japanese
architect Shigeru Ban.

Canali
28 | 25 | 24 | VE

NEW **E 50s** | 625 Madison Ave. (59th St.) | 212-752-3131
Financial District | 25 Broad St. (Exchange Pl.) | 212-842-8700
www.canali.it
"If you're in FiDi, there's no better place to shop for fine Italian menswear" than this "beautiful" Milanese haberdashery, aglow in marble
and smoked glass and its new bi-level Madison Avenue sidekick; the

"expensive", "high-quality" suits and "elegant" shirts and separates, including made-to-measure options, are crafted from luxurious textiles, many created exclusively for the third-generation family-owned label; P.S. on-site perks include a master tailor and an espresso bar.

Canvas
27 | 25 | 24 | E

Flatiron | 123 W. 17th St. (6th Ave.) | 212-372-7706
Little Italy | 199 Lafayette St. (Broome St.) | 646-873-6698
www.canvashomestore.com

"Walk in on a whim" and "restore your faith" in retail at this Flatiron–Little Italy do-gooder duo offering "wonderful finds" with a conscience, like reclaimed wood furniture, recycled glass pieces and hand-woven textiles promoting the shop's Fair Trade and green principles; customers concur service is "excellent", and while wallet-watchers warn "items are expensive", most agree the sustainability ethos justifies high prices.

Capezio
24 | 21 | 22 | M

E 90s | Ballet Academy East | 1651 Third Ave., 3rd fl. (93rd St.) | 212-348-7210
E Village | Peridance Capezio Ctr. | 126 E. 13th St. (bet. 3rd & 4th Aves.) | 212-388-0876
W 50s | 1650 Broadway, 2nd fl. (51st St.) | 212-245-2130
W 60s | 201 Amsterdam Ave. (69th St.) | 212-586-5140
www.capeziodance.com

For the "budding ballerina to the seasoned professional", "everything a dancer might need" is on offer at this performance wear "institution" boasting an "extensive selection" of leotards, tights and tap shoes, overseen by "knowledgeable" staffers; if a few quip it's "cost-prohibitive for anyone in the arts", and stage moms watch for dwindling supplies "around Nutcracker season", most agree the merch is applause-worthy.

Cappellini
26 | 25 | 25 | E

SoHo | 152 Wooster St. (Houston St.) | 212-966-0669 | www.cappellini.it
When seeking "to-die-for" furniture that's equally at home in a collector's living room as in the Museum of Modern Art, design buffs head to the SoHo outpost of this iconic Italian brand; the inventive contemporary designs are "exquisite" against the startling red wash of the "sleek" store, and though the "gorgeous stuff" might be "out of price range", big spenders say "you only live once."

Carhartt
▽ 28 | 22 | 22 | M

SoHo | 119 Crosby St. (bet. Houston & Prince Sts.) | 212-219-2934 | www.carhartt-wip.com
Bringing the "top-quality" brand for "made-to-last" menswear to SoHo, this "stylish" spacious shop features industrial decor – think reclaimed wood and exposed brick – that makes "proletarians who work with their hands" and casual-seekers alike feel right at home; prices aren't quite as working class, but this stuff "can take a beating."

Carlo Pazolini
- | | - | E

SoHo | 543 Broadway (bet. Prince & Spring Sts.) | 212-792-5855 | www.carlopazolini.com
Russian retail czar Ilya Reznik offers his take on the Italian shoemaking tradition at this SoHo leviathan, showcasing his contemporary de-

signer brand of "extremely comfortable" made-in-Italy footwear, accessories for men and a "wonderful collection of handbags"; the space age-y interior, detailed with curvy shelves, inset lighting and pop-colored seating, is a fitting backdrop for the house collections that range from moderate to stratospheric prices.

Carlos Miele

▽ 23 | 22 | 19 | VE

Meatpacking | 408 W. 14th St. (bet. 9th Ave. & Washington St.) | 646-336-6642 | www.carlosmiele.com

Find yourself something slinky at the Brazilian designer's Meatpacking District outpost, decked out with a futuristic sculpture and filled with silky, delicate gowns and party dresses that manage to be "gorgeous and funky all in one"; shoppers "love" the sexy, Rio-ready styles, which are perfect "for a very special occasion", though a few lament that prices are as sky-high as the thigh-revealing slits on his skirts.

Carolina Herrera

29 | 28 | 27 | VE

E 70s | 954 Madison Ave. (75th St.) | 212-249-6552 | www.carolinaherrera.com

What "class!" crow acolytes – "if you've money to spend" this eponymous designer's Madison Avenue showcase "is the place" to go for "pricey, elegant, gorgeous" getups, including "wonderful" dresses and bridal wear; season after season, this "wonderful, talented" maven's style "exhilarates" – in fact, wearing her creations is a rite of passage to some luxury-lovers who insist "we should all own a piece at some point in our lives."

Carol's Daughter

26 | 25 | 25 | M

Harlem | 24 W. 125th St. (bet. 5th & Lenox Aves.) | 212-828-6757
Downtown Bklyn | Atlantic Terminal | 139 Flatbush Ave. (Atlantic Ave.) | Brooklyn | 718-622-4514 ◗
877-540-2101 | www.carolsdaughter.com

"From the bottom of your feet to the top of your head", this "neat, modern" Harlem–Brooklyn duo specializing in natural beauty products "made for women of color" has you covered; "smell and touch" the "high-quality hair supplies", "fragrant creams, lotions and soaps" and "girlie gifts" – "how amazing and beneficial" exclaim enthusiasts who also tout the "knowledgeable" staff that "takes time with you."

NEW Carson Street Clothiers

- | - | - | E

SoHo | 63 Crosby St. (bet. Broome & Spring St.) | 212-925-2627 | www.carsonstreetclothiers.com

This SoHo menswear store targets the city's most stylish guys with its solid selection of shoes, accessories and apparel from both well-known and obscure designers like Michael Bastian, Ian Velardi and Wings + Horns, plus its own house label; the clubby, 2,000-sq.-ft. space hews to a masculine aesthetic with antique wooden tables, worn-in leather couches, tapestry rugs and a dry bar to the rear.

Cartier

29 | 29 | 27 | VE

E 50s | 653 Fifth Ave. (52nd St.) | 212-753-0111
E 60s | 828 Madison Ave. (69th St.) | 212-472-6400
800-227-8437 | www.cartier.com

For "discerning clientele with plenty of moolah" and aspirants alike, it's a "thrill to shop" at the "mansion on Fifth" with its "carriage-trade setting and service" and the smaller, equally "high-end" Madison Avenue mecca, both boasting "beautifully constructed displays" of "jaw-dropping jewels", "sublime" watches ("everyday and diamond encrusted, to last a lifetime"), "timeless classics" like the Love bracelet and Trinity ring and "fabulous engagement sparklers"; expect "unmatched style and quality" – this is "true luxury" sigh sybarites.

Catbird
28 | 28 | 26 | M

Williamsburg | 219 Bedford Ave. (N. 4th St.) | Brooklyn | 718-599-3457 | www.catbirdnyc.com

You can "always find something lovely and unique" in this "tiny gem of a shop" in Williamsburg, a "stylish girl's dream" for "modern, quirky-yet-classic" jewelry "at all price levels" from emerging and beloved local designers, plus "cute" gift ideas like notecards, candles and picture frames; the "helpful staff" and "chic" black-and-gold exterior, a nod to Versailles, further explain why it's catnip to "hip" shoppers.

Catherine Malandrino
27 | 27 | 25 | VE

Meatpacking | 652 Hudson St. (bet. Gansevoort & W. 13th Sts.) | 212-929-8710
SoHo | 468 Broome St. (Greene St.) | 212-925-3415
www.catherinemalandrino.com

"Beautifully designed", "finely crafted" womenswear from the namesake French designer lures "stylish", "bohemian-chic" types to these Meatpacking-SoHo branches, "lovely" spaces with "interesting architecture" and a relaxed vibe that makes it easy to "enjoy shopping here"; while the price tags of the draped, dramatic and effortlessly chic creations are decidedly uptown, given the "quality" most "only regret that they can't buy one of everything."

Catimini
28 | 23 | 26 | VE

E 80s | 1125 Madison Ave. (bet. 84th & 85th Sts.) | 212-987-0688 | www.catimini.com

Mixing and matching is made easy at the Madison Avenue flagship of this French childrenswear outfit, whose "fun" and spirited approach to dressing the kiddie crowd – "especially little girls" – translates to fashion-forward sportswear in lively colors and prints; the "exquisite" clothes are of "excellent" quality but très "pricey", so "*maman's* budget may end up mini-sized after a spree here."

Caudalie
- | - | - | E

E 70s | 1031 Lexington Ave. (bet. 73rd & 74th Sts.) | 212-308-3551
NEW Caudalie
W Village | 315 Bleecker St. (Grove St.) | 212-308-3552
us.caudalie.com

The French couple behind this Bordeaux-born beauty brand chose the West Village and Upper East Side as the settings for their first-ever boutiques, where guests can indulge in free facials, customize their own exfoliating scrubs and splurge on any number of signature organic products that harness the antioxidant-rich properties of the grapevine; the white-on-wood interior makes for a spalike experience.

CB2
19 | 23 | 19 | M

E 50s | 979 Third Ave. (bet. 58th & 59th Aves.) | 212-355-7974

(continued)

(continued)

CB2

SoHo | 451 Broadway (bet. Grand & Howard Sts.) | 212-219-1454 ●
800-606-6252 | www.cb2.com

Crate and Barrel's "hip little brother" offers "a bit of everything" at its East 50s and SoHo chain links, with "creative displays" of "modern" housewares "from sofas to paper clip" containers in "bright and bold patterns"; staffers can be "elusive", and "don't expect the stuff to last a long time", but the "playful accents" at "inexpensive prices" allow you to "consistently refresh your surroundings."

Céline

25 | 24 | 22 | VE

E 70s | 870 Madison Ave. (71st St.) | 212-535-3703 | www.celine.com

Chic shoppers set their sights on this legendary French brand's Madison Avenue boutique, reveling in "beautifully put-together outfits" for elegant, artsy affairs; sleek marble cubes showcase accessories, while "splendid" displays spotlight "classic with a modern twist" designs: sharp, slouchy and "stylish" looks with that certain *je ne sais quoi* that have made creative director Phoebe Philo one of fashion's most revered talents; it all costs *beaucoup* de euros, but you get "excellent quality for the price."

Century 21 ●

21 | 13 | 12 | M

Financial District | 22 Cortlandt St. (bet. B'way & Church St.) | 212-227-9092
W 60s | 1972 Broadway (bet. 66th & 67th Sts.) | 212-518-2121
Bay Ridge | 472 86th St. (bet. 4th & 5th Aves.) | Brooklyn | 718-748-3266
Rego Park | 61-01 Junction Blvd. (bet. Horace Harding Expy. & 62nd Dr.) | Queens | 718-699-2121
877-350-2121 | www.c21stores.com

No matter whether you call it "a madhouse" or a "mecca beyond compare", bargain-hunters happily brave "mind-boggling disorganization" and "nonexistent service" at this 10,000-sq.-ft. "cave of discounted fashion" in the Financial District and its citywide branches in hopes of finding "fabulous buys on top-label brands"; shoppers with "commitment" don't mind "pushing through hordes of tourists" and "scouring every rack" if it means "hitting the jackpot" and unearthing a "special treasure."

Cesare Attolini

- | - | - | E

E 60s | 798-800 Madison Ave. (bet. 67th & 68th Sts.) | 646-707-3006 | www.cesareattolini.com

Nurtured by three generations of family over a span of 82 years, this menswear purveyor with a deep Neapolitan soul suits East 60s shoppers demanding craftsmanship with a modern edge; under the watch of meticulous Master Cesare, each suit takes at least 30 hours to create, with one tailor dedicated to each step of the process.

Cesare Paciotti

∇ 25 | 22 | 20 | VE

E 60s | 833 Madison Ave. (bet. 69th & 70th Sts.) | 212-452-1222 | www.cesare-paciotti.com

For "beautiful, well-made" footwear Italian-style, look no further than this Madison Avenue outpost of the Milan-based brand known for its sexy, "innovative, inspiring" designs; the sleek, two-level space done up in red, white and black showcases "cutting-edge" styles for men

QUALITY | DISPLAY | SERVICE | COST

and women as well as high-end leather goods like wallets, belts and handbags, most costing euros aplenty, as befits a *bellissimo* luxury label.

NEW Chacott by Freed of London
`- | - | - | E`

Gramercy | 20 E. 20th St. (bet. B'way & Park Ave.) | 212-432-4414 | www.freedusa.com

Dilettantes and performers alike can now find dance footwear, tights, leotards and accessories from both Japanese brand Chacott and its English counterpart Freed of London, all arranged in one spare, high-ceilinged Gramercy space; pointe shoes and ballet slippers, favored by members of the New York City Ballet, line the long wall, and service extends to professional fittings and custom costumes.

Chanel
`29 | 28 | 24 | VE`

E 50s | 15 E. 57th St. (bet. 5th & Madison Aves.) | 212-355-5050
E 60s | 737 Madison Ave. (bet. 64th & 65th Sts.) | 212-535-5505
SoHo | 139 Spring St. (Wooster St.) | 212-334-0055
800-550-0005 | www.chanel.com

"All hail Karl" – Lagerfeld – the brains behind the "holy grail of fashion" at the "house that Coco Chanel built"; from the "ne plus ultra" of ballet flats to bouclé suits that "set the international standard for the impeccably dressed" to "timeless" "chained bags and clutches", this outfit remains an "icon for the elite", with "absurd" prices part of the package; even aspirants who "can't afford" the "stunning couture" goods confide it's a "lovely experience" just to browse.

Chanel Fine Jewelry
`▽ 29 | 29 | 27 | VE`

E 60s | 733 Madison Ave. (64th St.) | 212-535-5828 | 800-550-0005 | www.chanel.com

"If camellias and clovers and comets" – just a few of Coco's favorite things – and other "magnificent" motifs strike your fancy, this Madison Avenue boutique, styled to resemble the French designer's Paris apartment, "is the place" to indulge; the "beautiful", whimsical baubles, fashioned from white and yellow gold, onyx, platinum and diamonds, are rendered with "wonderful quality", showcased in "elegant displays" and served up by a "civilized and educated" staff – just what you "would expect at these prices."

Charles P. Rogers
`24 | 20 | 22 | E`

Flatiron | 26 W. 17th St. (bet. 5th & 6th Aves.) | 212-675-4400 | 800-582-6229 | www.charlesprogers.com

Rest assured you'll find "beautiful beds", from the day variety to platform mattresses, plus "unique brass", antique iron and other "costly" headboards and frames of "very high quality" at this Flatiron loft space, a must-stop for decorators that's been ticking since 1855; no need to search for covers: this bedroom master also offers Egyptian cotton and European linen bedding and accessories.

Charles Tyrwhitt
`24 | 22 | 22 | E`

E 40s | 377 Madison Ave. (46th St.) | 212-286-8988
NEW W 40s | 1177 Sixth Ave. (bet. 45th & 46th Sts.) | 212-901-1050
W 50s | 745 Seventh Ave. (50th St.) | 212-764-4697 ◑
866-797-2701 | www.ctshirts.com

"Beautiful, clean, crisp shirts" are the hallmark of this British-born men's retailer with three Midtown locations, where "excellent-quality" button-downs and other "business-professional attire" at "affordable" prices are sure to please "Anglophiles" and "make your wife pause" in admiration; staffers are "attentive", and "expert in-house tailors" and "difficult-to-beat" sales sweeten the deal.

Charlotte Olympia — | — | — | VE

E 60s | 22 E. 65th St. (Madison Ave.) | 212-744-1842 | www.charlotteolympia.com

Take a romp back to Hollywood's Golden Age at Charlotte Dellal's East 60s salon, an elegant art deco-ish showcase for her celeb-approved creations worn by the likes of Katy Perry and Keira Knightley; both the venue and shoe soles boast the British designer's trademark spiderweb motif, with investment-worthy styles ranging from sexy ankle boots with metallic platforms to towering leopard affairs, all made in Italy.

CH Carolina Herrera 28 | 28 | 25 | E

E 60s | 802 Madison Ave. (bet. 67th & 68th Sts.) | 212-744-2076 | www.carolinaherrera.com

"Great selection, great service, great style" is the word at this Venezuelan designer's "exceptional", "elegant" Madison Avenue boutique where cubbyholes display offerings from her less-pricey lifestyle spin-off line, including accessories, menswear, childrenswear, "romantic evening dresses" and other flowy, pretty things; yes, the goods are "expensive", but when you want to "treat" yourself, what can be better than a timeless piece from this iconic talent?

Chelsea Garden Center ▽ 25 | 24 | 21 | M

W 40s | 580 11th Ave. (44th St.) | 212-727-7100
Red Hook | 444 Van Brunt St. (bet. Beard & Reed Sts.) | Brooklyn | 718-875-2100
www.chelseagardencenter.com

Unearth "the right botanical" for you at this Hell's Kitchen flora authority and its Red Hook offshoot, which market "healthy" indoor and outdoor plants "to please any season", along with pottery, garden furniture and other alfresco decoratives; the cultivated staff's "level of expertise" also extends to landscape-design services, though less-sunny sorts snipe they're "overpriced"; P.S. hours are seasonal.

Chelsea Guitars 26 | 23 | 25 | E

Chelsea | 224 W. 23rd St. (bet. 7th & 8th Aves.) | 212-675-4993 | www.chelseaguitars.com

Since 1989, strummers and shredders have frequented this legendary "tiny little store" in Chelsea, packed to the rafters with "excellent" instruments and staffed with "knowledgeable" staffers offering advice on purchases or repairs; "some axes here are as old as this shop", some truly vintage and others spanking new, but all are of "very high quality"; "expensive", yes, but maybe "they should be."

Chloé 28 | 25 | 25 | VE

E 70s | 850 Madison Ave. (70th St.) | 212-717-8220
NEW SoHo | 93 Greene St. (bet. Prince & Spring Sts.) | 646-350-1770
www.chloe.com

"The dreamiest handbags this side of heaven" agree luxury-lovers who fall for the French insouciance and "old-world class" of this status label helmed by creative director Clare Waight Keller and sold at its "chic"

UES-SoHo boutiques; completing the fantasy: romantic, feminine ready-to-wear ranging from "classic" to "eccentric", proffered by an "attentive, but not pushy" staff; *oui,* the "exorbitant" prices make these investment items, but everyone "must have at least one piece in their lifetime."

Chopard
29 | 28 | 27 | VE

E 60s | 709 Madison Ave. (63rd St.) | 212-223-2304 | www.chopard.com
Serious "bling" entices the elite to this Upper East Side showcase for the esteemed Swiss maker of "gorgeous" watches and jewelry, where the gem-encrusted wares – including timepieces with "floating diamonds" under the glass – are tended by a "lovely" staff in "very elegant" environs; it's the "ultimate splurge", but the big bucks buy "wonderful" work "that will be passed down for generations."

Christian Louboutin
28 | 27 | 25 | VE

E 70s | 965 Madison Ave. (bet. 75th & 76th Sts.) | 212-396-1884
W Village | 59 Horatio St. (Greenwich St.) | 212-255-1910
NEW Christian Louboutin Men's
Meatpacking | 808 Washington St. (bet. Gansevoort & Horatio Sts.) | 212-255-2056
www.christianlouboutin.com
"Shoe-lovers dream" about the "exquisite", "cult-status skyscraper heels" with "gorgeous red" soles from the "world-famous" French designer, housed in these "little stores" on Madison Avenue and Horatio Street; the "luxury" lairs are "always full" of "fashionistas", so you may have to squeeze in, and you're sure to "drop a pretty penny", but the payoff is those wearable "pieces of art" – "can one ever have too many?"; P.S. the men's Meatpacking shop also boasts a tattoo parlor.

NEW Christian Siriano
- | - | - | E

NoLita | 252 Elizabeth St. (bet. Houston & Prince Sts.) | 212-775-8494 | www.christianvsiriano.com
Project Runway's youngest winner with the 'fiercest' personality lures trendsetters to his orchid-filled, black-and-white boutique in NoLita; Payless fans can zoom in on the designer's style-for-less footwear while acolytes who prefer eveningwear with edge, à la Victoria Beckham and Sarah Jessica Parker, find head-turning numbers, and there's even sportswear for daring dressers, all exclusive to the store.

Christofle
29 | 27 | 25 | VE

E 70s | 846 Madison Ave. (70th St.) | 212-308-9390 | www.christofle.com
For "fine china the French way" visit this Parisian legend's "high-end" UESider, now in splashy quarters, to place "custom orders of exclusive merchandise" or peruse "heirloom-quality" "beautiful silverware", "elegant" sterling frames and "exquisite" crystal that make "terrific" "host or hostess gifts"; high prices mean it's "where you buy flatware after you win the lottery", but these wares are "guaranteed to impress."

Christopher Fischer
▽ 24 | 21 | 24 | E

E 80s | 1225 Madison Ave. (bet. 88th & 89th Sts.) | 212-831-8880
SoHo | 80 Wooster St. (bet. Broome & Spring Sts.) | 212-965-9009
888-234-6287 | www.christopherfischer.com
Founded in Hawick, the birthplace of Scottish cashmere, this posh brand plies its trade at these SoHo-Madison offshoots, outfitting men,

women and babies in soft styles that change with the seasons; the "elegant updated classics", ranging from cardigans and open-stitch sweaters to wraps and booties, come in a plentiful palette of hues and strike a special chord with fashionistas.

Chrome Hearts
29 | 28 | 27 | VE

E 70s | 870 Madison Ave. (71st St.) | 212-794-3100 | www.chromehearts.com

If you've got rocker taste and an investment banker's wallet, park your hog at this East 70s favorite for "drool-worthy leather jeans and jackets", "very cool, hip eyewear" and "expensive biker jewelry"; the "couture-quality" sterling-studded products are "insanely well designed", and the "service is great", making it the "ultimate shopping destination" for the "leatherman" with money to burn; P.S. the East 60s branch is closed for renovation.

Chuckies New York
▽ 25 | 20 | 18 | VE

E 60s | 1073 Third Ave. (bet. 63rd & 64th Sts.) | 212-593-9898
NEW E 70s | 1052 Lexington Ave. (bet. 74th & 75th Sts.) |
212-861-1415
E 80s | 1169 Madison Ave. (86th St.) | 212-249-2254
www.chuckiesnewyork.com

Find "what young women should be wearing" at this UES shoe trio stocking "trendy" designer footwear confections and "up-to-the-minute" accessories in "gorgeous and memorable" styles from its own house line along with labels like Belstaff, Lanvin and Valentino; prices are high, but "good sales" can temper the sticker shock.

Church's Shoes
27 | 21 | 22 | E

E 60s | 689 Madison Ave. (62nd St.) | 212-758-5200 | www.church-footwear.com

Fine, bench-crafted English footwear's the thing at this Madison Avenue home of the venerable Northampton-based "signature British" brand, offering "solid styles" of the "classics", including men's and women's oxfords, loafers and boots; sure, it's "costly", and service can be "highbrow", but few of the dapper lads and ladies who shop here mind given that "quality" is evident in every pair.

NEW Civilianaire
- | - | - | E

NoLita | 53-55 E. Houston St. (Mott St.) | 212-219-9966 | www.civilianaire.com

Basics are reborn at this airy NoLita outpost of the California-based brand, where the LA-made raw and colored denim, chinos, military-style wovens and knit henley shirts are hung on white pegboards or neatly stacked for easy access; a lone guitar parked beside a leather chair and tapestry rug lend warmth to the sparse white window-framed space.

Clarins
26 | 22 | 24 | E

W 70s | 247 Columbus Ave. (bet. 71st & 72nd Sts.) | 212-362-0190 | 866-325-2746 | www.clarins.com

Treat yourself to an "unparalleled selection" of this French cosmetics company's botanical-based skincare products, including "staples" that "emphasize anti-aging and skin softening", at its West 70s branch, a "beautiful, serene space very much like the brand it represents"; the "lovely" staff is "never pushy", and the attached spa is the place to "splurge" on facials – it's all expensive but well "worth the cost."

Clarks
24 | 20 | 22 | M

E 40s | 363 Madison Ave. (45th St.) | 212-949-9545
E 50s | 997 Third Ave. (59th St.) | 212-207-4115 ●
NEW Kings Plaza | Kings Plaza Shopping Ctr. | 5364 Kings Plaza (Flatbush Ave.) | Brooklyn | 718-338-2841 ●
Elmhurst | Queens Center Mall | 90-15 Queens Blvd. (bet. 57th & 58th Aves.) | Queens | 718-271-7505 ●
www.clarksusa.com

For "comfy" shoes for the whole clan, why "look anywhere else" crow champions of this British standby, who trek to borough-wide branches for "classic" Wallabees, desert boots and styles with "modern flair"; these kicks "hold up well to the wear and tear" of city streets – and may find a "permanent home" on your feet.

Clay Pot
26 | 25 | 22 | E

Park Slope | 162 Seventh Ave. (bet. 1st St. & Garfield Pl.) | Brooklyn | 718-788-6564 | 800-989-3579 | www.clay-pot.com

"Lovely, tried and true", this Park Slope "old reliable", a neighborhood fixture since 1969, is "the go-to spot for jewelry, gifts", wedding rings and "terrific", often handmade and "unexpected" home accoutrement, particularly "if you're in the market for artisanal, funky" finds like ceramics, serving pieces and knickknacks; warning: you may have to "take out a small loan for interesting, unique items."

Club Monaco
21 | 23 | 20 | M

Flatiron | 160 Fifth Ave. (21st St.) | 212-352-0936
SoHo | 121 Prince St. (bet. Greene & Wooster Sts.) | 212-533-8930
SoHo | 520 Broadway (bet. Broome & Spring Sts.) | 212-941-1511 ●
W 50s | 6 W. 57th St. (bet. 5th & 6th Aves.) | 212-459-9863
W 60s | 211 Columbus Ave. (bet. 69th & 70th Sts.) | 212-724-4076
W 80s | 2376 Broadway (87th St.) | 212-579-2587
Elmhurst | Queens Center Mall | 90-15 Queens Blvd. (bet. 57th & 59th Aves.) | Queens | 718-760-9282 ●
www.clubmonaco.com

The "go-to" chain for "clean" and "minimalist" "trendy-classic" pieces, this Canadian import peddles garments just right for "going out" and "office wear"; the "designs aren't too extreme, but funky enough to feel like you're wearing something special", and the "slim-fit" "monotone" pieces "work together" effortlessly, plus you can usually find a "repository of excellent fresh-looking jewelry for a song" to further advance your "updated" look.

Clyde's
27 | 24 | 23 | E

E 70s | 926 Madison Ave. (74th St.) | 212-744-5050 | 800-792-5933 | www.clydesonline.com

Perhaps one of the "most expensive drugstores in Manhattan", this 7,000-sq.-ft. Madison Avenue behemoth is "fun to browse" while waiting for prescription refills; the shelves are brimming with "everything for the makeup-obsessed woman", along with "high-end" skincare and haircare imports from Europe and a "fabulous selection of soaps, body lotions" and "all sorts of hard-to-find" beauty items, all peddled by a "knowledgeable" sales staff.

	QUALITY	DISPLAY	SERVICE	COST

Coach

26 | 25 | 24 | E

E 50s | Fuller Bldg. | 595 Madison Ave. (57th St.) | 212-754-0041 |
888-262-6224 | www.coach.com
Additional locations throughout the NY area

The "smell of sumptuous leather" wafts across the threshold of this
"enduring standard-bearer" of "impeccably made" handbags, wallets,
"cool shoes and accessories", which always impresses with its
"timeless" yet "creative designs" that "hold up through thick and
thin"; factor in "elegant displays" and "old-school customer service",
and it's no wonder that shopping for these "affordable luxuries" is
such a "positive experience."

Coach Legacy

26 | 25 | 25 | E

W Village | 372-374 Bleecker St. (bet. Charles & Perry Sts.) |
212-206-8343 | 888-262-6224 | www.coach.com

Selling "classic" handbags and leather goods inspired by legendary
Coach designer Bonnie Cashin's 1960s creations, this West Village
offshoot of the mainstream brand offers accessories with "elegance"
and careful "finishing"; boasting a small-boutique feel that contrasts
with the primary line's locations, the horseshoe-shaped space is "well
organized" with "interesting displays", and the "professional" "service
to crown it all is over the top."

C.O. Bigelow Chemists ◑

27 | 23 | 24 | M

G Village | 414 Sixth Ave. (bet. 8th & 9th Sts.) | 212-533-2700 |
800-793-5433 | www.bigelowchemists.com

Unearth "history on every counter" at this "old-school" Greenwich
Village "apothecary" dating back to 1838, where "knowledgeable"
staffers guide customers through "high-end" toiletries, "homeopathic
remedies", "hard-to-find knickknacks" and the pharmacy's namesake
line of salves and scents; entering the "tight" "wood-paneled" space
feels like taking "a step back in time", but the "too-expensive" prices
still reflect present day.

Coclico

▽ 23 | 24 | 20 | E

NoLita | 275 Mott St. (bet. Houston & Prince Sts.) | 212-965-5462 |
www.shopcoclico.com

Following a full-on renovation, French expat Sandra Canselier switched
the focus of her NoLita boutique, concentrating almost solely on the
eponymous house label of eco-friendly leather shoes designed in New
York and made in Spain, and placing less emphasis on kindred designers; fashionistas still get their kicks, splurging on the "best platform
sandals (versatile, stable, not clunky)" plus boots and heels in offbeat
styles and colors.

Cole Haan

26 | 23 | 23 | E

E 50s | Rockefeller Ctr. | 620 Fifth Ave. (50th St.) | 212-765-9747
Flatiron | 141 Fifth Ave. (21st St.) | 212-677-4693
SoHo | 128 Prince St. (Wooster St.) | 212-219-8240
W 60s | Shops at Columbus Circle | 10 Columbus Circle, ground fl.
(B'way & 60th St.) | 212-823-9420 ◑
800-488-2000 | www.colehaan.com

"Put your best foot forward" in the "fine leather" shoes crafted by
this American brand, known for its "timeless designs", "from practical
to fanciful" to on-trend capsule collections, that deliver "all-day"

comfort for the "modern city gal" and guy – "nothing beats" that "wonderful Nike Air technology"; loyalists who also "love" the "fabulous" handbags, outerwear and "unhurried" vibe can't stop praising the "accommodating" staff.

Comme des Garçons

28 | 28 | 25 | VE

Chelsea | 520 W. 22nd St. (bet. 10th & 11th Aves.) | 212-604-9200 | www.comme-des-garcons.com

"Worth visiting for the shop's design alone" declare devotees who "marvel" at the "insane architecture" of this Chelsea provocateur, where an "amazing" brushed-aluminum tunnel entrance leads to a spare white space showcasing Japanese designer Rei Kawakubo's "cutting-edge" yet "chic" collection, tended by "super-friendly" staffers; novices deem it "the weirdest clothing on the planet", but seasoned shoppers assert "treat it like a gallery and you won't be as shocked" by the unconventional creations and "astronomical" prices.

Comptoir des Cotonniers

25 | 23 | 23 | E

SoHo | 155 Spring St. (bet. W. B'way & Wooster St.) | 212-274-0830
W 60s | 184 Columbus Ave. (bet. 68th & 69th Sts.) | 212-874-0983
www.comptoirdescotonniers.com

"Ooh-la-la" – style-savvy moms and daughters love the "wonderful" house line of "chic, sexy" finds at the Upper West Side and SoHo branches of this French "gem"; "fashionable" and "eye-catching", the apparel "fits like a dream" and makes all ages "feel like a million" – these are clothes for "living confidently" and they're sold by a staff that's totally "down to earth."

Converse

22 | 23 | 18 | M

SoHo | 560 Broadway (Prince St.) | 212-966-1099 | www.converse.com

All the Cons "you could ever dream of" are afoot at this SoHo flagship for "iconic" sneaks ("gotta love" Chuck Taylors) and "reasonably priced clothing" that "keeps you in touch with your younger side"; the space's gymlike accents and shoes assembled into an outsized Stars 'n' Bars do justice to "an American classic" – "who doesn't need a pair in their life?"

Co-Op 87 Records ◑

- | - | - | M

Greenpoint | 87 Guernsey St. (bet. Nassau & Norman Aves.) | Brooklyn | 347-294-4629 | www.coop87.org

Co-owned by the people behind independent music label Captured Tracks, this Greenpoint record store offers a handpicked selection of vinyl that includes local artists, collector's items and bootleg concerts in addition to all of its own releases; the space may be small but the collection certainly isn't and prices are decent to boot.

Cosabella

28 | 25 | 25 | E

SoHo | 220 Lafayette St. (bet. Broome & Spring Sts.) | 212-405-1190 | www.cosabella.com

"Love" this "sexy lingerie" rendered in "gorgeous colors" and housed in "elegant" SoHo quarters, a garage-turned-boutique done up with white couches and chandeliers; the girlie backdrop offsets the "extensive selection" of shelf-bra tanks, thong undies and other unmentionables that "hold up well over time", all dreamed up by Ugo and Valeria

Campello in Miami, stitched in Italy and sold at "reasonable prices, given the quality."

Costco Warehouse ●

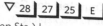 24 | 16 | 16 | I

Harlem | East River Plaza | 517 E. 117th St. (FDR Dr.) | 212-896-5873
Sunset Park | 976 Third Ave. (bet. 37th & 39th Sts.) | Brooklyn | 718-965-7603
LIC | 32-50 Vernon Blvd. (B'way) | Queens | 718-267-3680
New Springville | 2975 Richmond Ave. (Independence Ave.) |
Staten Island | 718-982-9525
800-774-2678 | www.costco.com

"Stock up" and "save a bundle" at this big-box megachain, which "redefines shopping" by offering grocery and household items "across many categories" at "unbelievable" discounts that are "well worth" the $55 yearly membership – provided you're prepared to buy "in bulk" and "schlep the stuff home"; the warehouse venues can be a "zoo" with "sparse" service and "long lines" of "carts as wide as Hummers", but most agree you "can't afford not" to go.

Costume National

▽ 28 | 27 | 25 | E

SoHo | 150 Greene St. (bet. Prince & W. Houston Sts.) |
212-431-1530 | www.costumenational.com

Minimalist, "chic street-sexy apparel" and footwear with its own cult following made from the softest leather imaginable await shoppers at this Milanese export in SoHo; the environs are "clean and a bit sparse", mirroring the sharp, edgy black and gray wardrobe wonders that fit like a glove and "so worth the money"; it's "oh-so-fun" to wander through, "if only to look and touch."

Cotélac

- | - | - | VE

NEW **E 70s** | 983 Lexington Ave. (71st St.) | 212-288-0400
SoHo | 92-94 Greene St. (bet. Prince & Spring Sts.) | 212-219-8065
www.cotelac.us

Francophiles brush up on their Parisian style at this French brand's wood and cement SoHo space and East 70s arrival, where whisper-thin tanks, ingénue-worthy dresses, cuffed denim and effortless trousers, for men, women and teens, all boast a je ne sais quoi that's perfect for a country picnic or day of urban *flânerie*; score a free CD by emerging musicians with every purchase.

Cotton Candy Machine

27 | 27 | 26 | M

Williamsburg | 235 S. First St. (bet. Havemeyer & Roebling Sts.) |
Brooklyn | 718-387-3844 | www.thecottoncandymachine.com

"An art gallery and clothing store in one", this "must-visit" Williamsburg boutique offers limited-edition prints, rock posters, books, novelty items and "truly unique shirts" from "a rotation of incredible local artists"; fans are also sweet on the modest prices for signed and numbered works, as well as the bona fide cotton candy machine on-site.

Courtshop ●

 - | - | - | E

NoLita | 168 Mott St. (Broome St.) | 212-925-1022 |
www.courtshop.com

When boutique fatigue hits, pay court to this NoLita staple, which recently moved into digs large enough to hold its design studio, just a few blocks from its original locale; denim is king here, with the house line of high-waisted jeans (including leather-trimmed styles), cropped jackets and flattering shorts filling the racks, plus cool-girl finds from other indie lines.

Crate & Barrel

`23` `24` `21` `M`

E 50s | 650 Madison Ave. (59th St.) | 212-308-0011
NoHo | Cable Bldg. | 611 Broadway (Houston St.) | 212-780-0004 ●
800-967-6696 | www.crateandbarrel.com

A "go-to place for everything household-related", these East 50s–NoHo chain links boast "everything from furniture to dishes to home decor", all "dazzlingly displayed" in "color-coordinated and themed" sets that let shoppers "have a whole made-up life in every corner of the store"; stocked with "tasteful designs", it's a wedding registry "stalwart" and "where you set up house post-Ikea."

Creatures of Comfort

▽ `22` `24` `20` `E`

NoLita | 205 Mulberry St. (bet. Kenmare & Spring Sts.) | 212-925-1005 | www.creaturesofcomfort.us

"Original, upscale funky stuff" is the stock in trade at this sprawling, gallery-esque brick-walled NoLita boutique, an offshoot of the LA original that merchandises its "unique" goods for guys and girls in small groupings; start your treasure hunt with cult favorites like Acne, Hope and United Bamboo, then take comfort in cool footwear from Aurora and Rachel Comey and a quirky mix of jewelry, housewares and accessories.

NEW Creel and Gow

`-` `-` `-` `VE`

E 70s | 131 E. 70th St. (Lexington Ave.) | 212-327-4281 | www.creelandgow.com

Housed in the former stables of a historic Upper East Side townhouse, this curiosities shop stocks nature-related oddities like vintage narwhal tusks, taxidermy peacocks and silver-plated seashells plus Moroccan textiles and terra-cotta figurines; the space itself is as striking and transporting as the inventory, with items artfully arranged on floor-to-ceiling shelves and atop a fireplace mantel.

Crewcuts

`24` `24` `22` `M`

E 80s | 1190 Madison Ave. (87th St.) | 212-348-9803
SoHo | 99 Prince St. (bet. Greene & Mercer Sts.) | 212-966-2739
www.jcrew.com

"Just classic and so cute!" gush parents and gift-givers who zip over to J.Crew's SoHo–East 80s offshoots, scooping up "preppy" and some-times "trendy" American sportswear "for the younger set" that's a dead-ringer for the grown-up collection; "great sales" may make the "pricey" merch more palatable, but still leave some wishing "the kids didn't grow out of it so fast."

Crumpler Bags

`27` `22` `24` `M`

NoLita | 45 Spring St. (bet. Mott & Mulberry Sts.) | 212-334-9391
W Village | 49 Eighth Ave. (bet. Horatio & W. 4th Sts.) |
212-242-2535
www.crumpler.com

Function trumps flash at these West Village and NoLita branches of the "popular" Aussie firm, where the "selection of the latest offerings" in camera, laptop and messenger bags (plus luggage from totes to duffels) represents quality that'll last "for years to come"; consult the "helpful" staffers for "the rundown" – you'll "want to take one of each home."

QUALITY DISPLAY SERVICE COST

Cursive ●

▽ 27 | 25 | 24 | E

E 40s | Grand Central Terminal | 87 E. 42nd St., Lexington Passage (Vanderbilt Ave.) | 212-867-5550 | www.cursivenewyork.com

"A gem of a store" tucked into "Grand Central's underrated retail corridor", this gifty stationer cherry-picks a "beautiful" collection including elegant paper from indie designers, letterpress cards and quotation-inscribed Jeanine Payer jewelry; the "very well-curated" lineup of arty curiosities makes it a fail-safe source of "lovely" presents for home and bath; P.S. there's also a kiosk inside ABC Carpet & Home.

NEW Cutler and Gross

– | – | – | E

SoHo | 110 Mercer St. (Spring St.) | 212-431-4440 | www.cutlerandgross.com

Ranging from iconic round sunnies to classic square tortoiseshell and angled cat's eye numbers, the handmade specs are something special at this British eyewear company's new flagship, a minimalist concept shop inspired by SoHo's cast iron urban architecture; scope out the exhibition of 4,000 frames dating back to 1969, and don't overlook the exclusive styles made in collaboration with designers like Giles Deacon and Jonathan Saunders.

Cut25

– | – | – | E

SoHo | 129 Grand St. (bet. B'way & Crosby St.) | 212-966-5080 | www.cut25.com

Cool and conceptual, Yigal Azrouël's shop on the edge of SoHo is devoted to his secondary, on-trend women's line, featuring silk dresses, printed pants and moto jackets that are as much about drape as structure, with prices hovering below $500; conceived with design provocateur Dror Benshetrit, the minimal space features cubic dressing rooms and angular mirrors, with pieces displayed on suspended racks and giant sawhorses; P.S. a Lexington Avenue branch is slated to open.

C. Wonder ●

21 | 27 | 21 | M

SoHo | 72 Spring St. (bet. B'way & Crosby St.) | 212-219-3500
NEW W 60s | Shops at Columbus Circle | 10 Columbus Circle, 2nd fl. (bet. 59th & 60th Sts.) | 212-956-9760
www.cwonder.com

Christopher Burch – Tory's ex – knows from retail, as evidenced by his "whimsical" SoHo and Time Warner Center emporiums; "bright and exciting", this "prep explosion" of inexpensive "classic" apparel, "hostess gifts" and personal gadgetry delivers an *Alice in Wonderland* experience that'll have you "smiling in a New York minute"; if kvetchers quibble "quality isn't top-notch", ravers retort the "mood-inspired dressing rooms" alone "make a visit mandatory"; P.S. a Flatiron branch is in the works.

Cynthia Rowley

28 | 26 | 25 | E

NEW E 70s | 43 E. 78th St. (bet. Madison & Park Aves.) | 212-288-1141
W Village | 376 Bleecker St. (bet. Charles & Perry Sts.) | 212-242-3803
www.cynthiarowley.com

Shoppers struggle "to leave without buying something" from this "lovely" West Villager and new East 70s townhouse, offering the eponymous designer's "irresistible" frocks, blouses and accessories in "whimsical styles" that stick "season after season"; staffers offer "attention even if you're just browsing", and while prices are high, these pieces can take you "from client meeting to date night"; P.S. the UES addition houses a sweets store called CuRious Candy upstairs.

Dagny & Barstow

– | – | – | E

NoLita | 264 Bowery (bet. Houston & Prince Sts.) | 212-675-2346 | www.dagnyandbarstow.com

Adding another style notch to the Bowery, Meredith Blank and Emily Titelman's brick-walled haven offers womenswear and accessories from international, local and emerging designers like Devastee and Emma Mulholland, exclusive lines not often found on boutique crawls, plus artwork from NYC talents; the mix may prompt shoppers to dance · for joy – after all, this space, replete with a bar, DJ booth and chandelier, once housed Lenny Kravitz's club, Kos.

Dalaga NYC

– | – | – | M

NoLita | 85 Kenmare St. (bet. Lafayette & Mulberry Sts.) | 646-449-8716
Greenpoint | 150 Franklin St. (bet. Greenpoint Ave. & Kent St.) | Brooklyn | 718-389-4049
www.dalaganyc.com

At their Greenpoint go-to and NoLita spin-off, pioneering owners Michelle and Mary Mangiliman cover all the "fashion needs" of budget-conscious girlie girls, offering a "fabulous selection" of dainty and down-right sexy dresses and separates, largely from local designers; staffers make you "feel at ease", and the environs, bedecked with gilt-edged mirrors, vintage furniture and family photos, are equally charming.

Danny's Cycles

26 | 23 | 25 | E

E 80s | 1690 Second Ave. (bet. 87th & 88th Sts.) | 212-722-2201
NEW **Gramercy** | 240 E. 23rd St. (2nd Ave.) | 212-213-6272
www.dannyscycles.com

Bikers of every pedaling level – from training wheels to triathlon – can saddle up and resupply at this Yorkville shop in the former Larry's Bicycle Plus locale and its Gramercy offshoot, where cycles of every description share a neat showroom with gear and road clothing; "great service" via amiable pros includes free lifetime tune-ups for any new set of wheels you buy.

Dave's Army Navy

23 | 17 | 22 | I

Chelsea | 581 Sixth Ave. (bet. 16th & 17th Sts.) | 212-989-6444 | 800-543-8558 | www.davesnewyork.com

"One of the last bastions of cheap chic", this "good ol'" Chelsea "institution" is a stockpile of "sturdy" "work" and "basic casual clothing", dealing in "no-nonsense" "Levi's, Lee, Carhartt" and other "manly" labels suitable for "building Habitats for Humanity"; it also supplies outdoorsy boots and womenswear, and earns extra medals for "super-nice" service and "very fair prices."

David Webb

29 | 29 | 27 | VE

E 70s | 942 Madison Ave. (bet. 74th & 75th Sts.) | 212-421-3030 | www.davidwebb.com

From pavé cocktail rings to the menagerie of chunky floral and animal-themed jewelry that caught fire in the '50s and '60s to "gorgeous" bracelets, brooches, earrings and necklaces, "no one designs jewelry" like this fabled Madison Avenue jeweler, with roots going back to 1948; "even the

QUALITY DISPLAY SERVICE COST

estate pieces are highly valued" and "always look special" – little wonder collectors exclaim these "exciting" keepers will "live forever."

David Yurman
28 | 27 | 25 | VE

E 60s | 712 Madison Ave. (bet. 63rd & 64th Sts.) | 212-752-4255 | 877-226-1400 | www.davidyurman.com

"Few others elicit this much confidence from nervous husbands" believe gift-givers who "sip champagne" and browse this namesake jeweler's "breathtaking designs" in signature silver and gold at his "must-visit" three-story UES townhouse; the "beautifully conceived and exquisitely executed" creations "never go out of style", all versatile enough to wear with "jeans or black tie", and while "really expensive", it's almost within reach: "this is Harry Winston for the rest of us."

DaVinci Artist Supply
▽ 25 | 18 | 23 | M

Chelsea | 132 W. 21st St. (bet. 6th & 7th Aves.) | 212-871-0220
Murray Hill | 137 E. 23rd St. (bet. Lexington & 3rd Aves.) | 212-982-8607
www.davinciartistsupply.com

"Frequented by students at SVA" and other latter-day Leonardos, this Chelsea and Murray Hill pair provisions "real artists and the hobbyist" with an "accessible" inventory of paper, paints, canvas and the like, bolstered by niche necessities you "couldn't find elsewhere"; they're staffed by "helpful" sorts, and the whopping Westsider adds custom framing to the repertoire.

Davis & Warshow
27 | 22 | 19 | E

E 50s | A&D Bldg. | 150 E. 58th St., 4th fl. (bet. Lexington & 3rd Aves.) | 212-688-5990
Harlem | 207 E. 119th St. (bet. 2nd & 3rd Aves.) | 212-369-2000
Harlem | 251 W. 154th St. (bet. 8th Ave. & Macombs Pl.) | 212-234-5100
SoHo | 96 Spring St. (bet. B'way & Mercer St.) | 212-680-9000
Maspeth | 57-22 49th St. (bet. 56th Rd. & Maspeth Ave.) | Queens | 718-391-4936
www.dwny.com

Your place "will be gorgeous" thanks to this venerable kitchen-and-bath biz, whose showrooms boast "beautiful displays" that plumb a "wide range" of "the more important lines in fixtures", including some "very high-end" options; however, as the 150-brand selection can be "overwhelming" and the service "nonchalant", consider "bringing your designer"; P.S. closed weekends.

DeBeers
28 | 28 | 26 | VE

E 50s | 703 Fifth Ave. (55th St.) | 212-906-0001 | 800-929-0889 | www.debeers.com

"Diamonds are a girl's best friend" at this Fifth Avenue venture from LVMH and the eponymous South African company where an "excellent" staff is gifted at making "wishes come true"; the prices of the "gorgeous", "perfectly cut" gems, starting at $1,000, are in plain sight, making it "a sightseeing stop in and of itself", and there's also a scanner that gauges the sparkle factor, ensuring there's "no buyer's remorse."

Dempsey & Carroll
28 | 22 | 20 | VE

E 70s | 1049 Lexington Ave. (bet. 74th & 75th Sts.) | 212-570-4800 | 877-750-1878 | www.dempseyandcarroll.com

"Super-luxurious" stationery both "classic" and "playful" is the thing at this venerable Upper Eastsider that's been a supplier of "beautiful" notecards, greeting cards, engraved announcements and other "elegant writing materials from a bygone era" since 1878; true, it's "wildly expensive", but those who can afford such "quality" declare it "worth the price" – and they do "save the plates so you can reorder" forever.

NEW Denim & Supply, Ralph Lauren   − | − | − | M

G Village | 99 University Pl. (12th St.) | 212-677-1895 | www.denimandsupply.com

Ralph Lauren fans who can't afford to shop at the mother ship can now stock up on jeans and casualwear from the designer's somewhat more wallet-friendly Americana brand, all showcased in the University Place space once devoted to the discontinued Rugby line; the feel is vintage Ralph, with an urban loft twist, including brick walls, wood-plank flooring, leather furniture, industrial lighting and denim to the rafters.

Derek Lam   27 | 27 | 22 | VE

E 60s | 764 Madison Ave. (bet. 65th & 66th Sts.) | 212-493-4454 | www.dereklam.com

Lam, who began his career at Michael Kors, makes "excellent" American classics with a vaguely '70s retro vibe, very feminine leanings and "one-of-a-kind fabrics", resulting in "gorgeous" dresses and sportswear that might "max out your credit card"; the "amazing" acrylic displays at this modern East 60s boutique "showcase the art of fashion", while "friendly" staffers keep a "sharp eye" out without hovering.

Dermalogica   ▽ 26 | 21 | 24 | E

SoHo | 110 Grand St. (bet. B'way & Mercer St.) | 212-219-9800

Dermalogica Academy

Chelsea | 140 W. 22nd St. (bet. 6th & 7th Aves.) | 212-243-3000 800-345-2761 | www.dermalogica.com

"Love their products" proclaim glamour girls who've allowed these beauty treatment centers in Chelsea and SoHo to get under their skin with a "special" collection of irritant-free cleansers, toners, exfoliants, masques, groomers and other "ultracalming", anti-aging lotions and potions; the "lovely" aestheticians pay close attention to your "personal" skincare "history" and concerns, while offering a heavenly facial, exfoliation or touch therapy session within state-of-the-art facilities.

Design Within Reach   25 | 23 | 20 | E

E 60s | 27 E. 62nd St. (bet. Madison & Park Aves.) | 212-888-4539
Flatiron | 903 Broadway (20th St.) | 212-477-1155
SoHo | 110 Greene St. (bet. Prince & Spring Sts.) | 212-475-0001
W 70s | 341 Columbus Ave. (76th St.) | 212-799-5900
Brooklyn Heights | 76 Montague St. (Hicks St.) | Brooklyn | 718-643-1015
800-944-2233 | www.dwr.com

This "brilliant" home-design chain spotlights "iconic modern furniture pieces" from the likes of Milo Baughman and Charles and Ray Eames – so you can get the look "without buying vintage" – plus "creative new" furnishings too; if the cautious counsel "don't be fooled by the name", the converted contend it's worth "going into your reserve account or eating ramen noodles" because "you'll probably keep" these "real McCoys" forever.

QUALITY DISPLAY SERVICE COST

de Vera
▽ 27 | 26 | 27 | E

E 80s | 26 E. 81st St. (Madison Ave.) | 212-288-2288
SoHo | 1 Crosby St. (Howard St.) | 212-625-0838
www.deveraobjects.com

"A little jewel box" on the UES and a larger one in SoHo are where designer Federico de Vera curates his singular collections of old and new – everything from architectural remnants to contemporary glass; most of the jewelry on show is by this namesake talent, who's famous for his work with rose-cut diamonds, so it's clearly a source for "the most desirable of objects."

NEW Devorado
- | - | - | E

E Village | 436 E. Ninth St. (Ave. A) | 917-280-0649 |
www.devoradonyc.com

Vintagiers on the hunt for collectable yet relevant pieces from some of fashion's most arresting talents find a standout selection, hand-plucked from Europe, Los Angeles and beyond, at this East Village venue; the array includes apparel and accessories from yesteryear's heavyweights like Adolfo, Claude Montana, Guy Laroche and Halston, with most pieces from the 1940s–1990s.

Diana Kane
▽ 25 | 21 | 20 | E

Park Slope | 229B Fifth Ave. (bet. Carroll & President Sts.) | Brooklyn | 718-638-6520 | www.dianakane.com

At this Park Slope staple owned by the eponymous jewelry designer, fashionistas with an understated style find cases filled with simple-yet-elegant sparkly stuff, a wealth of lingerie, plus scarves, bags and gift-y items arranged in wooden cubbyholes; rounding out the casual-chic wares: hand-plucked dresses, casualwear and swimsuits, many from eco-friendly labels like Matta, Prairie Underground and Velvet.

Diane von Furstenberg
27 | 27 | 23 | VE

(aka DVF the Shop)

Meatpacking | 874 Washington St. (14th St.) | 646-486-4800
SoHo | 135 Wooster St. (bet. Houston & Prince Sts.) | 212-542-5754
800-472-2382 | www.dvf.com

"That's a wrap" quip "fashionistas" who fall for DVF's "fabulous" and, yes, "expensive" signature dresses in "brightly colored prints", and other "timeless" creations, all "beautifully" displayed at these Meatpacking-SoHo outposts, deemed the "epitome of NYC cool"; this iconic designer "knows how to complement a woman's body", and when you visit her "awesome" shops you "truly understand her vibe", making a purchase "irresistible."

Dienst + Dotter
- | - | - | VE

NoHo | 411 Lafayette St. (bet. 5th & 6th Sts.) | 212-861-1200 |
www.dienstanddotter.com

Travel to Neoclassical times at Jill Dienst's Nordic-inspired NoHo antiques store featuring traditional and modern, one-of-a-kind pieces from Scandinavian cabinets and drop-leaf sideboards, to baroque tables and other age-old Northern European furnishings; while browsing here might feel like a stroll through the Metropolitan Museum of Art (the owner's a former employee), you'll need the inheritance of a Swedish prince to afford most items.

	QUALITY	DISPLAY	SERVICE	COST

Diesel
24 | **24** | **20** | **E**

SoHo | 135 Spring St. (bet. Greene & Wooster Sts.) | 212-625-1555
SoHo | 281 Lafayette St. (Prince St.) | 212-226-5055
Union Sq | 1 Union Sq. W. (14th St.) | 646-336-8552 ◗

Diesel Planet

E 50s | 685 Fifth Ave. (54th St.) | 212-755-3555 ◗
E 60s | 770 Lexington Ave. (60th St.) | 212-308-0055
www.diesel.com

Feels like you're "goin' to da club" as a "live DJ spins" while you stop at the "denim bar" to drink in the "expensive assortment" at this Italian trendsetter that's never "afraid to push the envelope"; diehards insist that you "can't go wrong" with "funky" sportswear (even the "basic tees" are "unique") or the "classic and wild" premium jeans that "make your butt look great, and last forever."

Diesel Black Gold
27 | **25** | **25** | **E**

SoHo | 68 Greene St. (bet. Broome & Spring Sts.) | 212-966-5593 | www.dieselblackgold.com

Diesel fans go into overdrive at this "very cool" SoHo stop showcasing the Italian label's high-end Black Gold line of "excellent" rocker-chic leather and denim; the "fun staff" helps you "pull all kinds of looks off", and the dark, sexy space itself, done up with Ultrasuede walls, zebra-skin rugs and metal accents, the vision of Ryan Korban, interior decorator darling du jour, is worth a go-see.

Diesel Kids
27 | **27** | **24** | **E**

SoHo | 416 W. Broadway (bet. Prince & Spring Sts.) | 212-343-3863 | www.diesel.com

Kick your kid's wardrobe into high gear at this SoHo tot shop featuring shrunken versions of the Italian denim brand's sophisticated streetwear duds, from "the cutest" jeans and jackets to T-shirts and sneakers for babies to tweens; while the "expensive" prices give some the blues, most don't mind paying more for such "durable", "quality" goods.

Dinosaur Hill
28 | **27** | **24** | **M**

E Village | 306 E. Ninth St. (2nd Ave.) | 212-473-5850 | www.dinosaurhill.com

"One of the few independently owned toy stores", this "charming" East Village dinosaur's "well-curated selection" of "quality" playthings upholds tradition with its carved wooden collections, musical instruments, kiddie clothing and "especially unique and pleasing" imported marionettes; for "a memorable gift" that's "something different", the slightly "high-end" prices are "totally worth it."

Dior Homme
26 | **25** | **23** | **VE**

E 50s | 17 E. 57th St. (bet. 5th & Madison Aves.) | 212-421-6009
SoHo | 133 Greene St. (bet. Houston & Prince Sts.) | 212-421-6009
www.dior.com

Belgian creative director Kris Van Assche designs some of the "best-cut men's clothing in the world", and it's all on view at this status label's Midtown HQ, boasting an LED-lit exterior, and its pop-up-gone-permanent SoHo satellite; the "quality stuff", including signature slim suits, is equally minimal but, *oui*, incredibly "expensive", and deep-pocketed shoppers jest that "you may have to hold up something shiny, like diamonds, to get the attention of the staff."

Dior New York
29 | 26 | 26 | VE

E 50s | 21 E. 57th St. (bet. 5th & Madison Aves.) | 212-931-2950 |
www.dior.com

With creative director Raf Simons at the helm, this storied French
fashion house continually keeps its "fashionable" offerings, from the
iconic Lady Dior bag to art-inspired dresses and gowns, "updated,
modern and relevant"; the multilevel East 50s showcase boasts "a layout as exquisite as the items inside" while the "helpful, unintimidating
staff" can recite "every detail" of the "beautiful" goods, so "at least
you know what you're paying those incredible prices for."

Diptyque
29 | 27 | 22 | E

E 70s | 971 Madison Ave. (bet. 75th & 76th Sts.) | 212-879-3330
W Village | 377 Bleecker St. (bet. Charles & Perry Sts.) | 212-242-2333
www.diptyqueparis.com

"Fancy candles for even fancier folks" is the signature of this "French
haven" of "lush scents" in the West Village and UES that embodies the
"elegance of Paris" with its design-forward "romantic setting"; the
"iconic packaging is stunning", as are the "sublime" waxy creations,
bath products and perfume that make "exquisite" "host/hostess and
housewarming gifts" – just be prepared to "burn through stacks of
cash", since everything costs "top dollar."

Dixon's Bicycle Shop
26 | 22 | 24 | M

Park Slope | 792 Union St. (bet. 6th & 7th Aves.) | Brooklyn |
718-636-0067

A Park Slope "go-to" for "a really long time" (since 1982), this old-
school bike depot keeps its rep pumped up by peddling a "nice selection" of basic cycles and gear at "reasonable prices"; its "stalwart"
style extends to repairs, with "excellent customer service" from a
"welcoming" crew that's sometimes "willing to fix" your ride right
"on the spot."

DKNY
23 | 23 | 22 | E

E 60s | 655 Madison Ave. (60th St.) | 212-223-3569
NEW Flatiron | 168 Fifth Ave. (22nd St.) | 212-989-3438
SoHo | 420 W. Broadway (bet. Prince & Spring Sts.) | 646-613-1100
www.dkny.com

Donna Karan's "fashion staples" in SoHo, the UES and now the Flatiron
too, offer "hot-off-the-runway" clothing and "fresh and contemporary" accessories, shoes, bags and perfume tended by "surprisingly
friendly" staffers; though "expensive" prices earn some detractors,
"sweet off-season deals" and an "impressive" three-story Madison
Avenue location with a snack bar keep fans coming.

Dolce & Gabbana
26 | 25 | 24 | VE

NEW E 50s | 715 Fifth Ave. (bet. 55th & 56th Sts.) | 212-207-8391
E 60s | 825-827 Madison Ave. (bet. 68th & 69th Sts.) |
212-249-4100
www.dolcegabbana.com

Attention-grabbing garb takes center stage at Italian design duo
Stefano Gabbana and Domenico Dolce's intimate, always-"excellent"
Madison Avenue standby and Fifth Avenue addition, a marble-and-
glass flagship boasting Venetian chandeliers and gilt-framed mirrors;
glamorous corset dresses and exquisitely crafted men's suits are the

luxury brand's stock in trade, plus "stunning" leather goods in bright colors and exotic skins, but you might "need a second mortgage" to buy the "insanely expensive" wares.

Dolce Vita
23 | 25 | 23 | M

NoLita | 255 Elizabeth St. (bet. Houston & Prince Sts.) | 212-226-0635 | www.dolcevita.com

Get your fix of the house brand's "seriously addictive" footwear at its NoLita boutique, offering "price-interesting products", from "comfortable" colorful "wedges to trendy boots" and sandals, that "look like they cost a lot more" but don't skimp on "quality"; the "cute" womenswear, a mix of the proprietary and indie labels, completes the edgy toe-to-head ensemble.

Donna Karan
26 | 26 | 24 | VE

E 60s | 819 Madison Ave. (bet. 68th & 69th Sts.) | 212-861-1001 | www.donnakaran.com

"One of New York's favorite designers", the legendary woman who introduced seven easy mix-and-match pieces back in the 1980s is still in "a class by herself", creating "classic", chic and sculptural ready-to-wear and accessories, all housed in a three-story Madison Avenue fashion fortress; the Zen backdrop of this airy stone-and-glass haven – replete with a bamboo forest and Japanese sculptures – provides a "wonderful, serene atmosphere" that's just as timeless.

Doyle & Doyle
27 | 25 | 25 | E

LES | 189 Orchard St. (bet. Houston & Stanton Sts.) | 212-677-9991 | www.doyledoyle.com

"Just the place for a special, individual piece of jewelry", this "small, quiet" LES shop owned by the Doyle sisters "stocks only estate and vintage" standouts, "beautifully" presented "gallery-style" in framed wall displays and in cases; there's a "huge price range", plus "pitch-perfect" service that's "not at all pushy" makes it easier to find that "unique" art deco, Georgian or Victorian find.

D. Porthault
29 | 28 | 26 | VE

E 50s | 470 Park Ave. (58th St.) | 212-688-1660 | www.dporthaultparis.com

You'll find the "finest of the fine" at this Park Avenue purveyor of "pristine, elegant" French linens for the boudoir, bath and table, known for its "classic" signature patterns, sky-high thread counts and "fantastic" service; these sheets "last forever and are priced accordingly", but those looking to spend even more can splurge on the "customized" designs.

Dr. Martens
28 | 26 | 22 | M

NEW **Flatiron** | 888 Broadway (bet. 17th & 18th Sts.) | 646-449-0086

SoHo | 148 Spring St. (bet. W. B'way & Wooster St.) | 212-226-8500 800-810-6673 | www.dmusastore.com

Oi! – "they're back in style" say mavens of the Brit boot brand once favored by the '70s punk set and now "upgraded for the 21st century" and available at these Flatiron-SoHo outposts; the "wonderful" line of his-and-hers footwear includes flashy designs (flora, leopard prints) and "endless colors" along with "the classic" heavy-duty lace-ups, all "very comfortable" "once broken in" and built to "last forever."

Dunhill

 28 | 26 | 25 | VE

E 50s | 545 Madison Ave. (55th St.) | 212-753-9292 | www.dunhill.com

A "traditional British" "class" act, this London-based emporium on Madison Avenue is famed for "sleek" clothing for the "upper-crust" gent, matched with "high-quality" leather goods and "beautiful men's accessories" ("lighters, pens, cuff links", etc.); it's teddibly "expensive", but for merch "that'll truly last" and "never go out of style", fanciers pay up with "no regrets."

Duxiana

 29 | 23 | 24 | VE

E 50s | 235 E. 58th St. (bet. 2nd & 3rd Aves.) | 212-755-2600
TriBeCa | 161 Hudson St. (Laight Sts.) | 212-777-0771
www.duxiana.com

If you're willing to spring for "a great night's sleep", this Swedish brand's East 50s–TriBeCa shops, rated NYC's No. 1 in the Home/Garden category, showcase "the most luxurious beds" (and "amazing linens"), even providing rooms to test-rest the "incredible" technologically advanced mattresses; "you need to take out a mortgage to pay", but it's "worth the investment" for those with the bux since it "truly stands by its products."

DwellStudio

- | - | - | E

SoHo | 77 Wooster St. (bet. Broome & Spring Sts.) | 646-442-6000 | www.dwellstudio.com

After 13 years of offering its adult and kids' wares via catalog, online and wholesale, the furniture, bedding and tabletop accessories company known for its bold textiles and modern silhouettes unveiled its first stand-alone retail location in SoHo; the 2,700-sq.-ft. space boasts a dusty-blue exterior and perfectly styled displays inside.

The Earnest Sewn Co.

28 | 27 | 21 | VE

LES | 90 Orchard St. (Broome St.) | 212-979-5120
Meatpacking | 821 Washington St. (bet. Gansevoort & Little W. 12th Sts.) | 212-242-3414

The Earnest Sewn Outpost

NEW **NoLita** | 32 Prince St. (bet. Mott & Mulberry Sts.) | 212-947-2281
www.earnestsewn.com

"Expensive stuff but worth it" declare denim purists who find a "fantastic selection" of premium jeans at the brand's general-storelike LES-Meatpacking duo and a smaller sampling displayed in a 19th-century schoolhouse at the Outpost; there are "tons of washes" on hand and other "casual clothes" too, all arranged in a "comfortable" old-timey setting and sold by "helpful" staffers – a plus since "jeans shopping can be rather daunting."

E.A.T. Gifts

22 | 21 | 17 | E

E 80s | 1062 Madison Ave. (80th St.) | 212-861-2544 | www.elizabar.com

"Splurge on silly things you just can't resist" at Eli Zabar's UES variety store, where the "well-displayed" array of "cute, quirky" toys and novelties yields "small gifts and party favors" that are "surefire hits" with tots, "tweens" and "adults with fanciful temperaments"; it's "always fun" – especially at "holiday" time when it's *the* place for "high-end stocking stuffers" – even if some find the "outrageous" prices hard to swallow.

Edit
▽ 26 | 24 | 23 | E

E 90s | 1368 Lexington Ave. (bet. 90th & 91st Sts.) | 212-876-1368 | www.editnewyork.com

What a "delight" to shop the "perfectly edited collection" of "chic womenswear and accessories" along with the "gorgeous" Little Edit kids' line at this two-story East 90s townhouse exclaim style-hounds who pounce on names like baby Dior, Derek Lam and Proenza Schouler; the "very upscale and trendy" merchandise is "exactly what you wish your closet looked like", plus the "lovely" owners "never steer you wrong!"

Editions de Parfums Frédéric Malle
▽ 25 | 26 | 22 | E

E 70s | 898 Madison Ave. (bet. 72nd & 73rd Sts.) | 212-249-7941 | www.editionsdeparfums.com

"Create your own special scent" at French perfume provocateur Malle's sweet-smelling Madison Avenue boutique for lotions, candles and eau de parfums, where antique art and vintage sofas offset the futuristic 'smelling columns', refrigerated display cases and minimalist packaging; prices are high, but staffers "really take the time to work with you" in creating a signature fragrance that's all your own.

Eileen Fisher
26 | 24 | 24 | E

E 50s | 521 Madison Ave. (bet. 53rd & 54th Sts.) | 212-759-9888
E 70s | 1039 Madison Ave. (bet. 79th & 80th Sts.) | 212-879-7799
E Village | 314 E. Ninth St. (bet. 1st & 2nd Aves.) | 212-529-5715
Flatiron | 166 Fifth Ave. (bet. 21st & 22nd Sts.) | 212-924-4777
SoHo | 395 W. Broadway (bet. Broome & Spring Sts.) | 212-431-4567
W 60s | Shops at Columbus Circle | 10 Columbus Circle, 2nd fl. (B'way & 60th St.) | 212-823-9575 ●
W 70s | 341 Columbus Ave. (bet. 76th & 77th Sts.) | 212-362-3000
800-345-3362 | www.eileenfisher.com

The quest for that perfect balance of "comfortable yet chic" apparel ends at this "favorite" chain for the "fashionable over-40" set, with "confident, timeless" separates for "work and play" crafted from "excellent fabrics"; "helpful" staffers and "beautiful displays" enhance the experience, and, yes, it's "expensive", but the sales offer "real savings."

Elie Tahari
26 | 23 | 24 | E

SoHo | 417 W. Broadway (bet. Prince & Spring Sts.) | 212-334-4441 | www.elietahari.com

Offering "coverage and elegance" in clothes that "look great on petites" and "those of us who are size 14", the "beautifully tailored" dresses and other pieces in this designer's SoHo flagship shows that he "knows women"; while a few yawn that the pricey items lack "personality", most usually find "something unique" – and even the basics make "great wardrobe essentials" for the professional.

Elizabeth Charles
- | - | - | VE

Meatpacking | 639½ Hudson St. (bet. Gansevoort & Horatio Sts.) | 212-243-3201 | www.elizabeth-charles.com

One of the retail pioneers of the Meatpacking District, this salonlike boutique continues to deliver high-end frocks and frills from designers that Melbourne native Elizabeth Charles finds on trips back home, plus luxe European labels; the "cozy" space sports inviting dressing rooms, while the "relaxed" staff is as refreshingly "no-pressure" as ever, giving the post-brunch crowd time to digest the "tad pricey" "stunning international selection."

Emporio Armani

29 26 24 VE

NEW E 50s | 601 Madison Ave. (bet. 57th & 58th Sts.) | 212-317-0800
SoHo | 410 W. Broadway (bet. Prince & Spring Sts.) | 646-613-8099
www.emporioarmani.com

"Like shopping in Rome" gush fashionable globe-trotters who fly over to Giorgio's sleek spin-offs in SoHo and the East 50s; what an "extensive collection" – "love" the "excellent-quality", classic yet on-trend pieces for men and women that "never go out of style"; another reason to say *grazia*: an "accommodating" staff that "presents you with additional choices not readily visible on the sales floor."

Environment

- | - | - | E

NoHo | 350-352 Bowery (bet. 3rd & 4th Sts.) | 212-780-0051 |
www.environmentfurniture.com

Merging style and sustainability, this furniture-maker uses largely reclaimed, recycled or repurposed wood and canvas to create eco-friendly designs that are both livable and sophisticated; the NoHo showroom displays the brand's low-slung beds and distressed tables alongside lighting and accessories from like-minded companies.

Epaulet

▽ 25 25 26 E

LES | 144 Orchard St. (bet. Rivington & Stanton Sts.) | 212-228-3626
Carroll Gardens | 231 Smith St. (bet. Butler & Douglass Sts.) | Brooklyn |
718-522-3800
www.epauletshop.com

For classic American and British menswear with an "authentic, individual flavor", in-the-know gents head to these Carroll Gardens and LES haunts of "timeless style"; the "fashionable" array includes sportcoats, trousers, shirts and footwear boasting "impeccable construction" from the house label, plus heritage stalwarts like Alden, Gitman Vintage and Johnstons and a smattering of "interesting" women's items, all sold by "ready-to-help" owners who ably earn "customer loyalty."

Equinox Energy Wear ◑

25 20 18 E

E 60s | 817 Lexington Ave. (63rd St.) | 212-750-4900 | www.equinox.com
Additional locations throughout the NY area

"Great associates help you find perfect outfits for the gym and after" at this activewear chain located inside the upscale fitness clubs, offering "fantastic quality" work-out wear by Lululemon, James Perse and its own Equinox collaboration lines, plus Kiehl's skincare stuff; it's "definitely not catering to the bargain-shopper", so those on a budget may need to "wait for sales."

NEW Equipment

- | - | - | E

SoHo | 110 Wooster St. (bet. Prince & Spring Sts.) | 646-277-6496 |
www.equipmentfr.com

Founded in the late '70s, this French brand has been reborn under the aegis of Serge Azria who's made the signature line of effortlessly chic silk blouses wardrobe staples once more, showcasing the collection at this SoHo boutique, one of two in the States; the minimalist setting boasts a rainbow of choices, plus dresses, knitwear and a collection for guys as well.

	QUALITY	DISPLAY	SERVICE	COST

Erica Weiner
| - | - | - | M |

NoLita | 173 Elizabeth St. (bet. Kenmare & Spring Sts.) | 212-334-6383
NEW **Boerum Hill** | 360 Atlantic Ave. (bet. Bond & Hoyt Sts.) |
Brooklyn | 718-855-2555
www.ericaweiner.com

The designer's "whimsical", affordable jewelry, ranging from dainty to big and bold, including her 1909 collection, named for her grandma's birth year, are made locally and sold at this NoLita sliver and spacious Boerum Hill addition; the old-timey cases also brim with curated curios and vintage finds like "reasonably priced" lockets, coin necklaces and Victorian rings from scouting trips to Morocco, London and the U.S.

Ermenegildo Zegna
| 28 | 27 | 25 | VE |

E 50s | 663 Fifth Ave. (bet. 52nd & 53rd Sts.) | 212-421-4488 |
www.zegna.com

Whether it's the sleek architecture or "beautiful, superb craftsmanship and tailoring" of the "top-notch", "cutting-edge" sartorial pleasures, no lapel goes unscrutinized at this brand's East 50s "one-stop shop for the elegant man with panache"; now helmed by head of design Stefano Pilati, the "quality wares" are particularly appealing if "you have a bulge in your money clip" – "a bank loan is needed here" – but there's no denying, if guys "want to dress well, this is the place!"

Escada
| 25 | 24 | 24 | VE |

E 50s | 7 E. 55th St. (bet. 5th & Madison Aves.) | 212-755-2200 |
www.escada.com

Founded in 1970s Germany, the womenswear brand is kept on-trend nowadays by design directors Karen Schoeller and Daniel Wingate, whose "pretty", entrance-making silky evening gowns and modern suits take center stage at this newly relocated bi-level East 50s boutique with gold-lacquered walls and a swanky lounge area; 'luxurious' sums it up, from the colorful clothes to the classy decor to the professional service and ultra–high-end prices.

Etro
| 27 | 26 | 27 | VE |

E 60s | 720 Madison Ave. (bet. 63rd & 64th Sts.) | 212-317-9096
SoHo | 89 Greene St. (Spring St.) | 646-329-6929
www.etro.com

"Classic cuts with a little va-va-voom" and vivid "accents that pop" make this Italian label's art-filled SoHo and UES boutiques a go-to "for the woman who doesn't like plain" and the peacock who prefers to strut in a "unique shirt or blazer"; the "high-quality" luxury goods are "super-expensive", but *amici* agree that this "fashion house's" "beautiful use of color" "makes you stand out, in a good way."

NEW Everything But Water
| - | - | - | E |

E 80s | 1060 Madison Ave. (80th St.) | 212- 249-4052 |
www.everythingbutwater.com

The mega-swimwear chain finally surfaces in the Big Apple, setting up shop at this splashy new branch in the East 80s; bathing beauties find everything from colorful bandeau-top one-piece suits and sexy bikinis to resort essentials like maxi dresses, cover-ups, tote bags and thong sandals from a vast array of makers including Jantzen, Mara Hoffmann and Zimmermann.

QUALITY DISPLAY SERVICE COST

Evolution Store
`27` `29` `23` `E`

SoHo | 120 Spring St. (bet. Greene & Mercer Sts.) | 212-343-1114 | www.theevolutionstore.com

"When you want the unusual", head to this SoHo shop and explore the "mysteries of the natural world", with two floors of "exotic gifts" including "lovely shells", "taxidermy", jewelry fashioned from fossils, "curiousities" and "skeletons and skulls of animals" – "and (erp) people"; despite the temptation to "unleash your inner mad scientist", the "extremely helpful" staff makes it all "fascinating rather than creepy."

Express ●
`21` `22` `20` `M`

Garment District | 7 W. 34th St. (bet. 5th & 6th Aves.) | 212-629-6838 | 888-397-1980 | www.express.com
Additional locations throughout the NY area

It's not easy to please the "working professional *and* the sassy fashionista", but this chain hits the mark, delivering "conservative" office attire (including the ever-popular "editor pants") and "night-out" outfits for the "young or young at heart"; "happy to help" staffers make sure the racks are "well kept", and if some pout it's "too expensive for what you're getting", fast-trackers retort it's "generous with coupons."

Fabergé
`-` `-` `-` `VE`

E 60s | 694 Madison Ave. (bet. 62nd & 63rd Sts.) | 646-559-8848 | www.faberge.com

Channel your inner oligarch at the storied Russian brand's sumptuous Madison Avenue mecca, an opulent jewel box modeled after its flagship sibling in Geneva; silk curtains, regal purple walls and oak floors hint at the brand's Romanov roots, while the posh luxury goods, including those fabled collectible eggs, silver, and exclusive collections of gem-laden jewelry, handmade timepieces and cuff links, summon plenty of rubles.

Fabulous Fanny's
▽ `24` `22` `24` `M`

E Village | 335 E. Ninth St. (bet. 1st & 2nd Aves.) | 212-533-0637 | www.fabulousfannys.com

"Worth the trip from anywhere", this "quirky" East Village eyewear boutique boasts a "floor-to-ceiling" selection of "vintage and vintage-inspired" frames and sunglasses; it "takes some time and patience" to sort through the hundreds of styles housed in antique drawers, but the "excellent choices and prices" make the "treasure hunt" pay off, and though there's no optician-on site, staffers can suggest one.

FACE Stockholm ●
`23` `24` `21` `M`

W 60s | Shops at Columbus Circle | 10 Columbus Circle, ground fl. (B'way) | 212-823-9415 | 888-334-3223 | www.facestockholm.com

It's "fun" to browse the seemingly endless color selection at this sleek, "chic" makeup store in the Time Warner Center, an outpost of the Swedish cosmetics chain with its own line of beauty products, helmed by a mother-daughter duo; while it "never quite went mainstream" in this city, easy-to-shop displays and helpful service explain why it's a "favorite" of many in the know.

Façonnable
`26` `24` `23` `E`

E 50s | 636 Fifth Ave. (51st St.) | 212-319-0111 | www.faconnable.com
The "Euro-fresh designs" at "expensive but not outrageous prices" make it "easy to spend" *beaucoup* de bucks at this French maker's "beauti-

QUALITY DISPLAY SERVICE COST

fully laid-out" two-floor beaux arts Midtown flagship, featuring "quite current" looks for madame and monsieur; the fabrics are "still wonderful" and miraculously hold up "after continual wear", plus the designs are "really a cut above" others', prompting partisans to pronounce it a fashionable "favorite."

Fair Folks & a Goat `-` `-` `-` `E`

G Village | 96 W. Houston St. (bet. LaGuardia Pl. & Thompson St.) | 212-420-7900 | www.fairfolksandagoat.com

Run by a husband-and-wife team, this quirky Village outpost offers a tightly edited mix of offbeat jewelry, clothing and home furnishings plus original artwork, all arranged to feel as if you've stepped inside someone's stylish apartment; plunk down $25 per month for unlimited cups of coffee and invitations to cool cultural events and it may even become your home away from home.

FAO Schwarz `26` `27` `21` `E`

E 50s | 767 Fifth Ave. (58th St.) | 212-644-9400 | 800-426-8697 | www.fao.com

An "NYC institution", this famed "toy wonderland" on Fifth Avenue is "as much an amusement park as a store" (you "gotta go for the *Big* piano") and never fails to "wow" with its "massive" selection encompassing everything from the "basics" to those "over-the-top" items (think "larger-than-life stuffed animals") that "dreams are made of"; if a few nostalgists claim it's "not what it used to be", the steadfast swear its a "magical" experience, "especially during the holidays" – but just "have your wallet ready."

Fendi `28` `27` `25` `VE`

E 50s | 677 Fifth Ave. (bet. 53rd & 54th Sts.) | 212-759-4646 | www.fendi.com

Logo fiends with a penchant for interlocking F's fawn over the "bags and shoes, the true stars" of the show, while clotheshorses leap for the "fashionable and classic Italian" apparel at this locus of luxury where you "get what you pay for"; boasting "elegant woodwork" and travertine marble, this "spacious" Peter Marino–designed emporium evokes an aquatic idyll that "does Fifth Avenue proud"; P.S. when you're "looking to make a splash, check out the divine furs."

Film Biz Prop Shop `-` `-` `-` `M`

Gowanus | 540 President St. (bet. 3rd & 4th Aves.) | Brooklyn | 347-384-2336 | www.filmbizrecycling.org

Behind a gated parking lot on a Gowanus side street lies this "amazing" basement trove of "kooky" treasures that once helped make movie magic; film industry vet Eva Radke takes in post-wrap "donations that are headed to landfills" and resells them here, offering "whosits and whatsits" along with cameras, typewriters, street signs and furniture from recent television, motion picture, theater and video productions at "affordable prices."

NEW Fine and Dandy `-` `-` `-` `M`

W 40s | 445 W. 49th St. (bet. 9th & 10th Aves.) | 212-247-4847 | www.fineanddandyshop.com

Modern day dandies visit this Hell's Kitchen haberdasher to top off their outfits with swashbuckling accessories, from belts, ties and

QUALITY DISPLAY SERVICE COST

socks to ascots, suspenders and pocketwatches; though there are a few exceptions, most items are F&D originals, and the retro setting and nostalgic playlist fit the old-school offerings.

Fiorentini + Baker
| – | – | – | E |

SoHo | 54 Mercer St. (bet. Broome & Grand Sts.) | 212-226-7229 | www.fiorentini-baker.com

At this SoHo stomping ground, fans scoop up the British-born footwear brand's rugged, Italian-made men's and women's biker boots and shoes, bearing such hallmarks of expert craftsmanship as oft-distressed leathers, buckle and zipper treatments and nailed-in soles; the earthy-colored kicks are displayed on wire racks near bohemian bags and studded belts, with a red divan to the rear heightening the trying-on experience.

Fishs Eddy
| 22 | 20 | 19 | I |

Flatiron | 889 Broadway (19th St.) | 212-420-9020 ●
NEW Staten Island | Staten Island Mall | 2555 Richmond Ave. (Richmond Hill Rd.) | 718-494-7020
877-347-4733 | www.fishseddy.com

"The place to go for funky dishes", this "bustling" Flatiron fixture (and Staten Island Mall outlet) specializes in that "fun vintage look", including "handmade glass masterpieces and old tea cups" along with "diner-white and whimsical NYC-themed dinnerware", but "stock revolves" so "if you see something you love, buy it"; the staff gives a "warm welcome", and "there's always a gem" in the "back cove" sale area – if you're willing to go fishing.

Fivestory
| – | – | – | E |

E 60s | 18 E. 69th St. (bet. 5th & Madison Aves.) | 212-288-1338 | www.fivestoryny.com

Set in an East 60s townhouse, this enchanting two-floor boutique, owned by a young gallerist, appeals to globe-trotters bored of the same old, same old, with an expertly edited array of unique apparel, jewelry and shoes; the razor-sharp merchant zeroes in on untapped talents from near and abroad, including Anndra Neen and Vika Gazinskaya, and offers exclusive pieces plucked for guys with direction from the owner of LA's Union.

Fjällräven
| ▽ 23 | 23 | 23 | E |

NoLita | 262 Mott St. (bet. Houston & Prince Sts.) | 212-226-7846 | www.fjallraven.us

"Famous" for their merger of form and function ("love the bold colors"), Kånken backpacks from this Swedish activewear giant show up stateside at this NoLita flagship, which also equips the outward-bound with jackets, sweaters, parkas and other durable duds; however, while most are busy räven over the "quality" goods, a few groan about "backbreaking prices."

Flight 001
| 22 | 23 | 20 | M |

W Village | 96 Greenwich Ave. (bet. Jane & 12th Sts.) | 212-989-0001
Boerum Hill | 132 Smith St. (bet. Bergen & Dean Sts.) | Brooklyn | 718-243-0001
877-354-4481 | www.flight001.com

"Make traveling more chic" with a visit to this West Village and Boerum Hill duo, the "ideal destination" to secure "neat stuff" for your flight, from well-designed luggage to "whimsical and practical" accessories and "gadgets" you "never knew you needed"; the retro "airport"–inspired setups are a "cute" warm-up for both current excursions and "fun trips in the future."

Fogal
▽ 27 | 23 | 25 | VE

E 50s | 611 Madison Ave. (58th St.) | 212-207-3080
E 60s | 785 Madison Ave. (bet. 66th & 67th Sts.) | 212-535-8510
NEW SoHo | 155 Spring St. (bet. W. B'way & Wooster St.) | 212-775-7400
www.fogal.com

Hosiery aficionados flock to the tiny Madison Avenue and SoHo outposts of this Swiss legwear brand for some of "the best pantyhose in the city", stocking up on "very beautiful", "comfortable" tights, sheers and garters in "lots of colors"; the goods are "long-wearing, and should be for the price" – in fact, anyone who can afford the steep sums "should indulge at least once."

Fool's Gold Records
▽ 22 | 22 | 23 | M

Williamsburg | 536 Metropolitan Ave. (bet. Lorimer St. & Union Ave.) | Brooklyn | 347-294-4224 | 888-810-4242 | www.foolsgoldrecs.com
Founded in 2007 by two DJs with a "great knack for talent", Brooklyn-based record label Fool's Gold opened its Williamsburg retail location a few years later, selling merch and music from its "incredible roster of artists" and a "great selection of old vinyl" at "competitive" prices; staffers are "genuinely nice people", and the "easy-to-navigate" space acts as a venue for gallery shows and live performances.

42nd Street Photo
23 | 20 | 20 | M

Garment District | 378 Fifth Ave. (bet. 35th & 36th Sts.) | 212-594-6565 | 888-810-4242 | www.42photo.com
Shutterbugs swarm to this "popular" 50-year-old Herald Square outfit that features "all the major brands" of "anything photo-related"; heavy "tourist" traffic makes it "a bit of a madhouse", but it's still a snap to find "what you want" from the "dependable" inventory, plus "knowledgeable" service and "competitive" pricing make it "worth a visit."

Foscarini Spazio Soho
- | - | - | VE

SoHo | 17 Greene St. (Grand St.) | 212-257-4412 | www.foscarini.com
The directional Italian lighting company brightens up the SoHo home furnishings landscape with this newly reconceived loftlike pillared showcase featuring statement-making wall, floor, desk and ceiling fixtures in modern envelope-pushing shapes and materials, colors like bright white or red, and site-specific installations; many of the pieces are created in collaboration with leading edge artists, making it a must-stop for interior decorators, architects and house-proud customers.

Fountain Pen Hospital
29 | 22 | 26 | E

TriBeCa | 10 Warren St. (bet. B'way & Church St.) | 212-964-0580 | 800-253-7367 | www.fountainpenhospital.com
A discerning scribe's "mecca" in TriBeCa since 1946, this "very welcome" "throwback" stocks a pen for "every budget", with a "large selection" that draws "serious" collectors seeking "vintage" instruments and "high-quality limited editions"; inks, cases, desk sets and other writerly frills also figure, and besides being "generous with advice",

the staff of ur-media mavens provides "wonderful repairs"; P.S. closed Saturdays and Sundays.

Fragments
▽ 24 | 23 | 22 | E

SoHo | 116 Prince St. (bet. Greene & Wooster Sts.) | 212-334-9588 | 888-637-2463 | www.fragments.com

Long before designer spots took Downtown by sparkly storm, this SoHo "must for unique jewelry" was serving up oodles of gilded accessories underneath a Baccarat chandelier and in artfully arranged window displays; the "many designers showcased" here, both mainstream and under-the-radar types, mean you can find "something special for everyone at almost any style and price!"

Frank Stella, Ltd.
24 | 20 | 21 | E

W 50s | 921 Seventh Ave. (58th St.) | 212-957-1600
W 80s | 440 Columbus Ave. (81st St.) | 212-877-5566
www.frankstellanyc.com

What "tasteful yet fashionable stuff" agree guys who gravitate to this Westside duo for casual staples along with "high-quality suits and coats", some from its own house label; if nitpickers pout that prices are "more appropriate for Madison Avenue", most Frank fans who've "shopped here for many years" applaud its "fine service" and "frequent sales" that are "worth waiting for."

Fratelli Rossetti
29 | 23 | 24 | VE

E 50s | 625 Madison Ave. (58th St.) | 212-888-5107 | www.rossetti.it

"Classic" and "beautiful", the shoes are like "practical works of art" claim sole-mates who also clamor for the "tasteful, fashion-forward" leather goods for men and women at this Italian luxury label's swanky Madison Avenue mecca; sure, it's pricey, but the "wonderful" wares are "comfortable", "wear well" and "invariably draw compliments"; in fact, some may "last a lifetime", prompting customers to "keep going back for more."

Fred Leighton
29 | 29 | 25 | VE

E 60s | 773 Madison Ave. (66th St.) | 212-288-1872 | www.fredleighton.com

"Dreams are made of" the "Oscar-worthy" jewels "to befit a queen" of the movie screen at this art deco Madison Avenue salon of glittering temptations; "just looking in the window is a thrill, but you better bring bags of dollars" if "you absolutely must buy it and have the money to do it and lack the sense not to" – the antique, estate and signature collection "gems" are "nothing you ever need, but the sparkle" is dazzling.

Fred Perry
28 | 25 | 23 | E

SoHo | 133 Wooster St. (bet. Houston & Prince Sts.) | 212-260-4770
Fred Perry Surplus Shop
Williamsburg | 306 Grand St. (Havemeyer St.) | Brooklyn | 347-689-2096
www.fredperry.com

High Street meets Main Street at this "curiously capable" inventor of sportswear with a British swagger and fashionable flair; the "hip" SoHo branch stays true to its tennis "heritage", offering "super-well-made" men's polos and and women's dresses that read demure with a splash of "sexy", all adorned with that laurel wreath logo, plus sporty bags, while the Williamsburg surplus shop serves up bargains on past-seasons' wares.

Freemans Sporting Club  ▽ 26 | 24 | 21 | E

LES | 8 Rivington St. (bet. Bowery & Chrystie St.) | 212-673-3209
W Village | 343 Bleecker St. (bet. Christopher & W. 10th Sts.) | 212-255-5509
www.freemanssportingclub.com
Barber & Supply
NEW **Williamsburg** | 101 N. Eighth St. (Wythe Ave.) | Brooklyn | 718-522-4959 | www.fscbarber.com

Selling mostly products made within 10 miles of their LES and West Village shops, this "hip but accessible" menswear purveyor aims to please the on-trend urban gentleman, offering slim-fitting ties, tees and made-to-measure suiting in a "cool atmosphere" of vintage para-phernalia and old-school barber chairs; "excellent" service, on-site tonsorialists and a grooming/apothecary offshoot in Williamsburg ramp up its appeal.

Free People 22 | 23 | 20 | E

E 40s | 79 Fifth Ave. (16th St.) | 212-647-1293 ◗
E 70s | 1319 Third Ave. (bet. 75th & 76th Sts.) | 212-744-0379
SoHo | 99 Spring St. (Mercer St.) | 212-226-7497 ◗
Boerum Hill | 113 Smith St. (Pacific St.) | Brooklyn | 718-250-0050
www.freepeople.com

"Find your inner hippie goddess" at this Urban Outfitters spin-off, an "inviting" chain offering teens and twentysomethings "accessible boho chic" in the form of floaty, "feminine" peasant tops, retro bell-bottoms and rocker jackets and other "eye-catchers"; if granola girls grumble that it's a "little pricey for the quality", most maintain it's the place to "try a trend without a hefty price tag."

Fresh 26 | 24 | 24 | E

E 70s | 1367 Third Ave. (78th St.) | 212-585-3400
Flatiron | 872 Broadway (18th St.) | 212-477-1100
NoLita | 57 Spring St. (bet. Lafayette & Mulberry Sts.) | 212-925-0099
W 60s | 159 Columbus Ave. (67th St.) | 212-787-3505
W Village | 388 Bleecker St. (bet. 11th & Perry Sts.) | 917-408-1850
800-373-7420 | www.fresh.com

"Create your own spa experience" at this "feel-good" bath and body chain, where "helpful" staffers "pamper" shoppers with "fresh" scents, "life-changing" lip treatments and "effective" bath products; serene surrounds create "Zen in the crazy city", and while it's "not the cheapest bar of soap in the world", beauty buffs rave about Spa Week specials.

Frette 29 | 25 | 24 | VE

E 60s | 799 Madison Ave. (bet. 67th & 68th Sts.) | 212-988-5221 | 800-353-7388 | www.frette.com

"There's nothing better to sleep with" – ok, "almost nothing" – than the "gorgeous" bedding from this "high-end" Italian master's Upper East Side emporium, where the "heavenly" sheets, spreads and other linens, not to mention towels, are as "stunning to look at" as they are to "sink into"; spendthrifts rest easy since "the best" is "worth every penny", but anyone fretting over the "splurge" might want to wait for a sale.

Frick Collection Shop

27 | 25 | 23 | M

E 70s | The Frick Collection | 1 E. 70th St. (5th Ave.) | 212-547-6848 | www.frick.org

"In character" with the esteemed Upper East Side museum in which it resides, this "small" shop is "a sanctuary" for "lovely merchandise" – be it books, prints, "paper items" or "arty gifts" – that'll make you seem "more cultured than you are"; though there's "not a wide selection", it's "not to be missed" for "quality" "memorabilia" from a "magnificent collection."

Frye

28 | 25 | 22 | E

SoHo | 113 Spring St. (bet. Greene & Wooster Sts.) | 212-226-3793 | www.thefryecompany.com

"What's not to love?" quip loyalists who gallop over to this venerable American company's SoHo flagship to lasso footwear for the entire family; rustic details like old photographs, leather chairs and reclaimed barn doors create a "beautifully designed" backdrop for the main draw: "excellent-quality" "drool-worthy boots" for men, women and children, crafted from fine leather, in "all colors and styles" from "hot" cowboy kicks to "motorcycle" mama.

The Future Perfect

- | - | - | E

NoHo | 55 Great Jones St. (bet. Bowery & Lafayette St.) | 212-473-2500
Williamsburg | 115 N. Sixth St. (Berry St.) | Brooklyn | 718-599-6278
877-388-7373 | www.thefutureperfect.com

Truly a "bridge between art and home furnishings", this Williamsburg original and its NoHo offshoot curate an "all-star cast" of emerging designers and "indie products"; the "edgy" mix, including Piet Hein Eek furniture, colorful pouffes, modular chandeliers and bold-patterned wallpaper, is ideal for "window-shopping" since it's "often expensive."

Galeria Melissa

- | - | - | E

(aka Melissa Shoes)

SoHo | 102 Greene St. (bet. Prince & Spring Sts.) | 212-775-1950 | www.melissa.com.br

Joining the Brazilian fashion invasion, this São Paolo cobbler brings "beautifully designed" shoes to SoHo, with footwear ranging from brightly colored sky-high wedges to metallic flats, all in the brand's signature "high-quality" plastic, arranged on conelike pedestals in a modern, white space; collaborations with top-notch designers such as Vivienne Westwood make this "creative talent's" innovative line all the more "desirable."

NEW Gamine

- | - | - | E

Williamsburg | 439 Metropolitan Ave. (bet. N. 5th & 6th Sts.) | Brooklyn | 347-541-4652 | www.gamine.co

While hyper-local is the name of the Brooklyn game, this Williamsburg boutique goes against the trend with its globally sourced array of women's and men's clothing and accessories, some of which are exclusive to the shop; the spare, light-filled space also hosts events and art exhibitions.

	QUALITY	DISPLAY	SERVICE	COST

Gant

| | 25 | 23 | 21 | E |

E 50s | 645 Fifth Ave. (bet. 51st & 52nd Sts.) | 212-813-9170

Gant Rugger

NoLita | 25 Prince St. (bet. Elizabeth & Mott Sts.) | 646-559-0170
W Village | 353 Bleecker St. (bet. Charles & W. 10th Sts.) |
212-620-5949
www.gant.com

"Be prepared to pay lots" for this Swiss brand's Euro take on sporty Americana at this trio of retro, design-y Manhattan shops; the "cool, classic rugby shirts and polos", plaid button-downs and oxfords, preppily rugged blazers and khakis, and limited-edition one-offs somehow "turn your boyfriends metro", plus women can also get their Gant on without borrowing from the guys.

Gap 1969 ●

| | 23 | 22 | 21 | M |

SoHo | 513 Broadway (bet. Broome & Spring Sts.) | 212-431-2686 |
800-427-7895 | www.gap.com

"What jeans should be" declare devotees of the "covetable" premium denim pieces stocked by this SoHo spin-off of the popular chain; a "streamlined selection" focused on essential fits like 'super skinny' and 'long & lean' means most find the "perfect cut" for their figure, and although "slightly pricier than regular Gap" stuff, it's "worth it" considering "the quality you get."

Garber Hardware

| | 25 | 15 | 23 | M |

W Village | 710 Greenwich St. (bet. Charles & W. 10th Sts.) |
212-242-9807 | www.garberhardware.com

A West Village "staple" since 1884, this "quintessential" "old-style" hardware store "has everything" for home improvement, including tools, paints, electrical and plumbing supplies and hard-to-find odds and ends; between the ample stock and family ownership that's "unfailingly helpful even to neophytes", DIY types "feel lucky it's in the neighborhood."

Generation Records ●

| | ∇ 26 | 22 | 24 | M |

G Village | 210 Thompson St. (bet. Bleecker & 3rd Sts.) | 212-254-1100 |
www.generationrecords.com

"Still standing" as a "top-shelf" destination for devotees of "metal, rock, Goth-industrial, punk, etc.", this Villager vends used and new CDs and vinyl with an ear for the esoteric, plus "a huge selection of" music tees and posters; insiders advise "real bargains are found" on "vintage" platters "down in the basement", which also hosts "occasional appearances by bands."

Georg Jensen

| | 29 | 27 | 26 | VE |

E 60s | 687 Madison Ave. (bet. 61st & 62nd Sts.) | 212-759-6457 |
800-546-5253 | www.georgjensen.com

Loyalists who love this luxurious UES Danish outpost laud the "timeless" and "classic Scandinavian styling" and "gorgeous everything", including the "unique jewelry design, much of it ageless", and "wonderful silver" serving pieces, cutlery and vases that make perfect "wedding gifts"; from the "exquisite quality and service" to the "elegant" Nordic merchandise, it's "a real class act" – and one of the "best" places to invest in "antiques of the future."

QUALITY DISPLAY SERVICE COST

Ghurka   ▽ 29 | 24 | 25 | VE

E 50s | The Sherry-Netherland | 781 Fifth Ave. (59th St.) | 212-826-8300
NEW **SoHo** | 65 Prince St. (bet. Crosby & Lafayette Sts.) | 212-826-8300 800-587-1584 | www.ghurka.com

Remember the Raj in high style at this leather merchant's flagship in The Sherry-Netherland and new SoHo sidekick, which pay homage to the Crown's Ghurka regiments with luggage, briefcases and handbags that are tough as nails yet so "classy" you may hesitate to "let the airlines handle" them; even commoners who lament it's all "so expensive" still "like to look."

Giggle   26 | 24 | 24 | E

E 70s | 1033 Lexington Ave. (74th St.) | 212-249-4249
SoHo | 120 Wooster St. (bet. Prince & Spring Sts.) | 212-334-5817
W 70s | 352 Amsterdam Ave. (bet. 76th & 77th Sts.) | 212-362-8680
800-495-8577 | www.giggle.com

If big-box stores aren't your speed, swing into one of these "fashion-forward" tot shops, links of an SF company vending "modern" nursery furnishings, gear and apparel in a fresh boutique setting presided over by "helpful" staffers who'll "hold the hand" of first-timers fretting over their registries; naturally all of this "cute"-ness "isn't cheap", but if you're seeking "unique" gifts sure to "impress", this is the spot.

GiGi K   - | - | - | M

G Village | 42 University Pl. (9th St.) | 212-777-2211
G Village | 60 W. Eighth St. (6th Ave.) | 212-677-1122
www.gigik.us

Add some style to your stems with a visit to Parsons grad Gigi Kwon's Greenwich Village duo stocked with unique Japanese-made leggings, knee-highs, leg warmers and pantyhose that run the gamut from lace to leopard and from subdued to wild; the small digs also boast a limited selection of clothing and accessories to the rear.

Girard Perregaux   ▽ 29 | 28 | 29 | VE

E 60s | 701 Madison Ave. (63rd St.) | 646-495-9915 | www.girard-perregaux.com

The first name in "beautiful" timepieces and one of the greatest and most elite of Swiss watchmakers, this prestige brand proffers its exclusive wares, including coveted limited editions, at this spacious Midtown flagship; the luxe digs have a spare art deco style, but the brand dates much further back, to 1791, and prices reflect its considerable expertise: they soar into the hundreds of thousands of dollars.

Giuseppe Zanotti Design   27 | 27 | 24 | VE

E 60s | 806 Madison Ave. (bet. 67th & 68th Sts.) | 212-650-0455 | www.giuseppezanottidesign.com

It's easy to become "addicted" to this "innovative" Italian designer's "gorgeous", "beautifully made" stilettos, booties and platform peep-toes, which are temptingly displayed at his tasteful Madison Avenue digs; like jewelry for the feet, these "limousine shoes" are glammed up with Swarovski crystals, jewels, feathers and other finery, making you feel so fabulous and "chic" you hardly notice "the dent they make in your wallet."

Goorin Bros.

| 26 | 26 | 27 | M |

W Village | 337 Bleecker St. (Christopher St.) | 212-256-1895
Park Slope | 195 Fifth Ave. (bet. Berkeley Pl. & Union St.) | Brooklyn | 718-783-4287
www.goorin.com

They've got a chapeau to suit just about everyone at these West Village and Park Slope branches of a well-established California hatter, whose quaint shops brim "wall-to-wall" with "the coolest" fedoras, straws and caps for him or her; the rates run from "pricey" to "more reasonable", while staffers are "very helpful" for picking a lid "that fits both your head and style."

Gotham Bikes

| 26 | 19 | 24 | E |

TriBeCa | 112 W. Broadway (bet. Duane & Reade Sts.) | 212-732-2453 | www.gothambikes.com

With a location "convenient for Brooklyn Bridge and West Side" Greenway tours, this TriBeCa cycle sanctum trades in "high-quality bikes" for sale or rental in a straightforward setting stocked full of serious rides and gear; tune-ups and repairs are done on-site by an "easygoing" but "super-professional" crew who "know the best" wheels for you.

Gracious Home

| 25 | 20 | 21 | E |

Chelsea | 45 W. 25th St. (bet. 5th & 6th Aves.) | 212-414-5710
E 70s | 1201 Third Ave. (bet. 69th & 70th Sts.) | 212-517-6300
E 70s | 1220 Third Ave. (70th St.) | 212-517-6300
W 60s | 1992 Broadway (67th St.) | 212-231-7800 ◑
800-338-7809 | www.gracioushome.com

"Things you need, things you want and things you never even thought of" are found at this "gracious" quartet "where Manhattanites shop for high-quality home products and appliances"; the "jam-packed" layout brims with a "little bit of everything", from "esoteric nuts and bolts", "fine linens", "snappy tableware" and "lightbulbs to a $1,000 chandelier", and luckily the "top-drawer" staff can "have it delivered" – just what the "pampered apartment-dweller" needs.

Graff

| ▽ 29 | 29 | 29 | VE |

E 60s | 710 Madison Ave. (63rd St.) | 212-355-9292 | www.graffdiamonds.com

"I'd pay to just look at the incredible window candy" admit admirers who deem the London jeweler's four-story emporium on Madison Avenue pure "heaven"; whether you're searching for "investment-grade stones", from royal blue sapphires to heart-shaped diamonds, magnificently set in cocktail rings, statement cuffs or glittering earrings or stunning bridal jewelry, you'll find "simply the best on offer."

GRDN Bklyn

| ▽ 26 | 24 | 24 | M |

Boerum Hill | 103 Hoyt St. (bet. Atlantic & Pacific Sts.) | Brooklyn | 718-797-3628 | www.grdnbklyn.com

The gardening season "lasts all year" at this "charming" Boerum Hill go-to for green thumbs, where the "beautiful flowers, plants and home accessories" – including a "wide variety" of "lovely pots" and planters plus horticultural "gadgets" and patio furniture – are sure to "fit your needs"; beyond the earthy interior, "check out the backyard" to "visualize your own" patch.

	QUALITY	DISPLAY	SERVICE	COST

Green Depot
25 | 22 | 23 | M

SoHo | 222 Bowery (bet. Prince & Spring Sts.) | 212-226-0444
Greenpoint | 1 Ivy Hill Rd. (Rewe St.) | Brooklyn | 718-782-2991
www.greendepot.com

Fix-it folks get eco-conscious at these Greenpoint and SoHo outlets of a conservationist hardware chain, where the paints, cleaning supplies, lumber and building materials are all chosen for their earth-friendly impact; green-leaners report it "just feels good to walk through" the showrooms and get tips you "can trust" from a "considerate" team.

GreenFlea Market ⇗
20 | 17 | 21 | M

W 70s | Columbus Ave. (77th St.) | 212-239-3025 |
www.greenfleamarkets.com

The "eclectic mix" of crafts, clothing, furniture, jewelry and "lots of vintage everything" means you "never know what you'll find" at this year-round Sunday flea market in an Upper West Side "schoolyard and cafeteria"; both "quality and price range from high to low", but "if you have patience" it's a "colorful" way to "kill a few hours."

Greenhouse
28 | 26 | 28 | E

Downtown Bklyn | 387 Atlantic Ave. (bet. Bond & Hoyt Sts.) |
Brooklyn | 718-422-8631 | www.thegreenhouselifestyle.com

It's easy to be green at this sprawling lifestyle store with a conscience on Atlantic Avenue; the clean, comfortable space boasts wood-plank floors and a handpicked mix of handsome, high-style furniture, bedding, tableware and bath products that are both sustainable and tasteful, all strictly sourced from eco-friendly companies.

Greenwich Letterpress
▽ 29 | 24 | 24 | M

W Village | 39 Christopher St. (bet. 7th Ave. & Waverly Pl.) |
212-989-7464 | www.greenwichletterpress.com

"Quality old-fashioned printing" is still in style at this "darling little" West Village shop, whose clean-energy presses turn out "beautifully made" stationery, invitations and cards that rank "hands down" with "the most clever, unusual and gorgeous" around; the owners are "pleasant" and "informed", and "recipients always seem thrilled", so patrons come "willing to pay."

NEW G Shock
– | – | – | M

SoHo | 454 W. Broadway (bet. Houston & Prince Sts.) | 212-533-8700 |
www.gshock.com

A mainstay since the '80s, this Casio brand is known for durable resin-band digital watches that are shock-resistant, waterproof and even solar powered; the two-story art-filled SoHo flagship displays new inventory and current collaborations in display cases peppered with vintage timepieces from the line's early days.

G-Star Raw
▽ 22 | 23 | 21 | E

Flatiron | 873 Broadway (bet. 18th & 19th Sts.) | 212-253-1117
SoHo | 270 Lafayette St. (Prince St.) | 212-219-2744 ◗
SoHo | 441 Broadway (bet. Grand & Howard Sts.) | 212-625-3702
www.g-star.com

"Hipster-chic clothing" with a Euro twist is the province of this Dutch denim outfit with three modern, spacious city stores under its belt; don't expect any ol' five-pockets: these "great urban fashion" statements range from baked, molded jeans to "basic but stylish" Western-style chambray shirts, plus offerings go beyond the blues, like khaki flight jackets and tapered cargo pants; P.S. there's even a customization service to boot.

Gucci

28 | 27 | 25 | VE

E 50s | Trump Tower | 725 Fifth Ave. (56th St.) | 212-826-2600
E 60s | 840 Madison Ave. (bet. 69th & 70th Sts.) | 212-717-2619
www.gucci.com

Customers prosperous enough to be "greeted by name" and aspirants alike are gluttons for Gucci, agreeing it's worth a visit to Trump Tower to take in the "awesome" marble madness and the "beautiful" bonanza of "ultimate status items": "excellent" shoes (possibly the "best men's loafers in town"), "timeless" bags, "great sunglasses" and "lasting fashions"; the Madison Avenue location is the spot "if you don't want to feel like a tourist", but in either case, staffers "dote" "hand and foot" while you contemplate the perilously posh array.

Gucci Kids

- | - | - | VE

E 50s | Trump Tower | 725 Fifth Ave. (56th St.) | 212-826-2600 |
www.gucci.com

Conveniently located alongside the Italian brand's East 50s adult shop, this luxury children's boutique echoes the grown-up emporium with its sleek black-and-white interior, gold accents and tiny chairs in plush fabrics; on the racks are finely made clothing and accessories for the well-heeled tot, from cozy coats, pleated frocks, pint-sized purses and colorful sunglasses to fur and leather jackets priced in the thousands.

NEW Gudrun Sjödén

- | - | - | M

SoHo | 50 Greene St. (bet. Broome & Grand Sts.) | 212-219-2510 |
www.gudrunsjoden.com

Founded in Sweden in 1976, this cheerful source for colorful, comfy womenswear plus bedding, towels and tabletop wares plants its Scandinavian-design flag in SoHo; eco-conscious, durable cottons are the stock in trade and the expansive all-green, rustic-chic environs, replete with stenciled floors, are as bright as the Land of the Midnight Sun.

Guess by Marciano

▽ 22 | 27 | 25 | E

SoHo | 514 Broadway (bet. Broome & Spring Sts.) | 212-925-0817 |
www.guessbymarciano.com

Guess Jeans' more upscale sibling, this flamboyantly fashion-forward SoHo store offers "nice looks" with plenty of "trendy, well-made clothing and accessories", all offered by solid staffers against a splashy backdrop of mirrors and animal prints; while there are plenty of edgy styles to fall for, some label the garments too "expensive."

Guggenheim Museum Store

24 | 21 | 17 | E

E 80s | Guggenheim Museum | 1071 Fifth Ave. (89th St.) |
212-423-3615 | 800-329-6109 | www.guggenheimstore.org

After "spiraling" through the Upper East Side art institution, "round out your day" with a "cool" keepsake from this museum shop's "quite interesting" "jumble", which appeals especially to "Frank Lloyd Wright freaks" since his designs inspire "everything from ties to teapots";

alas, a few critics cavil there's "not enough space" and it's "under-staffed" ("less is less").

NEW Halston Heritage

`- | - | - | E`

E 80s | 1122 Madison Ave. (bet. 83rd & 84th Sts.) | 646-863-4188
Once synonymous with '70s-era Studio 54, the label first conceived by the late American designer Roy Halston Frowick has since been reborn via its Heritage collection, and now it's expanding with boutiques nationwide, including this two-floor Madison Avenue outpost; while the bright drapey designs, including dressy dresses, stay true to the brand's roots they're also completely contemporary and the right fit for the 21st century.

Hammacher Schlemmer & Co.

`25 | 23 | 22 | E`

E 50s | 147 E. 57th St. (bet. Lexington & 3rd Aves.) | 212-421-9002 | 800-421-9002 | www.hammacher.com
"A toy store for grown-ups", this recently renovated, "tried-and-true" East 50s "gadget-lover's Eden" is stocked with "really cool stuff" ranging from the "useful to the bizarre", making it the gift go-to "for the person who has everything"; whether browsing or buying, it's "super-fun", and while some "gizmos" may be too "dear to buy", others are "not as expensive as you might think."

H&M

`15 | 18 | 14 | I`

E 50s | 640 Fifth Ave. (51st St.) | 212-489-0390 | 800-466-7467 | www.hm.com
Additional locations throughout the NY area
"'Affordability' is the key word" at this Swedish megachain known for its "disposable" "cheap-chic" trendwear including eco-conscious and designer capsule collections (like Isabel Marant) offered at "bargain-basement" prices in an "ever-changing" array that keeps diehards dropping by "at least weekly"; "disorganized" racks, "lacking" service and "long lines" can be a hassle though, so those in a hurry skip the "backed-up dressing rooms" and head straight for the "funky" and "whimsical" statement accessories.

NEW HAN KJØBENHAVN

`- | - | - | E`

NoLita | 27 Prince St. (bet. Elizabeth & Mott Sts.) | www.hankjobenhavn.com
Tim Faith Hancock and Jannik Wikkelso Davidsen bring their Danish style to this small, über-minimalist NoLita shop where their menswear, specs and accessories share the clean, white space with glossy art books and photographs; a few classic pieces from furniture designers like Arne Jacobsen and Hans Wegner complete the Nordic picture.

NEW Hanro of Switzerland

`- | - | - | E`

Meatpacking | 806 Washington St. (bet. Gansevoort & Horatio Sts.) | 646-810-8687 | www.hanrousa.com
Before splurging on clothing from the surrounding designer shops in the Meatpacking, pick up your foundation essentials at this 125-year-old brand's first stateside shop, a high-ceilinged affair with sculptural lighting fixtures; though renowned for its delicate yet long-lasting un-derthings like camis, panties and bras, the Austrian-based company recently added tasteful casualwear to the mix, and even covers the guys with boxers, briefs and sleepwear.

	QUALITY	DISPLAY	SERVICE	COST

NEW Happy Socks
— | — | — | M

SoHo | 436 W. Broadway (bet. Prince & Spring Sts.) | 212-966-9692 | www.happysocks.com

Everyday accessories become a source of smiles at this all-white SoHo outpost of the Swedish retailer, where there's a bright sock in every shape, color and pattern to warm the toes of men, women and children; the company also offers tights for women and occasionally collaborates with brands like Keds and Opening Ceremony.

Harlem Haberdashery
— | — | — | E

Harlem | 245 Lenox Ave. (122nd St.) | 646-707-0070 | www.harlemhaberdashery.com

Set in Lenox Avenue brownstone, this boutique hawks its own brand of locally made, urban-meets-preppy his-and-hers attire, offering modern pieces that riff on the spiffy style of the Harlem Renaissance, plus accessories from other designers; with its navy walls, animal skin rugs and ruby-red chandelier, the space is as handsome as the dashing apparel.

Harry's Shoes
25 | 18 | 20 | E

W 80s | 2299 Broadway (83rd St.) | 212-874-2035 | 866-442-7797 | www.harrys-shoes.com

"Broadway wouldn't be the same without" this "venerable" footwear palace, which recently more than doubled its size and continually stocks an "unsurpassed selection" spanning "all price points"; it's helmed by staffers who won't quit until "the fit is just right", and while the array isn't "necessarily for the fashion-minded", it's an "incredible" source for "comfy", "sensible" options (think Dansko, Ecco and Teva) "you can actually walk in."

Harry's Shoes for Kids
24 | 20 | 24 | M

W 80s | 2315 Broadway (bet. 83rd & 84th Sts.) | 212-874-2034 | www.harrys-shoes.com

One of "the best spots in town for kids' shoes", this West 80s standby – just steps from its parent store – has a well-rounded selection covering all the bases, from sturdy school shoes to gym sneakers to cozy winter boots, overseen by a "fantastic" staff that "gets you in and out" fast – a good thing, since it gets pretty "crowded", especially "on weekends."

Harry Winston
29 | 29 | 27 | VE

E 50s | 718 Fifth Ave. (56th St.) | 212-399-1000 | 800-988-4110 | www.harrywinston.com

The neo-classical interior of this Fifth Avenue "Cadillac of jewelry stores" dazzles with its "off-the-charts beauty", spotlighting "giant diamonds" and "drool-worthy" gems designed for the "discriminating"; though the staff is by turns "arrogant", "truly gracious" and "willing to help you learn", the shop's reputation precedes itself as it's a "legend in both the world and the history of the finest" sparklers imaginable – in fact, "the name says it all . . . sigh"; P.S. it's now owned by the Swatch Group.

Haute Hippie
24 | 25 | 23 | E

E 80s | 1070 Madison Ave. (81st St.) | 212-535-0914
NoLita | 9 Prince St. (bet. Bowery & Elizabeth St.) | 212-431-0101
www.hautehippie.com

Fashionable "hippies" bring peace, love and money to this UES-Nolita duo, slipping svelte bodies into "fabulous" boho-inspired, wide-legged pants, hand-embellished dresses, slouchy graphic tees, fringed suede jackets and neutral-hued, nomadic basics; the welcoming environment somehow feels like a vintage-inspired library and, at the same time, a "fun" Wild West hideaway, replete with cowhide rugs; P.S. there are also some items for the dudes.

Hell's Kitchen Flea Market

20 | 18 | 19 | I

Garment District | W. 39th St. (9th Ave.) | 212-243-5343 | www.hellskitchenfleamarket.com

"Bargain"-hunters hit this open-air weekend market near the Port Authority to browse "everything and anything" a frequent flea-er would expect, namely vintage clothing, jewelry, home goods, furniture and miscellaneous "weird and odd items"; however, while foragers with "a creative eye" may "find some hidden treasures", others are left itching for "more vendors and a better selection."

Helmut Lang

▽ 26 | 25 | 25 | E

SoHo | 93 Mercer St. (bet. Broome & Spring Sts.) | 212-242-3240
W 70s | 230 Columbus Ave. (bet. 70th & 71st Sts.) | 212-877-3450
www.helmutlang.com

The namesake designer left the label eons ago, but his minimalist aesthetic lives on in the form of skinny jeans, suits and jackets for him and her, all on view at these understated SoHo-UWS boutiques; long-limbed women are sure to "turn heads without being too flashy" in figure-enhancing dresses and tunics boasting "architectural draping that always flatters", and also swear by the comfy, clean-lined wardrobe staples.

Henri Bendel

26 | 26 | 23 | VE

W 50s | 712 Fifth Ave. (56th St.) | 212-247-1100 | 800-423-6335 | www.henribendel.com

Though clothing is no longer a part of the mix, this "iconic" Fifth Avenue department store is still "a girl's shopping mecca" for those with "generous discretionary income" to spend on the "best bangles, baubles and accessories" or at the "beautiful makeup counters"; while the less bedazzled say this century-old outfit "seems to have lost its identity", Bendel-ites believe "turning it into a specialty gift boutique was absolutely genius."

Henry Beguelin

- | - | - | VE

W Village | 30 Charles St. (Waverly Pl.) | 212-647-8415 | www.henrybeguelinbycn.com

Cultists of this Italian leather goods steer over to its light-filled West Village boutique to shop for subtle yet impactful pieces, such as bags and cobbler-chic sandals embellished with tassels and beads; rounding out the supple mix: washed-suede trenches and home accessories, like woven baskets, plus equally luxe lines, many also made from sumptuous skins.

Hermès

30 | 28 | 24 | VE

E 60s | 691 Madison Ave. (62nd St.) | 212-751-3181
Financial District | 15 Broad St. (Exchange Pl.) | 212-785-3030
800-441-4488 | www.hermes.com

The "crème de la crème" of "luxury purveyors, hands down", this legendary French brand's "museumlike" boutiques are rated No. 1 for

Quality – scoring a rare 30 – in NYC's Fashion/Beauty category; "nothing feels better than walking down Madison" – or the FiDi's Broad Street – "with a distinctive orange bag full of beautifully designed goodies", be it "timeless scarves" and "outstanding" ties in "delicious prints", "impeccably constructed" handbags (ah, that "irresistible Birkin"), "elegant" apparel or jewelry; oui, "prices are in the upper galaxy", and service ranges from "excellent" to "snooty", but there's no more "indulgent gift to oneself or a loved one."

Hermès Men

29 | 28 | 27 | VE

E 60s | 690 Madison Ave. (62nd St.) | 212-308-3585 | www.hermes.com

"You know you've made it" when you can shop this handsome, four-floored, men's-only boutique on Madison Avenue housing some of the "finest ties in town", as well as a "beautiful" collection of ready-to-wear from the "iconic" French luxury brand; despite "astronomical" bills, when you factor in the "impeccable" service and quality of merchandise, including custom-made creations, it's "worth the price" – besides, you'll feel so "spoiled", you won't want to go anywhere else.

Hervé Leger
26 | 24 | 22 | VE

E 60s | 804 Madison Ave (bet. 64th & 65th Sts.) | 212-794-7008
SoHo | 409 W. Broadway (Spring St.) | 212-991-4740
www.herveleger.com

"Minimal is immediately what you think when you walk into" this label's ode to the iconic, "skintight bandage dress" of the '80s, now owned by Max Azria of BCBG fame; "there's a modicum of hanging in the lavender-walled Madison Avenue boutique and its SoHo offshoot, and "barely any material", but the "fantastic" "celeb favorites with A-list price tags" "make you feel as if you're one of the gods or goddesses – just for a few moments."

Hickey Freeman
27 | 24 | 26 | VE

E 50s | 543 Madison Ave. (bet. 54th & 55th Sts.) | 212-586-6481 | 800-537-4976 | www.hickeyfreeman.com

For "incredible suits and sport coats that last through time", depend on this East 50s men's clothing shop that boasts "American tailoring that rivals European standards" and proves "you don't have to look boring as a result"; service is "excellent" and the selection is "top-notch" – from off-the-rack "sportswear to made-to-measure, they do it right" – while the "high" "quality matches the price."

Hickoree's Hard Goods

– | – | – | M

Williamsburg | 109 S. Sixth St., 2nd fl. (bet. Bedford Ave. & Berry St.) | Brooklyn | 347-294-0005 | www.hickorees.com

Housing a "vast" collection of vests, jeans, handkerchiefs and ties, this sunlit Williamsburg destination, set aloft on the second floor, attracts guys in search of goods with a story, including many distinctive items made in the U.S.; poring over finds like 1950s-inspired work shirts, patchwork tote bags and wool coats crafted from Italian military blankets, low-key sartorialists admit "I truly buy my entire wardrobe here."

H.L. Purdy
25 | 21 | 25 | VE

E 50s | 501 Madison Ave. (bet. 52nd & 53rd Sts.) | 212-688-8050
(continued)

(continued)

H.L. Purdy

E 80s | 1171 Madison Ave. (86th St.) | 212-249-3997
E 80s | 1195 Lexington Ave. (81st St.) | 212-737-0122
www.hlpurdy.com

Right on the nose with classy glasses for those "who live in them", these optical Eastsiders carry "the latest in frame styles" from a host of "high-quality" designers, as well as specialty specs for night driving and computer sessions and even hand-painted models; with "excellent" service, they cater to those with an eye to "the best" – but just make sure "you can afford it."

Honora

▽ 25 | 26 | 24 | E

E 50s | 30 E. 57th St. (bet. Madison & Park Aves.) | 212-308-8707 | www.honora.com

Bauble-lovers need not look any further than this Midtown East showroom, cheered as being "the best place in Manhattan for pearls" including Chinese cultured freshwater and South Sea varieties; with a "wonderful selection" of classic pieces and more "creative", colored gems "not seen anywhere else", it's the go-to "when you can't afford Mikimoto."

Hoodie Shop ◐

26 | 23 | 25 | E

LES | 181 Orchard St. (bet. Houston & Stanton Sts.) | 646-559-2716 | www.thehoodieshop.com

Hooded his-and-hers clothing is the specialty at this LES boutique-cum-event space cofounded by (among others) Questlove and Peter Shapiro, owner of Williamsburg's performance venue Brooklyn Bowl; the casual crew reports "everything about this place is excellent" including the funky feathered theme painted on the walls, plus the lighted marquee, huge screen for projecting retro concert footage and DJ booth in the back.

NEW House of Horology

- | - | - | E

SoHo | 193 Prince St. (Sullivan St.) | 212-203-3384 | www.houseofhorology.com

Founded on the belief that timepieces should be sturdy but not cumbersome, fashionable but not over-the-top and, above all, accessible without breaking the bank, this line of chronographs, sold at a subterranean SoHo shop, also boasts Swiss-style trappings like water-resistant stainless-steel casings; the collection, along with a smattering of vintage watches, is arranged in floating art-galleresque display cases.

Housing Works Thrift Shop

20 | 18 | 16 | I

Chelsea | 143 W. 17th St. (bet. 6th & 7th Aves.) | 718-838-5050 | www.housingworks.org
Additional locations throughout the NY area

"Tremendous finds" await the patient picker at this "never stagnant" local chain considered the "Bergdorf" of thrift outfits, where browsers happen upon "super-fashionable" "vintage and contemporary" clothing and "designer" furniture, all tended by "pleasant, unobtrusive" staffers; each branch "has its own personality", and though displays are "chaotic" and prices can be "all over the map", there's "no junk", plus proceeds go to charity, making this the "best feel-good shopping in NYC."

	QUALITY	DISPLAY	SERVICE	COST

H. Stern
29 | 27 | 27 | VE

E 50s | 645 Fifth Ave. (51st St.) | 212-655-3910 | 800-747-8376 | www.hstern.net

"Be prepared to be pampered with a cocktail", an "attentive staff" and a caliber of "exquisite" service that is as "rare as the H. Stern stones" that glitter and beckon from the exclusive counters of this cosmopolitan Fifth Avenue phenomenon; what a "wonderful selection" attest admirers who lavish themselves and loved ones with "gorgeous" Brazilian-designed watches and "unique jewelry designs" boasting the "finest colored gemstones", all of "incredible quality"; in a word, simply "fabuloso!"

Hugo Boss
27 | 24 | 24 | VE

Meatpacking | 401 W. 14th St. (9th Ave.) | 646-336-8170
SoHo | 132 Greene St. (bet. Houston & Prince Sts.) | 212-965-1300
SoHo | 555 Broadway (bet. Prince & Spring Sts.) | 212-334-9001 ●
W 60s | Shops at Columbus Circle | 10 Columbus Circle, ground fl. (bet. B'way & 60th St.) | 212-485-1900 ●
800-484-6267 | www.hugoboss.com

"Love the style, love the fits" gush gents and ladies who fall for the German label's multiple color-coded collections at this urbane quartet, including the Meatpacking mecca and expanded Columbus Circle triple-decker; the "simple" yet on-trend suits and jackets make you "look like a boss", the "shirts and jeans are perfect for going out to a swanky nightclub", plus "super-helpful" salespeople help you find "last-minute gifts", especially "for the guy in your life"; P.S. Jason Wu now helms BOSS womenswear.

NEW H.W. Carter and Sons
- | - | - | E

Williamsburg | 127 N. Sixth St. (bet. Bedford & Berry Sts.) | Brooklyn | 718-599-7091 | www.hwcarterandsons.com

Resembling a general store of yore but with Williamsburg edge, this neighborhood newcomer dresses dudes of all stripes in its house brand, a sturdy collection of workwear and dungarees with a heritage reaching back 152 years; the expansive space is also stocked with like-minded lines like Engineered Garments, Hancock and Woolrich, punctuated by apothecary goods up front and stained-glass detailing.

IF
29 | 25 | 25 | VE

SoHo | 94 Grand St. (bet. Greene & Mercer Sts.) | 212-334-4964 | www.ifsohonewyork.com

"Always stocking a well-edited selection for the high-end hipster set", this spendy SoHo boutique provides the "avant-garde" items that the cool crowd wears to "galas at BAM or Downtown openings", with a focus on Japanese and Belgian designers; staffers can be standoffish but "they seem to warm up", and even those who deem the offerings "difficult" sometimes find that "occasional all-time favorite" piece here.

Ikea ●
16 | 21 | 14 | I

Red Hook | 1 Beard St. (Otsego St.) | Brooklyn | 718-246-4532 | 888-888-4352 | www.ikea.com

It's worth a trip to this "irreplaceable" Scandinavian chain when in the market for "well-designed furniture" and "cheerful, cheap, colorful stuff for your home"; the "expansive spaces" can "make you dizzy" and these "cool" housewares "aren't made to go the distance", but even so, the "bargains" here are hard to "pass up."

QUALITY | DISPLAY | SERVICE | COST

Ilori ●

- | - | - | E

SoHo | 138 Spring St. (Wooster St.) | 212-226-8276 | www.iloristyle.com
When you're craving designer frames and shades from cult names like Chrome Hearts and Loree Rodkin or style heavyweights like Tom Ford, follow the well-heeled tastemakers to this SoHo wonderland, the flagship of Luxottica, a Milan-based luxury eyewear brand; the performance and high-fashion specs are appealingly displayed on aubergine-tinged Mondrian-like shelves, and opticians are on hand to fill prescriptions.

Il Papiro

▽ 28 | 23 | 20 | E

E 70s | 1021 Lexington Ave. (bet. 73rd & 74th Sts.) | 212-288-9330 | www.ilpapirofirenze.it
"An Italian paper shop from another time and place", this Upper East Side fixture imports "wonderful" hand-marbleized Florentine stationery and cards, along with "everything you need to keep it all organized" (desk accessories, journals, scrapbooks, photo albums, etc.); quaint and well stocked, it's a favored fallback for "small gifts."

Ina

25 | 17 | 16 | E

NEW Chelsea | 207 W. 18th St. (bet. 7th & 8th Aves.) | 212-334-6572
NoHo | 15 Bleecker St. (Elizabeth St.) | 212-228-8511
NoLita | 21 Prince St. (bet. Elizabeth & Mott Sts.) | 212-334-9048
SoHo | 101 Thompson St. (bet. Prince & Spring Sts.) | 212-941-4757
Ina Men
NoLita | 19 Prince St. (bet. Elizabeth & Mott Sts.) | 212-334-2210
www.inanyc.com
Among "the best secondhand stores in the city", this "exciting" consignment chainlet carries "just the right call" – a mix of "gently worn" and vintage designer wear "from eras gone by" for men and women (in separate locations); "I'm wowed every time I walk in and always find something perfect", but the "the good items go quick" – think "50% off Manolos and Hervé Léger dresses."

Inglot Cosmetics

26 | 26 | 22 | M

Chelsea | Chelsea Mkt. | 75 Ninth Ave., 5th fl. (bet. 15th & 16th Sts.) | 212-672-7124
W 40s | 1592 Broadway (48th St.) | 212-247-8169 ●
www.inglotcosmetics.com
Painted ladies head to a "candy shop" of "beautifully displayed", "rainbow-colored cosmetics" at this Chelsea Market–Times Square makeup wonderland, a Polish import brimming with a prism of formaldehyde-free "glitter and matte eye shadows", "powders, blushes, lip glosses" and "custom palettes" with "amazing pigmentation"; adventurers willing to "venture out of their comfort zone" are rewarded with "great-quality" products and tips from a "helpful staff."

In God We Trust

▽ 23 | 21 | 23 | E

NoLita | 265 Lafayette St. (bet. Prince & Spring Sts.) | 212-966-9010
Greenpoint | 70 Greenpoint Ave. (bet. Franklin & West Sts.) | Brooklyn | 718-389-3545
Williamsburg | 129 Bedford Ave. (bet. 9th & 10th Sts.) | Brooklyn | 718-384-0700
www.ingodwetrust.com
Spanning Williamsburg, Greenpoint and NoLita, these "awesome", "friendly and accommodating" boutiques for guys and gals offer "sim-

ple", "smart New York style" including "vintage-inspired designs that look great without screaming 'I'm trying to be a hipster'" and its own IGWT jewelry line; the "well-made" namesake collections just might hit you on a feel-good level too, since they're designed and produced in Brooklyn.

Intermix
24 | 21 | 19 | E

E 70s | 1003 Madison Ave. (bet. 77th & 78th Sts.) | 212-249-7858
Flatiron | 125 Fifth Ave. (bet. 19th & 20th Sts.) | 212-533-9720
Meatpacking | 812 Washington St. (Gansevoort St.) | 646-480-5762
NEW **NoHo** | 332 Bowery (bet. Bond & Great Jones Sts.) | 212-228-8531
SoHo | 98 Prince St. (Mercer St.) | 212-966-5303
W 60s | 210 Columbus Ave. (bet. 69th & 70th Sts.) | 212-769-9116
W Village | 365 Bleecker St. (Charles St.) | 212-929-7180
www.intermixonline.com

Fashionistas agree that this "very New York" boutique chain (including a new Bowery branch) is "hip, hip, hip" and "easy to shop", with a "well-edited collection" of "chic" handbags, "trendy" shoes and "colorful" clothing and accessories from the likes of Equipment, IRO and Giuseppe Zanotti; some say service could be "friendlier", and while the "slim, stylish" customers drop *beaucoup* bucks to "dress like celebrities", others need shades to face the "blinding price tags."

International Center of Photography Store
27 | 23 | 20 | M

W 40s | International Center of Photography | 1133 Sixth Ave. (43rd St.) | 212-857-9725 | www.icp.org

For "anyone interested in photography", this Midtown museum shop is a "gold mine" given its carefully curated selection of "the best books" covering the field, taking in many "hard-to-find" and special-edition tomes; the fun but "selective" lineup of pop cameras, T-shirts and "photo-related gifts" is also worthy of exposure.

Intimacy
26 | 19 | 25 | E

E 60s | 1051 Third Ave. (bet. 62nd & 63rd Sts.) | 646-395-3885
E 90s | 1252 Madison Ave. (90th St.) | 212-860-8366
www.myintimacy.com

"Can a bra change your life? the answer is yes" declare "the well-endowed, barely there and everyone in between" who head to this Eastside lingerie duo for "beautiful", "expensive" brassieres "you don't want to hide"; "make an appointment" and "prepare to be fondled a bit" by the "knowledgeable salespeople" – "it's amazing what the proper fit can do for one's figure"; P.S. they also make custom creations.

NEW Iosselliani
- | - | - | E

Chelsea | 4 W. 29th St. (bet. B'way & Fifth Ave.) | 212-686-2211 | www.iosselliani.com

The Italian jewelry design brand's first U.S. flagship supplies NoMad folk with its signature Swarovski-studded bracelets, stacked rings and bold statement necklaces; spare yet dramatic displays accentuate the selection, but the store's real eye-catcher is a huge statue of King Kong that overlooks the space, the company's own quirky homage to the Big Apple.

QUALITY | DISPLAY | SERVICE | COST

NEW Ippolita

−|−|−| VE

E 60s | 796 Madison Ave. (bet. 67th & 68th Sts.) | 646-664-4240 | www.ippolita.com

The high-end jewelry brand's first stateside store stocks a candy-colored array of high-end but ultrawearable necklaces, bracelets and earrings, all arranged in a snug UES setting built to resemble designer Ippolita Rostagno's own Brooklyn abode; the baubles are eye-catching, but the porcelain chandelier and elaborate, ever-changing window displays also steal the show.

NEW IRO

−|−|−| E

SoHo | 450 Broome St. (Mercer St.) | 212-925-2290 | www.iro.fr

Gallic-fashion fever reaches new heights of chicdom with the arrival of this contemporary brand's SoHo branch, a black-white-and-mirrored corner enclave just steps away from fellow French trendsetters like Isabel Marant and Jerome Dreyfuss; in between massive pillars, floating racks are hung with edgy Euro essentials, including moto jackets, skinny jeans and slouchy tees for guys and girls, with cool footwear to boot.

Isabel Marant

▽ 25 | 26 | 23 | VE

SoHo | 469 Broome St. (Greene St.) | 212-219-2284 | www.isabelmarant.com

"The queen of Paris", renowned for her upmarket, effortlessly cool "French boho wear", lures legions of style mavens to this airy, gallery-esque SoHo outpost, her first store in the U.S.; the "simply fun young clothes" reveal the designer's "imaginative styling of classics" and they're all tempting to "a more contemporary girl", while the jewelry and accessories, particularly the booties, are a huge favorite with fashion editors.

Issey Miyake

28 | 29 | 25 | VE

TriBeCa | 119 Hudson St. (N. Moore St.) | 212-226-0100 | www.isseymiyake.com

Consider it free admission to "an ever-changing museum of style": Frank Gehry's gloriously massive titanium sculpture dominates the "fabulous", "beautifully designed" space that still looks cutting-edge after a decade-plus in TriBeCa, while the namesake designer's innovative, "unbelievably cool" Japanese pieces for 21st-century men and women always win accolades; devoted disciples of this master of minimalism swear "you really don't need anything else in your wardrobe."

IWC Schaffhausen

−|−|−| VE

E 50s | 535 Madison Ave. (54th St.) | 212-355-7271 | www.iwc.com

Specializing in haute horlogerie since 1868, this Schaffhausen, Switzerland–based watchmaker caters to luxury lovers at its Madison Avenue mecca, a sleek and modern cubelike two-level showcase that's also the brand's largest store yet; all of its signature standouts are on hand, including the Portuguese Automatic, the Portofino hand-wound and a special edition of the Big Pilot timepiece, released in tribute to Muhammad Ali's 70th birthday.

Jacadi

28 | 25 | 25 | VE

E 70s | 1260 Third Ave. (72nd St.) | 212-717-9292
E 80s | 1242 Madison Ave. (89th St.) | 212-369-1616

(continued)

Jacadi

W 60s | 1841 Broadway (60th St.) | 212-246-2753
www.jacadi.us

"Your little ones will look like royalty" in "beautiful" outfits from this French childrenswear chain, made with such "exquisite taste" they could easily "become heirlooms"; the "amazing" mix-and-match styles make "absolutely perfect" gifts, but it takes some awfully "deep pockets" to build this baby-sized wardrobe, prompting a few euro-counters to advise "watch for the sales", then "scoop up as much as you can."

JackRabbit Sports

26 | 22 | 27 | M

E 80s | 1255 Lexington Ave. (bet. 84th & 85th Sts.) | 212-727-2981 ◗
Union Sq | 42 W. 14th St. (bet. 5th & 6th Aves.) | 212-727-2980 ◗
W 70s | 140 W. 72nd St. (bet. B'way & Columbus Ave.) | 212-727-2982
Park Slope | 151 Seventh Ave. (bet. Carroll St. & Garfield Pl.) |
Brooklyn | 718-636-9000
www.jackrabbitsports.com

"Be prepared to hit the treadmill" at this chainlet for "avid runners" – the "expert staff" watches your running style to get you into "the right pair of shoes"; it's also a "go-to" for all your cycling, swimming and yoga needs, and though items are "not cheap", shoppers enjoy "awesome" extras, like classes for first-time marathoners and 10%–off incentives.

Jack Rogers

– | – | – | E

E 80s | 1198 Madison Ave. (bet. 87th & 88th Sts.) | 212-259-0588 |
www.jackrogersusa.com

There's more afoot at this longtime label's new East 80s quarters than its Navajo sandal, a colorful favorite of beach-goers once coveted by such 1960s style icons as Jackie Kennedy and Talitha Getty: the sprawling shop boasts Moroccan-style wood screens and black oak floors with well-spaced tables and shelves showcasing ballet flats, wedge espadrilles, pumps and moccasins, all inspired by the iconic thong-toe classic; rounding out the resort-ready, jet-set array are swimsuits, caftans, straw hats and girls' footwear and dresses.

Jack Spade

25 | 24 | 22 | E

SoHo | 56 Greene St. (bet. Broome & Spring Sts.) | 212-625-1820
W Village | 400 Bleecker St. (11th St.) | 212-675-4085
877-917-5225 | www.jackspade.com

The "manbags just can't be beaten" profess professionals who scoop up "gorgeous" "gear for guys" at Andy and Kate Spade's chainlet branches in SoHo and the West Village; the "super–high-quality" accessories exude "functional male chic" and artfully avoid looking "like a purse", plus the digs are homey and the "unbelievably helpful" staff can assist in choosing from the "solid selection" of "restrained" sportswear.

James Perse

24 | 20 | 20 | E

SoHo | 60 Mercer St. (Broome St.) | 212-334-3501
W Village | 361 Bleecker St. (bet. Charles & W. 10th Sts.) | 212-255-5801
W Village | 411 Bleecker St. (bet. Bank & W. 11th Sts.) | 212-620-9991
www.jamesperse.com

"Casualwear never had it so good" agree admirers who descend on this LA designer's West Village and SoHo branches for "beautiful" separates in "top-notch soft cottons" that always have you looking "unfussily fantastic"; some say the lovely apparel "doesn't justify overly high prices", but others are willing to "pay through the nose" for tees that are "the comfiest you will ever wear."

James Robinson
▽ 29 | 26 | 29 | VE

E 50s | 480 Park Ave. (58th St.) | 212-752-6166 | www.jrobinson.com
There's "true artistry" in the "exquisite handmade English silver" (the "more you use it, the better it looks"), George III porcelain and "especially attractive antique jewelry" at this Park Avenue stalwart with roots dating back to 1912; "wonderful" staffers can assist with restoration and direct you to "very original pieces" or reproductions, still made in an 18th-century manner; these are "once-in-a-lifetime purchases for most of us, but they last multiple lifetimes!"

J&R Jr.
24 | 22 | 23 | M

Financial District | 1 Park Row (Ann St.) | 212-238-9000 | www.jr.com
"Kidz rule" at this 15,000-sq.-ft. "funhouse" for the junior set, "conveniently" sited upstairs from the Financial District's electronics superstore J&R Music & Computer World; its "huge inventory" is arrayed in "playful displays" of "trendy", "fairly priced" baby merchandise spanning cribs, car seats and strollers to toys, clothes and other "cool shower gifts"; P.S. should snack time strike, there's a mezzanine cafe.

J&R Music & Computer World
24 | 18 | 19 | M

Financial District | 23 Park Row (bet. Ann & Beekman Sts.) | 212-238-9000 | 800-221-8180 | www.jr.com
"Long live" the "candy store" of "all things techy" cheer champions of this Park Row "staple" that "makes your head spin" with its "huge variety" of "anything that uses electricity" (plus "CDs and DVDs of all kinds") in "multiple" stores spanning a "city block"; between the "sprawling" setup and "spotty service" it's "nothing glamorous", but for "reliable" choices and "competitive pricing", you "gotta love it."

Janovic Plaza
23 | 18 | 19 | M

Hudson Square | 161 Sixth Ave. (Spring St.) | 212-627-1100 | www.janovic.com
Additional locations throughout the NY area
With "lots of locations" this is "the place to go for paint", along with "wonderful" wallpapers, window treatments and "decor ideas" for "nonprofessionals" from folks who "know their stuff", but be prepared to "wait an eternity to have someone who can help you"; despite the "crowded aisles" and "uncomfortable check-out area", "there is a reason the pros shop here" – for the "quality goods" and "competitive prices."

Jay Kos
▽ 29 | 28 | 26 | VE

NoLita | 293 Mott St. (Houston St.) | 212-319-2770 | www.jaykos.com
If you're a Downtown celeb or looking to resemble one, hit this "eclectic" appointment-only "foppish" haberdasher in NoLita, where you'll "slither into the best-fitting and flattering leathers for men" or strut in peacock-hued blazers and, if necessary, escape the paparazzi with a "cigar and scotch in the made-to-measure room downstairs"; the namesake designer is "frequently about and "will fit you himself" – sartorial service "doesn't get any better than this."

| | QUALITY | DISPLAY | SERVICE | COST |

Jazz Record Center
QUALITY 29 | DISPLAY 27 | SERVICE 26 | COST M

Chelsea | 236 W. 26th St., 8th fl. (bet. 7th & 8th Aves.) | 212-675-4480 |
www.jazzrecordcenter.com

"For jump-starting or juicing up your jazz collection", this Chelsea
store is the place to go as choices abound for the aficionado, and it's a
"great place to learn" "for the neophyte" as staffers "know their stuff";
proprietor "Fred Cohen understands what things are worth", buying
and selling LPs and CDs as well as books, videos and ephemera.

J.B. Prince
28 | 20 | 21 | E

Murray Hill | 36 E. 31st St., 11th fl. (bet. Madison & Park Aves.) |
212-683-3553 | 800-473-0577 | www.jbprince.com

"If you're not a chef but want to pretend", this Murray Hill supplier to
"professional" kitchens is the source for cutting-edge cookware à la imported cutlery, pots, pastry molds and other "quality restaurant stuff";
it's all presented in an industrial-style display "on the 11th floor of a non-
descript building", but be ready to fork up since "the best" is "expensive."

J.Crew
22 | 22 | 20 | M

Flatiron | 91 Fifth Ave. (bet. 16th & 17th Sts.) | 212-255-4848
SoHo | 99 Prince St. (bet. Greene & Mercer Sts.) | 212-966-2739
W 50s | Rockefeller Ctr. | 30 Rockefeller Plaza (bet. 5th & 6th Aves.) |
212-765-4227
W 60s | Shops at Columbus Circle | 10 Columbus Circle, 2nd & 3rd fls.
(bet. B'way & 60th St.) | 212-823-9302 ●
800-562-0258 | www.jcrew.com

"Preppy Manhattanites" "never walk out without making a purchase"
from this "stylishly chic" chain peddling "basics, classics and clean lines"
in "bright colors" (plus the bridal collection in the Flatiron); under creative director Jenna Lyons it's become a "trendsetting force", delivering
"perfect for the young professional" ensembles and "adorable" weekend
wear, and if some deem it "pricey", most admit "you can hit the jackpot" at sale time; P.S. a Cobble Hill branch is in the works.

J.Crew Collection
25 | 26 | 22 | E

E 60s | 769 Madison Ave. (66th St.) | 212-824-2500
E 70s | 1035 Madison Ave. (79th St.) | 212-249-3869
www.jcrew.com

For fans of J.Crew, this Madison Avenue offshoot offers a "curated",
"high-fashion" version of the "classic" merchandise at "moderate to expensive" prices; the "swoon-worthy" shops feature "gorgeous" wood
floors and "boudoirlike" dressing rooms tended by "helpful salespeople", "without the overstimulating atmosphere" of the regular stores.

J.Crew Men's
25 | 24 | 20 | E

E 70s | 1040 Madison Ave. (79th St.) | 212-453-2677
SoHo | 484 Broadway (bet. Broome & Grand Sts.) | 212-343-1227
TriBeCa | 235 W. Broadway (White St.) | 212-226-5476
W 60s | Shops at Columbus Circle | 10 Columbus Circle, 2nd fl. (B'way &
60th St.) | 212-956-1120 ●
Ludlow Shop
TriBeCa | 50 Hudson St. (Thomas St.) | 212-587-3139
www.jcrew.com

Specializing in "classics with an updated touch", this chain knows what
fellas want, presenting its "smart", "urban" gear in "cool hangouts",

including the TriBeCa liquor store–cum-boutique, complete with a bar repurposed as a check-out counter, and the antiques-laden Ludlow Shop, specializing in slim-cut suits; collaborations with brands including Sperry Top-Sider and Timex appeal to heritage buffs, while its own oxford shirts "get better with every wash."

Jean-Michel Cazabat

W Village | 350 Bleecker St. (W. 10th St.) | 646-669-8508 | www.jeanmichelcazabat.com

The New York–based French king of "rock 'n' roll shoes" presents his "cutting-edge" designs in a cozy West Village space kitted out with a limestone fireplace, red armchairs and a living-roomlike feel; statement kicks abound, from crocodile boots and metallic oxfords for guys and towering wedge sandals and sparkly evening shoes for ladies, plus exotic-skin purses and other glam goodies.

Jean Shop
▽ 26 | 23 | 23 | E

Meatpacking | 435 W. 14th St. (bet. 9th & 10th Aves.) | 212-366-5326 | www.worldjeanshop.com

"What a memorable experience" exult jeans fans who flock to this Meatpacking mecca for "excellent-quality" raw denim, custom-woven in Japan with its own signature selvedge; the "first-class" staff helps you "find your perfect fit", educating you on wash and wear and narrowing the "overwhelming" choices – no wonder "wowed" customers "cannot understand why anyone would go back" to run-of-the-mill options.

Jeffrey New York ●
27 | 25 | 23 | VE

Meatpacking | 449 W. 14th St. (bet. 9th & 10th Aves.) | 212-206-1272 | www.jeffreynewyork.com

"Like a contemporary museum of clothing" sigh breathless admirers of Jeffrey Kalinsky's "tightly curated" Meatpacking "haunt" brimming with "ultrachic" womenswear, the likes of which "you've just seen in the latest edition of *Vogue*", "high-end" menswear and one of the "best shoe selections in the city", all from "innovative designers" galore; expect "astronomical prices" and a tad of "fashion attitude", but rest assured whatever you purchase will be "the talking piece for your whole outfit."

Jerome Dreyfuss
– | – | – | E

SoHo | 473-475 Broome St. (bet. Greene & Wooster Sts.) | 212-334-6920 | www.jerome-dreyfuss.com

This eponymous French designer presents his chic yet practical handbags, plus a new collection for guys, in this tree house-esque shop with modular Ron Arad seating cubes steps away from his wife Isabel Marant's SoHo boutique; every bag bears a man's name and – whether sporty or slouchy, satchellike or safari-inspired, python or lambskin – boasts jaunty colors and details like pockets, straps and buckles.

Jewish Museum Stores
26 | 24 | 24 | M

E 90s | Jewish Museum | 1 E. 92nd St. (bet. 5th & Madison Aves.) | 212-423-3260
E 90s | Jewish Museum | 1109 Fifth Ave. (92nd St.) | 212-423-3211
www.thejewishmuseum.org

"You don't have to be Jewish to love" this twosome's "wonderful array of Judaica", with the main museum store showcasing "desirable" "books and baubles" (often "reflecting the current exhibit"), while its neighbor is "nice" for "high-quality" "holiday and ritual" pieces; "look no further" for a "meaningful" "remembrance", especially if money's "no object."

Jil Sander
`28 | 27 | 23 | VE`

E 60s | 818 Madison Ave. (bet. 68th & 69th Sts.) | 212-838-6100
SoHo | 30 Howard St. (Crosby St.) | 212-925-2345
www.jilsander.com

Jil herself is back at the design house she built, inspiring renewed pilgrimages to the brand's "gorgeous" SoHo and UES showcases offering "high-end clothing at a premium", from beautifully cut dresses and jackets to a tailored men's collection impeccably crafted in the "most luxurious of fabrics" with structured bags to boot; tended by "unassuming" staffers, the "modern, minimalist" digs "offer a consistent point of view" that matches the spare aesthetic.

Jimmy Choo
`28 | 27 | 26 | VE`

E 50s | 645 Fifth Ave. (51st St.) | 212-593-0800
E 60s | 716 Madison Ave. (bet. 63rd & 64th Sts.) | 212-759-7078
W Village | 407 Bleecker St. (bet. Bank & W. 11th Sts.) | 212-366-1305
www.jimmychoo.com

"Carrie Bradshaw wasn't making this stuff up": the "designer" heels and handbags decking the shelves of these shoe temples are simply "fabulous" and "ooze with sexiness" – "no woman" can resist such "exquisite" designs; "excellent" service makes it all the easier to "fork over" half your "paycheck" to take home these treasures, but your "wardrobe will reach a new level of chic."

J.J. Hat Center
`▽ 28 | 20 | 27 | E`

Garment District | 310 Fifth Ave. (bet. 31st & 32nd Sts.) |
212-239-4368 | 800-622-1911 | www.jjhatcenter.com

As one of the "last great hatters" and among NYC's oldest, this centurian in the Garment District rates a doff of the homburg for its "incredible" collection of "classic", mainly "gents'" headwear including fedoras, newsboys and "Borsalinos galore"; the "old-world" staff ("like you just stepped out of 1959") provides custom-fitting with "unparalleled expertise", but as there's "none finer", these lids "don't come cheap."

J. McLaughlin
`23 | 24 | 22 | E`

E 70s | 1004 Lexington Ave. (72nd St.) | 212-879-9565
E 70s | 1008 Lexington Ave. (bet. 72nd & 73rd Sts.) | 212-879-2240
E 90s | 1311 Madison Ave. (bet. 92nd & 93rd Sts.) | 212-369-4830
Brooklyn Heights | 218 Hicks St. (bet. Montague & Remsen Sts.) |
Brooklyn | 347-599-2818
www.jmclaughlin.com

"Before heading to Nantucket" or the Hamptons, "preppy" practitioners zip over to this "lovely" chainlet championing "quality" men's and women's staples and staffed with "helpful" salespeople; the khakis, blazers and button-downs are turned out in "great colors" galore and "go from day to night with ease", plus it's "all displayed so perfectly."

J. Mendel
`▽ 28 | 26 | 24 | VE`

E 60s | 723 Madison Ave. (bet. 63rd & 64th Sts.) | 212-832-5830 |
www.jmendel.com

"Drop-dead stunning" outerwear and the "most gorgeous dresses" attract luxury-fashion fanatics to the fifth-generation fur house on the

Upper East Side; patrons "love" the displays and chandelier-clad interior, though some find it "intimidating", with "exorbitant" prices fit for the celebrity circuit and affluent Uptown crowd.

NEW JNRL X STR
`- | - | - | M`

LES | 55 Clinton St. (Stanton St.) | 212-729-1655 | www.jnrlstr.com
Pronounced 'general store', this quirky Lower East Side gallery and retail shop specializing in innovative everyday items will fill your gift-giving needs whether you're looking for clever kitchen tools, high-end grooming gear or old-school View-Master slides from the 1960s; the brightly colored inventory pops against stark white walls hung with original artwork.

Joe Fresh
`20 | 21 | 20 | I`

E 40s | 510 Fifth Ave. (43rd St.) | 212-764-1730 ◑
E 80s | 1055 Madison Ave. (80th St.) | 212-472-1505
Flatiron | 110 Fifth Ave. (16th St.) | 212-366-0960 ◑
Garment District | 215 W. 34th St. (bet. 7th & 8th Aves.) | 646-692-9046 ◑
888-495-5111 | www.joefresh.com
Style sleuths "who shop at stores like Zara", "Uniqlo" and other fast-fashion chains "appreciate" the "classic cuts, fresh colors", "edgy versions of trends" and "twists on basics" at this "refreshing addition to the NYC shopping experience", masterminded by Joe Mimran, former owner of Club Monaco; the Canadian chain's "confetti for the eyes" may outfit the family but "will not last forever" – at these "crazy-cheap" prices, "that's ok."

Joe's Jeans
`28 | 24 | 23 | E`

SoHo | 77 Mercer St. (bet. Broome & Spring Sts.) | 212-925-5727 | 877-528-5637 | www.joesjeans.com
A visit to this "iconic" LA-based premium denim brand's "small, cute" SoHo branch is a total "necessity" for blues addicts who find an extensive selection ranging from playful prints to distressed variations, balanced by moto jackets, flannel shirts, tees and casual knitwear; the jeans offer such "great quality for the price" that you may "only need a pair or two, because they'll last you forever."

John Derian Company
`27 | 27 | 22 | E`

E Village | 6 E. Second St. (bet. Bowery & 2nd Ave.) | 212-677-3917
John Derian Dry Goods
E Village | 10 E. Second St. (bet. Bowery & 2nd Ave.) | 212-677-8408
www.johnderian.com
"So creative", these East Village namesakes of the home-decor "genius" show off "beautifully designed and displayed" decoupage plates and glassware in the "lovely" Company shop, balanced by antique furniture and posh bedding, pillows and throws at its Dry Goods sidekick; it's "a don't-miss" duo for "unusual and interesting gifts", though wallet-watchers daresay the "treat" can be a bit "too precious."

John Fluevog Shoes
`28 | 23 | 26 | E`

NoLita | 250 Mulberry St. (Prince St.) | 212-431-4484 | www.fluevog.com
For made-from-scratch, "exquisitely done" kicks "that get noticed", footwear fanatics flock to this corner NoLita shop designed by John Fluevog himself; styles run the gamut from "fashion trendy" to the "funkiest" imaginable, and the staff is "super-attentive" – some have

even been known to "plop down on the floor to lace up your shoes for you"; little wonder cultists gush "you can't go wrong" here.

John Lobb ▽ 29 | 28 | 29 | VE

E 60s | 800 Madison Ave. (bet. 67th & 68th Sts.) | 212-888-9797 | www.johnlobb.com

"Stunning workmanship" characterizes the "classic", "handmade" men's footwear at this Madison Avenue standby; whether you choose custom pairs crafted in Paris that "you will cherish for years" or off-the-shelf styles like loafers, boots and oxfords, yes, "you pay more", but Lobb loyalists proclaim it's "worth every penny" for some of "the best shoes you can put on your feet."

John Varvatos 26 | 26 | 24 | VE

E Village | 315 Bowery (bet. 1st & 2nd Sts.) | 212-358-0315
SoHo | 122 Spring St. (bet. Greene & Mercer Sts.) | 212-965-0700
www.johnvarvatos.com

"Trendy, fashionable", "beautifully cut" menswear draws the "hip and stylish" to this *Fashion Star* mentor/designer's Downtown duo; the airy SoHo shop is "worth a look" but most talk up the Bowery outpost, housed in the former club where Blondie and The Ramones once ruled the stage, exclaiming "CBGB is still alive"; vinyl records, guitars, hi-fi equipment and vintage motorcycle jackets further ramp up the "rock 'n' roll vibe."

Joie ▽ 24 | 24 | 22 | E

E 80s | 1196 Madison Ave. (bet. 87th & 88th Sts.) | 212-837-2220
NEW **Meatpacking** | 429 W. 14th St. (Washington St.) | 212-897-1878
NEW **SoHo** | 114 Wooster St. (bet. Prince & Spring Sts.) | 646-284-9081
www.joie.com

Fans warn: "you won't be able to walk in without coveting" several of designer Serge Azria's "feminine" chiffon pieces that are simply "beautiful"; women "of all ages" love the "flowy, flattering fashions" housed in this "lovely", flower-filled Uptown-Downtown trio, including dreamy sweaters and wear-anywhere dresses that are often spotted on celebs ranging from Diane Kruger to Vanessa Hudgens.

Joinery - | - | - | E

Williamsburg | 263 S. First St. (Havemeyer St.) | Brooklyn | 347-889-6164 | www.joinerynyc.com

Hard-to-find housewares and fashion brands mingle in equal measure at this pine-floored, wood-fronted Williamsburg boutique; former life-style blogger Angela Silva stocks her shop with an offbeat assortment of womenswear, accessories and soft furnishings from international designers, including handmade wovens from Brazil (she's half Brazilian); P.S. there are some guy goods to keep the boys occupied.

Jo Malone 28 | 28 | 26 | E

E 70s | 946 Madison Ave. (bet. 74th & 75th Sts.) | 212-472-0074
W Village | 330 Bleecker St. (Christopher St.) | 212-242-1454
866-566-2566 | www.jomalone.com

"From candles to bath oil, soap to cologne", beauty buffs "can't get enough" of the "gorgeous, unusual fragrance combinations" for body and home at these UES–West Village outposts of the London-based parfumerie; the "exceptional" staff makes you feel like a "welcomed friend" and is "generous with samples", while the products with "chic"

QUALITY | DISPLAY | SERVICE | COST

packaging "deliver as promised" – no wonder scent-ualists become "customers for life."

Jonathan Adler
23 | 24 | 21 | E

E 80s | 1097 Madison Ave. (83rd St.) | 212-772-2410
SoHo | 47 Greene St. (bet. Broome & Grand Sts.) | 212-941-8950
W 70s | 304 Columbus Ave. (74th St.) | 212-787-0017
W Village | 37 Greenwich Ave. (bet. Charles & W. 10th Sts.) | 212-488-2803
Boerum Hill | 378 Atlantic Ave. (bet. Bond & Hoyt Sts.) | Brooklyn | 718-855-0017
877-287-1910 | www.jonathanadler.com

For "retro righteousness" that's "just the right side of twee", hit the "talented designer's" "cute" convoy offering "colorful" "conversation-starters" including "funky, hip ceramics, pillows, furniture and accessories"; "employees are quick and genuine", and the merry merch makes for "cheerful hostess gifts for your favorite quirky friend", though shopping here "requires a substantial dip into the kids' college funds", so consider "saving up to buy something" and then "take three!"

Joseph
▽ 27 | 24 | 26 | E

E 60s | 816 Madison Ave. (bet. 68th & 69th Sts.) | 212-570-0077 | www.joseph.co.uk

When "you need to look fabulous, you need to stop by" this Brit brand's Madison Avenue venue for "the best women's trousers" in town; such urbane sophistication doesn't come cheap and a few lament the "limited" selection, but fashion fiends find these "quality" pants, which come low-slung and extra-long, a perfect fit.

Journelle
29 | 27 | 25 | E

E 70s | 1266 Third Ave. (73rd St.) | 212-255-7804
Flatiron | 3 E. 17th St. (bet. B'way & 5th Ave.) | 212-255-7800
SoHo | 125 Mercer St. (bet. Prince & Spring Sts.) | 212-255-7803
888-885-6876 | www.journelle.com

"It's the only place I buy my bras" proclaim the "modern women" who indulge at this trio of "small, cozy and utterly feminine" "gems" for the "most gorgeous lingerie", loungewear, shapewear and "everyday under-garments" with "more flair" than most; if the "unparalleled" service doesn't make you a convert, the "free decadent chocolate" in the "fantastic dressing rooms" may have you dancing in your birthday suit.

J. Press
25 | 23 | 23 | E

E 40s | 380 Madison Ave. (47th St.) | 212-687-7642 | 888-757-7377 | www.jpressonline.com

If you're after "that cobweb Wasp look", ditch the bush leagues and join the Ivy at this "last bastion of old-fashioned good taste", an East 40s redoubt that's been "serving preppies" since 1902; partisans proclaim that the "American classics" (think khakis, madras blazers, bow ties) are of "superb quality", while the staffers "really know their craft."

NEW J. Press – York Street ◐
- | - | - | E

W Village | 304 Bleecker St. (bet. Barrow & Grove Sts.) | 212-255-6151 | www.jpressonline.com

A descendant of the New Haven tailor that first appeared on Yale's campus in 1902, this preppy menswear line outfits men in attire commensurate with their Ivy League status, but with an updated, slim-cut twist, courtesy of Shimon and Ariel Ovadia, the brother-designers behind the label Ovadia & Sons; the West Village boutique evokes the storied secret societies of the academic elite, replete with worn bookshelves, leather couches and handsome furniture.

Judith Ripka

| 28 | 27 | 26 | VE |

E 60s | 673 Madison Ave. (61st St.) | 212-355-8300
E 60s | 777 Madison Ave. (bet. 66th & 67th Sts.) | 212-517-8200
800-575-3935 | www.judithripka.com

"Stunning" bejeweled baubles in candy colors bring big spenders to the jewelry designer's UES outposts, where diamond-encrusted 18-karat gold rings, earrings, necklaces and bracelets share shelf space with more "affordable" "sterling-silver items", all sure to "go with any outfit"; the gleaming, mirrored spaces make for a serene shopping experience, and so does that "helpful" staff that's on hand to offer "great suggestions."

NEW Juliette Longuet

| - | - | - | E |

E 70s | 153 E. 70th St. (bet. Lexington & 3rd Aves.) | 646-360-3300 | www.juliettelonguet.com

Bringing her brand of Parisian chic to the Upper East Side, the FIT-educated French designer offers dresses, separates and accessories in styles that are both buttoned-up and bohemian; customers can expect to receive personalized service in a tony townhouse adorned with high ceilings, chandeliers and a fireplace.

Jumelle

| - | - | - | E |

Williamsburg | 148 Bedford Ave. (bet. N. 8th & 9th Sts.) | Brooklyn | 718-388-9525 | www.shopjumelle.com

Williamsburg style mavens feel "instant sartorial lust upon entering" this spare-yet-elegant Bedford Avenue boutique offering a "comprehensive" mix of "feminine and timeless" indie brands like A Détacher, A.P.C., Isabel Marant and Rachel Comey complemented by shoes from Dieppa Restrepo and handcrafted jewelry; "warm" service elevates the experience, as does its "unique" luxe boudoir look.

NEW Jung Lee

| - | - | - | E |

Chelsea | 25 W. 29th St. (bet. B'way & 6th Ave.) | 212-257-5655 | www.jungleeny.com

Located in emerging NoMad, near the Ace Hotel, this expansive home decor store boasts a tasteful assortment of high-end porcelain and stemware, offbeat pieces, like decanters corked with animal heads, and affordable plastic goblets – everything hosts need to stage unforgettable dinner parties; the namesake co-owner, a globe-trotting event planner, showcases her wares via imaginative tables settings, flanked by floor-to-ceiling shelves and a library/gift registry to the rear.

Karkula

| - | - | - | E |

Williamsburg | 98 S. Fourth St. (bet. Bedford Ave. & Berry St.) | Brooklyn | 212-645-2216 | www.karkula.com

Parsons grad John Erik Karkula curates the work of influential and lesser known designers at his showroom, which recently crossed the bridge to Williamsburg; furniture, fixtures, artwork and accessories both modern and whimsical are displayed in a spare yet stunning art-gallery-style space, and going forward, the owner also plans to offer pieces of his own design.

	QUALITY	DISPLAY	SERVICE	COST

Kate Spade

| | 25 | 26 | 23 | E |

NEW E 70s | 789 Madison Ave. (67th St.) | 212-988-0259
Flatiron | 135 Fifth Ave. (20th St.) | 212-358-0420 ◑
SoHo | 454 Broome St. (Mercer St.) | 212-274-1991 ◑
866-999-5283 | www.katespade.com

This "ace of style" gives shoppers a "mood lift" at her shops in the Flatiron, East 70s, SoHo and soon, on the UWS, "vibrant", "playful" displays of "super-cute", "ladylike" dresses and jewelry, plus "handbags galore" served up for "sophisticated" dames looking to show their "colorful" side; some wallet-watchers frown at the designer price tags, but there's no denying that the "classic" styles will "last you awhile."

Kate's Paperie

| | 26 | 24 | 20 | E |

NEW SoHo | 188 Lafayette St. (Broome St.) | 212-966-3904
SoHo | 435 Broome St. (bet. B'way & Crosby St.) | 212-941-9816 |
800-809-9880
www.katespaperie.com

"A cornucopia of paper-related goods" "inspire" crafters and gift-givers at this SoHo stationery-and-more store, where "great" staffers tend to "beautifully displayed" boxes, rubber stamps and ribbons that "make you want to throw a party just so you can create cute invitations"; "you sure pay for" the pretty products, but they add "the artful flair that make any present pop"; P.S. the Lafayette Street spin-off specializes in custom printing.

Kathryn Amberleigh

| | - | - | - | E |

NEW Meatpacking | 13 Gansevoort St. (bet. Hudson & W. 4th Sts.) |
212-729-0488
NoLita | 219 Mott St. (bet. Prince & Spring Sts.) | 212-842-2134 ◑
www.kathrynamberleigh.com

Shape matters at Kathryn (and husband Howard) Kim's minimalist NoLita nook and Meatpacking arrival boasting original columns and wood ceiling beams, each filled with footwear in a dizzying array of colors, skins and silhouettes; drawstring slouch booties, '80s-informed neon-colored pumps and leopard peep-toed stilettos sit side by side, but usually not for long, since the designer makes limited numbers of each style.

NEW Khirma Eliazov

| | - | - | - | E |

W Village | 102 Charles St. (bet. Bleecker & Hudson Sts.) |
212-529-1408 | www.khirmaeliazov.com

The former fashion editor launched her line of luxe handbags in 2009 and now, thanks to the arrival of her flagship in a Charles Street brownstone, the upscale inventory is available beyond high-end department stores; the arresting array includes tantalizingly tactile clutches and colorful carryalls crafted from exotic skins and buttery Italian leather, along with clothing and accessories from like-minded designers.

Kid Robot

| | 25 | 26 | 21 | M |

SoHo | 118 Prince St. (bet. Greene & Wooster Sts.) | 212-966-6688 |
877-762-6543 | www.kidrobot.com

When you've "graduated from Hello Kitty", prowl this "hip" SoHo store that salutes Japanese anime with its "clever" "art toys" designed "for and by grown-ups" (think "Smorkin' Labbit, the cigarette-smoking bunny"), including "cool" figurines, limited-edition "collector's" items and "original" tees, hoodies and accessories; no, "the merchandise ain't cheap", but besides having "a bit of character", it's "really a blast."

Kiehl's
27 | 24 | 25 | E

E 60s | 841 Lexington Ave. (64th St.) | 917-432-2511
E Village | 109 Third Ave. (13th St.) | 212-677-3171
Meatpacking | 400 W. 14th St. (9th Ave.) | 212-337-0406
W 60s | 154 Columbus Ave. (bet. 66th & 67th Sts.) | 212-799-3438
800-543-4571 | www.kiehls.com

Bringing dull complexions "back to life" since 1851, this "time-warp chemist of yore" peddles "hard-to-live without" products like "unique cosmetics", "natural" shampoo, "refreshing" "cucumber-herbal" toners and "lovely" body butter ("Creme de Corps: nothing moisturizes better") in an "old-school" setting; "as luxuries go, it's comparatively cheap", and the "ego-boosting" staff is "generous" with both kind words and free samples.

Kiki de Montparnasse
▽ 28 | 29 | 26 | VE

SoHo | 79 Greene St. (bet. Broome & Spring Sts.) | 212-965-8150 | 888-965-5454 | www.kikidm.com

"Seductively naughty" meets sublimely "classy" at this "fabulous" den of decadence in SoHo dedicated to "sexy" things ranging from luxe lingerie and beauty products to instruments of pleasure (silver-tipped riding crop or 24-karat-gold handcuffs, anyone?) that "will make you both lose your breath"; the "beautiful" interior and "welcoming staff" are equally "inviting" – if you have the bucks and a "heartbeat, you need to shop here."

Kirna Zabête
▽ 26 | 24 | 21 | VE

SoHo | 477 Broome St. (bet. Greene & Wooster Sts.) | 212-941-9656 | www.kirnazabete.com

Gladiators of glam bow down to Beth Buccini and Sarah Easley, the "prophetic" proprietors of this "fashion-forward" SoHo boutique who always "hit the right note", even after a decade-plus of being stylishly on the mark; the "fabulously edited collections" of "high-end" womenswear, footwear and accessories from designers like Alexander Wang, Christopher Kane, Lanvin and Thakoon are "all displayed freshly" in the expansive quarters with a "point of view", in fact, "you'll always find something here that you don't see elsewhere."

Kiton
▽ 29 | 29 | 27 | VE

E 50s | 4 E. 54th St. (bet. 5th & Madison Aves.) | 212-813-0272 | www.kiton.it

There's no "going back" after slipping on the "über-fine classic clothing" at this East 50s purveyor of "unsurpassed quality"; in an instant, shoppers are "spoiled for life" with "splurge"-worthy Italian shirts plus off-the-rack and made-to-measure suits that make you feel like a "millionaire"; *sí*, it's "painfully expensive" for many sartorialists, but if you're planning to "wear the hell out of it", look no further.

Kleinfeld
25 | 21 | 24 | E

Chelsea | 110 W. 20th St. (bet. 6th & 7th Aves.) | 212-352-2180 | www.kleinfeldbridal.com

"Wedding dresses, tons of tulle and their own TV show" ensure you'll "say yes to the dress" at Chelsea's "pristine-white", by-appointment-only "ultimate bridal source", offering a "gigantic selection" from designers like Anne Barge, Amsale and Monique Lhuillier, plus shoes, headpieces and eveningwear; the "professional" staff can "fit up a bride and her entourage" and "work within your budget", whether you stick to it or spend "as much as a car that gets great gas mileage"; P.S. grooms can also find top-notch tuxes and suits here.

Knitty City

| 27 | 22 | 27 | M |

W 70s | 208 W. 79th St. (bet. Amsterdam Ave. & B'way) | 212-787-5896 | www.knittycity.com

With "tons of colors", "excellent advice", an "extensive selection of books", "needles, crochet hooks, notions and anything else" "beginners and pros" need, this "homey" West 70s "paradise for knitters" is "hands down" one of "the most down-to-earth, helpful and charming yarn shops in the city"; it's "more of a neighborhood hangout than a store" suggests the purl set – in fact, this "cornerstone" is a "community in itself."

Knoll

| 29 | 22 | 24 | VE |

Chelsea | 76 Ninth Ave., 11th fl. (bet. 15th & 16th Sts.) | 212-343-4000
NEW **W 50s** | 1330 Sixth Ave. (54th St.) | 212-343-4190
800-343-5665 | www.knoll.com

The "real deal" "from the beginning", this furniture icon's midcentury masterworks are "classics of modern design", making its Chelsea showroom an enduring "favorite" for "chic" residential and "office decor" and its new West 50s showcase (spotlighting designer collaborations) well worth a look-see; naturally "perfection" comes "at a price", and the whole kaboodle is sold by staffers who "know every piece in and out."

Korin

| 29 | 24 | 25 | E |

TriBeCa | 57 Warren St. (bet. W. B'way & Church St.) | 212-587-7021 | 800-626-2172 | www.korin.com

"If you're a home chef" seeking "top-notch" knives, you'll know "you've arrived" once you peruse the "amazing selection of Japanese cutlery" laid out in a "museum-quality display" at this TriBeCa outlet of an Osaka supplier to the pros; after your spending appetite's whetted, browse the "sharpening tools", "serving pieces", flatware, "sake sets" and other "imports" sold by the "helpful staff."

Krizia

| ▽ 25 | 25 | 25 | VE |

Meatpacking | 446 W. 14th St. (bet. 9th & 10th Aves.) | 212-879-1211 | www.krizia.it

All chrome, glass and black enamel, the swank Milanese label's starkly modernist Meatpacking home makes a fitting foil to the "beautiful Italian elegance" of the apparel here; aficionados can "always find a great piece" in these richly designed collections, where unorthodox fabric juxtapositions and unusual color palettes come together for a look that's "everything a girl could dream of."

NEW Kurt Geiger

| - | - | - | E |

W Village | 375 Bleecker St. (bet. Charles & Perry Sts.) | 212-367-0830 | us.kurtgeiger.com

The London-based footwear and accessory designer makes his NYC debut with this slim West Village storefront, where guys and girls score styles from four different lines under the brand's umbrella; the inventory is smartly displayed in the mirrored space, complete with an eye-catching shoe chandelier and a red couch where your sidekicks can chill while you strut.

NEW Labor Skateshop | - | - | - | M |

LES | 46 Canal St. (Ludlow St.) | 646-351-6792 | www.laborskateshop.com
Gear up for outings at the the freshly redesigned Coleman Oval Skatepark at this small but impactful LES arrival owned by a longtime skateboarder; gleaming decks, wheels, accessories and apparel from the likes of 5boro, Independent, Alien Workshop and Brixton are displayed like pieces of art against stark white walls.

Lacoste | 24 | 22 | 19 | E |

E 40s | 608 Fifth Ave. (49th St.) | 212-459-2300 ●
E 50s | 575 Madison Ave. (bet. 56th & 57th Sts.) | 212-750-8115
Gramercy | Gansevoort Park Ave. | 420 Park Ave. S. (29th St.) | 646-380-5224
SoHo | 134 Prince St. (bet. W. B'way & Wooster St.) | 212-226-5020
SoHo | 541 Broadway (bet. Prince & Spring Sts.) | 212-219-9203 ●
800-452-2678 | www.lacoste.com
"The croc is still the best" at this "upscale" stalwart that continues to hold court 80 years after French tennis star René Lacoste embroidered the creature on his polo shirt; the pricey sportswear includes men's and women's "classic" separates, from polos and skirts to watches and belts, in bright colors that "get you noticed" and are "suitable for many years after purchase."

Lalique | 29 | 28 | 27 | VE |

E 50s | 609 Madison Ave. (58th St.) | 212-355-6550 | 800-214-2738 | www.lalique.com
"Glass with class!" exult crystal collectors who find it a "pure pleasure" to shop at this Madison Avenue leviathan; whether you're searching for a "high-end wedding or housewarming gift", "lovely" stemware "to toast with", "beautiful quality" figurines, desk accessories or vases, or "exquisite" jewelry such as an art deco pendant or cabochon ring, this storied French company proffers "endless options" that are "both functional and for display."

Lanvin | 28 | 27 | 25 | VE |

E 60s | 815 Madison Ave. (bet. 68th & 69th Sts.) | 646-439-0380 | www.lanvin.com
Designer "Alber Elbaz is a genius" and his women's couture and ready-to-wear creations for this storied French label are both "beautiful" and "interesting" enthuse fans who discover "some of the chicest fashions in the world" at this elegant, multifloor Madison Avenue outpost; the "very helpful staff" and plush decor (think marble floors and antique chandeliers) complete the luxurious shopping experience.

NEW Lanvin Men | - | - | - | VE |

E 60s | 807 Madison Ave. (bet. 67th & 68th Sts.) | 212-812-2866 | www.lanvin.com
Sartorialists scoop up statement designwear at the legendary French brand's first men's stateside store, a handsome townhouse close to the women's UES boutique; mirroring the Parisian gentlemen's outpost with dark wood and metal accents, the first floor boasts sporty polos, hoodies

	QUALITY	DISPLAY	SERVICE	COST

and jackets in luxe fabrics and a wall of fashion-forward signature sneakers (worn by everyone from Jay-Z to Justin Bieber), while the second floor spotlights elegant suitings and a luxe eveningwear salon.

La Perla
	28	27	25	VE

E 60s | 803 Madison Ave. (bet. 67th & 68th Sts.) | 212-570-0050
Meatpacking | 425 W. 14th St. (bet. 9th Ave. & Washington St.) | 212-242-6662
SoHo | 93 Greene St. (bet. Prince & Spring Sts.) | 212-219-0999
877-305-7872 | www.laperla.com

The "sexy windows" lure you into this innerwear brand's Uptown-Downtown branches showcasing "beautiful lingerie" "like the works of art that they are"; yes, it's "expensive" ("can only afford one bra strap"), but "nothing can make you feel more like a woman" than donning these "ooh-la-la" negligees, camis and panties that "leave your better half with unforgettable images" – "you can bet you will get your money's worth."

La Petite Coquette
	28	24	26	E

G Village | 51 University Pl. (bet. 9th & 10th Sts.) | 212-473-2478 | 888-473-5799 | www.thelittleflirt.com

"Women on the hunt" for "beautiful underthings" set their sights on this "super-cute", boudoir-esque Village boutique; whether you're full-figured or less-endowed, owner Rebecca Apsan and her "helpful staff" size you up in a heartbeat, delivering "lingerie to die for"; the panties and such may be "pricey", but it's "worth every single pretty penny" – even better, "buy on your significant other's account."

Layla
	-	-	-	E

Downtown Bklyn | 86 Hoyt St. (bet. Atlantic Ave. & State St.) | Brooklyn | 718-222-1933 | www.layla-bklyn.com

"You can't leave empty-handed" from this stylish "treasure trove of textiles from India" just off booming Atlantic Avenue; the colorful quarters showcase "one-of-a-kind merchandise" including an eponymous natural-material clothing line, "exquisite" brightly-colored and -patterned "towels, bedding and accessories", plus "exceptional jewelry" and exotic footwear from Calleen Cordero.

Lazzoni
	-	-	-	E

Chelsea | 154 W. 18th St. (bet. 6th & 7th Aves.) | 212-242-0606 | www.lazzoni.us

This furniture company's roots extend back to 1950s Turkey, but you'd never know it by the modern designs showcased at its Chelsea showroom; the directional collection on view, including steel-frame sectionals, black lacquer coffee tables and modular shelving, feature Italian leather, Turkish textiles and Austrian hardware, plus there's also a Euro-crafted line that's designed in NYC with the city's notoriously small apartments in mind.

Lederer de Paris
	▽ 26	25	23	E

E 50s | 625 Madison Ave. (bet. 58th & 59th Sts.) | 212-355-5515 | www.ledererdeparis.com

Known for its "fine selection" of handcrafted ladies' bags, plus a "colorful" array of luggage, scarves, ties, shoes and wallets, this East 50s leather goods stalwart offers "attentive" service paired with luxe old-world craftsmanship befitting its 115-year-old heritage; sure, it's expensive, but loyalists attest the merchandise will "still look great in 30 years."

Lee's Art Shop

| 26 | 22 | 21 | M |

W 50s | 220 W. 57th St. (bet. B'way & 7th Ave.) | 212-247-0110 | www.leesartshop.com

If you're "feeling creative", the "cornucopia" of "anything remotely artistic" at this multilevel Midtown "landmark" "has you covered", with a "courteous" staff tending "tons" of "hard-core" "craft supplies", pens, frames, stationery and whatever else "you need to express yourself" ("kids' toys" included); while the "mega-selection" is "tempting", "be careful not to get carried away" since such "quality" can be "pricey."

Lee's Studio

| 25 | 21 | 20 | E |

W 50s | 220 W. 57th St., 2nd fl. (bet. B'way & 7th Ave.) | 212-581-4400 | 877-544-4869 | www.leesstudio.com

A "convenient way to see" lighting options from "lots of manufacturers", this adjunct on the second floor of Lee's Art Shop shines with an "outstanding selection" of some 1,000 "cool and funky" contemporary lamps alongside "top-notch" home and office furniture; maybe it's "not as cheap as" some, but prices are relatively "competitive", and a bright staff is on hand "when you have questions."

Leffot

| - | - | - | VE |

W Village | 10 Christopher St. (bet. Gay St. & Waverly Pl.) | 212-989-4577 | www.leffot.com

"Calm the shakes in between commissions from London custom" specialists at this "minimalist" West Village dandy offering men's shoes that are "guaranteed to last and age with character", from exclusives on Euro lines like Alfred Sargent, Gaziano & Girling and Pierre Corthay to high-enders like Alden, Church's and Edward Green to made-to-order styles; the "superb quality" goods are "exquisite without being too swanky" and sure to "get you started on the right foot."

LEGO

| 26 | 27 | 20 | E |

W 40s | Rockefeller Ctr. | 620 Fifth Ave. (bet. 49th & 50th Sts.) | 212-245-5973
Elmhurst | Queens Center Mall | 90-15 Queens Blvd. (bet. 57th Ave. & 90th St.) | Queens | 718-699-4565 ◑
800-453-4652 | www.lego.com

Imaginations run wild at this "must-see" Rockefeller Center "attraction" and Queens Center offshoot, where "nerds and tourists" spend "hours" exploring the toy-filled space; you'll "want to build something, even if you're over the age of 10" after perusing the flagship's Master Builder bar, "tiny" NYC dioramas and computer stations for designing custom kits – as long as you don't mind quarters "so packed" you "start to feel like a LEGO brick" yourself.

NEW Leica

| - | - | - | E |

SoHo | 460 W. Broadway (bet. Houston & Prince Sts.) | 212-475-7799 | www.leicastoresoho.com

A pacesetter on the camera front for nearly 100 years, the iconic German brand offers its entire portfolio of hand-assembled equipment at its new SoHo digs, including the celeb 'accessory', the M-System range finder, plus sport optics devices like binoculars and telescopes;

QUALITY DISPLAY SERVICE COST

striking in black and white with red lighting, the sleek space doubles as a photo gallery and high-end items are displayed in cases like precious artwork.

Leonard Opticians

27 | 23 | 27 | VE

E 70s | 1264 Third Ave. (bet. 72nd & 73rd Sts.) | 212-535-1222
W 50s | 24 W. 55th St. (bet. 5th & 6th Aves.) | 212-246-4452
www.leonardopticians.com

"They get you seeing and looking good" at this crosstown pair of eyewear boutiques, where a "wonderful selection" of some 8,000 frames from the most voguish names is custom-fit with a "personal" touch by an "attentive, professional" team; yes, their specs may "cost the mint", but if your sights are set on "top quality" it's "worth every cent" ("love these folks").

Les Petits Chapelais

- | - | - | E

SoHo | 146 Sullivan St. (bet. Houston & Prince Sts.) | 212-625-1023 |
www.lespetitschapelaisnyc.com

French owner Dominique Simonneaux recently relocated her childrenswear standby to larger, splashier SoHo digs, offering cheerful goods that run the gamut from the whimsical to the practical; the concept shop is carefully arranged by age, highlighting covetable, lesser-known European lines such as Toit de la Lune along with reliable basics from Petit Bateau, capped with super-stylish shoes and boots in bright colors and metallics.

Lester's

23 | 17 | 20 | E

E 80s | 1534 Second Ave. (80th St.) | 212-734-9292
Sheepshead Bay | 1120 Ave. U (bet. Coney Island Ave. & 12th St.) |
Brooklyn | 718-375-7337
866-666-8766 | www.lestersnyc.com

"Best known for its tween-and-under offerings", this "one-stop-shopping" Sheepshead Bay–UES resource remains "mom heaven", "maintaining its fashion sense" with "head-turning" clothes, accessories and shoes from labels like Billabong, Splendid and Superga; "get them set for camp with customized" gear here, or up to speed on "all the latest trends" in juniors' sportswear and even formalwear (and don't overlook the "fantastic baby department").

Levi's Store

23 | 20 | 19 | M

E 50s | 750 Lexington Ave. (bet. 59th & 60th Sts.) | 212-826-5957
Flatiron | 414 W. 14th St. (bet. 5th & 6th Aves.) | 212-242-2128 ●
Garment District | 45 W. 34th St. (bet. 5th & 6th Aves.) |
212-643-4358 ●
Meatpacking | 25 W. 14th St. (bet. 9th Ave. & Washington St.) |
212-367-2110
SoHo | 495 Broadway (bet. Broome & Spring Sts.) | 646-613-1847 ●
W 40s | 1501 Broadway (bet. 43rd & 44th Sts.) | 212-944-8555 ●
800-872-5384 | www.levisstore.com

"The daddy" of denim offers "all-American casualwear" at "reasonable prices" in these citywide storefronts, where the "classic" brand is "still rocking" after 160 years and focuses on premium, cutting-edge blueswear at its Meatpacking outpost; "kind and willing" salespeople help navigate aisles that are understandably "overrun with tourists" – after all, "everyone should have a pair" of these jeans.

Lexington Gardens

24 | 26 | 23 | E

E 70s | 1011 Lexington Ave. (bet. 72nd & 73rd Sts.) | 212-861-4390 | www.lexingtongardensnyc.com

Private Park Avenue terraces and garden-apartment plots are prettied up by this "charming" Upper East Side store, where there is "something new to catch the eye" in "always"-changing displays of "quirky" topiaries, elegant urns and "attractive" dried floral arrangements that are elevated to art; the owners also offer styling services, executing transformations of outdoor spaces into urban oases.

NEW Liebeskind Berlin

- | - | - | M

SoHo | 276 Lafayette St. (bet. Houston & Prince Sts.) | 212-993-7894 | www.liebeskind-berlin.com

Designed in – where else – but Berlin, this urbane, handcrafted collection of leather goods is displayed in a SoHo shop with cement floors, copper tables, high museum cabinets and an industrial feel inspired by its native city; the curated range includes sporty buckled handbags, metallic clutches and studded bowling styles along with phone accessories, wallets, shoes and belts, each revealing unique characteristics and priced somewhat within reach.

Lighting By Gregory

23 | 16 | 16 | M

LES | 158 Bowery (bet. Broome & Delancey Sts.) | 212-226-1276 | 800-807-1826 | www.lightingbygregory.com

The "best on the Bowery" for "modern" illuminations, this "busy" LES lighting shop has "cutting-edge" designs and a "fabulous collection" of "brand names", making it "one of the best lamp stores in existence"; the space is "jammed to the gills with fixtures and sconces", so "it helps to know what you want", since service sometimes leaves you in the dark.

Ligne Roset

26 | 23 | 23 | VE

Flatiron | 250 Park Ave. S. (20th St.) | 212-375-1036
SoHo | 155 Wooster St. (Houston St.) | 212-253-5629
800-297-6738 | www.lignerosetny.com

"Temples of modernism", this family-owned French label's SoHo and Flatiron stores are home to "gorgeous furniture" with "great style" and "killer quality" – and "prices to match"; fine service and the fact that their designs, particularly the sleek sofa beds and chic storage systems, "fit in New York apartments" mean most think a visit is well worth it when feathering your nest.

Lilly Pulitzer

27 | 26 | 24 | E

E 70s | 1020 Madison Ave. (bet. 78th & 79th Sts.) | 212-744-4620 | 888-725-4559 | www.lillypulitzer.com

"Pretend you're a Palm Beach heiress" like its late namesake founder at this "tried-and-true" brand's "beautiful" two-floor branch, a Madison Avenue "must-stop" for any country club aspirant; "it's impossible not to be cheered up by the colorful togs" for women, men and kids, with preppy patterns that make you "look and feel special" – "you want to think you're too trendy for it, but the hot pink is irresistible."

Lisa Perry

- | - | - | VE

E 70s | 988 Madison Ave. (77th St.) | 212-334-1956 | www.lisaperrystyle.com

This "store is an outfit" say admirers of this bold designer's starkly white Madison Avenue digs, the perfect backdrop – complete with retro "lounge chairs and spacious areas for browsing" – to show off the "colorful", whimsical wares inside; a curated cache of vintage clothes mixes with Perry's own Pop Art–inspired creations, including home accessories, "knickknacks" and those mod "shades-of-the-'60s" shift dresses, "standards at any event in the Village."

Little Eric   ▽ 26 | 25 | 26 | E

E 80s | 1118 Madison Ave. (bet. 83rd & 84th Sts.) | 212-717-1513
"Perfect in every way", this brightly colored Madison Avenue standby with a playful amusement park feel, horsey ride and train sets has everything for junior's feet, and a few styles (some matching) for mom and dad too; the "very fashionable" footwear, including its signature walking shoes, is handcrafted in Italy from top-notch leathers and sold by "helpful personnel."

L.K. Bennett   23 | 22 | 23 | E

W 50s | Shops at Columbus Circle | 10 Columbus Circle, 2nd fl. (B'way) | 212-309-7559 | www.lkbennett.com
Hit your fashion stride at Londoner Linda Bennett's "beautiful" glossy-white Time Warner Center shop spotlighting the "luxury" brand's signature footwear collection; styles run the gamut from Lurex sandals to patent kitten heels, while the ladylike accessories and apparel are "very complementary"; another Ben-efit: shoppers are "very impressed" by the way "attentive" staffers "approach everyone."

L'Occitane ●   26 | 24 | 24 | E

E 80s | 180 E. 86th St. (bet. Lexington & 3rd Aves.) | 212-722-5141 | www.loccitane.com
Additional locations throughout the NY area
The "closest you'll get to Provence" in NYC, this "aromatherapy haven" purveys some of the "best body care potions" around, including "gorgeous shower gels" and "lovely, long-lasting" lemon verbena and lavender soaps and hand creams "enriched with shea butter" that "smell like the South of France"; these "balms" "come at a price", but they're an "affordable luxury", and the "attractive packaging" makes for "welcome hostess gifts."

Loehmann's ●   20 | 12 | 11 | M

Chelsea | 101 Seventh Ave. (bet. 16th & 17th Sts.) | 212-352-0856
W 70s | 2101 Broadway (74th St.) | 212-882-9990
Kingsbridge | 5740 Broadway (236th St.) | Bronx | 718-543-6420
Sheepshead Bay | Sheepshead Bay Marina | 2807 E. 21st St. (Emmons Ave.) | Brooklyn | 718-368-1256
855-563-4626 | www.loehmanns.com
Loyalists are "literally addicted" to this "quintessential" discounter offering popular brands at "amazing prices" in a setting that "has all the charm of a supermarket"; salespeople "can't be bothered", dressing areas are communal and scouring the "hit-or-miss" racks is "a chore", but bargain-seekers say it's worth the "treasure hunt", especially if you "snag" a "top-designer" deal in the Back Room.

Longchamp   27 | 24 | 24 | E

E 60s | 713 Madison Ave. (bet. 63rd & 64th Sts.) | 212-223-1500
SoHo | 132 Spring St. (bet. Greene & Wooster Sts.) | 212-343-7444

(continued)

Longchamp

W 40s | Rockefeller Ctr. | 610 Fifth Ave. (bet. 49th & 50th Sts.) |
212-315-1365
877-566-4242 | www.longchamp.com

This "Paris saddlemaker does a *bon* job" delivering "more than just those ubiquitous leather and cloth bags for sorority girls" at its trio of shops in Midtown, the East 60s and SoHo; the "popular staples of quality and practicality" – "durable, waterproof and light" "signature fabric totes" and a duffel that "folds up to nothing but is there when you need it" – come "without the hackneyed logos" of other status houses, plus these keepers "last and last!"

Lord & Taylor ❶

| 25 | 23 | 22 | M |

Murray Hill | 424 Fifth Ave. (bet. 38th & 39th Sts.) | 212-391-3344 |
800-223-7440 | www.lordandtaylor.com

A "class act", this venerable Murray Hill department store mixes "old-time retailing with a modern-day appeal", making it the "go-to spot" for savvy shoppers who appreciate the "cordial, attentive" service and "wonderful selection" that runs the gamut from "awesome" shoes and "wardrobe basics – lingerie, cosmetics, gloves" – to "beautiful gowns and party dresses"; fans "love the animated Christmas windows", and when it's sale time and you're "armed with your coupons", well, it's "the best."

Loro Piana

| 29 | 27 | 26 | VE |

E 60s | 748 Madison Ave. (bet. 64th & 65th Sts.) | 212-980-7961 |
www.loropiana.com

"You have to pet everything here to believe how amazing" it is agree tactile sorts who give the "exquisite merchandise" at this four-story Madison Avenue mecca a big hand; from his-and-hers "chic wardrobe staples in gorgeous Italian fabrics" to bespoke menswear and "the best cashmere in the world", all with a "European flair", this is where "haute couture" meets "haughty service", and the steep price tags are "worth every penny."

Louis Vuitton

| 28 | 28 | 25 | VE |

E 50s | 1 E. 57th St. (5th Ave.) | 212-758-8877
SoHo | 116 Greene St. (bet. Prince & Spring Sts.) | 212-274-9090
866-884-8866 | www.vuitton.com

"Exquisite, expensive and exclusive", the "very high-end" French brand's "must-visit" emporiums "ooze luxury" with "timeless" handbags and luggage bearing "traditional LV logos" "that will get passed down the generations" and "beautiful" Marc Jacobs–designed apparel; the Midtown flagship, with its "lavish" windows, is "as much a museum as it is a store", while the recently expanded SoHo satellite is "hipper", and both offer "speedy" if sometimes "snooty" service and covetables that set "a standard by which others can be judged."

Love Adorned

| 27 | 27 | 25 | E |

NoLita | 269 Elizabeth St. (bet. Houston & Prince Sts.) | 212-431-5683 |
www.loveadorned.com

Lori Leven's "fabulous" skylit NoLita loft, an offshoot of New York Adorned ("one of the best tattoo and piercing parlors in the city"), exudes a tough, earthy feel, stocking a "uniquely edited mix" of leather goods, ceramics and vintage and "beautifully handcrafted jewelry" from an "ever-changing roster" of artisans; the "eclectic" wares are "displayed in such a way that everything seems special" – in fact, you'll "feel like you won a prize with your purchase."

Lovely

| - | - | - | E |

W Village | 313 W. Fourth St. (bet. Bank & W. 12th Sts.) | 212-924-2050 | www.lovelybride.com

"If you're looking for an intimate" bridal shopping "experience" book an appointment at this "small" West Village brownstone offering gowns from specialists like Carol Hannah, Nicole Miller and Lea Ann Belter, at moderate to budget-busting prices; faux jewels, hair ornaments, veils and sashes round out the lovely selection, all sold by "super-helpful" assistants who are "not pushy at all"; P.S. a TriBeCa addition is in the works.

Lower East Side Tenement Museum Bookshop

| 26 | 25 | 24 | M |

LES | 103 Orchard St. (bet. Broome & Delancey Sts.) | 212-982-8420 | www.tenement.org

Now in a more "spacious location", this Lower East Side museum store "takes you back in time" with its "outstanding book selection" that "represents the immigrant experience" as well as "the history of this fabulous city"; add "NY-oriented" "tchotchkes" that offer "maximum learning opps", and it's a "unique" source of "classy" keepsakes "for tourists and residents" alike.

Lucky Wang

| 24 | 22 | 23 | E |

Chelsea | 82 Seventh Ave. (bet. 15th & 16th Sts.) | 212-229-2900
NEW **E 90s** | 1435 Lexington Ave. (bet. 93rd & 94th Sts.) | 212-360-6900
G Village | 799 Broadway (bet. 10th & 11th Sts.) | 212-353-2850
866-353-2850 | www.luckywang.com

"When you need a baby gift to impress" or just want to outfit your offspring in "really cute" Asian-inspired togs, get lucky at this Uptown/Downtown trio; with "charming" kimonos packaged in Chinese-takeout-type containers and "window displays that invariably bring a smile", it's one of the "most adorable" destinations for children's attire; other fortunate finds: fuzzy tinsel accessories, table lamps and pillows.

Lulu Guinness

| ∇ 24 | 24 | 23 | E |

W Village | 394 Bleecker St. (bet. 11th & Perry Sts.) | 212-367-2120 | www.luluguinness.com

"Funky and offbeat" accessories are the specialty at this Brit wit's West Villager featuring "whimsical" and "one-of-a-kind" items with cleverly printed handbags, wallets, umbrellas and other tchotchkes that are "fun for the younger set" and perfect "if you want to be different"; the gleaming white storefront, quirky displays and creative wares are designed to "make you smile."

Lululemon Athletica

| 27 | 23 | 25 | E |

E 80s | 1146 Madison Ave. (85th St.) | 212-452-1909
NEW **Meatpacking** | 408 W. 14th St. (bet. 9th Ave. & Washington St.) | 212-255-2978
SoHo | 481 Broadway (bet. Broome & Grand Sts.) | 212-334-8276
Union Sq | 15 Union Sq. W. (bet. 14th & 15th Sts.) | 212-675-5286
W 60s | 1928 Broadway (64th St.) | 212-712-1767 ◗

(continued)

Lululemon Athletica

W 70s | 2139 Broadway (75th St.) | 212-362-5294
NEW **Cobble Hill** | 166 Smith St. (Wyckoff St.) | Brooklyn | 718-852-6713
Park Slope | 472 Bergen St. (bet. 5th & Flatbush Aves.) | Brooklyn |
718-636-6298
877-263-9300 | www.lululemon.com

"Get your sweat on in style" at this "yoga heaven", where the "extremely versatile" "high-end" "amazing activewear" is like a "gift to your self image" since it "actually makes you look good", plus the "staff of perky yogis" is "skilled and sweet"; sure, it's "spendy", but "clotheshorses" delight in the "regularly released" new colors and designs, claiming "there's a fit for everyone."

Lush

25 | 24 | 24 | M

NEW **E 80s** | 206A E. 86th St. (3rd Ave.) | No phone
Garment District | 1293 Broadway (bet. 33rd & 34th Sts.) | 212-564-9120 ◗
SoHo | 529 Broadway (bet. Prince & Spring Sts.) | 212-925-2323 ◗
Union Sq | 7 E. 14th St. (bet. 5th Ave. & University Pl.) | 212-255-5133 ◗
W 70s | 2165 Broadway (bet. 76th & 77th Sts.) | 212-787-5874 ◗
888-733-5874 | www.lush.com

"Fancy" soaps, "fresh" cosmetics and "heavenly" shower jellies and bubble bars are "as natural as possible" at this "socially responsible" bath and beauty chainlet, where the "goodies" smell so "fresh and tasty" that buyers "don't know whether to rub them on their hands or lick them off their fingers"; "all price points are available" and staffers are "consistently amazing", though some say the "vibrant, colorful" shops can be "aggressively" fragrant.

Lyric Hi-Fi, Inc.

∇ 29 | 24 | 27 | VE

E 80s | 1221 Lexington Ave. (bet. 82nd & 83rd Sts.) | 212-439-1900 |
www.lyricusa.com

Hard-core fidelity freaks wax lyrical over this Upper East Side fixture's "top-of-the-line" audio and "(some) video" equipment, displayed in a "refined" setting with six sound rooms to "let the buyer test a broad range" of systems; you "don't come here looking for moderately priced" goods, but the "big bucks" buy "excellent service", including installation of "really complicated setups."

M.A.C. Cosmetics

26 | 24 | 22 | M

SoHo | 506 Broadway (bet. Broome & Spring Sts.) | 212-334-4641 |
800-588-0070 | www.maccosmetics.com
Additional locations throughout the NY area

Makeup junkies go wild at this cosmetics chain that's a "grown-up's play-land" with its house brand of "all the new lipstick colors", "richly pigmented" blushes and "a rainbow assortment of look-at-me shadows and liners"; stylists "know their stuff" and stand ready "to give you a new look" – they'll even do makeovers on the spot, though you may feel "obligated to buy something."

Mackage

- | - | - | M

SoHo | 123 Mercer St. (Prince St.) | 212-925-1455 | 866-973-5287 |
www.mackage.com

At the first sign of cool weather, fashionistas flock to this Canadian outerwear maven's SoHo offshoot for sleek, well-tailored pieces that

QUALITY DISPLAY SERVICE COST

belie just how warm they are; with its myriad styles for guys and gals, including luxe shearlings, belted trenches, rugged leather bombers and puffy down jackets, this shop's got everyone covered – and now there's women's apparel too.

MacKenzie-Childs
27 | 27 | 25 | VE

W 50s | 20 W. 57th St. (bet. 5th & 6th Aves.) | 212-570-6050 | 888-665-1999 | www.mackenzie-childs.com
It's "whimsy all the way" at this "wonderful" West 50s boutique, starting with the "unusual and charming" china accessories it's famed for and going straight through to "over-the-top" furniture, garden accessories and "unique" gifts, all "lovingly displayed"; loyalists long to "get lost in the checks and florals" but rue that you "have to be in the one-percent bracket" to buy these "beautiful" items; still, "everyone needs at least one M-C piece."

Maclaren
27 | 23 | 24 | E

SoHo | 150 Wooster St. (bet. Houston & Prince Sts.) | 212-677-2700 | 888-805-0100 | www.shopmaclarenbaby.com
"Every parent needs one!" declare devotees of this British stroller brand that "sets itself apart" from the pack with its "high-quality", lightweight models, plus designer buggies from the likes of Dylan's Candy Bar by Volo and Cath Kidston, all on display at its SoHo showroom; accessories like footmuffs and mosquito nets will keep little ones comfy in all climes, while tune-ups come courtesy of an on-site repair shop.

Macy's ◑
23 | 21 | 18 | M

Garment District | 151 W. 34th St. (bet. B'way & 7th Ave.) | 212-695-4400
Parkchester | 1441 Metropolitan Ave. (Wood Ave.) | Bronx | 718-828-7000
Downtown Bklyn | 422 Fulton St. (bet. Gallatin Pl. & Hoyt St.) | Brooklyn | 718-875-7200
Kings Plaza | Kings Plaza Shopping Ctr. | 5400 Ave. U (Flatbush Ave.) | Brooklyn | 718-253-3100
Douglaston | 242-02 61st Ave. (Douglaston Pkwy.) | Queens | 718-225-7300
Flushing | 136-50 Roosevelt Ave. (bet. Main & Union Sts.) | Queens | 718-358-9000
Rego Park | 90-01 Queens Blvd. (90th St.) | Queens | 718-271-7200
New Springville | Staten Island Mall | 112 Richmond Hill Rd. (Richmond Ave.) | Staten Island | 718-761-3000
800-289-6229 | www.macys.com
Rated NYC's Most Popular department store, the "behemoth" Herald Square "landmark" (and its myriad branches) sells "anything you could possibly want", including clothing, accessories and housewares at prices "for every pocketbook"; staffers "could be more attentive", and "overwhelmed" visitors hiss it's a "perennial zoo", suggesting you "bring a map" to navigate the "many wings"; still, shoppers rave about the flagship's "outstanding" holiday displays and "fantastic" sales and, with the opening of its new women's shoe floor, billed as the world's largest, they can now find infinite footwear choices to boot.

Madewell ●

| 23 | 22 | 21 | M |

Flatiron | 115 Fifth Ave. (19th St.) | 212-228-5172
SoHo | 486 Broadway (Broome St.) | 212-226-6954
www.madewell.com

J.Crew's "younger sister" brand attracts a "hipster" crowd to its expansive, Corinthian-columned Flatiron flagship and cozier SoHo outpost, both of which have an intimate, "'I'm in someone's closet' feel", with antiques and knickknacks scattered among the faded jeans and shrunken oxford shirts; the merch boasts a "little edginess" – there's always something to "intrigue the buyer" – plus on-site denim alterations keep 'em coming back for more.

Maison Kitsuné ●

| - | - | - | VE |

Chelsea | NoMad Hotel | 1170 Broadway (28th St.) | 212-481-6010 | www.kitsune.fr

Deep-pocketed hipsters who prefer their oxford shirts, cashmere sweaters and trousers cut just so with a soupçon of elegance lay down significant greenage for this Parisian label's cult goods, all housed at this bright NoMad Hotel boutique; the owners – a Daft Punk vet and a Japanese architect – also sell music from their same-name record label and inform the space with graceful Gallic touches like parquet floors and prints of French landmarks.

Maison Martin Margiela

| - | - | - | VE |

W Village | 801-803 Greenwich St. (bet. Jane & W. 12th Sts.) | 212-989-7612 | www.maisonmartinmargiela.com

Though the namesake designer is no longer with this fashion house, his labels and provocative style sensibility forge on at this "superb" sub-rosa West Villager boasting connected-but-separate storefronts for men and women; the understated yet conceptual "special threads" like deconstructed cashmere sweaters are artfully arranged in an all-white, unfinished space that's more "gallery than store" – another reason why tastemakers say it tops their "list of must-things to visit in NYC."

Maje

| - | - | - | E |

NEW E 80s | 1070 Madison Ave. (81st St.) | 212-288-2550
NoLita | 10 Prince St. (bet. Bowery & Elizabeth St.) | 212-226-0426
SoHo | 145 Spring St. (Wooster St.) | 212-775-8330
W Village | 417 Bleecker St. (Bank St.) | 646-666-0000
www.maje.com

"Totally Gallic in style" gush Francophiles who "want each one" of the approachable women's designs from this hip French brand, including cape dresses, fringed leather jackets and standout accessories, all displayed at its Uptown-Downtown branches (most located near Sandro, owned by the designer's relatives); the goods cost a pretty euro, but the store decor is as chic as a Parisian apartment and service is "personal", which help soften the blow.

NEW Makerbot Store

| - | - | - | M |

NoHo | 298 Mulberry St. (bet. Bleecker & Houston Sts.) | 347-457-5758 | www.makerbot.com

The future has arrived, at least at this NoHo retailer/workshop that introduces customers to the wonders of its namesake 3-D printer, a groundbreaking device that allows users to design their own gadgets and doodads and produce real-life creations by heating special plastics that harden in a nano-second; techies can shop for bot-made gifts and supplies for said machines, watch live demos or take classes.

Make Up For Ever   ▽ 28 | 26 | 25 | M

G Village | 8 E. 12th St. (bet. 5th Ave. & University Pl.) |
212-941-9337 | 877-757-5175 | www.makeupforever.com

Makeup artists and beauty buffs find "everything they need" at this Greenwich Village cosmetics mecca, where the brand's "professional"-grade foundations, powders, liners and lipsticks are "the best"; potions might be pricey, but coverage is flawless, leading theatrical enthusiasts to say "they're not just selling makeup, they're selling hope."

Malcolm Shabazz Harlem Market ❶⇆   20 | 21 | 21 | M

Harlem | 52 W. 116th St. (bet. 5th Ave. & Malcom X Blvd.) |
212-987-8131

A canopied bazaar devoted to African handicrafts and textiles, this "Harlem staple" has vendors aplenty dealing in "imported" "goodies" like leather bags, jewelry, traditional clothes, fabrics, wooden masks and more; it helps to know "what's authentic and what's mass-produced", but "cheap exotic goods" abound once you "learn the lay of the land."

Malia Mills Swimwear   26 | 18 | 25 | E

E 70s | 1031 Lexington Ave. (bet. 73rd & 74th Sts.) | 212-517-7485
E 80s | 1225 Madison Ave. (bet. 88th & 89th Sts.) | 212-410-4787
NoLita | 199 Mulberry St. (bet. Kenmare & Spring Sts.) |
212-625-2311
W 70s | 220 Columbus Ave. (70th St.) | 212-874-7200
Boerum Hill | 375 Atlantic Ave. (bet. Bond & Hoyt Sts.) | Brooklyn |
347-799-1600
800-685-3479 | www.maliamills.com

"The secret" to this designer's eponymous swimwear biz is the "incredibly helpful" staff, which "works with you to find the perfect" suit, whether you're 30A or 40DDD; fans do back flips over the "timeless", "supremely made" "mix-and-match" styles available in "fantastic" fabrics with "funky yet tasteful" cover-ups, dresses, hats and flip-flops to go with, so the only downside is "paying for each piece separately (sigh)."

Malin + Goetz ❶   28 | 26 | 27 | E

Chelsea | 177 Seventh Ave. (bet. 20th & 21st Sts.) | 212-727-3777
W 80s | 455 Amsterdam Ave. (82nd St.) | 212-799-1200
877-777-2021 | www.malinandgoetz.com

Groupies gush over the "indie skincare" products purveyed at this minimalist, lablike Chelsea-UWS duo, citing "smooth", hydrating lotions, "wonderful" shampoos and grooming goodies with "fabulous scents" such as "cilantro and peppermint" that "linger for a moment"; the stores are "as pristine as the packaging", and though prices are on the high side, the "knowledgeable, friendly" staff is "super-generous" with free samples.

M&J Trimming/Bridal ❶   25 | 21 | 20 | M

Garment District | 1008 Sixth Ave. (bet. 37th & 38th Sts.) |
212-391-6200 | 800-965-8746 | www.mjtrim.com

With "oceans of notions", you "could lose hours browsing for the perfect button", ribbon or trim at this Garment District veteran known for its "amazing" inventory ("if you can't find it here, it probably doesn't exist"); "there aren't many like this anymore" so few mind that "prices

are on the higher side"; P.S. "crafty brides on a budget" should inves-
tigate their "DIY sashes and hairpieces."

Manolo Blahnik

29 | 27 | 26 | VE

W 50s | 31 W. 54th St. (bet. 5th & 6th Aves.) | 212-582-3007 |
www.manoloblahnik.com

"Once you're done looking at the real art at MoMA", cross the street
and check out the "wearable art" by the "original king of luxury footwear", lining this "elegant" West 50s "jewel box"; the "gorgeous",
"fancy" heels are "comfortable enough to climb Mount Everest" and
come at prices "equivalent to buying a Picasso", but if you want to "indulge your inner Carrie Bradshaw", this "shoe nirvana" is where it's at.

Marc by Marc Jacobs Mens

▽ 26 | 23 | 22 | E

W Village | 382 Bleecker St. (Perry St.) | 212-929-0304 |
877-707-6272 | www.marcjacobs.com

Quirky threads at "low-ish prices" draw dapper dudes to this Bleecker
Street counterpoint to the mega-designer's wildly popular women's
collection of the same name, with "fun" menswear – think plenty of
stripes, checks and "colorful" accents – that wins accolades; just don't
expect the staff to roll out the red carpet in these cramped quarters –
the service style is distinctly "not uptown."

Marc by Marc Jacobs Womens

25 | 24 | 21 | E

W Village | 403-5 Bleecker St. (W. 11th St.) | 212-924-0026 |
877-707-6272 | www.marcjacobs.com

For an "excellent selection" of the eponymous star designer's "stylish,
trendy apparel", fashion fiends flock to the chic West Village outpost
of his lower- (but still not low!) priced line for flirty, girlie frocks,
sportswear and "fabulous" handbags and accessories; maybe the
salespeople could stand to "lose the attitude", nevertheless the lust-
worthy wares still mark this haunt as a "must-go."

Marc by Marc Jacobs
Womens Accessories

26 | 24 | 23 | E

W Village | 301 W. Fourth St. (Bank St.) | 212-929-9455

Marc Jacobs Collection Accessories

W Village | 385 Bleecker St. (Perry St.) | 212-924-6126
www.marcjacobs.com

"If this store were a person, they'd have a legal document keeping me
at least 30 feet away" quip "psycho MJ enthusiasts" that "push past"
"groups of NYU students" and tourists to stalk this "small" West Village
"favorite" filled with totes, charms, wallets and tees from a "name you
can afford"; the nearby Bleecker Street boutique boasts a "beautiful
selection" of "classy" handbags and leather goods from the luxer, pricier line, all made in Italy.

Marc Jacobs

26 | 25 | 25 | VE

SoHo | 163 Mercer St. (bet. Houston & Prince Sts.) | 212-343-1490 |
877-707-6272 | www.marcjacobs.com

American fashion's Downtown don and his "friendly staff" have been
holding court in this loftlike SoHo space since 1997, offering a consistently "gorgeous selection" of just-edgy-enough men's and women's
clothing, "unique" pieces, "basics" and legendarily "distinct" handbags; followers who swear he's "still one of the best designers in NYC"

fantasize "if I could buy everything in any one brand and not look at the price tag, it would be Marc Jacobs."

Little Marc Jacobs   27 | 25 | 24 | E

W Village | 298 W. Fourth St. (Bank St.) | 212-206-6644 |
www.marcjacobs.com

Parked within a stone's throw of Marc Jacobs' Bleecker Street boutiques, this wee West Village corner store is "perfect if you want your mini-me to be as fashion-forward as you are"; say what you may about the "super-stylish", "totally overpriced outfits" and other adorable tchotchkes like stuffed animals and picture books, the "wonderfully willing salespeople and imaginative product make it worthwhile."

Marimekko   27 | 26 | 24 | E

E 70s | 1262 Third Ave. (bet. 72nd & 73rd Sts.) | 212-628-8400
Flatiron | 200 Fifth Ave. (bet. 23rd & 24th Sts.) | 212-843-9121
888-246-6665 | us.marimekko.com

An "oasis of color and pattern", this Finnish brand "dresses up" its Flatiron flagship and East 70s standby with "marvelous" "big and bold" designs in fabrics, sheets and housewares, even "fashions for people who like to have fun"; the "riot of prints" "adds a pop of color" in an "otherwise restrained world", and while "expensive", they're also "timeless" – just remember "a little goes a long way."

Mark Ingram Bridal Atelier   ▽ 29 | 25 | 28 | VE

E 50s | 110 E. 55th St., 8th fl. (bet. Lexington & Park Aves.) |
212-319-6778 | www.markingramatelier.com

Brides-to-be "fall in love" with the "quality" gowns at this by-appointment-only boutique in the East 50s, offering dresses by top-tier designers like Carolina Herrera, Angel Sanchez, Oscar de la Renta and Jenny Packham; "attentive" service that leaves shoppers "feeling pampered" and an elegant ambiance further explain why, despite high price points, the aisle-bound "feel good" about spending here.

Marni   28 | 28 | 26 | VE

E 60s | 21 E. 67th St. (bet. 5th & Madison Aves.) | 212-257-6907
SoHo | 161 Mercer St. (bet. Houston & Prince Sts.) | 212-343-3912
Marni Edition
Meatpacking | 1 Gansevoort St. (13th St.) | 646-532-6015
www.marni.com

"If one has lots of money to spend" and a "love" for Consuelo Castiglioni's "over-the-top Italian couture" creations, there's no better place to splash out than her futuristic SoHo storefront, East 60s outpost housed in a former art gallery and the slightly less-pricey Edition spin-off in a triangular Meatpacking space; acolytes "adore" the "amazing construction and design" of her garments and accessories, notably the "innovative materials" and playful prints and agree, *sí*, the staff is "helpful."

NEW Massimo Dutti ◗   – | – | – | M

E 50s | 689 Fifth Ave. (54th St.) | 212-371-2555 |
www.massimodutti.com

This Spanish retailer showcases its men's and women's clothing in a 13,000-sq.-ft. East 50s space formerly occupied by sister company Zara; known for classic, well-tailored threads, the brand offers pieces that are attractive but affordable for the fashionable folks strolling Fifth Avenue.

	QUALITY	DISPLAY	SERVICE	COST

Matt Bernson
| - | - | - | M |

TriBeCa | 20 Harrison St. (bet. Greenwich & Hudson Sts.) |
212-941-7634 | www.mattbernson.com

City girls in the know covet this eponymous designer's collection of
wedge sandals, suede booties, patterned smoking shoes and other
subtly stylish, super-comfy kicks, all displayed at his restored 1820s
carriage house in TriBeCa; handmade in artisanal workshop factories
from ecologically responsible materials like vegetable-tanned leathers, each pair is built to last with many priced for shoestring budgets.

Matt Umanov Guitars
▽ | 28 | 25 | 24 | E |

G Village | 273 Bleecker St. (bet. Cornelia & Jones Sts.) |
212-675-2157 | www.umanovguitars.com

"Beautiful instruments" lure strummers to this West Village purveyor
of new and vintage guitars, mandolins, banjos and ukuleles, offering
an incredible selection, plus "expert repairs", since 1965; the atmosphere is "relaxed", with "helpful" staffers (musicians themselves)
who will "encouragingly let you play anything" – yes, "there are
cheaper places", but admirers attest "they're not in the same league."

Mauboussin
▽ | 28 | 26 | 28 | E |

E 60s | 714 Madison Ave. (bet. 63rd & 64th Sts.) | 212-752-4300 |
www.mauboussin.us

Founded in France in 1827, this "luxury" jeweler brings its "great tradition" to NYC via its "sophisticated" David Rockwell–designed Madison
Avenue townhouse flagship; each floor is decorated in a distinctly different style, all the better to showcase the "beautiful", "unusual" baubles with "distinctive styling", from "cool" timepieces and colored
gems to "finely crafted" engagement rings and diamonds.

Max Mara
| 28 | 24 | 25 | VE |

E 60s | 813 Madison Ave. (68th St.) | 212-879-6100 | www.maxmara.com
The "chic Italian designs" for women at this "elegant" three-story flagship on Madison are the "type of clothing that will last a lifetime and
never go out of fashion"; the label is particularly known for its top-
stitched tailored suits and the "best", most luxurious coats, all "high-
quality", "beautifully crafted" and "stratospherically expensive."

Me&Ro
▽ | 25 | 24 | 22 | E |

NoLita | 241 Elizabeth St. (bet. Houston & Prince Sts.) | 917-237-9215 |
877-632-6376 | www.meandrojewelry.com

A "go-to" boutique for "beautiful" rings, necklaces and bracelets inspired by nature, this NoLita hideaway offers gold and silver collections crafted by head designer Robin Renz, with prices as "on-trend"
as the jewelry; the wares are displayed in an intimate, wood-clad
space complete with a flower pond in the window.

Memorial Sloan-Kettering Cancer Center Thrift Shop
| 23 | 18 | 20 | M |

E 80s | 1440 Third Ave. (bet. 81st & 82nd Sts.) | 212-535-1250 |
mskcc.convio.net

A "well-curated" thrift store "run by committed and friendly volun-
teers" since the '40s, this Upper Eastsider remains a "great resource
for high-end clothing" and accessories, along with "wonderful" home
furnishings and antiques, some offered through pop-up shop part-

QUALITY DISPLAY SERVICE COST

ners; rummagers report "few bargains" among the "finds", but the inventory's always "changing", so "you have to go back – for a good cause" of course.

NEW MenScience — | — | — | E

NoHo | 329 Lafayette St. (bet. Bleecker & Houston Sts.) | 800-608-6367 | www.menscience.com

Previously only available at high-end retailers, this men's grooming brand is now on offer at a sleek NoHo storefront; the skincare and nutrition lotions and potions are stacked ceiling-high in a window-fronted space lined with reclaimed wood, and there's an old-school barber chair where guests can get a haircut, shave and mini-facial.

Met Opera Shop ● 26 | 23 | 21 | E

W 60s | Metropolitan Opera House at Lincoln Ctr. | 136 Columbus Ave. (bet. 62nd & 65th Sts.) | 212-580-4090 | www.metoperashop.org

"Denizens of Lincoln Center" give the Metropolitan Opera's "fabulous" lobby shop a standing O for its "stylish jewelry and clothing", "exclusive" knickknacks and "excellent selection" of "favorite opera performances" on CD and DVD; the "top quality" guarantees a gift that "will be well received", and "take comfort" – if you "can afford going to the Met, you can afford to pay their prices."

Metropolitan Museum of Art Store 26 | 25 | 21 | E

E 80s | The Metropolitan Museum of Art | 1000 Fifth Ave. (82nd St.) | 212-570-3894

Washington Heights | The Cloisters Museum & Gdns. | 799 Fort Washington Ave. (190th St.) | 212-650-2277

W 40s | Rockefeller Ctr. | 15 W. 49th St. (5th Ave.) | 212-332-1360 800-468-7386 | store.metmuseum.org

"Almost as interesting as the museum itself", these "distinctive" stores are a "prime" source for an "incredible" range of "irresistible", "mostly affordable" "art for the ages", notably "wonderful" replica jewelry and accessories, home-"design finds", "special exhibition" items and "tons" of "coffee-table books"; the "courteous" employees may be "frazzled" by "Grand Central"-like throngs, but to "treat yourself" or score "a gift that will be remembered", "start here."

Michael Aram 27 | 26 | 24 | E

Chelsea | 136 W. 18th St. (bet. 6th & 7th Aves.) | 212-461-6903 | www.michaelaram.com

A "high-style space" in a Chelsea carriage house makes it "a pleasure to peruse" the "exquisite" line from the eponymous "design genius", who lends "distinctive" "organic" flair to handmade metal furnishings, "tableware, serving pieces" and other "elegant" items that'll "beautify any home"; the "cost will depend", but it's failsafe for "a housewarming or bridal gift" you'll "be proud to give."

Michael C. Fina ● 27 | 25 | 23 | E

E 50s | 500 Park Ave. (59th St.) | 212-557-2500 | 800-289-3462 | www.michaelcfina.com

"Popular" with brides "who don't want to battle the department store crowds", this "manageable" "classic", recently relocated to Park Avenue, remains "one of the best places to register" for "fine" flatware, "casual dinnerware" and "all the designers'" china at competitive prices; a "helpful staff" guides you through the "organized displays", and "if you haven't said yes yet, send your hubby-to-be here to check out the ring selection."

Michael Kors

| 27 | 26 | 25 | E |

E 60s | 667 Madison Ave. (bet. 60th & 61st Sts.) | 212-980-1550
E 60s | 790 Madison Ave. (67th St.) | 212-452-4685
Flatiron | 133 Fifth Ave. (20th St.) | 212-228-2043 ◐
SoHo | 101 Prince St. (bet. Greene & Mercer Sts.) | 212-965-0401 ◐
W 40s | Rockefeller Ctr. | 610 Fifth Ave. (bet. 49th & 50th Sts.) |
212-582-2444 ◐
W Village | 384 Bleecker St. (Perry St.) | 212-242-0700 ◐
Elmhurst | Queens Center Mall | 90-15 Queens Blvd. (bet. 57th &
59th Aves.) | Queens | 718-760-1500 ◐
New Springville | Staten Island Mall | 2655 Richmond Ave.
(bet. Platinum Ave. & Richmond Hill Rd.) | Staten Island |
718-494-3811 ◐
www.michaelkors.com

"It's tough to leave empty-handed" from this American designer's "impeccable" covey of around-town stores, where the "quality is off the charts" and the choices are "fantastic", whether you're searching for "classic" sportswear or "elegant, slightly flashy" handbags and shoes that "never go out of style"; add in a staff that's "dying to help", and it's little wonder most count themselves "very happy customers"; P.S. branches are slated to open at 520 Broadway and Brookfield Place.

Michael's,
The Consignment Shop for Women

| 23 | 15 | 14 | E |

E 70s | 1041 Madison Ave., 2nd fl. (bet. 79th & 80th Sts.) |
212-737-7273 | www.michaelsconsignment.com

"Kept women" and ladies who want to look like them frequent this "very reliable", "well-organized" family-owned consignment mainstay that's been located in the same Madison Avenue digs since 1954; treasure-hunters scour the racks of "authentic", "better-label" fashions, furs and accessories from designer names including Chanel, Gucci and Prada and "always find something magnificent", adding, just "be prepared to drop some cash."

NEW Miguel Antoinne

| – | – | – | E |

SoHo | 39 Wooster St. (bet. Broome & Grand Sts.) | 212-219-8200 |
www.miguelantoinne.com

Hop up the metal steps and into this sizable stark-white sanctum set away from the maddening SoHo crowds, where the namesake FIT grad showcases his cutting-edge creations crafted from sumptuous leather, silk and jersey fabrics; the statement pieces are hung on standing racks beneath a skylight, with austere shelves and a wood-slab table displaying other items like luxe accessories and arty coffee table books.

Mikimoto

| 29 | 28 | 28 | VE |

E 50s | 730 Fifth Ave. (bet. 56th & 57th Sts.) | 212-457-4600 |
888-701-2323 | www.mikimotoamerica.com

"A store where one can go to wish", this contemporary East 50s gem houses fine jewelry, including "exquisite" pearls in "the most amazing combinations"; "every strand" should be from this venerable Japanese mainstay sigh luxe-lovers who dive into necklaces, earrings and bracelets made from traditional white and black

South Sea varieties; rounding out the world-class experience: an "excellent staff and repair services."

Milly
28 | 26 | 24 | E

E 70s | 900 Madison Ave. (73rd St.) | 212-395-9100 | 877-645-5969 | www.millyny.com

"Bright", fun-loving colors and prints help make Michelle Smith's "beautiful", "well-made" apparel and accessories for women and girls stand out among the Madison Avenue crowd of shops; a "fantastic layout", wallpapered fitting rooms, black hardwood floors and pops of pink add to the upbeat atmosphere, while the "sweet, laid-back" staff is agreeably "attentive"; P.S. the designer's bridal collection is housed in an on-site salon.

Missoni
29 | 27 | 24 | VE

E 70s | 1009 Madison Ave. (78th St.) | 212-517-9339 | www.missoni.com

What "wonderful window shopping" agree admirers who peruse this Madison Avenue outpost of the Italian legend, snagging "really special garments in colorful, imaginative fabrics"; its trademark designs, recognized by fashion pacesetters worldwide, are "still the most original and beautiful knitwear for any season", hewing to a "family-based tradition" that hearkens back to 1953; then, as now, the "lovely" womenswear and accessories of unimpeachable quality appeals to "nonfrugal" shoppers with "extremely deep pockets."

Mitchell Gold + Bob Williams ◑
26 | 23 | 20 | E

SoHo | 210 Lafayette St. (Kenmare St.) | 212-431-2575 | www.mgbwhome.com

The "terrific" signature line of "upper-midrange" furniture is "artfully presented" at this sizable SoHo showroom, where the "beautiful", comfortably contempo samples "can be customized" with upholstery of your choice; luckily the solicitous salespeople let you "take as much time as you need", because you may "want everything in the store."

Miu Miu
26 | 26 | 24 | VE

E 50s | 11 E. 57th St. (bet. 5th & Madison Aves.) | 212-641-2980
SoHo | 100 Prince St. (bet. Greene & Mercer Sts.) | 212-334-5156
www.miumiu.com

"Lesser (priced) cousins to Prada", this sassy SoHo and 57th Street pair pop with Miuccia's mostly understated, occasionally overstated brand of glam; fashion mavens "love everything here", from the moddish store decor to the sweet, helpful staffers, and adore the "cool-looking" shoes and clothing that just jump with "great style", especially the pieces that dazzle with "so much glitter."

NEW MM6 Maison Martin Margiela
– | – | – | E

W Village | 363 Bleecker St. (bet. Charles & W. 10th Sts.) | 646-664-1655 | www.maisonmartinmargiela.com

With carpeting that resembles a sidewalk, movable shelves fashioned from pressed tin and a wacky mirrored light fixture, the first stand-alone store devoted to Margiela's spin-off line gives shoppers yet another reason to bop down Bleecker Street; the womenswear, including signature multifunctional pieces, hews to the experimental script, delivering envelope-pushing style for less dough than the main Maison collection.

Mociun

— | — | — | E

Williamsburg | 224 Wythe Ave. (4th St.) | Brooklyn | 718-387-3731 | www.mociun.com

California girl/renaissance woman Caitlin Mociun, renowned for her handcrafted, uniquely patterned dresses, offers up a world of goods at her sparsely decorated, gallery-esque Williamsburg shop, including her own jewelry creations boasting geometric-shaped gems, and artisan-crafted home goods and objets d'art; the modular corner space allows for ever-changing display possibilities – which seems to fit this free-spirited merchant to a tee.

Molton Brown

27 | 24 | 23 | E

E 50s | 515 Madison Ave. (53rd St.) | 212-755-7194
SoHo | 128 Spring St. (bet. Greene & Wooster Sts.) | 212-965-1740
866-933-2344 | www.moltonbrown.com

"Where else would hotels furnish their bathrooms?" wonder fans who've "fallen in love" with the British brand's "cut-above" collection of bath and body products sold by "knowledgeable" staffers at its "well-located" East 50s–SoHo branches; "recharge" or "relax" with candles and home fragrances that offer an "escape for the senses", and "smooth" lotions and shampoos that put "luxury in a bottle"; sure, it's "expensive", but "worth every penny."

MoMA Design and Book Store

26 | 24 | 19 | E

SoHo | 81 Spring St. (Crosby St.) | 646-613-1367
W 50s | The Museum of Modern Art | 11 W. 53rd St. (bet. 5th & 6th Aves.) | 212-708-9700
W 50s | 44 W. 53rd St. (bet. 5th & 6th Aves.) | 212-708-9669
800-851-4509 | www.momastore.org

"When you're feeling mod", these vending extensions of the Museum of Modern Art will "spice up your everyday existence" (and provide "hip" "gift ideas galore") with an array of "striking" "high-design house-wares", kitchen gizmos, furniture, toys and "incredible art book selection"; though "packed" with "tourists" and "not necessarily easy on the wallet", its "a summary of all that made the 20th century worthwhile."

Moncler

28 | 26 | 24 | VE

SoHo | 90 Prince St. (bet. Broadway & Mercer St.) | 646-350-3620 | www.moncler.com

Devotees of this storied French brand slalom over to the SoHo outpost for the "best quality" outerwear, particularly the "de rigueur" down jackets, perusing the "perfect selections each season", all sold by a "patient" staff; you may "blink twice" at the steep prices, nevertheless it's "worth a visit, at the very least" just to feast your eyes on the "cool window displays."

NEW Monique Lhuillier

— | — | — | VE

E 70s | 19 E. 71st St. (bet. 5th & Madison Aves.) | 212-683-3332 | www.moniquelhuillier.com

Before walking down the aisle or the red carpet, Manhattanites with money to burn turn to this designer's coveted collections, now show-cased at her first retail venue in an Upper East Side townhouse; the first floor features ready-to-wear while upstairs houses a plush bridal salon complete with pristine china and sparkly accessories.

QUALITY | DISPLAY | SERVICE | COST

Montblanc
28 | 26 | 25 | VE

E 50s | 598 Madison Ave. (bet. 57th & 58th Sts.) | 212-223-8888 |
800-581-4810 | www.montblanc.com

"Still the king" of "the art of writing", this "absolutely first-class"
Eastsider carries "beautiful, high-quality pens" with the "little star at
the tip", which "never fail to impress as prized personal possessions";
the "courteous" staff also oversees fine watches, leather goods, jewelry and sunglasses, though even the "status-obsessed" blanch it's
all "ridiculously priced."

Mood Designer Fabrics
26 | 18 | 19 | M

Garment District | 225 W. 37th St., 3rd fl. (bet. 7th & 8th Aves.) |
212-730-5003 | www.moodfabrics.com

"Oh, what a selection!" gush "fabric aficionados" who wend through
this tri-level Garment District "sewer's heaven", where the "amazing"
"array" of "quality" cloths "in all price ranges" – "extravagant materials" from "designer" names included – makes one "understand why
Project Runway" came running; yes, the layout's a "confusing mess",
but "if you know what you want you'll probably find it here."

Moon River Chattel
– | – | – | E

Williamsburg | 62 Grand St. (bet. Kent & Wythe Aves.) | Brooklyn |
718-388-1121 | www.moonriverchattel.com

"Worth a trip to Williamsburg just for the inspiration" insist nesters
enamored by this home store's antique, used and repro furniture with
"built-in patina" and "unique household must-haves" ranging from
salvaged doors, bathroom fixtures, "beautful" towels and industrial
lights to enamelware and classic-looking toys; much of this "incredible
stuff" "can't be found anywhere else", and it's all arranged in a welcoming space with a retro feel.

MooShoes
25 | 25 | 25 | E

LES | 78 Orchard St. (bet. Broome & Grand Sts.) | 212-254-6512 |
866-598-3426 | www.mooshoes.com

The "cruelty-free shoes and accessories" at this "lovely" LES standby
are "perfect for those who care about all living beings and the planet"
chorus vegan-ites who love the "high-quality" alternatives to leather
and appreciate the "very helpful staff"; while the "stylish" selection
can be "somewhat limited", it's "offset by its virtuousness", which extends to the "rescue cats" and dogs available for adoption.

Morgan Library & Museum Shop
26 | 23 | 21 | M

Murray Hill | The Morgan Library | 225 Madison Ave. (bet. 36th & 37th Sts.) |
212-590-0390 | www.themorgan.org

"Just like the Morgan" Library itself, this "classy" Murray Hill gift shop
is a "rare find" for "impressive" books and reproductions from the collections, "lovely" jewelry and "unusual" decorative knickknacks with
an "aesthetic factor" that "befits the museum"; veterans of "many visits" disclose it's "expensive overall, but don't hesitate" – you'll be
"helping support a gem of the city."

Morgenthal Frederics
27 | 24 | 25 | VE

E 60s | 699 Madison Ave. (bet. 62nd & 63rd Sts.) | 212-838-3090
E 70s | 944 Madison Ave. (bet. 74th & 75th Sts.) | 212-744-9444
SoHo | 399 W. Broadway (Spring St.) | 212-966-0099

(continued)

Morgenthal Frederics

W 60s | Shops at Columbus Circle | 10 Columbus Circle, ground fl.
(B'way & 60th St.) | 212-956-6402 ●
www.morgenthalfrederics.com

"See in style" with "fashionable" frames from these "sophisticated" optical boutiques, where the "top-quality" house line (the "horn glasses are unparalleled") and "well-edited selection" from chichi designers are "curated" with "professionalism" in tony David Rockwell-designed quarters; expect to "spend *beaucoup* bucks", but farsighted sorts say the wares are "so very timeless" you'll be "set for life."

Moroso
– | – | – | VE

SoHo | 146 Greene St. (bet. Houston & Prince Sts.) | 212-334-7222 |
www.morosousa.com

Designed by Milan-based architect Patricia Urquiola, this U.S. flagship of the venerable Italian furniture concern in SoHo showcases the company's entire fine furniture collection; Maharam textiles are highlighted here along with sublime seating and tremendous tables from high-end heavies like Marc Newson, Ron Arad and Tord Boontje.

Moschino
∇ 25 | 22 | 22 | VE

Meatpacking | 401 W. 14th St. (bet. 9th & 10th Aves.) |
212-243-8600 | www.moschino.com

"My obsession has grown with the years" admit fashion aficionados who shop for the Italian design house's eccentric creations at this shiny red-and-white marble Meatpacking destination boasting heart-shaped lighting fixtures and an air of glossy glamour; "love" the funky window displays and funkier fashions – the designs are all so "very different and wonderful" and, of course, command some mighty deep pockets.

Moscot
25 | 20 | 23 | E

LES | 108 Orchard St. (Delancey St.) | 212-477-3796
Union Sq | 69 W. 14th St. (6th Ave.) | 212-647-1550
Cobble Hill | 159 Court St. (bet. Dean & Pacific Sts.) | Brooklyn |
718-551-0591
866-667-2687 | www.moscot.com

Dating back to 1915, this "classic", "family-run" operation staffed with "people-friendly" salesfolk is famed for its "fabulously authentic retro eyewear", including "iconic" house-crafted frames that "instantly add character" to your visage, and it's all on view at its nostalgia-trip branches, including the LES mainstay, now in new Orchard Street quarters; budget-minded types sigh "if only they had old-timey pricing", but the specs are so "universally flattering", the "compliments you'll get" are "worth it."

Moss Bureau
28 | 29 | 21 | VE

Garment District | 256 W. 36th St., 10th fl. (bet. 7th & 8th Aves.) |
212-204-7100 | www.mossbureau.com

Relocated from its original SoHo digs to a no-nonsense office-cum-showroom in the Garment District, Murray Moss' "wonderment" of a "high-end design store" remains "ahead of the pack" with "off-the-charts originality"; though now with a more modest scope, it still offers "carefully curated" displays of globally sourced furniture, lighting, tableware and "artsy knickknacks" from "the cutting-edge" – visit, and you may "come away with a whole new direction" in decorating.

Mr. Throwback   – | – | – | E

E Village | 428 E. Ninth St. (bet. Ave. A & 1st Ave.) | 646-410-0310 | www.mrthrowback.com
Children of the '90s happily nostalgia trip at this closet-sized East Village shop, where owner Michael Spitz hawks old-school stuff that he's been collecting since he was 13 years old, plus consignment items; the bounty includes acid-washed jeans, jerseys, Air Jordans, vintage video games and an extensive collection of Knicks paraphernalia.

Muji ●   22 | 23 | 18 | M

NEW **E Village** | 52 Cooper Sq. (bet. 6th & 7th Sts.) | 212-358-8693
Flatiron | 16 W. 19th St. (bet. 5th & 6th Aves.) | 212-414-9024
SoHo | 455 Broadway (bet. Grand & Howard Sts.) | 212-334-2002
W 40s | New York Times Bldg. | 620 Eighth Ave. (40th St.) | 212-382-2300
www.muji.us
"Keep your life ordered and serene" at these chain purveyors of "Japanese simplicity", where "form follows function" via "well-designed" wares "in a minimalist vein" made accessible "without the hype or price"; whether it's for "Zen home goods", "super" storage containers, "fantastic stationery", "functional" apparel or "smart" "travel products", go in "just to explore" and you'll "walk out with more than you intended to."

Mulberry   28 | 26 | 25 | VE

E 50s | 605 Madison Ave. (bet. 57th & 58th Sts.) | 212-256-0632
SoHo | 134 Spring St. (bet. Greene & Wooster Sts.) | 646-669-8380
W Village | 387 Bleecker St. (Perry St.) | 917-261-4394
888-685-6856 | www.mulberry.com
The woodsy, "whimsical displays" alone make this English luxury brand's Midtown, SoHo and West Village branches "lovely places to browse" agree deep-pocketed shoppers who snap up the "beautiful" iconic handbags and "trendy", well-crafted leather goods; the "quality is superb", and the luxe offerings are priced accordingly, but considering them "good investment pieces" helps soften the blow.

Muléh   – | – | – | E

Chelsea | 500 W. 22nd St. (10th Ave.) | 212-524-0220 | www.muleh.com
Owner Christopher Reiter draws inspiration from his travels through Southeast Asia when curating the handpicked mix of fashion and furniture at this minimalist haven, fittingly located in Chelsea's gallery district; on-trend women's fashions from sought-after names like Hache, Ter Et Bantine and Vivienne Westwood Anglomania steal the show, punctuated by contemporary interior design pieces and lighting fixtures, many made from sustainable materials.

Museum of Arts & Design Store   26 | 24 | 22 | E

W 50s | Museum of Arts and Design | 2 Columbus Circle (bet. B'way & 8th Ave.) | 212-299-7700 | thestore.madmuseum.org
"Perfectly reflecting the functional art found in the museum", this Columbus Circle gift shop is a "retail oasis" of the "highest caliber", where the "beautiful" jewelry, glassware, "ceramic objects" and

"artsy" home accents are often "handcrafted" in "unique designs"
from featured artists; while "a tad pricey", it's a cache of "lovely" gift
ideas for "that special someone."

Museum of the City of New York Shop | 26 | 24 | 21 | I |

E 100s | Museum of the City of New York | 1220 Fifth Ave. (103rd St.) |
212-534-1672 | www.mcny.org

For Gothamite goodies "you don't see everywhere", this snug Museum
Mile shop is "definitely worth a visit", with its creative assortment of
prints, clothes and accessories, knickknacks and "nice range of books",
all reflecting serious "NYC interest"; the merch is "not expensive", so
geez, "every New Yorker should go at least once."

My Little Sunshine | - | - | - | E |

Chelsea | 177 Ninth Ave. (bet. 20th & 21st Sts.) | 212-929-0887
NEW **TriBeCa** | 145 Hudson St. (bet. Beach & Hubert Sts.) | 212-966-8840
www.mylittlesunshinenyc.com

Put on your multitasking hat and steer over to this Chelsea bright spot
and new TriBeCa sidekick to shop for junior; while you're browsing
through the racks of kids' clothing from labels like Blu Pony Vintage
and Imps & Elfs, hugging the ever-squeezable Jellycat animals and
mulling over bedding items, your moptop can get his/her hair cut
while seated in a cheery red airplane.

Nanette Lepore | 26 | 26 | 24 | E |

E 70s | 958 Madison Ave. (bet. 75th & 76th Sts.) | 212-452-3056
SoHo | 423 Broome St. (bet. Crosby & Lafayette Sts.) | 212-219-8265
www.nanettelepore.com

When feminine girls "need a dress for a party or event" and convince
themselves that their "closet is empty", they scoot over to this "spacious", birdcage-bedecked SoHo standby that feels like a "ballroom
with clothes", and its Madison Avenue offshoot; both boast the namesake designer's "really innovative", mostly NYC-made creations, imbued with a "stylish retro feel" that still manages to "look fresh and
perfect" years hence.

NARS | 25 | 25 | 25 | E |

W Village | 413 Bleecker St. (bet. Ban & 11th Sts.) | 646-459-2323 |
888-788-6277 | www.narscosmetics.com

"From the coveted nail polish" and "really cool foundation shades" to
"eye crayons, mascara, lip liner and lipstick" in "kaleidoscopic" colors,
fans "swear" by François Nars' "fun, flirty" collection showcased at his
West Village beauty boutique; the "amazing" products are served up
in a "high-end" yet cozy atmosphere, replete with a marble fireplace
mantle, and makeup artists are "very generous in giving demos."

NBA Store ⚫ | 21 | 23 | 19 | E |

W 40s | 590 Fifth Ave. (bet. 47th & 48th Sts.) | 212-515-6221 |
866-746-7622 | store.nba.com

"Paradise" for "basketball fans", this Midtowner has "everything you
could want" in the way of officially licensed team apparel for kids and
adults, along with roundball paraphernalia galore; just "be prepared to
pay" and to be "surrounded" by "overwhelming" "teenage" crowds,
"especially during the NBA season"; P.S. a move to roomier digs is
in the works.

QUALITY DISPLAY SERVICE COST

Neue Galerie Shop

26 | 23 | 22 | E

E 80s | Neue Galerie | 1048 Fifth Ave. (86th St.) | 212-628-6200 |
www.neuegalerie.org

From Adolf Loos to Joseph Hoffmann, this "refined" UES museum
shop showcases a "unique collection" of "quality reproductions" of
Austrian and German designs, including serving pieces, jewelry and
the Neue Hund collection of "outrageously expensive accoutrements
for the dog who has everything"; though "stellar", some merchandise
is "priced at astronomical levels", so just sip a Viennese hot chocolate
at the cafe until you "get rich."

New Balance Experience Store

23 | 20 | 21 | M

Flatiron | 150 Fifth Ave. (20th St.) | 212-727-2520 | www.newbalance.com
Fitness fanatics come running to this footwear mainstay's Flatiron
flagship, where the latest updates on its "traditional" athletic shoes
for cross-training, hiking, walking and other activities are balanced by
branded activewear; the roomy display floor sports a mini test track
and a station where workers also turn out colorful, custom-designed
kicks from scratch.

New London Pharmacy

27 | 25 | 24 | M

Chelsea | 246 Eighth Ave. (23rd St.) | 212-243-4987 | 800-941-0490 |
www.newlondonpharmacy.com

"One of the few small, independent pharmacies left in the city", this
"adorable" Chelsea apothecary boasts an "amazing selection" of
makeup, toiletries, fragrances and homeopathic and natural remedies
handpicked by owners/licensed pharmacists Abby and John Fazio; staffers are "helpful", and a full-time nutritionist offers private consultations,
leading fans to ask "why go to the chains when these guys have it all?"

New Museum of Contemporary Art Store

25 | 24 | 22 | E

LES | New Museum of Contemporary Art | 235 Bowery (Prince St.) |
212-343-0460 | www.newmuseumstore.org

For something "refreshingly different from the typical", this "innovative"
LES museum lobby nook stocks "specialty art and design books" centered on the contempo scene, plus "irreverent and clever" "nifty-gifties"
and limited-edition items like plates and skateboards conceived by
rising and iconic talents; critics dis the "uninformed" staff, but even
they concede it's "totally worth a look-see" for an edgy keepsake.

New York Botanical Garden Shop

25 | 24 | 22 | M

Fordham | New York Botanical Gdn. | 2900 Southern Blvd. (Fordham Rd.) |
Bronx | 718-817-8073 | www.nybgshop.org

"If you're a fan of foliage and flowers", this "gorgeous" "oasis in da Bronx"
will make your "green thumb itch" given its "rare" plants, "tempting
garden supplies", "lovely" home decor, "jewelry with floral designs"
and "wonderful range of books" on sale in a "beautiful" skylit pavilion;
horticulturalists dig all the "really neat things", but note that the prices
can shoot "way out of sight."

New York Central Art Supply

27 | 17 | 20 | M

E Village | 62 Third Ave. (11th St.) | 212-473-7705 | 800-950-6111 |
www.nycentralart.com

"Professional artists" are "like kids in a candy store" at this old-time
East Village "treasure" given its "extensive" lineup of "high-quality"

paints, brushes, canvas, "odd" tools and "absolutely amazing" paper "from around the world"; particulars may be "hard to find" in its poky setting, but the staffers supply "patient service and advice."

The New York Public Library Shop   24 | 22 | 20 | M

E 40s | 476 Fifth Ave. (42nd St.) | 212-930-0641
Harlem | Schomburg Ctr. | 515 Malcolm X Blvd. (135th St.) | 212-491-2206
www.nypl.org

Sure "to suit a word-lover's fancy", this "gem" in the Midtown main branch's "cool old-world surrounds" has "much to choose from" with its "mix of books", pens and stationery, "interesting jewelry", "New Yorky" souvenirs and "arty items" featuring the twin lion mascots; the Harlem sibling (aka the Schomburg Shop) adds African artifacts to the mix – both are "awesome" if you're gift shopping "for your favorite bookworm."

New York Running Company ◑   27 | 23 | 26 | E

E 60s | 1059 Third Ave. (bet. 62nd & 63rd Sts.) | 212-223-8109
W 60s | Shops at Columbus Circle | 10 Columbus Circle, 2nd fl. (B'way & 60th St.) | 212-823-9626
www.therunningcompany.net

"If you're going to start running, here is your starting line" say fans of this "very specialized" Uptown pair, where "knowledgeable" staffers observe your walking style and give "honest appraisals" of your sneaker needs; it also offers "really nice apparel", daily group runs and "wonderful" yoga classes, and though "it's expensive, your feet will appreciate it."

Nicholas Kirkwood   - | - | - | VE

Meatpacking | 807 Washington St. (Gansevoort St.) | 646-559-5239 | www.nicholaskirkwood.com

Stay one step ahead of the fashion pack with statement footwear from this eponymous British designer who showcases his collection in a sun-dappled Meatpacking shop with a back garden, modeled after his Mayfair, London, boutique; the objects of desire, constructed of snakeskin, satin, lace and luxe leathers, with towering heels, are tucked into wall insets and set atop white cubes like museum pieces, commanding the attention of worshipers.

Nicole Miller   26 | 25 | 24 | E

E 60s | 780 Madison Ave. (bet. 66th & 67th Sts.) | 212-288-9779
SoHo | 77 Greene St. (bet. Broome & Spring Sts.) | 212-219-1825
000-300-6250 | www.nicolemiller.com

"Beyond terrific!" crow acolytes who hotfoot it to this eponymous designer's airy SoHo flagship and equally "popular" UES offshoot; "love the styles" – her "very chic" body-con pieces "fit like a glove", and the "special" (yes, "pricey") bright, colorful dresses are just right for that "very special event"; P.S. the Greene Street location features a bridal salon.

Nike   25 | 24 | 19 | E

SoHo | 21 Mercer St. (bet. Grand & Howard Sts.) | 212-226-5433
Nike Running ◑
Flatiron | 156 Fifth Ave. (20th St.) | 212-243-8560

(continued)

QUALITY DISPLAY SERVICE COST

(continued)

Niketown New York

E 50s | 6 E. 57th St. (bet. 5th & Madison Aves.) | 212-891-6453
www.nike.com

The five-story Midtown "sneakerhead's" "mecca" from the athletic footwear "front-runner" sports an "impressive" array of kicks "for everyone" – "go ahead and design your own" with NikeID – as well as activewear and sporting goods, so most take the "tourist throngs" and "distracted staff" in stride; meanwhile, "collectors" sprint to the SoHo boutique for "the latest" limited releases, and marathon mavens race over to the Flatiron store specializing in running shoes.

NEW Norman & Jules   - | - | - | M

Park Slope | 158 Seventh Ave. (bet. 1st St. & Garfield Pl.) | Brooklyn | 347-987-3323 | www.normanandjules.com

Committed to nurturing young minds, the owners of this Park Slope shop stock a colorful selection of handmade toys and playthings crafted by local and international artisans using sustainable materials; the hands-on displays keep kids entertained, and a portion of the profits go to charity.

No. 6   - | - | - | E

Little Italy | 6 Centre Market Pl. (bet. Broome & Grand Sts.) | 212-226-5759 | www.no6store.com

"Well-priced, original pieces" and some of the "best" wooden-heeled clogs from the house line coexist with midcentury vintage clothing at this airy Little Italy venue; insiders agree that the "sharp"-eyed owners have your number – they're not only "fashion curators par excellence" but often act like "your personal stylists, making you feel like a million bucks."

Oak   ∇ 24 | 24 | 21 | E

NoHo | 28 Bond St. (bet. Bowery & Lafayette St.) | 212-677-1293 ●
Greenpoint | 55 Nassau Ave. (bet. Guernsey & Lorimer Sts.) | Brooklyn | 718-782-0521
www.oaknyc.com

Have "cash to burn"? shop among "models" and other "in-the-know" folks at this minimalist NoHo-Greenpoint duo offering an "incredible selection" of menswear and womenswear from its house label and über-hip brands like Alexander Wang, Rick Owens and Won Hundred, much of it in dark shades and all sure to "improve your wardrobe"; rounding out the mix: less-pricey items like jewelry, scarves and candles.

Obscura Antiques & Oddities   26 | 28 | 25 | E

E Village | 207 Ave. A (13th St.) | 212-505-9251 | www.obscuraantiques.com

"History" buffs can "spend hours" at this "unique" East Village antiquery, an "ideal" resource for "one-of-a-kind furniture, paintings and other decorative items" such as anatomical drawings and taxidermy displayed inside glass domes; yes, the wares may be pricey, but devotees declare it's "a treat to visit" for the "streetside freak show" displays alone.

Obsessive Compulsive Cosmetics   - | - | - | M

LES | 174 Ludlow St. (Houston St.) | 212-675-2404 | 888-622-0504 | www.occmakeup.com

Being OCD has never been better since this laid-back, low-key cosmetics shop opened on the LES, providing beauty addicts with 100%

vegan nail lacquer, brushes, bold eye shadow, airbrush foundation, tinted moisturizer and the famed Lip Tar with amazing "staying power"; ask one of the staffers for a private consultation or a trip through the mixing bar, where you can create your own shades.

Odin
27 | 26 | 24 | E

NoLita | 199 Lafayette St. (bet. Broome & Kenmare Sts.) | 212-966-0026 ●
W Village | 106 Greenwich Ave. (bet. Jane & 13th Sts.) | 212-243-4724

Odin on 11th ●

E Village | 328 E. 11th St. (bet. 1st & 2nd Aves.) | 212-475-0666
www.odinnewyork.com

The house of hipster "high fashion" serves up a novel "mix of established and new designers" including Burkman Bros., Engineered Garments and a raft of store-exclusive items, all geared toward the guys; the "inspiring" menswear styles run the gamut from "classic to more current", with dress pants and jackets sharing space with hoodies, army fatigues and a house line of fragrances – in sum, "pretty sweet" stuff.

Oliver Peoples
28 | 24 | 22 | VE

E 60s | 812 Madison Ave. (68th St.) | 212-585-3433
SoHo | 366 W. Broadway (Broome St.) | 212-925-5400
www.oliverpeoples.com

"Avoid the librarian look" with "high-quality eyewear" from these East Side–SoHo branches of LA's "classic" name in celeb-sanctioned shades, famed for "vintage-inspired" specs and sunglasses that "stunningly frame your best features" and "let you stand out", bolstered by its Paul Smith and Mosley Tribe collections; the "exceptional" staff "encourages you to try unique looks" so play away – "there's definitely a pair for everyone – though not every budget."

Omega
▽ 28 | 24 | 27 | VE

E 50s | 711 Fifth Ave. (55th St.) | 212-207-3333 | www.omegawatches.com
"If James Bond chooses Omega, do you really have to contemplate?" quip arbiters of chronometer cachet who steal over to this tony Midtown boutique, where the Swiss watchmaker's illustrious his-and-hers timepieces share a gallerylike display with jewelry and leather accessories; the VIP treatment extends to the "secret" service center upstairs, but just be ready to spend megabucks.

OMO Norma Kamali
25 | 26 | 24 | VE

W 50s | 11 W. 56th St. (bet. 5th & 6th Aves.) | 212-957-9797 |
800-852-6254 | www.normakamali.com

This American icon opened her multifloor Midtown boutique in 1978 post-divorce (OMO = On My Own), and it remains a testament to her signature style, displaying everything from "classic bathing suits" to convertible dresses; adorers agree "even if you can't afford to buy, it pays to just come and ogle" because this "talented" designer "gets it and she always has"; P.S. The Wellness Cafe on-site offers organic treats.

Onassis
- | - | - | E

SoHo | 71 Greene St. (bet. Broome & Spring Sts.) | 212-966-8869
NEW **W 40s** | 61 W. 49th St. (bet. 5th & 6th Aves.) | 212-586-8688
www.onassisclothing.com

Drop anchor at this emerging menswear label's SoHo flagship and Rockefeller Center offshoot, specializing in woven shirts along with

QUALITY DISPLAY SERVICE COST

denim, chinos, slub tees and other Platonic basics for the office or yacht club; the apparel fuses vintage American designs with Tokyo crafts-manship, evident in its anchor-stitched buttons, made by the oldest button-maker in Japan, and it's all displayed amid rustic wooden tables and accents like tobacco tins and framed nautical prints.

Opening Ceremony
25 | 22 | 21 | VE

Chelsea | Ace Hotel | 1190-92 Broadway (bet. 28th & 29th Sts.) | 646-695-5680 ●
SoHo | 35 Howard St. (bet. B'way & Crosby St.) | 212-219-2688
www.openingceremony.us

Humberto Leon and Carol Lim's "off-the-beaten-path" SoHo "bohemian general store" and smaller Ace Hotel spin-off are "too cool for school", but both "can actually back it up" with "world-class" goods that annually spotlight one country; achingly hip staffers can be "grumpy" or "amazing", and prices border on "mind-blowing", nevertheless acolytes agree it's "worth searching out" for "fantastic designs from often-unheard-of" talents and limited-run collaborations.

Orchard Corset Center
▽ 25 | 4 | 24 | M

LES | 157 Orchard St. (bet. Rivington & Stanton Sts.) | 212-674-0786 | 866-456-7411 | www.orchardcorset.com

"Not really a store, it is an experience" to shop at this "no-frills, no-fuss" LES specialist where "you tell the stern-looking saleswoman what you're looking for, get whisked into a back room and instantly fitted" from the countless boxes stacked floor to ceiling; whether you're searching for "basic lingerie" or a corset to go under a wedding gown, the "extremely efficient" staffers will have you sorted and rung up "in about 15 minutes", and you'll pay a "discounted price."

Organic Modernism
▽ 26 | 25 | 26 | E

Chelsea | 150 W. 26th St. (bet. 6th & 7th Aves.) | 212-989-4871
E 50s | 249 E. 57th St. (bet. 2nd & 3rd Aves.) | 212-546-9020
E Village | 43 Ave. A (bet. 3rd & 4th Sts.) | 212-387-7760
Flatiron | 124 W. 18th St. (bet. 6th & 7th Aves.) | 212-627-2087
Flatiron | 133 W. 22nd St. (bet. 6th & 7th Aves.) | 212-242-3004
TriBeCa | 353 Broadway (bet. Franklin & Leonard Sts.) | 212-431-2673
TriBeCa | 85 White St. (bet. B'way & Lafayette St.) | 212-966-6711
Williamsburg | 174 N. 11th St. (bet. Bedford Ave. & Berry St.) | Brooklyn | 718-388-2036
Williamsburg | 203 N. 11th St. (bet. Driggs Ave. & Roebling St.) | Brooklyn | 718-388-2036
www.organicmodernism.com

This modernist furniture outfit started in Brooklyn in 2009 and quickly mushroomed to several locations across Manhattan, all dedicated to the company mission of bringing good design to the masses with pieces that are "somehow classic and modern at the same time"; partisans applaud the "friendly service", non-designer prices and the brand's dedication to environmentally responsible practices.

Origins
25 | 22 | 23 | M

E 40s | Grand Central Terminal | 87 E. 42nd St., main concourse (Vanderbilt Ave.) | 212-808-4141 ●
Flatiron | Flatiron Bldg. | 175 Fifth Ave. (22nd St.) | 212-677-9100
SoHo | 402 W. Broadway (Spring St.) | 212-219-9764 ●

(continued)

Origins

W 80s | 2327 Broadway (bet. 84th & 85th Sts.) | 212-769-0970
900-674-4467 | www.origins.com

No matter your complexion type, the paraban-free products offered at this "natural" skincare serenity stop-off will leave you beautiful and virtuous; the "smell good, feel good" cosmetics, and corporate commitment to sustainability, are a hit with the "under-25 set"; add "take-home samples" and spontaneous facials from the "amazing staff", and you'll be ready to glow.

Oscar de la Renta

| 29 | 27 | 27 | VE |

E 60s | 772 Madison Ave. (66th St.) | 212-288-5810 | 866-782-6357 | www.oscardelarenta.com

Oscar's "clothing never ceases to amaze" the chic crowd that shops his "elegant" cream-carpeted East 60s boutique for "sophisticated" suits and beautiful "cocktail attire" that's both fashion-forward and "classic" and always "stunning"; as you'd expect, service is "excellent" and the price tags are as arresting as the clothes, but since a piece from this designer is a "timeless" addition to any wardrobe, few who can afford it mind.

NEW Osswald Parfumerie + Luxury Skincare Boutique

| - | - | - | E |

SoHo | 311 W. Broadway (bet. Canal & Grand Sts.) | 212-625-3111 | www.osswaldnyc.com

Founded in Zurich in 1921, this Swiss beauty mainstay branches out with a new destination on the edge of SoHo that effortlessly conveys a European feel; the gleaming space is anchored by a sizable collection of vintage perfume bottles, plus makeup and skincare products and an olfactory gallery of niche brands arranged in neat rows, including some store exclusives.

Other Music

| ∇ | 29 | 24 | 26 | M |

NoHo | 15 E. Fourth St. (bet. B'way & Lafayette St.) | 212-477-8150 | www.othermusic.com

One of the "last of the independent record stores", this NoHo mainstay "run by music-lovers" is heaven "for those who still appreciate holding a CD or piece of vinyl" rejoice aficionados who browse the packed bins filled with "outstanding selections" of rare, indie and import music; it's definitely not "the place to go for Top 40", but "perfect for those with expanding musical horizons."

Otte

| ∇ | 24 | 23 | 23 | E |

NEW E 70s | 1232 Third Ave. (bet. 71st & 72nd Sts.) | 212-744-4002
E 90s | 1281 Madison Ave. (bet. 91st & 92nd Sts.) | 212-289-2644
TriBeCa | 37 N. Moore St. (bet. Hudson & Varick Sts.) | 212-431-8501
W Village | 121 Greenwich Ave. (bet. Jane & 13th Sts.) | 212-229-9424
www.otteny.com

It's "one-stop chic shopping" at this quartet of "cheerful boutiques chock-full of the latest names and looks", with everything a girl needs from "everyday wearable clothes to a party outfit" by international labels, "emerging designers" and the new house line of luxe basics; a "really lovely" sales staff and upbeat pink-and-white decor add to the "fun."

QUALITY DISPLAY SERVICE COST

Owen

Meatpacking | 809 Washington St. (bet. Gansevoort & Horatio Sts.) | 212-524-9770 | www.owennyc.com

FIT prodigy Phillip Salem's Meatpacking boutique hosts a painstakingly curated mix of new designers and established names, with trendsetting guy/girl wear from Carven, Ohne Titel and Suno arranged by color for easy browsing; the sleek store prides itself on customer service – the training manual says 'everyone should be treated like Beyoncé' – and design: the airy space is lined with an arc of artfully arranged paper bags.

Paige Premium Denim
▽ 25 | 22 | 24 | E

Meatpacking | 869 Washington St. (bet. 13th & 14th Sts.) | 212-807-1400
SoHo | 71 Mercer St. (bet. Broome & Spring Sts.) | 212-625-0800
W 70s | 245 Columbus Ave. (bet. 71st & 72nd Sts.) | 212-769-1500
www.paigeusa.com

When on the hunt for the perfect fit, this "way cool" trio featuring the designs of denim guru Paige Adams Geller could be your one and only stop to find the "best jeans for your butt", as well as lots of options without "obnoxious designs on the pockets"; the selection can be overwhelming, so ask the "helpful" staff when it comes to picking the winning pair(s).

ꞏ NEW ꞏ Pamela Gonzales
- | - | - | E

SoHo | 311 W. Broadway (bet. Canal & Grand Sts.) | 212-966-3113 | www.pamela-gonzales.com

Set on the fringes of SoHo, the Peruvian designer's concept store showcases her risqué, body-conscious attire in an airy, all-white space punctuated with colorful objets d'art; the diverse mix includes dramatic, event-ready and understated looks from a global array of guest independent designers, each with a distinctive style perspective, so shoppers can easily expand their fashion horizons with each excursion.

Papyrus
26 | 23 | 19 | E

Flatiron | 940 Broadway (22nd St.) | 212-228-2877 | www.papyrusonline.com
Additional locations throughout the NY area

For "creative" paper goods head to this chain of "swanky little shops" specializing in all kinds of "pretty things for special people", with "unique" greeting cards, stationery and wrapping paper arranged in "glowing, themed" displays; staffers leave you "on your own", and penny-pinchers say "you really have to love someone" to spend this much on a card, so watch out for the "generous" seasonal sales.

Paragon Sporting Goods
26 | 18 | 20 | M

Union Sq | 867 Broadway (18th St.) | 212-255-8889 | 800-961-3030 | www.paragonsports.com

"Sweat it out in style" with "real outfitting" from this "trusted" Union Square "sports mecca", where "impressive" departments for "every activity known to man" equip everything "from baseball to yoga" in "less-corporate" fashion than "the big chains"; it's "not cheap" and the "unusual floor plan" leads to "terrible traffic flow", but it's "unsurpassed" for "top-shelf" variety all "under the same roof."

	QUALITY	DISPLAY	SERVICE	COST

NEW Pas de Calais
- | - | - | E

SoHo | 482 Broome St. (Wooster St.) | 212-938-1973 |
www.pasdecalais-int.com

Its roots are in Japan and its new galleryesque showcase is set in SoHo, but this company's name and style inspiration can be traced to a region in Northern France famed for its delicate lace and lovely landscape; the subtly colored textural guy-and-girl garments are fashioned from natural cotton, silk and linen and hung on floating racks, surrounded by an intricate string installation reminiscent of a giant loom.

Patagonia
27 | 22 | 23 | E

NEW Meatpacking | 414 W. 14th St. (bet. 9th Ave. & Washington St.) | 212-929-6512
SoHo | 101 Wooster St. (bet. Prince & Spring Sts.) | 212-343-1776
W 80s | 426 Columbus Ave. (81st St.) | 917-441-0011
800-638-6464 | www.patagonia.com

"Outdoorsy" sorts can "brave the elements" with a conscience thanks to these Meatpacking, SoHo and UWS branches of the "superior" international chain, a "top choice" for "practical" activewear that's "stylish" yet "rugged" enough to "get adventurous" in, and manufactured with the "environment" in mind; it'll cost some "green", but the "crunchy-granola staff" provides "helpful" assistance, and "these clothes perform."

Patricia Field ◐
23 | 26 | 21 | E

NoHo | 306 Bowery (bet. Bleecker & Houston Sts.) | 212-966-4066 |
www.patriciafield.com

Owned by the legendary "costume designer of *Sex and the City*" fame, this "wild and crazy" Bowery destination for "fierce fashions", accessories and tchotchkes is a "go-to" when you're going "all out"; it's just the thing when you need a "unique piece for a costume" or just something "fun, fun, fun", though regulars warn prices are "all over the map", from affordable to downright "inaccessible."

Paul Smith
27 | 25 | 21 | VE

Flatiron | 108 Fifth Ave. (16th St.) | 212-627-9770
SoHo | 142 Greene St. (bet. Houston & Prince Sts.) | 646-613-3060
www.paulsmith.co.uk

Get "Saville Row–worthy tailoring" without crossing the pond at this English designer's SoHo and Flatiron "feasts for the fashion senses", offering "quintessential British style" in a sometimes "wacky assemblage" of pricey merchandise, including "preppy" clothing, "colorful" accessories and "sleek" suiting; the staff is "friendly" and "funky", and "it's always a joy to stop in", even if just to bask in the "varying levels of cheekiness."

Paul Smith Sale Shop
▽ 25 | 23 | 21 | E

Williamsburg | 280 Grand St. (bet. Havemeyer & Roebling Sts.) |
Brooklyn | 718-218-0020 | www.paulsmith.co.uk

Fashion fanciers on a budget are "loving it" at this "excellent" Williamsburg outpost, where the "overflow" of "top-quality" men's and women's threads from "the famous British designer's" Flatiron and SoHo namesakes is racked "at a reduced price" (typically 40 to 50% off); with such "hard-to-beat" styles "always on discount", the "sophisticated rummaging" involved is a "special treat."

	QUALITY	DISPLAY	SERVICE	COST

Paul Stuart

29	27	27	VE

E 40s | 10 E. 45th St. (bet. 5th & Madison Aves.) | 212-682-0320 | 800-678-8278 | www.paulstuart.com

"The Great Gatsby" would feel at home in this "classic" Midtown haberdashery that's been making "preppy" menswear "kinda cool since 1938"; the gentlemanly atmosphere perfectly showcases the "superb suits and shirts" and "eclectic" accessories ranging from braces to pocket squares, prompting partisans to pronounce it the "ultimate" for "high-end", "bar none" and "worth every penny."

Pearl Paint

24	16	18	M

Chinatown | 308 Canal St. (bet. B'way & Church St.) | 212-431-7932 | 800-451-7237 | www.pearlpaint.com

They have "exactly what you need", and more than "you could ever use" at this "legendary" C-town "behemoth of art supplies", where the "mind-expanding palette" of products spread over six floors ("hope you've been using the StairMaster") is "affordable for struggling" talents; though the setup's "haphazard" and the staffers sometimes "too hip to assist", it's "the real deal"; P.S. custom framing available.

Pearl River Mart

18	19	13	I

SoHo | 477 Broadway (bet. Broome & Grand Sts.) | 212-431-4770 | 800-878-2446 | www.pearlriver.com

Aficionados of "all things Asian" "hit the jackpot" at this SoHo multilevel "megastore" "celebrating the Far East" with its "colorful" abundance of "neat Chinese stuff" ("some tacky, some delightful") at prices most "can't resist"; you "could get lost perusing" the "huge variety", including clothing, accessories, housewares and an upstairs furniture department likened to "the Ikea of the Orient."

P.E. Guerin

▽ 29	19	25	VE

W Village | 23 Jane St. (bet. 8th & Greenwich Aves.) | 212-243-5270 | www.peguerin.com

"If nothing but the best will do", this West Village family outfit, founded in 1857, is "unmatched" for "beautiful" architectural hardware (e.g. ornate knobs, knockers, bathroom fixtures and "furniture mountings") and will reproduce antique fittings or craft custom pieces to order; available by appointment only, it offers "unbelievable stuff" – "if you can afford it."

Perrin Paris

-	-	-	E

E 70s | Carlyle Hotel | 987 Madison Ave. (77th St.) | 212-585-1893 | www.perrinparis.com

This storied French brand has crafted leather accessories since 1893, and with the opening of its tiny shop inside the Carlyle Hotel, luxe lovers can now access the goods sans airfare; the structured clutches, shoulder bags and satchels are displayed like museum pieces on gleaming glass shelves, though the exotic skins and textural materials, including raffia, python and crocodile, may prompt browsers to look and to touch.

Personnel of New York

-	-	-	E

W Village | 9 Greenwich Ave. (bet. Christopher & 10th Sts.) | 212-924-0604 | www.personnelofnewyork.com

Kristi Paras recently unveiled her new guy-girl concept, setting up shop in the West Village space once inhabited by the last branch of her much loved, now-defunct vintage enterprise, Zachary's Smile; the expansive digs feature concrete floors and saw-tablelike displays, a fitting showcase for cool, indie labels like Black Crane, Courtshop, Creatures of Comfort and Mary Meyer.

Peter Elliot

28 | 26 | 25 | VE

E 80s | 1071 Madison Ave. (81st St.) | 212-570-1551

Peter Elliot Blue

E 70s | 997 Lexington Ave. (72nd St.) | 212-570-2301

Peter Elliot Boots, Etc.

E 80s | 1179 Lexington Ave. (bet. 80th & 81st Sts.) | 212-776-1925
www.peterelliot.com

"Beautiful, tasteful" and exclusive menswear is the hallmark of this string of UES stores, including dapper duds for boys (and women at the 1071 Madison Avenue location) and a boot-centric offshoot; sartorially speaking, the "well-curated selection" leans to the "traditional", though the "high prices" are decidedly up-to-date, but few mind given the quality, staffers who are "lovely to work with" and a civilized atmosphere.

Piaget

▽ 29 | 27 | 26 | VE

E 50s | 730 Fifth Ave. (bet. 56th & 57th Sts.) | 212-246-5555 | www.piaget.com

It's a "pleasure to shop" the "gorgeous" jewelry and luxury timepieces at this venerable Swiss horologist's elegantly understated Fifth Avenue flagship; from its accessibly priced Rose jewelry collection to over-the-top diamond-encrusted watches, every piece represents the "excellent craftsmanship" it's been known for since 1874, and the superb level of service further gilds its "fabulous" reputation.

Pierre Hardy

- | - | - | VE

W Village | 30 Jane St. (W. 4th St.) | 646-449-0070 | www.pierrehardy.com

Renowned for his architectural shapes, this French shoe designer presents looks like towering platforms, natural wood-grain spike heels and shiny patent trainers in a West Village carriage house that's been converted with modern-day trappings, from wood and leather flooring to clear, gray glass displays; the high-fashion mix also includes couture styles for women, a few men's options and distinctively structured handbags.

Pilgrim Surf & Supply

- | - | - | E

Williamsburg | 68 N. Third St. (Wythe Ave.) | Brooklyn | 718-218-7456 | www.pilgrimsurfsupply.com

Urban surfers land everything from trunks, sunnies and colorful chinos to boards, neoprene wetsuits and art books at this inviting Williamsburg shop from the guy behind the now-closed Mollusk; with laid-back staffers and an airy space boasting wood-plank floors and filled with all things water-related, this bright spot brings a bit of California to Brooklyn, while launch parties and photo installations help engage the community.

Pink Chicken

- | - | - | E

E 80s | 1223 Madison Ave. (88th St.) | 212-722-9090 | www.pinkchicken.com

This Amagansett children's atelier ducks into the Upper East Side, bringing striped leggings, ruffled skirts and colorful cotton frocks in twee prints to Madison Avenue, with a few items for moms who want to match their daughters; the boutique has a Hamptons flair, with white walls, funky light fixtures and a beachy feel.

Pintchik
19 | 14 | 21 | M

Park Slope | 478 Bergen St. (Flatbush Ave.) | Brooklyn | 718-783-3333 | 866-290-5334 | www.acehardware.com

It's "been around for a century", so this Park Slope fixer-upper's "fixture" combines long-term "professional" cred with "lots of selection" spanning "paints and related equipment" as well as a "decent assortment of hardware" ("they always have everything – somewhere"); "community" boosters call it a "friendly neighborhood alternative" to the big-box boys.

NEW Piperlime
- | - | - | E

SoHo | 121 Wooster St. (bet. Prince & Spring Sts.) | 212-343-4284 | www.piperlime.com

Fans of the Gap-owned e-commerce site get a real-life retail experience at this SoHo boutique, stocked with a high/low mix of clothing and accessories merchandised by color, with some collections curated by boldface guest editors like Olivia Palermo and Rachel Zoe; temptations abound from names like BB Dakota, Free People and Tibi, plus there's a curved shoe wall to the rear featuring kicks for every budget.

Pippin
▽ 27 | 25 | 28 | M

Chelsea | 112 W. 17th St. (bet. 6th & 7th Aves.) | 212-505-5159 | www.pippinvintage.com

"You never know what you'll find" at this Chelsea vintage jewelry shop harking back to "a time of graciousness and craftsmanship that's almost gone from our world"; it's "lovely" to "browse the trays" of "fairly priced" wares "laid out by type, era or color", and the "attentive" service is "as exquisitely period as the goods"; P.S. the vintage furniture store "tucked away" down the alley from the original is a "gem" too.

Pixie Market ●
- | - | - | M

LES | 100 Stanton St. (Ludlow St.) | 212-253-0953 | www.pixiemarket.com

Funky meets feminine at this quirky LES boutique boasting an indie mix inspired by hip London markets like Spitalfields; the cutting-edge looks, culled from a global array of underground labels and sorted by color, are as likely to boast ruffles as sailor-striped T-shirt dresses and buckled boots; bonus: the salespeople are as "young and adorable" as the mostly moderately priced goods.

Pompanoosuc Mills
28 | 24 | 26 | E

TriBeCa | 124 Hudson St. (Ericsson Pl.) | 212-226-5960 | 800-718-8608 | www.pompy.com

Lend your city digs a little Green Mountain sensibility with "beautiful", "well-crafted furniture" from this handsome TriBeCa showroom, whose solid, country-style pieces for the bedroom, living room, dining room "and beyond" are made to order in Vermont; it's tended by an "excellent" team, but the penny-wise still protest it's "overpriced when compared to similar options."

Pork Pie Hatters ●
- | - | - | M

E Village | 440 E. Ninth St. (bet. Ave. A & 1st Ave.) | 212-260-0408

(continued)

Pork Pie Hatters

NEW Williamsburg | 441 Metropolitan Ave. (bet. Marcy & Meeker Aves.) | Brooklyn | 347-457-6519
www.porkpiehatters.com

An extension of the century-old J.J. Hat Center, this East Village and Williamsburg duo outfits modern-day dandies with cashmere caps, derby toppers, woven fedoras and, yes, nattily trimmed pork-pies, from well-respected brands like Borsalino and Phrenology NYC; both locations are handsomely decorated with masculine furniture, and the Brooklyn outpost has a workshop for crafting custom orders.

Prada
28 | 27 | 24 | VE

E 50s | Fuller Bldg. | 45 E. 57th St. (bet. Madison & Park Aves.) | 212-308-2332
E 50s | 724 Fifth Ave. (bet. 56th & 57th Sts.) | 212-664-0010
E 70s | 841 Madison Ave. (70th St.) | 212-327-4200
SoHo | 575 Broadway (Prince St.) | 212-334-8888
www.prada.com

"Gold-standard" styles, "lip-smacking" bags and "can't-live-without" shoes keep customers coming to Miuccia Prada's SoHo flagship and its scattered sibs despite "break-the-bank" prices, but the "superior merchandise" is only half the pleasure; the Rem Koolhaas–designed attraction, set in Broadway's former Guggenheim building, is "a work of art in itself", making it "part museum, part amusement park", and with "very helpful" staffers too, it's truly "the ultimate shopping experience."

Pratesi
29 | 25 | 24 | VE

E 60s | 829 Madison Ave. (69th St.) | 212-288-2315 | www.pratesi.com

"Treat yourself like royalty" at the venerable Italian company's outpost where Upper Eastsiders who "never want to sleep on anything else" snap up "luxurious bed and bath linens that will spoil you for life"; "despite the formality, the sales staff will not bite", and everything is the "finest quality" and "priced accordingly", though well-rested fans point out "you only pay once, but you enjoy it forever."

NEW Private Stock
- | - | - | E

SoHo | 76 Wooster St. (bet. Broome & Spring Sts.) | 212-219-9889 | www.privatestockbrand.com

Previously available at select fashion-forward retailers, this globally influenced menswear brand by designer Jon Koon is now showcased in his own striking, all-white SoHo destination that's curated like an edgy art gallery; luxe leather accessories are set behind frosted glass and limited-edition jeans are pinned to sliding panels, complete with museum cards, plus there's a koi pond below in an appointment-only subterranean parlor that holds the exotic skins collection.

NEW Procell
- | - | - | E

LES | 5 Delancey St. (bet. Bowery & Chrystie St.) | 212-226-2315 | www.brianprocell.com

Vintage collector Brian Procell displays the fruits of his labor at this LES shop, where his years of scouring flea markets and thrift shops have netted an impressive array of men's and women's attire from the '80s and '90s; the white space provides a spare backdrop for the brightly colored collection of concert tees, backpacks and other old-school ephemera.

	QUALITY	DISPLAY	SERVICE	COST

NEW Proenza Schouler

| - | - | - | VE |

E 60s | 822 Madison Ave. (bet. 68th & 69th Sts.) | 212-585-3200 | www.proenzaschouler.com

Jack McCollough and Lazaro Hernandez's refined collection, named for their mothers' maiden monikers, boasts a hip, downtown sensibility, and yet their retail showcase is located on the Upper East Side, closer to where the designers' deep-pocketed clients reside; steel shelves, exposed beams and pipes create a modern backdrop for store exclusives and runway looks, tailored yet edgy pieces with a subtle 'wow' factor.

Pronovias

| ▽ 25 | 22 | 23 | E |

E 50s | 14 E. 52nd St. (bet. 5th & Madison Aves.) | 212-897-6393 | www.pronovias.us

The aisle-bound adore the super-romantic, sometimes glamorous and always "beautifully made" wedding gowns from this by-appointment-only, Barcelona-based bridal brand; "top-notch" service and "reasonable" prices at the dazzling, seven-story East 50s flagship, which also stocks dresses for mothers of the bride and cocktail frocks, further explain why most brides-to-be deem it "a wonderful shopping experience."

Pucci

| 29 | 27 | 26 | VE |

E 70s | 855 Madison Ave. (71st St.) | 212-230-1135 | www.emiliopucci.com

This iconic Italian design house's "must-place to shop for the fashionista" recently made its move to Madison Avenue, unveiling a sleek space that offers a modern take on the palazzo courtesy of architect Joseph Dirand; informed by the 1960s yet still "timeless", the "fabulous, colorful, on-trend" ready-to-wear, signature prints and eveningwear are of the "highest quality" and sure to "make you drool", plus attentive staffers are "always on hand to assist."

Puma

| 23 | 22 | 20 | M |

Meatpacking | 421 W. 14th St. (bet. 9th & 10th Aves.) | 212-206-0109
SoHo | 521 Broadway (bet. Broome & Spring Sts.) | 212-334-7861
Union Sq | 33 Union Sq. W. (bet. 16th & 17th Sts.) | 212-206-7761
www.puma.com

Jocks "usually do find something" to pounce on at these ambassadors of the German footwear brand, which deliver a "positive experience" with stylish activewear to augment its snazzy sneakers; expect a "trendy setting" that replicates NYC's streets with crumbling brick walls and neon lights at the renovated SoHo flagship, a more exclusive selection on Union Square and classy kicks conceived by various designers at Meatpacking's Black Store.

Purl Soho

| 28 | 27 | 23 | E |

SoHo | 459 Broome St. (bet. Greene & Mercer Sts.) | 212-420-8796 | www.purlsoho.com

A "yarn connoisseur's delight", this "chic little" SoHo store is enough to "give heart palpitations to crafters everywhere", as it's "packed" with "wispy kid mohair, decadent cashmere, soft merino" and other "unexpected yarns in a huge variety of colors", all "stunningly" displayed; for quilters and sewing fans there's a similarly spectacular array of fabrics; sure, it's "expensive" – everything is "high quality" and so "beautiful."

Rachel Riley

–	–	–	E

E 90s | 1286 Madison Ave. (bet. 91st & 92nd Sts.) | 212-534-7477 | www.rachelriley.com

What started as a mother handcrafting clothing for her three children has evolved into a British luxury line of kids' clothing from this eponymous designer, inspired by retro styles of the '40s, '50s and '60s; the whole caboodle is sold at her cozy UES shop along with traditional-style footwear and accessories tweaked for the times and a few pieces for mums as well.

Rag & Bone ☻

26	24	21	E

NEW **Meatpacking** | 425 W. 13th St. (Washington St.) | 212-249-3331
NoLita | 73 E. Houston St. (Elizabeth St.) | 212-777-2210
SoHo | 119 Mercer St. (bet. Prince & Spring Sts.) | 212-219-2204
W 60s | 182 Columbus Ave. (bet. 68th & 69th Sts.) | 212-362-7138
W Village | 100-104 Christopher St. (bet. Bedford & Bleecker Sts.) | 212-727-2990
www.rag-bone.com

David Neville and Marcus Wainwright's "burgeoning super-brand of high-quality" streetwear continues to gain ground, with cool shops Uptown and Downtown, including an industrial-feel, brick-walled Meatpacking addition, equipped with an in-house java bar serving Jack's Stir Brew Coffee; loyalists "love the cuts and fabrics" of these "well-fitted American fashions" ("two words: colored denim"), and if a few find it "a bit expensive", even they admit the pieces "last a long time" – and there's "always something unusual" on the racks.

NEW Raleigh

–	–	–	E

NoLita | 211 Elizabeth St. (Prince St.) | 212-334-1330 | www.raleighworkshop.com

Founded by a husband-and-wife team, this Raleigh, North Carolina–based brand creates its collection the old-fashioned way, making small batches of limited-edition jeans from locally sourced selvedge denim on vintage machines; its new NoLita showcase adds a modern design element to that rustic sensibility, with flocks of paper airplanes covering metal grates, countered by bright chandeliers and a warm tapestry rug.

Ralph Lauren

26	27	24	VE

E 70s | 867 Madison Ave. (bet. 71st & 72nd Sts.) | 212-606-2100
E 70s | 888 Madison Ave. (bet. 71st & 72nd Sts.) | 212-434-8000
SoHo | 109 Prince St. (Greene St.) | 212-625-1660
888-475-7674 | www.ralphlauren.com

"Magnificent all around", the Rhinelander mansion is an "enchanted" setting for the flagship of Ralph Lauren's "classic American brand", with "gorgeous" displays offering a "mind-boggling selection" of "timeless", "high-end" men's fashion, and staffers who "go out of their way to help"; the women's and home store across the street at 888 Madison is "fabulous" too, as is the SoHo offshoot – all are "stocked wall-to-wall" with the "preppy", "expensive/casual" clothes the designer is famous for; P.S. a Polo addition is slated to open at 711 Fifth Avenue.

Ralph Lauren Children's

28 | 27 | 25 | VE

E 70s | 878 Madison Ave. (bet. 71st & 72nd Sts.) | 212-606-3376 | 888-475-7674 | www.ralphlauren.com

When city kids need to dress to impress – you know, for "those kindergarten interviews" – this classic American label delivers with its "imaginative, eye-catching" collection of children's sportswear and special-occasion finery, showcased at this UES destination; a few quibble the tony togs are too "expensive" for everyday, but the faithful find it's "worth a visit" for those "special" outfits.

Ralph Lauren RRL

26 | 27 | 21 | VE

SoHo | 31 Prince St. (Mott St.) | 212-343-0841
SoHo | 381 W. Broadway (bet. Broome & Spring Sts.) | 212-625-3480
W Village | 381 Bleecker St. (Perry St.) | 646-638-0684
W Village | 383 Bleecker St. (Perry St.) | 212-645-5513
www.ralphlauren.com

"Gold mines for lovers of vintage-inspired workwear", this West Village-SoHo quartet is home to the designer's Western-style men's clothing line (think denim, jackets, rugged boots and other "fashionable" essentials for the urbane cowboy); the shops are "beautiful" and "worth seeing" for their retro fittings, and if some bemoan the "pricey" tags, loyalists insist it's "worth it" for such ruggedly "classic" pieces.

Ray Beauty Supply

23 | 11 | 17 | M

W 40s | 721 Eighth Ave. (45th St.) | 212-757-0175 | 800-253-0993 | www.raybeauty.net

Ballerinas, hair stylists and fashionistas visit this no-frills Hell's Kitchen cosmetology and "hair product emporium" to grab the latest styling tools, salon equipment, barber supplies and "any type of professional makeup that exists"; some say staffers are "super-helpful", while others call customer service "nonexistent" and complain that the "chaotic displays" can be a bit "messy."

Rebecca Taylor

24 | 26 | 21 | E

NEW **E 70s** | 980 Madison Ave. (bet. 76th & 77th Sts.) | 646-560-2515
Meatpacking | 34 Gansevoort St. (bet. Greenwich & Hudson Sts.) | 212-243-2600
NoLita | 260 Mott St. (bet. Houston & Prince Sts.) | 212-966-0406
www.rebeccataylor.com

"Unique" designs that manage to be "classic yet trendy", "flirty" but with an "air of relaxation", are what keep clients coming back to this outfit in NoLita, the Meatpacking and Madison Avenue, for "feminine" dresses, separates and sweet seasonal coats; a "beautiful" ambiance and a model-esque staff complete the experience, prompting shoppers to proclaim their "love, love, love!" for the namesake New Zealand designer.

Red Lantern Bicycles ●

- | - | - | E

Clinton Hill | 345 Myrtle Ave. (bet. Adelphi St. & Carlton Ave.) | Brooklyn | 347-889-5338 | www.redlanternbicycles.com

Urban pedalers, from commuters to messengers, flock to this funky Clinton Hill cycle stop for new, refurbished and custom rides plus classes and repairs; the industrial digs also boast a cafe/bar where house-roasted coffee, homemade nut milks and Brooklyn-brewed beer add to the hipster groove – just remember, don't drink and drive.

Reed Krakoff
▽ 28 | 26 | 25 | VE

E 60s | 831 Madison Ave. (bet. 69th & 70th Sts.) | 212-988-0560 | 877-733-3511 | www.reedkrakoff.com

Tailored lines and "simple but practical styling" define Coach executive director Reed Krakoff's eponymous line, which includes luxe sportswear and "truly beautiful" handbags at luxury prices; the Madison Avenue flagship is modern, sleek and spacious with white walls and flattering lighting allowing the coveted "quality" pieces to shine.

Reem Acra
- | - | - | VE

E 50s | 730 Fifth Ave. (bet. 56th & 57th Sts.) | 212-308-8760 | www.reemacra.com

Before walking the red carpet or gliding down the aisle, celebs, royals and tuned-in fashion folk head to this Lebanese designer's Fifth Avenue salon to choose a knockout number; the head-turning, boldly embellished eveningwear, ready-to-wear and bridalwear is arranged amid exotic poufs, chandeliers and pillars and priced for ladies with deep pocketbooks.

Reformation
- | - | - | M

LES | 156 Ludlow St. (bet. Rivington & Stanton Sts.) | 646-448-4925 ●

NEW **SoHo** | 23 Howard St. (bet. Crosby & Lafayette Sts.) | 212-510-8455 www.thereformation.com

Creative director Yael Aflalo is the mastermind behind this eco-conscious enterprise that peddles its own modified and repurposed vintage pieces and au courant standouts refashioned from dead stock materials, all made locally; the brick-walled LES original features old-timey dummies that seem to wink at Ludlow's tenement past while the mammoth Howard Street store boasts a photo booth, juice presses and a mix that's a tad more posh.

REI ●
26 | 24 | 25 | M

NoLita | Puck Bldg. | 303 Lafayette St. (Houston St.) | 212-680-1938 | www.rei.com

"Get your outdoor fix" at this "terrific" branch of Seattle's sporting goods champ in NoLita's Puck Building, a tri-level brick-and-iron behemoth that "preserves artifacts" of the historic edifice and offers "excellent" activewear and gear "galore", sure to propel you "into the wild"; "top-notch" staffers can "truly guide you to what you need" and pricing is "fair" (with "a healthy rebate" for members) – so fans "couldn't be happier."

Resurrection Vintage
- | - | - | VE

NoLita | 217 Mott St. (bet. Prince & Spring Sts.) | 212-625-1374 | www.resurrectionvintage.com

"When you see vintage [garb] in the fashion magazines, chances are it's from this top-quality shop" in NoLita say admirers of this LA sibling's crème-de-la crème collection of avant-garde 1960s–1990s clothing, housed in a chic, uncluttered red-and-black space; true, prices may be dead expensive, but devoted resurrectionists contend that once you "swan around in a Halston gown or snag a Chanel jacket for your skinny jeans", no other venue will do.

QUALITY DISPLAY SERVICE COST

Rick Owens

‐ | ‐ | ‐ | VE

Hudson Square | 250 Hudson St. (bet. Broome & Dominick Sts.) | 212-627-7222 | www.rickowens.eu

The expat Parisian designer really makes a statement in his stark semi-industrial Hudson Square space, oddly adorned with a fog machine; expect dramatic, intricately knotted "black, cool things" for men and women – some cut asymmetrically, others on the bias, all imbued with plenty of artistic attitude (an air also possessed by the shop's beautiful salespeople).

Ricky's ❂

19 | 17 | 16 | M

SoHo | 590 Broadway (bet. Houston & Prince Sts.) | 212-226-5552 | www.rickys-nyc.com
Additional locations throughout the NY area

When "you're looking for off-the-wall, you'll likely find it" at this "quirky" beauty chainster found mostly in New York City, where employees hawk "funky" cosmetics, toiletries, gags and gifts, "erotic" items and even Halloween costumes; still, some customers cite "a love/hate relationship" with this spot, complaining of "crowded" displays, "teenage girl" clientele and "especially long lines" near October 31.

Rico

‐ | ‐ | ‐ | E

Gowanus | 546 Third Ave. (bet. 13th & 14th Sts.) | Brooklyn | 718-797-2077 | www.shoprico.com

"If you want great furniture" in a modern vein, trek to Rico Espinet's Gowanus Goliath, a three-story wonderland of contemporary finds that recently relocated from Atlantic Avenue; each floor is worth exploring, offering a mix of design-forward lighting and made-to-order sofas and chairs from high-end, expertly crafted American and European lines, including DellaRobbia, American Leather and the owner's own innovative collection.

Ride Brooklyn

23 | 22 | 23 | M

Park Slope | 468 Bergen St. (bet. 5th & Flatbush Aves.) | Brooklyn | 718-857-7433
NEW **Williamsburg** | 50 N. Seventh St. (Kent Ave.) | Brooklyn | 718-387-2453
www.ridebrooklynny.com

Skate Brooklyn

Park Slope | 78 St. Marks Pl. (4th Ave.) | Brooklyn | 718-857-5283 | www.skatebrooklynny.com

Ride off with "new bikes for the family" from this "neighborhood" specialist in Park Slope and now Williamsburg too, where its team of "super-friendly" "experts" pairs "novice and pro cyclists alike" with wheels and getups from brands that "strike a good balance between casual and fancy"; meanwhile, its "neat" sidekick on St. Marks Place fully equips skaters at "reasonable prices."

Roberta Freymann

∇ 23 | 24 | 20 | M

E 70s | 958 Lexington Ave. (70th St.) | 212-717-7373 | www.robertafreymann.com

"Elegant, yet unpretentious" resortwear and "unique" accessories that are happily "not too expensive" make this globe-trotting designer's UES brownstone a "favorite" with seekers of the exotic; brightly colored walls set the perfect backdrop for "interesting items with an Indian flavor", including caftans and shawls sourced directly from world bazaars and created in partnership with local artisans in Thailand, Nepal, Peru and beyond.

Roberta Roller Rabbit

 ▽ 25 | 25 | 25 | E

E 70s | 1019 Lexington Ave. (73rd St.) | 212-772-7200
NEW **TriBeCa** | 176 Duane St. (bet. Greenwich & Hudson Sts.) | 212-966-0076
www.robertafreymann.com

A "wonderful design sense" pervades designer Roberta Freymann's East 70s and TriBeCa storefronts where her Indian-inspired line of pretty, colorful screen-printed linens, "unique" furniture and other "attractive" home furnishings makes some "want to redecorate their whole apartment"; others settle for her "comfy weekend wear", like pajamas and tunics for men, women and children, made with wonderfully "light and airy fabrics."

Robert Lee Morris Gallery

27 | 27 | 26 | E

SoHo | 400 W. Broadway (bet. Broome & Spring Sts.) | 212-431-9405 | www.robertleemorrisgallery.com

Jewelry designer Robert Lee Morris continues his four-decade-long run as a purveyor of "unique" sculptural cuffs, charms and chokers in hammered silver and gold, hawking his wares via "great displays" in a SoHo storefront; shoppers "adore his sensibility" and praise his "craftsmanship", saying his stuff is "worth every penny."

Robert Marc

25 | 23 | 23 | VE

E 40s | 400 Madison Ave. (bet. 47th & 48th Sts.) | 212-319-2900
E 50s | 551 Madison Ave. (bet. 55th & 56th Sts.) | 212-319-2000
E 60s | 782 Madison Ave. (bet. 66th & 67th Sts.) | 212-737-6000
E 70s | 1046 Madison Ave. (bet. 79th & 80th Sts.) | 212-988-9600
E 80s | 1225 Madison Ave. (bet. 88th & 89th Sts.) | 212-722-1600
SoHo | 436 W. Broadway (bet. Prince & Spring Sts.) | 212-343-8300
W 60s | 190 Columbus Ave. (bet. 68th & 69th Sts.) | 212-799-4600
W Village | 386 Bleecker St. (Perry St.) | 212-242-6668
www.robertmarc.com

"No matter the trends", the "classy specs" from this fashion-forward visionary will fetch "a bunch of compliments" for their "elegant" styling, thanks to the "house brand's" "flattering" lineup of designer frames and "well-made sunglasses"; the chainlet is also marked by "excellent" guidance from pros who "know their inventory", so though you'll "spend a bundle", it's "worth it."

Roberto Cavalli

28 | 27 | 25 | VE

E 60s | 711 Madison Ave. (63rd St.) | 212-755-7722 | www.robertocavalli.com

A distinctly "rock 'n' roll" vibe (think python-print furniture) pervades the Madison Avenue boutique of this "one-of-a-kind" Florentine designer known for his ample use of animal patterns and leather in his womens- and menswear; it's easy to imagine this "cool" garb on "bronzed and toned" jet-setter types who are pampered by the stylish staff and who don't bat a (fake) eyelash at the aspirational price tags.

Roche Bobois
25 | 26 | 21 | VE

 NEW **E 50s** | 207 E. 57th St. (bet. 2nd & 3rd Aves.) | 212-980-2574
Murray Hill | 200 Madison Ave. (35th St.) | 212-889-0700
www.roche-bobois.com

Très "attractive" designs are the hallmark of this French furniture company that's offered lovely modern decor at its Madison Avenue address since 1961; salespeople can be "very intimidating" and price tags that are "out of reach for many" mean some stick to "window shopping", but given the quality of its furnishings fans say "if you can afford it, do it."

Roger Vivier
28 | 27 | 25 | VE

E 60s | 750 Madison Ave. (65th St.) | 212-861-5371 |
www.rogervivier.com

In the careful hands of creative director Bruno Frisoni, this legendary French footwear label continues to step out, offering covetable, cutting-edge stilettos and boots together with more "timeless", "feminine" designs like the late namesake designer's "classic" pilgrim flats "with the square buckle"; adding to their allure, the "elegant" shoes are artfully displayed in the brand's "beautiful", museum-style Madison Avenue salon.

Room & Board
24 | 25 | 23 | E

SoHo | 105 Wooster St. (bet. Prince & Spring Sts.) | 212-334-4343 |
800-301-9720 | www.roomandboard.com

"Do a one-stop shop" for your pad at this Minnesota-born chain link in SoHo advise home improvers who praise the "excellent-quality" "modern classics", including "timeless" couches, home accessories and bedding; the "inspiring" displays "show great possibilities", the multifloor setup is "easy to navigate" and "professional" staffers also help you "maximize your space" – even "the delivery service treats your merchandise like gold."

Rothman's
25 | 21 | 25 | E

Union Sq | 222 Park Ave. S. (18th St.) | 212-777-7400 |
www.rothmansny.com

Situated in sprawling 11,000-sq.-ft. quarters, this Union Square haberdasher carries "everything you need to keep your man's wardrobe current" at "sometimes sale prices", offering "beautiful suits, coats, ties and casual pieces" from labels like Canali, Hugo Boss and Earnest Sewn; a fixture since its pushcart days in the 1920s, this "family-owned" enterprise is "ahead of the game for a reason: they know their customers."

Rubin Museum of Art Shop
26 | 23 | 22 | M

Chelsea | Rubin Museum of Art | 150 W. 17th St. (bet. 6th & 7th Aves.) |
212-620-5000 | www.rmanyc.org

"Perfectly befitting" its site in the Chelsea museum of Himalayan art, this "lovely gift shop" merges "quality" with "spiritual resonance" in a selection of "treasures" "from the Far East", including "exotic jewelry", "beautiful scarves", "unusual" "books on Buddhism" and a dharma-friendly "line of toys"; while occasionally "costly", it's "a real find" for "inspiring and enlightening" splurges.

Rudy's Music Shop
▽ 29 | 23 | 24 | E

SoHo | 461 Broome St. (bet. Greene & Mercer Sts.) | 212-625-2557

	QUALITY	DISPLAY	SERVICE	COST

(continued)

Rudy's Music Shop

W 40s | 169 W. 48th St. (bet. 6th & 7th Aves.) | 212-391-1699
www.rudysmusic.com

A "standard for pros" and wannabes alike, this Midtown mainstay and its "beautiful" SoHo encore are "musician's musician shops" mostly noted for "dazzling" high-end guitars, vintage and new; the "down-to-earth service" is "as well tuned as the gear", and the prices "work for any serious player", so "when you get that record contract" "take a good look" – it's "worth every penny."

Sabon ◑ | 26 | 26 | 27 | E |

SoHo | 93 Spring St. (B'way) | 212-925-0742 | 866-697-2266 |
www.sabonnyc.com
Additional locations throughout the NY area

Cleansing "never felt so sinful" claim "overstressed New Yorkers" who are "totally hooked" on this "heavenly", "high-end Israeli" sudster pushing "Dead Sea salt" scrubs, "handmade" soaps, "luscious creams" and other "nose candy"; you're welcomed by a "pampering" staff that performs a "luxurious hand-washing session", so just "hand over your wallet" and succumb to the "soapalicious" temptations.

Saint James Boutique   ▽ | 25 | 24 | 21 | VE |

W Village | 319 Bleecker St. (bet. Christopher & Grove Sts.) |
212-741-7400 | www.saintjamesboutique.com

Bringing a "slice" of French style to the West Village, this offshoot of the legendary Lower Normandy–based company outfits modern-day mariners in "beautiful", colorful iterations of the classic Breton striped T-shirts favored by fashion plates like Gwyneth Paltrow; rounding out the functional yet fashionable Francophile mix: fisherman's sweaters, duffle coats and sailor-inspired accessories.

Saint Laurent Paris | 28 | 27 | 26 | VE |
(aka Yves St. Laurent)

E 50s | 3 E. 57th St. (bet. 5th & Madison Aves.) | 212-980-2970
NEW **SoHo** | 80 Greene St. (bet. Broome & Spring Sts.) | 212-431-3240
800-399-0929 | www.ysl.com

"Fabulous, fabulous, fabulous" swoon fans of the "gorgeous" men's and women's apparel and accessories from this iconic French phenomenon, all laid out against a sophisticated black-and-white backdrop at the 57th Street mecca and its brand-new marble-and-chrome SoHo addition; while a recent changeover rendered "heir" to the YSL throne Stefano Pilati out and artistic director Hedi Slimane in, and the name itself has been officially rebranded Saint Laurent Paris, "elegance" abounds and you'll still pay top dollar for the ultra-"chic" experience.

Saks Fifth Avenue | 27 | 26 | 23 | VE |

E 50s | 611 Fifth Ave. (50th St.) | 212-753-4000 | 877-551-7257 |
www.saks.com

Deemed the "queen of department stores", this Fifth Avenue "institution" has "everything you ever dreamt of under one roof", with "top-notch" designer duds, an "excellent cosmetics" floor, "a shoe section that's as close to heaven as possible" ("there is a reason" it "has its own zip code") and "massive sale racks" that can temper "prohibitively expensive" tabs; "impeccable" service and "breathtaking displays" "delight and inspire" – especially around Christmas, when "windows are remarkably dressed – not unlike the patrons."

Salvatore Ferragamo
29 | 28 | 26 | VE

E 50s | 655 Fifth Ave. (52nd St.) | 212-759-3822 | 800-628-8916 | www.ferragamo.com

An "exquisite" experience, this 20,000-sq.-ft. Fifth Avenue showboat is the Italian brand's largest store and leather goods "heaven" for aficionados; the "deliciously comfortable" footwear (notably the ribbon-bowed Vara) and "best of the best" scarves, ties, handbags and apparel "are always ace", while the "excellent craftsmanship means these luxury goods last and last"; add in an "impeccable" staff that "helps you narrow down" your "haul" and it's little wonder that "loyal customers" feel it's "worth every penny."

Sam Ash
26 | 22 | 22 | M

Garment District | 333 W. 34th St. (bet. 8th & 9th Aves.) | 212-719-2299
Kings Plaza | 2600 Flatbush Ave. (Hendrickson Pl.) | Brooklyn | 718-951-3888 ●
Forest Hills | 113-25 Queens Blvd. (bet. 75th Ave. & 76th Rd.) | Queens | 718-793-7983 ●
800-472-6274 | www.samashmusic.com

A "necessity" for anyone "creating music", this chainster is a "legend" for its "broad selection" of "fantastic instruments": guitars, drums, keyboards, winds and strings or "devices for all your DJ" needs, plus "related items"; also expect "in-the-know" service from "dedicated (even obsessed)" staffers who "look like extras from *Spinal Tap*."

NEW Sam Edelman
– | – | – | M

SoHo | 109 Spring St. (bet. Greene & Mercer Sts.) | 212-226-7800 | www.samedelman.com

Planting his first flagship in the middle of SoHo, this cool cobbler trades in fashion-forward footwear, bags and jackets at prices as sunny as the bright setting; the collection is displayed in three chandeliered salons that match the mood of the casual, dressy and rocker-style looks, with plenty of room to move – catnip for Carrie Bradshaws-in-training clogging the nabe's cobblestone streets.

Sam Flax
23 | 17 | 17 | M

E 50s | 900 Third Ave. (bet. 54th & 55th Sts.) | 212-813-6666
Flatiron | 3 W. 20th St. (bet. 5th & 6th Aves.) | 212-620-3000
800-628-9512 | www.samflaxny.com

"Whatever your art needs", this East 50s–Flatiron pair carries a "complete range" including design supplies, stationery, an "excellent" framing department and "streamlined" furniture and office goods to "add distinction to your work world"; it catches flack for being "pricey", but it has "that unique item" you need "even if you're not an artist."

Sandro
– | – | – | E

NEW E 70s | 986 Madison Ave. (bet. 76th & 77th Sts.) | 212-772-8500
NoLita | 8 Prince St. (bet. Bowery & Elizabeth St.) | 212-226-3226
NEW SoHo | 150 Spring St. (bet. W. B'way & Wooster St.) | 212-226-2090
W Village | 415 Bleecker St. (Bank St.) | 646-438-9335
www.sandro-paris.com

For effortless style, head to these Big Apple offshoots from the popular Paris-based juggernaut; designed by a mother-and-son duo, the "trendy" label is staking its claim on the fashion set with its romantic, modern and always "on-point" "high-quality" womenswear and city-chic looks for guys; P.S. the stores are located near Maje, another French staple, created by the owners' sister/aunt.

Santa Maria Novella

29 | 29 | 24 | E

(aka LAFCO NY)

NoLita | 285 Lafayette St. (bet. Houston & Prince Sts.) | 212-925-0001 | 800-362-3677 | www.lafcony.com

Like a "little slice of Italy" "transported to Lafayette Street", this beauty sanctuary, rated No. 1 in NYC for Display, offers "truly amazing" "wares made from centuries-old recipes", "from colognes and room sprays to candles" and "gorgeous soaps"; "the aroma will lure you" into a dark wooden and iron-pillared space that's as "hard to resist" as the Florence original – just bring lots of euros for this "utterly exquisite" "splurge."

Saturdays Surf NYC

- | - | - | E

SoHo | 31 Crosby St. (bet. Broome & Grand Sts.) | 212-966-7875
W Village | 17 Perry St. (Waverly Pl.) | 347-246-5830
www.saturdaysnyc.com

Perhaps the "most elegant surf shops ever", this surfboard-bedecked SoHo-Village duo draws waveriders looking to "add to their wardrobes" with "ever-so-cool" attire including house-line tees and boardshorts and Vans sneakers, plus Patagonia wet suits and scuba gear; the Crosby Street original boasts an "amazing" espresso bar and "quaint garden", giving the hang-10 set even more reason to, well, hang.

NEW Schutz

- | - | - | E

E 60s | 655 Madison Ave. (64th St.) | 212-257-4366 | www.schutz-shoes.com

The coveted Brazilian shoe label brings its head-turning style state-side, opening its first store outside of its homeland on well-traveled Madison Avenue; the graphic gallery-inspired black-and-white space boasts geometric tables and backlit cubes, the better to showcase de-signer Giovanni Bianco's bejeweled platforms, velvety slippers and strappy sandals that reflect the brand's sexy South American roots.

Scoop Men's

23 | 22 | 20 | E

E 70s | 1277 Third Ave. (bet. 73rd & 74th Sts.) | 212-535-5577
Meatpacking | 873 Washington St. (14th St.) | 212-929-1244
www.scoopnyc.com

Hailed as a "godsend for the well-dressed man", Scoop's sibs offer a "great mix" of "hip, cutting-edge designer clothes" from the likes of Billy Reid and John Varvatos, in Meatpacking and UES digs adjacent to their womenswear counterparts; the convenience factor makes "higher-end" prices worth it – guys can get in, "get all the essentials" and get out.

Scoop NYC

24 | 22 | 17 | E

E 70s | 1273-1275 Third Ave. (bet. 73rd & 74th Sts.) | 212-535-5577
Meatpacking | 861 Washington St. (14th St.) | 212-691-1905
SoHo | 473-475 Broadway (bet. Broome & Grand Sts.) | 212-925-3539
877-726-6777 | www.scoopnyc.com

"Shop like a true New Yorker", as do "waify models" and "Waspy social-ites", at this "hip" chainlet with Uptown-Downtown branches, where "bold, refreshing, out-of-the-box" finds from DVF, Theory and Zac Posen abound alongside über-directional jeans; service ranges from "insightful" to sorta "rude", but all agree it's still the spot to "pick up an outfit for tonight"; P.S. the SoHo boutique also stocks some guywear.

Scotch & Soda
▽ 27 | 26 | 27 | E

NEW **Flatiron** | 866 Broadway (bet. 17th & 18th Sts.) | 646-561-9676
NoLita | 273 Lafayette St. (Prince St.) | 212-966-3300
www.scotch-soda.com

Get a taste of Dutch style at this Amsterdam-based brand's Flatiron-NoLita branches brimming with some of the "best clothes" around; guys and girls "love" this outfit for its "fantastic" fashions and "unique pieces", some inspired by classic, military and vintage styles, and toast the "really friendly staff" for providing "great service."

Scully & Scully
28 | 26 | 27 | VE

E 50s | 504 Park Ave. (bet. 59th & 60th Sts.) | 212-755-2590 |
800-223-3717 | www.scullyandscully.com

For a glimpse of "old-guard NYC", head to this Park Avenue stalwart that's been purveying heirloom-ready furniture and home furnishings, plus ever-chic jewelry, since 1934; aspirants and well-heeled society ladies alike find American and European treasures galore to re-create a kinder, gentler era, from emerald-green leather recliners and brass candlestick lamps to Herend figurines, china, crystal and sterling flatware.

Selima Optique
25 | 24 | 25 | E

E 70s | 899 Madison Ave. (bet. 72nd & 73rd Sts.) | 212-988-6690
SoHo | 59 Wooster St. (Broome St.) | 212-343-9490
www.selimaoptique.com

Sucre

W Village | 357 Bleecker St. (bet. Charles & 10th Sts.) |
212-352-1640 | www.sucrenyc.com

For pacesetters in pursuit of "new and updated eyeglasses", visionary designer Selima Salaun's boutiques boast a "wonderful selection" of her signature frames (notably colorful takes on classic shapes) plus models from elite French, Italian and Japanese names; yes, such "great quality" can be "expensive", but the staff's "not pushy" and Sucre sweetens the deal with womenswear, jewelry and accessories.

Sephora ☽
25 | 24 | 22 | M

E 40s | 597 Fifth Ave. (bet. 48th & 49th Sts.) | 212-980-6534 |
877-737-4672 | www.sephora.com
Additional locations throughout the NY area

All hail the "candy store of cosmetics" carrying "your favorite brands" and hot "newcomers" in makeup, skin treatments, haircare, fragrance and beauty tools for every age and ethnicity; reviewers adore the "well-trained" staff, "deluxe" free samples (the "perfect fix for a crisis"), loyalty card "perks" and return policy, not to mention the on-site paint artists; just "be careful, it's a seductive place and the tendency to impulse buy" reigns supreme.

7 For All Mankind
25 | 23 | 22 | E

Flatiron | 73 Fifth Ave. (15th St.) | 212-924-4146 ☽
SoHo | 394 W. Broadway (bet. Broome & Spring Sts.) | 212-226-8615
W Village | 347 Bleecker St. (W. 10th St.) | 212-255-2705
877-427-1114 | www.7forallmankind.com

Jeans lovers appreciate the sheer "simplicity of shopping" at this premium denim brand's boutiques boasting a "deep assortment" of "every possible cut-and-color combo" imaginable, sold by staffers who don't "bat an eye when you attempt to try on" every number; the "super-cute booty" styles "help flat bums" and the "taller crowd" also scores big-time – whatever your body type "be prepared to shell out" for "pairs that fit perfectly."

718 Cyclery ❷   - | - | - | E

Gowanus | 254 Third Ave. (bet. President & Union Sts.) | Brooklyn | 347-457-5760 | www.718c.com

Owned by former bike messenger Joseph Nocella, an architect by day and full-time cycle geek, this community-minded Gowanus enterprise serves up two-wheelers from Brooklyn Cruiser, Public, Torker and other hard-to-track-down makers in an open layout kitted out with living room–type furniture; enthusiasts can ride over for tune-ups or sign up for a collaborative-build experience, creating custom vehicles alongside seasoned mechanics.

Shabby Chic Couture   ▽ 25 | 27 | 24 | E

SoHo | 117 Mercer St. (bet. Prince & Spring Sts.) | 212-334-3500 | www.shabbychic.com

Followers of British trailblazer Rachel Ashwell "love every piece" at her SoHo home furnishings "dreamland", where the "beautiful" house-label line of slipcovered seating, bedding, lighting and decor accents is fabricated in a lived-in vein (per the moniker) to "look like you've had it forever"; no wonder it's so tempting to "spend lots of money."

The Shade Store   ▽ 27 | 21 | 24 | M

E 50s | 200 E. 59th St. (3rd Ave.) | 212-645-2424
E 80s | 1100 Madison Ave. (bet. 82nd & 83rd Sts.) | 212-645-2424
SoHo | 198 Spring St. (bet. Sullivan & Thompson Sts.) | 212-645-2424
800-754-1455 | www.theshadestore.com

Keeping the indoors out of the sun, these branches of a bicoastal outfit display a tasteful lineup of "quality" window shades, wood blinds and drapery, presenting "lots of choices" including varieties you "couldn't find anywhere else"; the "helpful" sales team specializes in custom treatments tailored to your panes and will provide "samples" free of charge.

Shen Beauty   - | - | - | E

Cobble Hill | 315 Court St. (bet. Degraw & Sackett Sts.) | Brooklyn | 718-576-2679 | www.shen-beauty.com

The brainchild of a former stylist/beauty writer, this white-and-pink apothecary brings a covey of niche, natural and organic cosmetics and toiletries from Britain and beyond to Cobble Hill; boost your routine with Amanda Lacey's skincare products and Mrs. White's cold cream, usually near-impossible to find stateside, and check out the grooming goods too, like Recipe for Men's low-foam shaving cream.

Shoe Market ❷   25 | 24 | 24 | M

Williamsburg | 160 N. Sixth St. (Bedford Ave.) | Brooklyn | 718-388-8495 | www.shoemarketnyc.com

Sole-searchers on shoestring budgets score big at this semi-"affordable" Williamsburg staple, where the handpicked footwear for grown-ups and kids includes classic Bass styles, "hip-and-now" finds from Dolce Vita and Jeffrey Campbell and off-the-beaten-path labels like Senso Diffusion; with such a "range of prices", the shoes are ripe for the picking.

The Shop@Scandinavia House
▽ 25 | 19 | 20 | M

Murray Hill | Scandinavia House | 58 Park Ave. (38th St.) | 212-847-9737 | www.scandinaviahouse.org

Score those "Marimekko hostess gifts" at this "charming little" Murray Hill haven, an "attractive" smorgasbord of "Scandinavian style" where the "unique" merch features "wonderful" designs in tableware, clothing, jewelry and "tchotchkes"; prices run "reasonable" to "expensive" "depending", but these "tempting goodies" are "hard to find elsewhere."

Silver Lining Opticians
- | - | - | E

SoHo | 92 Thompson St. (bet. Prince & Spring Sts.) | 212-274-9191 | www.silverliningopticians.com

Jordan Silver and optician Erik Sacher "really know their way around glasses" exclaim loyalists who discover an "incredible selection" that's "completely unlike anything you'll find" elsewhere at the owners' brick-walled SoHo boutique; the thoughtful array includes "classic, handcrafted" frames and sunnies from directional labels like Barton Perreira and Garrett Leight, "cool" never-worn vintage treasures from Carrera and Persol and a popular house collection, plus most can be fitted with prescription lenses on the spot.

Simon's Hardware & Bath
26 | 19 | 19 | E

Murray Hill | 421 Third Ave. (bet. 29th & 30th Sts.) | 212-532-9220 | 888-274-6667 | www.simonshardwareandbath.com

"If it's a knob or pull" or an "unusual" bauble for the kitchen and bath you're after, you'll find "gorgeous quality hardware" aplenty at this Murray Hill mainstay, the "first stop" for home renovators; "browsing is wonderful", "prices are competitive" (if "expensive") and "service is excellent and knowledgeable" – though a few pout it's "rare" to find "assistance."

NEW SlapBack ●
- | - | - | M

Williamsburg | 490 Metropolitan Ave. (Rodney St.) | Brooklyn | 347-227-7133 | www.slapbacknyc.com

Retro fiends get their fill at this black, white and leopard-accented Williamsburg boutique, where vintage replications of *Mad Men*-era styles (think circle skirts, high-waisted shorts and sireny dresses) fill the racks and old movie posters adorn the walls; the quirky spot still manages to keep things modern with punky shop girls and tough accessories.

Smythson of Bond Street
29 | 26 | 24 | VE

W 50s | 4 W. 57th St. (5th Ave.) | 212-265-4573 | 877-769-8476 | www.smythson.com

When "only the best will do", this tip-top Midtown envoy of the circa-1887 London landmark trades in "timeless elegance" with its "absolutely lovely" bespoke stationery and lustrous leather goods, notably handbags and cases in vibrant hues, "the most beautiful" bound diaries and posh personal accessories for him or her; the prices are predictably "astronomic", but these "goods last forever" ("technology be damned").

QUALITY | DISPLAY | SERVICE | COST

Soapology

25 | 24 | 21 | E

W Village | 67 Eighth Ave. (13th St.) | 212-255-7627 |
www.soapologynyc.com

"So many choices, but there are only so many body parts to wash"
quip patrons who lather up at this West Village beauty destination,
choosing natural and organic soaps, shower gels, lotions and potions
in over 50 scents and, for the fragrance-adverse, unscented options;
it's all presented in a vintage-y setting awash in distressed wood, and
sold by "kind" staffers who dispense plenty of "free samples."

Sony Store

27 | 23 | 20 | E

E 50s | Sony Plaza | 550 Madison Ave. (bet. 55th & 56th Sts.) |
212-833-8800 | www.sony.com

A "great display environment" for "all the newest Sony equipment",
this expansive East Side flagship of the "consumer electronics" colos-
sus boasts an eye-filling array of cameras, computers, gaming con-
soles and home theater equipment ("especially check out the TV"
section to "get the real experience"); it skews "expensive", but the
"knowledgeable" salespeople "won't rush you" – most techies "couldn't
be more pleased."

Space Kiddets

25 | 21 | 23 | E

Flatiron | 26 E. 22nd St. (bet. B'way & Park Ave.) | 212-420-9878 |
www.spacekiddets.com

"There's a lovely whimsy about" this far-out Flatiron kids' shop, making it a go-to for gift-givers who know they'll discover that "special
present" amid the "unusual" jumble of toys, games and clothing "full
of attitude"; if the out-of-this-world prices have some grumbling "the
stuff gets a lot less charming when it's so expensive", rocketeers say
they sure know what makes kids "tick."

Space.NK apothecary

27 | 25 | 24 | E

E 70s | 968 Lexington Ave. (71st St.) | 212-288-3212
SoHo | 99 Greene St. (bet. Prince & Spring Sts.) | 212-941-4200
W 70s | 217 Columbus Ave. (70th St.) | 212-362-2840
www.spacenk.com

Truly "a little treasure of a shop" with three Manhattan locations,
this "great English import" offers a "terrific", if pricey, selection of
"high-quality" "unusual beauty brands" like Philip B, Chantecaille and
Hourglass, plus an edited assortment of other "fantastic" cult favorites, all tended by a "very knowledgeable" staff; items are prettily displayed in a "modern and futuristic" setting, which some fawn over and
others find "intimidating."

Sperry Top-Sider

26 | 23 | 22 | M

Flatiron | 103 Fifth Ave. (bet. 17th & 18th Sts.) | 212-675-7248 |
800-247-6575 | www.sperrytopsider.com

Boaters (or those who just want to look the part) cruise over to
this preppy nautical brand's Flatiron District flagship for "very
comfortable" classic rubber-sole deck shoes – a "summer must-
have" available in "every imaginable" color and pattern – plus
"chukka boots", ballet flats, wedges and some apparel; an open-
stockroom setup offers a convenient self-serve option, making shopping here smooth sailing.

QUALITY DISPLAY SERVICE COST

Splendid
▽ - | - | - | M

SoHo | 111 Spring St. (bet. Greene & Mercer Sts.) | 212-966-6600 | www.splendid.com

The whole family can get comfy at this SoHo outpost of the popular LA-based label renowned for its super-soft, understated T-shirts, tanks, hoodies, swimsuits and beach-ready dresses in neutral and vivid bright colors and stripes; the setting – whitewashed exposed-brick walls, natural wood displays, playful pinwheel accents – is just as laid-back as these easy-wear jersey and woven pieces.

Sportmax
▽ 27 | 26 | 23 | E

SoHo | 450 W. Broadway (bet. Houston & Prince Sts.) | 212-674-1817 | www.sportmax.it

Chichi ladies and European tourists "keep coming back" to MaxMara's pristine SoHo sibling for Italian silk party dresses, luxe leather jackets, flowy pants and "charming" accessories; "attentive" salespeople tend to the sleek setting and "interesting" displays, and though prices are high, "great clearance and regular sales" calm sticker shock.

Stella McCartney
26 | 24 | 24 | VE

SoHo | 112 Greene St. (bet. Prince & Spring Sts.) | 212-255-1556 | www.stellamccartney.com

"Even if she weren't Paul's daughter", the U.K. designer's sporty, "high-end" duds for the "daring" woman, marked with "unique and individual style" (and no leather, ever), would be "unequalled" according to avid admirers who shop the collection along with out-of-the-ordinary children's apparel at this spacious, bi-level SoHo flagship; completing the luxe package: an "accommodating" crew that "goes the extra mile."

Stereo Exchange
▽ 28 | 20 | 21 | E

NoHo | 627 Broadway (bet. Bleecker & Houston Sts.) | 212-505-1111 | 800-833-0071 | www.stereoexchange.com

Audiophiles with an ear for the "good stuff" turn to this NoHo outfit for "top-end stereo" and home theater equipment shown in a sprawling space with seven sound rooms; the ample inventory ranges from big-ticket to "less expensive", though critics who contend the salespeople "push their pet" preferences hint "go there knowing what you want."

Steven Alan
28 | 24 | 24 | E

NoLita | 229 Elizabeth St. (bet. Houston & Prince Sts.) | 212-226-7482
W Village | 69 Eighth Ave. (13th St.) | 212-242-2677 ●
Downtown Bklyn | 347-349 Atlantic Ave. (bet. Bond & Hoyt Sts.) | Brooklyn | 718-852-3257

Steven Alan Annex
NEW **Chelsea** | 140 10th Ave. (bet. 18th & 19th Sts.) | 646-664-0606
TriBeCa | 103 Franklin St. (bet. Church St. & W. B'way) | 212-343-0692

Steven Alan Home Shop
NEW **TriBeCa** | 158 Franklin St. (bet. Hudson & Varick Sts.) | 646-402-9661

Steven Alan Outpost
W 80s | 465 Amsterdam Ave. (bet. 82nd & 83rd Sts.) | 212-595-8451
877-978-2526 | www.stevenalan.com

"An NYC original", this chainlet with a general store feel offers a "fantastic, well-curated" (if pricey) selection of effortlessly "stylish" menswear and womenswear that's "ahead of the curve", including "hipster goods" from Daryl K, No. 6 and the namesake owner's "preppy-ish" line, "truly unique" leather bags and apothecary finds, plus tabletop items and more at the newly hatched home shop; the crowning touch: staffers with a "genuine love for the product."

Stickley, Audi & Co.

26 | 26 | 24 | VE

Chelsea | 207 W. 25th St. (bet. 7th & 8th Aves.) | 212-337-0700 | www.stickleyaudi.com

"They have the quality you want" at this tri-level Chelsea showroom, a specialist in "simply beautiful" Mission furniture, where savvy staffers "help you choose the right piece, wood and fabric" ("nothing is cookie-cutter"), complemented by fine rugs and Craftsman seating; though the "high" cost is a sticking point, "if you like this style" it's "well worth every cent you spend."

St. John

28 | 26 | 27 | VE

E 50s | 665 Fifth Ave. (bet. 53rd & 54th Sts.) | 212-755-5252 | www.discoverstjohn.com

"Even if you're not a size two" or a "governor's wife", the "modern woman" can find both "beautiful, classic" knitwear and "sophisticated" items at this storied label's "elegant" Fifth Avenue flagship; while society and business types collect the "gorgeous" attire for their walk-in closets aided by "wonderful salespeople", some note that its rebranding efforts have yet to attract "younger customers", dubbing the designs "matronly."

Stone Fox Bride

- | - | - | E

SoHo | 611 Broadway (bet. Bleecker & Houston Sts.) | 212-260-8600 | www.stonefoxbride.com

For an untraditional wedding-day ensemble, visit Molly Guy's sun-filled SoHo salon, where the former *Nylon* magazine beauty/style editor teams up with directional designers like Ohne Titel and showcases her own line of froufrou-free wedding gowns, bridesmaid dresses and accessories, plus vintage finds too, all geared toward brides with a bohemian-punk sensibility; the shop also offers unique services, including referrals for financial counselors, nutritionists and even sex therapy.

NEW Store One One 4

- | - | - | E

LES | 114 Stanton St. (bet. Essex & Ludlow Sts.) | 212-780-0227 | www.storeoneone4.com

The designers behind labels Some Odd Rubies and Lindsey Thornburg team up at this Lower East Side boutique, where both brands are on view alongside jewelry and accessories from other indie-oriented New York–based designers; the decor matches the attire's bohemian aesthetic, and there's a workshop on-site as well.

Story

22 | 20 | 22 | E

Chelsea | 144 10th Ave. (19th St.) | 212-242-4853 | www.astartupstore.com

"Very casual, yet chic and upscale", this Chelsea upstart is one part store, one part gallery, with a magazine's point of view; marketing consultant/mastermind Rachel Shechtman collaborates with guest curators from diverse industries, conjuring up revolving themes that change every four–six weeks, with apparel, jewelry, beauty products and gift items culled from local and established brands; the result: "wonderful!"

QUALITY | DISPLAY | SERVICE | COST

String
29 | 28 | 26 | E

E 60s | 33 E. 65th St. (bet. Madison & Park Aves.) | 212-288-9276 |
www.stringyarns.com

"Knitting nirvana" is found at this Victorian East 60s brownstone,
rated NYC's No. 1 in the Lifestyle category; "novices" and pros alike
swoon over the "gorgeous displays" of "luxurious fibers", from alpaca
and silk to "scrumptious cashmere" (the "proprietary lines are the
best") and applaud the "trunk shows from top yarn-makers"; the finishing touch: a "skilled staff" that "knows their products" and can
deftly "teach a new stitch or fix a goof-up."

Stuart Weitzman
28 | 26 | 24 | E

E 50s | 625 Madison Ave. (bet. 58th & 59th Sts.) | 212-750-2555
E 50s | 675 Fifth Ave. (53rd St.) | 212-759-1570
NEW SoHo | 118 Spring St. (bet. Greene & Mercer Sts.) | 212-226-3440
W 60s | Shops at Columbus Circle | 10 Columbus Circle, ground fl.
(B'way & 60th St.) | 212-823-9560 ●
W 70s | 2151 Broadway (bet. 75th & 76th Sts.) | 212-873-0983
www.stuartweitzman.com

"Put your best foot forward" at this namesake designer's sleek shops
around town, a footwear "favorite" brimming with "great staples",
"classy, comfortable" and "fashion-forward" offerings and "superb"
wedding styles, all available in hard-to-find sizes – "a godsend for
women with small feet"; "polite, helpful" staffers help find looks "you
can wear forever", and though prices are "moderate to expensive",
you can always "wait for the sales."

The Studio Museum in Harlem Gift Shop
25 | 25 | 25 | M

Harlem | The Studio Museum in Harlem | 144 W. 125th St.
(bet. Adam Clayton Powell Jr. Blvd. & Lenox Ave.) | 212-864-4500 |
www.studiomuseum.org

African and African-American art are "reflected in the merch" at this
"small" but "exciting" shop catering to Harlem-centric tastes with "interesting stock", from "phenomenal" books to an "excellent selection
of jewelry", prints and other cultured curios; as one might gather from
perusing the "unusual" wares, "the museum is also incredible."

Sugar Cookies ●
27 | 24 | 24 | E

Chelsea | 203 W. 19th St. (bet. 7th & 8th Aves.) | 212-242-6963 |
www.sugarcookiesnyc.com

Whether you're looking for something sweet or sexy, this Chelsea lingerie shop has it in store, with flirty nighties, lacy bra-and-panty
sets, sensual accessories and swimwear from the likes of Eberjey,
Hanky Panky and Chantelle; the petite boutique is full of fresh flowers
and chandeliers, with proprietor Susanne doling out sugar cookies
to lucky shoppers.

Suitsupply ●
- | - | - | E

SoHo | 453 Broome St., 2nd fl. (Mercer St.) | 212-404-6182 |
855-784-8464 | www.suitsupply.com

In its first U.S. foray, this Amsterdam brand brings fine details like Italian
wool and colored linings to SoHo's young, budget-friendly suit-set at
prices starting around $400; guys choose from styles including con-
temporary, classic and luxury, adding a bold-hued tie, slim-fitting shirt
and a pocket square along the way to complete the European look.

QUALITY DISPLAY SERVICE COST

Superga ●

| – | – | – | E |

SoHo | 78 Crosby St. (bet. Prince & Spring Sts.) | 212-625-8290 |
www.superga-usa.com

Courting the style set, the Italian sneaker company named Alexa
Chung as the brand's face, appointed the Olsen twins as creative directors and now seals the deal with the Downtown crowd with this dis-
creet SoHo storefront, the first U.S. outpost of the 100-year-old
brand; the kaleidoscopic array of kicks is arranged in librarylike rows,
with classic colors, canvas platforms and floral footwear reachable
by rolling ladder.

Supreme

| 23 | 23 | 17 | E |

SoHo | 274 Lafayette St. (bet. Houston & Prince Sts.) | 212-966-7799 |
www.supremenewyork.com

"A center of New York City skate wear", this SoHo boutique to the "hip
and trendoid" gets customers fitted up with "quality" house-designed
duds and boards, plus other "cool", sometimes "exclusive" items from
other streetwear brands; a few "nice discounts" can be found among
the "expensive" selections, just beware the staff can be on the "snotty"
side, especially "if you aren't a young surfer."

Surface to Air

| – | – | – | E |

SoHo | 27 Mercer St. (bet. Grand & Howard Sts.) | 212-256-0340 |
www.surfacetoair.com

This Parisian creative collective with projects in music, art and apparel
tackles retail too with boutiques in Paris, São Paolo and SoHo; the
group's own brand of "cool, modern French fashion", which includes
collabs with rockers like Kim Gordon and Kid Cudi, echoes the minimalist feel of the large flagship, and since prices tend to be "a bit expensive", you may need to "surface for air" post-purchase.

Sur La Table ●

| 25 | 22 | 20 | E |

E 70s | 1320 Third Ave. (bet. 75th & 76th Sts.) | 646-843-7984
SoHo | 75 Spring St. (bet. Crosby & Lafayette Sts.) | 212-966-3375
W 50s | 306 W. 57th St. (8th Ave.) | 212-574-8334
800-243-0852 | www.surlatable.com

Amateurs and enthusiasts alike "feel like a kid in a candy store" at this
"foodie paradise" offering a "first-rate" selection of "kitchen paraphernalia", from "pretty-colored spatulas" and small appliances to
"gadgets and gorgeous linens", all proffered by a "gracious staff";
"come for the cookware and stay for the demos", and partisans promise "you'll become a chef" or at least "feel inspired" to whip up a meal
"when you leave."

Swarovski

| 26 | 26 | 23 | E |

E 40s | Rockefeller Ctr. | 30 Rockefeller Plaza (bet. 49th & 50th Sts.) |
212-332-4300 | 888-207-9873 | www.swarovski.com
Additional locations throughout the NY area

It's hard to "resist all the bling" at this glittery chain agree acolytes
who consider the "gorgeous" crystal-spangled jewelry "the next best
thing to diamonds"; the Austrian sparklers are "always on trend",
while the "beautiful" figurines, home accessories and sunglasses also
dazzle; though some items are "not that expensive" ("but look it"),
others require a "huge wad of cash."

QUALITY DISPLAY SERVICE COST

NEW Swords-Smith
| - | - | - | E |

Williamsburg | 98 S. Fourth St. (bet. Bedford Ave. & Berry St.) |
Brooklyn | 347-599-2969 | www.swords-smith.com
Owned by a former art gallery director and graphic designer, this
South Williamsburg newcomer is spare yet striking, with white walls,
soaring ceilings, dark-wood rafters and a thoughtful mix of girl-and-
guywear that steps well outside the box; the apparel, accessories and
androgynous jewelry are sourced from 50 local, lesser-known and
creative-minded labels, including Feral Childe, K/LLER and Titania
Inglis, and the modernist setting is just as arresting.

Target ◑
| 19 | 19 | 16 | I |

Harlem | 517 E. 117th St. (Pleasant Ave.) | 212-835-0860
Mott Haven | Gateway Center at Bronx Terminal Mkt. | 700 Exterior St.
(150th St.) | Bronx | 718-401-5651
Riverdale | River Plaza | 40 W. 225th St. (Exterior St.) | Bronx | 718-733-7199
Downtown Bklyn | Atlantic Terminal | 139 Flatbush Ave. (Atlantic Ave.) |
Brooklyn | 718-290-1109
East NY | Gateway Mall | 519 Gateway Dr. (Erskine St.) | Brooklyn |
718-235-6032
Flatbush | Junction | 1598 Flatbush Ave. (Ave. H) | Brooklyn |
718-637-5005
College Point | College Point Shopping Ctr. | 135-05 20th Ave. (132nd St.) |
Queens | 718-661-4346
Elmhurst | Queens Pl. | 88-01 Queens Blvd. (bet. 55th & 56th Aves.) |
Queens | 718-760-5656
Charleston | South Shore Commons | 2900 Veterans Rd. W. (Tyrellan Ave.) |
Staten Island | 718-701-6205
800-440-0680 | www.target.com
Find "everything under the sun" within your "budget target" at this
"mass-market" chain, which distinguishes itself as a "best bet"
given its abundance of housewares, clothing ("designer partner-
ships" included), personal-care products, groceries and much more;
snipers take aim at the "disarray", "madhouse" crowds and "almost-
nonexistent" service, but for scoring lotsa "bargains" "in one trip", it's
a "secret passion."

Tarzian Hardware
| 23 | 16 | 21 | M |

Park Slope | 193 Seventh Ave. (bet. 2nd & 3rd Sts.) | Brooklyn |
718-788-4120 | www.tarzianhardware.com
It's "been in Park Slope since the beginning of time" (well, 1921), and
this "local" "throwback" remains a cherished resource given its "wide
selection" of "basic" hardware, tools, paint and gardening supplies
shoehorned into a "small space"; its "old-fashioned" values include
"hands-on" service from a "generally knowledgeable and friendly"
staff – "if you don't see it, they'll find it."

Tarzian West
| 25 | 16 | 19 | E |

Park Slope | 194 Seventh Ave. (2nd St.) | Brooklyn | 718-788-4213 |
www.tarzian-west.com
"They could use elasticized walls" at this "tiny", locally owned Slope
fixture that's "stuffed" till seemingly "on the verge of bursting" with a
"useful selection" of "fine" kitchen and household goods, from cookware and utensils to bath products; yes, it's a bit "disorganized", but
"dig a lot and you'll find" anything you "absolutely need" – "for a price."

	QUALITY	DISPLAY	SERVICE	COST

Ted Baker
26 | 24 | 22 | E

NEW **E 40s** | 595 Fifth Ave. (48th St.) | 212-317-1514
Meatpacking | 34 Little W. 12th St. (bet. Greenwich & Washington Sts.) |
212-647-0991
SoHo | 107 Grand St. (Mercer St.) | 212-343-8989
www.tedbaker.com

Guys and girls in the market for "well-made" separates and outerwear
"with an edgy Brit twist" pop over to the London-based brand's 1920s-
inspired, new Fifth Avenue townhouse and Downtown outposts, zero-
ing in on pieces with "fine tailoring" and "cheeky details" that "achieve
a refined style without the risk of being a bore"; the "sexy" stores are
"surprisingly accessible", likewise the "friendly" staffers who "make
suggestions without any pressure."

Tekserve ●
27 | 16 | 26 | M

Chelsea | 119 W. 23rd St. (bet. 6th & 7th Aves.) | 212-929-3645 |
888-929-3645 | www.tekserve.com

Have your "peace of mind restored along with your hard drive" at this
"pioneering" Chelsea "indie guru" devoted to "all things Apple", which
comes "to the rescue" with "excellent tech support" and repairs for
anything "from iPods and iPads to MacBooks and more"; while it "specializes in" service, the rambling space is also "easy to shop" for add-
ons and software at "fair prices."

Tender Buttons ⌀
28 | 24 | 24 | E

E 60s | 143 E. 62nd St. (bet. Lexington & 3rd Aves.) | 212-758-7004 |
www.tenderbuttons-nyc.com

"What specialty retailing is all about", this "one-of-a-kind" UESider
houses a staggering array of "premium, collector's item" buttons to "fit
every buttonhole and every wallet", with staffers who find your match
"without blinking an eye"; the "exquisite displays" and "quaint" space
are "a throwback to another era" – as is the cash-or-check-only policy.

Theory
26 | 24 | 21 | E

E 60s | 755 Madison Ave. (bet. 65th & 66th Sts.) | 212-744-0141
E 80s | 1157 Madison Ave. (86th St.) | 212-879-0265
Meatpacking | 40 Gansevoort St. (bet. Greenwich & Hudson Sts.) |
212-524-6790
SoHo | 151 Spring St. (bet. W. B'way & Wooster St.) | 212-226-3691
W 70s | 201-203 Columbus Ave. (bet. 69th & 70th Sts.) | 212-362-3676
www.theory.com

The "go-to place" for "urban-professional" clothing for men and women,
this "stylish" chainlet spotlights Belgian artistic director/designer
Olivier Theyskens' own collection, Theyskens' Theory, along with
"quality basics" "that feel current but not too trendy"; it's "expensive
but worth it" – from "blazers to dresses to skinny jeans", this outfit
"delivers" say loyalists, who also theorize that the "very helpful and
charming" staff will "have you looking great in no time."

30th Street Guitars
26 | 25 | 25 | E

Garment District | 236 W. 30th St. (bet. 7th & 8th Aves.) |
212-868-2660 | www.30thstreetguitars.com

A mecca for rock stars and Eric Clapton wannabes since 1997, this
Garment District longtimer offers "an interesting and affordable
stock" of new and used amps and gear, but the real draw here is the

"extensive inventory of pre-loved", "vintage guitars"; "the helpful staff knows its stuff" when it comes to repairs, prompting fans to pledge "I wouldn't trust my axe with anyone else."

3x1.Made Here | 24 | 22 | 22 | E |

SoHo | 15 Mercer St. (bet. Grand & Howard Sts.) | 212-391-6969 | www.3x1.us

"Worth the extra cost", especially for "petite or super-tall girls" attest diehards who descend on denim guru Scott Morrison's SoHo blues haven for "fashionable" bespoke, "custom-style" and limited-edition jeans, made right there in an on-site manufacturing facility; the "excellent-quality" bottoms, cut from primo selvedge, may not be for dilettantes, but "if you play in this price range, this is the place to go!"

3.1 Phillip Lim | 24 | 22 | 22 | E |

SoHo | 115 Mercer St. (bet. Prince & Spring Sts.) | 212-334-1160 | www.31philliplim.com

The feel is "more of a museum than a store", making this SoHo showcase pitch-perfect for spotlighting the namesake designer's "simple yet modern and tastefully done" line for men and women; "whether you like to ogle handbags", "well-cut clothing in every shade of gray in the rainbow" or downright colorful attire, you'll find "newness and unique combinations"; the "helpful" staff also has your number, "letting you browse without feeling judged."

Tibi | ▽ 23 | 22 | 22 | E |

SoHo | 120 Wooster St. (bet. Prince & Spring Sts.) | 212-226-5852 | www.tibi.com

Inspiring island dreams, this girlie SoHo shop boldly goes where most New Yorkers don't dare – to the bright side, with designer Amy Smilovic's flowy silhouettes and brilliant color palettes; "gorgeous" color-blocked maxis, striped camis and pleated skirts leave fans saying "I am surprised when there is something in this store that I *don't* want to buy", though high prices keep shopping sprees in check.

Tiffany & Co. | 28 | 28 | 26 | VE |

E 50s | 727 Fifth Ave. (57th St.) | 212-755-8000
Financial District | 37 Wall St. (bet. Broad & William Sts.) | 212-514-8015
 NEW **SoHo** | 97 Greene St. (bet. Prince & Spring Sts.) | 212-226-6136
800-843-3269 | www.tiffany.com

A "New York legend", this "iconic" jeweler with a "beautiful" Fifth Avenue flagship and SoHo–Wall Street satellites sets the "gold standard" for "classic" jewelry including "sparkling" engagement rings, plus silver and crystal "gifts to impress"; the floors can be "full with tourists" so "make an appointment to see a personal shopper" if you're serious about buying, and while there's definitely "a markup for the name", most say the joy that that "distinctive blue box" brings makes it "well worth it."

Tip Top Kids | ▽ 25 | 19 | 25 | M |

W 70s | 149 W. 72nd St. (bet. Amsterdam & Columbus Aves.) | 212-874-1003 | 800-925-5464 | www.tiptopshoes.com

"Very popular" with parents and tykes, this offshoot of the veteran family-owned UWS shoe store stocks "good-quality" sneakers, sandals, cozy boots and loafers up to men's size seven, plus backpacks and those all-important hair accessories; the staff knows how to fit small feet and entertain their wriggling owners, and "they won't try to sell you the most pricey" pair.

Tip Top Shoes

25 | 17 | 21 | E

W 70s | 155 W. 72nd St. (bet. Amsterdam & Columbus Aves.) | 212-787-4960 | 800-925-5464 | www.tiptopshoes.com

A "classic" since 1940, this West 70s shoe store draws 'em in droves with its impressive "stock" and a "seasoned staff" "that measures feet" the "old-school" way; it's not high fashion, but you'll find a "wide range" of "comfort" and casual styles from "the best" European and American brands, most at "reasonable prices", making it hard to "leave empty-footed."

Tocca

- | - | - | E

W Village | 605 Hudson St. (bet. Bethune & W. 12th Sts.) | 212-255-3801 | www.tocca.com

Australian Emma Fletcher, the former Lyell designer, is the creative force behind this beloved brand, which rebounded with its own tiny West Village boutique; fans find lacey, retro-infused frocks and separates reminscent of the feminine looks that first put the label on the fashion map, supplemented by flirty fragrance and cosmetics lines in tasteful packaging.

Tom Ford

28 | 28 | 26 | VE

E 70s | 845 Madison Ave. (70th St.) | 212-359-0300 | www.tomford.com

An "emporium of cool", this namesake designer's Madison Avenue flagship is a dual-level affair replete with ebony staircase and other luxe trimmings; there are men's suits (both ready-to-wear and custom), shirts, "fabulous" accessories and "amazing scents", plus sunglasses and other lovely odds-and-ends for women; designs and prices are "not for the faint of heart", but then it costs to achieve the "height of sophistication"; P.S. serious shoppers should call ahead for a private appointment.

NEW Tommy Bahama ◐

- | - | - | E

E 50s | 551 Fifth Ave. (45th St.) | 212-537-0956 | www.tommybahama.com

Embrace that endless summer feeling at this two-floor Midtown mecca of mellow filled with the breezy brand's signature tropical print shirts, weekend-ready pants and sunny home accessories, all celebrating the laid-back life; between potted palms, ceiling fans and bright lighting, the only thing missing from the beachy digs is a flock of seagulls, but after cocktails at the in-store restaurant, those Fifth Avenue pigeons might just fool you.

Topshop/Topman ◐

19 | 19 | 14 | M

SoHo | 478 Broadway (bet. Broome & Grand Sts.) | 212-966-9555 | www.topshop.com

"London-trendy to the max", the mega-sized SoHo offshoot of this popular U.K. chain has "floors of fun fashions" including "awesome" shoes and accessories for men and women; the "super-unique" clothing has a "wonderful European flavor" but may be "a bit out-there" for some, and prices can be "kind of expensive for the quality."

Tory Burch
26 | 25 | 23 | E

E 60s | 797 Madison Ave. (bet. 67th & 68th Sts.) | 212-510-8371
Meatpacking | 38-40 Little W. 12th St. (bet. 9th Ave. & Washington St.) | 212-929-0125
NoLita | 257 Elizabeth St. (bet. Houston & Prince Sts.) | 212-334-3000
www.toryburch.com

Like stepping into a "Cape Cod beach house in the middle of Manhattan" exclaim loyalists who "love the feel" of Burch's posh, gold-accented shops showcasing her burgeoning empire of bohemian-"chic" womenswear, bags, jewelry and shoes, including the "medallion"-adorned ballet flats that started it all; it's hard to resist the "great color schemes" and "beautiful" fabrics – just remember that the "exceptional quality" goods command "matching prices."

Tourneau
27 | 26 | 23 | VE

E 50s | 510 Madison Ave. (bet. 52nd & 53rd Sts.) | 212-758-5830
W 60s | Shops at Columbus Circle | 10 Columbus Circle, ground fl. (B'way & 60th St.) | 212-823-9425

Tourneau TimeMachine
E 50s | 12 E. 57th St. (bet. 5th & Madison Aves.) | 212-758-7300
www.tourneau.com

"Whatever the price point, one can count on quality and style" from these "temples of timekeeping", where the "widest array of watches" going encompasses "both popular and hard-to-find" brands (including "ultra-high-end" models to "drool over") plus pre-owned pieces; it charges "top dollar", but "be unafraid to ask" the "courteous" salespeople "to do better" costwise; P.S. the TimeMachine flagship bills itself as the largest watch store on the globe.

Town Shop
25 | 14 | 22 | E

W 80s | 2270 Broadway (82nd St.) | 212-787-2762 | www.townshop.com

Loyalists "wouldn't buy their bras anyplace" but this UWS "institution", especially now that it's moved from "crammed" quarters to spacious digs across the street; it's one of the "best spots for big-busted women", offering "sizes nobody else carries" and a staff that's "wonderful at fitting you", plus you don't have to "ferret out the right styles" – they bring them into the dressing room for you – and you can boost your wardrobe with PJs and swimwear too.

Toy Tokyo
24 | 25 | 19 | M

E Village | 91 Second Ave. (bet. 5th & 6th Sts.) | 212-673-5424 | www.toytokyo.com

A "mind-boggling selection of everything pop culture and plastic" awaits up a flight of "narrow stairs" at this East Village vinyl toy "mecca", which imports a "collectible" array of "virtually any Japanese anime figure" ("hard-to-find classics" included) to "satisfy all your kaiju wants and needs"; the wall-to-wall display alone is a total "experience", so "hop on your hoverboard and race" over.

Tracy Reese
▽ 27 | 27 | 26 | E

Meatpacking | 641 Hudson St. (bet. Gansevoort & Horatio Sts.) | 212-807-0505 | www.tracyreese.com

This designer's eponymous sprawling flagship in the Meatpacking is as sophisticated and ladylike as the pieces she sells, which always have a touch of unmistakable New York glamour; every bit high fashion, her "absolutely amazing", brightly colored and intricately patterned dresses and upbeat pieces still wear well on women with 'real' bodies, like Michelle Obama.

Trash and Vaudeville ❷   22 | 21 | 21 | M

E Village | 4 St. Marks Pl. (bet. 2nd & 3rd Aves.) | 212-982-3590 | www.trashandvaudeville.com
"Goths and metalheads aren't the only ones diving into the fun, flirty and fatal fashions" – this "piece of punk rock history" on St. Marks Place is also a "must-stop" for teens trolling for "cutting-edge" styles; kick out the jams with "Ramones" T-shirts, walk this way in "novel" platforms or channel Blondie with a vinyl mini – whatever you buy, it'll be "something downtown."

Treasure & Bond ❷   - | - | - | E

SoHo | 350 W. Broadway (bet. Broome & Grand Sts.) | 646-669-9049 | www.treasureandbond.com
"Love that all the proceeds go to charity" declare do-gooders who frequent this "beautiful", two-floor Nordstrom-owned emporium/art gallery in SoHo, peddling a "wonderful assortment of this and that"; there's lots to treasure, including "a really interesting collection" of men's and women's apparel and accessories for the home from indie and under-the-radar labels, plus a smattering of store-exclusive childrenswear.

Treillage   ∇ 24 | 23 | 22 | E

E 70s | 1015 Lexington Ave. (73rd St.) | 212-988-8800
E 70s | 418 E. 75th St. (bet. 1st & York Aves.) | 212-535-2288
www.treillageonline.com
The "beautiful displays" alone are "worth a visit" to this Upper East Side twosome from antiques whiz John Rosselli and interior designer Bunny Williams, who select home furnishings "for the garden" that can also bring the alfresco indoors with a stylish blend of "traditional and trendy, practical and fancy"; the wares come at "many price points", but count on spending some green.

Trina Turk   27 | 25 | 24 | VE

Meatpacking | 67 Gansevoort St. (bet. Greenwich & Washington Sts.) | 212-206-7383 | www.trinaturk.com
This Meatpacking boutique's bold and colorful '70s decor, courtesy of Jonathan Adler, makes a fitting backdrop for the West Coast–based namesake designer's "pretty" version of California surf-chic, including "bohemian tunic dresses" and "fun swimsuits and cover-ups"; although Turk's cheerful fashions are "not for everyone", they're perfect for grown-up beach bums willing to pay for "quality" items with a smidge of retro kitsch.

NEW Trinity Place   - | - | - | M

Financial District | 61 Broadway (bet. Exchange Plaza & Rector St.) | 917-300-1184 | www.trinityplaces.com
A Euro-influenced specialty store comes to the style-starved Wall Street area offering indie, retro-esque threads, shoes, jewelry and more for women plus sophisticated duds and accessories for the gents and a collection for kids; quirky home furnishings round out the wares, and with bearable prices, you don't need a bull market to indulge.

	QUALITY	DISPLAY	SERVICE	COST

True Religion
24 | 21 | 22 | E

E 60s | 1122 Third Ave. (bet. 65th & 66th Sts.) | 212-288-8001
Financial District | 14 Wall St. (bet. Broad & Williams Sts.) |
212-791-5930
SoHo | 132 Prince St. (bet. W. B'way & Wooster St.) |
212-966-6011
Union Sq | 863 Broadway (17th St.) | 212-741-1401 ●
W 60s | Shops at Columbus Circle | 10 Columbus Circle, 2nd fl. (B'way &
60th St.) | 212-209-5970 ●
866-427-1119 | www.truereligionbrandjeans.com

Guys and gals with a serious jones for jeans know this woodsy-looking
outfit is *the* spot for the latest trends in premium denim – including short
shorts, slim-fit, flares and boyfriend-style; the trademark back flap
pockets with horseshoe stitching make your behind look butt-alicious,
however, you may be singing the blues given the sky-high prices.

NEW Trunk Show Designer Consignment
– | – | – | E

Harlem | 275-277 W. 113th St. (bet. 7th & 8th Aves.) | 212-662-0009 |
www.trunkshowconsignment.com

A luxury haven in Harlem, this designer consignment shop stocks like-
new pieces from the highest caliber of designers, with men's and
women's clothing and accessories by big names like Louis Vuitton,
Missoni and Jimmy Choo; while vintage boutiques are often cluttered,
this place keeps it clean with tightly edited racks and spare displays.

Tucker
– | – | – | E

SoHo | 355 W. Broadway (bet. Broome & Grand Sts.) | 212-938-0811 |
www.tuckerbygabybasora.com

Set on a busy stretch, this SoHo gem boasts a rotating display of artwork along with designer Gaby Basora's eminently wearable collection of gorgeously printed dresses, pants, jackets and tops; prized by
fashion-followers, the forgiving, flowing cuts walk the line between
sex kitten and bohemian rocker and are all made in NYC; completing
the look: a small supply of covetable shoes and jewelry.

TUMI
28 | 24 | 24 | VE

E 40s | Grand Central Terminal | 87 E. 42nd St., Lexington Passage
(Vanderbilt Ave.) | 212-973-0015
E 50s | 520 Madison Ave. (bet. 53rd & 54th Sts.) | 212-813-0545
E 80s | 1100 Madison Ave. (83rd St.) | 212-288-8802
Financial District | 67 Wall St. (Pearl St.) | 212-742-8020
Flatiron | 125 Fifth Ave. (bet. 19th & 20th Sts.) | 212-228-7155 ●
SoHo | 102 Prince St. (bet. Greene & Mercer Sts.) | 646-613-9101
W 40s | Rockefeller Ctr. | 53 W. 49th St. (bet. 5th & 6th Aves.) |
212-245-7460
W 60s | Shops at Columbus Circle | 10 Columbus Circle, ground fl.
(B'way & 60th St.) | 212-823-9390 ●
W 70s | 2205 Broadway (bet. 78th & 79th Sts.) | 212-877-1121
800-322-8864 | www.tumi.com

"You just feel cool" toting "fab" bags from this global standout, known
for furnishing "the best of the best for the hard-core road warrior" with
"sturdy and fashionable" luggage in "stylish" designs, along with
"beautiful" leather goods and accessories; they're "over-the-top
pricewise", but given "attentive" service and "impeccable" quality
that "truly lasts", "you won't regret" the "investment."

	QUALITY	DISPLAY	SERVICE	COST

Turnbull & Asser   28 | 25 | 23 | VE

E 50s | 50 E. 57th St. (bet. Madison & Park Aves.) | 212-752-5700 |
877-887-6285 | www.turnbullandasser.com

"High-end old-world" attire is the order of the day at this "charming
townhouse" in Midtown, where Anglophiles find luxe cashmere and
mostly U.K.-made custom shirts proffered by an "extremely compe-
tent" staff; the posh setting and marble floors are so "quintessentially
English", "you'd expect to see Prince Charles himself" shopping the
unrivaled sock selection, and the prices are fit for royalty too.

25 Park   23 | 22 | 22 | E

E 70s | 1296 Third Ave. (bet. 74th & 75th Sts.) | 212-585-2525
NEW **E 70s** | 998 Madison Ave. (bet. 77th & 78th Sts.) |
646-649-3125
www.25park.com

"Love" the "wonderful selection" from labels like Suno, Matthew
Williamson and Thakoon Addition – this East 70s duo is really
"well edited for the modern woman" and "offers a nice change" of
pace agree clotheshorses who also scoop up stylish accessories;
"eager-to-help" staffers and elegant digs bedecked with crystal
chandeliers, antique mirrors and plushy couches further enhance the
luxury shopping experience.

23rd Street Hardware   25 | 20 | 23 | M

Gramercy | 152 E. 23rd St. (bet. Lexington & 3rd Aves.) | 212-475-1883 |
www.23rdstreethardware.com

When "you're looking for a thingum", this venerable Gramercy "treasure trove" upholds its rep as a local hardware "go-to" that's "always
stocked" with "any nail, hook or gadget" under the sun; it "may not
look as flashy" as its big-name rivals, but it's "cheap" and "there when
you need it" – and the "smiling staff" knows "every item by heart."

UGG Australia   25 | 22 | 21 | E

E 50s | 600 Madison Ave. (58th St.) | 212-845-9905
NEW **Meatpacking** | 405 W. 14th St. (bet. 9th Ave. & Washington St.) |
212-863-9209
SoHo | 79 Mercer St. (bet. Broome & Spring Sts.) | 212-226-0602
W 60s | 160 Columbus Ave. (bet. 67th & 68th Sts.) | 212-671-1190
888-432-8530 | www.uggaustralia.com

A "steady stream of fur-footed admirers" beats a path to these Uptown-
Downtown branches of the super-popular California brand with Aussie
surf roots; in addition to its "cozy", "warm" sheepskin boots, you'll
find "footwear for your entire family and for all seasons", including
sandals, slippers, accessories and more that fans go all fuzzy for.

Uniqlo ●   21 | 22 | 19 | I

E 50s | 666 Fifth Ave. (53rd St.)
Garment District | 31 W. 34th St. (bet. 5th & 6th Aves.)
SoHo | 546 Broadway (bet. Prince & Spring Sts.)
877-486-4756 | www.uniqlo.com

"Beats the pants" off other fast-fashion chains in true "Japanese style"
gush groupies who "stock up" on "fresh-looking" "basics with a stylish
twist" at these "bright, neat" megabranches; loyalists "love" the "perfectly stacked" "towers of sweaters", "special" collaborations with unexpected designers like Suno, "excellent boy-girl versions of jeans"

and "innovative products like heat-tech" shirts; best of all, it's "insanely cheap" "without sacrificing quality."

Uno de 50

– | – | – | M

SoHo | 135 Prince St. (bet. W. B'way & Wooster St.) | 646-490-5070 | www.unode50.com

In business for over 20 years, this Spanish gem finally brings its made-in-Madrid jewelry, watches, belts, bags and gifts to SoHo; thanks to materials like silver, resin, crystal and leather, the collection has an edgy, artisanal feel, and while the limited-edition concept on which it was founded (and named) has succumbed to demand, collectors can still find certain pieces made in small batches.

Urban Archaeology

▽ 25 | 24 | 22 | VE

E 50s | 239 E. 58th St. (bet. 2nd & 3rd Aves.) | 212-371-4646
TriBeCa | 143 Franklin St. (bet. Hudson & Varick Sts.) | 212-431-4646
www.urbanarchaeology.com

Classic American designs are given new life at these TriBeCa–East 50s all-stars of salvage, where the "interesting" antique accents – bath and kitchen fixtures, tiles, lighting, ironwork, etc. – are excavated from their original settings or faithfully rendered in replica; decorators with traditional tastes and deep pockets "love the stuff"; P.S. closed weekends.

Urban Outfitters ◑

18 | 20 | 16 | M

Chelsea | 526 Sixth Ave. (14th St.) | 646-638-1646 | 800-282-2200 | www.urbanoutfitters.com
Additional locations throughout the NY area

For "young, funky threads" with a "hippie-chic twist" and "quirky, off-beat home decor", hit this "hipster haven" chain with locations citywide, all offering "clever displays" of "constantly changing stock"; staffers are "not very helpful", and some say it's all "thrift store knockoffs at boutique prices", but an "excellent sale section" brings "stampedes" of shoppers; P.S. a Williamsburg branch is in the pipeline.

Urban Zen

20 | 22 | 21 | E

W Village | 705 Greenwich St. (bet. Charles & W. 10th Sts.) | 212-206-3999 | www.urbanzen.com

Donna Karan's nonprofit Urban Zen Foundation gets 10% of the proceeds from everything sold in this "coolly Zen" West Village shop full of "absolutely gorgeous jewelry" and clothing that "feels so fabulous that you won't want to take it off"; some feel it's "on the pricey side", but the boutique's charitable nature makes the designer's fans comfortable splurging, saying "this isn't a store but a social project."

Vacheron Constantin

29 | 28 | 27 | VE

E 60s | 729 Madison Ave. (64th St.) | 855-729-1755 | www.vacheron-constantin.com

Chronometry connoisseurs confide "my next big gift to myself" will be a "classic timepiece" from this luxe new Upper East Side outpost of the 18th-century Swiss watchmaker, whose "superb" tickers are storied among those who know "the best"; between precision engineering and ultra-blinged-out assembly (think solid gold, diamond-bedizened), it's not for the faint of wallet.

QUALITY | DISPLAY | SERVICE | COST

Valentino

28 | **27** | **25** | **VE**

E 60s | 746 Madison Ave. (65th St.) | 212-772-6969 |
www.valentino.com

When you need to hit the red carpet, head to the "beautiful" East 60s
home of this renowned Italian design house famed for its "gorgeous"
special-occasion wear, including incredible evening gowns sold by a
super-professional, helpful staff; sure, the collection is "majorly expensive", but fans consider the clothing investments, not just outfits;
P.S. a Fifth Avenue branch housed in Takashimaya's former space is
in the works.

Van Cleef & Arpels

29 | **28** | **26** | **VE**

E 50s | 744 Fifth Ave. (57th St.) | 212-896-9284 | 877-826-2533 |
www.vancleefarpels.com

"He either really loves you or really screwed up if you're getting" an
"exquisite piece" from this "reenergized" Parisian jeweler with an "illustrious past"; the plush interior of its Fifth Avenue shop "just
screams money", and the "window displays are a must-see", as are
the au courant, bold arrangements of the Alhambra collection, its
"cloverleaf trademark" that now "speaks to a whole new generation"
and "is only found here."

Vera Wang

28 | **27** | **26** | **VE**

SoHo | 158 Mercer St. (bet. Houston & Prince Sts.) | 212-382-2184 |
www.verawang.com

While still best known for her wedding gowns, this designer also
garners praise for the "beautiful" ready-to-wear collection that's
showcased at her all-white, two-tiered flagship in SoHo; the "well-
made" clothing has a sculptural, artistic feel, and also on view are
accessories and fragrance – all dramatically lit in a theatrical space
that earns accolades for its "heavenly" vibe (and suitably, prices are
"out of this world").

Vera Wang Bridal Salon

29 | **27** | **28** | **VE**

E 70s | 991 Madison Ave. (77th St.) | 212-628-3400 |
www.verawang.com

It's "a dream come true" to shop the "gorgeous" gowns from one of the
most famous names in the bridal biz at her by-appointment-only
Madison Avenue salon, where there's an "extensive selection" of
dresses characterized by lush materials, impeccable finishing and
unique detailing; the "pampering" service "patiently" accommodates
all your needs, and while "prices are high", few mind given that you'll
"feel like a movie star" on your wedding day.

Verdura

▽ **28** | **26** | **26** | **VE**

E 50s | 745 Fifth Ave., 12th fl. (bet. 57th & 58th Sts.) | 212-758-3388 |
www.verdura.com

"Yes, the Maltese cross" bracelets and earrings and "gold-wrapped ruby
heart" brooches are "signatures", but this "old-time, upper-upper-
class" Fifth Avenue establishment is also a "marvelous resource" for
vintage and one-of-a-kind pieces that "defy anyone else's standards
for imagination and uniqueness"; "if you want to invest in something
for life", "bring your trust fund" – the "staff will help you choose the
thing that you will cherish forever"; P.S. closed weekends.

	QUALITY	DISPLAY	SERVICE	COST

Versace

26 | 26 | 23 | VE

E 50s | 647 Fifth Ave. (bet. 51st & 52nd Sts.) | 212-317-0224
NEW **SoHo** | 160 Mercer St. (bet. Houston & Prince Sts.) | 212-966-8111
www.versace.com

"The ultimate in sexy for men and women both", Donatella Versace's Italian luxury label offers "excellent quality and great design" via "very expensive" "leathers and silks that shine" and "slinky" "pieces that travel the world", all sold by "attentive, attractive" staffers; "well-tanned and -toned" patrons file into the Fifth Avenue mecca, while downtown types shop for store-exclusive items at the splashy SoHo addition, decked out with a mosaic floor and Plexiglass panels.

Victoria's Secret ●

22 | 23 | 20 | M

SoHo | 565 Broadway (bet. Houston & Prince Sts.) | 212-219-3643 |
www.victoriassecret.com
Additional locations throughout the NY area

It's "Valentine's Day every day" at this one-stop chain for "everything lingerie and everything sexy"; men swoon that it's "the place where gifts keep on giving", women swear "I am almost Giselle when wearing" styles that range "from basics to lacy and racy", and both adore the "pretty swell" staff and "stimulating" pink-hued surroundings; if critics confide it's a lotta "media hype" for "just fluff", for most it remains a "love" affair.

Victorinox Swiss Army

▽ 27 | 23 | 21 | E

SoHo | 99 Wooster St. (bet. Prince & Spring Sts.) | 212-431-4950 |
www.victorinox.com

You "never knew there were so many different types", sizes and colors of pocket knives before viewing the wall displays at this Swiss brand's newly relocated SoHo quarters, also stocked with "cool gadgets" geared for travel, including "nice luggage", "wonderful clothing" and, of course, those "great watches"; if some find prices "higher than the Alps" sharp shoppers insist you get "value for what you pay", and find the staff "generally helpful."

Vilebrequin

25 | 22 | 22 | VE

E 80s | 1007 Madison Ave. (bet. 77th & 78th Sts.) | 212-650-0353
SoHo | 436 W. Broadway (Prince St.) | 212-431-0673
888-458-0051 | www.vilebrequin.com

Men, meet "your new swim trunks" at these Saint Tropez–meets–Madison Avenue and SoHo swimwear stores peddling a "Wall Street at the sea" aesthetic of "bright" shorts in "vibrant yet tasteful prints", available in "father and son styles"; also on offer in these beachy boutiques are "super-colorful" towels and "great summer linen shirts", all quite pricey but "worth the money."

Vince

24 | 18 | 21 | E

NEW **E 70s** | 980 Madison Ave. (bet. 76th & 77th Sts.) |
646-560-2897
Meatpacking | 833 Washington St. (Little W. 12th St.) |
212-924-0370
NoLita | 16 Prince St. (Elizabeth St.) | 212-343-1945
866-601-2528 | www.vince.com

Urbanites agree it's "easy to love" the "high-quality" "contemporary" sportswear with "surprising and flattering cuts" that fill the racks of this popular label's NoLita, Meatpacking and UES branches; both men and women can readily put together outfits with these "solid, every-day designs" and while perhaps optimal for those with "some cash to spare", the "on-point trends" definitely up their style.

Vince Camuto
▽ 24 | 24 | 23 | M

E 40s | Grand Central Terminal | 87 E. 42nd St., main concourse (Vanderbilt Ave.) | 646-588-4444
NEW **E 60s** | 667 Madison Ave. (bet. 60th & 61st Sts.) | 646-998-4454
NEW **Garment District** | 30 W. 34th St. (bet. 5th & 6th Aves.) | 212-239-9271
SoHo | 532 Broadway (bet. Prince & Spring Sts.) | 646-532-2684 ◗
www.vincecamuto.com

Now that it's opened its own stores around town, it's "ohh-so-easy" to find this popular brand's "very stylish boots, shoes" and accessories, including the super-glam VC Signature collection, all in one place; rea-sonably priced slinky, sexy dresses, sportswear and swimwear in trend-forward silhouettes further con-Vince fans there's lots to "love" about this hot property.

VPL
- | - | - | E

SoHo | 5 Mercer St. (Howard St.) | 646-912-6141 | www.vplnyc.com

British designer Victoria Bartlett's SoHo loft has the feel of a chic gym-nasium, complete with ropes and rings, gymnast-ready vintage leather pommel horses and wooden bars hung with her femme-yet-tough, ballet-inspired confections; the bra acts as a leitmotif for crisscross bodiced dresses, tunics and tank tops made of feather-light fabrics and elasticized straps, while other pieces – snug leggings, slouchy sweaters – walk the line between sporty and edgy streetwear, but are definitely too pricey for sweat-inducing activities.

Warby Parker
27 | 24 | 27 | I

NEW **SoHo** | 121 Greene St. (bet. Houston & Prince Sts.) | 646-568-3720
NoLita | Puck Bldg. | 295 Lafayette St. (Houston St.) | 888-492-7297
www.warbyparker.com

Gain "instant hipster-chic cred" with "vintage-style specs" from this eyewear e-retailer's library-inspired, book-bedecked Greene Street flagship and Puck Building office/showroom, where "awesome" house-designed frames either "functional" or "fun" are priced "for everyone" at $95; adherents hope "this is the future", especially given the "socially conscious" business model that supports a charitable nonprofit

Warm
- | - | - | E

NoLita | 181 Mott St. (bet. Broome & Kenmare Sts.) | 212-925-1200 | www.warmny.com

Add some sizzle to your urban-nomad style with clothing, jewelry, ac-cessories and home items from off-the-beaten-path Euro and American designers and artisans at this NoLita nook, a former olive oil factory with a backyard garden; the effortlessly chic collection is culled by surfer-chick owner Winnie Beattie and her husband, photographer Rob Magnotta, both warm-weather–lovers who embrace the spirit of discovery and craftsmanship.

QUALITY | DISPLAY | SERVICE | COST

Waterworks

26 | 26 | 20 | VE

E 50s | 215 E. 58th St. (bet. 2nd & 3rd Aves.) | 212-371-9266
Flatiron | 7 E. 20th St. (bet. B'way & 5th Ave.) | 212-254-6025
800-899-6757 | www.waterworks.com

"If price is no object", visit this tony pair of showrooms in the East 50s and Flatiron displaying "luxury bath hardware" including "stunning fixtures, faucets and fittings" and "unusual" tiles "of the highest quality"; just stroll through and it's easy to "fantasize about sitting in their bathtubs" and the "many possibilities of fine living", but the staff's sometimes "snotty attitude" may bring you down to earth.

Wempe

29 | 28 | 29 | VE

E 50s | 700 Fifth Ave. (55th St.) | 212-397-9000 | 800-513-1131 |
www.wempe.com

"Search for the watch of your dreams" at this Fifth Avenue boutique, where a "knowledgeable staff" curates the German namesake's own "best-of-the-best timepieces" as well as a sampling from other luxury trademarks; jewelry is also on offer, but the "prices are beyond high" and the milieu's so "intimidating", it takes some "gumption to just walk in and browse."

NEW West Elm Market

- | - | - | M

Dumbo | 50 Washington St. (bet. Front & Water Sts.) | Brooklyn |
718-522-3498 | www.westelm.com

The affordable home furnishings chain brings its first housewares-focused concept to Dumbo stocked with gadgets and gizmos for the kitchen, bath and garden plus cleaning supplies and artisanal specialty foods, many locally sourced; the funky-industrial digs suit the waterfront nabe, and if browsing makes you hungry, there's an in-store coffee bar; P.S. a partnership with Skillshare provides cooking classes.

West 25th Street Market ⊄

∇ 16 | 16 | 16 | M

Chelsea | West 25th St. (bet. B'way & 6th Ave.) | 212-243-5343 |
www.hellskitchenfleamarket.com

Bargain-hunters agree "one of the best ways to spend a weekend morning" is table-hopping at this year-round flea market (an alfresco adjunct of the nearby Antiques Garage), where seasoned vendors sprawled around a Chelsea lot hawk a grab bag of vintage merch; one "never knows what one may find", so be ready to "walk around" – and to haggle.

What Goes Around Comes Around

22 | 21 | 21 | E

SoHo | 351 W. Broadway (bet. Broome & Grand Sts.) | 212-343-1225 |
www.whatgoesaroundnyc.com

"Designer duds from eons past find a second home" at this SoHo shop "frequented by socialites and models" searching for some of "the best vintage clothing on the planet", including jeans, "poofy ballet skirts, '80s costume jewelry" and Chanel finds; while the array is solid and staffers are "professional", some find it "too pricey" for secondhand stuff.

Whisk

∇ 21 | 20 | 21 | E

Flatiron | 933 Broadway (bet. 21st & 22nd Sts.) | 212-477-8680
Williamsburg | 231 Bedford Ave. (4th St.) | Brooklyn | 718-218-7230
www.whisknyc.com

"The neighborhood's chefs" whisk through this "adorable" Flatiron-Williamsburg duo, whose "well-curated" lineup of "kitchen essentials and gadgets" from fine specialty makers ranges from cutlery, cookware and culinary paraphernalia to bar and tabletop extras; service "with an attitude (a good one, that is)" makes it a "fun" place to "restock" whatever's "on the wish list."

Whitney Museum Store 24 | 19 | 18 | E

E 70s | Whitney Museum of American Art | 945 Madison Ave. (75th St.) | 212-570-3600 | 800-944-8639 | www.shopwhitney.org

"Take some affordable art home with you" from this UES shop, which "reflects the museum's mission" of celebrating the American scene with coffee-table books and "some very clever" knickknacks conceived by "very famous artists"; even with space limitations, it's failsafe for "unique gifts that you really can't find anywhere" else.

Williams-Sonoma 27 | 26 | 23 | E

Chelsea | 110 Seventh Ave. (bet. 16th & 17th Sts.) | 212-633-2203
E 50s | 121 E. 59th St. (bet. Lexington & Park Aves.) | 917-369-1131
E 80s | 1175 Madison Ave. (86th St.) | 212-289-6832
W 60s | Shops at Columbus Circle | 10 Columbus Circle, ground fl. (B'way & 60th St.) | 212-581-1146 ◗
877-812-6235 | www.williams-sonoma.com

An "indispensable" source of "kitchen fantasy fulfillment" for the "avid" home chef, this nationwide chain is guaranteed to "lend culinary cachet" with a "comprehensive selection" of "first-rate" cookware "classics" and "obscure" gadgets and tools to "salivate over", whether you're "newly wedded or empty-nesting"; between the "outstanding customer service" and "enticing displays", "discerning" food-lovers "don't mind paying top dollar" – "case closed."

William-Wayne & Co. 25 | 26 | 23 | E

E 60s | 846-850 Lexington Ave. (bet. 64th & 65th Sts.) | 212-737-8934
G Village | 40 University Pl. (9th St.) | 212-533-4711
800-318-3435 | www.william-wayne.com

It's like "having a high-caliber personal shopper" at this Village-UES duo, where owners with "impeccable taste" in home decorating proffer "beautiful" new and vintage furnishings, linens and tabletop accessories "at a variety of price points"; the display's "tightly packed", but "you can't go wrong" for a "hostess gift" or even an "unusual" find for yourself.

Willoughby's 25 | 19 | 21 | M

Garment District | 298 Fifth Ave. (31st St.) | 212-564-1600 | 800-378-1898 | www.willoughbys.com

Recognized as the city's "original camera store", this Garment District outfit dates to 1898 as a "wonderful" fallback for well-known brands of photo and video equipment overseen by staffers who'll answer "every question you ever had"; still, the less-enthused snap it can be "high-priced" depending "on what you want" and these days seems "more like a tourist" destination.

Wink 19 | 19 | 18 | E

E 70s | 1330 Third Ave. (76th St.) | 212-249-2033
SoHo | 129 Prince St. (Wooster St.) | 212-334-3646
W 60s | 188 Columbus Ave. (bet. 68th & 69th Sts.) | 212-877-7727
(continued)

(continued)

Wink

NEW **W Village** | 305 Bleecker St. (bet. Grove St. & 7th Ave. S.) |
212-433-0161
www.winknyc.com

"Love the accessories" and "interesting clothing" at this "adorable"
quartet – it's "always a treat to check out when you're in the mood for
retail therapy"; the "mix of high- and low-priced items" runs the gamut,
from outfit-completers like colorful scarves and silicone watches to
Seychelles footwear, making it the "perfect" place "to find a splurge
or a steal."

Wolford

28 | 22 | 22 | VE

E 50s | 619 Madison Ave. (bet. 58th & 59th Sts.) | 212-688-4850
E 70s | 997 Madison Ave. (bet. 77th & 78th Sts.) | 212-327-1000
SoHo | 122 Greene St. (Prince St.) | 212-343-0808
W 60s | Shops at Columbus Circle | 10 Columbus Circle, ground fl.
(B'way & 60th St.) | 212-265-7814 ☽
800-965-3673 | www.wolford.com

It's "well worth the extra bucks to make your legs feel like a million dollars" gush "loyalists" who go out on a limb to praise this Austrian import's "high-end luxury" hosiery; "every woman should treat herself to
at least a sexy pair or two" of these "heavenly stockings, tights" and
pantyhose – they're "by far the best you will find" for "everyday-into-
eveningwear" and they seem to "last forever."

The Yarn Company

23 | 21 | 17 | E

W 80s | 2274 Broadway (bet. 81st & 82nd Sts.) | 212-787-7878 |
888-927-6261 | www.theyarnco.com

"Inviting" and "open", this second-floor knitting, sewing, spinning and
weaving store on the UWS is "filled to the brim" with a "great selection", including lots of "independent yarn companies" in a "varied
price range"; scale the "steep" staircase and you'll find that sibling
owners Tavy and Assaf Ronen have "given this formerly cliquey shop
new life" rewarding crafters with "modern and stylish knitwear workshops" and finishing classes.

Yigal Azrouël

25 | 24 | 20 | E

E 70s | 1011 Madison Ave. (78th St.) | 212-929-7525 |
www.yigal-azrouel.com

Known for his quietly seductive gowns and edgy career cuts, the
namesake Israeli designer is a master of form, and his most unusual
designs, as well as exclusives, are showcased at his recently relocated
Madison Avenue boutique, a modern, modular, yet welcoming ex-
panse designed by Dror Benshetrit; some find the prices "expensive",
but the "really cool designs" will "make you look like a million bucks."

Yoya

▽ 23 | 22 | 22 | M

W Village | 636 Hudson St. (Horatio St.) | 646-336-6844

Yoya Mart

Meatpacking | 15 Gansevoort St. (bet. W. 4th & Hudson Sts.) | 212-242-5511
www.yoyamart.com

It's "such fun" to browse at these effortlessly cool tot shops, just blocks
apart on the West Village–Meatpacking District border, "even if you
don't have kids", as "friendly" staffers encourage customers to "play

around" with the merchandise; the Hudson Street site caters to younger kiddos with clothes and accessories, while its dad-designed sibling on Gansevoort carries "killer" sneakers, activewear, "collectible toys" and gadgets geared to an older crowd.

Y-3
26	24	19	E

SoHo | 92 Greene St. (bet. Prince & Spring Sts.) | 212-966-9833 | www.y-3store.com
"Yohji Yamamoto meets the three-stripe" at this sleek SoHo spot showcasing the Japanese master's "very, very cool" line of active-influenced sportswear for Adidas, including some hip swimsuits and club-worthy casual shoes that "cost a small fortune but will reap dividends for years"; prices may be high, but you feel like you've scored with these "unique" designer duds.

Yummy Mummy
23	23	22	E

E 80s | 1201 Lexington Ave. (bet. 81st & 82nd Sts.) | 212-879-8669 | 855-879-8669 | www.yummymummystore.com
A mecca for breast-feeding mums, this "stroller-friendly" East 80s spot, the brainchild of lactation expert Amanda Cole, is both boutique and community gathering place, offering "organized displays" that are a complete checklist of high-quality nursing necessities, including apparel, bras, pillows and ointments, together with support groups and classes like prenatal yoga and baby safety; throw in a knowledgeable, "attentive" staff, and you've got a yummy experience all around.

Yves Delorme
28	25	24	VE

E 70s | 985 Madison Ave. (bet. 76th & 77th Sts.) | 212-439-5701 | www.yvesdelorme.com
It's "complete heaven" to have your bed bedecked in the "beautiful linens" with the swan silhouette logo from this French brand's Madison Avenue boutique, a thread-count wonderland where the "luxurious" sheets, comforters and towels are the "comfiest and chicest ever", and the Provençal-inspired furniture used to display the bedding is for sale too; while it's "high-priced", most feel it's a small cost for such "sweet dreams."

Zabar's Mezzanine
28	20	19	M

W 80s | 2245 Broadway (80th St.) | 212-787-2000 | 800-697-6301 | www.zabars.com
"The source for all things cookware", the upstairs Mezzanine of the UWS's "ultimate" gourmet "extravaganza" offers "house-proud" homemakers and "professional caterers" alike an "incredibly wide selection" of pots and pans, "hard-to-find gadgets" and "small appliances and knives at pretty competitive prices"; the displays can be "rather helter-skelter" and it "doesn't carry lower-end" merch ("only quality abounds"), but it's worth the "pilgrimage" from anywhere (and open 365 days a year) so "sharpen your elbows and jump in."

Zacky's ●
27	23	22	M

NoHo | 686 Broadway (bet. 3rd & 4th Sts.) | 212-533-2005 | 855-492-2597 | www.zackys.com
European tourists and NYU kids alike find "shoes, shoes and more shoes" – close to 2,000 "reasonably priced" styles "under one roof" – including heavy-hitter brands like Converse, Frye and Steve Madden, and

a "wonderful selection" of must-have sneakers, at this loftlike, brick-walled NoHo shop; rounding out the affordable mix: stacks of Levi's jeans and "stylish" casualwear, all sold by a "helpful, knowledgeable" staff.

Zadig & Voltaire
▽ 26 | 25 | 19 | E

E 60s | 992 Madison Ave. (77th St.) | 212-396-3800
Meatpacking | 831 Washington St. (bet. Gansevoort & Little W. 12th Sts.) | 212-989-7300
SoHo | 153 Mercer St. (bet. Houston & Prince Sts.) | 212-965-8700
W Village | 409 Bleecker St. (bet. Bank & W. 11th Sts.) | 212-414-8470
www.zadig-et-voltaire.com

The French invasion continues to gain traction Uptown and Down with help from this contemporary Parisian import, renowned for its rock 'n' roll-inspired glitter-flecked sweaters and skull-print T-shirts for gamines, guys and kids; rounding out the Euro mix: snug-fitting cords, requisite scarves, scuff-me-to-perfection suede booties and biker-inspired pieces like black waxed-denim jeans that subtly communicate Gallic panache.

Zara
19 | 20 | 16 | M

E 40s | 500 Fifth Ave. (42nd St.) | 212-302-2677 ●
E 50s | 750 Lexington Ave. (bet. 59th & 60th Sts.) | 212-754-1120 ●
Garment District | 39 W. 34th St. (6th Ave.) | 212-868-6551 ●
SoHo | 580 Broadway (bet. Houston & Prince Sts.) | 212-343-1725 ●
W 50s | 666 Fifth Ave. (52nd St.) | 212-765-0477 ●
W 60s | 1963 Broadway (66th St.) | 212-362-4272
855-635-9272 | www.zara.com

"A Spanish staple that's taken the U.S. by storm", with a gigantic Midtown flagship and satellites, this "affordable Euro-chic" retailer combines a "healthy mix of edgy and classical styles", whether you want to "dress the part" of a "fashion-forward Parisian or a toned-down Lady Gaga"; the "constantly changing offerings" for men, women and children "make it a must-browse", but beware of "feisty fashionistas" and "messy" shelves come sale time.

Z'Baby Company
24 | 18 | 19 | E

E 70s | 996 Lexington Ave. (72nd St.) | 212-472-2229
W 70s | 100 W. 72nd St. (Columbus Ave.) | 212-579-2229
www.zbabycompany.com

City babes build their power wardrobes at this "cool" Uptown two-some, a "terrific" source for "urban kidwear" "with character" from the most exclusive labels, including "exciting stuff for boys"; the displays may be a little "haphazard", but with "so many cute styles", you "can always find" the perfect "last-minute gift", though some command "grandpa prices."

Zero + Maria Cornejo
26 | 24 | 22 | E

NoHo | 33 Bleecker St. (bet. Bowery & Lafayette St.) | 212-925-3849 | www.zeromariacornejo.com

Shoppers with a taste for intellectually engaging fashion "love, love, love" the "great styling" and architectural shapes at the Chilean-born designer's sparsely decorated NoHo outpost; the unusual cuts are popular with high-minded celebrities whose tastes skew toward the offbeat (and expensive), and if you need help with some of the more challenging items, "the service here will rock your world."

	QUALITY	DISPLAY	SERVICE	COST

Zimmermann
24 | **23** | **22** | **E**

SoHo | 87 Mercer St. (Spring St.) | 212-226-6440 |
www.zimmermannwear.com

Australian sisters Nicky and Simone Zimmermann bring their ethereal, ultrafeminine brand of swimwear, dresses and accessories to this airy SoHo space, where "excellent displays" showcase dreamy confections that would seem at home on the beaches of Sydney; salespeople are "polite", and though items are "expensive, you need to pay for quality."

Zitomer
25 | **22** | **21** | **E**

E 70s | 969 Madison Ave. (bet. 75th & 76th Sts.) | 212-737-5560 |
888-219-2888 | www.zitomer.com

Z Chemists

W 50s | 40 W. 57th St. (bet. 5th & 6th Aves.) | 212-956-6000 |
www.zchemists.com

The "Neiman Marcus of apothecaries", this "Madison Avenue landmark" and its West 50s counterpart attract "rich" locals and "drugstore-lovers" alike; it's a "fairly wacky" "one-stop-shopping" pharmacy experience given the "cornucopia of goodies", from "fur headbands" to "Chanel perfume and emery boards", plus the "staff is so helpful" you may "forget you're in New York."

Zoë ◗
23 | **21** | **22** | **E**

Dumbo | 68 Washington St. (bet. Front & York Sts.) | Brooklyn |
718-237-4002 | www.shopzoeonline.com

High-end labels like Céline, Lanvin and The Row commingle with contemporary must-haves from Helmut Lang and Rag & Bone plus leading-edge accessories and footwear at this Dumbo destination, an offshoot of the Princeton trendsetter – all the "good stuff" you'd expect to find in an upscale, artsy Brooklyn neighborhood; the expansive industrial space is made for easy browsing, and staffers are always happy to bring you that next size.

SHOPPING INDEXES

Special Features

Listings cover the best in each category.

ADDITIONS

(Properties added since the last edition of the book)

Amelia Toro | **Chelsea** ⌐|

Anne et Valentin | **NoLita** ⌐|

Armani Jr. | **E 80s** ⌐|

Askel Project | **SoHo** ⌐|

Baggu | **W'burg** ⌐|

The Bar at Baublebar | **Chelsea** ⌐|

Belstaff | **E 60s** ⌐|

Brian Atwood | **E 60s** ⌐|

Brooklyn Tailors | **W'burg** ⌐|

CADET | **multi.** ⌐|

Carson St. Cloth. | **SoHo** ⌐|

Chacott | **Gramercy** ⌐|

Christian Siriano | **NoLita** ⌐|

Civilianaire | **NoLita** ⌐|

Creel/Gow | **E 70s** ⌐|

Cutler and Gross | **SoHo** ⌐|

Denim & Supply, Ralph Lauren | ⌐|
   G Vill

Devorado | **E Vill** ⌐|

Environment | **NoHo** ⌐|

Equipment | **SoHo** ⌐|

Everything/Water | **E 80s** ⌐|

Fine/Dandy | **W 40s** ⌐|

Gamine | **W'burg** ⌐|

G Shock | **SoHo** ⌐|

Gudrun Sjödén | **SoHo** ⌐|

Halston Heritage | **E 80s** ⌐|

HAN KJØBENHAVN | **NoLita** ⌐|

Hanro | **Meatpacking** ⌐|

Happy Socks | **SoHo** ⌐|

Harlem Haberdashery | **Harlem** ⌐|

House of Horology | **SoHo** ⌐|

H.W. Carter | **W'burg** ⌐|

Iosselliani | **Chelsea** ⌐|

Ippolita | **E 60s** ⌐|

IRO | **SoHo** ⌐|

JNRL X STR | **LES** ⌐|

J. Press - York St. | **W Vill** ⌐|

Juliette Longuet | **E 70s** ⌐|

Jung Lee | **Chelsea** ⌐|

Khirma Eliazov | **W Vill** ⌐|

Kurt Geiger | **W Vill** ⌐|

Labor Skate | **LES** ⌐|

Lanvin Men | **E 60s** ⌐|

Lazzoni | **Chelsea** ⌐|

Leica | **SoHo** ⌐|

Liebeskind | **SoHo** ⌐|

Makerbot | **NoHo** ⌐|

MenScience | **NoHo** ⌐|

Miguel Antoinne | **SoHo** ⌐|

MM6 | **W Vill** ⌐|

Monique Lhuillier | **E 70s** ⌐|

Mr. Throwback | **E Vill** ⌐|

Norman/Jules | **Park Slope** ⌐|

Osswald | **SoHo** ⌐|

Pamela Gonzales | **SoHo** ⌐|

Pas de Calais | **SoHo** ⌐|

Perrin Paris | **E 70s** ⌐|

Personnel of NY | **W Vill** ⌐|

Pilgrim Surf | **W'burg** ⌐|

Piperlime | **SoHo** ⌐|

Pork Pie Hats | **multi.** ⌐|

Private Stock | **SoHo** ⌐|

Procell | **LES** ⌐|

Proenza Schouler | **E 60s** ⌐|

Rachel Riley | **E 90s** ⌐|

Raleigh | **NoLita** ⌐|

Red Lantern Bicycles | **Clinton Hill** ⌐|

Sam Edelman | **SoHo** ⌐|

Schutz | **E 60s** ⌐|

SlapBack | **W'burg** ⌐|

Store 114 | **LES** ⌐|

Swords-Smith | **W'burg** ⌐|

Tommy Bahama | **E 50s** ⌐|

Trunk Show | **Harlem** ⌐|

West Elm Mkt. | **Dumbo** ⌐|

AVANT-GARDE

Agt. Provocateur | **multi.** 26|

Alain Mikli | **multi.** 29|

Alexander McQueen | **Meatpacking** — 29

Aloha Rag | **Hudson Square** — 26

NEW Amelia Toro | **Chelsea** — –

Bape | **SoHo** — 27

Barneys NY | **E 60s** — 28

Cappellini | **SoHo** — 26

Comme/Garçons | **Chelsea** — 28

Costume Nt'l | **SoHo** — 28

Design Within Reach | **multi.** — 25

Editions/Parfums | **E 70s** — 25

Fivestory | **E 60s** — –

Future Perfect | **W'burg** — –

IF | **SoHo** — 29

Issey Miyake | **TriBeCa** — 28

NEW JNRL X STR | **LES** — –

Kirna Zabête | **SoHo** — 26

Love Adorned | **NoLita** — 27

Maison Kitsuné | **Chelsea** — –

Maison/Margiela | **W Vill** — –

NEW Makerbot | **NoHo** — –

Marni | **multi.** — 28

NEW MM6 | **W Vill** — –

Moss Bureau | **Garment** — 28

Muléh | **Chelsea** — –

Oak | **multi.** — 24

Opening Ceremony | **multi.** — 25

Other Music | **NoHo** — 29

NEW Pamela Gonzales | **SoHo** — –

Pierre Hardy | **W Vill** — –

Resurrection Vintage | **NoLita** — –

Rick Owens | **Hudson Square** — –

Story | **Chelsea** — 22

VPL | **SoHo** — –

Y-3 | **SoHo** — 26

Zero/Maria Cornejo | **NoHo** — 26

Zoë | **Dumbo** — 23

CELEBRITY CLIENTELE

Aaron Basha | **E 60s** — 28

ABC Carpet/Home | **Flatiron** — 26

Aedes/Venustas | **W Vill** — 29

Alain Mikli | **multi.** — 29

Alexander McQueen | **Meatpacking** — 29

Alexander Wang | **SoHo** — 26

Alexis Bittar | **multi.** — 26

Alice/Olivia | **multi.** — 24

Armani | **multi.** — 28

Balenciaga | **SoHo** — 29

Barneys NY | **E 60s** — 28

NEW Belstaff | **E 60s** — –

Bergdorf | **W 50s** — 29

Bergdorf Men | **E 50s** — 29

bliss | **multi.** — 25

Blue Tree | **E 90s** — 28

Bonpoint | **multi.** — 28

Bottega Veneta | **multi.** — 29

Bottega Veneta Men's | **E 60s** — –

Breguet | **E 60s** — 29

Breitling | **E 50s** — 29

NEW Brian Atwood | **E 60s** — –

Brioni | **E 50s** — 29

Burberry Brit | **multi.** — 28

Burton | **SoHo** — 26

Calypso | **multi.** — 23

Carolina Herrera | **E 70s** — 29

Catherine Malandrino | **multi.** — 27

Céline | **E 70s** — 25

Chanel | **multi.** — 29

Chanel Jewelry | **E 60s** — 29

Charlotte Olympia | **E 60s** — –

Chloé | **multi.** — 28

Christian Louboutin | **multi.** — 28

NEW Christian Siriano | **NoLita** — –

David Yurman | **E 60s** — 28

Derek Lam | **E 60s** — 27

de Vera | **multi.** — 27

Dior Homme | **E 50s** — 26

Dior | **E 50s** — 29

DKNY | **multi.** — 23

Dolce/Gabbana | **E 60s** — 26

Donna Karan | **E 60s** — 26

Editions/Parfums | **E 70s** — 25

Etro | **multi.** — 27

Fendi | **E 50s** — 28

Fivestory | **E 60s** — –

Fred Leighton | **E 60s** — 29

Girard Perregaux | **E 60s** — 29

Giuseppe Zanotti | **E 60s** — 27

Gucci | **multi.**	28
Haute Hippie | **multi.**	24
Helmut Lang | **multi.**	26
Hermès | **multi.**	30
Hervé Leger | **multi.**	26
Isabel Marant | **SoHo**	25
Jeffrey | **Meatpacking**	27
Jerome Dreyfuss | **SoHo**	-
Jil Sander | **multi.**	28
Jimmy Choo | **multi.**	28
J. Mendel | **E 60s**	28
Kate Spade | **multi.**	25
Kiki/Montparnasse | **SoHo**	28
Lanvin | **E 60s**	28
La Petite Coquette | **G Vill**	28
NEW Leica | **SoHo**	-
Longchamp | **multi.**	27
Louis Vuitton | **multi.**	28
M.A.C. | **SoHo**	26
Maje | **multi.**	-
Manolo Blahnik | **W 50s**	29
Marc Jacobs | **SoHo**	26
Marc Jacobs Access. | **W Vill**	26
Marni | **multi.**	28
Michael Kors | **multi.**	27
Miu Miu | **multi.**	26
Moncler | **SoHo**	28
Moss Bureau | **Garment**	28
Mulberry | **multi.**	28
NARS | **W Vill**	25
Nicholas Kirkwood | **Meatpacking**	-
Oliver Peoples | **multi.**	28
Oscar/Renta | **E 60s**	29
Prada | **multi.**	28
NEW Proenza Schouler | **E 60s**	-
Purl Soho | **SoHo**	28
Rag/Bone | **multi.**	26
Ralph Lauren | **multi.**	26
Ralph Lauren RRL | **multi.**	26
Reed Krakoff | **E 60s**	28
Rick Owens | **Hudson Square**	-
Robert Lee Morris | **SoHo**	27
Robert Marc | **multi.**	25
Roberto Cavalli | **E 60s**	28
Roger Vivier | **E 60s**	28

St. James | **W Vill**	25
Saks Fifth Ave. | **E 50s**	27
Salvatore Ferragamo | **E 50s**	29
Sandro | **multi.**	-
Santa Maria Novella | **NoLita**	29
Silver Lining | **SoHo**	-
Space.NK | **multi.**	27
Stella McCartney | **SoHo**	26
St. Laurent Paris | **multi.**	28
Stuart Weitzman | **multi.**	28
Superga | **SoHo**	-
Swarovski | **E 40s**	26
Tibi | **SoHo**	23
Tom Ford | **E 70s**	28
Tracy Reese | **Meatpacking**	27
Trina Turk | **Meatpacking**	27
True Religion | **multi.**	24
Tucker | **SoHo**	-
Urban Archaeology | **multi.**	25
Valentino | **E 60s**	28
Vera Wang | **SoHo**	28
Versace | **multi.**	26
Zero/Maria Cornejo | **NoHo**	26
Zimmermann | **SoHo**	24

GREEN GOODS

(Carries eco-conscious items)

A&G Merch | **W'burg**	27
ABC Carpet/Home | **Flatiron**	26
ABC | **Flatiron**	26
ABC Carpet/Outlet | **Soundview**	23
Aesop | **multi.**	26
Arcadia | **Chelsea**	26
Arhaus | **Meatpacking**	27
Aveda | **multi.**	26
NEW Baggu | **W'burg**	-
Bare Escentuals | **multi.**	26
bliss | **multi.**	25
Canvas | **multi.**	27
Caudalie | **multi.**	-
Equinox Energy | **E 60s**	25
Future Perfect | **multi.**	-
Green Depot | **multi.**	25
Greenhouse | **Downtown Bklyn**	28
NEW Gudrun Sjödén | **SoHo**	-

HIP/HOT

Future Perfect | **multi.**	-|
Gant | **multi.**	25|
Giuseppe Zanotti | **E 60s**	27|
Goorin Bros. | **multi.**	26|
H&M | **E 50s**	15|
Haute Hippie | **multi.**	24|
Helmut Lang | **multi.**	26|
Housing Works | **Chelsea**	20|
NEW H.W. Carter | **W'burg**	-|
Ikea | **Red Hook**	16|
Ilori | **SoHo**	-|
Ina | **multi.**	25|
Intermix | **multi.**	24|
NEW Ippolita | **E 60s**	-|
Isabel Marant | **SoHo**	25|
Jack Spade | **multi.**	25|
J.Crew | **multi.**	22|
J.Crew Men's | **multi.**	25|
Jean-Michel Cazabat | **W Vill**	-|
Jean Shop | **Meatpacking**	26|
Jeffrey | **Meatpacking**	27|
Jerome Dreyfuss | **SoHo**	-|
Jimmy Choo | **multi.**	28|
Joe Fresh | **multi.**	20|
John Derian | **E Vill**	27|
John Varvatos | **multi.**	26|
Joie | **multi.**	24|
Jonathan Adler | **multi.**	23|
Jumelle | **W'burg**	-|
Kate Spade | **multi.**	25|
Kiehl's | **multi.**	27|
Kirna Zabête | **SoHo**	26|
NEW Kurt Geiger | **W Vill**	-|
Lanvin | **E 60s**	28|
NEW Lanvin Men | **E 60s**	-|
NEW Leica | **SoHo**	-|
Lisa Perry | **E 70s**	-|
L.K. Bennett | **W 50s**	23|
Love Adorned | **NoLita**	27|
Lululemon | **multi.**	27|
M.A.C. | **SoHo**	26|
Mackage | **SoHo**	-|
Madewell | **multi.**	23|
Maison Kitsuné | **Chelsea**	-|
Maison/Margiela | **W Vill**	-|
Maje | **multi.**	-|
Malia Mills | **multi.**	26|
Manolo Blahnik | **W 50s**	29|
Marc/Marc Jacobs Men | **W Vill**	26|
Marc/Marc Jacobs Women | **W Vill**	25|
Marc Jacobs Access. | **W Vill**	26|
Marc Jacobs | **SoHo**	26|
Mauboussin | **E 60s**	28|
Me&Ro | **NoLita**	25|
Michael Kors | **multi.**	27|
Miu Miu | **multi.**	26|
Mood | **Garment**	26|
Moroso | **SoHo**	-|
Moscot | **multi.**	25|
Muji | **multi.**	22|
Mulberry | **multi.**	28|
My Little Sunshine | **multi.**	-|
Nanette Lepore | **multi.**	26|
NARS | **W Vill**	25|
Nicholas Kirkwood | **Meatpacking**	-|
Nike | **multi.**	25|
No. 6 | **L Italy**	-|
Oak | **multi.**	24|
Odin | **multi.**	27|
Opening Ceremony | **multi.**	25|
Organic Mod. | **multi.**	26|
Other Music | **NoHo**	29|
Otte | **multi.**	24|
Owen | **Meatpacking**	-|
Paragon | **Union Sq**	26|
Patricia Field | **NoHo**	23|
Pierre Hardy | **W Vill**	-|
Pilgrim Surf | **W'burg**	-|
NEW Piperlime | **SoHo**	-|
Pixie Mkt. | **LES**	-|
Prada | **multi.**	28|
NEW Proenza Schouler | **E 60s**	-|
Purl Soho | **SoHo**	28|
Rag/Bone | **multi.**	26|
NEW Raleigh | **NoLita**	-|
Ricky's | **SoHo**	19|
Ride/Skate | **multi.**	23|
Roberta Freymann/Ro's | **E 70s**	23|
Roberta Roller | **multi.**	25|

IN-STORE DINING

LONGTIMERS

1858	Macy's	**multi.**	23
1861	Bloomingdale's	**E 50s**	26
1862	FAO Schwarz	**E 50s**	26
1899	Bergdorf	**W 50s**	29
1900	Beacon Paint	**W 70s**	26
1905	NY Central Art	**E Vill**	27
1905	Simon's	**Murray Hill**	26
1908	Paragon	**Union Sq**	26
1912	Pintchik	**Park Slope**	19
1912	23rd St. Hardware	**Gramercy**	25
1915	Moscot	**LES**	25
1920	Altman Luggage	**LES**	26
1920	Harry Winston	**E 50s**	29
1921	Tarzian	**Park Slope**	23
1923	Mus./City of NY	**E 100s**	26
1924	A.W. Kaufman	**LES**	25
1924	Saks Fifth Ave.	**E 50s**	27
1925	Davis/Warshow	**E 50s**	27
1929	A.I. Friedman	**Flatiron**	25
1930	Whitney Mus. Store	**E 70s**	24
1932	H.L. Purdy	**E 50s**	25
1933	Albee Baby	**W 90s**	27
1933	Pearl Paint	**Chinatown**	24
1934	Scully/Scully	**E 50s**	28
1936	M&J	**Garment**	25
1938	Paul Stuart	**E 40s**	29
1939	Verdura	**E 50s**	28
1940	Tip Top	**W 70s**	25
1946	Fountain Pen	**TriBeCa**	29
1946	Mem. Sloan-Kettering	**E 80s**	23
1948	Lester's	**Sheepshead**	23
1950	Leonard Opticians	**W 50s**	27
1950	Ray Beauty	**W 40s**	23
1950	Zitomer/Z Chem.	**E 70s**	25

REGISTRY

(B=Baby; W=Wedding)

ABC Carpet/Home	W	**Flatiron**	26
ABC	W	**Flatiron**	26
Acorn	B, W	**Downtown Bklyn**	24
Aero	W	**SoHo**	24
Agt. Provocateur	W	**multi.**	26
Alessi	W	**multi.**	28
Area Kids	B, W	**W'burg**	24

Asprey	W	**E 70s**	28
babycottons	B, W	**E 80s**	28
Baccarat	W	**E 50s**	29
Barneys NY	W	**E 60s**	28
Bed Bath Beyond	W	**Flatiron**	22
Bergdorf	B, W	**W 50s**	29
Bernardaud	W	**E 50s**	29
Bloomingdale's	W	**E 50s**	26
Boomerang	W	**multi.**	25
B'way Panhandler	W	**G Vill**	25
Bklyn. Kitchen	W	**W'burg**	26
buybuy BABY	B, W	**Chelsea**	23
Calypso Home	W	**L Italy**	26
CB2	W	**multi.**	19
Christofle	W	**E 70s**	29
Crate/Barrel	B, W	**multi.**	23
D. Porthault	W	**E 50s**	29
DwellStudio	B, W	**SoHo**	-
Fishs Eddy	W	**multi.**	22
Frette	W	**E 60s**	29
Georg Jensen	W	**E 60s**	29
Giggle	B, W	**multi.**	26
Gracious Home	W	**multi.**	25
Greenhouse	W	**Downtown Bklyn**	28
Hermès	W	**multi.**	30
Honora	W	**E 50s**	25
Jacadi	B, W	**multi.**	28
J&R Jr.	B, W	**Financial**	24
Jewish Mus. Stores	W	**E 90s**	26
John Derian	W	**E Vill**	27
Jonathan Adler	W	**multi.**	23
Journelle	W	**multi.**	29
NEW Jung Lee	W	**Chelsea**	-
Kiki/Montparnasse	W	**SoHo**	28
Lalique	W	**E 50s**	29
Lanvin	W	**E 60s**	28
La Perla	W	**multi.**	28
Les Petits Chap.	B	**SoHo**	-
Lester's	B, W	**multi.**	23
Longchamp	W	**multi.**	27
Lucky Wang	B	**multi.**	24
MacKenzie-Childs	W	**W 50s**	27
Macy's	B, W	**multi.**	23
Met. Museum Store	W	**multi.**	26

Michael C. Fina | W | **E 50s** — 27

Pratesi | W | **E 60s** — 29

Scully/Scully | W | **E 50s** — 28

Shop@Scandinavia | W | **Murray Hill** — 25

Space Kiddets | B | **Flatiron** — 25

Sur La Table | W | **multi.** — 25

Target | W | **multi.** — 19

Tiffany's | W | **multi.** — 28

Wm.-Sonoma | W | **multi.** — 27

Wm.-Wayne | W | **multi.** — 25

Yoya/Mart | B, W | **multi.** — 23

Zabar's Mezz. | W | **W 80s** — 28

Z'Baby Co. | B | **multi.** — 24

STATUS GOODS

Aaron Faber | **W 50s** — 27

ABC Carpet/Home | **Flatiron** — 26

Aedes/Venustas | **W Vill** — 29

Agt. Provocateur | **multi.** — 26

Akris | **E 60s** — 29

Alan Moss | **E Vill** — 28

A La Vieille Russie | **E 50s** — 28

Alexander McQueen | **Meatpacking** — 29

Alexander Wang | **SoHo** — 26

Allen Edmonds | **multi.** — 28

Aloha Rag | **Hudson Square** — 26

Ann Sacks | **multi.** — 28

Apple | **multi.** — 29

Armani | **multi.** — 28

NEW Armani Jr. | **E 80s** — -

Artistic Tile | **Flatiron** — 27

Ascot Chang | **W 50s** — 27

Asprey | **E 70s** — 28

Audemars Piguet | **E 50s** — 29

Baccarat | **E 50s** — 29

Balenciaga | **SoHo** — 29

Bally | **E 50s** — 26

B&B Italia | **multi.** — 27

Bang/Olufsen | **multi.** — 28

Barbour | **multi.** — 28

Barneys NY | **E 60s** — 28

BDDW | **SoHo** — 25

Belgian Shoes | **E 50s** — 28

NEW Belstaff | **E 60s** — -

Bergdorf | **W 50s** — 29

Bergdorf Men | **E 50s** — 29

Bernardaud | **E 50s** — 29

Bisazza | **SoHo** — 25

Black Fleece | **W Vill** — 24

Blue Tree | **E 90s** — 28

Bogner | **SoHo** — 29

Bonpoint | **multi.** — 28

Bose | **multi.** — 27

Bottega Veneta | **multi.** — 29

Bottega Veneta Men's | **E 60s** — -

Breguet | **multi.** — 29

Breitling | **E 50s** — 29

NEW Brian Atwood | **E 60s** — -

Brioni | **E 50s** — 29

Brunello Cucinelli | **multi.** — 29

Buccellati | **E 60s** — 29

Bulgari | **E 50s** — -

Burberry | **multi.** — 28

Calvin Klein | **E 60s** — 26

Canali | **Financial** — 28

Cappellini | **SoHo** — 26

Carolina Herrera | **E 70s** — 29

Cartier | **multi.** — 29

Catimini | **E 80s** — 28

Céline | **E 70s** — 25

Cesare Attolini | **E 60s** — -

Cesare Paciotti | **E 60s** — 25

Chanel | **multi.** — 29

Chanel Jewelry | **E 60s** — 29

Charlotte Olympia | **E 60s** — -

Chloé | **multi.** — 28

Chopard | **E 60s** — 29

Christian Louboutin | **multi.** — 28

Christofle | **E 70s** — 29

Chrs. Fischer | **multi.** — 24

Chrome Hearts | **E 70s** — 29

Comme/Garçons | **Chelsea** — 28

NEW Creel/Gow | **E 70s** — -

Cynthia Rowley | **E 70s** — 28

David Webb | **E 70s** — 29

David Yurman | **E 60s** — 28

DeBeers | **E 50s** — 28

Dempsey/Carroll | **E 70s** — 28

Derek Lam | **E 60s** — 27

Design Within Reach	**multi.**	25	John Lobb	**E 60s**	29
de Vera	**multi.**	27	John Varvatos	**SoHo**	26
Diesel Black Gold	**SoHo**	27	Judith Ripka	**E 60s**	28
Dior Homme	**E 50s**	26	**NEW** Khirma Eliazov	**W Vill**	-
Dior	**E 50s**	29	Kirna Zabête	**SoHo**	26
Dolce/Gabbana	**multi.**	26	Kiton	**E 50s**	29
Donna Karan	**E 60s**	26	Kleinfeld	**Chelsea**	25
D. Porthault	**E 50s**	29	Knoll	**Chelsea**	29
Dunhill	**E 50s**	28	Lalique	**E 50s**	29
Duxiana	**multi.**	29	Lanvin	**E 60s**	28
Editions/Parfums	**E 70s**	25	**NEW** Lanvin Men	**E 60s**	-
Ermenegildo Zegna	**E 50s**	28	Lederer/Paris	**E 50s**	26
Escada	**E 50s**	25	Leffot	**W Vill**	-
Etro	**multi.**	27	**NEW** Leica	**SoHo**	-
Fabergé	**E 60s**	-	Lexington Gdns.	**E 70s**	24
FAO Schwarz	**E 50s**	26	Ligne Roset	**multi.**	26
Fendi	**E 50s**	28	Longchamp	**multi.**	27
Fivestory	**E 60s**	-	Loro Piana	**E 60s**	29
Fogal	**multi.**	27	Louis Vuitton	**multi.**	28
Fratelli Rossetti	**E 50s**	29	Lyric Hi-Fi	**E 80s**	29
Fred Leighton	**E 60s**	29	Maclaren	**SoHo**	27
Frette	**E 60s**	29	Maison Kitsuné	**Chelsea**	-
Georg Jensen	**E 60s**	29	Manolo Blahnik	**W 50s**	29
Ghurka	**multi.**	29	Marc Jacobs	**SoHo**	26
Girard Perregaux	**E 60s**	29	Marni	**multi.**	28
Giuseppe Zanotti	**E 60s**	27	Mauboussin	**E 60s**	28
Graff	**E 60s**	29	Max Mara	**E 60s**	28
Gucci	**multi.**	28	Michael C. Fina	**E 50s**	27
Gucci Kids	**E 50s**	-	Michael Kors	**multi.**	27
Harry Winston	**E 50s**	29	Missoni	**E 70s**	29
Henri Bendel	**W 50s**	26	Miu Miu	**multi.**	26
Hermès	**multi.**	30	Moncler	**SoHo**	28
Honora	**E 50s**	25	Montblanc	**E 50s**	28
H. Stern	**E 50s**	29	Morgenthal Frederics	**multi.**	27
Hugo Boss	**multi.**	27	Moroso	**SoHo**	-
Ilori	**SoHo**	-	Moschino	**Meatpacking**	25
NEW Ippolita	**E 60s**	-	Nicholas Kirkwood	**Meatpacking**	-
Isabel Marant	**SoHo**	25	Oliver Peoples	**multi.**	28
Issey Miyake	**TriBeCa**	28	Oscar/Renta	**E 60s**	29
IWC Schaff.	**E 50s**	-	Paul Smith	**multi.**	27
James Robinson	**E 50s**	29	P.E. Guerin	**W Vill**	29
Jerome Dreyfuss	**SoHo**	-	Piaget	**E 50s**	29
Jil Sander	**multi.**	28	Prada	**multi.**	28
Jimmy Choo	**multi.**	28	Pratesi	**E 60s**	29
J. Mendel	**E 60s**	28	**NEW** Proenza Schouler	**E 60s**	-

Pronovias | **E 50s**	25
Ralph Lauren | **multi.**	26
Ralph Lauren Child | **E 70s**	28
Reed Krakoff | **E 60s**	28
Rick Owens | **Hudson Square**	-
Robert Lee Morris | **SoHo**	27
Robert Marc | **multi.**	25
Roche Bobois | **Murray Hill**	25
Roger Vivier | **E 60s**	28
Saks Fifth Ave. | **E 50s**	27
Salvatore Ferragamo | **E 50s**	29
Santa Maria Novella | **NoLita**	29
Scully/Scully | **E 50s**	28
Smythson | **W 50s**	29
Sportmax | **SoHo**	27
Stella McCartney | **SoHo**	26
Stickley/Audi | **Chelsea**	26
St. Laurent Paris | **E 50s**	28
Tiffany's | **multi.**	28
Tom Ford | **E 70s**	28
Tory Burch | **multi.**	26
Tourneau | **multi.**	27
Turnbull/Asser | **E 50s**	28
Vacheron Constantin | **E 60s**	29
Valentino | **E 60s**	28
Van Cleef | **E 50s**	29
Vera Wang | **SoHo**	28
Vera Wang Bridal | **E 70s**	29
Verdura | **E 50s**	28
Versace | **multi.**	26
Waterworks | **multi.**	26
Wempe | **E 50s**	29
Wolford | **multi.**	28
Yigal Azrouël | **E 70s**	25
Yves Delorme | **E 70s**	28
Zoë | **Dumbo**	23

TWEEN/ TEEN APPEAL

Adidas | **multi.**	25
Alphabets | **E Vill**	25
Annie's Blue Ribbon | **Downtown Bklyn**	27
Anthropologie | **multi.**	23
Apple | **multi.**	29
Artists/Fleas | **W'burg**	24

Beacon's Closet | **multi.**	19
Billionaire Boys | **SoHo**	24
Bookmarc | **W Vill**	24
Brandy Melville | **SoHo**	-
Bklyn. Flea | **Ft Greene**	21
Bklyn. Industries | **W'burg**	21
Buffalo Exchange | **multi.**	20
Burton | **SoHo**	26
Converse | **SoHo**	22
Crumpler | **multi.**	27
Diesel | **multi.**	24
Dr. Martens | **multi.**	28
E.A.T. | **E 80s**	22
Evolution | **SoHo**	27
Express | **Garment**	21
Fjällräven | **NoLita**	23
Free People | **multi.**	22
Frye | **SoHo**	28
GiGi K | **G Vill**	-
Goorin Bros. | **multi.**	26
GreenFlea Mkt. | **W 70s**	20
H&M | **E 50s**	15
HK Flea Mkt. | **Garment**	20
Int'l Ctr./Photo. Store | **W 40s**	27
John Fluevog | **NoLita**	28
Kate Spade | **multi.**	25
Kate's Paperie | **SoHo**	26
Kid Robot | **SoHo**	25
Lester's | **multi.**	23
Levi's | **multi.**	23
Lilly Pulitzer | **E 70s**	27
Lush | **multi.**	25
M.A.C. | **SoHo**	26
Malcolm Shabazz | **Harlem**	20
Marc Jacobs Access. | **W Vill**	26
Marc Jacobs | **SoHo**	26
Marimekko | **multi.**	27
Muji | **multi.**	22
Nike | **multi.**	25
Paragon | **Union Sq**	26
Pearl River | **SoHo**	18
Pork Pie Hats | **multi.**	-
Puma | **multi.**	23
Ride/Skate | **multi.**	23
Rudy's Music | **multi.**	29

Sabon	**SoHo**	26	Trash/Vaudeville	**E Vill**	22
Sam Ash	**multi.**	26	UGG	**multi.**	25
Sephora	**E 40s**	25	Uniqlo	**multi.**	21
Soapology	**W Vill**	25	Urban Outfitters	**Chelsea**	18
Sony Store	**E 50s**	27	Vince Camuto	**multi.**	24
Sperry	**Flatiron**	26	W. 25th St. Mkt.	**Chelsea**	16
Supreme	**SoHo**	23	What Goes Around	**SoHo**	22
Topshop	**SoHo**	19	Zacky's	**NoHo**	27

Merchandise

Includes store names, locations and Quality ratings.

ACCESSORIES

(See also Department Stores)

Alexander Wang | **SoHo**	26
Alice/Olivia | **multi.**	24
Allen Edmonds | **W 40s**	28
Amarcord | **multi.**	24
Anna Sui | **SoHo**	23
Anthropologie | **Flatiron**	23
Anya Hindmarch | **E 60s**	27
Armani | **E 60s**	28
Ascot Chang | **W 50s**	27
Ash | **SoHo**	25
NEW Baggu | **W'burg**	-
Bally | **E 50s**	26
Barneys Co-Op | **multi.**	26
NEW Belstaff | **E 60s**	-
Brooks Bros. | **multi.**	26
Burberry | **multi.**	28
Céline | **E 70s**	25
Chanel | **multi.**	29
Charles Tyrwhitt | **W 40s**	24
Chloé | **multi.**	28
Chrs. Fischer | **SoHo**	24
Chuckies New York | **multi.**	25
Clarks | **multi.**	24
Club Monaco | **multi.**	21
Coach | **E 50s**	26
Coach Legacy | **W Vill**	26
Coclico | **NoLita**	23
Cole Haan | **multi.**	26
Derek Lam | **E 60s**	27
DVF | **Meatpacking**	27
Dior Homme | **SoHo**	26
Dior | **E 50s**	29
Dunhill | **E 50s**	28
Fair Folks | **G Vill**	-
NEW Fine/Dandy | **W 40s**	-
Free People | **E 40s**	22
NEW Gamine | **W'burg**	-
Giuseppe Zanotti | **E 60s**	27
Gucci | **E 60s**	28
NEW Halston Heritage | **E 80s**	-
Henry Beguelin | **W Vill**	-
Hermès | **multi.**	30
Hickoree's | **W'burg**	-
NEW H.W. Carter | **W'burg**	-
Intermix | **multi.**	24
Jeffrey | **Meatpacking**	27
Jerome Dreyfuss | **SoHo**	-
Jimmy Choo | **multi.**	28
J. McLaughlin | **E 90s**	23
J. Press | **E 40s**	25
Jumelle | **W'burg**	-
Kirna Zabête | **SoHo**	26
Krizia | **Meatpacking**	25
NEW Kurt Geiger | **W Vill**	-
Lacoste | **multi.**	24
NEW Liebeskind | **SoHo**	-
Lisa Perry | **E 70s**	-
Longchamp | **W 40s**	27
Lulu Guinness | **W Vill**	24
Madewell | **multi.**	23
Maje | **multi.**	-
Marc Jacobs Access. | **W Vill**	26
Michael Kors | **multi.**	27
Milly | **E 70s**	28
Missoni | **E 70s**	29
Miu Miu | **E 50s**	26
NEW Monique Lhuillier | **E 70s**	-
MooShoes | **LES**	25
Mulberry | **multi.**	28
Nanette Lepore | **multi.**	26
Nicole Miller | **multi.**	26
Odin | **multi.**	27
Utte | **multi.**	24
Patricia Field | **NoHo**	23
Perrin Paris | **E 70s**	-
Pierre Hardy | **W Vill**	-
Prada | **multi.**	28
NEW Proenza Schouler | **E 60s**	-
Pucci | **E 70s**	29
Ralph Lauren | **multi.**	26
Rebecca Taylor | **E 70s**	24
Reed Krakoff | **E 60s**	28

Resurrection Vintage | **NoLita**	–
Rick Owens | **Hudson Square**	–
Roger Vivier | **E 60s**	28
NEW Sam Edelman | **SoHo**	–
Sandro | **multi.**	–
Saturdays Surf | **multi.**	–
NEW Schutz | **E 60s**	–
NEW SlapBack | **W'burg**	–
Stella McCartney | **SoHo**	26
Stuart Weitzman | **multi.**	28
Theory | **multi.**	26
Tocca | **W Vill**	–
Tory Burch | **multi.**	26
Treasure/Bond | **SoHo**	–
Trina Turk | **Meatpacking**	27
Turnbull/Asser | **E 50s**	28
25 Park | **E 70s**	23
Wink | **multi.**	19
Zara | **multi.**	19

ANTIQUES

ABC Carpet/Home | **Flatiron**	26
ABC | **Flatiron**	26
Aero | **SoHo**	24
Alan Moss | **E Vill**	28
Antiques Garage | **Chelsea**	21
Bklyn. Flea | **multi.**	21
de Vera | **multi.**	27
Dienst/Dotter | **NoHo**	–
GreenFlea Mkt. | **W 70s**	20
Moon River | **W'burg**	–
Obscura | **E Vill**	26
W. 25th St. Mkt. | **Chelsea**	16

APPAREL

ACTIVEWEAR

Adidas | **multi.**	25
ASICS | **W 40s**	26
Athleta | **multi.**	25
Capezio | **multi.**	24
NEW Chacott | **Gramercy**	–
Equinox Energy | **E 60s**	25
JackRabbit | **multi.**	26
Lacoste | **multi.**	24
Lululemon | **multi.**	27
Moncler | **SoHo**	28

NBA | **W 40s**	21
NY Running | **multi.**	27
Nike | **multi.**	25
Paragon | **Union Sq**	26
Patagonia | **multi.**	27
Puma | **multi.**	23
REI | **NoLita**	26
Ride/Skate | **multi.**	23
Supreme | **SoHo**	23
Target | **multi.**	19
Y-3 | **SoHo**	26

CHILDREN'S
(See also Department Stores)

Area Kids | **W'burg**	24
NEW Armani Jr. | **E 80s**	–
babycottons | **E 80s**	28
Bonpoint | **multi.**	28
Brooks Bros. | **multi.**	26
Catimini | **E 80s**	28
Crewcuts | **multi.**	24
Diesel Kids | **SoHo**	27
Giggle | **multi.**	26
Gucci Kids | **E 50s**	–
Jacadi | **multi.**	28
James Perse | **W Vill**	24
Joe's Jeans | **SoHo**	28
Lacoste | **multi.**	24
Les Petits Chap. | **SoHo**	–
Lester's | **multi.**	23
Little Marc Jacobs | **W Vill**	27
Lucky Wang | **multi.**	24
NEW Massimo Dutti | **E 50s**	–
My Little Sunshine | **multi.**	–
Peter Elliot | **E 70s**	28
Pink Chicken | **E 80s**	–
Rachel Riley | **E 90s**	–
Ralph Lauren Child | **E 70s**	28
Reformation | **LES**	–
Space Kiddets | **Flatiron**	25
Yoya/Mart | **multi.**	23
Z'Baby Co. | **multi.**	24

MEN'S
(See also Apparel, Men's/Women's, Department Stores)

Ascot Chang | **W 50s**	27
NEW Askel Project | **SoHo**	–

Atelier NY | **Hudson Square**	25
Behaviour | **Chelsea**	26
Ben Sherman | **SoHo**	24
Beretta | **E 60s**	29
Billionaire Boys | **SoHo**	24
Bonobos | **multi.**	-
Bottega Veneta Men's | **E 60s**	-
Brioni | **E 50s**	29
Bklyn. Circus | **Boerum Hill**	25
Brooklyn Tailors | **W'burg**	-
By Robert James | **multi.**	-
NEW CADET | **multi.**	-
Canali | **multi.**	28
Carhartt | **SoHo**	28
NEW Carson St. Cloth. | **SoHo**	-
Cesare Attolini | **E 60s**	-
Charles Tyrwhitt | **multi.**	24
Diesel | **SoHo**	24
Dior Homme | **multi.**	26
Dunhill | **E 50s**	28
Ermenegildo Zegna | **E 50s**	28
Frank Stella | **multi.**	24
Freemans Sport | **multi.**	26
Gant | **multi.**	25
NEW HAN KJØBENHAVN | **NoLita**	-
Hermès Men | **E 60s**	29
Hickey Freeman | **E 50s**	27
Hickoree's | **W'burg**	-
NEW H.W. Carter | **W'burg**	-
Jay Kos | **NoLita**	29
J.Crew Men's | **multi.**	25
John Varvatos | **multi.**	26
J. Press | **E 40s**	25
NEW J. Press - York St. | **W Vill**	-
NEW Lanvin Men | **E 60s**	-
Marc/Marc Jacobs Men | **W Vill**	26
Odin | **multi.**	27
Onassis | **multi.**	-
Paul Stuart | **E 40s**	29
Peter Elliot | **E 70s**	28
NEW Private Stock | **SoHo**	-
Ralph Lauren RRL | **multi.**	26
Rothman's | **Union Sq**	25
Scoop Men's | **multi.**	23

Suitsupply | **SoHo**	-
Turnbull/Asser | **E 50s**	28
Vilebrequin | **multi.**	25

MEN'S/WOMEN'S
(Stores carrying both;
see also Department Stores)

Adidas SLVR | **SoHo**	23
Agnès B. | **multi.**	25
AllSaints | **multi.**	23
Alter | **Greenpt**	26
American Two Shot | **SoHo**	-
Armani | **multi.**	28
Assembly NY | **LES**	24
Atrium/KITH | **multi.**	23
Balenciaga | **SoHo**	29
Barbour | **multi.**	28
NEW Belstaff | **E 60s**	-
Billy Reid | **NoHo**	25
Bird | **multi.**	27
Blue/Cream | **E Vill**	25
Bogner | **SoHo**	29
Bottega Veneta | **E 50s**	29
Bklyn. Industries | **W'burg**	21
Brooks Bros. | **multi.**	26
Buffalo Exchange | **multi.**	20
Burberry | **multi.**	28
Burberry Brit | **multi.**	28
Calvin Klein | **E 60s**	26
CH Carolina | **E 60s**	28
Chrs. Fischer | **multi.**	24
Club Monaco | **multi.**	21
Comme/Garçons | **Chelsea**	28
Cotélac | **multi.**	-
Dave's Army | **Chelsea**	23
NEW Denim & Supply, Ralph Lauren | **G Vill**	-
Diesel | **multi.**	24
DKNY | **multi.**	23
Dolce/Gabbana | **multi.**	26
Emporio Armani | **multi.**	29
Epaulet | **multi.**	25
NEW Equipment | **SoHo**	-
Etro | **multi.**	27
Express | **Garment**	21
Fendi | **E 50s**	28
Fjällräven | **NoLita**	23

Fred Perry | **SoHo**	28
Gucci | **E 50s**	28
H&M | **E 50s**	15
Haute Hippie | **multi.**	24
Helmut Lang | **multi.**	26
Hermès | **multi.**	30
Hoodie Shop | **LES**	26
Hugo Boss | **multi.**	27
IF | **SoHo**	29
In God We Trust | **multi.**	23
Issey Miyake | **TriBeCa**	28
James Perse | **multi.**	24
J.Crew | **multi.**	22
J. McLaughlin | **multi.**	23
Joe Fresh | **multi.**	20
Joe's Jeans | **SoHo**	28
Lacoste | **multi.**	24
Levi's | **multi.**	23
Loehmann's | **multi.**	20
Loro Piana | **E 60s**	29
Mackage | **SoHo**	–
Macy's | **multi.**	23
Maison Kitsuné | **Chelsea**	–
Marc Jacobs | **SoHo**	26
🆕 Massimo Dutti | **E 50s**	–
Michael Kors | **multi.**	27
🆕 Miguel Antoinne | **SoHo**	–
Missoni | **E 70s**	29
Oak | **multi.**	24
Opening Ceremony | **multi.**	25
Owen | **Meatpacking**	–
🆕 Pas de Calais | **SoHo**	–
Paul Smith | **multi.**	27
🆕 Personnel of NY | **W Vill**	–
Peter Elliot | **E 80s**	28
Rag/Bone | **multi.**	26
🆕 Raleigh | **NoLita**	–
Roberto Cavalli | **E 60s**	28
Sandro | **multi.**	–
Scotch/Soda | **multi.**	27
Splendid | **SoHo**	–
Steven Alan | **multi.**	28
St. Laurent Paris | **multi.**	28
🆕 Swords-Smith | **W'burg**	–
Ted Baker | **multi.**	26

Theory | **multi.**	26
🆕 Tommy Bahama | **E 50s**	–
Topshop | **SoHo**	19
Trash/Vaudeville | **E Vill**	22
Treasure/Bond | **SoHo**	–
Trina Turk | **Meatpacking**	27
Uniqlo | **multi.**	21
Urban Outfitters | **Chelsea**	18
Valentino | **E 60s**	28
Versace | **multi.**	26
Vince | **multi.**	24
Zadig/Voltaire | **multi.**	26
Zara | **multi.**	19

VINTAGE/RESALE

Alter | **multi.**	26
Amarcord | **multi.**	24
American Two Shot | **SoHo**	–
Antiques Garage | **Chelsea**	21
Artists/Fleas | **W'burg**	24
Beacon's Closet | **multi.**	19
Bklyn. Flea | **multi.**	21
Buffalo Exchange | **multi.**	20
🆕 Devorado | **E Vill**	–
GreenFlea Mkt. | **W 70s**	20
HK Flea Mkt. | **Garment**	20
Housing Works | **Chelsea**	20
Ina | **multi.**	25
Michael's | **E 70s**	23
Mr. Throwback | **E Vill**	–
No. 6 | **L Italy**	–
🆕 Procell | **LES**	–
Reformation | **multi.**	–
Resurrection Vintage | **NoLita**	–
🆕 Store 114 | **LES**	–
🆕 Trunk Show | **Harlem**	–
W. 25th St. Mkt. | **Chelsea**	16
What Goes Around | **SoHo**	22

WOMEN'S
(See also Apparel, Men's/Women's, Department Stores)

A Détacher | **NoLita**	27
Akris | **E 60s**	29
Alice/Olivia | **multi.**	24
Alter | **Greenpt**	26
🆕 Amelia Toro | **Chelsea**	–
Anna Sui | **SoHo**	23

Annelore | **multi.**	24
Anthropologie | **multi.**	23
Aritzia | **multi.**	23
BCBG | **multi.**	24
Blue Tree | **E 90s**	28
Bond 07/Selima | **NoHo**	27
Bottega Veneta | **E 70s**	29
Calypso | **multi.**	23
Carlos Miele | **Meatpacking**	23
Carolina Herrera | **E 70s**	29
Catherine Malandrino | **multi.**	27
Céline | **E 70s**	25
Century 21 | **multi.**	21
Chanel | **multi.**	29
Chloé | **multi.**	28
NEW Christian Siriano | **NoLita**	-
Club Monaco | **multi.**	21
Comptoir | **multi.**	25
Courtshop | **NoLita**	-
Creatures/Comfort | **NoLita**	22
Cut25 | **SoHo**	-
C. Wonder | **multi.**	21
Cynthia Rowley | **multi.**	28
Dagny/Barstow | **NoLita**	-
Dalaga | **multi.**	-
Derek Lam | **E 60s**	27
Diana Kane | **Park Slope**	25
DVF | **multi.**	27
Dior | **E 50s**	29
DKNY | **Flatiron**	23
Dolce Vita | **NoLita**	23
Donna Karan | **E 60s**	26
Edit | **E 90s**	26
Eileen Fisher | **multi.**	26
Elie Tahari | **SoHo**	26
Elizabeth Charles | **Meatpacking**	-
Escada | **E 50s**	25
Fivestory | **E 60s**	-
Free People | **multi.**	22
NEW Gudrun Sjödén | **SoHo**	-
Guess/Marciano | **SoHo**	22
NEW Halston Heritage | **E 80s**	-
Hervé Léger | **multi.**	26
Ina | **Chelsea**	25

Intermix | **multi.**	24
NEW IRO | **SoHo**	-
J.Crew Coll. | **multi.**	25
Joie | **multi.**	24
Joinery | **W'burg**	-
Joseph | **E 60s**	27
NEW Juliette Longuet | **E 70s**	-
Jumelle | **W'burg**	-
Kate Spade | **multi.**	25
Kirna Zabête | **SoHo**	26
Krizia | **Meatpacking**	25
Levi's | **multi.**	23
Lilly Pulitzer | **E 70s**	27
Lisa Perry | **E 70s**	-
L.K. Bennett | **W 50s**	23
Madewell | **multi.**	23
Maje | **multi.**	-
Malia Mills | **E 80s**	26
Marc/Marc Jacobs Women | **W Vill**	25
Marimekko | **multi.**	27
Marni | **multi.**	28
Max Mara | **E 60s**	28
Milly | **E 70s**	28
Miu Miu | **multi.**	26
NEW MM6 | **W Vlll**	-
NEW Monique Lhuillier | **E 70s**	-
Nanette Lepore | **SoHo**	26
Nicole Miller | **multl.**	26
No. 6 | **L Italy**	-
OMO | **W 50s**	25
Oscar/Renta | **E 60s**	29
Otte | **multi.**	24
NEW Pamela Gonzales | **SoHo**	-
Patricia Field | **NoHo**	23
NEW Piperlime | **SoHo**	-
Pixie Mkt. | **LES**	-
NEW Proenza Schouler | **E 60s**	-
Pucci | **E 70s**	29
Ralph Lauren | **E 70s**	26
Rebecca Taylor | **multi.**	24
Reed Krakoff | **E 60s**	28
Reformation | **multi.**	-
Roberta Freymann/Ro's | **E 70s**	23

Sandro | **multi.** | _-_
Scoop | **multi.** | 24
NEW SlapBack | **W'burg** | _-_
Sportmax | **SoHo** | 27
Stella McCartney | **SoHo** | 26
St. John | **E 50s** | 28
Target | **multi.** | 19
3.1 Phillip Lim | **SoHo** | 24
Tibi | **SoHo** | 23
Tocca | **W Vill** | _-_
Tory Burch | **multi.** | 26
Tracy Reese | **Meatpacking** | 27
Tucker | **SoHo** | _-_
25 Park | **E 70s** | 23
Urban Zen | **W Vill** | 20
Vera Wang | **SoHo** | 28
Vince Camuto | **multi.** | 24
VPL | **SoHo** | _-_
Warm | **NoLita** | _-_
Wink | **multi.** | 19
Yigal Azrouël | **E 70s** | 25
Zero/Maria Cornejo | **NoHo** | 26
Zoë | **Dumbo** | 23

ART SUPPLIES

A.I. Friedman | **Flatiron** | 25
Blick Art | **NoHo** | 26
DaVinci | **multi.** | 25
Lee's Art | **W 50s** | 26
NY Central Art | **E Vill** | 27
Pearl Paint | **Chinatown** | 24
Sam Flax | **multi.** | 23

BABY GEAR

Acorn | **Downtown Bklyn** | 24
Albee Baby | **W 90s** | 27
babycottons | **E 80s** | 28
buybuy BABY | **Chelsea** | 23
Giggle | **multi.** | 26
J&R Jr. | **Financial** | 24
Maclaren | **SoHo** | 27

BATHROOM & KITCHEN FIXTURES/TILES

Ann Sacks | **multi.** | 28
Artistic Tile | **Flatiron** | 27

Bed Bath Beyond | **Flatiron** | 22
Bisazza | **SoHo** | 25
Blackman | **multi.** | 26
Davis/Warshow | **multi.** | 27
Simon's | **Murray Hill** | 26
Urban Archaeology | **multi.** | 25
Waterworks | **multi.** | 26

BEAUTY/GROOMING

(See also Department Stores)
Aedes/Venustas | **W Vill** | 29
Aesop | **multi.** | 26
Arcadia | **Chelsea** | 26
Art/Shaving | **multi.** | 26
Aveda | **multi.** | 26
Freemans Sport | **W'burg** | 26
Bare Escentuals | **multi.** | 26
Barneys Co-Op | **multi.** | 26
Bathroom | **W Vill** | 25
Benefit | **multi.** | 27
bliss | **multi.** | 25
Bluemercury | **multi.** | 26
Bond/9 | **multi.** | 27
Carol's Dghtr. | **multi.** | 26
Caudalie | **multi.** | _-_
Chanel | **multi.** | 29
Clarins | **W 70s** | 26
Clyde's | **E 70s** | 27
C.O. Bigelow | **G Vill** | 27
Dermalogica | **multi.** | 26
Editions/Parfums | **E 70s** | 25
FACE | **W 60s** | 23
Fresh | **multi.** | 26
Inglot | **multi.** | 26
Jeffrey | **Meatpacking** | 27
Jo Malone | **multi.** | 28
Kiehl's | **multi.** | 27
L'Occitane | **E 80s** | 26
Lush | **multi.** | 25
M.A.C. | **SoHo** | 26
Make Up For Ever | **G Vill** | 28
Malin/Goetz | **multi.** | 28
NEW MenScience | **NoHo** | _-_
Molton Brown | **multi.** | 27
NARS | **W Vill** | 25

CHINA/CRYSTAL/SILVER

(See also Department Stores)

A La Vieille Russie | **E 50s**	28
Baccarat | **E 50s**	29
Bernardaud | **E 50s**	29
Buccellati | **E 60s**	29
Cartier | **multi.**	29
Christofle | **E 70s**	29
Georg Jensen | **E 60s**	29
James Robinson | **E 50s**	29
NEW Jung Lee | **Chelsea**	-
Lalique | **E 50s**	29
Michael C. Fina | **E 50s**	27
NEW Monique Lhuillier | **E 70s**	-
Scully/Scully | **E 50s**	28
Swarovski | **E 40s**	26
Tiffany's | **multi.**	28
Vera Wang Bridal | **E 70s**	29

COOKWARE

(See also Department Stores)

A Cook's Cmpn. | **Bklyn Hts**	26
Alessi | **multi.**	28
Bed Bath Beyond | **Flatiron**	22
Bowery Kitchen | **Chelsea**	24
B'way Panhandler | **G Vill**	25
Bklyn. Kitchen | **W'burg**	26
Fishs Eddy | **multi.**	22
Gracious Home | **E 70s**	25
J.B. Prince | **Murray Hill**	28
Korin | **TriBeCa**	29
Sur La Table | **multi.**	25
Tarzian | **Park Slope**	25
NEW West Elm Mkt. | **Dumbo**	-
Whisk | **multi.**	21
Wm.-Sonoma | **multi.**	27
Zabar's Mezz. | **W 80s**	28

DEPARTMENT STORES

Barneys Co-Op | **multi.**	26
Barneys NY | **E 60s**	28
Bed Bath Beyond | **Flatiron**	22
Bergdorf | **W 50s**	29
Bergdorf Men | **E 50s**	29
Bloomingdale's | **multi.**	26
Gracious Home | **Chelsea**	25
Henri Bendel | **W 50s**	26
Jeffrey | **Meatpacking**	27
Lord/Taylor | **Murray Hill**	25
Macy's | **multi.**	23
Pearl River | **SoHo**	18
Saks Fifth Ave. | **E 50s**	27
Target | **multi.**	19
NEW Trinity Place | **Financial**	-

DISCOUNT STORES/MASS MERCHANTS

BJ's | **multi.**	20
Century 21 | **multi.**	21
Costco | **multi.**	24
Loehmann's | **multi.**	20
Paul Smith Sale | **W'burg**	25
Target | **multi.**	19

ELECTRONICS

AC Gears | **G Vill**	25
Adorama | **Flatiron**	27
Apple | **multi.**	29
B&H Photo-Video | **Garment**	28
Bang/Olufsen | **multi.**	28
BJ's | **multi.**	20
Bose | **multi.**	27
Camera Land | **E 50s**	24
Costco | **multi.**	24
42nd St. Photo | **Garment**	23
Hammacher | **E 50s**	-
J&R Music | **Financial**	24
NEW Leica | **SoHo**	-
Lyric Hi-Fi | **E 80s**	29
NEW Makerbot | **NoHo**	-
Matt Umanov | **G Vill**	28
Sam Ash | **multi.**	26
Sony Store | **E 50s**	27
Stereo Exch. | **NoHo**	28
Tekserve | **Chelsea**	27
Willoughby's | **Garment**	25

EYEWEAR

Alain Mikli | **multi.**	29
NEW Anne et Valentin | **NoLita**	-
Bond 07/Selima | **NoHo**	27
NEW Cutler and Gross | **SoHo**	-

SHOPPING

MERCHANDISE

FURS

J. Mendel	**E 60s**	28
Lanvin	**E 60s**	28

GARDEN ACCESSORIES/ FURNITURE

Bed Bath Beyond	**Flatiron**	22
Bklyn. Botanic Garden Shop	**Prospect Hts**	-
Chelsea Gdn. Ctr.	**multi.**	25
GRDN Bklyn	**Boerum Hill**	26
Lexington Gdns.	**E 70s**	24
Treillage	**E 70s**	24
NEW West Elm Mkt.	**Dumbo**	-

GIFTS/NOVELTIES

Alphabets	**E Vill**	25
Annie's Blue Ribbon	**Downtown Bklyn**	27
Arcadia	**Chelsea**	26
Blue Tree	**E 90s**	28
Bookmarc	**W Vill**	24
Boomerang	**TriBeCa**	25
Bklyn. Superhero	**Park Slope**	24
By Brooklyn	**Cobble Hill**	23
Cotton Candy Mach.	**W'burg**	27
NEW Creel/Gow	**E 70s**	-
Cursive	**E 40s**	27
Diptyque	**multi.**	29
E.A.T.	**E 80s**	22
Evolution	**SoHo**	27
Fair Folks	**G Vill**	-
Il Papiro	**E 70s**	28
NEW JNRL X STR	**LES**	-
John Derian	**E Vill**	27
Met Opera Shop	**W 60s**	26
Montblanc	**E 50s**	28
My Little Sunshine	**Chelsea**	-
Pearl River	**SoHo**	18
Shop@Scandinavia	**Murray Hill**	25
Story	**Chelsea**	22
Treasure/Bond	**SoHo**	-

HARDWARE

Beacon Paint	**W 70s**	26
Garber Hardware	**W Vill**	25
Green Depot	**multi.**	25

Janovic	**Hudson Square**	23
P.E. Guerin	**W Vill**	29
Pintchik	**Park Slope**	19
Simon's	**Murray Hill**	26
Tarzian	**Park Slope**	23
23rd St. Hardware	**Gramercy**	25

JEANS

Acne	**SoHo**	25
AG	**multi.**	26
A.P.C.	**multi.**	25
Atrium/KITH	**multi.**	23
Barneys Co-Op	**multi.**	26
Bklyn. Denim Co.	**W'burg**	24
NEW Civilianaire	**NoLita**	-
Diesel	**multi.**	24
Diesel Black Gold	**SoHo**	27
Earnest Sewn	**multi.**	28
Gap 1969	**SoHo**	23
G-Star	**multi.**	22
Guess/Marciano	**SoHo**	22
Jean Shop	**Meatpacking**	26
Joe's Jeans	**SoHo**	28
Levi's	**multi.**	23
Madewell	**multi.**	23
Oak	**multi.**	24
Paige Denim	**multi.**	25
Rag/Bone	**multi.**	26
NEW Raleigh	**NoLita**	-
Scoop	**multi.**	24
7/Mankind	**multi.**	25
3x1	**SoHo**	24
True Religion	**multi.**	24
What Goes Around	**SoHo**	22

JEWELRY

(*Antique/Vintage specialist)

Aaron Basha	**E 60s**	28
Aaron Faber*	**W 50s**	27
A La Vieille Russie*	**E 50s**	28
Alexis Bittar	**multi.**	26
AsiaStore	**E 70s**	25
Asprey	**E 70s**	28
Audemars Piguet	**E 50s**	29
NEW The Bar at Baublebar	**Chelsea**	-
Breguet	**multi.**	29

Buccellati	**E 60s**	29
Bulgari	**E 50s**	-
Calypso	**multi.**	23
Cartier	**multi.**	29
Catbird	**W'burg**	28
Chanel Jewelry	**E 60s**	29
Chrome Hearts	**E 70s**	29
Clay Pot	**Park Slope**	26
C. Wonder	**multi.**	21
David Webb	**E 70s**	29
David Yurman	**E 60s**	28
DeBeers	**E 50s**	28
de Vera*	**multi.**	27
Diana Kane	**Park Slope**	25
Doyle/Doyle*	**LES**	27
Erica Weiner*	**multi.**	-
Fabergé	**E 60s**	-
Fragments	**SoHo**	24
Fred Leighton*	**E 60s**	29
Graff	**E 60s**	29
Harry Winston	**E 50s**	29
Henri Bendel	**W 50s**	26
Honora	**E 50s**	25
H. Stern	**E 50s**	29
NEW Iosselliani	**Chelsea**	-
NEW Ippolita	**E 60s**	-
James Robinson*	**E 50s**	29
Judith Ripka	**E 60s**	28
Lalique	**E 50s**	29
Layla	**Downtown Bklyn**	-
Love Adorned	**NoLita**	27
Mauboussin	**E 60s**	28
Me&Ro	**NoLita**	25
Mikimoto	**E 50s**	29
Miu Miu	**SoHo**	26
Mociun	**W'burg**	-
MoMA Store	**multi.**	26
Neue Galerie Shop	**E 80s**	26
Piaget	**E 50s**	29
Pippin*	**Chelsea**	27
Robert Lee Morris	**SoHo**	27
Selima/Sucre*	**W Vill**	25
Swarovski	**E 40s**	26
Tiffany's	**multi.**	28

Uno de 50	**SoHo**	-
Urban Zen	**W Vill**	20
Van Cleef	**E 50s**	29
Verdura	**E 50s**	28
Wempe	**E 50s**	29
Wink*	**multi.**	19

KNITTING

Knitty City	**W 70s**	27
Pearl Paint	**Chinatown**	24
Purl Soho	**SoHo**	28
String	**E 60s**	29
Yarn Co.	**W 80s**	23

LEGWEAR/LINGERIE

(See also Department Stores)

Agt. Provocateur	**multi.**	26
A.W. Kaufman	**LES**	25
Bra Smyth	**multi.**	27
Bra*Tenders	**W 40s**	25
CK Underwear	**SoHo**	26
Cosabella	**SoHo**	28
Diana Kane	**Park Slope**	25
Fogal	**multi.**	27
GiGi K	**G Vill**	-
NEW Happy Socks	**SoHo**	-
Intimacy	**multi.**	26
Journelle	**multi.**	29
Kiki/Montparnasse	**SoHo**	28
La Perla	**multi.**	28
La Petite Coquette	**G Vill**	28
Orchard Corset	**LES**	25
Sugar Cookies	**Chelsea**	27
Town Shop	**W 80s**	25
Victoria's Secret	**SoHo**	22
Wolford	**multi.**	28

LIGHTING

Arhaus	**Meatpacking**	27
Foscarini Spazio	**SoHo**	-
Gracious Home	**multi.**	25
Jonathan Adler	**multi.**	23
Lee's Studio	**W 50s**	25
Lighting/Gregory	**LES**	23
Rico	**Gowanus**	-
Urban Archaeology	**multi.**	25

LUGGAGE

Altman Luggage | **LES**	26
Bric's | **E 50s**	26
Crumpler | **multi.**	27
Flight 001 | **multi.**	22
Ghurka | **multi.**	29
Jack Spade | **multi.**	25
Lederer/Paris | **E 50s**	26
Longchamp | **multi.**	27
Louis Vuitton | **multi.**	28
Patagonia | **Meatpacking**	27
TUMI | **multi.**	28

MATERNITY

Bump | **Park Slope**	26
Yummy Mummy | **E 80s**	23

MUSEUM SHOPS

Amer. Mus./Nat. History Shop | **W 70s**	27
AsiaStore | **E 70s**	25
Bklyn. Botanic Garden Shop | **Prospect Hts**	-
Bklyn. Mus. Shop | **Prospect Hts**	25
Frick Shop | **E 70s**	27
Guggenheim Store | **E 80s**	24
Int'l Ctr./Photo. Store | **W 40s**	27
Jewish Mus. Stores | **E 90s**	26
LES Tenement Mus. Books | **LES**	26
Met. Museum Store | **multi.**	26
MoMA Store | **multi.**	26
Morgan Library Shop | **Murray Hill**	26
Mus./City of NY | **E 100s**	26
Mus. Arts/Design Store | **W 50s**	26
Neue Galerie Shop | **E 80s**	26
New Museum Store | **LES**	25
NY Botanic Garden Shop | **Fordham**	25
NYPL Shop | **multi.**	24
Rubin Mus./Art Shop | **Chelsea**	26
Studio Mus./Harlem Shop | **Harlem**	25
Whitney Mus. Store | **E 70s**	24

MUSIC

Academy Records | **multi.**	25
Black Gold Rec. | **Carroll Gdns**	25
Bleecker St. Records | **W Vill**	24
Co-Op 87 | **Greenpt**	-
Fool's Gold | **W'burg**	22
Generation Records | **G Vill**	26
J&R Music | **Financial**	24
Jazz Record Ctr. | **Chelsea**	29
Met Opera Shop | **W 60s**	26
Met. Museum Store | **Wash. Hts**	26
Other Music | **NoHo**	29

MUSICAL INSTRUMENTS

Chelsea Guitars | **Chelsea**	26
Matt Umanov | **G Vill**	28
Rudy's Music | **multi.**	29
Sam Ash | **multi.**	26
30th St. Guitars | **Garment**	26

SHOES

(See also Apparel, Children's, Department Stores)

Alden | **E 40s**	29
Alice/Olivia | **multi.**	24
Allen Edmonds | **multi.**	28
Aritzia | **SoHo**	23
Armani | **multi.**	28
Ash | **SoHo**	25
Freemans Sport | **multi.**	26
BCBG | **multi.**	24
Belgian Shoes | **E 50s**	28
NEW Brian Atwood | **E 60s**	-
Burberry | **multi.**	28
Burberry Brit | **multi.**	28
Calypso | **multi.**	23
Camper | **multi.**	24
Canali | **multi.**	28
Carlo Pazolini | **SoHo**	-
Carlos Miele | **Meatpacking**	23
Cesare Paciotti | **E 60s**	25
NEW Chacott | **Gramercy**	-
Chanel | **multi.**	29
Charlotte Olympia | **E 60s**	-
Christian Louboutin | **multi.**	28
Chuckies New York | **multi.**	25
Church's | **E 60s**	27
Clarks | **multi.**	24
Coach | **E 50s**	26
Coclico | **NoLita**	23

SHOPPING

MERCHANDISE

SPORTING GOODS

Adeline Adeline | **TriBeCa** — 24
Bicycle Habitat | **multi.** — 27
Burton | **SoHo** — 26
Danny's Cycles | **multi.** — 26
Dixon's | **Park Slope** — 26
Gotham Bikes | **TriBeCa** — 26
JackRabbit | **multi.** — 26
Paragon | **Union Sq** — 26
Pilgrim Surf | **W'burg** — -
Red Lantern Bicycles | **Clinton Hill** — -
REI | **NoLita** — 26
Ride/Skate | **multi.** — 23
Saturdays Surf | **multi.** — -
718 Cyclery | **Gowanus** — -
Supreme | **SoHo** — 23

STATIONERY

Arthur Brown | **W 40s** — 27
Cursive | **E 40s** — 27
Dempsey/Carroll | **E 70s** — 28
Fountain Pen | **TriBeCa** — 29
G'wich Letter | **W Vill** — 29
Il Papiro | **E 70s** — 28
Kate's Paperie | **SoHo** — 26
Smythson | **W 50s** — 29
Tiffany's | **multi.** — 28

SWIMWEAR

(See also Department Stores)
Bra Smyth | **multi.** — 27
Calypso | **multi.** — 23
Diana Kane | **Park Slope** — 25
NEW Everything/Water | **E 80s** — -
Jack Rogers | **E 80s** — -
La Perla | **multi.** — 28
Malia Mills | **multi.** — 26
OMO | **W 50s** — 25
Paragon | **Union Sq** — 26
Trina Turk | **Meatpacking** — 27
Victoria's Secret | **SoHo** — 22
Vilebrequin | **multi.** — 25
Zimmermann | **SoHo** — 24

TOYS

Acorn | **Downtown Bklyn** — 24
American Girl Pl. | **E 40s** — 26
Area Kids | **W'burg** — 24
Balloon Saloon | **TriBeCa** — 22
Blue Tree | **E 90s** — 28
Boomerang | **multi.** — 25
Dinosaur Hill | **E Vill** — 28
E.A.T. | **E 80s** — 22
FAO Schwarz | **E 50s** — 26
Giggle | **multi.** — 26
Kid Robot | **SoHo** — 25
Lee's Art | **W 50s** — 26
LEGO | **multi.** — 26
Little Marc Jacobs | **W Vill** — 27
My Little Sunshine | **multi.** — -
NEW Norman/Jules | **Park Slope** — -
Toy Tokyo | **E Vill** — 24
Yoya/Mart | **Meatpacking** — 23

WATCHES

Aaron Faber | **W 50s** — 27
Audemars Piguet | **E 50s** — 29
Breguet | **multi.** — 29
Breitling | **E 50s** — 29
Bulgari | **E 50s** — -
Cartier | **multi.** — 29
Chopard | **E 60s** — 29
Fabergé | **E 60s** — -
Fred Leighton | **E 60s** — 29
Girard Perregaux | **E 60s** — 29
NEW G Shock | **SoHo** — -
Harry Winston | **E 50s** — 29
NEW House of Horology | **SoHo** — -
H. Stern | **E 50s** — 29
IWC Schaff. | **E 50s** — -
Kate Spade | **multi.** — 25
Mauboussin | **E 60s** — 28
MoMA Store | **multi.** — 26
Montblanc | **E 50s** — 28
Omega | **E 50s** — 28
Piaget | **E 50s** — 29
Tiffany's | **multi.** — 28
Tourneau | **multi.** — 27
Vacheron Constantin | **E 60s** — 29
Van Cleef | **E 50s** — 29
NEW Victorinox | **SoHo** — 27
Wempe | **E 50s** — 29

Locations

Includes store names, merchandise type (if necessary) and Quality ratings.

SHOPPING

LOCATIONS

Ted Baker | *Mens/Womenswear* 26

TUMI | *Luggage* 28

Vince Camuto | *Shoes* 24

Zara | *Mens/Womenswear* 19

EAST 50s

Alain Mikli | *Eyewear* 29

A La Vieille Russie | *Jewelry* 28

Allen Edmonds | *Shoes* 28

Amsale | *Bridal* 29

Ann Sacks | *Hardware* 28

Apple | *Electronics* 29

Aritzia | *Womenswear* 23

Armani | *Mens/Womenswear* 28

Art/Shaving | *Beauty/Groom.* 26

Audemars Piguet | *Watches* 29

Baccarat | *China/Crystal* 29

Bally | *Accessories* 26

B&B Italia | *Furniture/Home* 27

Belgian Shoes | *Shoes* 28

Bergdorf Men | *Dept. Stores* 29

Bernardaud | *China/Crystal* 29

Bloomingdale's | *Dept. Stores* 26

Bottega Veneta | *Accessories* 29

Breguet | *Jewelry* 29

Breitling | *Watches* 29

Bric's | *Luggage* 26

Brioni | *Menswear* 29

Bulgari | *Jewelry* -

Burberry | *Mens/Womenswear* 28

Burberry Brit | *Mens/Womenswear* 28

Camera Land | *Electronics* 24

Camper | *Shoes* 24

Canali | *Menswear* 28

Cartier | *Jewelry* 29

CB2 | *Furniture/Home* 19

Chanel | *Womenswear* 29

Clarks | *Shoes* 24

Coach | *Accessories* 26

Cole Haan | *Shoes* 26

Crate/Barrel | *Furniture/Home* 23

Davis/Warshow | *Hardware* 27

DeBeers | *Jewelry* 28

Diesel | *Jeans* 24

Dior Homme | *Menswear* 26

Dior | *Womenswear* 29

Dolce/Gabbana | *Mens/Womenswear* 26

D. Porthault | *Bed/Bath* 29

Dunhill | *Accessories* 28

Duxiana | *Bed/Bath* 29

Eileen Fisher | *Womenswear* 26

Emporio Armani | *Mens/Womenswear* 29

Ermenegildo Zegna | *Mens/Womenswear* 28

Escada | *Womenswear* 25

Façonnable | *Mens/Womenswear* 26

FAO Schwarz | *Toys* 26

Fendi | *Mens/Womenswear* 28

Fogal | *Legwear/Lingerie* 27

Fratelli Rossetti | *Shoes* 29

Gant | *Menswear* 25

Ghurka | *Luggage* 29

Gucci | *Mens/Womenswear* 28

Gucci Kids | *Childrenswear* -

Hammacher | *Electronics* -

H&M | *Mens/Womenswear* 15

Harry Winston | *Jewelry* 29

Hickey Freeman | *Menswear* 27

H.L. Purdy | *Eyewear* 25

Honora | *Jewelry* 25

H. Stern | *Jewelry* 29

IWC Schaff. | *Watches* -

James Robinson | *Jewelry* 29

Jimmy Choo | *Shoes* 28

Kiton | *Menswear* 29

Lacoste | *Mens/Womenswear* 24

Lalique | *China/Crystal* 29

Lederer/Paris | *Accessories* 26

Levi's | *Jeans* 23

Louis Vuitton | *Mens/Womenswear* 28

Mark Ingram | *Bridal* 29

NEW Massimo Dutti | *Mens/Womenswear* -

Michael C. Fina | *China/Crystal* 27

Mikimoto | *Jewelry* 29

Miu Miu | *Womenswear* 26

Molton Brown | *Beauty/Groom.* 27

Montblanc | *Stationery* 28

SHOPPING

LOCATIONS

Graff | *Jewelry* 29

Gucci | *Mens/Womenswear* 28

Hermès | *Mens/Womenswear* 30

Hermès Men | *Menswear* 29

Hervé Leger | *Womenswear* 26

Intimacy | *Legwear/Lingerie* 26

NEW Ippolita | *Jewelry* -

J.Crew Coll. | *Womenswear* 25

Jil Sander | *Mens/Womenswear* 28

Jimmy Choo | *Shoes* 28

J. Mendel | *Furs* 28

John Lobb | *Shoes* 29

Joseph | *Mens/Womenswear* 27

Judith Ripka | *Jewelry* 28

Kiehl's | *Beauty/Groom.* 27

Lanvin | *Womenswear* 28

NEW Lanvin Men | *Menswear* -

La Perla | *Legwear/Lingerie* 28

Longchamp | *Accessories* 27

Loro Piana | *Accessories* 29

Marni | *Womenswear* 28

Mauboussin | *Jewelry* 28

Max Mara | *Womenswear* 28

Michael Kors | *Mens/Womenswear* 27

Morgenthal Frederics | *Eyewear* 27

NY Running | *Sneakers* 27

Nicole Miller | *Womenswear* 26

Oliver Peoples | *Eyewear* 28

Oscar/Renta | *Womenswear* 29

Pratesi | *Bed/Bath* 29

NEW Proenza Schouler | *Womenswear* -

Reed Krakoff | *Womenswear* 28

Robert Marc | *Eyewear* 25

Roberto Cavalli | *Womenswear* 28

Roger Vivier | *Shoes* 28

NEW Schutz | *Shoes* -

String | *Knitting/Needlept.* 29

Tender Buttons | *Fabrics* 28

Theory | *Mens/Womenswear* 26

Tory Burch | *Womenswear* 26

True Religion | *Jeans* 24

Vacheron Constantin | *Watches* 29

Valentino | *Womenswear* 28

Vince Camuto | *Shoes* 24

Wm.-Wayne | *Furniture/Home* 25

Zadig/Voltaire | *Womenswear* 26

EAST 70s

Alain Mikli | *Eyewear* 29

Anthropologie | *Womenswear* 23

AsiaStore | *Mus. Shops* 25

Asprey | *Accessories* 28

Bang/Olufsen | *Electronics* 28

BCBG | *Womenswear* 24

Benefit | *Beauty/Groom.* 27

Bluemercury | *Beauty/Groom.* 26

Bond/9 | *Beauty/Groom.* 27

Bottega Veneta | *Mens/Womenswear* 29

Bra Smyth | *Legwear/Lingerie* 27

Calypso | *Womenswear* 23

Carolina Herrera | *Womenswear* 29

Caudalie | *Beauty/Groom.* -

Céline | *Womenswear* 25

Chloé | *Womenswear* 28

Christian Louboutin | *Shoes* 28

Christofle | *China/Crystal* 29

Chrome Hearts | *Jewelry* 29

Chuckies New York | *Shoes* 25

Clyde's | *Beauty/Groom.* 27

Cotélac | *Mens/Womenswear* -

NEW Creel/Gow | *Furniture/Home* -

Cynthia Rowley | *Womenswear* 28

David Webb | *Jewelry* 29

Dempsey/Carroll | *Stationery* 28

Diptyque | *Gifts/Novelties* 29

Editions/Parfums | *Beauty/Groom.* 25

Eileen Fisher | *Womenswear* 26

Free People | *Womenswear* 22

Fresh | *Beauty/Groom.* 26

Frick Shop | *Mus. Shops* 27

Giggle | *Childrenswear* 26

Gracious Home | *Bed/Bath* 25

Il Papiro | *Stationery* 28

Intermix | *Womenswear* 24

Jacadi | *Childrenswear* 28

J.Crew Coll. | *Womenswear* 25

J.Crew Men's | *Menswear* 25

Robert Marc | *Eyewear* 25
Shade Store | *Furniture/Home* 27
Theory | *Mens/Womenswear* 26
TUMI | *Luggage* 28
Vilebrequin | *Swimwear* 25
Wm.-Sonoma | *Cookware* 27
Yummy Mummy | *Maternity* 23

EAST 90s & 100s
(90th to 110th Sts.)
Blue Tree | *Mens/Womenswear* 28
Bonpoint | *Childrenswear* 28
Capezio | *Activewear* 24
Edit | *Womenswear* 26
Intimacy | *Legwear/Lingerie* 26
Jewish Mus. Stores | *Mus. Shops* 26
J. McLaughlin | 23
  Mens/Womenswear
Lucky Wang | *Childrenswear* 24
Mus./City of NY | *Mus. Shops* 26
Otte | *Womenswear* 24
Rachel Riley | *Childrenswear* -

EAST VILLAGE
(14th to Houston Sts., east of B'way, excluding NoHo)
Academy Records | *Music/DVDs* 25
Alan Moss | *Furniture/Home* 28
Alphabets | *Gifts/Novelties* 25
🆕 Bettie Page | *Womenswear* -
Blue/Cream | *Mens/Womenswear* 25
Buffalo Exchange | *Vintage* 20
🆕 CADET | *Menswear* -
Capezio | *Activewear* 24
🆕 Devorado | *Vintage* -
Dinosaur Hill | *Toys* 28
Eileen Fisher | *Womenswear* 26
Fabulous Fanny's | *Eyewear* 24
John Derian | *Furniture/Home* 27
John Varvatos | *Menswear* 26
Kiehl's | *Beauty/Groom.* 27
Mr. Throwback | *Vintage* -
Muji | *Furniture/Home* 22
NY Central Art | *Art* 27
Obscura | *Antiques* 26
Odin | *Menswear* 27
Organic Mod. | *Furniture/Home* 26

Pork Pie Hats -
Toy Tokyo | *Toys* 24
Trash/Vaudeville | 22
  Mens/Womenswear

FINANCIAL DISTRICT
(South of Murray St.)
Canali | *Menswear* 28
Century 21 | *Discount* 21
Hermès | *Mens/Womenswear* 30
J&R Jr. | *Baby Gear* 24
J&R Music | *Electronics* 24
Tiffany's | *Jewelry* 28
🆕 Trinity Place | -
  Mens/Womenswear
True Religion | *Jeans* 24
TUMI | *Luggage* 28

FLATIRON
(14th to 26th Sts., 6th Ave. to Park Ave. S., excluding Union Sq.)
ABC Carpet/Home | 26
  Furniture/Home
ABC | *Furniture/Home* 26
Academy Records | *Music/DVDs* 25
Adorama | *Electronics* 27
A.I. Friedman | *Art* 25
Ann Sacks | *Hardware* 28
Anthropologie | *Womenswear* 23
Artistic Tile | *Hardware* 27
Aveda | *Beauty/Groom.* 26
Bang/Olufsen | *Electronics* 28
BCBG | *Womenswear* 24
Bed Bath Beyond | *Dept. Stores* 22
Blackman | *Hardware* 26
Bluemercury | *Beauty/Groom.* 26
Bonobos | *Menswear* -
Brooks Bros. | *Mens/Womenswear* 26
Canvas | *Furniture/Home* 27
Charles Rogers | *Bed/Bath* 24
Club Monaco | 21
  Mens/Womenswear
Cole Haan | *Shoes* 26
Design Within Reach | 25
  Furniture/Home
DKNY | *Womenswear* 23
Dr. Martens | *Shoes* 28

Eileen Fisher	*Womenswear*	26
Fishs Eddy	*Furniture/Home*	22
Fresh	*Beauty/Groom.*	26
G-Star	*Jeans*	22
Intermix	*Womenswear*	24
J.Crew	*Mens/Womenswear*	22
Joe Fresh	*Mens/Womenswear*	20
Journelle	*Legwear/Lingerie*	29
Kate Spade	*Accessories*	25
Levi's	*Jeans*	23
Ligne Roset	*Furniture/Home*	26
Madewell	*Mens/Womenswear*	23
Marimekko	*Bed/Bath*	27
Michael Kors	*Mens/Womenswear*	27
Muji	*Furniture/Home*	22
New Balance	*Sneakers*	23
Nike	*Sneakers*	25
Organic Mod.	*Furniture/Home*	26
Origins	*Beauty/Groom.*	25
Papyrus	*Stationery*	26
Paul Smith	*Mens/Womenswear*	27
Sam Flax	*Art*	23
Scotch/Soda	*Mens/Womenswear*	27
7/Mankind	*Jeans*	25
Space Kiddets	*Childrenswear*	25
Sperry	*Shoes*	26
TUMI	*Luggage*	28
Waterworks	*Hardware*	26
Whisk	*Cookware*	21

GARMENT DISTRICT

(30th to 40th Sts., west of 5th)

B&H Photo-Video	*Cameras/Video*	28
Bare Escentuals	*Beauty/Groom.*	26
BCBG	*Womenswear*	24
Express	*Womenswear*	21
42nd St. Photo	*Electronics*	23
HK Flea Mkt.	*Flea Mkts.*	20
J.J. Hat Ctr.	*Accessories*	28
Joe Fresh	*Mens/Womenswear*	20
Levi's	*Jeans*	23
Lush	*Beauty/Groom.*	25
Macy's	*Dept. Stores*	23
M&J	*Fabrics*	25
Mood	*Fabrics*	26

Moss Bureau	*Furniture/Home*	28
Sam Ash	*Music Instruments*	26
30th St. Guitars	*Music Instruments*	26
Uniqlo	*Mens/Womenswear*	21
Vince Camuto	*Shoes*	24
Willoughby's	*Cameras/Video*	25
Zara	*Mens/Womenswear*	19

GRAMERCY PARK

(14th to 23rd Sts., east of Park Ave. S.)

NEW Chacott	*Activewear*	–
Danny's Cycles	*Sporting Gds.*	26
Lacoste	*Mens/Womenswear*	24
23rd St. Hardware	*Hardware*	25

GREENWICH VILLAGE

(Houston to 14th Sts., west of B'way, east of 6th Ave.)

AC Gears	*Electronics*	25
Aesop	*Beauty/Groom.*	26
Beacon's Closet	*Vintage*	19
B'way Panhandler	*Cookware*	25
C.O. Bigelow	*Beauty/Groom.*	27
NEW Denim & Supply, Ralph Lauren	*Mens/Womenswear*	–
Fair Folks	*Gifts/Novelties*	–
Generation Records	*Music/DVDs*	26
GiGi K	*Legwear/Lingerie*	–
La Petite Coquette	*Legwear/Lingerie*	28
Lucky Wang	*Childrenswear*	24
Make Up For Ever	*Beauty/Groom.*	28
Matt Umanov	*Music Instruments*	28
Wm.-Wayne	*Furniture/Home*	25

HARLEM/ EAST HARLEM

(110th to 155th Sts., excluding Columbia U. area)

Carol's Dghtr.	*Beauty/Groom.*	26
Costco	*Discount*	24
Davis/Warshow	*Hardware*	27
Harlem Haberdashery	*Menswear*	–
Malcolm Shabazz	*Flea Mkts.*	20
NYPL Shop	*Mus. Shops*	24

Studio Mus./Harlem Shop | *Mus. Shops* 25

Target | *Mass Merch.* 19

NEW Trunk Show | *Vintage* -

HUDSON SQUARE
(Canal to Houston Sts.,
west of 6th Ave.)

Aloha Rag | *Mens/Womenswear* 26

Atelier NY | *Menswear* 25

Janovic | *Hardware* 23

Rick Owens | *Mens/Womenswear* -

LITTLE ITALY
(Canal to Kenmare Sts.,
Bowery to Lafayette St.)

Calypso Home | *Furniture/Home* 26

Canvas | *Furniture/Home* 27

No. 6 | *Vintage* -

LOWER EAST SIDE
(Houston to Canal Sts.,
east of Bowery)

Adriennes | *Womenswear* 24

Altman Luggage | *Luggage* 26

Assembly NY | *Menswear* 24

A.W. Kaufman | *Legwear/Lingerie* 25

By Robert James | *Menswear* -

Doyle/Doyle | *Jewelry* 27

Earnest Sewn | *Jeans* 28

Epaulet | *Mens/Womenswear* 25

Freemans Sport | *Menswear* 26

Hoodie Shop | *Mens/Womenswear* 26

NEW JNRL X STR | *Gifts/Novelties* -

NEW Labor Skate | *Sporting Gds.* -

Lighting/Gregory | *Lighting* 23

LES Tenement Mus. Books | *Mus. Shops* 26

MooShoes | *Shoes* 25

Moscot | *Eyewear* 25

New Museum Store | *Mus. Shops* 25

Obsessive Compulsive | *Beauty/Groom.* -

Orchard Corset | *Legwear/Lingerie* 25

Pixie Mkt. | *Womenswear* -

NEW Procell | *Vintage* -

Reformation | *Womenswear* -

NEW Store 114 | *Vintage* -

MEATPACKING
(Gansevoort to 15th Sts.,
west of 9th Ave.)

Alexander McQueen | *Womenswear* 29

Alice/Olivia | *Womenswear* 24

AllSaints | *Mens/Womenswear* 23

Apple | *Electronics* 29

Arhaus | *Furniture/Home* 27

Bond/9 | *Beauty/Groom.* 27

Carlos Miele | *Womenswear* 23

Catherine Malandrino | *Womenswear* 27

Christian Louboutin | *Shoes* 28

DVF | *Womenswear* 27

Earnest Sewn | *Jeans* 28

Elizabeth Charles | *Womenswear* -

NEW Hanro | *Legwear/Lingerie* -

Hugo Boss | *Mens/Womenswear* 27

Intermix | *Womenswear* 24

Jean Shop | *Jeans* 26

Jeffrey | *Mens/Womenswear* 27

Joie | *Womenswear* 24

Kathryn Amberleigh | *Shoes* -

Kiehl's | *Beauty/Groom.* 27

Krizia | *Womenswear* 25

La Perla | *Legwear/Lingerie* 28

Levi's | *Jeans* 23

Lululemon | *Activewear* 27

Marni | *Womenswear* 28

Moschino | *Mens/Womenswear* 25

Nicholas Kirkwood | *Shoes* -

Owen | *Mens/Womenswear* -

Paige Denim | *Jeans* 25

Patagonia | *Activewear* 27

Puma | *Sneakers* 23

Rag/Bone | *Mens/Womenswear* 26

Rebecca Taylor | *Womenswear* 24

Scoop Men's | *Menswear* 23

Scoop | *Mens/Womenswear* 24

Ted Baker | *Mens/Womenswear* 26

Theory | *Mens/Womenswear* 26

Tory Burch | *Womenswear* 26

Tracy Reese | *Womenswear* 27

Trina Turk | *Womenswear* 27

UGG | *Shoes* 25

Vince | *Mens/Womenswear* 24

Yoya/Mart | *Childrenswear* 23

Zadig/Voltaire | *Womenswear* 26

MURRAY HILL

(26th to 40th Sts., east of 5th; 23rd to 26th Sts., east of Park Ave. S.)

DaVinci | *Art* 25

J.B. Prince | *Cookware* 28

Lord/Taylor | *Dept. Stores* 25

Morgan Library Shop | *Mus. Shops* 26

Roche Bobois | *Furniture/Home* 25

Shop@Scandinavia | *Gifts/Novelties* 25

Simon's | *Hardware* 26

NOHO

(Houston to 4th Sts., Bowery to B'way)

Adidas | *Sneakers* 25

Atrium/KITH | *Jeans* 23

Billy Reid | *Mens/Womenswear* 25

Blick Art | *Art* 26

Bond/9 | *Beauty/Groom.* 27

Bond 07/Selima | *Womenswear* 27

Crate/Barrel | *Furniture/Home* 23

Dienst/Dotter | *Antiques* ⌐

Environment | *Furniture/Home* ⌐

Future Perfect | *Furniture/Home* ⌐

Ina | *Vintage* 25

Intermix | *Womenswear* 24

NEW Makerbot | *Electronics* ⌐

NEW MenScience | *Beauty/Groom.* ⌐

Oak | *Mens/Womenswear* 24

Other Music | *Music/DVDs* 29

Patricia Field | *Womenswear* 23

Stereo Exch. | *Electronics* 28

Zacky's | *Shoes* 27

Zero/Maria Cornejo | *Womenswear* 26

NOLITA

(Houston to Kenmare Sts., Bowery to Lafayette St.)

A Détacher | *Womenswear* 27

Aesop | *Beauty/Groom.* 26

NEW Anne et Valentin | *Eyewear* ⌐

Armor-Lux | *Womenswear* 29

Calypso | *Womenswear* 23

NEW Christian Siriano | *Womenswear* ⌐

NEW Civilianaire | *Jeans* ⌐

Coclico | *Shoes* 23

Courtshop | *Womenswear* ⌐

Creatures/Comfort | *Womenswear* 22

Crumpler | *Luggage* 27

Dagny/Barstow | *Womenswear* ⌐

Dalaga | *Womenswear* ⌐

Dolce Vita | *Shoes* 23

Erica Weiner | *Jewelry* ⌐

Fjällräven | *Accessories* 23

Fresh | *Beauty/Groom.* 26

Gant | *Menswear* 25

NEW HAN KJØBENHAVN | *Menswear* ⌐

Haute Hippie | *Mens/Womenswear* 24

Ina | *Vintage* 25

In God We Trust | *Mens/Womenswear* 23

Jay Kos | *Menswear* 29

John Fluevog | *Shoes* 28

Kathryn Amberleigh | *Shoes* ⌐

Love Adorned | *Jewelry* 27

Maje | *Womenswear* ⌐

Malia Mills | *Swimwear* 26

Me&Ro | *Jewelry* 25

Odin | *Menswear* 27

Rag/Bone | *Mens/Womenswear* 26

NEW Raleigh | *Jeans* ⌐

Rebecca Taylor | *Womenswear* 24

REI | *Sporting Gds.* 26

Resurrection Vintage | *Vintage* ⌐

Sandro | *Womenswear* ⌐

Santa Maria Novella | *Beauty/Groom.* 29

Scotch/Soda | *Mens/Womenswear* 27

Steven Alan | *Mens/Womenswear* 28

Earnest Sewn | *Jeans* 28

Tory Burch | *Womenswear* 26

Vince | *Mens/Womenswear* 24

Warby Parker | *Eyewear* 27

Warm | *Womenswear* ⌐

SHOPPING

LOCATIONS

SOHO

(Canal to Houston Sts.,
west of Lafayette St.)

Acne	*Mens/Womenswear*	25
Adidas	*Sneakers*	25
Adidas SLVR	*Mens/Womenswear*	23
Aero	*Furniture/Home*	24
Aesop	*Beauty/Groom.*	26
AG	*Jeans*	26
Agt. Provocateur	*Legwear/Lingerie*	26
Agnès B.	*Mens/Womenswear*	25
Alessi	*Cookware*	28
Alexander Wang	*Womenswear*	26
Alexis Bittar	*Jewelry*	26
Alice/Olivia	*Womenswear*	24
AllSaints	*Mens/Womenswear*	23
Amarcord	*Vintage*	24
American Two Shot	*Mens/Womenswear*	-
Anna Sui	*Womenswear*	23
Anthropologie	*Womenswear*	23
A.P.C.	*Mens/Womenswear*	25
Apple	*Electronics*	29
Aritzia	*Womenswear*	23
Ash	*Shoes*	25
NEW Askel Project	*Menswear*	-
Aveda	*Beauty/Groom.*	26
Balenciaga	*Mens/Womenswear*	29
B&B Italia	*Furniture/Home*	27
Bang/Olufsen	*Electronics*	28
Bape	*Sneakers*	27
Barbour	*Mens/Womenswear*	28
Barneys Co-Op	*Mens/Womenswear*	26
BCBG	*Womenswear*	24
BDDW	*Furniture/Home*	25
Benefit	*Beauty/Groom.*	27
Ben Sherman	*Menswear*	24
Bicycle Habitat	*Sporting Gds.*	27
Billionaire Boys	*Menswear*	24
Bisazza	*Hardware*	25
bliss	*Beauty/Groom.*	25
Bloomingdale's	*Dept. Stores*	26
Bogner	*Mens/Womenswear*	29
Bonobos	*Menswear*	-
Bose	*Electronics*	27
Brandy Melville	*Womenswear*	-
Burberry	*Mens/Womenswear*	28
Burton	*Sporting Gds.*	26
CK Underwear	*Legwear/Lingerie*	26
Calypso	*Womenswear*	23
Camper	*Shoes*	24
Cappellini	*Furniture/Home*	26
Carhartt	*Menswear*	28
Carlo Pazolini	*Shoes*	-
NEW Carson St. Cloth.	*Menswear*	-
Catherine Malandrino	*Womenswear*	27
CB2	*Furniture/Home*	19
Chanel	*Womenswear*	29
Chloé	*Womenswear*	28
Chrs. Fischer	*Mens/Womenswear*	24
Club Monaco	*Mens/Womenswear*	21
Cole Haan	*Shoes*	26
Comptoir	*Womenswear*	25
Converse	*Shoes*	22
Cosabella	*Legwear/Lingerie*	28
Costume Nt'l	*Mens/Womenswear*	28
Cotélac	*Mens/Womenswear*	-
Crewcuts	*Childrenswear*	24
NEW Cutler and Gross	*Eyewear*	-
Cut25	*Womenswear*	-
C. Wonder	*Accessories/Womenswear*	21
Davis/Warshow	*Hardware*	27
Dermalogica	*Beauty/Groom.*	26
Design Within Reach	*Furniture/Home*	25
de Vera	*Furniture/Home*	27
DVF	*Womenswear*	27
Diesel	*Jeans*	24
Diesel Black Gold	*Jeans*	27
Diesel Kids	*Childrenswear*	27
Dior Homme	*Menswear*	26
DKNY	*Womenswear*	23
Dr. Martens	*Shoes*	28
DwellStudio	*Furniture/Home*	-
Eileen Fisher	*Womenswear*	26
Elie Tahari	*Womenswear*	26
Emporio Armani	*Mens/Womenswear*	29

SHOPPING

LOCATIONS

Paige Denim	*Jeans*	25	Sur La Table	*Cookware*	25
NEW Pamela Gonzales	*Womenswear*	–	Ted Baker	*Mens/Womenswear*	26
		Theory	*Mens/Womenswear*	26
NEW Pas de Calais	*Mens/Womenswear*	–	3x1	*Jeans*	24
		3.1 Phillip Lim	*Mens/Womenswear*	24
Patagonia	*Activewear*	27		
Paul Smith	*Mens/Womenswear*	27	Tibi	*Womenswear*	23
Pearl River	*Gifts/Novelties*	18	Tiffany's	*Jewelry*	28
NEW Piperlime	*Womenswear*	–	Topshop	*Mens/Womenswear*	19
Prada	*Mens/Womenswear*	28	Treasure/Bond	*Mens/Womenswear*	–
NEW Private Stock	*Menswear*	–		
Puma	*Sneakers*	23	True Religion	*Jeans*	24
Purl Soho	*Knitting/Needlept.*	28	Tucker	*Womenswear*	–
Rag/Bone	*Mens/Womenswear*	26	TUMI	*Luggage*	28
Ralph Lauren	*Mens/Womenswear*	26	UGG	*Shoes*	25
Ralph Lauren RRL	*Mens/Womenswear*	26	Uniqlo	*Mens/Womenswear*	21
		Uno de 50	*Accessories*	–
Reformation	*Womenswear*	–	Vera Wang	*Womenswear*	28
Ricky's	*Beauty/Groom.*	19	Versace	*Mens/Womenswear*	26
Robert Lee Morris	*Jewelry*	27	Victoria's Secret	*Legwear/Lingerie*	22
Robert Marc	*Eyewear*	25	**NEW** Victorinox	*Watches*	27
Room/Board	*Furniture/Home*	24	Vilebrequin	*Swimwear*	25
Rudy's Music	*Music Instruments*	29	Vince Camuto	*Shoes*	24
Sabon	*Beauty/Groom.*	26	VPL	*Womenswear*	–
NEW Sam Edelman	*Shoes*	–	Warby Parker		27
Sandro	*Womenswear*	–	What Goes Around	*Vintage*	22
Saturdays Surf	*Sporting Gds.*	–	Wink	*Accessories*	19
Scoop	*Mens/Womenswear*	24	Wolford	*Legwear/Lingerie*	28
Selima/Sucre	*Eyewear*	25	Y-3	*Mens/Womenswear*	26
7/Mankind	*Jeans*	25	Zadig/Voltaire	*Womenswear*	26
Shabby Chic	*Furniture/Home*	25	Zara	*Mens/Womenswear*	19
Shade Store	*Furniture/Home*	27	Zimmermann	*Swimwear*	24

TRIBECA

(Canal to Murray Sts., west of B'way)

Silver Lining	*Eyewear*	–
Space.NK	*Beauty/Groom.*	27
Splendid	*Mens/Womenswear*	–
Sportmax	*Womenswear*	27
Stella McCartney	*Womenswear*	26
St. Laurent Paris	*Mens/Womenswear*	28
Stone Fox	*Bridal*	–
Stuart Weitzman	*Shoes*	28
Suitsupply	*Menswear*	–
Superga	*Sneakers*	–
Supreme	*Activewear*	23
Surface/Air	*Mens/Womenswear*	–

Adeline Adeline	*Sporting Gds.*	24
Annelore	*Womenswear*	24
Balloon Saloon	*Toys*	22
Boomerang	*Toys*	25
Brooks Bros.	*Mens/Womenswear*	26
Calypso	*Womenswear*	23
Duxiana	*Bed/Bath*	29
Fountain Pen	*Stationery*	29
Gotham Bikes	*Sporting Gds.*	26
Issey Miyake	*Mens/Womenswear*	28
J.Crew Men's	*Menswear*	25

Korin | *Cookware* 29

Matt Bernson | *Shoes* – |

My Little Sunshine | – |
   Childrenswear

Organic Mod. | *Furniture/Home* 26

Otte | *Womenswear* 24

Pompanoosuc | *Furniture/Home* 28

Roberta Roller | *Furniture/Home* 25

Steven Alan | 28
   Furniture/Mens/Womenswear

Urban Archaeology | *Hardware* 25

UNION SQUARE

(14th to 17th Sts., 5th Ave. to
Union Sq. E.)

Agnès B. | *Mens/Womenswear* 25

Diesel | *Jeans* 24

JackRabbit | *Activewear* 26

Lululemon | *Activewear* 27

Lush | *Beauty/Groom.* 25

Moscot | *Eyewear* 25

Paragon | *Sporting Gds.* 26

Puma | *Sneakers* 23

Rothman's | *Menswear* 25

True Religion | *Jeans* 24

WASHINGTON HTS./ INWOOD

(North of W. 155th St.)

Met. Museum Store | *Mus. Shops* 26

WEST 40s

Alice/Olivia | *Womenswear* 24

Allen Edmonds | *Shoes* 28

Arthur Brown | *Stationery* 27

ASICS | *Sneakers* 26

Bare Escentuals | *Beauty/Groom.* 26

Bra*Tenders | *Logwear/Lingerie* 25

Charles Tyrwhitt | *Menswear* 24

Chelsea Gdn. Ctr. | *Garden* 25

NEW Fine/Dandy | *Accessories* – |

Int'l Ctr./Photo. Store | *Mus. Shops* 27

Inglot | *Beauty/Groom.* 26

LEGO | *Toys* 26

Levi's | *Jeans* 23

Longchamp | *Accessories* 27

Met. Museum Store | *Mus. Shops* 26

Michael Kors | 27
   Mens/Womenswear

Muji | *Furniture/Home* 22

NBA | *Gifts/Novelties* 21

Onassis | *Menswear* – |

Ray Beauty | *Beauty/Groom.* 23

Rudy's Music | *Music Instruments* 29

TUMI | *Luggage* 28

WEST 50s

Aaron Faber | *Jewelry* 27

Anthropologie | *Womenswear* 23

Ascot Chang | *Menswear* 27

Bergdorf | *Dept. Stores* 29

bliss | *Beauty/Groom.* 25

Bose | *Electronics* 27

Brooks Bros. | *Mens/Womenswear* 26

Capezio | *Activewear* 24

Charles Tyrwhitt | *Menswear* 24

Club Monaco | 21
   Mens/Womenswear

Frank Stella | *Menswear* 24

Henri Bendel | *Accessories* 26

J.Crew | *Mens/Womenswear* 22

Knoll | *Furniture/Home* 29

Lee's Art | *Art* 26

Lee's Studio | *Lighting* 25

Leonard Opticians | *Eyewear* 27

L.K. Bennett | *Shoes* 23

MacKenzie-Childs | 27
   Furniture/Home

Manolo Blahnik | *Shoes* 29

MoMA Store | *Mus. Shops* 26

Mus. Arts/Design Store | 26
   Mus. Shops

OMO | *Womenswear* 25

Smythson | *Stationery* 29

Sur La Table | *Cookware* 25

Zara | *Mens/Womenswear* 19

Zitomer/Z Chem. | *Beauty/Groom.* 25

WEST 60s

Apple | *Electronics* 29

Art/Shaving | *Beauty/Groom.* 26

Athleta | *Activewear* 25

Aveda | *Beauty/Groom.* 26

BCBG | *Womenswear* 24

Bose | *Electronics* 27

Brooks Bros. | *Mens/Womenswear* 26

Burberry Brit | *Mens/Womenswear* 28

Capezio | *Activewear* 24

Century 21 | *Discount* 21

Club Monaco | *Mens/Womenswear* 21

Cole Haan | *Shoes* 26

Comptoir | *Womenswear* 25

C. Wonder | 21
Accessories/Womenswear

Eileen Fisher | *Womenswear* 26

FACE | *Beauty/Groom.* 23

Fresh | *Beauty/Groom.* 26

Gracious Home | *Bed/Bath* 25

Hugo Boss | *Mens/Womenswear* 27

Intermix | *Womenswear* 24

Jacadi | *Childrenswear* 28

J.Crew | *Mens/Womenswear* 22

J.Crew Men's | *Menswear* 25

Kiehl's | *Beauty/Groom.* 27

Lululemon | *Activewear* 27

Met Opera Shop | *Gifts/Novelties* 26

Morgenthal Frederics | *Eyewear* 27

NY Running | *Sneakers* 27

Rag/Bone | *Mens/Womenswear* 26

Robert Marc | *Eyewear* 25

Stuart Weitzman | *Shoes* 28

Tourneau | *Watches* 27

True Religion | *Jeans* 24

TUMI | *Luggage* 28

UGG | *Shoes* 25

Wm.-Sonoma | *Cookware* 27

Wink | *Accessories* 19

Wolford | *Legwear/Lingerie* 28

Zara | *Mens/Womenswear* 19

WEST 70s

AG | *Jeans* 26

Alexis Bittar | *Jewelry* 26

Amer. Mus./Nat. History Shop | 27
Mus. Shops

Art/Shaving | *Beauty/Groom.* 26

Bang/Olufsen | *Electronics* 28

Barneys Co-Op | 26
Mens/Womenswear

Beacon Paint | *Hardware* 26

Bra Smyth | *Legwear/Lingerie* 27

Clarins | *Beauty/Groom.* 26

Design Within Reach | 25
Furniture/Home

Eileen Fisher | *Womenswear* 26

Giggle | *Childrenswear* 26

GreenFlea Mkt. | *Flea Mkts.* 20

Helmut Lang | *Mens/Womenswear* 26

JackRabbit | *Activewear* 26

Jonathan Adler | *Furniture/Home* 23

Knitty City | *Knitting/Needlept.* 27

Loehmann's | *Discount* 20

Lululemon | *Activewear* 27

Lush | *Beauty/Groom.* 25

Malia Mills | *Swimwear* 26

Paige Denim | *Jeans* 25

Space.NK | *Beauty/Groom.* 27

Stuart Weitzman | *Shoes* 28

Theory | *Mens/Womenswear* 26

Tip Top | *Childrenswear* 25

Tip Top | *Shoes* 25

TUMI | *Luggage* 28

Z'Baby Co. | *Childrenswear* 24

WEST 80s

Bluemercury | *Beauty/Groom.* 26

Brooks Bros. | *Mens/Womenswear* 26

Club Monaco | *Mens/Womenswear* 21

Frank Stella | *Menswear* 24

Harry's Shoes | *Shoes* 25

Harry's Shoes/Kids | *Childrenswear* 24

Malin/Goetz | *Beauty/Groom.* 28

Origins | *Beauty/Groom.* 25

Patagonia | *Activewear* 27

Steven Alan | *Mens/Womenswear* 28

Town Shop | *Legwear/Lingerie* 25

Yarn Co. | *Knitting/Needlept.* 23

Zabar's Mezz. | *Cookware* 28

WEST 90s

Albee Baby | *Baby Gear* 27

WEST VILLAGE

(Houston to 14th Sts., west of
6th Ave., excluding Meatpacking)

Aedes/Venustas | *Beauty/Groom.* 29

Alexis Bittar | *Jewelry* 26

Bronx

FORDHAM

KINGSBRIDGE

MOTT HAVEN

PARKCHESTER

SHOPPING

LOCATIONS

RIVERDALE

Target | *Mass Merch.* 19

SOUNDVIEW

ABC Carpet/Outlet | 23
Furniture/Home

Brooklyn

BAY RIDGE

Century 21 | *Discount* 21

BOERUM HILL

Bklyn. Circus | *Menswear* 25
Erica Weiner | *Jewelry* -
Flight 001 | *Luggage* 22
Free People | *Womenswear* 22
GRDN Bklyn | *Garden* 26
Jonathan Adler | *Furniture/Home* 23
Malia Mills | *Swimwear* 26

BROOKLYN HEIGHTS

A Cook's Cmpn. | *Cookware* 26
Design Within Reach | 25
Furniture/Home
J. McLaughlin | 23
Mens/Womenswear

CANARSIE

BJ's | *Discount* 20

CARROLL GARDENS

Black Gold Rec. | *Music/DVDs* 25
Epaulet | *Mens/Womenswear* 25

CLINTON HILL

Red Lantern Bicycles | -
Sporting Gds.

COBBLE HILL

Barneys Co-Op | 26
Mens/Womenswear
Bird | *Mens/Womenswear* 27
Buffalo Exchange | *Vintage* 20
By Brooklyn | *Gifts/Novelties* 23
Lululemon | *Activewear* 27
Moscot | *Eyewear* 25
Shen Beauty | *Beauty/Groom.* -

DOWNTOWN BROOKLYN

Acorn | *Toys* 24
Annie's Blue Ribbon | 27
Gifts/Novelties
Carol's Dghtr. | *Beauty/Groom.* 26
Greenhouse | *Furniture/Home* 28
Layla | *Bed/Bath* -
Macy's | *Dept. Stores* 23
Steven Alan | *Mens/Womenswear* 28
Target | *Mass Merch.* 19

DUMBO

NEW West Elm Mkt. | *Cookware* -
Zoë | *Womenswear* 23

EAST NEW YORK

BJ's | *Discount* 20
Target | *Mass Merch.* 19

FLATBUSH

Target | *Mass Merch.* 19

FORT GREENE

Bklyn. Flea | *Flea Mkts.* 21

GOWANUS

Film Biz Prop | *Furniture/Home* -
Rico | *Furniture/Home* -
718 Cyclery | *Sporting Gds.* -

GREENPOINT

Alter | *Mens/Womenswear* 26
Co-Op 87 | *Music/DVDs* -
Dalaga | *Mens/Womenswear* -
Green Depot | *Hardware* 25
In God We Trust | 23
Mens/Womenswear
Oak | *Mens/Womenswear* 24

KINGS PLAZA/ MARINE PARK

Clarks | *Shoes* 24
Macy's | *Dept. Stores* 23
Sam Ash | *Music Instruments* 26

PARK SLOPE

Beacon's Closet | *Vintage* 19
Bicycle Habitat | *Sporting Gds.* 27

Clarks | *Mens/Womenswear* 24

Club Monaco | *Mens/Womenswear* 21

LEGO | *Toys* 26

Michael Kors | *Mens/Womenswear* 27

Target | *Mass Merch.* 19

FLUSHING

Blackman | *Hardware* 26

Macy's | *Dept. Stores* 23

FOREST HILLS

Sam Ash | *Music Instruments* 26

LONG ISLAND CITY

Costco | *Discount* 24

MASPETH

Davis/Warshow | *Hardware* 27

MIDDLE VILLAGE

BJ's | *Discount* 20

QUEENS VILLAGE

Blackman | *Hardware* 26

REGO PARK

Century 21 | *Discount* 21

Macy's | *Dept. Stores* 23

Staten Island

CHARLESTON

Target | *Mass Merch.* 19

NEW SPRINGVILLE

Apple | *Electronics* 29

BCBG | *Womenswear* 24

Costco | *Mass Merch.* 24

Macy's | *Dept. Stores* 23

Michael Kors | *Mens/Womenswear* 27

STATEN ISLAND

Fishs Eddy | *Furniture/Home* 22

WEST BRIGHTON

Boomerang | *Toys* 25

FOOD LOVER'S

Top Quality

29 | Casa Della Mozz. | *Cheese*
Borgatti's | *Pasta*
Lady M Cake | *Baked Goods*
Le Dû's Wines | *Wine/Liquor*
Di Palo | *Cheese/Dairy*
Simchick, L. | *Meat/Poultry*
Russ & Daughters | *Smoked Fish*
Teuscher Chocolates | *Candy*
Murray's Cheese | *Cheese*
Florence Meat | *Meat*
Saxelby Cheese | *Cheese*
Staubitz Market | *Meat/Poultry*
Greenmarket | *Produce*
La Maison Chocolat* | *Candy*
Sherry-Lehmann | *Wine/Liquor*

Italian Wine | *Wine/Liquor*
28 | Lobel's Meats | *Meat/Poultry*
Ottomanelli & Sons | *Meat*
Harney & Sons | *Coffee/Tea*
Ottomanelli's Meats | *Meat*
Maison Ladurée | *Baked Goods*
Faicco's Pork | *Meat/Poultry*
Moore Brothers | *Wine*
Terranova* | *Baked Goods*
Dickson's Meats | *Meat*
Salumeria Rosi Parm. | *Meat*
Raffetto's | *Pasta*
Pisacane Midtown | *Seafood*
DavidsTea | *Coffee/Tea*
S&S Cheesecake | *Baked Goods*

Top Display

28 | Maison Ladurée | *Baked Goods*
Villabate-Alba | *Baked Goods*
Lady M Cake | *Baked Goods*
Moore Brothers | *Wine*
La Maison Chocolat | *Candy*
27 | Dylan's Candy Bar | *Candy*
Pomegranate | *Specialty Shop*
Pour | *Wine*
Teuscher Chocolates | *Candy*
Bottlerocket | *Wine*
Nespresso | *Coffee/Tea*
26 | Vosges | *Candy/Nuts*
Eataly | *Major Market*
Jacques Torres | *Candy*

MarieBelle's Treats | *Candy*
DavidsTea | *Coffee/Tea*
Le Dû's Wines* | *Wine/Liquor*
Puro Chile | *Specialty Shop*
Georget'wn Cup. | *Baked Goods*
Bedford Cheese | *Cheese*
One Girl Cookies | *Baked Goods*
Italian Wine | *Wine/Liquor*
Black Hound NY | *Baked Goods*
Bklyn Larder | *Specialty Shop*
Murray's Cheese | *Cheese*
Artopolis | *Baked Goods*
Ivy Bakery | *Baked Goods*
Sherry-Lehmann | *Wine/Liquor*
Dickson's Meats | *Meat*

Top Service

29 | Moore Brothers | *Wine*
28 | Le Dû's Wines* | *Wine/Liquor*
Pour | *Wine*
27 | Biancardi Meats | *Meat/Poultry*
DavidsTea | *Coffee/Tea*
Florence Meat | *Meat/Poultry*
Saxelby Cheese | *Cheese*
Enoteca Di Palo | *Wine/Liquor*
26 | Bottlerocket | *Wine*
Ottomanelli & Sons | *Meat*
Battery Place Mkt. | *Maj. Mkt.*
Dickson's Meats | *Meat*
Chambers St. | *Wine*
Staubitz Market | *Meat/Poultry*
Esposito Meat | *Meat*

Lobel's Meats | *Meat*
Italian Wine | *Wine/Liquor*
Sullivan St. Tea/Spice Co. | *Tea*
Ivy Bakery | *Baked Goods*
Harney & Sons | *Coffee/Tea*
Molly's Cupcakes | *Baked Goods*
D'Vine Taste | *Specialty Shop*
Piemonte Ravioli | *Pasta*
25 | Borgatti's | *Pasta*
Simchick, L. | *Meat/Poultry*
Di Palo | *Cheese/Dairy*
Bellocq Tea Atelier | *Tea*
Blue Apron | *Specialty Shop*
Bklyn Larder | *Specialty Shop*
Casa Della Mozz.* | *Cheese*

---

* Indicates a tie with place above; excludes those with low votes,
unless otherwise indicated

Visit zagat.com

TOPS BY CATEGORY

BEER
27│ Bierkraft
    Good Beer Store
    Breukelen Bier
25│ City Swiggers
23│ Eagle Provisions

BIALYS/BAGELS
26│ Absolute Bagels
    Kossar's Bialys
    Ess-a-Bagel
    Murray's Bagels
    Bagelworks, Inc.

BREAD
28│ Terranova Bakery
    Addeo Bakery
27│ Sullivan Street Bakery
    Balthazar Bakery
    Caputo's Bake Shop

CAKES
29│ Lady M Cake
28│ S&S Cheesecake
27│ Ladybird Bakery
    Villabate-Alba
26│ Black Hound NY

CANDY
(See also Chocolate)
29│ Minamoto Kitchoan
27│ The Sweet Life▽
25│ Economy Candy
    London Candy Co.
24│ Sockerbit∨
23│ Dylan's Candy Bar

CAVIAR/SMOKED FISH
29│ Russ & Daughters
28│ Zabar's
    Murray's Sturgeon
27│ Petrossian
    Sable's Smoked Fish

CHEESE/DAIRY
29│ Casa Della Mozz.
    Di Palo
    Murray's Cheese
    Saxelby Cheese
28│ Dean & DeLuca

CHOCOLATE
(See also Candy)
29│ Teuscher Chocolates
    La Maison Chocolat

28│ Kee's Chocolates
    Jacques Torres
    L.A. Burdick Chocolates

COFFEE
28│ McNulty's
27│ Porto Rico
    Nespresso Boutique
    D'Amico
26│ Zabar's

COOKIES
28│ Levain Bakery
27│ One Girl Cookies
    Artopolis
26│ Baked
    Silver Moon Bakery

CUPCAKES
27│ Ladybird Bakery
    Georgetown Cupcake
    Brooklyn Cupcake
    Molly's Cupcakes
26│ Sprinkles Cupcakes

DELIS/CHARCUTERIE
28│ Salumeria Rosi Parmacotto
    Marlow & Daughters
    Schaller & Weber
27│ Esposito & Sons
26│ Salumeria Biellese

GIFTS BASKETS
29│ Russ & Daughters
28│ Murray's Cheese
    Jacques Torres
    L.A. Burdick Chocolates
    The Orchard

HERBS AND SPICES
29│ Dean & DeLuca
27│ Kalustyan's
    Zabar's
26│ Sullivan St. Tea/Spice Co.
25│ Spices & Tease▽

MACARONS
28│ Maison Ladurée
    Kee's Chocolates
27│ Bouchon Bakery
26│ Almondine Bakery
25│ Financier Patisserie

MAJOR MARKETS

27 Eataly
Zabar's
26 Citarella
Dean & DeLuca
Agata & Valentina

MEATS/POULTRY

29 Simchick, L.
Florence Meat
Staubitz Market
28 Lobel's Meats
Ottomanelli & Sons

NUTS/DRIED FRUITS

28 Sahadi's
27 Kalustyan's
25 Economy Candy
24 Nut Box
Fairway

OLIVES/PICKLES

28 Sahadi's
27 Pickle Guys
Teitel Brothers
26 Titan Foods
25 Pickles, Olives Etc.

PASTAS

29 Borgatti's
28 Raffetto's
Eataly
Agata & Valentina
27 Piemonte Ravioli

PASTRIES

27 Bouchon Bakery
Balthazar Bakery

Dominique Ansel Bakery
Villabate-Alba
Artopolis

PRODUCE

27 Dean & DeLuca
26 Whole Foods Market
25 Manhattan Fruit Ex.
Agata & Valentina
Eli's Manhattan

SEAFOOD

28 Pisacane Midtown
Eataly
Citarella
27 Lobster Place
Fish Tales

SPECIALTY SHOPS

28 Sahadi's
Blue Apron
27 Bklyn Larder
Despaña Foods
D. Coluccio & Sons

TEA

28 Harney & Sons
DavidsTea
McNulty's
27 Porto Rico
26 Sullivan St. Tea/Spice Co.

WINES/BEER/LIQUOR

29 Le Dû's Wines
Sherry-Lehmann
Italian Wine
28 Moore Brothers
Burgundy Wine Company

TOPS BY LOCATION

CHELSEA

28 Dickson's Meats
DavidsTea
Jacques Torres
Burgundy Wine Company
27 Sullivan Street Bakery

CHINATOWN/ LITTLE ITALY

29 Di Palo
Alleva Dairy
27 Piemonte Ravioli
Despaña Foods
Enoteca Di Palo

EAST VILLAGE

27 Porto Rico
26 Black Hound NY
East Village Meat Market
25 ChikaLicious Dessert Club
Union Market

FLATIRON/MURRAY HILL

28 Moore Brothers
L.A. Burdick Chocolates
27 Beecher's Cheese
Eataly
Kalustyan's

GREENWICH VILLAGE

28 Raffetto's
27 Porto Rico
26 Sullivan St. Tea/Spice Co.
Citarella
Murray's Bagels

LOWER EAST SIDE

29 Russ & Daughters
Saxelby Cheese
27 Formaggio Essex
Porto Rico
Doughnut Plant

MIDTOWN EAST

29 Lady M Cake
Simchick, L.
Teuscher Chocolates
Murray's Cheese
La Maison Chocolat

MIDTOWN WEST

29 La Maison Chocolat
28 Kee's Chocolate
Jacques Torres
27 Sullivan Street Bakery
Bouchon Bakery

SOHO/HUDSON SQ.

28 Harney & Sons
Kee's Chocolates
Jacques Torres
27 Balthazar Bakery
Dominique Ansel Bakery

UPPER EAST SIDE

29 Lady M Cake
Teuscher Chocolates
La Maison Chocolat
28 Lobel's Meats
Maison Ladurée

UPPER WEST SIDE

28 Salumeria Rosi Parmacotto
Levain Bakery
Jacques Torres
Acker Merrall & Condit Co.
Murray's Sturgeon

WEST VILLAGE

29 Le Dû's Wines
Murray's Cheese
Florence Meat
28 Ottomanelli & Sons
Faicco's Pork

BX: ARTHUR AVE.

29 Casa Della Mozz.
Borgatti's
28 Terranova Bakery
Biancardi Meats
Addeo Bakery

BKLYN: BAY RIDGE/ BENSONHURST/ BOROUGH PARK

28 Faicco's Pork
27 Pastosa Ravioli
Villabate-Alba
D. Coluccio & Sons
Mike's Donuts & Coffee

BKLYN: BKLYN HTS./ CARROLL GDNS./ COBBLE HILL

29 Staubitz Market
28 Sahadi's
27 One Girl Cookies
Stinky Bklyn
Fish Tales

BKLYN: PARK SLOPE/ PROSPECT HEIGHTS

28 DavidsTea
Blue Apron
27 Bklyn Larder
Bierkraft
Ladybird Bakery

BKLYN: WILLIAMSBURG

28 Marlow & Daughters
Smorgasburg
Bedford Cheese
Breukelen Bier
Porto Rico

Best Buys

In order of Bang for the Buck rating.

1. Casa Della Mozz. | *Cheese*
2. Borgatti's | *Pastas*
3. Di Palo | *Cheese & Dairy*
4. Cannelle | *Baked Goods*
5. Greenmarket | *Produce*
6. Faicco's Pork | *Meat & Poultry*
7. McNulty's | *Coffee & Tea*
8. Sahadi's | *Specialty Shop*
9. Addeo | *Baked Goods*
10. Sullivan St. Bakery | *Baked Goods*
11. Villabate | *Baked Goods*
12. Porto Rico | *Coffee & Tea*
13. Pickle Guys | *Specialty Shop*
14. Caputo's | *Baked Goods*
15. D'Amico | *Coffee & Tea*
16. Madonia Bakery | *Baked Goods*
17. Randazzo's | *Seafood*
18. Damascas | *Baked Goods*
19. Economy Candy | *Candy & Nuts*
20. Fairway | *Major Market*

FOOD LOVER'S SOURCES DIRECTORY

QUALITY DISPLAY SERVICE COST

Absolute Bagels ●⌂⊅ *Baked Goods* `26` `15` `18` `I`

W 100s | 2788 Broadway (bet. 107th & 108th Sts.) | 212-932-2052
A "first choice" in the Columbia area, this "no-frills" storefront gets "back to the basics" with "awesome" "hand-rolled" bagels that meld "just the right amount of chewiness" with a "crispy" outside; "efficient" staffers slather the rounds with a "large variety" of "yummy" spreads, and despite the "chaotic-at-times" "morning rush", "carb-lovers" are absolutely convinced the "taste and price" are "worth traveling" for.

Acker Merrall & Condit Co. ● *Wines & Liquor* `28` `23` `25` `E`

W 70s | 160 W. 72nd St. (bet. B'way & Columbus Ave.) | 212-787-1700 |
www.ackerwines.com
"New, aged or hard-to-find" – "whatever you're looking for in the world of fine wines", from "French classics", Barbarescos and Riojas to California Cabernets and Super Tuscans, you'll likely find it at this UWS "top" shop, a fixture since 1820; the staff offers "recommendations you can trust", and its online and live auction offerings and hosted dinners are "simply incomparable" – little wonder oenophiles consider it a "quantum leap ahead" of most in the genre.

Acme Smoked Fish ⊅ *Smoked Fish* `25` `16` `19` `M`

Greenpoint | 30 Gem St. (15th St.) | Brooklyn | 718-383-8585 |
www.acmesmokedfish.com
"Go to the source" say smoked-fish fanatics who find it more than "worth the schlep" to this family-owned wholesaler/smokehouse among Greenpoint's "warehouses and factories" for "steal deals" on a "top-quality selection" of "loxilicious" goods, including whitefish, sturgeon, sable, herring and chubs (they even "give samples"); however, know that its "no-frills utilitarian retail shop" opens to civilians on Fridays from 8 AM–1 PM only, and "be prepared to wait on line" at holiday time.

Addeo Bakery ⊅ *Baked Goods* `28` `20` `23` `I`

Fordham | 2352 Arthur Ave. (bet. Crescent Ave. & 186th St.) | Bronx |
718-367-8316
Fordham | 2372 Hughes Ave. (186th St.) | Bronx | 718-367-8316
"Nothing has changed" at these "old-time" Bronx bakeries that remain as "authentic" and "friendly" as when your "great grandparents shopped here", turning out the same "wide variety" of "exceptionally good", "decent-priced" Italian breads, as well as biscotti "like momma made"; "oh, the aroma" – it's "worth" the "trek" to Hughes Avenue, where production takes place, though the goods are just as "fabulous" on Arthur Avenue; P.S. while you're there pick up some "fresh" "pre-made pizza dough", which is something of a regulars' "secret."

Agata & Valentina ● *Major Market* `25` `23` `22` `E`

E 70s | 1505 First Ave. (79th St.) | 212-452-0690
G Village | 64 University Pl. (bet. 10th & 11th Sts.) | 212-452-0690
www.agatavalentina.com
"Don't go hungry" to this UES "high-end purveyor" of Italian-accented "gourmet" goods and its newer Village offshoot, where devotees "dare you to leave with only what you came in for" once faced with the "outstanding" meats and seafood, "succulent" housemade pastas, "fresh and delicious" baked goods, "plentiful selection" of "first-rate" prepared foods and "exceptional" "spectrum of cheeses"; it "can get crazy"

at "peak hours" when "bustle" and "tussle" fill the "narrow aisles", but "eager" staffers and "fair" (for the zip code) prices mean for most it "can't be beat" for "one-stop shopping."

Alleva Dairy *Cheese & Dairy*   28 | 20 | 23 | M

Little Italy | 188 Grand St. (Mulberry St.) | 212-226-7990 | 800-425-5382 | www.allevadairy.com

They're "still doing it the old-fashioned way" at this "family-run" Little Italy "icon", a circa-1892 "throwback" that remains a "superb" source of "authentic Italian cheeses" ("fresh-made mozzarella", ricotta and "some unusual imports") along with salami, prosciutto and assorted "grocery items from Italy"; the staff "aims to please" and prices are "fair" – "hope they never change."

NEW All Good Things *Major Market*   - | - | - | E

TriBeCa | 102 Franklin St. (bet. 6th Ave. & W. B'way) | 212-966-3663 | www.allgoodthingsny.com

Purveyors of all things local and artisanal – from Dickson's Meats, Cavaniola's Cheese and Orwasher's to Blue Bottle Coffee, NuNu Chocolates and Blue Marble Ice Cream – are conveniently collected in one narrow, industrial-chic space at this TriBeCa craft food market; there are also flowers from Polux Fleuriste, and the market's chef/designer Ryan Tate (ex Savoy) runs fish and produce stands, a back coffee/wine bar for shopping breaks as well as a downstairs eatery, Le Restaurant.

Almondine Bakery *Baked Goods*   26 | 21 | 21 | M

Dumbo | 85 Water St. (bet. Dock & Main Sts.) | Brooklyn | 718-797-5026 | www.almondinebakery.com

"Beautiful" French pastries, croissants "worth walking the bridge for" and some of the "best baguettes" in town keep sweet tooths and carbophiles coming back to baker extraordinaire Hervé Poussot's "delightful", newly renovated Dumbo "jewel"; "delicate macarons, delectable sandwiches" and a friendly "French-speaking staff" complete the "little-bit-of-Paris-in-NY" picture.

Amy's Bread *Baked Goods*   26 | 22 | 21 | M

Chelsea | Chelsea Mkt. | 75 Ninth Ave. (bet. 15th & 16th Sts.) | 212-462-4338
W 40s | 672 Ninth Ave. (bet. 46th & 47th Sts.) | 212-977-2670 ❂
W Village | 250 Bleecker St. (Leroy St.) | 212-675-7802 ❂
www.amysbread.com

Amy Scherber's "constantly buzzing" bakery trio remains a "carb-lovers' dream" thanks to its "wonderful artisanal breads" – "iconic fennel-semolina-golden raisin" loaves, "addictive" black olive twists – that are "divine" as ever "after all these years"; its "sandwiches, pizzas and sweets" including "delicious" cakes are also voted "worth every calorie", and while seating is "limited", a bonus at the Chelsea Market branch is getting to watch the "bakers in action."

Artopolis ❂ *Baked Goods*   27 | 26 | 22 | M

Astoria | Agora Plaza | 23-18 31st St. (bet. 23rd Ave. & 23rd Rd.) | Queens | 718-728-8484 | 800-553-2270 | www.artopolis.net

It's as if an "upscale" Athenian bakery "dropped from the sky and landed in Astoria" agree admirers agog over the "fantastic selection" of "artistic" cakes and "so-very-fresh" pastries, plus "French-style desserts", "superb" cookies and "savory items" at this "modern" standout; the "wonderful" breads and Greek specialties are deemed "truly worth a special trip" – just "secure those boxes" of *kourabiedes* and baklava for the "subway home", lest you finish them off before arriving.

Astor Wines & Spirits ● *Wines & Liquor* | 26 | 24 | 23 | M |

NoHo | 399 Lafayette St. (4th St.) | 212-674-7500 | www.astorwines.com
With "mammoth" (11,000-sq.-ft.) proportions and an "encyclopedic" selection spanning "any kind of wine, bubbly, spirit" or sake imaginable at "some of the best prices in the city", this NoHo behemoth remains a NYC "favorite"; "you could spend a day roaming" the "user-friendly layout" in search of that "hard-to-find bottle" – or "geek out" with the "well-versed" staffers who'll guide you to "real treasures" – at this "stellar cellar" that "has all your imbibing needs" covered, from "frequent tastings" and "free delivery" to a "varied calendar" of classes at the "educational" Astor Center upstairs.

BabyCakes NYC ● *Baked Goods* | 24 | 22 | 22 | M |

LES | 248 Broome St. (bet. Ludlow & Orchard Sts.) | 212-677-5047 | www.babycakesnyc.com
"Heaven-sent for both vegans" and people with "food allergies and sensitivities", this "quaint little" LES "bakery experience" offers up "healthier" renditions of "birthday cakes", "cupcakes, cookies and treats" made without milk, soy, refined sugar and other trigger-point ingredients; if a few feel less than babied by "granddaddy prices", admirers retort "what's not to love?" – "gluten-free never tasted this good."

Bagelworks ● *Baked Goods* | 26 | 16 | 20 | I |

E 60s | 1229 First Ave. (bet. 66th & 67th Sts.) | 212-744-6444
Despite its modest size, this "no-nonsense" nook works up an "excellent selection" of "wonderful" "classic" bagels hailed as "some of the best" on the UES; the goods are "fresh"-baked and paired with "lots of spreads" at a "competitive price", and if the "very small" digs are often "crowded", to most it's well "worth the hassle for what you get in return."

Baked *Baked Goods* | 26 | 22 | 22 | M |

Red Hook | 359 Van Brunt St. (bet. Dikeman & Wolcott Sts.) | Brooklyn | 718-222-0345 | www.bakednyc.com
"Schlep to Red Hook?" – heck yeah, if you make this "charming, neighborhoody" bakery your "decadent" destination, with or without a "trip to Fairway"; "it's all about the chocolate chip cookies and brownies" here, not to mention the Brookster, an "illicit love child" of both, though the "sweet and salty caramel" "treats" and cupcakes are "also to die for" – dig in at the "comfortable" "large tables" where you can also "sit and read or chat"; P.S. a Manhattan offshoot is in the works.

Baked In Brooklyn *Baked Goods* | - | - | - | I |

Greenwood Heights | 755 Fifth Ave. (bet. 25th & 26th Sts.) | Brooklyn | 718-788-3164 | www.bibcatering.com
Follow the aroma of baking bread to this Greenwood Heights arrival, a retail storefront attached to the wholesale baker Alladin's production facility, with a few tables and big windows providing a view of the bakers and giant machines at work in the factory; its extensive array of carbs – from loaves (pumpernickel, whole wheat, ciabatta) to focaccia, rolls, bagels and tortillas – comes fresh out of the oven at seriously low

prices, along with dips, cheeses, charcuterie and other bread-friendly accompaniments, not to mention Stumptown coffee.

Balthazar Bakery *Baked Goods*   27 | 24 | 21 | E

SoHo | 80 Spring St. (bet. B'way & Crosby St.) | 212-965-1785 | www.balthazarbakery.com

"Even after all these years" this French bakery "addendum" to SoHo's Balthazar remains a "scene" with "crowds" spilling "out the door", all clamoring to "pay a pretty penny" for "absolutely top-drawer" "crusty and chewy baguettes" and other "exquisite" breads, "mouthwatering" pastries and "arguably the best croissants" around; it "smells like heaven" and is mightily "hard to resist" so "don't even try" – just "grab a tartine" and a "divine" hot chocolate and "pretend you're in Paris."

Bangkok Center Grocery *Specialty Shop*   ∇ 24 | 16 | 22 | I

Chinatown | 104 Mosco St. (bet. Mott & Mulberry Sts.) | 212-349-1979 | www.bangkokcentergrocery.com

"One of the only" options for "authentic Thai stuff" in town, this "compact" but "organized" Chinatown mart's wares include "all of the essentials for preparing" Siamese feasts, from imported sauces and fresh curry pastes to herbs and seasonings like fresh "kaffir lime leaves and Thai basil"; it's also a godsend "for newbies" since the "staff will cheerfully give you advice on just what you need."

Barnyard Cheese Shop *Cheese & Dairy*   ∇ 26 | 23 | 22 | E

E Village | 149 Ave. C (bet. 9th & 10th Sts.) | 212-674-2276 | www.barnyardcheese.com

It's "like going to a friend's" at this East Village "community cheese shop", where "extremely personable" types oversee an artisanal selection starring locally sourced varieties augmented by Swiss and Bavarian imports, plus charcuterie and other gourmet nibbles; loyalists "love their sandwiches" as well, and if tabs run "a little high for the neighborhood", it won't cost you the farm.

Battery Place Market ● *Major Market*   27 | 25 | 26 | M

Financial District | Goldman Sachs Bldg. | 240 Murray St. (bet. North End Ave. & West St.) | 212-323-6965
Financial District | 77 Battery Pl. (3rd Pl.) | 212-786-0077
www.batteryplacemarkets.com

With locations in the base of a Battery Park 'green' luxury condo and in the Goldman Sachs Building, this "much-needed" "upscale" Financial District grocer stocks the "finest-caliber" cheeses, prepared foods, bakery items, charcuterie and more, with focus on goods from "small producers and local artisans"; in a zone that's short on food markets, it's particularly appreciated for its grass-fed meat counter and "organic vegetables and fruit", though the pricing on some items is "definitely for the Wall Street banker" budget.

Bedford Cheese Shop ● *Cheese & Dairy*   27 | 26 | 24 | E

Gramercy | 67 Irving Pl. (bet. 18th & 19th Sts.) | 718-599-7588
Williamsburg | 229 Bedford Ave. (N. 4th St.) | Brooklyn | 718-599-7588 | 888-484-3243
www.bedfordcheeseshop.com

"One of the seven wonders of Williamsburg" – now with a roomier, every-bit-as-"adorable" Gramercy satellite – this corner "cheese lover's

QUALITY DISPLAY SERVICE COST

paradise" flaunts more than 150 "extraordinary" fromages "well chosen" "from around the world" by a "helpful" staff that's "quick to offer samples and suggestions"; it's "equally good" for upmarket, locavore-oriented groceries (jams, condiments, oils, vinegars), salumi and bread from the city's best bakeries, and while it'll "make a bit of a dent in your wallet", the "outstanding" quality keeps it ever "popular."

Beecher's Handmade Cheese Counter *Cheese & Dairy*

27 | 23 | 24 | M

Flatiron | 900 Broadway (bet. 19th & 20th Sts.) | 212-466-3340 | 877-907-1644 | www.beechershandmadecheese.com
Proving that "gourmet American cheese" is not an oxymoron, this "upscale", tri-level Flatiron "outpost of the Seattle favorite" offers an "unbeatable selection" of "fabulous" domestic "artisanal" fromages, including those "you can see them making" in-house before they travel to a downstairs aging cave; the goods can be on the "pricey" side, but to most it's "oh-so-worth-it" when you factor in the "courteous", "helpful" service and additive-free accompaniments – not to mention the "decadent" dishes from the adjacent cafe, packaged to go.

Beer Table Pantry ⦿ *Beer*

▽ 26 | 20 | 22 | M

E 40s | Grand Central Terminal | main concourse, Graybar Passage (42nd St. & Lexington Ave.) | 212-922-0008 | www.btpantry.com
You can "stock up on craft beer on your way on or off a train" at this tiny Grand Central offshoot of Park Slope's Beer Table, where shelves of "choice" bottled beers plus 64-oz. growlers – filled from a rotating on-tap selection – tempt many a commuter; the "limited" offerings include a few products from local producers, including beef jerky, jam, pickles and baked goods from Scratch Bread.

Bellocq Tea Atelier *Tea*

25 | 24 | 25 | E

Greenpoint | 104 West St. (Kent St.) | Brooklyn | 800-495-5416 | www.bellocq.com
"Wonderful aromas greet you" at this tea shop that got its start in London before crossing the pond to industrial Greenpoint, where its atmospheric, "deep purple–hued" space features reclaimed wood shelves lined with elegant, fragrant tins and brew accessories; its owners "know their stuff", creating a "wide selection" of custom artisanal blends with evocative names like White Wolf and Noble Savage, which are based on "exotic" leaves sourced from small producers around the globe and presented by folks who can "tell you everything" about 'em, "down to the name of the farmer."

Betty Bakery *Baked Goods*

▽ 26 | 23 | 23 | E

Boerum Hill | 448 Atlantic Ave. (bet. Bond & Nevins Sts.) | Brooklyn | 718-246-2402 | www.bettybakery.com
"Beautifully decorated" special-event "creations" for nuptials, birthdays and really "all occasions" crafted by wedding-cake pros Cheryl Kleinman and Bijoux Doux's Ellen Baumwoll are just the jumping-off point at this colorful, retro-inspired Boerum Hill bakery kitted out with a 1920s-era green stove; sweet tooths also turn to it for everyday "fresh, real and amazing" strawberry shortcake, "cute cookies and petit fours" and "really wonderful" cakes (coconut, red velvet), all of them "outstanding."

| | QUALITY | DISPLAY | SERVICE | COST |

NEW Beurre & Sel *Baked Goods* — | — | — | M

Harlem | La Marqueta | 1590 Park Ave. (115th St.) | no phone
LES | Essex Street Mkt. | 120 Essex St. (Rivington St.) | 917-623-3239
www.beurreandsel.com

Cookbook author Dorie Greenspan brings her legendary baking prowess to these bite-size, no-frills stalls in the Essex Street Market and East Harlem's La Marqueta; lined up on marble slabs are about a dozen varieties of cookies – including her trademark Jammers and World Peace chocolate sablés – offered solo in a three-inch size or in smaller rounds sold in pre-packed stacks.

Biancardi Meats *Meat & Poultry* 28 | 25 | 27 | M

Fordham | 2350 Arthur Ave. (bet. Crescent Ave. & 186th St.) | Bronx | 718-733-4058

"What an incredible place" rave carnivores of this family-owned Arthur Avenue "meat heaven", where the "high-quality" beef, lamb, pork, poultry and "outstanding" sausages are offered alongside harder-to-find viands like rabbit, pheasant, tripe and sweetbreads; in business since 1932, it's an Italian-style "throwback" to the days of meat "trimmed to order" by butchers with "excellent skills" – factor in "good prices", and no wonder you'll see "license plates from several states" parked outside.

Bien Cuit *Baked Goods* ▽ 23 | 22 | 18 | E

NEW W Village | 35 Christopher St. (Waverly Pl.) | 646-590-3341
Cobble Hill | 120 Smith St. (bet. Dean & Pacific Sts.) | Brooklyn | 718-852-0200
www.biencuit.com

"High-end" artisanal bread comes to Cobble Hill and Greenwich Village via these French bakeries from an alum of Philadelphia's Le Bec-Fin, whose "amazing" crusty loaves (the moniker means 'well done') are offered alongside "gorgeous, delicious" sweet and savory tarts and other pastries, plus "wonderful sandwiches"; the simple storefronts feature a few tables for on-site munching, and many a local "wakes up on Saturday mornings dreaming about this place."

Bierkraft ● *Beer* 27 | 21 | 24 | M

Park Slope | 191 Fifth Ave. (bet. Berkeley Pl. & Union St.) | Brooklyn | 718-230-7600 | www.bierkraft.com

"Wow, that's a lot of beer" – the "unbeatable" 1,000-plus selection at this "Park Slope gem" encompasses "fabulous" craft brews "from all over the world", plus the "frothy" favorites on tap lead sudsophiles to say "growlers are the way to go" ("who doesn't like refills?"); prices are on the "expensive" side, but with pluses like "hearty sandwiches" to "keep the drinkers nice and full" and a "really dedicated" staff, to most it's "worth" the "extra dough."

Bisous, Ciao *Baked Goods* ▽ 25 | 25 | 25 | E

LES | 101 Stanton St. (Ludlow St.) | 212-260-3463
W Village | 235 Bleecker St. (bet. Carmine & Leroy Sts.) | 212-675-6366 ●
www.bisousciao.com

Exquisite, "bite-of-heaven" French-style macarons are the *specialité* of this dainty Lower East Side boutique and its new West Village offshoot; arranged in rows in glass cases, the colorful treats come in "amazing" flavors both classic (chocolate, pistachio) and seasonal (fall cran-

QUALITY | DISPLAY | SERVICE | COST

berry, spring violet) and are packaged in "tasteful" sleek black boxes; P.S. it also does custom orders for bridal showers and other events.

Bklyn Larder ● *Specialty Shop*   27 | 26 | 25 | E

Park Slope | 228 Flatbush Ave. (bet. Bergen St. & St. Marks Ave.) | Brooklyn | 718-783-1250 | www.bklynlarder.com

A "terrific" player on the "Park Slope foodie scene", this gourmet pantry (co-owned by the Franny's folks) is "jam-packed" with "extraordinary" "artisanal foodwares" including "better-than-sex" cheeses (from an on-site cave), "seriously good" house-cured meats, chocolates, oils and condiments, plus "first-rate" prepared foods and sandwiches "as tasty as they look"; "ridiculous prices" draw some fire, but the "enthusiastic" staff's "generous with the samples" and for "amazing finds" you "won't see elsewhere" it's "so worth it"; P.S. a new pastry chef is stepping up the baked goods selection.

Black Hound New York ● *Baked Goods*   26 | 26 | 23 | E

E Village | 170 Second Ave. (bet. 10th & 11th Sts.) | 212-979-9505 | 800-344-4417 | www.blackhoundny.com

"Just taking a deep breath" at this "tiny" East Villager "can give a chocoholic a rush" agree "serious" sweet tooths who find the "indulgent", "expensive" jam-filled cookies, tarts, truffles and "really special" cakes – including "cute" mini-sizes – "worth the splurge"; a few sourpusses say the treats "under-deliver on flavor", but the tail-wagging majority insists the inventory here is "as pleasing to the taste buds as it is to the eye."

Blue Apron Foods *Specialty Shop*   28 | 24 | 25 | E

Park Slope | 814 Union St. (bet. 7th & 8th Aves.) | Brooklyn | 718-230-3180 | www.blue-apron-foods.com

A "little slice of luscious in Park Slope", this "small but wonderful" gourmet shop is "chock-full" of "all things delicious", notably a bounty of "lovely cheeses" and charcuterie and a "carefully selected" mix of "high-quality" goods from premium pastas to sweets from Nunu Chocolates and fresh bread from top bakeries; the "friendly" "pro" staff offers "great guidance" too, so while this nook is "expensive" and "a little overcrowded", it's a major "benefit" for the neighborhood that's considered well "worth visiting – and often."

Bond Street Chocolate *Candy & Nuts*   ▽ 27 | 26 | 23 | E

E Village | 63 E. Fourth St. (bet. Bowery & 2nd Ave.) | 212-677-5103 | www.bondstchocolate.com

It's a "delightful surprise in the East Village" gush sweet tooths who stumble upon Lynda Stern's tiny, brick-walled sweets shop producing "wonderful", quirky chocolates, from edible gold leaf–dusted statues of Jesus, Moses and the Virgin of Guadalupe and tins of metallic silver skulls to dark bonbons with boozy fillings like bourbon or elderflower liquor; works of art all, it's no wonder they're showcased in a lovely antique jewelry case.

Borgatti's Ravioli & Egg Noodles ⊅ *Pastas*   29 | 20 | 25 | I

Fordham | 632 E. 187th St. (bet. Belmont & Hughes Aves.) | Bronx | 718-367-3799 | www.borgattis.com

"Step back to the old days" at this "no-frills" Arthur Avenue-area "shrine" proffering "sublime" "creamy pillows" of ravioli "like nonna used to make", as well as "fresh, delicate" "outstanding" pastas rang-

QUALITY | DISPLAY | SERVICE | COST

ing from "light whole wheat" to squid ink; it's all "made and sold with a smile" by a "lovely" family that operates its business "with pride" – "no wonder it's been around for generations" ("please never stop!").

Bottlerocket Wine & Spirit *Wines & Liquor*   25 | 27 | 26 | M

Flatiron | 5 W. 19th St. (bet. 5th & 6th Aves.) | 212-929-2323 | www.bottlerocketwine.com

Perfect for those who "get overwhelmed" in traditional wine stores and "just plain fun" for the "savvy", this Flatiron shop's "brilliant setup" amounts to "smart" "kiosk" displays presenting its "well-curated" 365 labels sorted by theme or category ("value", "gift ideas", "region", etc.), with a "fact sheet" explaining each bottle; it's "really easy", but "if you can't navigate it", a staff willing to "bend over backwards" is "at your service."

Bouchon Bakery *Baked Goods*   27 | 24 | 22 | E

W 40s | Rockefeller Ctr. | 1 Rockefeller Plaza (bet. 48th & 49th Sts.) | 212-782-3890

W 60s | Shops at Columbus Circle | 10 Columbus Circle (bet. 58th & 60th Sts.) | 212-823-9366 ●

www.bouchonbakery.com

When you want to "embrace your inner cookie monster", head to Thomas Keller's bakery/take-out counter "just down the corridor" from his "casual" same-name cafe offering "dramatic" views of Columbus Circle, along with "delicate macarons" that may be the "best" "outside of Paris" and other "*fantastique*" "French-style treats" including "decadent", "beautiful" pastries, breads, sandwiches and soups; just "be prepared" for "long lines", minimal seating and "Time Warner Center prices" – "although compared to Per Se" upstairs, it's a "steal!"; P.S. there's also a smaller Rock Center offshoot.

NEW Breads Bakery *Baked Goods*   - | - | - | M

Union Sq | 18 E. 16th St. (bet. B'way & 5th Ave.) | 212-633-2253 | www.breadsbakery.com

A link of an Israeli chain specializing in the breads of Denmark and Northern Europe, this bright, high-ceilinged bakery off Union Square boasts a wide variety of premium loaves (100% rye, French sourdough, walnut) as well as sugary treats like babka, rugalach and pain au chocolat, arrayed in a wood-and-glass display case; amble past several cafe tables to pick up savory sandwiches or espresso drinks at the back register, where you can glimpse the gleaming kitchen beyond.

Bread Talk *Baked Goods*   25 | 24 | 24 | I

Chinatown | 47 Catherine St. (Madison St.) | 917-832-4784

"Everything's fresh and tasty" at this bargain Chinatown bakery boasting Asian pastries like coconut-filled 'cocktail buns', but it's the "lovely egg custard" tarts (two for a dollar) that are the talk of the neighborhood; a "friendly" crew makes the modest storefront all the more "inviting."

Breukelen Bier Merchants ● *Beer*   27 | 23 | 24 | M

Williamsburg | 182 Grand St. (Bedford Ave.) | Brooklyn | 347-457-6350 | www.breukelenbiermerchants.com

"Half beer store, half bar", this "mellow" Williamsburg merchant pours a rotating, "fairly eclectic" selection of "quality" brews – 16 on draft, 500 or so by the bottle or can – to be enjoyed on the premises (they do "flights to pair with cheese and meat plates") or taken to go; with "good prices", "friendly" employees who are "willing to educate", a few "wood tables to sit at" inside and a "backyard that you should seek out" in warm weather, sudsophiles muse "what's not to like?"

Brooklyn Brine *Specialty Shop* 23 | 19 | 21 | M

Gowanus | 574A President St. (4th Ave.) | Brooklyn | 347-223-4345 | www.brooklynbrineco.com

Now that it operates a retail shop within its Gowanus production facility, this greenmarket favorite's seasonally evolving array of "fresh", "savory", "interesting" pickles – from classic NYC deli spears and half-sours to whiskey-scented sauerkraut and Moroccan-spiced green beans – can be purchased right from the barrel (plus there's a front fridge that sometimes offers in-store-only finds); it's a strictly no-frills operation, but the staff's enthusiasm adds warmth.

Brooklyn Cupcake *Baked Goods* 27 | 24 | 23 | M

Dumbo | The Shops at 145 Front Street | 61 Pearl St. (bet. Front & Water Sts.) | Brooklyn | 718-576-3600

Williamsburg | 335 Union Ave. (bet. Grand & Maujer Sts.) | Brooklyn | 718-576-3600 ⊟

LIC | 5-43 48th Ave. (bet. 5th St. & Vernon Blvd.) | Queens | 718-482-8220 ◑ www.brooklyncupcake.com

"Why don't these cupcakes get more press?" wonder devotees of these bakeries – no longer just in Brooklyn – where "both the cake and the frosting are outstanding"; the "unique" flavors (guava con queso) and more traditional ones (red velvet) are "a slice of heaven" considered well "worth every pound you'll gain", so the only downside is "how hard it is to decide" which one you want.

NEW Brooklyn Harvest Market *Major Market* – | – | – | E

Williamsburg | The Edge | 155 Kent Ave. (bet. N. 4th & 5th Sts.) | Brooklyn | no phone

It's from the owner of Williamsburg's Foodtown, but this new super-market on the neighborhood's emerging Gold Coast boosts the quality level by a couple of notches (likewise the prices); packed into its sizable-for–New York City space are full-service butcher and seafood counters, fancy cheeses, upscale dry goods and a well-displayed section of fresh fruits and veggies.

Brooklyn Oenology *Wines & Liquor* ∇ 26 | 23 | 22 | M

Williamsburg | 209 Wythe Ave. (bet. N. 3rd & 4th Sts.) | Brooklyn | 718-599-1259 | www.brooklynoenology.com

This "wonderful" winery HQ housed in a converted Williamsburg warehouse offers "great" French and Bordeaux varietals made under contract with a host vineyard on LI's North Fork (even the labels on the bottles have been designed by neighborhood artists); it also vends other NY State wines, and has a tasting room where you can meet the "nice" vintners and taste their wares – "makes buying local" even more "pleasant."

Brooklyn Victory Garden ◑ *Specialty Shop* 26 | 25 | 23 | M

Clinton Hill | 920 Fulton St. (bet. St. James Pl. & Washington Ave.) | Brooklyn | 718-398-9100 | www.brooklynvictorygarden.com

Catering to Clinton Hill locavores, this "sweet little" self-styled 'urban general store' specializes in local, pastured and sustainable meats and cheeses (think Brooklyn Cured pork, Bo Bo head-on chickens, Jasper Hill cheese), "fresh breads" and other "high-quality products", many from NYC producers; it's all overseen by husband-and-wife owners who "really love what they do" – no wonder the feel is so "warm and welcoming."

Brouwerij Lane ●🗗 *Beer* ▽ 28 | 23 | 28 | M

Greenpoint | 78 Greenpoint Ave. (Franklin St.) | Brooklyn | 347-529-6133 | www.brouwerijlane.com

Offering "beers from everywhere", this "lesser-known" Greenpoint "gem" owned by brew broker Ed Raven carries some 170 "fantastic" imported and domestic labels with a focus on small, American craft brewers; 64-oz. growlers filled from one of the 19 taps dispensing a rotating selection of drafts (including house specialties Jever and Gaffel) can "elevate a night of hanging with your buds", and if you need help deciding, the "great guys" on staff "sure know what they're talking about."

BuonItalia *Specialty Shop* 26 | 20 | 18 | M

Chelsea | Chelsea Mkt. | 75 Ninth Ave. (bet. 15th & 16th Sts.) | 212-633-9090 | www.buonitalia.com

"Italophiles flock" to this Chelsea Market staple, an "excellent" resource for "authentic provisions of all kinds", most notably "artisanal pastas", "to-die-for" truffles, the "finest" cured meats, 50-plus cheeses and lots of "hard-to-find" "imported indulgences" direct from The Boot; the "service is a bit aloof", but for "stocking up on" delicacies you "don't see anywhere else", it's "heaven"; P.S. prepared foods are sold at the deli counter/cafe.

Burgundy Wine Company *Wines & Liquor* 28 | 23 | 24 | E

Chelsea | 143 W. 26th St. (bet. 6th & 7th Aves.) | 212-691-9092 | 888-898-8448 | www.burgundywinecompany.com

As the name suggests, this "cool niche for Pinot lovers" in Chelsea specializes in fine wines from, yes, the Bourgogne region in France, as well as Rhônes and Oregonians, all carefully chosen and, *naturelle-ment,* on the "pricey" side (although there's a "good selection" for under $20 too); bottles are displayed with short descriptions for the cognoscenti, or you can get one of the "friendly" "wine geeks" on staff to give you a hand, while daily tastings and live jazz on Wednesdays are other enticements.

Butterfield Market *Specialty Shop* 25 | 23 | 21 | E

E 70s | 1114 Lexington Ave. (bet. 77th & 78th Sts.) | 212-288-7800 | www.butterfieldmarket.com

"Year after year", this circa-1915 food market and caterer "keeps up its high standards", supplying the UES with a tasteful array highlighting "excellent" produce, "fresh sandwiches", "delicious prepared foods" and shelves stocked with "exquisite" "specialty items"; add "courteous and quick" service and it's "right up there with the best" for an "easy dinner at home", but "bring your wallet" – "you pay for" the "zip code"; P.S. the offshoot a few doors down specializes in cake-style donuts that are baked, not fried.

Butter Lane Cupcakes *Baked Goods* 25 | 21 | 22 | M

E Village | 123 E. Seventh St. (bet. Ave. A & 1st Ave.) | 212-677-2880 ●

(continued)

(continued)

Butter Lane Cupcakes
Park Slope | 240 Seventh Ave. (bet. 4th & 5th Sts.) | Brooklyn |
718-369-0466
www.butterlane.com

Its "French buttercream will change your world – at least on a bad day"
say sweet tooths enamored with these "adorable" East Village and
Park Slope bakeries, where you can "pick your own" cupcake flavor
and icing – "who could ask for anything more?"; these "totally moist"
"little treasures" pack "serious locavore" cred – they're made from organic and locally sourced ingredients – plus you can learn to make
your own at a baking class – "so much fun!"

Calandra Cheese Co. *Cheese & Dairy*   ▽ 27 | 19 | 25 | M
Fordham | 2314 Arthur Ave. (bet. Crescent Ave. & 187th St.) | Bronx |
718-365-7572

Dating from the 1930s, this unassuming Arthur Avenue shop "is truly
an artisan" when it comes to crafting the "very freshest" Italian
cheeses, and its housemade specialties – the "most delicate" ricotta
and "delicious" mozzarella in either the standard or the enriched
scamorza and caciocavallo varieties – "can't be beat"; with an imported selection also on hand, far-flung formaggio fanciers only "wish
this store were closer."

Calvisius Caviar ● *Caviar & Smoked Fish*   ▽ 29 | 25 | 25 | VE
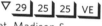
E 50s | Four Seasons Hotel | 58 E. 58th St. (bet. Madison &
Park Aves.) | 212-207-8222 | 885-225-8474 |
www.calvisiuscaviar.com

This chichi caviar boutique and lounge in the lobby of the Four Seasons
Hotel in Midtown puts a sustainable spin on all things eggs-cellent, offering the likes of farm-raised, imported-from-Italy osetra and white
sturgeon available in tins or, for those who eat in, served atop warm
potato purée with sips of Dom Perignon; tabs are in the *ka-ching* realm,
but then "is there such as thing as cheap caviar?"

Cannelle Patisserie *Baked Goods*   ▽ 29 | 22 | 19 | M
Jackson Heights | 75-59 31st Ave. (78th St.) | Queens | 718-565-6200 |
www.cannellepatisserie.com

Pastry chefs who honed their skills at the Waldorf-Astoria are behind
this "fantastic" bakery/cafe whose "highly unlikely" location in a Jackson
Heights strip mall has habitués exalting "finally" – Queens has a "top"-
quality patisserie; its "light, flaky croissants", "fabulous" gateaux
Breton, éclairs, tarts *et tout comme ça* "rival the best of France", and
while there are often "lines" out the door, devotees declare the goods
"worth the wait" – especially given "amazing-value" prices that are
"simply the icing on the cake."

Caputo's Bake Shop ⊟ *Baked Goods*   27 | 20 | 21 | I

Carroll Gardens | 329 Court St. (bet. Sackett & Union Sts.) | Brooklyn |
718-875-6871

"Crispy, warm loaves fly off the shelves" at this Carroll Gardens
"institution" that for more than a century has been baking "heavenly"
Italian breads (seeded or plain), ciabatta, olive and semolinas,
plus a prosciutto-packed lard version that aficionados deem down-
right "remarkable" ("forget the cardiologist"); low prices and a coun-

	QUALITY	DISPLAY	SERVICE	COST

ter crew that includes "entertaining older ladies" complete the "true Brooklyn-Italian experience."

Carry On Tea & Sympathy ❷ *Coffee & Tea* | 25 | 20 | 21 | M |

W Village | 110 Greenwich Ave. (bet. 12th & 13th Sts.) | 212-989-9735 | www.teaandsympathynewyork.com

Pop in "for everything British" at this next-door annex to the West Village's Tea & Sympathy, a carry-out shop that's "small" but "stocked so well" with "wonderful, eclectic U.K. products", from a "lovely tea" selection to "quaint" pots, condiments, biscuits, boiled sweets and scads of other "English goodies"; "cute" decor that's "worthy of a Monty Python sketch" and "cheeky, fun" employees well endowed with "wit" have the homesick saying it's "just like Blighty"; P.S. it also caters, with deliveries made via an authentic London cab.

Casa Della Mozzarella *Cheese & Dairy* | 29 | 25 | 25 | M |

Fordham | 604 E. 187th St. (Arthur Ave.) | Bronx | 718-364-3867

"Mozzarella doesn't get any better" than at this circa-1922 Arthur Avenue mecca – voted No. 1 for Quality in the NYC Food Lover's Survey – which is esteemed as "the definitive source" for the "freshest", "creamiest" "homemade" mozz "this side of the Atlantic"; with the house's own olive oil, imported cheeses and "ridiculously good" salumi from the "accommodating" "counter guys" to round out the "sensory overload" of "old-world Italian delights", this is the "real deal."

NEW Cavaniola's | - | - | - | E |
Gourmet Cheese Shop *Cheese & Dairy*

TriBeCa | All Good Things | 102 Franklin St. (bet. 6th Ave. & W. B'way) | 212-226-2083 | www.cavaniola.com

A spin-off of the family-owned Sag Harbor original, this fine fromage stand inside TriBeCa's All Good Things artisan food market specializes in imported and domestic artisanal cheeses, yogurts, jams and olive oils; for a savory lunchtime splurge, grab a pressed panini or cheese and charcuterie plate to go.

Ceci-Cela *Baked Goods* | 26 | 21 | 20 | M |

Little Italy | 55 Spring St. (bet. Lafayette & Mulberry Sts.) | 212-274-9179 | www.cecielanyc.com

"Sinfully delicious Napoleons", "to-die-for" éclairs, tarts, madeleines, "flakey, buttery croissants" and other "sweets and savories" looking like "works of art" add up to "a taste of Paris" at this Little Italy patisserie; a "pipsqueak of a place" it may be, but it's "the real thing", from the "good, strong coffee" served in the "quaint little sitting area" to the "dash" of "sassy" service "to spice it up" a bit; P.S. it also specializes in wedding cakes.

Chambers Street Wines ❷ *Wines & Liquor* | 27 | 24 | 26 | E |

TriBeCa | 148 Chambers St. (bet. Greenwich St. & W. B'way) | 212-227-1434 | www.chambersstwines.com

Perfect when you "need an impress-the-boss bottle", this "excellent" wine shop "buried" on a TriBeCa "backstreet" carries an "unusually good selection of Loire and biodynamic wines" among its "interesting" stock of small-producer and "hard-to-find" vintages; "decent" (if not cheap) prices lure "experienced wine-buyers", who can be found "ogling the aged stuff", but whether you're "a geek" or a "novice", the "passionate" staff will "happily guide you."

Cheese of the World *Cheese & Dairy*　26 | 21 | 21 | M

Forest Hills | 71-48 Austin St. (Queens Blvd.) | Queens | 718-263-1933
They've been "doing it right" "for ages" at this Forest Hills "mom-and-pop" cheesemonger, "iconic" in the area for its "amazing selection" of some 250 "hard-to-find" fromages "from around the globe", hewn from huge wheels at "incredibly good prices" by a "knowledgeable staff"; figure in charcuterie and "accoutrements like jam" and crackers, and the worldly-wise agree it's "sure to please."

Chelsea Market Baskets *Specialty Shop*　23 | 23 | 21 | M

Chelsea | Chelsea Mkt. | 75 Ninth Ave. (bet. 15th & 16th Sts.) | 212-727-1111 | 888-727-7887 | www.chelseamarketbaskets.com
Assemble an "eclectic" gift basket "for any person's passions" at this Chelsea Market "catch-all store", which custom-fills totes and hampers with a "super assortment" of "things you don't find everywhere", whether English preserves, candy and chocolates, cookies, tea and coffee, toys, "New York–centric" items or "you name it"; the goods are "cleverly displayed", and the "outstanding staff" "will accommodate" your choices so you only "pay as much as you can afford."

Chikalicious Dessert Club ● *Baked Goods*　25 | 22 | 23 | M

E Village | 204 E. 10th St. (bet. 1st & 2nd Aves.) | 212-475-0929 | www.dessertclubchikalicious.com
Sweet tooths "can't rave enough" about this "cute little" East Village "boutique" outlet of the well-known dessert bar across the street, where "the art" of treats is expressed in "cookies to kill for" and "cheesecake to die for", not to mention "incredible éclairs" and other "sublime" pastries to take out or eat at the stand-up counter; there's "always a line", but that's the price of "bliss."

Chocolate Works *Candy & Nuts*　26 | 25 | 24 | E

W 90s | 641 Amsterdam Ave. (91st St.) | 212-799-3630 | www.chocolateworksnyc.com
A "chocolate-lover's nirvana", this "friendly" West Side sweet spot vends "nicely presented", all-kosher treats like handmade truffles, bulk candies and "impossible-to-resist" Belgian chocolates in whimsical shapes from alligators to unicorns; "expensive" but "worth" it, the "cute" package includes a workshop space where kids can "create their own confections."

Choice Greene ● *Specialty Shop*　▽ 27 | 23 | 19 | M

Fort Greene | 214 Greene Ave. (bet. Cambridge Pl. & Grand Ave.) | Brooklyn | 718-230-1243

Choice Market ●⊄ *Specialty Shop*

Clinton Hill | 318 Lafayette Ave. (Grand Ave.) | Brooklyn | 718-230-5234
www.choicebrooklyn.com
This "gourmet" duo enjoys a "trendy" rep, with the Clinton Hill cafe vending "delightful" baked goods, sandwiches and prepared foods (it can get "hectic", especially "around lunchtime"), while the Fort Greene grocer stocks a full range of choice specialty items; it's further evidence that "Brooklyn has become the new Manhattan", so expect prices "similar to those in the city."

	QUALITY	DISPLAY	SERVICE	COST

Citarella ● *Major Market*

26 | 24 | 22 | E

E 70s | 1313 Third Ave. (bet. 75th & 76th Sts.) | 212-874-0383
G Village | 424 Sixth Ave. (9th St.) | 212-874-0383
W 70s | 2135 Broadway (75th St.) | 212-874-0383
www.citarella.com

"The best of everything under one roof" entices the faithful to this "top-quality" "gourmet purveyor", well known as "one of the most reliable" and "customer-oriented" sources for "fabulous", "swimmingly fresh" seafood and "exceptional" "prime meats" trimmed with the "friendly" humor of "a hometown butcher"; it's also a "treasure hunt" of "excellent produce", "superb prepared foods", "delicious" deli items, a "curated selection of cheeses" and "outta sight" breads and baked goods – despite the "commensurate" "hefty cost", seekers of "first-class" rations find it "hard to do better."

City Swiggers ● *Beer*

25 | 22 | 25 | M

E 80s | 320 E. 86th St. (bet. 1st & 2nd Aves.) | 212-570-2000 |
www.cityswiggers.com

Suds-swillers are almost "overcome" by the "wide selection" of brews at this "organized", "open" boutique "bringing beer back to Yorkville" with some 800 craft options by the bottle or can, plus 14 on tap to sample either by the pint on-premises or to take home in growlers (you can even bring your own to fill); the "attentive" service, frequent tastings and "fair prices" go down equally smoothly.

Colson Patisserie *Baked Goods*

▽ 24 | 22 | 19 | M

Park Slope | 374 Ninth St. (6th Ave.) | Brooklyn | 718-965-6400
NEW Sunset Park | Industry City | 220 36th St. (bet. 2nd & 3rd Aves.) |
Brooklyn | 347-637-6676
www.colsonpastries.com

A "wee gem", this "busy" French-Belgian Park Slope patisserie (with a Sunset Park satellite) is the "real deal", featuring "fantastic" pastries and croissants, pain au chocolat, brioche, "noteworthy financiers" and all the *classiques,* as well as "delectable" sandwiches and coffee, plus gelato in summertime; the "pleasant" staff and "child-friendly" vibe cement its status as a neighborhood standby.

Court Pastry Shop ⚐ *Baked Goods*

26 | 19 | 22 | I

Cobble Hill | 298 Court St. (bet. Degraw & Douglass Sts.) | Brooklyn |
718-875-4820

Almost "a picture of time standing still", this Cobble Hill Sicilian bakery "has been around forever" (actually since 1948) "and deservedly so", considering its "wow"-inducing "handmade" sweets all "done right", including cookies and "excellent biscotti", "outstanding cannoli", sfogliatelle and the like; although it can be "hard" to choose among the "not-to-be-missed" options, in summertime "the housemade ices are a cooling treat" while you make up your mind.

Court Street Grocers *Specialty Shop*

▽ 29 | 28 | 27 | E

Carroll Gardens | 485 Court St. (bet. Huntington & Nelson Sts.) |
Brooklyn | 718-722-7229 | www.courtstreetgrocers.com

An "expertly curated" selection of "high-end" packaged comestibles, "amazing sandwiches" and "seriously delicious" prepared foods, plus high-quality meats, cheeses and "outstanding produce", have Carroll Gardens locals calling this the "perfect neighborhood grocery"; "very friendly workers" and an all-around "great, casual" atmosphere are other reasons it's an area "favorite", though "not-cheap" prices mean you probably "won't do your weekly shopping here."

Croissanteria *Baked Goods* | - | - | - | M |

E Village | 66 Ave. A (bet. 4th & 5th Sts.) | 212-466-2860 | www.croissanterianyc.com

Regular and miniature croissants come in a host of sweet flavors – apricot, almond, cinnamon swirl – or as the base for savory sandwiches at this modestly priced East Village bake shop, which pours Brooklyn Roasting Company coffee, wine and beer into the evening; stone tables, cushioned seats and free WiFi encourage the laptop crowd to linger within its subway-tiled walls.

Crush Wine & Spirits ● *Wines & Liquor* | 27 | 25 | 25 | E |

E 50s | 153 E. 57th St. (bet. Lexington & 3rd Aves.) | 212-980-9463 | www.crushwineco.com

A "lovely, well-stocked shop" with a "modern feel", this "upscale" Midtown wine merchant focusing on small producers is "right up there" for oenophiles, while novices can count on "great recommendations" from a staff that "knows all there is to know"; the 3,000-odd labels include "high-end" and "rare" vintages stored in a temperature-controlled room called the Cube, but there's also a solid showing of everyday bottles, and it's all offered at "competitive prices."

Damascus Bread & Pastry Shop *Baked Goods* | 26 | 18 | 22 | I |

Brooklyn Heights | 195 Atlantic Ave. (bet. Clinton & Court Sts.) | Brooklyn | 718-625-7070

Known for the "best pita to be found" and other "authentic" Middle Eastern flatbreads, this circa-1930 Brooklyn Heights Syrian bakery also turns out "luscious" savory and sweet pastries – spinach pies, baklava and other "sticky delights" – so "delicious" you can "gain 10 pounds just looking in the window"; "charming owners" preside over the old-style, "no-frills" setting, where the dips, spreads, "wonderful feta cheese and nuts" are additional reasons it's "worth the trip."

D'Amico *Coffee & Tea* | 27 | 16 | 22 | I |

Carroll Gardens | 309 Court St. (bet. Degraw & Sackett Sts.) | Brooklyn | 718-875-5403 | 888-814-7979 | www.damicofoods.com

Still the neighborhood "standard to judge by", this circa-1948 Carroll Gardens "coffee lovers' oasis" perfumes the block with the "delicious aroma" of its "black gold" as a wide assortment of the "best beans" are "freshly roasted" daily and sold from sacks lining the floor; with a sandwich board and "fine" Italian groceries as well, it's a "homey" emporium that's a favorite local trip "back in time."

DavidsTea ● *Coffee & Tea* | 28 | 26 | 27 | M |

Chelsea | 688 Sixth Ave. (22nd St.) | 212-229-0002
E 60s | 1124 Third Ave. (66th St.) | 212-717-1116
W Village | 275 Bleecker St. (bet. Jones & Morton Sts.) | 212-414-8599
NEW **Park Slope** | 234 Seventh Ave. (4th St.) | Brooklyn | 347-223-4637
www.davidstea.com

Bringing a spot of "tea culture" to NYC, this Montreal-based loose-leaf company arrived with "flying colors" and is opening outlets around town; "gracious" staffers who "really know the merchandise" are "more than happy to help" customers navigate the "well-organized", "amazing assortment" of brews and tisanes, and they "know how to prepare" a cuppa properly too, so why not "save your Lipton pennies" and "splurge."

D. Coluccio & Sons *Specialty Shop*   27 | 21 | 22 | M

Borough Park | 1214 60th St. (bet. 12th & 13th Aves.) | Brooklyn | 718-436-6700 | www.dcoluccioandsons.com

"Here's the real deal" promise partisans of this family-run specialty grocer in "unfancy" Borough Park boasting an "extensive" array of "authentic Italian" goods "to make your mouth water", most of them imported "from all parts of the motherland"; it's an "excellent source" of "wonderful" cheeses, 80 varieties of pasta, olives, condiments, oils and other "favorites" "at the best prices" – no wonder "those in the know swear by this place."

Dean & DeLuca *Major Market*   26 | 25 | 21 | VE

E 80s | 1150 Madison Ave. (85th St.) | 212-717-0800
SoHo | 560 Broadway (Prince St.) | 212-226-6800
800-221-7714 | www.deandeluca.com

"Everything's a wow" at this dean of "fancy schmancy" gourmet grocers, an "inspiring" gastronomic showplace that goes "above and beyond" with the "gorgeously displayed" likes of "excellent" produce, "superior" prepared foods, "heavenly" baked goods "poised for a photo shoot", "luscious", "less-common" cheeses, an "encyclopedic" lineup of "hard-to-find" specialty items, "wonderful" spices, coffee and teas, "pristine seafood" and a "super selection" of "high-quality" cookware; it "caters to the rich and shameless" with notoriously "over-the-top" pricing, but even for "window shopping" this is "foodie" nirvana."

Delillo Pastry Shop *Baked Goods*   25 | 21 | 22 | M

Fordham | 610 E. 187th St. (bet. Arthur & Hughes Aves.) | Bronx | 718-367-8198 | www.delillopastryshop.com

An "Arthur Avenue treasure" since 1925, this "traditional Italian pasticceria" can be counted on for handmade "sfogliatelle that sing", cannoli, biscotti, sesame-seed cookies and all "the best recipes from the century-before-last" – you "can't really go wrong here"; far-flung devotees declare it's "worth trekking to the Bronx" for such "quality."

Dépanneur ● *Specialty Shop*   – | – | – | E

Williamsburg | 242 Wythe Ave. (N. 3rd St.) | Brooklyn | 347-227-8424 | www.depanneurbklyn.com

"You can find the best stuff" at this Williamsburg "amazing corner store" – it self-identities as a 'glorified bodega' – stocking a high-end "great selection of specialty foods, cheeses", charcuterie and other provisions, many of them made in the borough, from Mast Brothers Chocolate to Kings County Jerky; there's also a small cafe area vending Intelligentsia coffee, baked goods and "addictive" sandwiches – which are just the thing to "take along to scenic" Grand Ferry Park nearby.

Despaña Foods *Specialty Shop*   27 | 23 | 23 | E

Little Italy | 408 Broome St. (bet. Cleveland Pl. & Lafayette St.) | 212-219-5050 | www.despananyc.com

(continued)

(continued)
Despaña Foods
Jackson Heights | 86-17 Northern Blvd. (bet. 86th & 87th Sts.) | Queens | 718-779-4971 | www.despanabrandfoods.com
888-779-8617

"*Que bueno!*" cheer champions of these "top-notch importers" of "the best of Spain" in Jackson Heights and Little Italy, where "helpful" staffers oversee an "enticing" trove of "hard-to-find" "delicacies", notably "luxurious" Serrano and Ibérico ham, housemade chorizo and a "terrific" array of cheeses; given the "awesome" lineup of "wonderful olive oils", rice and grains, cooking implements and grocery "basics" "from the home country", it's something "really special"; P.S. the Manhattan store's back counter turns out "incredibly tasty" sandwiches and tapas too.

Despaña Vinos Y Mas *Wines & Liquor* ▽ 28 | 24 | 24 | E

Little Italy | 410 Broome St. (bet. Cleveland Pl. & Lafayette St.) | 212-219-1550 | www.despanafinewines.com
When "you need a cava that isn't Freixenet" or seek that vintage "you once had in San Sebastián", try this "wonderful" wine store spun off from the Spanish specialty-foods standout Despaña, sited next door to its Little Italy flagship; it's a "tiny" source for some 400 regional wines and sherries from Spain (50 or so under $25) – many of which otherwise "can't be found outside the mother country" – with helpful tasting notes and a staff ready to guide novices.

Dickson's 28 | 26 | 26 | E
Farmstand Meats *Meat & Poultry*
🆕 **Chelsea** | Foragers City Grocer | 300 W. 22nd St. (bet. 8th & 9th Aves.) | 212-243-8888
Chelsea | Chelsea Mkt. | 75 Ninth Ave. (bet. 15th & 16th Sts.) | 212-242-2630
🆕 **TriBeCa** | All Good Things | 102 Franklin St. (bet. 6th Ave. & W. B'way) | 212-226-0120
www.dicksonsfarmstand.com

"Foodies and locavores" applaud the "real butchery" at Jacob Dickson's sleek Chelsea Market meat mart (with counters inside TriBeCa's All Good Things and Chelsea's Foragers), where the "incredible display" of "outstanding" humanely raised beef, lamb, pork, goat and poultry from regional farms strikes most as "well worth" the "high prices"; housemade sausages are another specialty, not to mention "delicious", "freshly made" sandwiches at lunchtime, and it even offers butchering classes.

Di Palo *Cheese & Dairy* 29 | 24 | 25 | M
Little Italy | 200 Grand St. (bet. Mott & Mulberry Sts.) | 212-226-1033 | www.dipaloselects.com
"Absolutely the best" for "fabulous" Italian formaggio (some 300 varieties), this "old-world" Little Italy "classic" with five generations of family-owned history behind it is "cherished" as an "unsurpassed" showcase for housemade mozzarella ("a religious experience"), "delectable" parmigiano, pecorino and other imports, as well as "superior" Boot-style "goodies" from pasta to prosciutto; the "warm" staff "will take care of you" "when it's your turn", and even the weekend "mob scene" is "well worth the detour" when only "the real thing" will do.

	QUALITY	DISPLAY	SERVICE	COST

Dominique Ansel Bakery *Baked Goods*

27	25	25	E

SoHo | 189 Spring St. (Thompson St.) | 212-219-2773 |
www.dominiqueansel.com

Pastry chef Dominique Ansel has created a "glorious piece of heaven"
with his SoHo patisserie, where the canelés, "citrusy madeleines", tarts,
cookies, "must-try" kouign amann and other "amazing" seasonal French
treats are as "lovely to look at" as they are "delicious" – and the recently
debuted cronut (a croissant-donut hybrid) has sweet tooths lining up at
the door; factor in savories served by an "incredibly nice staff" in a slim
space augmented with the "surprise treat" of a roomy back garden, and
to most it's "worth every penny" of the somewhat "pricey" tab.

Dorian's Seafood Market *Seafood*

26	22	25	E

E 80s | 1580 York Ave. (83rd St.) | 212-535-2736 | www.doriansseafood.com

Appreciated as an "old-style fishmonger", this "small" Yorkville outfit
purveys "terrific" "fresh seafood" as well as smoked fish and "delicious"
prepared foods like poached salmon, chowders and more; the "superb
service" includes on-the-spot oyster shucking and free delivery, and
though it can "cost you a fin and a leg", "the best quality" means "you
get what you pay for."

Dough ⊞ *Baked Goods*

▽ 26	22	21	M

Bed-Stuy | 305 Franklin Ave. (Lafayette Ave.) | Brooklyn | 347-533-7544

This "friendly" Bed-Stuy standout from the Choice Market folks specializes in airy, delicate, "delicious" yeast donuts with a "rainbow" of
"creative" glazes like dulce de leche with almonds or bright-pink hibis-
cus, as well as filled versions plumped with the likes of chai cream,
Nutella or spiced plum; new batches come out often as the day goes
on, as do the pots of French-press coffee to go with – no wonder "long
lines form daily" at prime times.

Doughnut Plant *Baked Goods*

27	17	20	M

Chelsea | Chelsea Hotel | 220 W. 23rd St. (bet. 7th & 8th Aves.) |
212-675-9100
LES | 379 Grand St. (bet. Essex & Norfolk Sts.) | 212-505-3700 ⊞
www.doughnutplant.com

A "pioneer" when it comes to "decadent", "drool-worthy donuts", this
Lower East Side factory and its roomier sibling inside the Chelsea Hotel
supply "sublime" examples, "fried, baked, glazed and stuffed" in 35
seasonally rotating "marvelous", "wild flavors" like chestnut, tres
leches, blackout and PB&J, all made with "fresh, natural ingredients";
it's "kinda pricey" and you should "be prepared for long lines", but
"you'll forget about" all that "from bite one."

Dry Dock ◐ *Wines & Liquor*

▽ 28	27	28	M

Red Hook | 424 Van Brunt St. (Van Dyke St.) | Brooklyn | 718-852-3625 |
www.drydockny.com

Moored in Red Hook, this boutique liquor store "fills a void" with its
"excellent", Italian-leaning lineup of some 500 "smartly chosen"
wines ("biodynamic" offerings included) and "deep bench" of small-
batch bourbons and single-malt scotches; given the "fair prices",
"thoughtful suggestions" from a "friendly" staff, tastings on weekends
and free neighborhood delivery of cases, "thrilled" locals marvel "what
more could you ask?"

QUALITY DISPLAY SERVICE COST

Duane Park Patisserie *Baked Goods* | 25 | 18 | 18 | E |

TriBeCa | 179 Duane St. (bet. Greenwich & Hudson Sts.) | 212-274-8447 | 877-274-8447 | www.duaneparkpatisserie.com
"TriBeCa's favorite neighborhood patisserie" is this "quiet" veteran specializing in "excellent" Austrian, French and German treats like "petits fours to die for", "gorgeous", "artistic" special-occasion cakes, "beautifully decorated" cookies, lemon curd tarts and other "quality" goodies baked "with heart"; "service is iffy", especially when it's busy in the usually "relaxing" cafe, but there's a "little park across the street" to retreat to once you've nabbed your sweet.

NEW Du Jour *Baked Goods* | - | - | - | M |

Park Slope | 365 Fifth Ave. (bet. 5th & 6th Sts.) | Brooklyn | 347-227-8953 | www.dujourbakery.com
Its name may be French, but this bakery/cafe along Park Slope's bustling Fifth Avenue strip offers lots of American favorites (muffins, cookies, donuts) alongside the viennoiserie and Gallic pastries, plus it specializes in custom cakes in designs from elegant to whimsical; the minimalist exposed-brick digs outfitted with wood two-tops are spare but cozy, and there's a back patio to enjoy during the summer months.

Durso's Pasta & Ravioli Co. *Pastas* | 26 | 21 | 24 | M |

Flushing | 189-01 Crocheron Ave. (Utopia Pkwy.) | Queens | 718-358-1311 | www.dursos.com
"Good luck getting out" of this "lovely, family-owned" "local gem" in Flushing "without a big bag of goodies", notably "fresh, delicious light pastas" that'll "melt in your mouth", plus "incredible sauces", sausages and cheeses or a "spectacular selection" of Italian prepared dishes "better than your momma made"; it's all served up by a staff of "professionals" who are "animated" and "helpful" – regulars have "never been disappointed."

D'Vine Taste ❶ *Specialty Shop* | 26 | 20 | 26 | M |

Park Slope | 150 Seventh Ave. (bet. Carroll St. & Garfield Pl.) | Brooklyn | 718-369-9548 | www.dvine-taste.com
"For that ingredient you can't find anywhere", this Park Slope Middle Eastern mart plies a "terrific array" of "excellent cheeses" and specialty grocery "treats" like spreads, dried fruits and a "great selection of spices", all at "reasonable prices"; with counters also vending an "amazing selection of prepared and baked goods" and a staff of "the world's nicest people", the "lucky folks" in the neighborhood "can't praise this shop enough."

Dylan's Candy Bar ❶ *Candy & Nuts* | 23 | 27 | 19 | E |

E 60s | 1011 Third Ave. (60th St.) | 646-735-0078 | 866-939-5267 | www.dylanscandybar.com
This "real-life Candyland" on the East Side is a "delight for the senses" declared "worth a special trip" given its 5,000-strong selection of "unusual and classic" candies, many "sold in bulk", spread over three "heavenly" floors; it "takes you back to your childhood" – in fact, "nostalgia is all around you" in the form of Charleston Chews, Mallo Cups, etc. – but just know it all "comes with a hefty price tag"; P.S. there's an ice cream/coffee bar "to boot."

	QUALITY	DISPLAY	SERVICE	COST

Eagle Provisions *Meat & Poultry* | 23 | 18 | 21 | M |

Greenwood Heights | 628 Fifth Ave. (18th St.) | Brooklyn | 718-499-0026
Located just south of Park Slope in Greenwood Heights but "spiritually based in Krakow", this old-school "neighborhood grocery" specializes in "hard-to-find" Eastern European comestibles and "fine cured meats", including house-smoked kielbasa; its "little-of-everything" selection includes an "extensive" array of oils, vinegars and similar provisions at "fair" prices, but most "amazing" of all may be its 2,000-plus lineup of imported and microbrew beers.

East Village Meat Market *Meat & Poultry* | 26 | 20 | 22 | M |

E Village | 139 Second Ave. (bet. 9th St. & St. Marks Pl.) | 212-228-5590
"The last of the great Ukrainian butchers" in the East Village, this "friendly", "old-fashioned" meatery "entices" with "prime" viands, "wonderful smoked meats" (including "the best kielbasa in the world"), plus "good-quality" poultry and "delicious fresh-baked tur-key"; imported Eastern European comestibles and "reasonable prices" are other lures for devoted customers, many of whom "have been shopping here since the '70s."

Eataly ● *Major Market* | 27 | 26 | 22 | E |

Flatiron | 200 Fifth Ave. (bet. 23rd & 24th Sts.) | 212-229-2560 | www.eataly.com
"Mamma mia!" – the Batali-Bastianich team's "Disneyworld" of "all things Italian" in the Flatiron, a "vast" outpost of a Turin chain, pres-ents a "dazzling" array of stations dispensing artisanal bread and 400 cheeses from Italy plus housemade mozz, "heavenly" fresh or dry pas-tas, "top-notch" prepared foods (eat in or take out), countless "im-ported gourmet" goods, "incredible" meats and seafood and "fantastic" produce; there's also cookware, coffee bars, a gelateria and next-door wine shop, as well as a cooking school overseen by Lidia Bastianich, so despite "not-cheap" pricing and "madhouse" crowds, all agree it's a "NYC must."

Economy Candy *Candy & Nuts* | 25 | 20 | 20 | I |

LES | 108 Rivington St. (bet. Essex & Ludlow Sts.) | 212-254-1531 | www.economycandy.com
"Amazing" "candy nostalgia" is the "blockbuster" attraction at this circa-1937 Lower East Side "wonderland" that's "packed floor-to-ceiling" with "retro and international" "sugary treats", including innumerable "old-school brands you never knew were still in production", plus "fresh nuts, dried fruit and halvah" too; "bargain prices" are yet an-other reason it's the "perfect" place to show the "kids and grandkids" what a "classic" is all about.

Egidio Pastry Shop *Baked Goods* | 25 | 23 | 23 | M |

Fordham | 622 E. 187th St. (Hughes Ave.) | Bronx | 718-295-6077
"Holy cannoli" – it's a century old, and this Arthur Avenue–area pasticceria is still known for "excellent Italian pastries", cakes, biscotti and cookies, including what may be the "best" pignoli va-riety "on the continent"; but despite the "delicious" baked goods, in summer insiders insist "you're here for the ices" in a staggering array of "traditional" flavors, while at Christmastime it's the place to go for gingerbread houses.

	QUALITY	DISPLAY	SERVICE	COST

Eileen's Special Cheesecake ◐ *Baked Goods*   25 | 18 | 21 | M

NoLita | 17 Cleveland Pl. (Kenmare St.) | 212-966-5585 | 800-521-2253 |
www.eileenscheesecake.com

A "must for any cheesecake-lover", this "exceptional" NoLita bakery
has "been around forever" (well, since the 1970s) turning out "light",
"fluffy" versions in varieties from Key lime to dulce de leche – good
thing the individual-size ones allow you to sample different flavors
"without feeling too guilty"; though it does a big web-order business,
locals claim it as one of their own "hidden gems" that happily "isn't
priced for tourists."

Eli's Bread and Pastry   *Baked Goods*   26 | 21 | 19 | E

E 40s | Grand Central Mkt. | 89 E. 42nd St. (bet. Park & Vanderbilt Aves.) |
646-503-3535 | www.elizabar.com

"Bread for all occasions" tempts carbophiles at Eli Zabar's stall in
Grand Central Market ("finally, a location that's easy to get to") stocking his famously "delish" hearth-baked, predominently sourdough
loaves, plus rolls, pastries and crisps; maybe "just looking at all their
goodies will put on the pounds", but acolytes claim eating 'em warm
"verges on a religious experience" – even if for some it's an act of faith
to pay prices "high to the point of ridiculousness."

Eli's Manhattan ◐ *Major Market*   25 | 24 | 21 | VE

E 80s | 1411 Third Ave. (80th St.) | 212-717-8100 |
www.elizabar.com

Procure "everything you might want and then some" at Eli Zabar's "upmarket" market, which indulges Upper Eastsiders with a cornucopia of
"quality" gourmet goods taking in "fabulous breads" and other bakery
"delights", droves of "delicious" cheeses, an "excellent" stock of specialty items, "inspired" prepared foods, "wonderful meats", "dependable" fish and an "abundant display" of "lovely produce"; "superb"
"quality is assured" throughout, though "sticker shock" can be "an issue" for those who feel it's "really too expensive for everyday."

Eli's Vinegar Factory ◐ *Major Market*   24 | 22 | 18 | VE

E 90s | 431 E. 91st St. (bet. 1st & York Aves.) | 212-987-0885 |
www.elizabar.com

Though "a little out of the way" on the UES, Eli Zabar's gourmet market-
cum–cafe flagship rewards the schlep with an "extensive" choice of
"first-rate" comestibles, from pristine "fresh" produce and "dependably" "excellent" house-baked breads to "wonderful" specialty groceries, "prime meats" and seafood, a "great variety" of "interesting
cheeses" and "gorgeous sandwiches" and prepared foods; some are
sour on the "sky-high prices", but for followers the overall appeal is
"oftentimes worth it."

Empire Cake ◐ *Baked Goods*   26 | 25 | 25 | E

Chelsea | 112 Eighth Ave. (bet. 15th & 16th Sts.) | 212-242-5858 |
www.empirecake.com

This "cute" Chelsea baker uses high-quality ingredients to prepare
"creative and delicious" baked goods with a retro-snack twist, meaning it's the "perfect" place for those who "always wondered what a
Twinkie would taste like if it weren't made by a team of scientists";
there's also a "divine" lineup of more classic desserts, like Southern

red velvet and organic carrot cakes, and "formal" wedding gateaux are also a specialty.

Empire Mayonnaise *Specialty Shop*

`- | - | - | M`

Prospect Heights | 564 Vanderbilt Ave. (bet. Bergen & Dean Sts.) | Brooklyn | 718-636-2069 | www.empiremayo.com

The brainchild of chef Sam Mason (ex wd~50) and his business partner, Elizabeth Valleau, this oh-so-Brooklyn artisanal mayonnaise business operates out of a closet-size Prospect Heights storefront – the retail area consists of a counter and a single display shelf – turning out small-batch mayos in au courant flavors like black garlic, bacon, lime pickle or vadouvan; a four-oz. jar runs $7, but then it's made with non-GMO oils and local, cage-free, pasture-raised eggs.

Enoteca Di Palo *Wines & Liquor*

`27 | 25 | 27 | M`

Little Italy | 200 Grand St. (bet. Mott & Mulberry Sts.) | 212-680-0545

"Unusual" vintages turn up at this all-Italian vino vendor annex to Little Italy's Di Palo Fine Foods, where 250-odd labels representing every region of The Boot yield "some very interesting" varietals "from small producers" at the "right price point"; "to help you choose", the staffers provide "knowledgeable" assistance and host regular tastings in the handsome, wood-beamed space – *salute!*

Esposito & Sons Pork Store ⌿ *Meat & Poultry*

`27 | 19 | 24 | M`

Carroll Gardens | 357 Court St. (bet. President & Union Sts.) | Brooklyn | 718-875-6863

It's "quality all the way" at this "real-deal", "old-school", third-generation Carroll Gardens Italian butcher that's been plying "excellent" pork in its many forms since 1922, most notably via a selection of "standout" house-cured sausages (salami, pepperoni and sopressata "you can't stop eating"); it's also a "standby" for imported provisions, aged cheeses and fresh mozzarella, as well as sandwiches and prepared foods like lasagna, eggplant parm and "delicious" arancini.

Esposito Meat Market *Meat & Poultry*

`27 | 20 | 26 | M`

Garment District | 500 Ninth Ave. (38th St.) | 212-279-3298 | www.espositomeatmarket.com

"A true old-time butcher shop", this Garment District stalwart is "famous for its pork" but also offers "optimum-quality" veal, lamb and poultry, plus "hard-to-find" game meats like buffalo, rabbit and venison – "not to mention" some of the "best sausages in town"; a family-owned biz that's "been around forever", it's appreciated more for "wonderful service and value" than "fancy-dancy" displays.

Ess-a-Bagel ◑ *Baked Goods*

`26 | 16 | 18 | I`

E 50s | 831 Third Ave. (bet. 50th & 51st Sts.) | 212-980-1010
Gramercy | 359 First Ave. (21st St.) | 212-260-2252
www.ess-a-bagel.com

"Bagels the size of hubcaps" will "hold you all day" at this ess-ential East Side duo, where "superior", "incredibly fresh" rounds that earn "props" for "perfect texture" ("crisp on the outside, soft and chewy on the inside") are topped with a "mind-boggling" choice of spreads; the "salty" "counter guys" exhibit "plenty of NY 'tude", but there's "nothing ersatz" here and "major lines on the weekends" only confirm a "hands-down winner" – "'nuff said."

QUALITY | DISPLAY | SERVICE | COST

Faicco's Pork Store   *Meat & Poultry*   `28` `23` `25` `M`

W Village | 260 Bleecker St. (bet. 6th & 7th Aves.) | 212-243-1974
Bay Ridge | 6511 11th Ave. (bet. 65th & 66th Sts.) | Brooklyn |
718-236-0119

"If you're not Italian, you will be as soon as you walk through the door"
of these "old-world" butchers/salumerias, "go-to destinations" for
"terrific" housemade sausages (fresh, dried and cured) and "expertly
cut" pork and meats "of all varieties", plus "excellent" cheeses, oils,
vinegars, housemade sauces, "ready-made specialties" and more;
"fair prices" and "counter guys" who're "all smiles" ensure these "in-
stitutions" remain "perfect local" standbys; P.S. the circa-1940 West
Village branch is the original, while the Bay Ridge offshoot is roomier.

Fairway ◐ *Major Market*   `25` `19` `18` `M`

E 80s | 240 E. 86th St. (bet. 2nd & 3rd Aves.) | 212-327-2008
Harlem | 2328 12th Ave. (bet. 132nd & 133rd Sts.) | 212-234-3883
Murray Hill | 550 Second Ave. (30th St.) | 646-720-9420
W 70s | 2127 Broadway (74th St.) | 212-595-1888
Red Hook | 480-500 Van Brunt St. (Reed St.) | Brooklyn | 718-234-0923
Douglaston | Douglaston Plaza Shopping Ctr. | 242-02 61st Ave.
(Douglaston Pkwy.) | Queens | 718-432-2100
www.fairwaymarket.com

"If it exists, you can find it" at this UWS gourmet "mainstay" and its
"warehouse-size" offshoots, where shoppers are "spoiled" by the
"phenomenal selection", "reliable quality" and "fair prices" on produce
that's "perfection" "piled high", a "super" assortment of "enticing"
cheeses, "delicious prepared foods", a "profusion" of natural items, a
"world market" of "tempting" specialty goods, "outstanding" seafood
and "the freshest" prime meat; it takes "sterner stuff" to cope with the
"chaotic" "throngs", but loyalists "never tire" of this all-purpose "paradise"; P.S. a new Chelsea store at 766 Sixth Avenue is in the works.

Filling Station ◐ *Specialty Shop*   `25` `24` `23` `M`

Chelsea | Chelsea Mkt. | 75 Ninth Ave. (bet. 15th & 16th Sts.) |
212-989-3868 | www.thefillingstationnyc.com

Epicures fuel up at this Chelsea Market stall whose "amazing" oleaginous inventory features "excellent olive oils" – some 15 imported and
domestic varieties – which customers purchase in bottles that they
can bring back to refill at a 10% discount; other renewable offerings
include vinegars, "wonderful" sea salts (both flavored and not) and
unrefined sugars, not to mention growlers of "excellent craft brews" –
but, alas, those are for "take-away only, no samples."

Financier Patisserie   *Baked Goods*   `25` `24` `20` `M`

E 40s | Brookfield Property | 245 Park Ave. (47th St.) | 212-687-9000
E 40s | Grand Central Terminal | main concourse, 42nd St. Passage
(42nd St. & Vanderbilt Ave.) | 212-973-1010 ◐
E 50s | 983 First Ave. (54th St.) | 212-419-0100 ◐
E 50s | 989 Third Ave. (59th St.) | 212-486-2919
Financial District | Winter Garden | 3-4 World Financial Ctr. (Vesey &
West Sts.) | 212-786-3220
Financial District | 35 Cedar St. (bet. Pearl & William Sts.) |
212-952-3838 ◐
Financial District | 62 Stone St. (bet. Mill Ln. & William St.) |
212-344-5600 ◐

(continued)

Financier Patisserie
Financial District | 90 Nassau St. (Fulton St.) | 212-748-6000
NoHo | 2 Astor Pl. (Broadway) | 212-228-2787
W 40s | 1211 Sixth Ave. (48th St.) | 212-381-4418
www.financierpastries.com

These proliferating "taste-of-Paris" patisseries proffer "gorgeous" French sweets that "live up to their appearance", including "to-die-for" éclairs, tarts, "the best macarons" and "delicate" croissants, plus sandwiches and salads for the lunch crowd; "clean and bright-looking" digs make up for any service miscues, while the "delicious" "tiny" financiers given "free with coffee" further sweeten the deal.

Fish Tales *Seafood*   27 | 24 | 24 | E
Cobble Hill | 191A Court St. (bet. Bergen & Wyckoff Sts.) | Brooklyn | 718-246-1346 | www.fishtalesonline.com

Expect "fish so fresh you want to slap them" at this "classy" little Cobble Hill market, an "excellent" purveyor of "treasures from the sea" where "the best catch of the day" is lovingly laid out on ice and a slew of premade fin fare is "cooked to a tee"; "it's not cheap", but the "personal service" is "always a pleasure" and hey, "quality costs."

Flatiron Wines & Spirits ◐ *Wines & Liquor*   – | – | – | M
Flatiron | 929 Broadway (22nd St.) | 212-477-1315 |
www.flatiron-wines.com

This exposed-brick and natural wood–lined Flatiron vintner showcases small-producer wines and liquors, originating everywhere from Burgundy to Brooklyn, with a focus on organic and biodynamic selections; sensible prices (check out the 'grab and go' $15-and-under tables), online ordering and free neighborhood delivery are further endearments.

Fleisher's Grass-fed &   ▽ 29 | 24 | 28 | E
Organic Meats *Meat & Poultry*
Park Slope | 192 Fifth Ave. (bet. Sackett & Union Sts.) | Brooklyn | 718-398-6666 | www.fleishers.com

"What a thrill to have it here" enthuse Park Slopers of this offshoot of the renowned Upstate meatery practicing the utmost in "modern butchery" with its nose-to-tail treatment of "humanely raised", pastured, all-natural animals from small, local, sustainable farms, resulting in some of the "best-tasting" beef, pork, lamb and poultry going, not to mention "great sausages" in numerous varieties, bacon, cold cuts, dairy, pot pies and – proving nothing is wasted – tallow soap; "sure, it costs more", but given the "wonderful" quality and "excellent", "no-attitude" service, most declare "hang the expense."

Florence Prime Meat Market *Meat & Poultry*   29 | 18 | 27 | M
W Village | 5 Jones St. (bet. Bleecker & W. 4th Sts.) |
212-242-6531

A "NYC treasure" since 1936, this tiny West Village butcher shop is beloved for its "finest"-quality meats aged in-house and "cut to your exact specifications" by "friendly" countermen who show "superb attention" to their craft; the "charm" is enhanced by the "screen door", "sawdust on the floor" and "house cat", not to mention the "reasonable" prices (as a particular "bargain" the "Newport steak is a classic"); P.S. it also vends sausages, game and organic poultry, but whatever your order, consider calling ahead to "save time."

Foods of India   *Herbs & Spices*   `23` `17` `17` `I`
Murray Hill | 121 Lexington Ave. (bet. 28th & 29th Sts.) | 212-683-4419

"They have everything" to flavor a subcontinental spread at this Murray Hill spice shop, a long-standing "go-to for all things Indian" that "hasn't changed in years" according to fans of its broad array of "fresh", "exotic" seasonings; best of all, it'll put the kick in your curry at prices that are "often less" than the competition's.

Foragers City Grocer ◑   *Major Market*   ▽ `26` `23` `18` `E`
Chelsea | Gem Hotel | 300 W. 22nd St. (8th Ave.) | 212-243-8888
Dumbo | 56 Adams St. (Front St.) | Brooklyn | 718-801-8400
www.foragerscitygrocer.com

The bodega-size fancy-foods "favorite" in Dumbo has been joined by a roomy Chelsea offshoot, and both are strong on organic, regionally sourced and "unusual" items, including cheeses, grass-fed meat, sustainable seafood, vegetables harvested from a Columbia County farm, NYC-made goods and tempting prepared foods; however, the Manhattan location also boasts an on-site cafe and an adjacent wine store.

Formaggio Essex   *Cheese & Dairy*   `27` `21` `25` `E`
LES | Essex Street Mkt. | 120 Essex St. (bet. Delancey & Rivington Sts.) | 212-982-8200 | www.formaggioessex.com

In an Essex Street Market berth not much bigger than a "shoebox", this offshoot of a beloved Cambridge, MA, gourmet store squeezes in an "amazing selection" of the "highest-quality" imported European cheeses and "excellent" housemade charcuterie, plus high-end olive oils, pastas, beans, grains and baked goods; it's "not cheap", but "passionate", "personable" staffers who "share their expertise" – "no matter how busy" they are – compensate; P.S. it also does a big web-order business.

Fortunato Bros. ◑⊟   *Baked Goods*   `27` `23` `21` `M`
Williamsburg | 289 Manhattan Ave. (Devoe St.) | Brooklyn | 718-387-2281

"One of the great Italian pastry shops from the old school", this Williamsburg "institution" has been around since "way before the neighborhood got trendy", maintaining its reputation with "better-than-mama's" cannoli, sfogliatelle, lobster tails, cookies and marzipan treats almost "too gorgeous to eat"; the "unpretentious" vibe makes it a "nice place to sit with a cup of coffee", but just keep in mind the "step-back-in-time" milieu is complete with a "cash-only" policy.

Four & Twenty Blackbirds ⊟   *Baked Goods*   ▽ `26` `19` `24` `M`
Gowanus | 439 Third Ave. (8th St.) | Brooklyn | 718-499-2917 | www.birdsblack.com

Doing a "formidable job" with fruit pies and other "amazing" buttery-crusted creations, this "charming" shop "off the beaten path" in Gowanus offers a "daily changing" array of pies like "what grandma made but with a twist" – apple-cheddar, honeyed fig, salted caramel – crafted by hand in an open kitchen and sold by the slice ("call in advance" to order 'em whole); with its "homey" space sporting "rustic wood" tables, "sweet" service and Irving Farm coffee, it's perfect for on-site snacking.

Francois Payard Bakery *Baked Goods*   ▽ 27 | 25 | 21 | E

Financial District | 210 Murray St. (bet. North End Ave. & West St.) | 212-566-8300
G Village | 116 W. Houston St. (bet. Sullivan & Thompson Sts.) | 212-995-0888
W 50s | 1775 Broadway (58th St.) | 212-956-1775 ◐
www.fpbnyc.com

FP Patisserie *Baked Goods*

E 70s | 1293 Third Ave. (74th St.) | 212-717-5252 | www.fppatisserie.com ◐
W 50s | Plaza Food Hall | 1 W. 59th St., lower level (5th Ave.) | 212-759-1600 | www.fcchocolatebar.com

Rapturous fans of pâtissier extraordinaire François Payard and his "classic but casual" French bakeries and patisseries (the sleek Upper Eastsider is the flagship) insist the "fabulous" treats will "transport you from your troubles" – too-good-to-be-true" treats like macarons, tarts and "to-die-for" croissants that have devotees declaring "I'm back in Paris!"; "beautiful packaging and presentation" and "friendly, efficient" service ice the cake.

Georgetown Cupcake ◐ *Baked Goods*   27 | 26 | 25 | M

SoHo | 111 Mercer St. (bet. Prince & Spring Sts.) | 212-431-4504 | www.georgetowncupcake.com

The baker sisters from TLC's *DC Cupcakes* bring their "delectable" desserts to the Big Apple with this "cute" SoHo shop serving up "moist" "drool-worthy" creations in a "wide variety" of "playful" rotating flavors (plus coffee and tea) sure to "satisfy sweet tooths"; the "lines" and prices are what you'd expect, but devotees deem it a "true treat."

Good Beer Store ◐ *Beer*   ▽ 27 | 24 | 26 | M

E Village | 422 E. Ninth St. (bet. Ave. A & 1st Ave.) | 212-677-4836 | www.goodbeernyc.com

It's brewski bliss at this East Village beer bazaar whose nearly 600 labels (80% domestic craft brews, 20% imported) can make for an occasionally "overwhelming" shopping experience, but you can always "ask the staff to point you in the right direction"; there's also a dozen taps flowing with an ever-changing lineup that customers can buy by the refillable growler or sample at an in-store cafe serving charcuterie to go with pints and tasting flights – the smitten swear this place should be redubbed "Great Beer."

Grace's Marketplace ◐ *Major Market*   25 | 23 | 20 | VE

E 70s | 1237 Third Ave. (71st St.) | 212-737-0600 | www.gracesmarketplace.com

This enduring Upper East Side gourmet market stays in the neighborhood's good graces with "friendly" service and inventory that's "lovely to behold and taste", extending to "glorious" baked goods, an abundance of "the best cheeses", prepared foods "tasty" enough "to pass off as your own", "quality meats and poultry" from "helpful butchers", "always-fresh" produce and various "difficult-to-find" specialty items; granted, it's "crowded" and "expensive", but loyalists insist it's a "pleasure spending too much money" here.

Grandaisy Bakery *Baked Goods*   25 | 19 | 21 | M

TriBeCa | 250 W. Broadway (Beach St.) | 212-334-9435
W 70s | 176 W. 72nd St. (Amsterdam Ave.) | 212-334-9435
www.grandaisybakery.com

"Fantastic artisanal" breads are the showstoppers at these bakeries whose yeasty lineup ranges from "addictive" focaccia to one of the "best Pullman loaves in NY", and there are also "delightful nibbles" like the "terrific" olive rolls, "sublime" thin-crust pizzas and seasonal panettone; its TriBeCa-UWS storefronts are on the "small and simple" side, but never mind – they "always smell great."

The Greene Grape ❶ *Wines & Liquor*   22 | 19 | 23 | M

Fort Greene | 765 Fulton St. (bet. Portland Ave. & S. Oxford St.) | Brooklyn | 718-797-9463 | www.greenegrape.com

"Pick up a bottle" on "the trip home" at this Fort Greene wine merchant that's a "local favorite" for its "limited" but "excellent" stock centered on small, family-run vintners, as well as a "small choice of premium spirits"; it hosts tastings of "rarely seen" varietals and gets points for its "really reasonable price range" as well.

Greene Grape Provisions ❶ *Specialty Shop*   ▽ 27 | 21 | 25 | E

Fort Greene | 753 Fulton St. (S. Portland Ave.) | Brooklyn | 718-233-2700 | www.greenegrape.com

Bringing "more choice" to Fort Greene with its "variety of excellent foods", this "cute little" gourmet market "matchbox" (sib of the nearby Greene Grape wine shop) stocks an often-organic mix with highlights like fresh meat and fish, "local produce", "nice cheeses", baked goods and even microbrews; "it's going to cost you", but the staff is "warm and knowledgeable" and "you always know the quality's superb."

Greenmarket *Produce*   29 | 24 | 23 | M

Union Sq | Union Sq. | B'way & 17th St. | 212-788-7476 | www.grownyc.org | Mon./Wed./Fri./Sat., Year-round
For a full list of Greenmarket locations, see p. 307

"The farm comes to the city" via this "beloved" network of markets throughout the five boroughs (the Union Square "mecca" is the largest), where regional growers and producers vend "gorgeous", just-picked produce and "the freshest" meats, cheese, seafood, "homemade" baked goods, flowers and "fabulous" finds "you didn't know existed"; they're "a must-visit for foodies", chefs from "many of the top restaurants" and local-sustainable enthusiasts who concur quality "doesn't get better" – especially if you "get there early."

Gustiamo *Specialty Shop*   – | – | – | M

Fairmont-Claremont Village | 1715 W. Farms Rd. (Sheridan Expwy.) | Bronx | 718-860-2949 | 877-907-2525 | www.gustiamo.com

"Love their stuff" gush *amici* of this Bronx-based importer of Italian goods, where pricey but "wonderful artisanal foods" (many "not available anywhere else") – including top-quality pastas, oils, vinegars and jarred items - are carefully chosen from small suppliers and shipped exclusively from The Boot; while the store's situated well off the beaten path in Claremont Village, it's popular with online shoppers who can procure its regional delicacies and gift baskets through the website.

	QUALITY	DISPLAY	SERVICE	COST

Harney & Sons *Coffee & Tea*   28 | 25 | 26 | M

SoHo | 433 Broome St. (bet. B'way & Crosby St.) | 212-933-4853 |
888-427-6398 | www.harney.com

It's always tea time at this "beautiful" SoHo outpost of a Millerton, NY,
shop that has gained a wide following for its "marvelous", "reasonably
priced" teas, which can be sampled at a tasting bar, and there's also a
"nice little cafe in back" for enjoying a cuppa with scones and other
treats; its "bazillion varieties" (well, 250) – black, white, green, oolong,
herbal, fruit, decaf, kosher – are packaged in trademark tins and displayed on wooden shelves, along with pots and assorted accoutrements, and overseen by a "friendly", "über-knowledgeable" staff.

Heritage Meat Shop *Meat & Poultry*   ∇ 27 | 21 | 25 | M

LES | Essex Street Mkt. | 120 Essex St. (bet. Delancey & Rivington Sts.) |
212-539-1111 | www.heritagemeatshop.com

When you need to know the pedigree of your pork chop, this Essex
Street Market outpost of the online artisanal butcher Heritage Foods
USA fills the bill, with a "lovely" counter staff to shepherd conscientious carnivores as they select cuts from heirloom animals humanely
raised on independent farms, including beef, pork, goat, poultry and
more, plus bacon, "holy cow"–good salumi and sandwiches at lunchtime; no wonder meat-lovers declare it a "great place to buy" and "worth
every penny" of the unsurprisingly higher-than-supermarket prices.

Hester Street Fair *Specialty Shop*   21 | 20 | 20 | M

LES | Hester & Essex Sts. | 917-267-9496 | www.hesterstreetfair.com

"Walk, shop and chow down" at this seasonal Lower East Side weekend "street fair", where the 50-plus stalls include "friendly vendors" of
"so much yummy food", from cookies, brownies and pretzels to Luke's
Lobster rolls; it's on the "smaller" side (think a "mellow cousin to the
Brooklyn Flea"), but if you "go hungry" there's more than "enough to
keep yourself occupied" here.

Hot Bagels & Bialys ◑ *Baked Goods*   25 | 17 | 21 | I

Midwood | 1615 Kings Hwy. (E. 17th St.) | Brooklyn |
718-627-9868

Bagels "chewy and dense with a perfect crust" (the "nearest thing to
heaven") plus "can't-be-beat" bialys earn this unpretentious storefront a reputation as the carbophile's "Shangri-la of Midwood"; its
ever-steamy windows hint at the fact that its traditionally made
goods, available in the usual range of flavors, are made fresh throughout the day – and sold into the wee hours.

Hot Bread Almacen *Baked Goods*   - | - | - | M

Harlem | La Marqueta | 1590 Park Ave. (115th St.) | 212-369-3331 |
www.hotbreadkitchen.org

The retail arm of a nonprofit culinary training program for low-income
immigrant women, this airy stand in East Harlem's La Marqueta showcases multiethnic breads (Moroccan flatbread, Armenian lavash
crackers, tortillas) inspired by its diverse workforce, as well as standards like sourdough and a 'New Yorker' rye; sip espresso from the
window-side breakfast bar over an eggy 'Bialy al Barrio', or choose
from buttered toasts freshly fired in the on-site production facility, run
by Per Se baker Ben Hershberger.

	QUALITY	DISPLAY	SERVICE	COST

NEW House of Cupcakes ● *Baked Goods*

| - | - | - | M |

W Village | 101 Seventh Ave. S. (Grove St.) | 212-255-7102
Baychester | Bay Plaza Shopping Ctr. | 2100 Bartow Ave. (Co-Op City Blvd.) | Bronx | 718-379-4500
www.houseofcupcakes.com

Offshoots of a popular Princeton bakery that was a winner of the Food Network's *Cupcake Wars* a couple of years back, these Village-Baychester shops – links of a planned franchise – seek to set themselves apart from the copious competition with dozens of flavors both familiar (carrot cake, red velvet) and less so (rosebud, pistachio–white chocolate); options to personalize with photos or messages, weekly giveaways and bright, cheery interiors are further lures.

House of Spices *Herbs & Spices*

| ▽ 26 | 18 | 19 | M |

Flushing | 127-40 Willets Point Blvd. (Northern Blvd.) | Queens | 718-507-4600 | www.hosindia.com

An "interesting concept" for an out-of-the-way Flushing warehouse, this well-established Indian importer is home to a "tremendous array of spices for all" your South Asian culinary needs; it's also a bountiful cache of beans, nuts, oils, pickles, pastes, chutneys, sweets and frozen meals, typically sold wholesale but also retailed for nice prices to those willing to venture out.

Ideal Cheese *Cheese & Dairy*

| 27 | 21 | 23 | E |

E 50s | 942 First Ave. (52nd St.) | 212-688-7579 | 800-382-0109 | www.idealcheese.com

An "incredible assortment" of "luscious" cheeses "from around the world" plus an "excellent array" of "go-withs" (e.g. "meats, pâtés, crackers" and even beer) help this East Side shop "live up to its name", while "first-cabin" service from "knowledgeable" folk push it over the top; they'll even "pack goodies to take away for the weekend", so "you'll leave every time with a smile" – or at least saying 'cheese.'

Il Buco Alimentari e Vineria ● *Specialty Shop*

| ▽ 25 | 24 | 23 | E |

NoHo | 53 Great Jones St. (bet. Bowery & Lafayette St.) | 212-837-2622 | www.ilbucovineria.com

"Outstanding" house-cured salumi is the star at this Italian market inside Il Buco's "charming" wine bar/eatery in NoHo, which also dispenses artisanal cheeses, housemade breads, pastas and gelato, not to mention "some of the best sandwiches" around, plus dry goods like sea salt, olive oils and vinegars; it's all overseen by a "helpful, knowledgeable" counter crew, and for those who want to *mangia* on the spot, there's an adjacent cafe area that's a combination coffee bar/*vineria*.

Italian Wine Merchants *Wines & Liquor*

| 29 | 26 | 26 | E |

Union Sq | 108 E. 16th St. (bet. Irving Pl. & Union Sq. E.) | 212-473-2323 | www.italianwinemerchants.com

"Like a museum for wine", this Union Square boutique shop deals mostly in "fine Italian" vintages, showcasing an "amazing selection" from "all regions" (rare finds included) displayed "art-gallery" style and curated by a "most informed" staff that's ready with "wonderful service and recommendations"; insiders say "you'd better cash in a CD" first – but to most it's worth the "splurge" since if it's "on their shelves, you know it has to be good."

	QUALITY	DISPLAY	SERVICE	COST

Ivy Bakery ● *Baked Goods*   25 | 26 | 26 | M

G Village | 138 W. Houston St. (bet. MacDougal & Sullivan Sts.) |
347-598-3452 | www.ivybakery.com

Relocated from Bay Ridge to roomier exposed-brick quarters in the
Village, this reasonably priced bakery offers all the usual sweet sus-
pects ("moist" cookies, parfaits and by-the-slice cake and tart selections) along with "good savory pies" and more than 600 custom choices
for special diets or special occasions; factor in late-night hours, solid
service, weekly baking classes and live music and it's no surprise pro-
ponents pronounce it the "perfect neighborhood spot."

Jacques Torres Chocolate   *Candy & Nuts*   28 | 26 | 23 | E

Chelsea | Chelsea Mkt. | 75 Ninth Ave. (bet. 15th & 16th Sts.) |
212-229-2441
Hudson Square | 350 Hudson St. (King St.) | 212-414-2462
W 40s | Rockefeller Ctr. | 30 Rockefeller Plaza, concourse level
(bet. 49th & 50th Sts.) | 212-664-1804
W 70s | 285 Amsterdam Ave. (bet. 73rd & 74th Sts.) |
212-787-3256
Dumbo | 66 Water St. (bet. Dock & Main Sts.) | Brooklyn | 718-875-9772

Jacques Torres Ice Cream   *Ice Cream*

Dumbo | 62 Water St. (bet. Dock & Main Sts.) | Brooklyn | 718-875-9772
www.mrchocolate.com

"Willy Wonka has nothing" on "chocolate wizard" Jacques Torres and
his mini-empire, where the "mind-boggling variety" of "vaunted" confections runs from "glorious" truffles and other "grown-up" bonbons to
"chocolate-covered cornflakes" and "warm, melty" cookies; "snazzy
presentation" is a given, while the "high prices" are deemed "oh, so
worth it", especially when you can "watch the candy get made" at
some branches, and even the Chelsea Market stall serves the "incomparable" hot chocolate deemed so "heavenly" It's "sinful"; P.S. the
shop next to the Dumbo original specializes in "OMG" ice cream.

Japan Premium Beef, Inc.   *Meat & Poultry*   ∇ 29 | 25 | 26 | VE

NoHo | 57 Great Jones St. (Bowery) | 212-260-2333 |
www.japanpremiumbeef.jimdo.com

In-the-know carnivores question whether "there is a better cut of beef
in the city" than those exemplars found at this sleek NoHo Japanese
butcher, which specializes in domestically bred, Kobe-style Wagyu
beef; whether it's sold as rib-eyes, the "best strip steaks ever" or cuts
trimmed on request for Japanese BBQ, the luxurious, intensely marbled meat comes at a premium – "but man, is it worth it."

Kalustyan's   *Specialty Shop*   21 | 20 | 19 | M

Murray Hill | 123 Lexington Ave. (bet. 28th & 29th Sts.) | 212-685-3451 |
800-352-3451 | www.kalustyans.com

Dubbed "the mother lode of spices" for its "endless variety" of "superb" Indian and Mideastern seasonings, this "amazing" Murray Hill
"bazaar" is also a "staggering" grocery "cornucopia" where "chefs
looking for inspiration" can browse a "brilliant selection" of items both
"common and exotic" – "wonderful dried fruit", nuts, rice, beans, frozen
foods, "teas galore", fresh flatbreads, cookware or "you name it" – all
at "pretty reasonable prices"; add a "hidden" "cafe upstairs" serving
"delish" prepared specialties, and there's "always a lot to discover."

QUALITY DISPLAY SERVICE COST

Kam Man *Specialty Shop*   21 | 15 | 11 | I

Chinatown | 200 Canal St. (bet. Mott & Mulberry Sts.) | 212-571-0330 | www.newkamman.com

"No matter what you need for an Asian kitchen, they've got it" at this Chinatown vet, still a "best bet" for "authentic" Eastern eats (dried goods, frozen items, sweets, teas and prepared specialties like BBQ duck) along with the equipment to cook them with and "dishes to serve them in" from the housewares section downstairs; it takes "patience to hunt" around and there's "very little service", but the "great buys" make for many happy kampers all the same; P.S. the upper level deals in beauty supplies.

Kee's Chocolates *Candy & Nuts*   28 | 21 | 22 | E

Garment District | 315 W. 39th St. (bet. 8th & 9th Aves.) | 212-967-8088
SoHo | 80 Thompson St. (bet. Broome & Spring Sts.) | 212-334-3284
W 40s | HSBC Bldg. | 452 Fifth Ave. (40th St.) | 212-525-6099
www.keeschocolates.com

"Chocolate goddess" Kee Ling Tong offers "the most gastronomically forward" bonbons of "any chocolatier in the city" according to acolytes of her tiny SoHo storefront and Midtown offshoots, where the "dreamlike" handcrafted confections' "smooth texture" and "exotic" flavors – from "addictive" crème brûlée and passion fruit to "particularly sinful" Asian-accented "black sesame" – "satisfy even the most discriminating palates"; just "get there early" as the "best ones are gone by midday" – "that's how fresh they are, and how popular."

Kossar's Bialys ⌀ *Baked Goods*   26 | 13 | 17 | I

LES | 367 Grand St. (bet. Essex & Norfolk Sts.) | 212-253-2138 | www.kossarsbialys.com

It doesn't get "better", "fresher" or "more authentic" for bagels, bulkas and bialys than at this circa-1935 Lower East Side "landmark", a "bare-bones" storefront turning out "superb" "old-country" carbs "baked daily" (they're "hot! hot! hot!") the way "bubbie's bubbie used to make"; here "nothing changes" and you "can't beat the prices", so "get down" to Grand Street and sample the "real thing" – but just "don't go on Saturdays because they're closed."

Kusmi Tea *Coffee & Tea*   ▽ 26 | 24 | 24 | E

E 50s | Plaza Food Hall | 1 W. 59th St. (5th Ave.) | 212-486-2843
E 60s | 1037 Third Ave. (bet. 61st & 62nd Sts.) | 212-355-5580
www.kusmitea.com

A "gem" on the East Side, this "inviting Parisian import" (with a sibling inside the Plaza Food Hall) specializes in "absolutely delicious" teas of the "highest quality" packaged in "beautiful", colorful tins and presented in a sleekly "gorgeous" space; 140-plus years of "integrity" goes into the "large selection of flavored and herbal" blends – detox, "Russian-style" Prince Vladimir, etc. – while "friendly" staffers who "know their tea" ensure it's a prime "place for a gift", but "oh, those prices!"

La Bergamote *Baked Goods*   26 | 25 | 19 | E

Chelsea | 177 Ninth Ave. (20th St.) | 212-627-9010
W 50s | 515 W. 52nd St. (bet. 10th & 11th Aves.) | 212-586-2429
www.labergamotenyc.com

Find the "true French cafe experience" at this Chelsea patisserie whose "gorgeous and delicious pastries" are showcased in "pretty"

quarters in Chelsea and at a "lovely" West Hell's Kitchen offshoot; regulars praise the likes of "jewellike tarts" and "irresistible" *souris au chocolat* (chocolate mice) as well as some of the "best croissants in NYC", even if it's all offered up with a bit of "attitude."

La Boîte à Epice *Herbs & Spices*   - | - | - | M

W 50s | 724 11th Ave. (bet. 51st & 52nd Sts.) | 212-247-4407 | www.laboiteny.com

From a chef who has worked for big names like Daniel Boulud, this Hell's Kitchen sliver specializes in unusual spice blends inspired by the owner's travels, including some 40 mixtures, such as Mishmish (crystallized honey, saffron, lemon), Ararat (Urfa biber, smoked paprika, fenugreek) and Pierre Poivre (a mix of eight peppercorns); also on offer are biscuits – actually sweet and savory cookies – that change seasonally and are developed in collaboration with an artist whose work adorns the packages; P.S. open Wednesday to Friday, 3–7 PM.

L.A. Burdick Handmade   28 | 24 | 23 | E
Chocolates ● *Candy & Nuts*

Flatiron | 5 E. 20th St. (bet. B'way & 5th Ave.) | 212-796-0143 | www.burdickchocolate.com

The Flatiron's "charming" cafe/sweets shop from the New Hampshire-based confectioner is known for its "exquisitely crafted and flavored" artisanal chocolates, ranging from animal shapes (those trademark "tiny mice" are "conversation pieces") to "all sorts of truffles", bonbons, bars and dipped fruit; there are also "terrific pastries in a vaguely Viennese" style, perfect for nibbling on-site with some hot chocolate so "heavenly", the "Swiss Miss would hang up her apron if she tried it."

Ladybird Bakery *Baked Goods*   27 | 24 | 23 | E

Park Slope | 1112 Eighth Ave. (bet. 11th & 12th Sts.) | Brooklyn | 718-499-8108 | www.ladybirdbakery.com

A longtime "Park Slope treasure", this "teeny", "friendly" storefront is beloved by the neighborhood for its "top-quality baked goods" – "addictive" scones and cookies, "fantastically good" fruit tarts and cupcakes – that "taste just like granny's"; it specializes in "truly delicious" birthday and wedding cakes, and while there are a few grumbles about "Manhattan prices", most don't mind much considering that the decorations are "so freakin' beautiful."

Lady M Cake Boutique *Baked Goods*   29 | 28 | 23 | VE

E 70s | 41 E. 78th St. (bet. Madison & Park Aves.) | 212-452-2222
Lady M at The Plaza Food Hall *Baked Goods*

E 50s | Plaza Food Hall | 1 W. 59th St. (5th Ave.) | 646-755-3225 www.ladym.com

This "refined" UES boutique (with a Plaza Food Hall offshoot) is famed for its "exquisite" signature mille crêpes gateau, comprising numerous layers of custard and pastry, and other "light, delicious, dainty" Japanese-inspired cakes displayed like gems in a "jewel box"; it fairly "drips with elegance" – you may "feel like you have to be dressed-up" just to enter – and prices are accordingly "expensive", but "ladylike" devotees declare it "well worth the splurge"; P.S. a Bryant Park location is in the works at 32 West 40th Street.

	QUALITY	DISPLAY	SERVICE	COST

La Maison du Chocolat *Candy*

29 | 28 | 24 | VE

E 50s | Plaza Food Hall | 1 W. 58th St. (5th Ave.) | 212-355-3436
E 70s | 1018 Madison Ave. (bet. 78th & 79th Sts.) | 212-744-7117
Financial District | 63 Wall St. (bet. Hanover & Pearl Sts.) |
212-952-1123
W 40s | Rockefeller Ctr. | 30 Rockefeller Ctr. (49th St., bet. 5th & 6th Aves.) |
212-265-9404
www.lamaisonduchocolat.com

It's "the next best thing" to being in Paris sigh the smitten who "swoon over" the "spectacular variety" of "divine", "luxurious" French chocolates in *très* "unique" flavors, not to mention "perfect macarons", at this "upscale" Madison Avenue boutique/cafe and its siblings around town; prices are in the "investment-banker" range, but the "delectable" goods in "beautiful", haut packaging and "insanely smooth" hot chocolate are deemed "well worth it" – it's the "best way to self-medicate after a bad day."

La Maison du Macaron *Baked Goods*

▽ 28 | 25 | 22 | E

Chelsea | 132 W. 23rd St. (bet. 6th & 7th Aves.) | 212-243-2757 |
www.nymacaron.com

A "true macaron mecca", this Chelsea patisserie has earned favorable comparisons to "Laudurée in Paris" for its "amazing" meringue cookie sandwiches, whose wide variety of flavors includes caramel, pistachio and chocolate; savory treats like a "super" croque monsieur and "fantastic" ham-and-cheese croissant round out the offerings, and if they're served with *un peu* of "traditional French crankiness", at least "your mouth will be in heaven."

Lamazou *Cheese & Dairy*

26 | 19 | 24 | M

Murray Hill | 370 Third Ave. (bet. 26th & 27th Sts.) | 212-532-2009 |
www.lamazoucheese.com

"Treat yourself" at this "tiny" but "impressive" Murray Hill European cheese and prepared-foods shop that garners praise for its "spectacular variety" of fromage and draws "lunchtime lines" for its "excellent" sandwiches made with "fresh, authentic ingredients"; "charming" service and low prices have locals "loving this place."

NEW LeChurro ● *Baked Goods*

- | - | - | I

E 80s | 1236 Lexington Ave. (bet. 83rd & 84th Sts.) | 646-649-5253 |
www.lechurro.com

Madrid meets the Upper East Side at this sleek Spanish bakery where the made-to-order namesake sweets come stuffed with fillings or primed for dipping into a variety of sauces – like caramel and passion fruit – or dunking into hot cocoa and espresso; the modern, bite-size digs are equipped with a few two-tone tables, but otherwise a milkshake and a 'cone of churros' make a take-out treat for minimal dough.

Le Dû's Wines *Wines & Liquor*

29 | 26 | 28 | E

W Village | 600 Washington St. (bet. Leroy & Morton Sts.) |
212-924-6999 | www.leduwines.com

"When you can't find it anywhere else", this "excellent" West Village vintner run by "charming" "top sommelier" Jean-Luc Le Dû (a Daniel alum) lovingly displays a "carefully chosen stock" of "world-class wines" highlighting "hard-to-get or obscure" vintages "from all regions", plus spirits and sake; "informative" staffers are "happy to guide" greenhorns and conduct weekly tastings, but as this is "not just the same old" selection, don't be surprised if prices are "on the high side."

Lee Lee's ✍ *Baked Goods*   - | - | - | I

Harlem | 283 W. 118th St. (Frederick Douglass Blvd.) | 917-493-6633
'Rugalach by a brother' is the tagline for this Harlem bakery where the namesake owner, a local fixture, crafts his own take on the traditional Jewish pastry in apricot, raspberry and chocolate versions, alongside other sugary staples; housed in a modest red-and-white-tiled storefront, it sweetens the deal with budget-friendly prices and mail-order delivery.

Leonard's Market *Seafood*   26 | 21 | 25 | E

E 70s | 1437 Second Ave. (bet. 74th & 75th Sts.) | 212-744-2600 | 866-744-2600 | www.leonardsnyc.com
Family-operated for three generations, this circa-1910 Yorkville outfit remains a steadfast source of "off-the-boat-fresh" seafood and prime cut-to-order meats (with sidelines in smoked fish and game birds), proffered with "expert advice on how to prepare" any purchase; steep pricing can be a sticking point, but the neighborhood regulars know you "can't get better quality" or service.

Leonidas *Candy & Nuts*   26 | 24 | 23 | E

E 50s | 485 Madison Ave. (bet. 51st & 52nd Sts.) | 212-980-2608
Financial District | 120 Broadway (Thames St.) | 212-766-6100
Financial District | 3 Hanover Sq. (bet. Pearl & William Sts.) | 212-422-9600
Financial District | 74 Trinity Pl. (bet. Rector & Thames Sts.) | 212-233-1111
800-900-2462 | www.leonidas-chocolate.com
"Such a rich, tasty, luscious indulgence" – these links of the Brussels-based chain are a "favorite guilty pleasure" for "Belgian-chocolate aficionados" who "go often to satisfy" "cravings"; the "exquisite" bonbons come "beautifully wrapped" in Ballotin boxes ("excellent gifts"), and though they're "priced for people with deep pockets", big spenders say they're "reasonable" "compared to other fancy" shops; P.S. the "tiny espresso bars" Downtown (sharing space with Manon Cafe) "give out free pieces" with your java.

NEW Le Palais des Thés ● *Coffee & Tea*   - | - | - | M

SoHo | 156 Prince St. (bet. Thompson St. & W. B'way) | 646-513-4369
W 60s | 194 Columbus Ave. (bet. 68th & W. 69th Sts.) | 646-664-1902
www.palaisdesthes.com
The first U.S. outposts of a Paris-based chain, these brew shops on the Upper West Side and in SoHo supply a wide assortment of international single-estate teas – green, black, white, oolong and more – in bags, pouches and colorful tins; gift-friendly accessories and a range of price points (from accessible breakfast blends to extravagant small-batch selections) soothe sip-happy shoppers who may also attend tasting classes at the roomier Prince Street store.

Levain Bakery *Baked Goods*   28 | 18 | 23 | M

Harlem | 2167 Frederick Douglass Blvd. (117th St.) | 646-455-0952
W 70s | 167 W. 74th St. (bet. Amsterdam & Columbus Aves.) | 212-874-6080
www.levainbakery.com
This "minuscule" UWS bakery (with a slightly roomier Harlem off-shoot) "reigns supreme" with its "heavenly", "moist, rich", "gargan-

tuan" chocolate chip cookies ("more like a meal than a snack") that devotees claim "make life worth living" and repay "every penny and pound"; insiders also "don't pass up" the "fabulous" breads, "buttery" scones and brioche – and to sweeten the deal, each day's unsold goods are donated to charity.

Li-Lac Chocolates *Candy & Nuts*   26 | 24 | 23 | E

E 40s | Grand Central Mkt. | Lexington Ave. (43rd St.) | 212-370-4866 | 866-898-2462
W Village | 40 Eighth Ave. (Jane St.) | 212-924-2280
Sunset Park | 213 50th St. (2nd Ave.) | Brooklyn | 718-567-9500
www.li-lacchocolates.com

A "veteran" "all-American" confectioner, this West Village "institution" continues to produce "the best fudge", "unbeatable buttercrunch", "delicious caramels" and "marvelous handmade chocolates" in a multitude of "artistic" shapes "almost too good to eat"; a few still "miss the atmospheric Christopher Street store", but most focus on the treats' own "old-time" appeal, whether to satisfy a "craving" or as a "great hostess gift"; P.S. the Grand Central outpost is just the ticket for an "impulse" purchase, and there's also a retail shop at the Sunset Park factory.

Lioni Fresh Mozzarella *Cheese & Dairy*   27 | 18 | 19 | M

Bensonhurst | 7803 15th Ave. (bet. 78th & 79th Sts.) | Brooklyn | 718-232-1411 | www.lionimozzarella.com

This mom-and-pop deli in Bensonhurst will have you "hooked" on "super-fresh" mozzarella that's "soft", "delicious" and "dripping with cream", not to mention the smoked and dried varieties and ricotta; the massive sandwich menu has more than 125 "super-size" heros that are named for Italian celebrities, taste "terrific" and can "feed a family of four" – factor in "decent" prices, and "what more could you ask for?"

Lobel's Prime Meats *Meat & Poultry*   28 | 24 | 26 | VE

E 80s | 1096 Madison Ave. (bet. 82nd & 83rd Sts.) | 212-737-1373 | 800-556-2357 | www.lobels.com

Now in its fifth generation of family ownership, this "first-class" UES "institution" is still renowned for the "unquestionable quality" of its "sublime meats", from "awesome Wagyu", lamb and filet mignon to hot dogs and specialty items; each "unforgettable" cut is "custom" trimmed with genuine "graciousness" by "expert" butchers, and while it's notorious for charging "a king's ransom", don't hesitate to "rob a bank" – "you'll agree it's worth every penny"; P.S. the online ordering and shipping service "works like a Swiss clock."

Lobster Place *Seafood*   27 | 24 | 24 | M

Chelsea | Chelsea Mkt. | 75 Ninth Ave. (bet. 15th & 16th Sts.) | 212-255-5672 | www.lobsterplace.com

"One step away from buying your fish off the boat", this Chelsea Market staple provides an "overflowing bounty" of "amazingly fresh" seafood, whether it's the eponymous "excellent" lobsters or "just about anything else from the ocean" – and following a recent renovation and expansion, the selection has grown to include an even more "abundant" selection of sushi, soups and other prepared foods, not to mention a next-door eatery, Cull & Pistol; factor in "personal" service and "fair" prices, and "what more do you want?"

	QUALITY	DISPLAY	SERVICE	COST

London Candy Co. ● Candy & Nuts ▽ 25 | - | 25 | M

W Village | 267 Bleecker St. (bet. 6th & 7th Aves.) | 212-427-2129 | www.thelondoncandycompany.com

For sweets that are simply smashing, English expats and locals alike head for this "cheerful" British candy emporium specializing in hard-to-find dainties imported from Old Blighty, a "quite tempting array" spanning "old favorites" like Cadbury chocolates, Nestlé Lion Bars and Maynard Wine Gums to newer arrivals with a retro touch (e.g. treats from Hope & Greenwood), all considered a bite of U.K. "heaven"; it recently relocated to the Village, where it's now done up with a 'modern English garden' theme, and a back tearoom is in the works.

Lucy's Whey Cheese & Dairy ▽ 29 | 26 | 29 | E

Chelsea | Chelsea Mkt. | 425 West 15th St. (bet. 9th & 10th Aves.) | 212-463-9500 | www.lucyswhey.com

"Cheesemongers who care" offer a "personal shopping experience" at this "wonderful" little Chelsea Market fromage stall, an offshoot of the East Hampton shop that specializes in "top-quality" American farmstead cheeses "you won't find elsewhere" (no wonder it's "pricey"); if you "don't know what you want" they'll "happily cut you slivers" to try, and if you seek a party platter "they can take care of that too."

NEW Macaron Parlour - | - | - | M
Patisserie ● Baked Goods

E Village | 111 St. Marks Pl. (bet. Ave. A & 1st Ave.) | 212-387-9169 | www.macaronparlour.com

Husband-and-wife pastry chefs Christina Ha and Simon Tung put whimsical spins on the traditional French macaron at this modern East Village dessert den, transcending meringue and butter cream with flavors like candied bacon with maple cream cheese, green tea and (yes) Cheetos; sensible prices and late evening hours encourage the local crowd to linger over coffees and treats at the white cafe tables in back.

Madonia Bakery ⌿ Baked Goods 26 | 21 | 21 | I

Fordham | 2348 Arthur Ave. (187th St.) | Bronx | 718-295-5573 | www.madoniabakery.com

"Buy extra" because "you'll eat some on the way home" urge aficionados of this "family-owned" Arthur Avenue bakery, an "old-world" Italian holdout where the "fabulous" "specialty breads" (especially the "divine" olive and prosciutto loaves) emerge from the ovens "crusty but light as a feather"; "cannoli filled on the spot" and "amazing" cookies also account for its "must-stop" status in the neighborhood.

Magnolia Bakery ● Baked Goods 21 | 21 | 18 | M

E 40s | Grand Central Terminal | dining concourse (42nd St. & Vanderbilt Ave.) | 212-682-3588
E 50s | Bloomingdale's | 1000 Third Ave., 1st fl. (bet. 59th & 60th Sts.) | 212-265-5320
W 40s | 1240 Sixth Ave. (49th St.) | 212-767-1123
W 60s | 200 Columbus Ave. (69th St.) | 212-724-8101
W Village | 401 Bleecker St. (11th St.) | 212-462-2572
www.magnoliabakery.com

"Gimme sugar!" cry "the faithful" at this wildly "popular" West Village "destination" and its spin-offs around town, "cute", "old-fashioned" bakeries that "still rule" with "luscious" cupcakes "like June Cleaver used to bake" topped with "oh-so-buttery" pastel frosting sweet enough to "make your teeth ring", plus other "goodies" like "out-of-this-world" banana pudding; you may have to join the "tourists waiting in line" to experience the Bleecker Street original's "charm", but the other locations "don't have the crazy crowds."

NEW Maison Kayser ● *Baked Goods* — | — | — | E

E 60s | 1294 Third Ave. (74th St.) | 212-744-3100 | www.maison-kayser-usa.com

New to town and already the sole bread supplier to top-rated eatery Le Bernardin, this UES branch of a Parisian patisserie chain has been a hit from day one thanks to its broad, high-end selection of artisanal loaves and rolls, French pastries (both traditional and less so), viennoiserie, cookies and other sweets, not to mention its slim dining room that packs in the locals at lunchtime for salads, quiches and other light bites; P.S. three other locations are slated to open soon in the Flatiron, near Bryant Park and off Columbus Circle.

Maison Ladurée *Baked Goods* 28 | 28 | 25 | VE

E 70s | 864 Madison Ave. (bet. 70th & 71st Sts.) | 646-558-3157 | www.laduree.fr

"Do you wear these little jewels or eat them?" muse admirers of what may be "the most treasured macarons on the planet" at this UES outpost of the famed Parisian "luxury" confectioner – voted No. 1 for Display in the NYC Food Lover's survey – whose "*magnifique*" array of "crisp, airy", flown-in-from-France meringue cookies are displayed like bijoux and come in a "colorful" array of "decadent flavors"; devotees who brave the "lengthy lines" and "very expensive" prices declare the "superb" quality and "coddling" service "well worth" it – it's "the next best thing to a trip to Paris"; P.S. a roomier SoHo location is in the works.

Make My Cake *Baked Goods* 26 | 22 | 21 | M

Harlem | 121 St. Nicholas Ave. (116th St.) | 212-932-0833 ●
Harlem | 2380 Adam Clayton Powell Jr. Blvd. (139th St.) | 212-234-2344
www.makemycake.com

"Definitely among Harlem's best bakeries", this pair of Southern specialists makes its name with "homestyle" desserts like sweet potato cheesecake, "truly amazing" red velvet renditions, butter-cream and German chocolate cakes, cupcakes and other "tasty treats"; they're "not cheap", but given the "outstanding quality" and hospitality from a staff of "great folks", most count on them as "worthwhile stops" for birthdays, weddings and catering.

Malaysia Beef Jerky ⊄ *Meat & Poultry* ∇ 25 | 15 | 21 | I

Chinatown | 95A Elizabeth St. (bet. Grand & Hester Sts.) | 212-965-0796 | www.malaysiabeefjerky.com

"One of Chinatown's best-kept secrets", this simple storefront is devoted exclusively to "mouthwatering jerky" prepared Singapore-Malaysian style, with chunks of beef, pork and chicken coated in regular or spicy sauce, grilled to tenderness "right before your eyes" and purveyed as whole or thin-sliced tidbits; clued-in meat eaters who deem it a "must-try" gloat "this is the real stuff."

Malt & Mold *Specialty Shop*

QUALITY	DISPLAY	SERVICE	COST
–	–	–	M

LES | 221 E. Broadway (Clinton St.) | 212-227-2242 | www.maltandmold.com
Craft beer and artisanal cheeses are just the beginning at this pint-size Lower East Side gourmet pantry whose packed shelves hold a variety of locally sourced goods – from pickles and charcuterie to chocolates and ice cream – in addition to a fine fromage selection and microbrews in bottles, cans and three different sizes of take-home growlers poured from eight taps; frequent tastings and prudent prices keep the diminutive digs buzzing.

Manhattan Fruit Exchange ● *Produce*

QUALITY	DISPLAY	SERVICE	COST
25	22	17	I

Chelsea | Chelsea Mkt. | 75 Ninth Ave. (bet. 15th & 16th Sts.) | 212-989-2444
"If it grows in the earth, they'll have it" at this Chelsea Market "cornerstone", a "premier" purveyor of an "awesome" variety of "beautiful" fruits and veggies that's well stocked with "exotics" you'd have "trouble finding elsewhere", not to mention "assorted cheeses", coffee, candy, nuts and other "goodies"; locals find it "hard to shop anywhere else" given such "dirt-cheap" prices.

Manhattan Fruitier *Specialty Shop*

QUALITY	DISPLAY	SERVICE	COST
25	–	24	VE

LIC | 21-09 Borden Ave. (21st St.) | Queens | 212-686-0404 | www.mfruit.com
"One to go to" when you aim to "make an impression", this "first-class" veteran specializes in "beautiful" gift baskets laden with exotic fruit, filled out with a gourmet array of chocolates, caviar, artisanal cheeses, dried fruits and nuts; it has relocated to Long Island City from its longtime Murray Hill quarters, but since the "excellent" options include online ordering and delivery, it remains "just perfect" for that "very special" someone – though naturally going for such a "top choice" means paying "top dollar."

MarieBelle's Fine Treats & Chocolates *Candy & Nuts*

QUALITY	DISPLAY	SERVICE	COST
26	26	23	E

SoHo | 484 Broome St. (bet. W. B'way & Wooster St.) | 212-431-1768 | www.mariebelle.com
"Chocolate as art" sums up the ornate, "ladylike" confections at Maribel Lieberman's "delightful" SoHo shop, where the "delicious" morsels come "exquisitely presented" and are "worth every sou" of the "king's ransom" they cost; as for Cacao Bar, the "cute cafe" in back, aficionados say it's "like being in Paris" to sit there and sip "fabulous" "rich Aztec" hot chocolate.

Marlow & Daughters *Meat & Poultry*

QUALITY	DISPLAY	SERVICE	COST
28	24	25	E

Williamsburg | 95 Broadway (Berry St.) | Brooklyn | 718-388-5700 | www.marlowanddaughters.com
"Better than fantastic" is the word from meat mavens who "couldn't get along without" this Williamsburg butcher (from the team behind Diner and Marlow & Sons), where the sausage is made in-house and the beef, pork and poultry is sourced from local and sustainable suppliers "they vet" so carnivores can "enjoy eating with a clear conscience"; it also carries a few grocery items like local cheeses and produce, and while "it's on the expensive side", boosters advise "save up" – the quality's "just about the best."

Martine's Chocolates *Candy & Nuts*

25 | 23 | 23 | E

E 80s | 400 E. 82nd St. (bet. 1st & York Aves.) | 212-744-6289 |
www.martineschocolates.com

A "gift to the neighborhood", this Upper East Side confectioner con-
cocts "fresh", handmade "luxe" chocolates, marzipan and other treats
within view of customers in its "keyhole of a shop"; high prices are a
hallmark, as is the "vast selection" of "exotic shapes" (think dogs and
frogs), but it's the "brilliant quality" that has the smitten asking "may
I sleep here?"

Mast Brothers Chocolate *Candy & Nuts*

▽ 25 | 20 | 20 | E

Williamsburg | 111 N. Third St. (bet. Berry St. & Wythe Ave.) |
Brooklyn | 718-388-2625 | www.mastbrothers.com

"The smell is intoxicating" at this Williamsburg factory, where a pair
of "expert" siblings makes "superb" artisanal chocolate from scratch,
roasting and grinding cacao beans imported from small farms and
crafting "amazing" bars ("wrapped in beautiful paper") and bonbons,
plus now a back bakery turns out cakes and cookies too; a few skeptics
call the goods "ordinary and overpriced", but most who visit its vintage
warehouse–style space or pick up bars at gourmet markets around
town aver they're simply "awesome."

McNulty's Tea & Coffee Co. ❶ *Coffee & Tea*

28 | 23 | 25 | M

W Village | 109 Christopher St. (bet. Bleecker & Hudson Sts.) |
212-242-5351 | 800-356-5200 | www.mcnultys.com

"They've been here forever" (well, since 1895), and this West Village
"gem" remains a "nirvana for real coffee-lovers" given its "terrific inventory" of "high-quality" brews bolstered by "apothecary jars" filled
with "more teas than you can shake a stick at"; "pro" staffers will "steer
you" to the perfect blend at a "decent price", and the "wonderful aromas" suffusing the "vintage" digs are "an intoxicating experience" –
"some things never change, thank God!"

The Meadow *Specialty Shop*

▽ 29 | 28 | 26 | E

W Village | 523 Hudson St. (bet. Charles & 10th Sts.) | 212-645-4633 |
888-388-4633 | www.atthemeadow.com

An outpost of a Portland, OR, shop owned by Mark Bitterman, author
of *Salted: A Manifesto on the World's Most Essential Mineral,* not surprisingly this "beautiful", minuscule West Villager specializes in the
aforementioned seasoning, offering a "most impressive" selection of
some 130 artisan varieties hailing from more than 25 countries; the
rest of the eclectic goods overseen by a "helpful" staff includes high-
end chocolate bars, specialty cocktail bitters, syrups and even fresh
flowers; P.S. it also offers classes and workshops.

The Meat Hook *Meat & Poultry*

▽ 27 | 23 | 26 | M

Williamsburg | 100 Frost St. (bet. Leonard St. & Manhattan Ave.) |
Brooklyn | 718-349-5033 | www.the-meathook.com

"Noticeably tastier" meat is the métier of this "funky" Williamsburg
butcher that shares space with the cookware store Brooklyn Kitchen
and is renowned for its "knowledgeable" staff whose on-site butchering of "awesome" stock from small "local" producers yields "excellent" housemade sausages and charcuterie, as well as grass-fed beef,
lamb and pork; it's "not a huge selection", but cuts "of the highest

class" and "fair prices" hook "hordes" of carnivores who consider it "heaven on earth."

Mediterranean Foods ❶ *Specialty Shop*   26 | 20 | 22 | M

Astoria | Agora Plaza | 23-18 31st St. (bet. 23rd Ave. & 23rd Rd.) | Queens | 718-721-0221
Astoria | 30-12 34th St. (30th Ave.) | Queens | 718-728-6166
www.mediterraneanfoodsny.com

"This is where to shop" for "high-quality" Greek specialties agree hungry Hellenists at this Astoria duo, home to a "wide variety" of imported victuals including "fabulous" "fresh fetas" and other cheeses, olives "picked by those who know", oils, yogurts and packaged foods; with cordial service and "low, low prices", it's a "must-visit" for your next "ethnic-inspired" spread.

Mike's Donuts & Coffee ⊭ *Baked Goods*   27 | 24 | 25 | I

Bay Ridge | 6822 Fifth Ave. (bet. Bay Ridge Ave. & 68th St.) | Brooklyn | 718-745-6980 | www.mikesdonuts.com
Experience "old-school Brooklyn at its finest" at this basic Bay Ridge bake shop dispensing "any kind of donut you can imagine" (some 33 flavors) with "crunchy exteriors, satisfying crumb" and an "always fresh and delicious" taste enhanced by "even better prices"; the "fast" counter crew also proffers muffins, bagels and coffee for those who prefer their breakfasts without jelly, glaze or sprinkles.

Milk & Cookies Bakery ❶ *Baked Goods*   25 | 20 | 20 | M

W Village | 19 Commerce St. (bet. Bedford St. & 7th Ave.) | 212-243-1640 | www.milkandcookiesbakery.com

"Give yourself a little treat" at this "charming" West Village "gem", which custom-bakes "wonderful" "fresh" cookies to order once you name your preference of dough flavor and mix-ins; premade cookies, bars and brownies are on hand to sweeten the deal, and everything's a "divine" match for "delicious ice cream sandwiches", shakes and sundaes via Il Laboratorio del Gelato and Ronnybrook Farms Dairy milk.

Mille-Feuille *Baked Goods*   ▽ 25 | 18 | 23 | M

G Village | 552 La Guardia Pl. (bet. Bleecker & 3rd Sts.) | 212-533-4698 | www.millefeuille-nyc.com

"You'll think you've just landed in Paris" attest admirers of this "tiny", "very French" Greenwich Village patisserie from a classically trained Gallic pastry chef; it's a petite source for "outstanding" croissants and brioche, "fine macarons" in many hues and flavors and, *naturellement*, the namesake many-layered confection, with "good prices" further sweetening the deal.

Minamoto Kitchoan *Candy & Nuts*   ▽ 29 | 29 | 26 | E

W 40s | Swiss Center Bldg. | 608 Fifth Ave. (49th St.) | 212-489-3747 | www.kitchoan.com

"Delicate", "divine Japanese sweets" are oh-so-"beautifully displayed" at this "peaceful" Midtown "oasis" offering a taste of Tokyo via "traditional" wagashi – the "artistic" confections served at tea; given that these "unique" treats come "elegantly" wrapped "with the utmost precision" by "über-polite" staffers, they make "exceptional" if "expensive" gifts, but remember: "this is not your American candy, loaded with sugar", so it "may not suit all Western tastes."

Molly's Cupcakes ❶ *Baked Goods* 27 | 25 | 26 | M

W Village | 228 Bleecker St. (bet. Carmine & Downing Sts.) | 212-414-2253 | www.mollyscupcakes.com

Named after the owner's third grade teacher, this "cute" Chicago import in the West Village furthers the "premium cupcake" craze with its "wonderful sweet treats" available in five batter flavors, five frostings and a host of fillings (butterscotch caramel, peach cobbler) that combine "creativity" with "pure decadence"; a "friendly" crew further ensures that it's "worth the price" as well as the "wait" to "feel like a kid" within its "bright, cheery" yellow storefront digs.

Momofuku Milk Bar ❶ *Baked Goods* 25 | 19 | 19 | M

E Village | 251 E. 13th St. (bet. 2nd & 3rd Aves.) | 347-577-9504
W 50s | Chambers Hotel | 15 W. 56th St. (bet. 5th & 6th Aves.) | 347-577-9504
W 80s | 561 Columbus Ave. (87th St.) | 347-577-9504
Carroll Gardens | 360 Smith St. (2nd Pl.) | Brooklyn | 347-577-9504
Williamsburg | 382 Metropolitan Ave. (bet. Havemeyer St. & Marcy Ave.) | Brooklyn | 347-577-9504
www.milkbarstore.com

"Creative, cool and scrumptious" sums up David Chang's "non-typical" East Village bakery and its offshoots, where pastry chef Christina Tosi's "imagination" yields "fantastic" pork buns and "delightful" desserts including "sublime" cookies, "truly addicting" crack pie and soft-serve ice cream in "out-of-the-box" flavors; it's on the "expensive" side, and while you can "stand while you swoon" at "crowded" communal tables at the original location, the rest are takeout-only – "but you won't be sorry."

Monteleone *Baked Goods* ▽ 29 | 26 | 23 | M

Carroll Gardens | 355 Court St. (bet. President & Union Sts.) | Brooklyn | 718-852-5600 | www.fmonteleonebakery.com

"Excellent" cakes, pastries, the "best cannoli" and housemade gelato have made this sliver of an Italian bakery a beloved Carroll Gardens standby for decades, but it's the "wide variety" of traditional cookies that really stands out here; a "first-rate" staff is another reason this is such a "sweet place."

Moore Brothers Wine Co. ❶ *Wines & Liquor* 28 | 28 | 29 | M

Flatiron | 33 E. 20th St. (bet. B'way & Park Ave. S.) | 212-375-1575 | 866-986-6673 | www.moorebrothers.com

They "exhibit the highest degree of care" at this "one-of-a-kind" Flatiron vintner from Philly-area connoisseurs Greg and David Moore, voted No. 1 for Service in the NYC Food Lover's survey thanks to its "most knowledgeable" expert staff; the "terrific handpicked" wines from European "artisanal producers" are "shipped properly in refrigerated trucks" and displayed at the "correct temperature" in a "pristine", two-story space, and the fact that they're offered at "excellent value" gives those "not blessed with trust funds" moore reason to "love it all"; P.S. insiders tout its "tasting events."

Morrell & Co. *Wines & Liquor* 26 | 24 | 23 | E

W 40s | Rockefeller Ctr. | 1 Rockefeller Plaza (bet. 5th & 6th Aves.) | 212-688-9370 | 800-969-4637 | www.morrellwine.com

This handsome hideaway across from the Rockefeller Center rink "truly distinguishes itself" with an "amazing", 5,000-strong lineup of "fine wines", plus top-shelf liquors, made "accessible" by "classy", "amiable and informative" staffers; yes, the price tag is "top dollar", but "if you're willing to spend" you'll "always find something to satisfy"; P.S. along with "noteworthy" tastings and classes, it offers wedding registration, consignment and online futures sales.

Murray's Bagels ● *Baked Goods*   26 | 19 | 19 | M

Chelsea | 242 Eighth Ave. (bet. 22nd & 23rd Sts.) | 646-638-1335
G Village | 500 Sixth Ave. (bet. 12th & 13th Sts.) | 212-462-2830
www.murraysbagelschelsea.com

"Plump", "crispy on the outside, fluffy on the inside" rounds "exactly as a bagel should be" ignite carb cravings at these Greenwich Village–Chelsea twins, which also supply "all the schmears you can think of" and "fine" smoked fish; "quick service" keeps "out-the-door" lines moving on weekends – so "the only sad thing" is that "they won't toast."

Murray's Cheese Shop   *Cheese & Dairy*   29 | 26 | 25 | E

E 40s | Grand Central Mkt. | Lexington Ave. (43rd St.) | 212-922-1540 ●
W Village | 254 Bleecker St. (Cornelia St.) | 212-243-3289
888-692-4339 | www.murrayscheese.com

Among the city's top destinations "for all things cheesy", this West Village "mecca" – "complete with worshiping crowds" – lays out a "ridiculously expansive" lactic array, from Appenzeller to Zimbro, plus "fabulous" charcuterie and deli items, pastas, bread, nuts, chocolates and more; patrons praise "patient", "knowledgeable" staffers (they're "generous with the samples") and cite the in-house "caves", "classroom" and catering menu as more reasons to ignore your "cardiologist" and sing "cheese, glorious cheese"; P.S. the Grand Central annex is a boon to fromage-seeking commuters.

Murray's Sturgeon   *Caviar & Smoked Fish*   28 | 20 | 23 | E

W 80s | 2429 Broadway (bet. 89th & 90th Sts.) | 212-724-2650 | www.murrayssturgeon.com

The "stalwart sturgeon surgeons" at this "old-time" (since 1946) Upper Westsider serve up "excellent-quality" smoked fish, pickled herring, sturgeon and lox, plus kosher deli meats and other "Jewish soul food at its best" (the "chopped liver is to die for – and of!"); regulars rave these "real"-deal goods are "worth every dollar you spend", especially given the bonus of "wonderful, reliable" service and pleasing "throwback-to-old-NY" digs – just "how do they get so much great stuff into such a small store?"

Myers of Keswick   *Specialty Shop*   25 | 20 | 22 | M

W Village | 634 Hudson St. (bet. Horatio & Jane Sts.) | 212-691-4194 | www.myersofkeswick.com

"British expats and Anglophiles" hankering for "edible memories" flock to this "quaint" West Village shop, a "jolly good showcase" chockablock with "veddy" English specialties "of all sorts", from "top-notch" "household foods" to key "treats you can't live without"; whether you're "stocking up" on imports "in tins and packets" ("get your marmite fix") or "guilty pleasures" like "housemade bangers", "Scotch eggs, sausage rolls and pork pies", with "so many" "favorites in one place" it's the "best thing barring a trip to London."

Nespresso Boutique *Coffee & Tea*

27 | 27 | 24 | E

E 60s | 761 Madison Ave. (65th St.)
SoHo | 92 Prince St. (Mercer St.)
800-562-1465 | www.nespresso.com

"Take your coffee experience to a whole new level" at these "beautiful" SoHo–East Side branches of a global outfit, "pleasingly elite" oases for java "junkies" to "splurge" on "little sachets" of "out-of-this-world" espresso and pick up state-of-the-art machines to brew them in; they're also "sit-down" "respites" for "delish" snacks and "luxe" cuppas, though even "tony" types say it's "difficult paying their prices."

Neuchatel Chocolates *Candy & Nuts*

▽ 28 | 28 | 26 | VE

E 50s | Park Ave. Plaza | 55 E. 52nd St. (bet. Madison & Park Aves.) | 212-759-1388 | 800-597-0759 | www.neuchatelchocolates.com

"Now this is chocolate!" declare devotees of the "excellent truffles" and other "amazingly smooth", "sinful" Swiss confections that are the specialty of this East Side shop; naturally, such "fabulous" treats are costly, so you need to be "feeling flush", but those willing to "splurge" report that, "once inside", you'll "never want to leave."

Neuhaus *Candy & Nuts*

26 | 25 | 23 | E

E 40s | Grand Central Terminal | main concourse (42nd St. & Vanderbilt Ave.) | 212-972-3740
E 50s | 500 Madison Ave. (bet. 52nd & 53rd Sts.) | 212-644-4490
E 50s | 569 Lexington Ave. (bet. 50th & 51st Sts.) | 212-593-0848
NEW Elmhurst | Queens Center Mall | 9015 Queens Blvd. (bet. 57th & 59th Aves.) | Queens | 718-699-0701 ●
www.neuhauschocolate.com

Leave it to the "Belgians to fashion" the kind of "delicious", "decadent" chocolates on offer at these "charming" outposts of the Brussels-based chain, where "rich", "high-end" truffles and other confections come "in familiar as well as unusual flavors" ("the chocolate-covered potato chips are unbelievable"); they're predictably "expensive" and service can be "snobby" at times, but that's "worth putting up with" given their "made-to-order" assortments and "impressive" packaging "perfect for a special gift."

New Amsterdam Market *Specialty Shop*

28 | 23 | 25 | M

Seaport | 100 Peck Slip (South St.) | 212-766-8688 | www.newamsterdammarket.org

"Such a great concept", this outdoor market on the Seaport's old Fulton Fish Market site is a "locavore and gastronome heaven" with stalls specializing in a "wide variety" of "artisanal foods" from area providers, including "excellent produce", cheeses, pasture-raised meats, baked goods, ice cream and more; it's becoming a "favorite" of foodies in the know and shoppers in search of "something new and different."

New Beer *Beer*

▽ 26 | 15 | 19 | I

LES | 167 Chrystie St. (bet. Delancey & Rivington Sts.) | 212-260-4360 | www.newbeerdistributors.com

It's a beer bonanza at this family-owned LES "warehouse" stocking some 1,000 domestic and international brews, including the rare and hard to find, from arcane local bottlings to New Zealand imports; sudsophiles say new brews "will show up here before they do anywhere else", and prices are "fair", so never mind the "no-frills setup."

	QUALITY	DISPLAY	SERVICE	COST

Nordic Delicacies *Specialty Shop* ▽ 28 | 23 | 28 | M

Bay Ridge | 6909 Third Ave. (bet. Bay Ridge & Ovington Aves.) | Brooklyn | 718-748-1874 | www.nordicdeli.com

"One of the few Scandinavian grocery stores left in Brooklyn", this Bay Ridge outpost is a "real treat" for "delicious" Nordic "specialties you can't find anywhere else", whether imported jams, cheeses and pickled herring or fresh baked goods and other traditional comestibles like "homemade *polse,* liver *postei* and *julekake*"; it also can be counted on for clothing and gifts, and everything's tended by "helpful" følks.

Nunu Chocolates *Candy & Nuts* ▽ 25 | 20 | 23 | M

NEW **TriBeCa** | All Good Things | 102 Franklin St. (bet. 6th Ave. & W. B'way) | no phone

Downtown Bklyn | 529 Atlantic Ave. (bet. 3rd & 4th Aves.) | Brooklyn | 917-776-7102 ◕

www.nunuchocolates.com

Brooklynites are "falling in love with chocolate all over again" thanks to this "micro shop" on the Downtown–Boerum Hill border (with a counter inside TriBeCa's All Good Things) producing "amazing" varieties like "gourmet" ganaches filled with fruit purée, tea or liquor, as well as "scrumptious" caramels, all made on-site; those who agree that pairing beer and chocolate is a "win-win" can sit and sample one of the "hard-to-find" "craft brews" with their bonbons.

Nut Box ◕ *Candy & Nuts* 24 | 23 | 22 | M

Chelsea | Chelsea Mkt. | 75 Ninth Ave. (bet. 15th & 16th Sts.) | 212-243-2325

G Village | 49 E. Eighth St. (University Pl.) | 212-933-1018

Cobble Hill | 163 Smith St. (Wyckoff St.) | Brooklyn | 347-689-9948

www.thenutbox.com

Whether you hit the Cobble Hill original or the "wonderful" Chelsea Market and Village outposts, these nut emporiums are "fun to discover" given their "quality" selection, mostly from the U.S., which come plain, salted, roasted, honeyed or chocolate-covered; "excellent" dried fruits, including unusual and organic choices, plus ready-made and make-your-own trail mixes, seeds, granola, spices, colorful candies and house-roasted coffee beans round out the offerings, with "amazing prices" as the dried cherry on top.

O&CO. *Specialty Shop* 27 | 25 | 23 | E

E 40s | Grand Central Terminal | main concourse, Graybar Passage (42nd St. & Vanderbilt Ave.) | 212-973-1472

W 60s | Shops at Columbus Circle | 10 Columbus Circle (bet. 58th & 60th Sts.) | 212-757-9877 ◕

W Village | 249 Bleecker St. (bet. 6th & 7th Aves.) | 212-463-7710

www.oliviersandco.com

"Truly an olive oil mecca", these specialists in "spectacular" oleaginous imports offer a "wonderful selection" with variations for cooking or "dipping" curated by "friendly" staffers who'll let you "test your palate" to explore "subtle differences"; "lovely packaging" makes for "fabulous gifts", and the "highest quality" extends to its aged "balsamic vinegar", tapenades and accessories, so though the tab "can get pretty pricey" it's "well worth the cost."

QUALITY | DISPLAY | SERVICE | COST

One Girl Cookies *Baked Goods* 27 | 26 | 23 | E

Cobble Hill | 68 Dean St. (bet. Boerum Pl. & Smith St.) | Brooklyn |
212-675-4996
Dumbo | 33 Main St. (Water St.) | Brooklyn | 347-338-1268
www.onegirlcookies.com

"Definitely one girl who knows how to bake", this "adorable" Cobble
Hill shop-cum–espresso bar and its Dumbo offshoot have a flair for
"teeny", "exquisite-looking" cookies crafted in a mix of "delish" flavors
(e.g. "to-die-for Whoopie Pie") that "really make you want more"; the
cupcakes, brownies and cakes are "top-notch" too, and the "friendly"
staffers can also create upscale event favors and gift boxes.

The Orchard *Specialty Shop* 28 | 21 | 23 | E

Midwood | 1367 Coney Island Ave. (bet. Ave. J & Cary Ct.) | Brooklyn |
718-377-1799 | 800-222-0240 | www.orchardfruit.com

"Perfect for every occasion", this Midwood kosher "fixture" dates to
1955 as a purveyor of "fantastic" gourmet fruit in "huge, fresh baskets" filled out with chocolates and preserves, or "fabulous" platters
incorporating smoked fish and cheese; prices can quickly add up to
"breathtaking" levels, but "when you really want to impress", its
"beautiful arrangements" rank with "the very best."

Orwasher's Bakery *Baked Goods* 26 | 20 | 22 | M

E 70s | 308 E. 78th St. (bet. 1st & 2nd Aves.) | 212-288-6569 |
www.orwasherbakery.com

An "old-world bakery that still thrives", this circa-1916 "throwback"
on the Upper East Side is a kosher bakery "standout" producing
"memorable" Jewish-style breads ("love that raisin-pumpernickel")
in a "no-frills" "neighborhood" setting; between the "genial" service and "absolute quality", you "can't really go wrong" – "thank heaven
it's still here."

Ottomanelli & Sons *Meat & Poultry* 28 | 22 | 26 | E

W Village | 285 Bleecker St. (bet. Jones St. & 7th Ave.) |
212-675-4217
Woodside | 61-05 Woodside Ave. (61st St.) | Queens |
718-651-5544

"This is what a real butcher shop is" opine "old-fashioned" fans of
these "longtime" Italian "landmarks" in the West Village and Woodside,
separately run "family operations" famed for "superior", "well-
marbled meat" both "common and exotic", all "perfectly trimmed"
with a "smile" by a "terrific" counter staff that "will provision, educate
and charm you"; with a "wide" variety from dry-aged beef and homemade sausage to "game meats" like venison and kangaroo, they're
worth "a special trip."

Ottomanelli's Prime Meats *Meat & Poultry* 28 | 24 | 25 | E

Flushing | 190-21 Union Tpke. (192nd St.) | Queens | 718-468-2000 |
www.ottomanellibros.com

"Love these guys!" gush Flushing fanciers of this local meat market,
where the "fresh" "prime" cuts range from steaks, veal and poultry to
exotic game like pheasant, alligator, boar, deer, buffalo, ostrich – "you
name it"; add a "wonderful" prepared foods lineup featuring Italian favorites like chicken parm and baked ziti, and there's "something for
everyone", even if it is on the "pricey" side.

| | QUALITY | DISPLAY | SERVICE | COST |

Ovenly *Baked Goods* — — — **M**

Greenpoint | 31 Greenpoint Ave. (West St.) | Brooklyn | 347-512-2238 | www.oven.ly

Wholesale suppliers of salty-sweet snacks to gourmet grocers around town, baker buddies Agatha Kulaga and Erin Patinkin now craft clever treats and baked goods (spicy bacon-caramel popcorn, blue cheese-pecan scones) that are on offer at this sensibly priced brick-and-mortar retail location in Greenpoint; cafe tables facing huge windows make an ideal morning perch for Stumptown coffee and a pistachio-cardamom muffin or the like.

Pain D'Avignon *Baked Goods* ▽ **24** **20** **21** **M**

E 50s | Plaza Food Hall | 1 W. 59th St. (5th Ave.) | 646-755-3229
LES | Essex Street Mkt. | 120 Essex St. (bet. Delancey & Rivington Sts.) | 212-673-4950
www.paindavignon-nyc.com

"Totally addictive" to breadheads, this Long Island City–based bakery (by way of a Cape Cod original) packs its Essex Street Market and Plaza Food Hall berths to the rafters with a "wonderful line" of some 50 European-style variations on the staff of life; expect "fresh and tasty" French baguettes, seven-grain, caraway rye and cranberry-pecan, rounded out by croissants and brioche.

NEW Pain d'Epices *Baked Goods* — — — **M**

W 70s | 104 W. 70th St. (Columbus Ave.) | 212-496-1450

Taking over the space that formerly housed Soutine, this UWS bakery specializing in viennoiserie aims to draw fans of its predecessor with a modestly priced lineup of French pastries and breads, including a few made from recipes the new owners acquired along with the space; standout treats like lemon–poppy seed cake and pistachio scones may be sampled in diminutive digs that should feel familiar to longtime locals.

Paneantico Bakery & Café ● *Baked Goods* **26** **23** **21** **M**

Bay Ridge | 9124 Third Ave. (92nd St.) | Brooklyn | 718-680-2347

Among the "best reasons to go out to Bay Ridge", this Italian bakery/cafe "gem" is prized for its "fresh" house-baked breads, but it also boasts an "excellent variety" of pastries and prepared foods, not to mention "wonderful sandwiches"; according to "the locals" lingering over espresso, "anything you get, you know it's going to be delicious."

Papabubble ● *Candy & Nuts* ▽ **23** **23** **21** **M**

Little Italy | 380 Broome St. (bet. Mott & Mulberry Sts.) | 212-966-2599 | www.papabubbleny.com

Demonstrating "the definition of eye candy", artisans at this lablike Little Italy confectioner work in view, stretching and rolling molten sugar in a "rainbow" of colors to sculpt "fun", "unique shapes with un-usual flavors" from the fruit and herbal oils they use; the result is "so-phisticated" hard sweets that make it a "go-to" for gifts, even "cool, customized" ones – that is "if you can resist eating them all" yourself.

Park Avenue Liquor Shop *Wines & Liquor* **27** **20** **25** **E**

E 40s | 292 Madison Ave. (bet. 40th & 41st Sts.) | 212-685-2442 | www.parkaveliquor.com

Just the place "to pick up that special bottle" before "taking Metro-North to the 'burbs", this "old-world" Midtown wine seller near Grand

Central includes rare-vintage Burgundies and Bordeaux among its "stacked-to-the-ceiling" inventory, and it's also home to one of the "best selections of single-malt scotches" outside "Scotland" (400 labels); what's more, service is "helpful" and "without attitude" – no wonder tabs are so "pricey."

Pastosa Ravioli *Pastas*

27 | 22 | 24 | M

Throgs Neck | 3812 E. Tremont Ave. (Lamport Pl.) | Bronx | 718-822-2800
Bensonhurst | 7425 New Utrecht Ave. (75th St.) | Brooklyn | 718-236-9615
Mill Basin | 5223 Ave. N (53rd St.) | Brooklyn | 718-258-1002
Eltingville | 3817 Richmond Ave. (Wilson Ave.) | Staten Island | 718-356-4600
Grasmere | 1076 Richmond Rd. (Columbus Ave.) | Staten Island | 718-667-2194
West Brighton | 764 Forest Ave. (B'way) | Staten Island | 718-420-9000
800-457-2786 | www.pastosa.com

"Creamy, light" ravioli is "king" at this Bensonhurst "landmark" and its separately owned offshoots, but the "excellent breads, pastas" (including "gluten-free options"), sausages, "fresh housemade mozzarella" and a "wide selection" of Italian products also "don't disappoint"; it's a "real experience", and service is "on the money", "just like in the old Brooklyn days"; P.S. the Forest Avenue locale distinguishes itself with a "terrific" range of cheeses.

Patisserie Claude ♥ *Baked Goods*

26 | 16 | 19 | M

W Village | 187 W. Fourth St. (bet. 6th & 7th Aves.) | 212-255-5911

"Just as good as when Claude was the baker", this veteran Village pâtisserie – now run by the retired namesake's "longtime assistant" – remains a "master" of "spectacular" "buttery, flaky croissants" and "excellent basic French pastries"; combining a "low-key" milieu with "very high quality", it's "totally addictive" despite hints of "attitude" – this is "a true slice of Paris", after all.

Petrossian Boutique & Cafe *Caviar & Smoked Fish*

27 | 25 | 24 | VE

W 50s | 911 Seventh Ave. (bet. 57th & 58th Sts.) | 212-245-2217 | 800-828-9241 | www.petrossian.com

For "special occasions" or a "totally decadent splurge", fish-egg fanciers converge on the "crème de la crème" of "caviar purveyors" near Carnegie Hall to "lust after" "sublime" roe, smoked fish, foie gras, jarred comestibles and other "high-end" "delicacies" at "stratospheric prices"; there are also "mouthwatering" French breads and pastries, which, assuming your wallet is up to the task, complete the "simply splendid" experience.

Pickle Guys *Specialty Shop*

27 | 19 | 23 | I

LES | 49 Essex St. (bet. Grand & Hester Sts.) | 212-656-9739
Midwood | 1364 Coney Island Ave. (bet. Aves. J & K) | Brooklyn | 718-677-0639
888-474-2553 | www.pickleguys.com

"Pucker up" for "the real thing" at this LES "favorite" (and its Midwood outpost) producing "the freshest", most "mouthwatering" "traditional Jewish pickles" cured "the way God intended" and dispensed "direct from the barrel" with a "good-size helping of New York attitude" from a staff of "jocular" "characters"; it "packs a pungent punch" with varieties like full- and half-sour, sweet gherkin and horseradish, "along with other pickled items" – connoisseurs of fine brines "wouldn't buy them anywhere else."

Pickles, Olives Etc. *Specialty Shop*

25 | 18 | 25 | M

E 80s | 1647 First Ave. (86th St.) | 212-717-8966 | www.picklesandolives.com

"Like the name says", this "very friendly" Upper Eastsider "can't be beat" for "barrels" full of "fantastic pickles" in diverse styles "with just the right pucker", plus olives "of every type" including "delicacies" "stuffed with goat cheese, blue cheese, lemon rind, garlic", etc.; plus, when you're in a "pre-party shopping" pickle, "you can round out your appetizers" with "fresh baba ghanoush", hummus, grape leaves and more.

Piemonte Ravioli *Pastas*

27 | 18 | 26 | I

Little Italy | 190 Grand St. (bet. Mott & Mulberry Sts.) | 212-226-0475 | www.piemonteravioli.com

The "easiest way to make a restaurant-quality meal at home" is to head for this "old-fashioned" Little Italy stalwart and pick up some "pillow-soft gnocchi", squid-ink noodles or other "quality" pasta in a myriad of shapes, including filled versions like "top-notch" tortellini, ravioli or cannelloni (it's one of the "only places" around for those tasty cylinders), plus "cheeses to go with"; whatever your choice, it'll be dispensed by a "helpful" staff, but be warned: it's all "so good", you may "never want to eat dried noodles again."

Pino Prime Meats ♥ *Meat & Poultry*

▽ 29 | 21 | 28 | M

SoHo | 149 Sullivan St. (bet. Houston & Prince Sts.) | 212-475-8134

Pino Cinquemani is the "epitome of the neighborhood butcher", and his "old-school" SoHo shop "takes you back to a better time" with "excellent cuts" of the "freshest possible meat" including prime beef, homemade sausage, salami and game such as venison, wild boar and pheasant; citing "reliable" quality, "friendly" countermen who take "a personal interest" and "great prices to boot", locals and those in the know "love, love, love this place."

Pisacane Midtown *Seafood*

28 | 20 | 24 | E

E 50s | 940 First Ave. (bet. 51st & 52nd Sts.) | 212-355-1850

Ichthyophagous Eastsiders say "no one can hold a candle to" the "outstanding quality and freshness" at this "superb" family-run fish market, awash with a wide lineup of "impeccable" seafood overseen by an "excellent" crew who'll hospitably "tell you what to order"; the "prepared dishes to go" are "quite good" too, though not surprisingly such "top" offerings are on the "pricey" side.

PJ Wine ● *Wines & Liquor*

27 | 17 | 20 | M

Inwood | 4898 Broadway (bet. 204th & 207th Sts.) | 212-567-5500 | www.pjwine.com

You "can spend hours" at this "massive" (15,000-sq.-ft.) Inwood wine-and-spirits store that scores points for its "good values" on a "vast selection" of bottles "from all over", with a particular concentration on Spanish, Chilean and Argentinean producers; throw in "competitive" delivery rates, and it's "worth the slog" up there, although in-the-know customers encourage anyone who "can't make the trip" to visit its "great website."

QUALITY | DISPLAY | SERVICE | COST

The Ploughman ❶ *Specialty Shop*   26 | 19 | 22 | E

Park Slope | 438 Seventh Ave. (bet. 14th & 15th Sts.) | Brooklyn |
718-369-7595 | www.theploughmanbklyn.com

This pint-size South Slope specialty shop offers a "limited selection"
of "top-quality" foodstuffs, from "fantastic" artisanal cheeses and
charcuterie to baked goods, high-end chocolates, oils and vinegars
and lots of locally produced comestibles, along with beers offered by
the growler; prices are on the "steep" side, but "friendly and knowledgeable" service adds value.

Pomegranate ❶ *Specialty Shop*   26 | 27 | 20 | E

Midwood | 1507 Coney Island Ave. (Ave. L) | Brooklyn | 718-951-7112 |
www.thepompeople.com

"If you're kosher, you owe it to yourself to peruse" the "extraordinary
selection" at this "huge, upscale" Midwood supermarket offering an
enormous array of staple groceries, prime meats, fish, dairy, "fresh
fruits and veggies" and a "lovely assortment" of prepared foods and
baked goods from their three kitchens; "the price scale is higher" than
some, but with such "impressive" quality "in so many categories", "if
you can't find it here, you'd be hard-pressed to find it anywhere."

Porto Rico Importing Co. *Coffee & Tea*   27 | 22 | 22 | I

E Village | 40½ St. Marks Pl. (bet. 1st & 2nd Aves.) |
212-533-1982

G Village | 201 Bleecker St. (bet. MacDougal St. & 6th Ave.) |
212-477-5421 | 800-453-5908 ❶

LES | Essex Street Mkt. | 120 Essex St. (bet. Delancey & Rivington Sts.) |
212-677-1210

Williamsburg | 636 Grand St. (bet. Leonard St. & Manhattan Ave.) |
Brooklyn | 718-782-1200
www.portorico.com

"They're serious" about "java beans" at this "well-worn and well-loved"
Village "classic" and its offshoots, which cater to "discerning caffeine
addicts" with an "incredible selection" of "fresh" roasts "from around
the world" displayed in "giant" "burlap sacks", along with a "compara-
bly large" lineup of loose-leaf teas; the "heavenly" "aromas" alone are
"intoxicating" ("can this be legal?"), and there's the "added bonus" of
"bargain" prices and a staff that "would make a sommelier jealous."

Poseidon Bakery *Baked Goods*   25 | 18 | 23 | I

W 40s | 629 Ninth Ave. (bet. 44th & 45th Sts.) | 212-757-6173

"Fresh-made phyllo dough" earns "kudos" for this "funky, little" fourth-
generation family-owned bakery in Hell's Kitchen, a "bastion of Greek
goodies" turning out "flaky" "delicacies" "both savory and sweet",
e.g. "stellar baklava" and "delicious spanakopita"; with service as
"charming" as the goods are "authentic", admirers are "so glad" it's
around to spare them the "schlep to Astoria."

Pour ❶ *Wines & Liquor*   24 | 27 | 28 | M

W 70s | 321 Amsterdam Ave. (75th St.) | 212-501-7687 |
www.pourwines.com

Oenophiles pour on the praise for this near-"perfect neighborhood
wine store" on the UWS that's refreshingly "non-intimidating" thanks
to "superb service" from "chilled-out" salespeople who have a flair for
"helping you pair wine with food"; "high-end" and hard-to-find spirits

share floor space with "value" selections in "beautiful displays" in which "every bottle's a winner."

Puddin' by Clio ● *Baked Goods* ▽ 29 | 25 | 25 | M

E Village | 102 St. Marks Pl. (bet. Ave. A & 1st Ave.) | 212-477-3537 | www.puddinnyc.com

"Taking pudding to a whole new level", this minute East Villager from pastry chef Clio Goodman makes the humble namesake dessert a "surprising, delicious" "must-try" thanks to quality ingredients (organic dairy, high-end dark chocolate), an array of flavors from banana cream to caramel macchiato, and "yummy" toppings to seal the deal; with just seven seats in the simple, white-oak-clad space, those in the know opt for takeout.

Puro Chile *Specialty Shop* 26 | 26 | 25 | M

Little Italy | 221 Centre St. (bet. Grand & Howard Sts.) | 212-925-7871

Puro Wine *Wines & Liquor*

Little Italy | 161 Grand St. (bet. Centre & Lafayette Sts.) | 212-925-0090 www.puro-wine.com

A "piece of Chilean culture" set down "in the middle of" Little Italy, these adjacent stores seek to offer the best of the South American country's exports, in mod quarters designed by a Santiago architect; on one side are comestibles, like olive oil, honey and jam and housewares (including traditional clay pots and tableware), and next door are some 150 wines, ranging from affordable Valle Central labels to hard-to-find collectors' bottles.

Raffetto's ⊅ *Pastas* 28 | 21 | 24 | I

G Village | 144 W. Houston St. (bet. MacDougal & Sullivan Sts.) | 212-777-1261

"You can still watch the old-style pasta cutting" machine in action at this circa-1906 "NYC treasure", where loading up on "fantastic fresh pasta in a multitude of shapes and flavors" at "entirely fair prices" is a cherished "Village tradition"; in addition to the noodles ("so tender, so delicate"), ravioli and other filled versions "just like grandma's" and "dry pastas imported from Italy", there are "cheeses, sauces, bread" and prepared dishes (meatballs, lasagna, etc.) so "wonderful", you may be tempted to "claim them as your own."

Randazzo's Seafood *Seafood* 26 | 21 | 24 | M

Fordham | 2327 Arthur Ave. (bet. 183rd & 187th Sts.) | Bronx | 718-367-4139 | www.randazzoseafood.com

"If you're looking for fresh seafood", it's "worth the trip to Arthur Avenue" to be dazzo'd by this longtime fishmonger's "superb-quality", "excellent selection" (it's "great for shellfish" too) and service "of yesteryear" from family owners who "know their fish"; it specializes in "imported sardines and other ocean goodies from different regions of Italy", and "you can even eat clams standing on the sidewalk" at their raw bar out front.

Ronnybrook Milk Bar *Cheese & Dairy* 26 | 20 | 20 | M

Chelsea | Chelsea Mkt. | 75 Ninth Ave. (bet. 15th & 16th Sts.) | 212-741-6455 | 800-772-6455 | www.ronnybrook.com

This "dairy godmother" in the Chelsea Market is a wish-come-true for milk-lovers who are udderly delighted by the "exceptional" offerings in its "farmhouse"-inspired storefront, including many types of milk and cream, butter, "delicious" yogurt drinks and ice cream, plus "thick, frothy" milkshakes, sundaes and such are available at the counter; it's always a "fun" stop "for families and couples alike", but the cream-of-the-crop lineup is also on offer at the Greenmarket and in gourmet stores citywide.

NEW Royce' Chocolate *Candy & Nuts*

E 50s | 509 Madison Ave. (bet. 52nd & 53rd Sts.) | 646-590-0650
W 40s | 28 W. 40th St. (bet. 5th & 6th Aves.) | no phone
W Village | 253 Bleecker St. (Cornelia St.) | 646-296-7653
www.royceconfectusa.com

This Japanese confectioner brings its line of signature 'Nama chocolate' – small, cocoa-powder-dusted squares fattened up with rich cream from the northern island of Hokkaido – to America with sleek, white boutiques in Midtown (plus a stripped-down location in the West Village), carrying flavors like champagne and green tea; the premium lineup also includes solid sweets and chocolate-coated cookies and potato chips for the crunch-seeking contingent.

Russ & Daughters *Caviar & Smoked Fish*

| 29 | 24 | 25 | E |

LES | 179 E. Houston St. (bet. Allen & Orchard Sts.) | 212-475-4880 | 800-787-7229 | www.russanddaughters.com

This family-run LES "landmark" dating to 1914 is in a "class by it-self" thanks to the "new generation" there that's "keeping up the quality" with "drool-worthy displays" of "legendary offerings", no-tably sable and "lox to dream of", "herring perfection", "top-quality" caviar and more, from bagels and babka to dried fruits and choco-late; it's always a "mad scene", especially at holidays ("oy vey!"), but the counter folk are "super helpful", so "take a number" – "it's worth the lines" and "expensive" tab to "order some of the best" with a side of "history."

Sable's Smoked Fish *Caviar & Smoked Fish*

| 27 | 19 | 23 | E |

E 70s | 1489 Second Ave. (bet. 77th & 78th Sts.) | 212-249-6177 | www.sablesnyc.com

"You can't get out" of this "swimmingly good" UES smoked-fish bazaar without being offered a "generous" sample of the signature whitefish or lobster salad as you troll the "cramped" quarters for "wonderful ap-petizing" and other "high-quality" "Sunday morning" fixings; it's "worth the extra" coinage you pay for this level of "quality and fresh-ness", but just "don't forget to bring your gold bullion."

Sahadi's *Specialty Shop*

| 28 | 22 | 22 | I |

Brooklyn Heights | 187 Atlantic Ave. (bet. Clinton & Court Sts.) | Brooklyn | 718-624-4550 | www.sahadis.com

"It doesn't get any better" for seekers of "Middle Eastern provisions" than this "long-established", recently renovated and expanded Brooklyn Heights "labyrinth" of "exotic" "delights", an "institution to be trea-sured" for its "vast inventory" of "traditional" staples including nuts, dried fruits, spices, olives, coffee, grains, oils, jams, fresh cheeses and "excellent" prepared foods such as "hummus, grape leaves, etc." – in short, "everything you need"; it's a "zoo" at "peak times" ("get ready to take a number"), but with "efficient" service and "unbeatable prices", it's "worth the hassle" even if you're "schlepping from Manhattan."

QUALITY · DISPLAY · SERVICE · COST

Sakaya *Wines & Liquor*   ▽ 28 | 26 | 28 | M

E Village | 324 E. Ninth St. (bet. 1st & 2nd Aves.) | 212-505-7253 |
www.sakayanyc.com

Sake sippers swear by this "well-kept secret" in the East Village, a
"jewel box of a store" chock-full of "amazing choices" imported from
Japan, including a locally "unmatched" selection of some 100 varieties of rice wine plus a smaller sampling of the distilled spirit shochu;
ultra-"helpful" salesclerks are primed to "educate", and there are also
weekly in-store tastings as well as off-site ones that can be arranged
at customers' homes.

Salumeria Biellese *Meat & Poultry*   26 | 16 | 20 | M

Chelsea | 378 Eighth Ave. (29th St.) | 212-736-7376 |
www.salumeriabiellese.com

This 1925-vintage Chelsea salumeria is prized for its "terrific Italian-
style cured meats" and "outstanding fresh sausage", housemade
"with care" from "farm-raised" stock in 40-plus variations spanning
"the usual" to the unique; the products turn up at "forbidding" upscale
restaurants like Daniel Boulud's and Jean-Georges Vongerichten's,
but those coming straight to the source note the price tag "isn't
haute"; P.S. they also offer prepared foods, imported prosciutto and a
full line of sandwiches.

Salumeria Rosi Parmacotto ● *Specialty Shop*   28 | 24 | 23 | E

NEW **E 70s** | 903 Madison Ave. (bet. 72rd & 73rd Sts.) | 212-517-7700
W 70s | 283 Amsterdam Ave. (bet. 73rd & 74th Sts.) | 212-877-4800
www.salumeriarosi.com

"Like a little piece of Italy" in NYC, this "spectacular" UWS salumeria/
cafe and its new UES sibling are "gems" where chef Cesare Casella
oversees an "eclectic selection" showcasing "wonderful" cured meats
(think "authentic" salamis and prosciutto di Parma) "flown in daily"
from the old country along with "delicious cheeses", pastas, oils and
other "lovely" "specialty foods"; the "super-educated staff" also mans
an eating area "crowded" with cognoscenti sampling tapas-size
plates, and while it's admittedly "high-priced", the "superior taste is
worth every penny."

S&S Cheesecake *Baked Goods*   28 | 14 | 20 | M

Kingsbridge | 222 W. 238th St. (bet. Bailey Ave. & B'way) | Bronx |
718-549-3888 | 800-385-0546 | www.sscheesecake.com

Theirs is "the cheesecake you dream about" promise partisans of this
"still-incredible" bakery in the Kingsbridge section of the Bronx – "nothing comes close" to the legendarily "rich" "manna" that's the "ultimate
"calorie splurge"; even if you "need your GPS" to find its "no-frills" facility
(open Monday–Friday till 3 PM), it's worth "the trip from anywhere" –
though the wares can also be had at "fancy restaurants" around town.

Saxelby Cheesemongers *Cheese & Dairy*   29 | 24 | 27 | E

LES | Essex Street Mkt. | 120 Essex St. (bet. Delancey & Rivington Sts.) |
212-228-8204 | www.saxelbycheese.com

This "lovely little" "American-only" cheese stall in the Essex Street
Market is "locavore" heaven given its "small but superb" selection
of "regional" artisanal cheeses with a spotlight on those from the
Northeast as well as local "milk, yogurt, butter, eggs and bread"; it's

	QUALITY	DISPLAY	SERVICE	COST

all overseen by "very caring owners" Anne Saxelby and Benoit Breal, whose "fun" demeanor adds to the enjoyment and helps compensate for "costly" price tags.

Schaller & Weber *Meat & Poultry*

28 | 22 | 23 | M

E 80s | 1654 Second Ave. (bet. 85th & 86th Sts.) | 212-879-3047 | 800-847-4115 | www.schallerweber.com

"*Danke schön!*" cry thankful fans of this "remnant of the old Yorkville", a "real treasure" that "still sets the standard" with a "wide range" of the "finest" "old-world German" wursts, wieners and meats tendered by "butchers who know their trade"; it's also "a mini-grocery well stocked" with "excellent" imported sundries, and while it's "not cheap", for "hands-down" "authentic" goods "this is the spot" – may it "stay there forever."

Scratch Bread *Baked Goods*

▽ 27 | 21 | 25 | M

Bed-Stuy | 1069 Bedford Ave. (Lexington Ave.) | Brooklyn | no phone | www.scratchbread.com

Founded by baker Matthew Tilden, who has the store logo tattooed on his arm, this Bed-Stuy bakery is best known by carb connoisseurs for its rustic artisanal breads – made from scratch, natch – like Brownstone focaccia, Stuyvesant sour and whole wheat–spelt nut; the loaves, plus sandwiches, soups and more, are peddled from a take-out window, and are also available at Smorgasburg and at restaurants and gourmet stores around town.

Shelsky's Smoked Fish *Caviar & Smoked Fish*

24 | 19 | 25 | E

Boerum Hill | 251 Smith St. (bet. Degraw & Douglass Sts.) | Brooklyn | 718-855-8817 | www.shelskys.com

Ready to meet "all your smoked fish emergencies", Boerum Hill's old-style Jewish appetizing store is "the place" for those who "love a good sturgeon", whitefish, pickled herring or other "scrumptious" classic; add traditional schmears and spreads, not to mention bagels, bialys and Orwasher's bread, and most happily overlook prices on the "expensive" side – hey, it beats "schlepping" to Manhattan, and the service with "direct-from-Brooklyn humor" comes free.

Sherry-Lehmann *Wines & Liquor*

29 | 26 | 25 | E

E 50s | 505 Park Ave. (59th St.) | 212-838-7500 | www.sherry-lehmann.com

The "gold standard" for "well-rounded" wine emporiums, this Midtown imbiber's "Eden" makes it a "pleasure to shop" for vintages and liquor of all kinds "in person", "online" or from the mail-order catalog – a bacchanal's "dream book" – given the "superlative selection" of "high-end" libations (some 6,500 labels), "engaged", "knowledgeable" sales reps, "fast" delivery and in-house "educational seminars"; loads of glassware and accessories are also on hand, and if your sales slip is sky-high, at least you "get what you pay for."

Silver Moon Bakery *Baked Goods*

26 | 22 | 22 | M

W 100s | 2740 Broadway (105th St.) | 212-866-4717 | www.silvermoonbakery.com

"Breads and pastries that transport you to Paris" are the specialty of this "superior" UWS French bakery whose "delicious delights" – from baguettes to challah, cakes to macarons and frangipane tarts – always seem "fresh" "out of the oven"; locals who nearly "jump over the moon" as the "smells waft out to Broadway" warn "don't be put off by cramped quarters" and "weekend crowds" – just join the fray and try to "get noticed" by the counter crew.

Simchick, L. *Meat & Poultry* | 29 | 19 | 25 | VE |

E 50s | 988 First Ave. (bet. 54th & 55th Sts.) | 212-888-2299
With an "emphasis on top quality and personal service", this East Side "real old-fashioned butcher" supplies "high-end" meats that are simply "the finest", housemade sausages and "oven-ready" specialties including marinated steaks and roasts; naturally "you pay" for such "superb" stock, but it comes courtesy of "knowledgeable and friendly" staffers who dependably "deliver."

Smorgasburg *Specialty Shop* | 28 | 16 | 19 | I |

NEW **Dumbo** | Brooklyn Bridge Park | 30 Water St. (Dock St.) | Brooklyn | 718-928-6603
Williamsburg | East River State Park (Kent Ave. & N. 7th St.) | Brooklyn | 718-928-6603
www.smorgasburg.com
These outdoor, warm weather–only offshoots of the Brooklyn Flea offer "Manhattan skyline" views to go with the "fantastic", "deliciously cheap" eats from "local food purveyors", drawing "crazy crowds" of "yupsters" and "hipsters" to the Williamsburg waterfront (Saturdays) and Dumbo's Brooklyn Bridge Park (Sundays); "the sheer variety" – everything from hot dogs, tacos, BBQ, pizza, pickles and noodles to pops, donuts, cupcakes and cookies – "makes the trip essential" for foodies, but "go early as things tend to sell out."

Sockerbit ❶ *Candy & Nuts* ▽ 24 | 24 | 20 | E |

W Village | 89 Christopher St. (bet. Bleecker & W. 4th Sts.) | 212-206-8170 | www.sockerbit.com
"Call the dentist" before checking out the "fun selection" of more than 130 varieties of bulk "couture candy" imported from Scandinavia at this West Village confectionary that's the "perfect" source of "quirky gifts" for the "sweet tooth" in your life; it offers an "amazing range in gummies", sugary suckers and novelties within its minimalist, all-white digs, so the kinda "expensive" prices are the only sour note.

Spice Corner ❶ *Herbs & Spices* | 23 | 19 | 21 | M |

Murray Hill | 135 Lexington Ave. (29th St.) | 212-689-5182 | www.spicecorner29.com
Binge on "bargains galore" at this "small", "bodega-style" Murray Hill Indian food market, a "go-to" for "all sorts of" Mideastern and South Asian spices and "high-quality" groceries including rice, beans, nuts, dates, chutney and Bengali confections; run by staffers who "couldn't be friendlier", it keeps savvy shoppers in its corner with "better prices" and a "warmer welcome" than most.

Spices & Tease ❶ *Herbs & Spices* ▽ 25 | 24 | 26 | M |

Chelsea | Chelsea Mkt. | 75 Ninth Ave. (bet. 15th & 16th Sts.)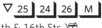
E 40s | Grand Central Mkt. | Lexington Ave. (45th St.) | 212-883-8327
W 90s | 2580 Broadway (bet. 97th & 98th Sts.) | 347-470-8327
www.spicesandtease.com
Now bringing its "heavenly aromas" to the UWS, Grand Central and Chelsea Market, this merchant offers the same "plethora" of "inter-

esting teas" and "fresh spices" (including 30 housemade blends) that have drawn raves at street markets for years; expect some 180 loose-leaf teas, including exotics like strawberry-rhubarb, plus an assortment of dried herbs, flavored sugars, salts and peppers, all overseen by a staff willing to "guide you" if the choices seem "overwhelming."

Sprinkles Cupcakes ● *Baked Goods*   26 | 25 | 25 | M

E 60s | 780 Lexington Ave. (bet. 60th & 61st Sts.) | 212-207-8375 | www.sprinkles.com

A leader in the "cupcake craze", this Beverly Hills bakery's UES outpost offers 14 daily changing varieties of the "melt-in-your-mouth", "moist, soft", "flavorful" "indulgences" topped with "fun decorations"; an "enthusiastic" crew oversees the "adorable" quarters, and although a been-there-done-that few yawn that these "chic", "calorific" concoctions are "not up to the hype", those who appreciate the "no-gimmicks-or-goop" "quality" suggest you "invoke your inner baker by bringing home their mixes."

Staubitz Market   *Meat & Poultry*   29 | 25 | 26 | E

Cobble Hill | 222 Court St. (bet. Baltic & Warren Sts.) | Brooklyn | 718-624-0014 | www.staubitz.com

A "wonderful throwback" "that can't be duplicated", this Cobble Hill "neighborhood" "classic" has "been around forever" (since 1917) and still perches near the "top of the butcher list" with its "fantastic" cuts of beef, pork, poultry and game, including a "terrific range of organic" meats; the prices may be "some of the highest" around, but "everything is prime" and "you can taste the difference"; P.S. "order early for Thanksgiving" and other holidays.

Steve's Authentic Key Lime Pies   *Baked Goods*   26 | 13 | 17 | M

Red Hook | Pier 40 | 185 Van Dyke St. (Ferris St.) | Brooklyn | 718-858-5333 | 888-450-5463 | www.stevesauthentic.com

Yes, essentially there's "only one thing" on offer, but when it comes to "delicious Key lime pie" you should "get it here" say acolytes of this eccentric dessert wholesaler that's "out of the way" in Red Hook – post-Sandy it moved a block from its original location – but is resoundingly voted "worth the search"; you can almost "see the sun setting" over the Florida Keys when "you take a bite" of its "delicious" sweet-tart treats, including the Swingle, a frozen pop version "dipped in chocolate" that's as "insane" as you imagine.

Stinky Bklyn   *Cheese & Dairy*   27 | 22 | 25 | M

Cobble Hill | 215 Smith St. (bet. Baltic & Butler Sts.) | Brooklyn | 718-522-7425 | www.stinkybklyn.com

This slice of "cheese heaven" in Cobble Hill emits "the best stench around" thanks to its "wonderful selection" of fromage in "peak-ripe" condition, plus an assortment of "good crusty breads" and "amazing" charcuterie to "go with"; the sharp, "friendly" staffers know their stuff, but they just might "make fun of you if you ask for Havarti."

Streit's Matzo Co. ⊄ *Baked Goods*   27 | 14 | 19 | I

LES | 148-154 Rivington St. (bet. Clinton & Suffolk Sts.) | 212-475-7000 | www.streitsmatzos.com

You can "watch the matzo being made" at this "wonderful" Lower East Side "holdover", a fifth-generation family business and factory turning out "authentic" "fresh-baked" unleavened crackers and vending a variety of kosher goods, from macaroons to matzo-ball-soup mix; it's a prime destination come Passover, and to such a "historical spot" devotees say *"l'chaim!"*

🆕 Sugar and Plumm ● *Candy & Nuts*   - | - | - | M

W 70s | 377 Amsterdam Ave. (bet. 78th & 79th Sts.) | 212-787-8778
W Village | 257 Bleecker St. (Cornelia St.) | 212-388-5757
www.sugarandplumm.com

Bakeries, ice cream parlors and candy shops all in one, these sweeteries, offshoots of a New Jersey outfit, showcase tempting treats like dainty salted caramel macarons, fluffy croissants, waffle-and-bacon milkshakes and whimsically shaped chocolates; it's all displayed in bright quarters, with the UWSer featuring an all-day sit-down bistro and the smaller West Village satellite catering to the grab-and-go crowd.

Sugar Shop *Candy & Nuts*   - | - | - | M

Cobble Hill | 254 Baltic St. (bet. Clinton & Court Sts.) | Brooklyn | 718-576-3591 | www.sugarshopbrooklyn.com

A rainbow of colorful treats fills the glass canisters at this white-tiled Cobble Hill candy store showcasing more than 150 types of bulk sweets, including chocolates, jelly beans and nostalgic goodies like Charleston Chews and Clark bars (which come at contemporary prices); a 'made in Brooklyn' section highlights local brands like Mast Brothers and Fine & Raw, and a separate room is available for children's parties.

Sugar Sweet Sunshine ● *Baked Goods*   26 | 20 | 23 | I

LES | 126 Rivington St. (bet. Essex & Norfolk Sts.) | 212-995-1960 | www.sugarsweetsunshine.com

Prepared with "love", the "awesome", "homemade-iest" cupcakes at this LES bakery are worth "daydreaming" over given their "moist, flavorful" base and "wonderful" icing "reminiscent of childhood birthdays", and there are also full-size cakes, cookies, bars and "to-die-for banana pudding"; factor in "cheap" prices that make for an affordable "fix", and this contender "simply outshines the rest" in the neighborhood.

Sullivan Street Bakery *Baked Goods*   27 | 21 | 21 | M

🆕 Chelsea | 236 Ninth Ave. (bet. 24th & 25th Sts.) | 212-929-5900 ●
W 40s | 533 W. 47th St. (bet. 10th & 11th Aves.) | 212-265-5580
www.sullivanstreetbakery.com

"Bless you, Jim Lahey" swoon disciples of the no-knead "master" baker and his "variety of artisanal loaves" with a "beautiful crust", "thin, crunchy" pizzas that "transport you to Rome" along with an "outstanding" lineup of "rolls, sandwiches, little pies, cakes" and more; those who complained that the West Hell's Kitchen store is "almost in New Jersey" now have a quicker trip to "bread heaven" via the newer Chelsea location – and of course the "divine" goods are also on offer at restaurants and gourmet markets around town.

Sullivan Street Tea & Spice Company *Coffee & Tea*   26 | 23 | 26 | M

G Village | 208 Sullivan St. (bet. Bleecker & W. 3rd Sts.) | 212-387-8702 | www.onsullivan.com

The "perfect spot" for a "spot of tea", this "charming" Greenwich Village storefront presents more than 80 different brews (green, black, white, oolong, rooibos) plus a wide selection of organic herbs and spices – from fiery sundried ghost peppers to fragrant lavender flowers – amid "cozy" confines that naturally "smell lovely"; pick up some loose leaves or let the "knowledgeable" staff steep you a cuppa to go.

The Sweet Life Candy & Nuts   ▽ 27 | 25 | 26 | M

LES | 63 Hester St. (Ludlow St.) | 212-598-0092 | 800-692-6887 | www.sweetlifeny.com

This "tiny" Lower East Side candy shop is "overflowing with temptations of the best quality", from old-time treats like licorice, gummies, caramels and lollipops to "fresh", housemade chocolate products ("try the marshmallow"); imports include an array of honey, syrups, spreads, nuts and halvah, while the health-conscious declare the assortment of dried fruits is a "delicious way to increase your fiber intake."

NEW **Tache Artisan**   - | - | - | E
Chocolate ● Candy & Nuts

LES | 254 Broome St. (Orchard St.) | 212-473-3200 | www.tachechocolate.com

The eponymous Parisian chocolatier teamed up with a NYC pastry chef to open this LES confectioner, where the made-fresh-daily truffles, bars, pastries, macarons and more are decidedly French, though some of the flavorings travel the globe a bit (tequila-infused ganache, anyone?); its petite, brick-walled space with a bright-pink awning houses a small seating area where the treats can be enjoyed on-premises along with Dallis Brothers coffee.

Tea & Honey Store Coffee & Tea   ▽ 29 | 28 | 26 | E

E 60s | 828 Lexington Ave. (63rd St.) | 212-355-2812 | www.theteaandhoneystore.com

This mod, honeycomb-shelved East 60s store has enthusiasts "humming like a bee" over its "incredible selection" of "flavorful teas" – including "unusual" imports – offered alongside "the best honeys" for an even sweeter deal, plus accoutrements if "you don't have a pot to brew in"; the staff is unwaveringly "helpful", and the goods make standout gifts "when you want to bring something other than a bottle of wine."

NEW **Teavana** ● Coffee & Tea   - | - | - | E

E 80s | 1291 Lexington Ave. (bet. 86th & 87th Sts.) | 212-831-5738
W 80s | 2261 Broadway (W. 81st St.) | 212-799-0724
www.teavana.com

Loose-leaf lovers seek nirvana at these bag-free tea emporiums, links in a Starbucks-owned chain stocking just about every brew imaginable – white, green, oolong, herbal, black, rooibos, maté and custom blends – plus ample accessories like ceramic pots, strainers and color-coded tins; free samples and bars serving hot and cold single cups make it easier to decide what type to take home with you.

Teitel Brothers Specialty Shop   27 | 19 | 22 | M

Fordham | 2372 Arthur Ave. (186th St.) | Bronx | 718-733-9400 | 800-850-7055 | www.teitelbros.com

The "heart and soul of Arthur Avenue" when it comes to "specialty Italian items", this circa-1915 "local" grocery is "crowded" to overflowing (the "sidewalk included") with "all sorts of" imports, embracing "hard-to-find" cheeses, "cured meats, dried pastas", olive oils and "anything else you need" for an old-world "feast"; despite occasionally "pushy" service, *amici* who feel enteitled to a "varied selection" at "fair prices" agree it's "worth a trip to the Bronx."

Ten Ren Tea & Ginseng Co. *Coffee & Tea*   25 | 21 | 18 | M

Chinatown | 75 Mott St. (bet. Bayard & Canal Sts.) | 212-349-2286 | 800-292-2049 | www.tenrenusa.com

A "dream come true" for the "aficionado of Chinese tea", this "atmospheric" C-town stalwart – not to be confused with its bubble tea bar offshoots around town – stocks an "amazing selection" of loose-leaf "exotics" imported in "many grades", with "prices based on the quality" (from "decent" to "eye-popping") to guarantee a brew "for every budget", plus there are also elegant tea sets and accessories; it couldn't be more "authentic", and it's all overseen by staffers who "know their stuff."

Terranova Bakery ⊅ *Baked Goods*   28 | 20 | 22 | I

Fordham | 691 E. 187th St. (bet. Beaumont & Cambreleng Aves.) | Bronx | 718-367-6985 | www.terranovabakery.com

Seekers of "fabulous" crusty Italian bread "go no further" than this "friendly" Arthur Avenue–area bakery whose "excellent" loaves, rolls, baguettes, focaccia, "the very best *pane di casa*" and other "fabulous" baked goods keep emerging "fresh" from the coal-fired brick oven "all day"; a pasta factory on the premises adds to the carb-tastic offerings, while nominal prices mean it won't set you back too much dough.

Teuscher Chocolates   29 | 27 | 25 | VE
of Switzerland *Candy & Nuts*

E 40s | 620 Fifth Ave. (bet. 49th & 50th Sts.) | 212-246-4416
E 60s | 25 E. 61st St. (bet. Madison & Park Aves.) | 212-751-8482
800-554-0924 | www.teuscher-newyork.com

Despite "new competition" in recent years, the "luxurious", "eye-pleasingly packed" Swiss chocolates dispensed by this East Side twosome "still reign supreme", and are rated "sensational" enough to "unlock the grumpiest of hearts"; yes, "you gotta pay" "heavily" and "put up with" occasional attitude from the capable staff, but that all melts away when you bite into one of those "divine champagne truffles" – "if you don't swoon, you're dead."

Three Tarts *Baked Goods*   ▽ 26 | 26 | 25 | M

Chelsea | 164 Ninth Ave. (20th St.) | 212-462-4392
E 50s | Plaza Food Hall | 1 W. 59th St. (5th Ave.) | 646-755-3232 ●
www.3tarts.com

"Beautiful sweets and treats" come in "small sizes" at this "cute" Chelsea confectioner/bakery (with a spin-off in the Plaza Food Hall) vending bite-size tarts, pretty petits fours, "the best" homemade marshmallows (some 30 flavors) and other "mini-indulgences" sold in optional tins, jars and trays; these diminutive treats "always impress", making them ideal "to bring to a party or give as gifts", but there are also a few seats for enjoying 'em right on the spot.

NEW **Tiberio Custom Meats** *Meat & Poultry*   – | – | – | E

LES | Sauce | 78 Rivington St. (Allen St.) | 718-374-5148 |
www.tiberiocustommeats.com

In the back of the Lower East Side Italian eatery Sauce dwells this full-service butcher shop from meat maven Adam Tiberio (ex Dickson's),

QUALITY DISPLAY SERVICE COST

a source for 100% grass-fed, pasture-raised beef, pork and poultry from small-scale farms in Vermont and New York State; custom trimming, a whole-animal CSA program and a nightly Butcher's Table dinner at Sauce help set it apart from the herd.

Titan Foods ◑ *Specialty Shops* — 26 | 22 | 20 | M
Astoria | 2556 31st St. (bet. Astoria Blvd. & 28th Ave.) | Queens | 718-626-7771 | www.titanfood.com

The "mother ship" of "all things Greek", this Astoria specialty supermarket is a "phenomenal" source of all that "you could wish for" in the way of "real-deal" imports, offering "outstanding" cheeses (including some 15 types of feta), "wonderful olives", baked goods and other "finds" at a "very fair" price; "don't expect much service", but Hellenists with time to "browse" "really don't have to go anywhere else."

Todaro Brothers ◑ *Specialty Shops* — 25 | 20 | 21 | E
Murray Hill | 555 Second Ave. (bet. 30th & 31st Sts.) | 212-532-0633 | 877-472-2767 | www.todarobros.com

A Murray Hill "lifesaver" "year after year", this "classic neighborhood" fixture is a "go-to" for "top-quality" Italian "gourmet" goods that packs "as much as possible" into a "limited space", including a "wide variety" of meat, fish, "fresh fruits and vegetables", "some of the best cheeses", pastas, olive oils and "excellent prepared foods" and sandwiches; the aisles are "sometimes very crowded", but the "informed" staff is "a big plus" – local seekers of "authentic" edibles "can't ask for more."

Trois Pommes Patisserie *Baked Goods* — ▽ 27 | 24 | 24 | M
Park Slope | 260 Fifth Ave. (bet. Carroll St. & Garfield Pl.) | Brooklyn | 718-230-3119 | www.troispommespatisserie.com

"Lovely and intimate", this Park Slope patisserie incorporates Greenmarket ingredients into a "delicious" lineup of cookies, cupcakes and ice cream, as well as "new takes on old favorites" (e.g. housemade 'Oreos' and red-velvet 'Twinkies'); "seasonal offerings", "personal and personable" service and "great-value" prices are other highlights; P.S. it also does special-order birthday and wedding cakes.

Tu-Lu's Gluten-Free Bakery ◑ *Baked Goods* — ▽ 25 | 24 | 23 | M
E Village | 338 E. 11th St. (bet. 1st & 2nd Aves.) | 212-777-2227 | www.tu-lusbakery.com

"Who needs gluten anyway?" muse mavens of this "much-needed" East Village niche bakery that devotes its entire menu to wheat- and gluten-free breads, brownies, cookies, cupcakes, muffins and panini, and they "taste great" – "wow"; the impressive options extend to custom cakes (including wedding versions) that can also be prepared to suit dairy-free or vegan predilections.

Two for the Pot ⌂ *Coffee & Tea* — ▽ 26 | 22 | 26 | M
Brooklyn Heights | 200 Clinton St. (bet. Atlantic Ave. & State St.) | Brooklyn | 718-855-8173

For Brooklyn Heights 'hoodies, this durable little shop may be "the best" choice around for premium coffees and "fantastic" "imported teas", quaintly curated by a "charming" owner who creates his own "custom-blended" brews; also chockablock with an "exotic" variety of spices and herbs, select specialty items, British pantry staples and "beautiful" accessories ("want a teapot?"), "this place has it all" as long as you have "plenty of cash, as they don't take cards."

Two Little Red Hens *Baked Goods* | 26 | 23 | 22 | E |

E 80s | 1652 Second Ave. (bet. 85th & 86th Sts.) | 212-452-0476 | www.twolittleredhens.com

Customers crow with delight over this "absolutely charming" Upper East Side bakery adored for its "gorgeous" "top-quality" cakes and cupcakes in "superlative flavors", which are "exquisitely decorated" and "delicious to eat" (a troublingly "rare combination"); it also proffers pies, and while some cry fowl over "steep" prices, "gracious" service helps tip the scale to "worth every penny" – just be sure to order "well ahead" for the holidays.

Union Market ● *Major Market* | 25 | 23 | 22 | E |

E Village | 240 E. Houston St. (Norfolk St.) | 212-677-2441
Cobble Hill | 288 Court St. (bet. Degraw & Douglass Sts.) | Brooklyn | 718-709-5100
Park Slope | 402 Seventh Ave. (bet. 12th & 13th Sts.) | Brooklyn | 718-499-4026
Park Slope | 754-756 Union St. (6th Ave.) | Brooklyn | 718-230-5152
www.unionmarket.com

"When you need everything in one place", these "lovely" markets fill the bill with an "incredible array" highlighting natural and organic goods, all organized into "pretty displays" featuring breads from artisanal bakeries, craft cheeses, "quality" meats and fish as well as "top-notch" produce; they're an "interesting work in progress", and while prices run "high", when your "appetite is stimulated" "convenience sometimes trumps cost."

Union Square | 25 | 23 | 22 | E |
Wines & Spirits ● *Wines & Liquor*

Union Sq | 140 Fourth Ave. (13th St.) | 212-675-8100 | www.unionsquarewines.com

Vinophiles return "again and again" to the "super" and "superbly edited" selection (some 2,500 labels) at this "spacious", "classy" wine emporium off Union Square that has earned a loyal following among "frequent buyers" who can "rack up points with purchases" and use "Enomatic wine cards" to get "free tastings"; some report "gouge"-level prices, but others citing "case discounts", a "well-educated" staff and "amazing events" chide "no wine-ing"; P.S. its wines can also be ordered through Fresh Direct.

Valley Shepherd Creamery *Cheese & Dairy*   ▽ | 28 | 24 | 25 | M |

Park Slope | 211 Seventh Ave. (bet. 3rd & 4th Sts.) | Brooklyn | 347-889-5508 | www.valleyshepherd.com

It's all about ewe, ewe, ewe, at this "locavore"-approved sheep-cheese monger in Park Slope (plus at the Greenmarket and other markets), a retail outlet of a NJ dairy that locals say is the next best thing to having "a farm in the neighborhood" given its lactic lineup of more than 30 "extremely delicious" fromages, alongside butter, yogurt, lamb meat, bread and specialty goods; "helpful" counter folk doling out "samples" will keep you coming baaack, not to mention the sandwiches at lunchtime.

QUALITY | DISPLAY | SERVICE | COST

Varsano's *Candy & Nuts*   ▽ 29 | 27 | 28 | M

W Village | 172 W. Fourth St. (bet. 6th & 7th Aves.) | 212-352-1171 | 800-414-4718 | www.varsanos.com

The "sweet" proprietor of this West Village bonbon shop is "always experimenting" with new "housemade specialties" to complement such popular signatures as caramel pretzel rods, chocolate-covered potato chips, "the best truffles" and "dark chocolate malted milk balls that will change your life"; even the "sugar-free selections are delicious", while the wide array of novelty molds include Porsches, tools, boxing gloves and other guy-friendly shapes along with ballet slippers and blow-dryers for the ladies.

Veniero's ● *Baked Goods*   25 | 23 | 19 | M

E Village | 342 E. 11th St. (bet. 1st & 2nd Aves.) | 212-674-7070 | www.venierospastry.com

The line outside "says it all" at this "venerable" Italian bakery, a "superior" pasticceria and East Village "fixture" since 1894 that's famed for its "amazing selection" of "authentic" cannoli, cheesecakes, rainbow cookies and other "old-school" favorites "made with love"; "reasonable prices" add to the "joyful experience" – no wonder diehards say it's a "must-go" for every sweet tooth.

Villabate-Alba Pasticceria ● *Baked Goods*   27 | 28 | 23 | M

Bensonhurst | 7001 18th Ave. (70th St.) | Brooklyn | 718-331-8430 | www.villabate.com

"Each item is a work of art" at this Bensonhurst Italian pastry emporium where the "attention to detail" is "evident" in all manner of "to-die-for" Sicilian cakes, cannoli, cookies and whimsically shaped marzipan in "amazingly beautiful" presentations; no surprise this "year-round favorite" has a line "out the door at Christmas" – and "don't forget the housemade gelato" – "if you're Italian or want to be", this is "the place."

Vosges Haut-Chocolat *Candy & Nuts*   27 | 26 | 23 | E

E 80s | 1100 Madison Ave. (bet. 82nd & 83rd Sts.) | 212-717-2929
SoHo | 132 Spring St. (bet. Greene & Wooster Sts.) | 212-625-2929
888-301-9866 | www.vosgeschocolate.com

"Adventurous" chocoholics "looking for something unusual" hit these SoHo–Upper East Side boutique confectioners where the "fantastic" creations feature unexpected "spices" and "extraordinary flavor combinations" (think bittersweet with Taleggio cheese or "wowza bacon bar"); "sleek" purple packaging and "haute prices" add to the "air of exclusivity", and though a few skeptics sigh it's all a little "over-the-top", even they admit you've "got to give points for gutsy" "innovation."

NEW Wedge ● *Cheese & Dairy*   – | – | – | M

Crown Heights | 728 Franklin Ave. (bet. Park & Sterling Pls.) | Brooklyn | 845-325-3145

Barely bigger than a wheel of Parmigiano, this bright, brick-and-tile-lined new cheesemonger in Crown Heights has managed to wedge an impressive selection into its petite fromage case, ranging from classics like Cabot Clothbound to lesser-known domestic farmstead offerings, and there's also charcuterie, bread from Bien Cuit, a daily changing sandwich lineup, high-end jams and other provisions, along with

Toby's Estate coffee; relatively reasonable prices and a regular roster of 'Wedge-ucate Yourself' classes should help keep the locals coming.

Whiskey Shop ◑ *Wines & Liquor* ▽ 27 | 27 | 25 | E |

Williamsburg | 44 Berry St. (on N. 11th St., bet. Berry St. & Wythe Ave.) | Brooklyn | 718-384-7467 | www.whiskeyshopbrooklyn.com

"No normal liquor store", this Williamsburg nook from the owners of the next-door bar Whiskey Brooklyn really "should be called whiskey heaven" given its "unbelievable selection" (a rotating mix of 99 labels) lined up on tall shelves, spanning scotch, bourbon, rye and more, with an emphasis on domestic and local distillers; there are also wines in stock, and it's all overseen by "super-friendly" staffers who "know their stuff", meaning this place offers just about "everything a booze-lover needs."

Whole Foods Market ◑ *Major Market* 25 | 25 | 21 | E |

Chelsea | 250 Seventh Ave. (24th St.) | 212-924-5969
NEW E 50s | 226 E. 57th St. (bet. 2nd & 3rd Aves.) | 646-497-1222
LES | 95 E. Houston St. (Bowery) | 212-420-1320
TriBeCa | 270 Greenwich St. (Warren St.) | 212-349-6555
Union Sq | 4 Union Square S. (bet. B'way & University Pl.) | 212-673-5388
W 50s | Shops at Columbus Circle | 10 Columbus Circle (bet. 58th & 60th Sts.) | 212-823-9600
W 90s | 808 Columbus Ave. (bet. 97th & 100th Sts.) | 212-222-6160
888-746-7936 | www.wholefoodsmarket.com

"Up there at the top of the food chain", these "big, beautiful" branches of the "eco-friendly" Texas empire "delight" with the "superior quality" and "amazing breadth" of their "wholesome" provisions, notably "fantastic" produce displayed like a "still life", a "treasure chest" of "fabulous" cheeses, coffee and tea, "choice" meats and poultry, "exceptional" seafood, "fresh" baked goods, an "excellent" beer selection heavy on "regional microbrews" and a "gazillion" "awesome" prepared foods; the "spacious aisles" and "organized check-out" will "make your day", and if the price tag "can be hefty", a "splurge" "doesn't get much better than this."

William Greenberg Desserts *Baked Goods* 25 | 22 | 22 | E |

E 50s | Plaza Food Hall | 1 W. 59th St. (5th Ave.) | 646-755-3235
E 80s | 1100 Madison Ave. (bet. 82nd & 83rd Sts.) | 212-861-1340
www.wmgreenbergdesserts.com

Though no longer in the Greenberg family, this "old-time" UES bakery (with a Plaza Food Hall offshoot) continues its "long history" of rolling out "classy", "delicious" kosher baked goods that are perfect "for that special occasion", including "tabulous" black-and-white cookies, schnecken, babka and brownies; these days, it's perhaps best known for its "unbelievable architectural" wedding cakes deemed "worth" the significant price and the "zillions of calories" – bring on the "butter."

Xocolatti *Candy & Nuts* ▽ 22 | 21 | 19 | E |

SoHo | 172 Prince St. (Thompson St.) | 212-256-0332 | www.xocolatti.com

Adventurous chocolate connoisseurs head to this sleek SoHo confectioner, a small but deluxe shop with candy box–covered walls that specializes in housemade truffles, clusters and crumbles offered in "delicious" exotic flavors (think passion fruit, sake, pomegranate), along with gelato and hot chocolate; yes, the goods are "expensive", but they make a "great gift option" for "special occasions."

Yonah Schimmel Knish Bakery *Baked Goods* | 24 | 11 | 16 | I |

LES | 137 E. Houston St. (bet. 1st & 2nd Aves.) | 212-477-2858 |
www.yonahschimmel.com

"A knish is still a knish" at this "one-and-only" LES "legend", a "vestige" of the old neighborhood that has been dispensing "heavy, calorie-filled" Jewish "comfort food" for more than a century, notably "melt-in-your-mouth" knishes "of every variety", plus "great kugel and pickles" and "egg creams too"; aesthetics-wise it's on the "shabby"-"shoddy" side, and you can "forget about service", but remember you're here "for a blast of old NY" – just "nosh!"

Zabar's *Major Market* | 27 | 21 | 21 | E |

W 80s | 2245 Broadway (bet. 80th & 81st Sts.) | 212-787-2000 |
www.zabars.com

It's worth a "move to the UWS to be near" this "iconic" one-stop gourmet "extravaganza", still proffering a "plethora" of "unbeatable" goods, from the legendarily "exceptional" smoked fish ("brave the lines" and "get it hand-cut") to "terrific baked goods", a "glorious", "mind-boggling" cheese selection, "outstanding coffee", a "wow" of a deli, "divine" prepared foods, plus "discount" cookware and gadgets "cluttered" together upstairs; it's a "jammed" "maze" that's "not for the faint of heart", but the experience "cannot be imitated" so "sharpen your elbows and jump in."

Zucker Bakery ⊅ *Baked Goods* | 24 | 21 | 23 | M |

E Village | 433 E. Ninth St. (bet. Ave. A & 1st Ave.) | 646-559-8425 |
www.zuckerbakery.com

Be prepared to succumb to "delicious aromas" at this "homey, friendly" bakery in the East Village that pastry pundits "love" for its "so-delicious" selection of delicacies reflecting the owner's Eastern European and Israeli roots, including signature sticky buns (known as 'roses'), rugalach and Friday-only challah; Stumptown coffee and other barista-made beverages that can be enjoyed on the premises seal the deal – this is a "gem worth coming back to."

Zucker's Bagels & Smoked Fish *Baked Goods* | 22 | 18 | 17 | M |

NEW **E 40s** | Grand Central Terminal | 370 Lexington Ave. (bet. 40th & 41st Sts.) | 212-661-1080

TriBeCa | 146 Chambers St. (W. B'way) | 212-608-5844
www.zuckersbagels.com

"Mouthwatering bagels" and traditional "appetizing" await at these shops in TriBeCa and Grand Central from the owners of Murray's Bagels; they "fill the bill" when you seek "Sunday brunch" fixings, notably "crispy-on-the-outside, soft-on-the-inside" bagels and all manner of "schmears", not to mention La Colombe coffee by the pound and pastries from Trois Pommes, though some say the service could "use some warming up."

Greenmarket Locations

For ratings and reviews, see p. 270. And for the most current information about Greenmarket locations, check www.grownyc.org.

Manhattan

E 40s | Dag Hammarskjold Plaza | 47th St. (2nd Ave.) | Wed., Year-round
E 80s | 82nd St. (bet. 1st & York Aves.) | Sat., Year-round
E 90s | First Ave. (bet. 92nd & 93rd Sts.) | Sun., June–Dec.
E 90s | Mt. Sinai Hospital | 99th St. (bet. Madison & Park Aves.) | Wed., June–Nov.
E Village | St. Mark's Church | 10th St. (2nd Ave.) | Tues., June–Dec.
E Village | Tompkins Sq. | E. Seventh St. (Ave. A) | Sun., Year-round
Financial District | Staten Island Ferry/Whitehall Terminal | 4 South St. | Tues./Fri., Year-round
Financial District | Bowling Green | Broadway (Battery Pl.) | Tues./Thurs., Year-round
Financial District | City Hall Park | Broadway (Chambers St.) | Tues./Fri., March–Dec.
Financial District | W. Broadway (bet. Barclay St. & Park Pl.) | Tues., Year-round
Gramercy | Stuyvesant Town Oval | 14th St. Loop (bet. Ave. A & 1st Ave.) | Sun., April–Dec.
Inwood | Isham St. (bet. Cooper St. & Seaman Ave.) | Sat., Year-round
TriBeCa | Greenwich St. (bet. Chambers & Duane Sts.) | Wed./Sat., Year-round
Union Sq. | Union Sq. | Broadway (17th St.) | Mon./Wed./Fri./Sat., Year-round
Washington Heights | 175th St. (bet. B'way & Wadsworth Ave.) | Thurs., June–Nov.
Washington Heights | 168th St. (Fort Washington Ave.) | Tues., June–Nov.
W 40s | Port Authority Bus Terminal | 42nd St. (8th Ave.) | Thurs., Year-round
W 40s | 42nd St. (bet. 11th & 12th Aves.) | Wed., July–Nov.
W 50s | Ninth Ave. (bet. 56th & 57th Sts.) | Wed., May–Dec., Sat., April–Dec.
W 50s | Rockefeller Ctr. | 50th St. (Rockefeller Plaza) | Wed./Thurs./Fri., July–Aug.
W 60s | Columbus Ave. (66th St.) | Thurs./Sat., Year-round
W 70s | Columbus Ave. (78th Sts.) | Sun., Year-round
W 90s | 97th St. (bet. Amsterdam & Columbus Aves.) | Fri., Year-round
W Village | Abingdon Sq. | Eighth Ave. & Hudson St. (bet. Bethune & W. 12th Sts.) | Sat., Year-round
W 100s | Columbia University | Broadway (bet. 114th & 115th Sts.) | Thurs./Sun., Year-round

Bronx

Bronx | Poe Park | 192nd St. (bet. Grand Concourse & Valentine Ave.) | Tues., July–Nov.
Bronx | Bronx Borough Hall | Grand Concourse (bet. 161st & 162nd Sts.) | Tues., June–Nov.
Bronx | New York Botanical Gdn. | Southern Blvd. (bet. Bedford Park Blvd. & Mosholu Pkwy.) | Wed., June–Nov.

GREENMARKET LOCATIONS

Bronx | Lincoln Hospital | 149th St. (bet. Morris & Park Aves.) | Tues./Fri., June–Nov.

Bronx | Virginia Park | Westchester Ave. (White Plains Rd.) | Fri., June–Nov.

Brooklyn

Bay Ridge | 95th St. (3rd Ave.) | Sat., June–Nov.

Bensonhurst | 81st St. (18th Ave.) | Sun., July–Nov.

Borough Park | 14th Ave. (bet. 49th & 50th Sts.) | Thurs., July–Nov.

Carroll Gardens | Carroll Park | Carroll St. (bet. Court & Smith Sts.) | Sun., Year-round

Downtown Bklyn | Brooklyn Borough Hall | Court & Montague Sts. | Tues./Thurs./Sat., Year-round

Flatbush | Cortelyou Rd. (bet. Argyle & Rugby Rds.) | Sun., Year-round

Fort Greene | Fort Greene Park | Washington Park (bet. DeKalb Ave. & Willoughby St.) | Sat., Year-round

Greenpoint | McCarren Park | Union Ave. (bet. Driggs Ave. & 12th St.) | Sat., Year-round

Park Slope | Bartel-Pritchard Sq. | Prospect Park W. (15th St.) | Wed., May-Nov.

Park Slope | Grand Army Plaza | Prospect Park, NW entrance | Sat., Year-round

Sunset Park | Fourth Ave. (bet. 59th & 60th Sts.) | Sat., June–Nov.

Williamsburg | Havemeyer St. (bet. B'way & Division St.) | Thurs., July–Nov.

Windsor Terrace | 11th Ave. (bet. Sherman St. & Windsor Pl.) | Sun., May–Dec.

Queens

Astoria | 14th St. (bet. 31st Ave. & 31st Rd.) | Wed., July–Nov.

Corona | Roosevelt Ave. (103rd St.) | Fri., July–Nov.

Elmhurst | 41st Ave. (bet. 80th & 81st Sts.) | Tues., June–Nov.

Forest Hills | 70th Ave. (Queens Blvd.) | Sun., April–Dec.

Jackson Heights | 34th Ave. (78th St.) | Sun., Year-round

LIC | Socrates Sculpture Park | Vernon Blvd. (B'way) | Sat., June–Nov.

Sunnyside | Skillman Ave. (bet. 42nd & 43rd Sts.) | Sat., June–Dec.

Staten Island

Staten Island | St. George at Borough Hall | St. Marks Pl. (Hyatt St.) | Sat., May–Nov.

Staten Island | Staten Island Mall | Richmond Ave. (main parking lot) | Sat., June–Nov.

FOOD LOVER'S INDEXES

Special Features

Listings cover the best in each category and include source names, locations and Quality ratings.

ADDITIONS

(Properties added since the last edition of the book)

All Good Things	**TriBeCa**	_]
Baked In Brooklyn	**Greenwood Hts**	_]
Beurre/Sel	**LES**	_]
Bklyn. Harvest Mkt.	**W'burg**	_]
Breads Bakery	**Union Sq**	_]
Cavaniola's	**TriBeCa**	_]
Du Jour	**Park Slope**	_]
Empire Mayo.	**Prospect Hts**	_]
House of Cupcakes	**multi.**	_]
LeChurro	**E 80s**	_]
Le Palais de Thés	**multi.**	_]
Macaron Parlour	**E Vill**	_]
Maison Kayser	**E 60s**	_]
Malt/Mold	**LES**	_]
Ovenly	**Greenpt**	_]
Pain d'Epices	**W 70s**	_]
Royce' Chocolate	**multi.**	_]
Sugar/Plumm	**multi.**	_]
Sugar Shop	**Cobble Hill**	_]
Sullivan St. Tea	**G Vill**	26]
Tache Artisan Choc.	**LES**	_]
Teavana	**E 80s**	_]
Tiberio Custom Meats	**LES**	_]
Wedge	**Crown Hts**	_]

BAGELS & BIALYS

Absolute Bagels	**W 100s**	26]
Bagelworks	**E 60s**	26]
Eli's Manhattan	**E 80s**	25]
Eli's Vinegar	**E 90s**	24]
Ess-a-Bagel	**multi.**	26]
Hot Bagels /Bialys	**Midwood**	25]
Kossar's	**LES**	26]
Murray's Bagels	**multi.**	26]
Murray's Sturgeon	**W 80s**	28]
Shelsky's	**Boerum Hill**	24]
Yonah Schimmel	**LES**	24]
Zabar's	**W 80s**	27]

Zucker's Bagels	**TriBeCa**	22]

BAKED GOODS

(See also Bagels & Bialys, Cakes & Cupcakes, Cookies, Pies/Tarts)

Addeo Bakery	**Fordham**	28]
Agata/Valentina	**E 70s**	25]
NEW All Good Things	**TriBeCa**	_]
Almondine	**Dumbo**	26]
Amy's Bread	**multi.**	26]
Artopolis	**Astoria**	27]
BabyCakes	**LES**	24]
Baked	**Red Hook**	26]
NEW Baked In Brooklyn	**Greenwood Hts**	_]
Balthazar Bakery	**SoHo**	27]
Battery Place Mkt.	**Financial**	27]
Bedford Cheese	**W'burg**	27]
Betty Bakery	**Boerum Hill**	26]
NEW Beurre/Sel	**multi.**	_]
Bien Cuit	**Cobble Hill**	23]
Bisous, Ciao	**LES**	25]
Bklyn. Victory Garden	**Clinton Hill**	26]
Black Hound	**E Vill**	26]
Blue Apron	**Park Slope**	28]
Bouchon Bakery	**W 60s**	27]
NEW Breads Bakery	**Union Sq**	_]
Bread Talk	**Chinatown**	25]
Brooklyn Cupcake	**W'burg**	27]
Butter Lane Cupcakes	**E Vill**	25]
Cannelle Patisserie	**Jackson Hts**	29]
Caputo's Bake Shop	**Carroll Gdns**	27]
Carry On Tea	**W Vill**	25]
Ceci-Cela	**L Italy**	26]
Chikalicious Dessert Club	**E Vill**	25]
Choice Mkt.	**Clinton Hill**	27]
Citarella	**multi.**	26]
Colson	**Park Slope**	24]
Court Pastry	**Cobble Hill**	26]
Croissanteria	**E Vill**	_]
Damascus	**Bklyn Hts**	26]

FOOD LOVER'S

SPECIAL FEATURES

Wm. Greenberg Desserts | **E 80s**	25
Yonah Schimmel | **LES**	24
Zabar's | **W 80s**	27
Zucker Bakery | **E Vill**	24

BEER SPECIALISTS

Beer Table Pantry | **E 40s**	26
Bierkraft | **Park Slope**	27
Breukelen Bier | **W'burg**	27
Brouwerij Ln. | **Greenpt**	28
City Swiggers | **E 80s**	25
Eagle Provisions | **Greenwood Hts**	23
Eataly | **Flatiron**	27
Fairway | **multi.**	25
Filling Station | **Chelsea**	25
Good Beer | **E Vill**	27
Grace's Mkt. | **E 70s**	25
Greene Grape | **Ft Greene**	27
Malt/Mold | **LES**	-
New Beer | **LES**	26
The Ploughman | **Park Slope**	26
Whole Foods Mkt. | **multi.**	25

BREAD

Addeo Bakery | **Fordham**	28
Amy's Bread | **multi.**	26
Artopolis | **Astoria**	27
NEW Baked In Brooklyn | **Greenwood Hts**	-
Balthazar Bakery | **SoHo**	27
Battery Place Mkt. | **Financial**	27
Bedford Cheese | **W'burg**	27
Bien Cuit | **Cobble Hill**	23
Bklyn. Victory Garden | **Clinton Hill**	26
Blue Apron | **Park Slope**	28
Bouchon Bakery | **W 60s**	27
NEW Breads Bakery | **Union Sq**	-
Cannelle Patisserie | **Jackson Hts**	29
Caputo's Bake Shop | **Carroll Gdns**	27
Citarella | **multi.**	26
Damascus | **Bklyn Hts**	26
Dean/DeLuca | **multi.**	26
Eataly | **Flatiron**	27

Eli's Bread | **E 40s**	26
Eli's Manhattan | **E 80s**	25
Eli's Vinegar | **E 90s**	24
Fairway | **multi.**	25
Foragers City | **multi.**	26
Grandaisy | **multi.**	25
Greenmarket | **Union Sq**	29
Hot Bread Almacen | **Harlem**	-
Il Buco Alimentari | **NoHo**	25
Kalustyan's | **Murray Hill**	27
Levain Bakery | **multi.**	28
Madonia Bakery | **Fordham**	26
NEW Maison Kayser | **E 60s**	-
Murray's Cheese | **W Vill**	29
New Amsterdam Mkt. | **Seaport**	28
Orwasher's | **E 70s**	26
Pain D'Avignon | **multi.**	24
NEW Pain d'Epices | **W 70s**	-
Paneantico | **Bay Ridge**	26
Petrossian | **W 50s**	27
The Ploughman | **Park Slope**	26
Pomegranate | **Midwood**	26
Saxelby | **LES**	29
Scratch Bread | **Bed-Stuy**	27
Shelsky's | **Boerum Hill**	24
Silver Moon | **W 100s**	26
Stinky Bklyn | **Cobble Hill**	27
Sullivan St. Bakery | **W 40s**	27
Terranova | **Fordham**	28
Tu-Lu's GF | **E Vill**	25
Union Mkt. | **multi.**	25
Villabate-Alba | **Bensonhurst**	27
Whole Foods Mkt. | **multi.**	25

CAKES & CUPCAKES

Amy's Bread | **multi.**	26
Artopolis | **Astoria**	27
BabyCakes | **LES**	24
Baked | **Red Hook**	26
Balthazar Bakery | **SoHo**	27
Betty Bakery | **Boerum Hill**	26
Black Hound | **E Vill**	26
Brooklyn Cupcake | **W'burg**	27
Butter Lane Cupcakes | **E Vill**	25
Cannelle Patisserie | **Jackson Hts**	29

Ceci-Cela	**L Italy**	26	

Ceci-Cela | **L Italy** — 26
Chikalicious Dessert Club | **E Vill** — 25
Court Pastry | **Cobble Hill** — 26
Dean/DeLuca | **multi.** — 26
Delillo Pastry | **Fordham** — 25
Dominique Ansel | **SoHo** — 27
Duane Pk. | **TriBeCa** — 25
NEW Du Jour | **Park Slope** — -
Egidio Pastry | **Fordham** — 25
Eileen's Cheesecake | **NoLita** — 25
Eli's Vinegar | **E 90s** — 24
Empire Cake | **Chelsea** — 26
Financier Patisserie | **E 50s** — 25
FPB | **G Vill** — 27
Grace's Mkt. | **E 70s** — 25
NEW House of Cupcakes | **multi.** — -
Ivy Bakery | **G Vill** — 25
La Bergamote | **multi.** — 26
Ladybird | **Park Slope** — 27
Lady M | **E 70s** — 29
Magnolia Bakery | **multi.** — 21
Make My Cake | **Harlem** — 26
Mast Bros. Choc. | **W'burg** — 25
Mille-Feuille | **G Vill** — 25
Molly's | **W Vill** — 27
Momofuku Milk Bar | **multi.** — 25
Monteleone | **Carroll Gdns** — 29
One Girl | **Cobble Hill** — 27
Paneantico | **Bay Ridge** — 26
Patisserie Claude | **W Vill** — 26
S&S Cheesecake | **Kingsbridge** — 28
Silver Moon | **W 100s** — 26
Sprinkles | **E 60s** — 26
Sugar Sweet | **LES** — 26
Trois Pommes | **Park Slope** — 27
Tu-Lu's GF | **E Vill** — 25
Two/Red Hens | **E 80s** — 26
Veniero's | **E Vill** — 25
Villabate-Alba | **Bensonhurst** — 27
Whole Foods Mkt. | **multi.** — 25
Wm. Greenberg Desserts | **E 80s** — 25
Zabar's | **W 80s** — 27

CANDY & NUTS

Black Hound | **E Vill** — 26
Blue Apron | **Park Slope** — 28
Bond St. Choc. | **E Vill** — 27
Chelsea Baskets | **Chelsea** — 23
Choc. Works | **W 90s** — 26
Citarella | **multi.** — 26
Dean/DeLuca | **multi.** — 26
Dylan's Candy | **E 60s** — 23
Eataly | **Flatiron** — 27
Economy Candy | **LES** — 25
Eli's Manhattan | **E 80s** — 25
Eli's Vinegar | **E 90s** — 24
Fairway | **multi.** — 25
FPB | **G Vill** — 27
Gustiamo | **Fairmont-Claremont Village** — -
Hester St. Fair | **LES** — 21
Jacques Torres | **multi.** — 28
Kalustyan's | **Murray Hill** — 27
Kee's | **multi.** — 28
L.A. Burdick | **Flatiron** — 28
La Maison/Choc. | **multi.** — 29
Leonidas | **multi.** — 26
Li-Lac Choc. | **multi.** — 26
London Candy Co. | **W Vill** — 25
Martine's Choc. | **E 80s** — 25
Mast Bros. Choc. | **W'burg** — 25
Meadow | **W Vill** — 29
Minamoto | **W 40s** — 29
Murray's Cheese | **W Vill** — 29
Neuchatel | **E 50s** — 28
Neuhaus | **E 40s** — 26
New Amsterdam Mkt. | **Seaport** — 28
Nunu Choc. | **Downtown Bklyn** — 25
Nut Box | **multi.** — 24
Papabubble | **L Italy** — 23
Petrossian | **W 50s** — 27
The Ploughman | **Park Slope** — 26
NEW Royce' Chocolate | **multi.** — -
Russ/Daughters | **LES** — 29
Sahadi's | **Bklyn Hts** — 28
Sockerbit | **W Vill** — 24
NEW Sugar/Plumm | **W 70s** — -
Sugar Shop | **Cobble Hill** — -

Sweet Life | **LES**	27
NEW Tache Artisan Choc. | **LES**	–
Teuscher | **multi.**	29
Varsano's | **W Vill**	29
Vosges | **multi.**	27
Whole Foods Mkt. | **multi.**	25
Xocolatti | **SoHo**	22
Zabar's | **W 80s**	27

CAVIAR & SMOKED FISH

Acme Fish | **Greenpt**	25
Agata/Valentina | **E 70s**	25
Blue Apron | **Park Slope**	28
Calvisius Caviar | **E 50s**	29
Citarella | **multi.**	26
Dean/DeLuca | **multi.**	26
Dorian's Seafood | **E 80s**	26
Eli's Manhattan | **E 80s**	25
Eli's Vinegar | **E 90s**	24
Fairway | **multi.**	25
Gustiamo | **Fairmont-Claremont Village**	–
Leonard's Mkt. | **E 70s**	26
Murray's Bagels | **multi.**	26
Murray's Sturgeon | **W 80s**	28
Petrossian | **W 50s**	27
Russ/Daughters | **LES**	29
Sable's | **E 70s**	27
Shelsky's | **Boerum Hill**	24
Todaro Bros. | **Murray Hill**	25
Union Mkt. | **Park Slope**	25
Whole Foods Mkt. | **multi.**	25
Zabar's | **W 80s**	27
Zucker's Bagels | **TriBeCa**	22

CHARCUTERIE

Agata/Valentina | **E 70s**	25
Battery Place Mkt. | **Financial**	27
Bedford Cheese | **multi.**	27
Bklyn Larder | **Park Slope**	27
Blue Apron | **Park Slope**	28
BuonItalia | **Chelsea**	26
Casa Della | **Fordham**	29
Cheese/World | **Forest Hills**	26
Citarella | **multi.**	26

Dean/DeLuca | **multi.**	26
Despaña | **multi.**	27
Di Palo | **L Italy**	29
Durso's Pasta | **Flushing**	26
Eagle Provisions | **Greenwood Hts**	23
East Vill. Meat | **E Vill**	26
Eataly | **Flatiron**	27
Eli's Manhattan | **E 80s**	25
Eli's Vinegar | **E 90s**	24
Esposito Pork | **Carroll Gdns**	27
Esposito Meat | **Garment**	27
Faicco's Pork | **multi.**	28
Fairway | **multi.**	25
Fleisher's | **Park Slope**	29
Foragers City | **multi.**	26
Formaggio | **LES**	27
Grace's Mkt. | **E 70s**	25
Il Buco Alimentari | **NoHo**	25
Lioni Fresh Mozz. | **Bensonhurst**	27
Malaysia Beef Jerky | **Chinatown**	25
Marlow/Daughters | **W'burg**	28
Meat Hook | **W'burg**	27
Murray's Cheese | **multi.**	29
Ottomanelli's | **Flushing**	28
Ottomanelli/Sons | **multi.**	28
Petrossian | **W 50s**	27
The Ploughman | **Park Slope**	26
Salumeria Biellese | **Chelsea**	26
Salumeria Rosi | **W 70s**	28
Schaller/Weber | **E 80s**	28
Simchick | **E 50s**	29
Stinky Bklyn | **Cobble Hill**	27
Todaro Bros. | **Murray Hill**	25
NEW Wedge | **Crown Hts**	–
Whole Foods Mkt. | **multi.**	25
Zabar's | **W 80s**	27

CHEESE & DAIRY

Alleva Dairy | **L Italy**	28
NEW All Good Things | **TriBeCa**	–
Barnyard Cheese | **E Vill**	26
Battery Place Mkt. | **Financial**	27
Bedford Cheese | **multi.**	27
Beecher's Cheese | **Flatiron**	27

Bklyn Larder | **Park Slope**	27
Bklyn. Victory Garden | **Clinton Hill**	26
Blue Apron | **Park Slope**	28
BuonItalia | **Chelsea**	26
Butterfield Mkt. | **E 70s**	25
Calandra Cheese | **Fordham**	27
Casa Della | **Fordham**	29
NEW Cavaniola's | **TriBeCa**	-
Cheese/World | **Forest Hills**	26
Citarella | **multi.**	26
D'Amico | **Carroll Gdns**	27
D. Coluccio/Sons | **Borough Pk**	27
Dean/DeLuca | **multi.**	26
Despaña | **multi.**	27
Di Palo | **L Italy**	29
Durso's Pasta | **Flushing**	26
D'Vine | **Park Slope**	26
Eataly | **Flatiron**	27
Eli's Manhattan | **E 80s**	25
Fairway | **multi.**	25
Foragers City | **multi.**	26
Formaggio | **LES**	27
Grace's Mkt. | **E 70s**	25
Greenmarket | **Union Sq**	29
Gustiamo | **Fairmont-Claremont Village**	-
Hester St. Fair | **LES**	21
Ideal Cheese | **E 50s**	27
Il Buco Alimentari | **NoHo**	25
Lamazou | **Murray Hill**	26
Lioni Fresh Mozz. | **Bensonhurst**	27
Lucy's Whey | **Chelsea**	29
Malt/Mold | **LES**	-
Med. Foods | **Astoria**	26
Murray's Cheese | **multi.**	29
New Amsterdam Mkt. | **Seaport**	28
Nordic Delicacies | **Bay Ridge**	28
Pastosa Ravioli | **multi.**	27
The Ploughman | **Park Slope**	26
Pomegranate | **Midwood**	26
Ronnybrook | **Chelsea**	26
Sahadi's | **Bklyn Hts**	28
Salumeria Rosi | **W 70s**	28
Saxelby | **LES**	29

Staubitz Mkt. | **Cobble Hill**	29
Stinky Bklyn | **Cobble Hill**	27
Titan Foods | **Astoria**	26
Todaro Bros. | **Murray Hill**	25
Union Mkt. | **multi.**	25
Valley Shepherd | **Park Slope**	28
NEW Wedge | **Crown Hts**	-
Whole Foods Mkt. | **multi.**	25
Zabar's | **W 80s**	27

COFFEE & TEA

Agata/Valentina | **E 70s**	25
NEW All Good Things | **TriBeCa**	-
Bellocq Tea | **Greenpt**	25
Blue Apron | **Park Slope**	28
BuonItalia | **Chelsea**	26
Carry On Tea | **W Vill**	25
Chelsea Baskets | **Chelsea**	23
Citarella | **multi.**	26
D'Amico | **Carroll Gdns**	27
DavidsTea | **multi.**	28
Dean/DeLuca | **multi.**	26
Eataly | **Flatiron**	27
Eli's Manhattan | **E 80s**	25
Eli's Vinegar | **E 90s**	24
Fairway | **multi.**	25
Gustiamo | **Fairmont-Claremont Village**	-
Harney/Sons | **SoHo**	28
Kalustyan's | **Murray Hill**	27
Kusmi Tea | **E 60s**	26
NEW Le Palais de Thés | **multi.**	-
London Candy Co. | **W Vill**	25
Manhattan Fruit Ex. | **Chelsea**	25
McNulty's | **W Vill**	28
Myers/Keswick | **W Vill**	25
Nespresso | **E 60s**	27
Nut Box | **multi.**	24
Porto Rico | **multi.**	27
Sahadi's | **Bklyn Hts**	28
Spices/Tease | **multi.**	25
Sullivan St. Tea | **G Vill**	26
Tea/Honey | **E 60s**	29
NEW Teavana | **multi.**	-
Ten Ren Tea | **Chinatown**	25

FOOD LOVER'S

SPECIAL FEATURES

Todaro Bros. | **Murray Hill**	25
Two for the Pot | **Bklyn Hts**	26
Union Mkt. | **Cobble Hill**	25
Whole Foods Mkt. | **multi.**	25
Zabar's | **W 80s**	27

COOKIES

Agata/Valentina | **E 70s**	25
Amy's Bread | **multi.**	26
Artopolis | **Astoria**	27
Baked | **Red Hook**	26
Balthazar Bakery | **SoHo**	27
Betty Bakery | **Boerum Hill**	26
NEW Beurre/Sel | **multi.**	-
Bisous, Ciao | **LES**	25
Black Hound | **E Vill**	26
Bouchon Bakery | **W 60s**	27
Cannelle Patisserie | **Jackson Hts**	29
Carry On Tea | **W Vill**	25
Ceci-Cela | **L Italy**	26
Court Pastry | **Cobble Hill**	26
Dean/DeLuca | **multi.**	26
Delillo Pastry | **Fordham**	25
Dominique Ansel | **SoHo**	27
Duane Pk. | **TriBeCa**	25
Eataly | **Flatiron**	27
Eli's Manhattan | **E 80s**	25
Eli's Vinegar | **E 90s**	24
Financier Patisserie | **multi.**	25
Fortunato | **W'burg**	27
FPB | **G Vill**	27
Grace's Mkt. | **E 70s**	25
La Bergamote | **multi.**	26
La Boîte à Epice | **W 50s**	-
Ladybird | **Park Slope**	27
La Maison/Macaron | **Chelsea**	28
Lee Lee's | **Harlem**	-
Levain Bakery | **multi.**	28
NEW Macaron Parlour | **E Vill**	-
Madonia Bakery | **Fordham**	26
Magnolia Bakery | **W Vill**	21
NEW Maison Kayser | **E 60s**	-
Maison Ladurée | **E 70s**	28
Mast Bros. Choc. | **W'burg**	25
Milk/Cookies | **W Vill**	25

Momofuku Milk Bar | **multi.**	25
Monteleone | **Carroll Gdns**	29
One Girl | **Cobble Hill**	27
Ovenly | **Greenpt**	-
Patisserie Claude | **W Vill**	26
Silver Moon | **W 100s**	26
NEW Sugar/Plumm | **W 70s**	-
Todaro Bros. | **Murray Hill**	25
Two/Red Hens | **E 80s**	26
Veniero's | **E Vill**	25
Villabate-Alba | **Bensonhurst**	27
Whole Foods Mkt. | **multi.**	25
Wm. Greenberg Desserts | **E 80s**	25
Zucker Bakery | **E Vill**	24

DELIS

Agata/Valentina | **E 70s**	25
NEW All Good Things | **TriBeCa**	-
Battery Place Mkt. | **Financial**	27
Bklyn Larder | **Park Slope**	27
BuonItalia | **Chelsea**	26
Butterfield Mkt. | **E 70s**	25
Choice Mkt. | **multi.**	27
Citarella | **multi.**	26
Court St. Grcs. | **Carroll Gdns**	29
D'Amico | **Carroll Gdns**	27
Despaña | **multi.**	27
Dickson's | **Chelsea**	28
Di Palo | **L Italy**	29
D'Vine | **Park Slope**	26
Eagle Provisions | **Greenwood Hts**	23
Eataly | **Flatiron**	27
Eli's Manhattan | **E 80s**	25
Eli's Vinegar | **E 90s**	24
Esposito Pork | **Carroll Gdns**	27
Fairway | **multi.**	25
Foragers City | **Dumbo**	26
Formaggio | **LES**	27
Lioni Fresh Mozz. | **Bensonhurst**	27
Murray's Cheese | **multi.**	29
Murray's Sturgeon | **W 80s**	28
Paneantico | **Bay Ridge**	26
Salumeria Biellese | **Chelsea**	26
Salumeria Rosi | **W 70s**	28

Stinky Bklyn | **Cobble Hill**   27

Todaro Bros. | **Murray Hill**   25

Union Mkt. | **Cobble Hill**   25

Whole Foods Mkt. | **multi.**   25

Zabar's | **W 80s**   27

GAME

(May need prior notice)

Agata/Valentina | **E 70s**   25

Biancardi Meats | **Fordham**   28

Dean/DeLuca | **multi.**   26

Eagle Provisions | 23
    Greenwood Hts

Eli's Manhattan | **E 80s**   25

Eli's Vinegar | **E 90s**   24

Esposito Meat | **Garment**   27

Florence Meat | **W Vill**   29

Grace's Mkt. | **E 70s**   25

Leonard's Mkt. | **E 70s**   26

Lobel's Meats | **E 80s**   28

Ottomanelli's | **Flushing**   28

Ottomanelli/Sons | **multi.**   28

Pino Meats | **SoHo**   29

Schaller/Weber | **E 80s**   28

Simchick | **E 50s**   29

Whole Foods Mkt. | **multi.**   25

GIFT BASKETS

Acker Merrall | **W 70s**   28

Agata/Valentina | **E 70s**   25

Bedford Cheese | **Gramercy**   27

Bklyn Larder | **Park Slope**   27

Black Hound | **E Vill**   26

Blue Apron | **Park Slope**   28

Butterfield Mkt. | **E 70s**   25

Chelsea Baskets | **Chelsea**   23

Choc. Works | **W 90s**   26

Citarella | **multi.**   26

Dean/DeLuca | **multi.**   26

Dominique Ansel | **SoHo**   27

Dylan's Candy | **E 60s**   23

Eataly | **Flatiron**   27

Economy Candy | **LES**   25

Eli's Manhattan | **E 80s**   25

Eli's Vinegar | **E 90s**   24

Fairway | **E 80s**   25

Financier Patisserie | **Financial**   25

Grace's Mkt. | **E 70s**   25

Gustiamo | -
    Fairmont-Claremont Village

Harney/Sons | **SoHo**   28

Jacques Torres | **multi.**   28

L.A. Burdick | **Flatiron**   28

London Candy Co. | **W Vill**   25

Manhattan Fruitier | **LIC**   25

MarieBelle's | **SoHo**   26

Minamoto | **W 40s**   29

Morrell & Co. | **W 40s**   26

Murray's Cheese | **W Vill**   29

Myers/Keswick | **W Vill**   25

Neuhaus | **multi.**   26

Nordic Delicacies | **Bay Ridge**   28

Nut Box | **multi.**   24

O&CO. | **multi.**   27

One Girl | **Cobble Hill**   27

Orchard | **Midwood**   28

The Ploughman | **Park Slope**   26

Russ/Daughters | **LES**   29

Sahadi's | **Bklyn Hts**   28

Sherry-Lehmann | **E 50s**   29

NEW Sugar/Plumm | **multi.**   -

Three Tarts | **Chelsea**   26

Vosges | **SoHo**   27

Whole Foods Mkt. | **multi.**   25

Wm. Greenborg Desserts | **E 80s**   25

Zabar's | **W 80s**   27

GIFT IDEAS

(See also Gift Baskets)

Bellocq Tea | **Greenpt**   25

Bisous, Ciao | **LES**   25

Despaña | **multi.**   27

FPB | **multi.**   27

Heritage Meat | **LES**   27

Kusmi Tea | **E 60s**   26

La Boîte à Epice | **W 50s**   -

NEW Le Palais de Thés | **multi.**   -

Maison Ladurée | **E 70s**   28

MarieBelle's | **SoHo**   26

Meadow | **W Vill**   29

Papabubble | **L Italy**   23

NEW Royce' Chocolate | **multi.**   -

Sockerbit	**W Vill**	24
Tea/Honey	**E 60s**	29
Three Tarts	**multi.**	26
Xocolatti	**SoHo**	22

HERBS & SPICES

Dean/DeLuca	**multi.**	26
D'Vine	**Park Slope**	26
Fairway	**multi.**	25
Foods/India	**Murray Hill**	23
Hester St. Fair	**LES**	21
House/Spices	**Flushing**	26
Kalustyan's	**Murray Hill**	27
La Boîte à Epice	**W 50s**	-
Nut Box	**multi.**	24
Puro Chile	**L Italy**	26
Sahadi's	**Bklyn Hts**	28
Spice Corner	**Murray Hill**	23
Spices/Tease	**multi.**	25
Sullivan St. Tea	**G Vill**	26
Two for the Pot	**Bklyn Hts**	26
Whole Foods Mkt.	**W 90s**	25
Zabar's	**W 80s**	27

HISTORIC INTEREST

(Year opened)

1820	Acker Merrall	**W 70s**	28
1890	Yonah Schimmel	**LES**	24
1892	Alleva Dairy	**L Italy**	28
1894	Veniero's	**E Vill**	25
1895	Hester St. Fair	**LES**	21
1895	McNulty's	**W Vill**	28
1898	Sahadi's	**Bklyn Hts**	28
1900	Faicco's Pork	**multi.**	28
1904	Caputo's Bake Shop	**Carroll Gdns**	27
1906	Raffetto's	**G Vill**	28
1907	Porto Rico	**G Vill**	27
1910	Leonard's Mkt.	**E 70s**	26
1910	Pisacane	**E 50s**	28
1912	Egidio Pastry	**Fordham**	25
1914	Russ/Daughters	**LES**	29
1915	Butterfield Mkt.	**E 70s**	25
1915	Teitel Bros.	**Fordham**	27
1916	Orwasher's	**E 70s**	26
1917	Staubitz Mkt.	**Cobble Hill**	29

1917	Todaro Bros.	**Murray Hill**	25
1918	Madonia Bakery	**Fordham**	26
1920	Piemonte Ravioli	**L Italy**	27
1922	Casa Della	**Fordham**	29
1922	Esposito Pork	**Carroll Gdns**	27
1923	Li-Lac Choc.	**multi.**	26
1923	Poseidon	**W 40s**	25
1925	Delillo Pastry	**Fordham**	25
1925	Di Palo	**L Italy**	29
1925	Randazzo's	**Fordham**	26
1925	Salumeria Biellese	**Chelsea**	26
1925	Streit's Matzo	**LES**	27
1929	Addeo Bakery	**Fordham**	28
1930	Damascus	**Bklyn Hts**	26
1931	Zabar's	**W 80s**	27
1932	Biancardi Meats	**Fordham**	28
1932	Esposito Meat	**Garment**	27
1934	Park Ave. Liquor	**E 40s**	27
1934	Sherry-Lehmann	**E 50s**	29
1935	Borgatti's	**Fordham**	29
1935	Kossar's	**LES**	26
1935	Ottomanelli/Sons	**W Vill**	28
1936	Florence Meat	**W Vill**	29
1937	Economy Candy	**LES**	25
1937	Schaller/Weber	**E 80s**	28
1940	Murray's Cheese	**W Vill**	29
1941	Ronnybrook	**Chelsea**	26
1944	Kalustyan's	**Murray Hill**	27
1946	Murray's Sturgeon	**W 80s**	28
1946	Wm. Greenberg Desserts	**E 80s**	25
1947	Astor Wines	**NoHo**	26
1948	Court Pastry	**Cobble Hill**	26
1948	D'Amico	**Carroll Gdns**	27
1948	Morrell & Co.	**W 40s**	26
1952	Calandra Cheese	**Fordham**	27
1952	Cheese/World	**Forest Hills**	26
1954	Acme Fish	**Greenpt**	25
1954	Fairway	**Douglaston**	25
1954	Ideal Cheese	**E 50s**	27

1954 | Lobel's Meats | **E 80s** 28

1957 | Orchard | **Midwood** 28

MAJOR MARKETS

Agata/Valentina | **E 70s** 25

NEW All Good Things | **TriBeCa** _|

Battery Place Mkt. | **Financial** 27

NEW Bklyn. Harvest Mkt. | **W'burg** _|

Citarella | **multi.** 26

Dean/DeLuca | **multi.** 26

Eataly | **Flatiron** 27

Eli's Manhattan | **E 80s** 25

Eli's Vinegar | **E 90s** 24

Fairway | **multi.** 25

Foragers City | **multi.** 26

Grace's Mkt. | **E 70s** 25

Union Mkt. | **Park Slope** 25

Whole Foods Mkt. | **multi.** 25

Zabar's | **W 80s** 27

MEAT & POULTRY

Agata/Valentina | **E 70s** 25

NEW All Good Things | **TriBeCa** _|

Battery Place Mkt. | **Financial** 27

Biancardi Meats | **Fordham** 28

Bklyn. Victory Garden | **Clinton Hill** 26

Citarella | **multi.** 26

Court St. Grcs. | **Carroll Gdns** 29

Dean/DeLuca | **multi.** 26

Dickson's | **multi.** 28

Eagle Provisions | **Greenwood Hts** 23

East Vill. Meat | **E Vill** 26

Eataly | **Flatiron** 27

Eli's Manhattan | **E 80s** 25

Eli's Vinegar | **E 90s** 24

Esposito Pork | **Carroll Gdns** 27

Esposito Meat | **Garment** 27

Faicco's Pork | **multi.** 28

Fairway | **multi.** 25

Fleisher's | **Park Slope** 29

Florence Meat | **W Vill** 29

Foragers City | **multi.** 26

Grace's Mkt. | **E 70s** 25

Greene Grape | **Ft Greene** 27

Greenmarket | **Union Sq** 29

Heritage Meat | **LES** 27

Hester St. Fair | **LES** 21

Japan Premium Beef | **NoHo** 29

Leonard's Mkt. | **E 70s** 26

Lobel's Meats | **E 80s** 28

Malaysia Beef Jerky | **Chinatown** 25

Marlow/Daughters | **W'burg** 28

Meat Hook | **W'burg** 27

New Amsterdam Mkt. | **Seaport** 28

Ottomanelli's | **Flushing** 28

Ottomanelli/Sons | **multi.** 28

Pino Meats | **SoHo** 29

Pomegranate | **Midwood** 26

Salumeria Biellese | **Chelsea** 26

Schaller/Weber | **E 80s** 28

Simchick | **E 50s** 29

Staubitz Mkt. | **Cobble Hill** 29

NEW Tiberio Custom Meats | **LES** _|

Todaro Bros. | **Murray Hill** 25

Union Mkt. | **multi.** 25

Whole Foods Mkt. | **multi.** 25

Zabar's | **W 80s** 27

OLIVES & PICKLES

D. Coluccio/Sons | **Borough Pk** 27

Eli's Manhattan | **E 80s** 25

Eli's Vinegar | **E 90s** 24

Fairway | **multi.** 25

Murray's Cheese | **multi.** 29

Pickle Guys | **multi.** 27

Pickles/Olives | **E 80s** 25

Sahadi's | **Bklyn Hts** 28

Teitel Bros. | **Fordham** 27

Titan Foods | **Astoria** 26

Todaro Bros. | **Murray Hill** 25

Union Mkt. | **multi.** 25

Whole Foods Mkt. | **multi.** 25

Zabar's | **W 80s** 27

OPEN LATE

BAGELS & BIALYS

Absolute Bagels | **W 100s** 26

Bagelworks | **E 60s** 26

Ess-a-Bagel | **multi.** 26

Hot Bagels /Bialys | **Midwood** 25

Murray's Bagels | **multi.** 26

BAKED GOODS

Amy's Bread | **multi.** 26

Artopolis | **Astoria** 27

BabyCakes | **LES** 24

Black Hound | **E Vill** 26

Bouchon Bakery | **W 60s** 27

Butter Lane Cupcakes | **E Vill** 25

Chikalicious Dessert Club | **E Vill** 25

Eileen's Cheesecake | **NoLita** 25

Empire Cake | **Chelsea** 26

Financier Patisserie | **multi.** 25

Fortunato | **W'burg** 27

G'town Cupcake | **SoHo** 27

Ivy Bakery | **G Vill** 25

La Bergamote | **W 50s** 26

Magnolia Bakery | **multi.** 21

Make My Cake | **Harlem** 26

Milk/Cookies | **W Vill** 25

Molly's | **W Vill** 27

Momofuku Milk Bar | **multi.** 25

Paneantico | **Bay Ridge** 26

Puddin' by Clio | **E Vill** 29

Sprinkles | **E 60s** 26

Sugar Sweet | **LES** 26

Sullivan St. Bakery | **Chelsea** 27

Tu-Lu's GF | **E Vill** 25

Veniero's | **E Vill** 25

Villabate-Alba | **Bensonhurst** 27

CANDY & NUTS

Dylan's Candy | **E 60s** 23

L.A. Burdick | **Flatiron** 28

Li-Lac Choc. | **E 40s** 26

London Candy Co. | **W Vill** 25

Nunu Choc. | **Downtown Bklyn** 25

Nut Box | **multi.** 24

Papabubble | **L Italy** 23

Sockerbit | **W Vill** 24

NEW Tache Artisan Choc. | **LES** -

CAVIAR & SMOKED FISH

Calvisius Caviar | **E 50s** 29

CHEESE & DAIRY

Bedford Cheese | **multi.** 27

Murray's Cheese | **E 40s** 29

COFFEE & TEA

Carry On Tea | **W Vill** 25

DavidsTea | **multi.** 28

McNulty's | **W Vill** 28

Nespresso | **SoHo** 27

Porto Rico | **G Vill** 27

NEW Teavana | **multi.** -

HERBS & SPICES

Spice Corner | **Murray Hill** 23

Spices/Tease | **W 90s** 25

ICE CREAM

Fortunato | **W'burg** 27

PREPARED FOODS

Choice Mkt. | **multi.** 27

PRODUCE

Manhattan Fruit Ex. | **Chelsea** 25

SPECIALTY SHOPS

Battery Place Mkt. | **Financial** 27

Bklyn Larder | **Park Slope** 27

Bklyn. Victory Garden | **Clinton Hill** 26

Dépanneur | **W'burg** -

D'Vine | **Park Slope** 26

Filling Station | **Chelsea** 25

Greene Grape | **Ft Greene** 27

Il Buco Alimentari | **NoHo** 25

Kam Man | **Chinatown** 21

Med. Foods | **Astoria** 26

O&CO. | **W 60s** 27

The Ploughman | **Park Slope** 26

Pomegranate | **Midwood** 26

Salumeria Rosi | **W 70s** 28

Titan Foods | **Astoria** 26

Todaro Bros. | **Murray Hill** 25

WINES, BEER & LIQUOR

Acker Merrall | **W 70s** 28

Astor Wines | **NoHo** 26

Beer Table Pantry | **E 40s** 26

Bierkraft | **Park Slope** 27

Breukelen Bier | **W'burg** 27

Brouwerij Ln. | **Greenpt** 28

Chambers St. Wines | **TriBeCa** 27
City Swiggers | **E 80s** 25
Crush Wine | **E 50s** 27
Dry Dock | **Red Hook** 28
Flatiron Wines | **Flatiron** -
Good Beer | **E Vill** 27
Greene Grape | **Ft Greene** 22
Moore Bros. | **Flatiron** 28
PJ Wine | **Inwood** 27
Pour | **W 70s** 24
Union Sq. Wines | **Union Sq** 25
Whiskey Shop | **W'burg** 27

OPEN SUNDAY

(Except for liquor stores, butchers and fish markets, most places are open Sunday; here are some sources in those hard-to-find categories)

Astor Wines | **NoHo** 26
Bierkraft | **Park Slope** 27
Chambers St. Wines | **TriBeCa** 27
Crush Wine | **E 50s** 27
Eagle Provisions | 23
   Greenwood Hts
Esposito Pork | **Carroll Gdns** 27
Faicco's Pork | **multi.** 28
Greene Grape | **Ft Greene** 22
Leonard's Mkt. | **E 70s** 26
Lobster Pl. | **Chelsea** 27
Union Sq. Wines | **Union Sq** 25

PASTAS

Agata/Valentina | **E 70s** 25
Borgatti's | **Fordham** 29
BuonItalia | **Chelsea** 26
Citarella | **multi.** 26
D. Coluccio/Sons | **Borough Pk** 27
Dean/DeLuca | **multi.** 26
Di Palo | **L Italy** 29
Durso's Pasta | **Flushing** 26
Eataly | **Flatiron** 27
Eli's Manhattan | **E 80s** 25
Eli's Vinegar | **E 90s** 24
Fairway | **multi.** 25
Gustiamo | -
   Fairmont-Claremont Village
Il Buco Alimentari | **NoHo** 25

Murray's Cheese | **multi.** 29
Pastosa Ravioli | **multi.** 27
Piemonte Ravioli | **L Italy** 27
Raffetto's | **G Vill** 28
Teitel Bros. | **Fordham** 27
Terranova | **Fordham** 28
Todaro Bros. | **Murray Hill** 25
Whole Foods Mkt. | **multi.** 25
Zabar's | **W 80s** 27

PIES/TARTS

Baked | **Red Hook** 26
Balthazar Bakery | **SoHo** 27
Bien Cuit | **Cobble Hill** 23
Black Hound | **E Vill** 26
Bouchon Bakery | **W 60s** 27
Cannelle Patisserie | **Jackson Hts** 29
Ceci-Cela | **L Italy** 26
Colson | **Park Slope** 24
Dean/DeLuca | **multi.** 26
Delillo Pastry | **Fordham** 25
Dominique Ansel | **SoHo** 27
Duane Pk. | **TriBeCa** 25
Egidio Pastry | **Fordham** 25
Fairway | **multi.** 25
Financier Patisserie | **multi.** 25
Four/Twenty Blackbirds | 26
   Gowanus
FPB | **G Vill** 27
Grace's Mkt. | **E 70s** 25
Grandaisy | **TriBeCa** 25
La Bergamote | **multi.** 26
Ladybird | **Park Slope** 27
Magnolia Bakery | **W Vill** 21
NEW Maison Kayser | **E 60s** -
Momofuku Milk Bar | **multi.** 25
Patisserie Claude | **W Vill** 26
Petrossian | **W 50s** 27
Silver Moon | **W 100s** 26
Steve's Pies | **Red Hook** 26
Sugar Sweet | **LES** 26
Three Tarts | **Chelsea** 26
Trois Pommes | **Park Slope** 27
Two/Red Hens | **E 80s** 26
Veniero's | **E Vill** 25

Whole Foods Mkt. | **TriBeCa**	25
Wm. Greenberg Desserts | **E 80s**	25

PRODUCE

Agata/Valentina | **E 70s**	25
Butterfield Mkt. | **E 70s**	25
Citarella | **multi.**	26
Dean/DeLuca | **E 80s**	26
Eataly | **Flatiron**	27
Eli's Manhattan | **E 80s**	25
Eli's Vinegar | **E 90s**	24
Fairway | **multi.**	25
Foragers City | **multi.**	26
Grace's Mkt. | **E 70s**	25
Greene Grape | **Ft Greene**	27
Greenmarket | **Union Sq**	29
Manhattan Fruit Ex. | **Chelsea**	25
New Amsterdam Mkt. | **Seaport**	28
Pomegranate | **Midwood**	26
Union Mkt. | **multi.**	25
Whole Foods Mkt. | **multi.**	25
Zabar's | **W 80s**	27

SEAFOOD

Agata/Valentina | **E 70s**	25
NEW All Good Things | **TriBeCa**	–
Citarella | **multi.**	26
Dean/DeLuca | **multi.**	26
Dorian's Seafood | **E 80s**	26
Eataly | **Flatiron**	27
Eli's Manhattan | **E 80s**	25
Eli's Vinegar | **E 90s**	24
Fairway | **multi.**	25
Fish Tales | **Cobble Hill**	27
Foragers City | **Dumbo**	26
Greene Grape | **Ft Greene**	27
Greenmarket | **Union Sq**	29
Leonard's Mkt. | **E 70s**	26
Lobster Pl. | **Chelsea**	27
New Amsterdam Mkt. | **Seaport**	28
Pisacane | **E 50s**	28
Randazzo's | **Fordham**	26
Todaro Bros. | **Murray Hill**	25
Union Mkt. | **multi.**	25
Whole Foods Mkt. | **multi.**	25

SPECIALTY SHOPS

NEW All Good Things | **TriBeCa**	–
Bangkok Grocery | **Chinatown**	24
Battery Place Mkt. | **Financial**	27
Bklyn Larder | **Park Slope**	27
Bklyn. Victory Garden | **Clinton Hill**	26
Blue Apron | **Park Slope**	28
Brooklyn Brine | **Gowanus**	23
BuonItalia | **Chelsea**	26
Butterfield Mkt. | **E 70s**	25
Chelsea Baskets | **Chelsea**	23
D. Coluccio/Sons | **Borough Pk**	27
Dépanneur | **W'burg**	–
Despaña | **multi.**	27
D'Vine | **Park Slope**	26
Empire Mayo. | **Prospect Hts**	–
Filling Station | **Chelsea**	25
Greene Grape | **Ft Greene**	27
Gustiamo | **Fairmont-Claremont Village**	–
Hester St. Fair | **LES**	21
Il Buco Alimentari | **NoHo**	25
Kalustyan's | **Murray Hill**	27
Kam Man | **Chinatown**	21
Manhattan Fruitier | **LIC**	25
Meadow | **W Vill**	29
Med. Foods | **Astoria**	26
Myers/Keswick | **W Vill**	25
New Amsterdam Mkt. | **Seaport**	28
Nordic Delicacies | **Bay Ridge**	28
O&CO. | **multi.**	27
Orchard | **Midwood**	28
Pickle Guys | **multi.**	27
Pickles/Olives | **E 80s**	25
The Ploughman | **Park Slope**	26
Pomegranate | **Midwood**	26
Puro Chile | **L Italy**	26
Sahadi's | **Bklyn Hts**	28
Salumeria Rosi | **W 70s**	28
Smorgasburg | **W'burg**	28
Teitel Bros. | **Fordham**	27
Titan Foods | **Astoria**	26
Todaro Bros. | **Murray Hill**	25

WINES & LIQUOR

(* Open Sunday)

Acker Merrall | **W 70s** 28

Astor Wines* | **NoHo** 26

Bottlerocket | **Flatiron** 25

Brooklyn Oenology | **W'burg** 26

Burgundy | **Chelsea** 28

Chambers St. Wines* | **TriBeCa** 27

Crush Wine* | **E 50s** 27

Despaña Vinos | **L Italy** 28

Dry Dock | **Red Hook** 28

Eataly | **Flatiron** 27

Enoteca Di Palo | **L Italy** 27

Flatiron Wines | **Flatiron** -

Foragers City | **Chelsea** 26

Greene Grape* | **Ft Greene** 22

Italian Wine | **Union Sq** 29

Le Dû's Wines | **W Vill** 29

Moore Bros. | **Flatiron** 28

Morrell & Co. | **W 40s** 26

Park Ave. Liquor | **E 40s** 27

PJ Wine | **Inwood** 27

Pour | **W 70s** 24

Puro Chile | **L Italy** 26

Sakaya | **E Vill** 28

Sherry-Lehmann | **E 50s** 29

Union Sq. Wines* | **Union Sq** 25

Whiskey Shop | **W'burg** 27

FOOD LOVER'S

SPECIAL FEATURES

Ethnic Focus

Listings cover the best in each category and include source names, categories and Quality ratings.

ASIAN

(See also Chinese, Japanese and Thai)
Foods/India | *Herbs/Spices* **23**
House/Spices | *Herbs/Spices* **26**
Kalustyan's | *Spec. Shop* **27**
Malaysia Beef Jerky | *Meat/Poultry* **25**
Spice Corner | *Herbs/Spices* **23**

BELGIAN

Colson | *Baked Gds.* **24**
Leonidas | *Candy/Nuts* **26**
Martine's Choc. | *Candy/Nuts* **25**
Neuhaus | *Candy/Nuts* **26**

CHINESE

Bread Talk | *Baked Gds.* **25**
Kam Man | *Spec. Shop* **21**
Ten Ren Tea | *Coffee/Tea* **25**

ENGLISH

Bellocq Tea | *Tea* **25**
Carry On Tea | *Coffee/Tea* **25**
London Candy Co. | *Candy/Nuts* **25**
Myers/Keswick | *Spec. Shop* **25**

FRENCH

Almondine | *Baked Gds.* **26**
Balthazar Bakery | *Baked Gds.* **27**
Bien Cuit | *Baked Gds.* **23**
Bouchon Bakery | *Baked Gds.* **27**
Burgundy | *Wine/Liq.* **28**
Cannelle Patisserie | *Baked Gds.* **29**
Ceci-Cela | *Baked Gds.* **26**
Colson | *Baked Gds.* **24**
Dominique Ansel | *Baked Gds.* **27**
Duane Pk. | *Baked Gds.* **25**
Financier Patisserie | *Baked Gds.* **25**
FPB | *Baked Gds.* **27**
Jacques Torres | *Candy/Nuts* **28**
Kusmi Tea | *Coffee/Tea* **26**
La Bergamote | *Baked Gds.* **26**
La Maison/Choc. | *Candy* **29**

La Maison/Macaron | *Baked Gds.* **28**
NEW Macaron Parlour | **−**
  Baked Gds.
NEW Maison Kayser | *Baked Gds.* **−**
Maison Ladurée | *Baked Gds.* **28**
Mille-Feuille | *Baked Gds.* **25**
Patisserie Claude | *Baked Gds.* **26**
Petrossian | *Caviar/Smoked* **27**
Silver Moon | *Baked Gds.* **26**
NEW Sugar/Plumm | *Candy/Nuts* **−**
NEW Tache Artisan Choc. | **−**
  Candy/Nuts
Trois Pommes | *Baked Gds.* **27**

GERMAN/AUSTRIAN

Duane Pk. | *Baked Gds.* **25**
Schaller/Weber | *Meat/Poultry* **28**

GREEK

Artopolis | *Baked Gds.* **27**
Med. Foods | *Spec. Shop* **26**
Poseidon | *Baked Gds.* **25**
Titan Foods | *Spec. Shops* **26**

INDIAN

Foods/India | *Herbs/Spices* **23**
House/Spices | *Herbs/Spices* **26**
Kalustyan's | *Spec. Shop* **27**
Spice Corner | *Herbs/Spices* **23**

ISRAELI

Zucker Bakery | *Baked Gds.* **24**

ITALIAN

Addeo Bakery | *Baked Gds.* **28**
Agata/Valentina | *Maj. Mkt.* **25**
Alleva Dairy | *Cheese/Dairy* **28**
Biancardi Meats | *Meat/Poultry* **28**
Borgatti's | *Pastas* **29**
BuonItalia | *Spec. Shop* **26**
Calandra Cheese | *Cheese/Dairy* **27**
Caputo's Bake Shop | *Baked Gds.* **27**
Casa Della | *Cheese/Dairy* **29**

Locations

Includes names, categories and Quality ratings.

Manhattan

CHELSEA

(26th to 30th Sts., west of 5th; 14th to 26th Sts., west of 6th)

Amy's Bread	*Baked Gds.*	26
BuonItalia	*Spec. Shop*	26
Burgundy	*Wine/Liq.*	28
Chelsea Baskets	*Spec. Shop*	23
DavidsTea	*Coffee/Tea*	28
Dickson's	*Meat/Poultry*	28
Doughnut Plant	*Baked Gds.*	27
Empire Cake	*Baked Gds.*	26
Filling Station	*Spec. Shop*	25
Foragers City	*Maj. Mkt.*	26
Jacques Torres	*Candy/Nuts*	28
La Bergamote	*Baked Gds.*	26
La Maison/Macaron	*Baked Gds.*	28
Lobster Pl.	*Seafood*	27
Lucy's Whey	*Cheese/Dairy*	29
Manhattan Fruit Ex.	*Produce*	25
Murray's Bagels	*Baked Gds.*	26
Nut Box	*Candy/Nuts*	24
Ronnybrook	*Cheese/Dairy*	26
Salumeria Biellese	*Meat/Poultry*	26
Spices & Tease		25
Sullivan St. Bakery	*Baked Gds.*	27
Three Tarts	*Baked Gds.*	26
Whole Foods Mkt.	*Maj. Mkt.*	25

CHINATOWN

(Canal to Pearl Sts., east of B'way)

Bangkok Grocery	*Spec. Shop*	24
Bread Talk	*Baked Gds.*	25
Kam Man	*Spec. Shop*	21
Malaysia Beef Jerky	*Meat/Poultry*	25
Ten Ren Tea	*Coffee/Tea*	25

EAST 40s

Beer Table Pantry	*Beer*	26
Eli's Bread	*Baked Gds.*	26
Financier Patisserie	*Baked Gds.*	25
Li-Lac Choc.	*Candy/Nuts*	26
Magnolia Bakery	*Baked Gds.*	21

Murray's Cheese	*Cheese/Dairy*	29
Neuhaus	*Candy/Nuts*	26
O&CO.	*Spec. Shop*	27
Park Ave. Liquor	*Wine/Liq.*	27
Spices/Tease	*Herbs/Spices*	25
Teuscher	*Candy/Nuts*	29
Zucker's Bagels & Smoked Fish	*Baked Gds.*	22

EAST 50s

Calvisius Caviar	*Caviar/Smoked*	29
Crush Wine	*Wine/Liq.*	27
Ess-a-Bagel	*Baked Gds.*	26
Financier Patisserie	*Baked Gds.*	25
Ideal Cheese	*Cheese/Dairy*	27
Kusmi Tea	*Coffee/Tea*	26
Lady M	*Baked Gds.*	29
La Maison/Choc.	*Candy*	29
Leonidas	*Candy/Nuts*	26
Magnolia Bakery	*Baked Gds.*	21
Neuchatel	*Candy/Nuts*	28
Neuhaus	*Candy/Nuts*	26
Pain D'Avignon	*Baked Gds.*	24
Pisacane	*Seafood*	28
NEW Royce' Chocolate	*Candy/Nuts*	-
Sherry-Lehmann	*Wine/Liq.*	29
Simchick	*Meat/Poultry*	29
Three Tarts	*Baked Gds.*	26
Whole Foods Market	*Maj. Mkt.*	25
Wm. Greenberg Desserts	*Baked Gds.*	25

EAST 60s

Bagelworks	*Baked Gds.*	26
DavidsTea	*Coffee/Tea*	28
Dylan's Candy	*Candy/Nuts*	23
Kusmi Tea	*Coffee/Tea*	26
NEW Maison Kayser	*Baked Gds.*	-
Nespresso	*Coffee/Tea*	27
Sprinkles	*Baked Gds.*	26
Tea/Honey	*Coffee/Tea*	29
Teuscher	*Candy/Nuts*	29

EAST 70s

Agata/Valentina | *Maj. Mkt.*	25
Butterfield Mkt. | *Spec. Shop*	25
Citarella | *Maj. Mkt.*	26
FPB | *Baked Gds.*	27
Grace's Mkt. | *Maj. Mkt.*	25
Lady M | *Baked Gds.*	29
La Maison/Choc. | *Candy*	29
Leonard's Mkt. | *Seafood*	26
Maison Ladurée | *Baked Gds.*	28
Orwasher's | *Baked Gds.*	26
Sable's | *Caviar/Smoked*	27
Salumeria Rosi | *Spec. Shop*	28

EAST 80s

City Swiggers | *Beer*	25
Dean/DeLuca | *Maj. Mkt.*	26
Dorian's Seafood | *Seafood*	26
Eli's Manhattan | *Maj. Mkt.*	25
Fairway | *Maj. Mkt.*	25
NEW LeChurro | *Baked Gds.*	–
Lobel's Meats | *Meat/Poultry*	28
Martine's Choc. | *Candy/Nuts*	25
Pickles/Olives | *Spec. Shop*	25
Schaller/Weber | *Meat/Poultry*	28
NEW Teavana | *Coffee/Tea*	–
Two/Red Hens | *Baked Gds.*	26
Vosges | *Candy/Nuts*	27
Wm. Greenberg Desserts | *Baked Gds.*	25

EAST 90s & 100s

(90th to 110th Sts.)

Eli's Vinegar | *Maj. Mkt.*	24

EAST VILLAGE

(14th to Houston Sts., east of B'way, excluding NoHo)

Barnyard Cheese | *Cheese/Dairy*	26
Black Hound | *Baked Gds.*	26
Bond St. Choc. | *Candy/Nuts*	27
Butter Lane Cupcakes | *Baked Gds.*	25
Chikalicious Dessert Club | *Baked Gds.*	25
Croissanteria | *Baked Gds.*	–
East Vill. Meat | *Meat/Poultry*	26
Good Beer | *Beer*	27
NEW Macaron Parlour | *Baked Gds.*	–
Momofuku Milk Bar | *Baked Gds.*	25
Porto Rico | *Coffee/Tea*	27
Puddin' by Clio | *Baked Gds.*	29
Sakaya | *Wine/Liq.*	28
Tu-Lu's GF | *Baked Gds.*	25
Union Mkt. | *Maj. Mkt.*	25
Veniero's | *Baked Gds.*	25
Zucker Bakery | *Baked Gds.*	24

FINANCIAL DISTRICT

(South of Murray St.)

Battery Place Mkt. | *Maj. Mkt.*	27
Financier Patisserie | *Baked Gds.*	25
FPB | *Baked Gds.*	27
La Maison/Choc. | *Candy*	29
Leonidas | *Candy/Nuts*	26

FLATIRON

(14th to 26th Sts., 6th Ave. to Park Ave. S., excluding Union Sq.)

Beecher's Cheese | *Cheese/Dairy*	27
Bottlerocket | *Wine/Liq.*	25
Eataly | *Maj. Mkt.*	27
Flatiron Wines | *Wine/Liq.*	–
L.A. Burdick | *Candy/Nuts*	28
Moore Bros. | *Wine/Liq.*	28

GARMENT DISTRICT

(30th to 40th Sts., west of 5th)

Esposito Meat | *Meat/Poultry*	27
Kee's | *Candy/Nuts*	28

GRAMERCY PARK

(14th to 23rd Sts., east of Park Ave. S.)

Bedford Cheese | *Cheese/Dairy*	27
Ess-a-Bagel | *Baked Gds.*	26

GREENWICH VILLAGE

(Houston to 14th Sts., west of B'way, east of 6th Ave.)

Agata/Valentina | *Maj. Mkt.*	25
Citarella | *Maj. Mkt.*	26
FPB | *Baked Gds.*	27
Ivy Bakery | *Baked Gds.*	25
Mille-Feuille | *Baked Gds.*	25
Murray's Bagels | *Baked Gds.*	26
Nut Box | *Candy/Nuts*	24

FOOD LOVER'S

LOCATIONS

Porto Rico | *Coffee/Tea* 27

Raffetto's | *Pastas* 28

Sullivan St. Tea | *Coffee/Tea* 26

HARLEM/EAST HARLEM

(110th to 155th Sts., excluding Columbia U. area)

NEW Beurre/Sel | *Baked Gds.* –

Fairway | *Maj. Mkt.* 25

Hot Bread Almacen | *Baked Gds.* –

Lee Lee's | *Baked Gds.* –

Levain Bakery | *Baked Gds.* 28

Make My Cake | *Baked Gds.* 26

HUDSON SQUARE

(Canal to Houston Sts., west of 6th Ave.)

Jacques Torres | *Candy/Nuts* 28

LITTLE ITALY

(Canal to Kenmare Sts., Bowery to Lafayette St.)

Alleva Dairy | *Cheese/Dairy* 28

Ceci-Cela | *Baked Gds.* 26

Despaña | *Spec. Shop* 27

Despaña Vinos | *Wine/Liq.* 28

Di Palo | *Cheese/Dairy* 29

Enoteca Di Palo | *Wine/Liq.* 27

Papabubble | *Candy/Nuts* 23

Piemonte Ravioli | *Pastas* 27

Puro Chile | *Spec. Shop* 26

LOWER EAST SIDE

(Houston to Canal Sts., east of Bowery)

BabyCakes | *Baked Gds.* 24

NEW Beurre/Sel | *Baked Goods* –

Bisous, Ciao | *Baked Gds.* 25

Doughnut Plant | *Baked Gds.* 27

Economy Candy | *Candy/Nuts* 25

Formaggio | *Cheese/Dairy* 27

Heritage Meat | *Meat/Poultry* 27

Hester St. Fair | *Spec. Shop* 21

Kossar's | *Baked Gds.* 26

Malt/Mold | *Spec. Shop* –

New Beer | *Beer* 26

Pain D'Avignon | *Baked Gds.* 24

Pickle Guys | *Spec. Shop* 27

Porto Rico | *Coffee/Tea* 27

Russ/Daughters | *Caviar/Fish* 29

Saxelby | *Cheese/Dairy* 29

Streit's Matzo | *Baked Gds.* 27

Sugar Sweet | *Baked Gds.* 26

Sweet Life | *Candy/Nuts* 27

NEW Tache Artisan Choc. | *Candy/Nuts* –

NEW Tiberio Custom Meats | *Meat/Poultry* –

Whole Foods Mkt. | *Maj. Mkt.* 25

Yonah Schimmel | *Baked Gds.* 24

MURRAY HILL

(26th to 40th Sts., east of 5th; 23rd to 26th Sts., east of Park Ave. S.)

Fairway | *Maj. Mkt.* 25

Foods/India | *Herbs/Spices* 23

Kalustyan's | *Spec. Shop* 27

Lamazou | *Cheese/Dairy* 26

Spice Corner | *Herbs/Spices* 23

Todaro Bros. | *Spec. Shops* 25

NOHO

(Houston to 4th Sts., Bowery to B'way)

Astor Wines | *Wine/Liq.* 26

Financier Patisserie | *Baked Gds.* 25

Il Buco Alimentari | *Spec. Shop* 25

Japan Premium Beef | *Meat/Poultry* 29

NOLITA

(Houston to Kenmare Sts., Bowery to Lafayette St.)

Eileen's Cheesecake | *Baked Gds.* 25

SOHO

(Canal to Houston Sts., west of Lafayette St.)

Balthazar Bakery | *Baked Gds.* 27

Dean/DeLuca | *Maj. Mkt.* 26

Dominique Ansel | *Baked Gds.* 27

G'town Cupcake | *Baked Gds.* 27

Harney/Sons | *Coffee/Tea* 28

Kee's | *Candy/Nuts* 28

NEW Le Palais de Thés | *Coffee/Tea* –

MarieBelle's | *Candy/Nuts* 26

Nespresso | *Coffee/Tea* 27

Pino Meats | *Meat/Poultry* 29

Vosges | *Candy/Nuts* 27

Xocolatti | *Candy/Nuts* 22

SOUTH STREET SEAPORT

New Amsterdam Mkt. | *Spec. Shop* — 28

TRIBECA

(Canal to Murray Sts., west of B'way)
NEW All Good Things | *Maj. Mkt.* — ⌐
NEW Cavaniola's | *Cheese/Dairy* — ⌐
Chambers St. Wines | *Wine/Liq.* — 27
Dickson's | *Meat/Poultry* — 28
Duane Pk. | *Baked Gds.* — 25
Grandaisy | *Baked Gds.* — 25
Nunu Choc. | *Candy/Nuts* — 25
Whole Foods Mkt. | *Maj. Mkt.* — 25
Zucker's Bagels | *Baked Gds.* — 22

UNION SQUARE

(14th to 17th Sts., 5th Ave. to Union Sq. E.)
NEW Breads Bakery | *Baked Gds.* — ⌐
Italian Wine | *Wine/Liq.* — 29
Union Sq. Wines | *Wine/Liq.* — 25
Whole Foods Mkt. | *Maj. Mkt.* — 25

WASHINGTON HTS./INWOOD

(North of W. 155th St.)
PJ Wine | *Wine/Liq.* — 27

WEST 40s

Amy's Bread | *Baked Gds.* — 26
Bouchon Bakery | *Baked Gds.* — 27
Financier Patisserie | *Baked Gds.* — 25
Jacques Torres | *Candy/Nuts* — 28
Kee's | *Candy/Nuts* — 28
La Maison/Choc. | *Candy* — 29
Magnolia Bakery | *Baked Gds.* — 21
Minamoto | *Candy/Nuts* — 29
Morrell & Co. | *Wine/Liq.* — 26
Poseidon | *Baked Gds.* — 25
NEW Royce' Chocolate | *Candy/Nuts* — ⌐
Sullivan St. Bakery | *Baked Gds.* — 27

WEST 50s

FPB | *Baked Gds.* — 27
La Bergamote | *Baked Gds.* — 26
La Boîte à Epice | *Herbs/Spices* — ⌐

Momofuku Milk Bar | *Baked Gds.* — 25
Petrossian | *Caviar/Smoked* — 27
Whole Foods Mkt. | *Maj. Mkt.* — 25

WEST 60s

Bouchon Bakery | *Baked Gds.* — 27
NEW Le Palais de Thés | *Coffee/Tea* — ⌐
Magnolia Bakery | *Baked Gds.* — 21
O&CO. | *Spec. Shop* — 27

WEST 70s

Acker Merrall | *Wine/Liq.* — 28
Citarella | *Maj. Mkt.* — 26
Fairway | *Maj. Mkt.* — 25
Grandaisy | *Baked Gds.* — 25
Jacques Torres | *Candy/Nuts* — 28
Levain Bakery | *Baked Gds.* — 28
NEW Pain d'Epices | *Baked Gds.* — ⌐
Pour | *Wine/Liq.* — 24
Salumeria Rosi | *Spec. Shop* — 28
NEW Sugar/Plumm | *Candy/Nuts* — ⌐

WEST 80s

Momofuku Milk Bar | *Baked Gds.* — 25
Murray's Sturgeon | *Caviar/Smoked* — 28
NEW Teavana | *Coffee/Tea* — ⌐
Zabar's | *Maj. Mkt.* — 27

WEST 90s

Choc. Works | *Candy/Nuts* — 26
Spices/Tease | *Herbs/Spices* — 25
Whole Foods Mkt. | *Maj. Mkt.* — 25

WEST 100s

(See also Harlem/East Harlem)
Absolute Bagels | *Baked Gds.* — 26
Silver Moon | *Baked Gds.* — 26

WEST VILLAGE

(Houston to 14th Sts., west of 6th Ave., excluding Meatpacking)
Amy's Bread | *Baked Gds.* — 26
Bien Cuit | *Baked Gds.* — 23
Bisous, Ciao | *Baked Gds.* — 25
Carry On Tea | *Coffee/Tea* — 25
DavidsTea | *Coffee/Tea* — 28

Faicco's Pork | *Meat/Poultry* 28

Florence Meat | *Meat/Poultry* 29

NEW House of Cupcakes -

Le Dû's Wines | *Wine/Liq.* 29

Li-Lac Choc. | *Candy/Nuts* 26

London Candy Co. | *Candy/Nuts* 25

Magnolia Bakery | *Baked Gds.* 21

McNulty's | *Coffee/Tea* 28

Meadow | *Spec. Shop* 29

Milk/Cookies | *Baked Gds.* 25

Molly's | *Baked Gds.* 27

Murray's Cheese | *Cheese/Dairy* 29

Myers/Keswick | *Spec. Shop* 25

O&CO. | *Spec. Shop* 27

Ottomanelli/Sons | *Meat/Poultry* 28

Patisserie Claude | *Baked Gds.* 26

NEW Royce' Chocolate |
Candy/Nuts -

Sockerbit | *Candy/Nuts* 24

NEW Sugar/Plumm | *Candy/Nuts* -

Varsano's | *Candy/Nuts* 29

Bronx

BAYCHESTER

NEW House of Cupcakes -

FAIRMONT-
CLAREMONT
VILLAGE

Gustiamo | *Spec. Shops* -

FORDHAM

Addeo Bakery | *Baked Gds.* 28

Biancardi Meats | *Meat/Poultry* 28

Borgatti's | *Pastas* 29

Calandra Cheese | *Cheese/Dairy* 27

Casa Della | *Cheese/Dairy* 29

Delillo Pastry | *Baked Gds.* 25

Egidio Pastry | *Baked Gds.* 25

Madonia Bakery | *Baked Gds.* 26

Randazzo's | *Seafood* 26

Teitel Bros. | *Spec. Shop* 27

Terranova | *Baked Gds.* 28

KINGSBRIDGE

S&S Cheesecake | *Baked Gds.* 28

THROGS NECK

Pastosa Ravioli | *Pastas* 27

Brooklyn

BAY RIDGE

Faicco's Pork | *Meat/Poultry* 28

Mike's Donuts | *Baked Gds.* 27

Nordic Delicacies | *Spec. Shop* 28

Paneantico | *Baked Gds.* 26

BEDFORD-
STUYVESANT

Dough | *Baked Gds.* 26

Scratch Bread | *Baked Gds.* 27

BENSONHURST

Lioni Fresh Mozz. | *Cheese/Dairy* 27

Pastosa Ravioli | *Pastas* 27

Villabate-Alba | *Baked Gds.* 27

BOERUM HILL

Betty Bakery | *Baked Gds.* 26

Shelsky's | *Caviar/Smoked* 24

BOROUGH PARK

D. Coluccio/Sons | *Spec. Shop* 27

BROOKLYN HEIGHTS

Damascus | *Baked Gds.* 26

Sahadi's | *Spec. Shop* 28

Two for the Pot | *Coffee/Tea* 26

CARROLL GARDENS

Caputo's Bake Shop | *Baked Gds.* 27

Court St. Grcs. | *Spec. Shop* 29

D'Amico | *Coffee/Tea* 27

Esposito Pork | *Meat/Poultry* 27

Momofuku Milk Bar | *Baked Gds.* 25

Monteleone | *Baked Gds.* 29

CLINTON HILL

Bklyn. Victory Garden |
Spec. Shop 26

Choice Mkt. | *Spec. Shop* 27

COBBLE HILL

Bien Cuit | *Baked Gds.* 23

Court Pastry | *Baked Gds.* 26

Fish Tales | *Seafood* 27
Nut Box | *Candy/Nuts* 24
One Girl | *Baked Gds.* 27
Staubitz Mkt. | *Meat/Poultry* 29
Stinky Bklyn | *Cheese/Dairy* 27
Sugar Shop | *Candy/Nuts* -
Union Mkt. | *Maj. Mkt.* 25

CROWN HEIGHTS

NEW Wedge | *Cheese/Dairy* -

DOWNTOWN BROOKLYN

Nunu Choc. | *Candy/Nuts* 25

DUMBO

Almondine | *Baked Gds.* 26
Brooklyn Cupcake | *Baked Gds.* 27
Foragers City | *Maj. Mkt.* 26
Jacques Torres | *Candy/Nuts* 28
One Girl | *Baked Gds.* 27
Smorgasburg | *Spec. Shop* 28

FORT GREENE

Choice Mkt. | *Spec. Shop* 27
Greene Grape | *Wine/Liq.* 22
Greene Grape | *Spec. Shop* 27

GOWANUS

Brooklyn Brine | *Spec. Shop* 23
Four/Twenty Blackbirds | 26
  Baked Gds.

GREENPOINT

Acme Fish | *Smoked Fish* 25
Bellocq Tea | *Tea* 25
Brouwerij Ln. | *Beer* 28
Ovenly | *Baked Gds.* -

GREENWOOD HEIGHTS

NEW Baked In Brooklyn -
Eagle Provisions | *Meat/Poultry* 23

MIDWOOD

Hot Bagels /Bialys | *Baked Gds.* 25
Orchard | *Spec. Shop* 28
Pickle Guys | *Spec. Shop* 27
Pomegranate | *Spec. Shop* 26

MILL BASIN

Pastosa Ravioli | *Pastas* 27

PARK SLOPE

Bierkraft | *Beer* 27
Bklyn Larder | *Spec. Shop* 27
Blue Apron | *Spec. Shop* 28
Butter Lane Cupcakes | *Baked Gds.* 25
Colson | *Baked Gds.* 24
DavidsTea | *Coffee/Tea* 28
NEW Du Jour | *Baked Gds.* -
D'Vine | *Spec. Shop* 26
Fleisher's | *Meat/Poultry* 29
Ladybird | *Baked Gds.* 27
The Ploughman | *Spec. Shop* 26
Trois Pommes | *Baked Gds.* 27
Union Mkt. | *Maj. Mkt.* 25
Valley Shepherd | *Cheese/Dairy* 28

PROSPECT HEIGHTS

Empire Mayo. | *Spec. Shop* -

RED HOOK

Baked | *Baked Gds.* 26
Dry Dock | *Wine/Liq.* 28
Fairway | *Maj. Mkt.* 25
Steve's Pies | *Baked Gds.* 26

SUNSET PARK

Colson | *Baked Gds.* 24
Li-Lac Choc. | *Candy/Nuts* 26

WILLIAMSBURG

Bedford Cheese | *Cheese/Dairy* 27
NEW Bklyn. Harvest Mkt. | -
  Maj. Mkt.
Breukelen Bier | *Beer* 27
Brooklyn Cupcake | *Baked Gds.* 27
Brooklyn Oenology | *Wine/Liq.* 26
Dépanneur | *Spec. Shop* -
Fortunato | *Baked Gds.* 27
Marlow/Daughters | 28
  Meat/Poultry
Mast Bros. Choc. | *Candy/Nuts* 25
Meat Hook | *Meat/Poultry* 27
Momofuku Milk Bar | *Baked Gds.* 25
Porto Rico | *Coffee/Tea* 27

Smorgasburg | *Spec. Shop* 28

Whiskey Shop | *Wine/Liq.* 27

Queens

ASTORIA

Artopolis | *Baked Gds.* 27

Med. Foods | *Spec. Shop* 26

Titan Foods | *Spec. Shops* 26

DOUGLASTON

Fairway | *Maj. Mkt.* 25

ELMHURST

Neuhaus | *Candy/Nuts* 26

FLUSHING

Durso's Pasta | *Pastas* 26

House/Spices | *Herbs/Spices* 26

Ottomanelli's | *Meat/Poultry* 28

FOREST HILLS

Cheese/World | *Cheese/Dairy* 26

JACKSON HEIGHTS

Cannelle Patisserie | *Baked Gds.* 29

Despaña | *Spec. Shop* 27

LONG ISLAND CITY

Brooklyn Cupcake | *Baked Gds.* 27

Manhattan Fruitier | *Spec. Shop* 25

WOODSIDE

Ottomanelli/Sons | *Meat/Poultry* 28

Staten Island

ELTINGVILLE

Pastosa Ravioli | *Pastas* 27

GRASMERE

Pastosa Ravioli | *Pastas* 27

WEST BRIGHTON

Pastosa Ravioli | *Pastas* 27